THE DIARY

OF THE

AMERICAN

REVOLUTION

1775-1781

Compiled by

FRANK MOORE

Abridged, Edited, and with an Introduction, by

JOHN ANTHONY SCOTT

WASHINGTON SQUARE PRESS

New York, 1967

The frontispiece is from an engraving specially prepared for the 1876 edition of the *Diary* from Joseph Duplessis' portrait which Moore purchased in France and brought to the United States in 1874.

CONTENTS

LIST OF SONGS, BALLADS, AND VERSE

LIST OF ILLUSTRATIONS

Portraits

Broadsides

EDITOR'S INTRODUCTION

FRANK MOORE's *Diary of the American Revolution* was first published in 1860 and re-issued in various editions between 1863 and 1876. A source book for innumerable students of the Revolution, the *Diary* has been out of general circulation for nearly a century; this, to the American public at large, has been no uncertain loss. The *Diary* was put together almost entirely from newspapers appearing during the years 1775–81; it is unique as a study of revolutionary life and literature. A new edition of this book is both timely and necessary. The second centennial of the Revolution approaches; the world is still agitated by the same fundamental issues of national freedom and self-determination which lie at the heart of the American revolutionary tradition. A work which illuminates this tradition is of both historical and contemporary significance. A new edition of the *Diary* is also important because it draws attention to the life and contribution of Frank Moore, one of the ablest of nineteenth-century American historians and a pioneer worker in the field of American folk literature.

I

Frank Moore, the third of six children of Jacob Bailey Moore and Mary Adams Hill, was born in Concord, New Hampshire, in 1828. His life—he died in 1904—spanned the swift evolution of the United States from rural society to great industrial empire.[1] Family tradition was an important factor in molding

[1] There is no biography of Frank Moore. The sketch given here is based upon the following: E. S. Stearns, *Genealogical and Family History of the State of New Hampshire* (New York: Lewis Co., 1908); two letterbooks for the period 1869–75 containing official, business and personal correspondence, in The New-York Historical Society; manuscript "notes and memoranda" in the form of 21 bound volumes and 5 boxes of unbound notes, for the period 1877–94, in the New Hampshire Historical Society; the Elihu B. Washburne papers in the Library of Congress; and biographical sketches

Moore's interests and in determining the precise nature of the literary contribution that he was to make. The founder of the New Hampshire branch of the family was Jonathan Moore, a British Army colonel of Scots origin who settled in Stratham, New Hampshire, in the seventeenth century. Over the years the Moores proliferated children with pronounced intellectual and musical interests and with a heritage of struggle during the birth years of the infant Republic. Frank's great-grandfather, Coffin Moore, was a naval surgeon during the Revolution, and his grandfather, Jacob Bailey Moore, Sr., was a surgeon in the War of 1812. His father, Jacob Bailey Moore, Jr., was a journalist, historical editor, and man of letters who had been renowned in his youth for violin playing and singing.[2] Frank's uncles, Henry Eaton and John Weeks Moore, were both noted musicologists.

Some years before Frank's birth his father had been publisher and co-editor of the *New Hampshire Patriot;* his partner in this venture was his brother-in-law Isaac Hill. The two men quarreled in the mid twenties and became bitter political enemies, Hill, a Democrat, championing Andrew Jackson, and Moore, a Whig, John Quincy Adams. In 1826 Moore established his own organ, the *New Hampshire Journal,* and campaigned for the re-election of Adams. But the triumph of his opponents made life in the state difficult for him. In 1836 Isaac Hill was elected governor; in 1839 Jacob Bailey Moore wound up his affairs and left New Hampshire for good. After a brief stay in New York the family moved to Washington, D.C., where Moore's fidelity to the Whig cause was rewarded with a position as chief clerk in the Post Office under the Tyler administration. In 1845 the victory of the Democrats resulted in Moore's being turned out along with other Whig officeholders, and the family began its wanderings again. Another period of residence in New York and temporary jobs

---

of Frank, George, and Jacob Bailey Moore by Alexander J. Wall in the *Dictionary of American Biography.*

[2] He published a spirited defense of John Quincy Adams, wrote a history of New Hampshire newspapers, helped found the New Hampshire Historical Society, and edited an edition of rare documents relating principally to New Hampshire history.

ensued, but this terminated with the victory of the Whigs in the election of 1848; and in 1849 the family moved to California, where Jacob Bailey Moore became deputy postmaster in San Francisco.

Frank Moore was twenty-one years of age when he went to California; we know almost nothing concerning the life that he lived there, except that he ran for State Senator in the first election under the constitution of 1849–50, and, later in life, described himself as "one of the pioneers of San Francisco."[3] We know, too, that it was in conversation with California immigrants and sailors that Moore first became aware of the old revolutionary songs, and first began to note them down.[4]

In 1853 the family returned east, Jacob Bailey Moore to die in Vermont, and Frank to take up residence in New York City. With the encouragement and cooperation of his brother George, who was the Librarian of The New-York Historical Society, Frank embarked upon the preparation of his first major work. In the few years between 1850 and publication of *Songs and Ballads of the American Revolution* in 1856, he succeeded in bringing together a remarkable collection of lyrics: some were copied from revolutionary broadsides and newspaper files, and some came from songbooks. Many of them were "taken down from the lips of veterans who remembered them as sung late in the last century or early in this."[5]

Moore's book consisted of the lyrics, without music, of nearly one hundred revolutionary songs and ballads composed in the period 1765–83. Re-issued in 1905 and 1964, *Songs and Ballads of the American Revolution* remains the funda-

[3] He described his candidacy as "an affair of fun only." Letter to Horace H. Moore. New York City, June 13, 1874. New-York Historical Society mss.

[4] Letter to Dr. Oliver Wendell Holmes. New York City, June 17, 1875. Here Moore states explicitly that he has been collecting the songs and ballads "for the past twenty-five years"; that is, in the period that began with his arrival in California. New-York Historical Society mss.

[5] *Ibid.*, and *Songs and Ballads of the American Revolution* (New York: Appleton Co., 1856), v.

mental published source for the songs of the revolutionary period and a pioneer work in the history of American folk-song and native American topical balladry. Frank Moore had set himself the task of conserving the record of the past, organizing it, and making it available to his own contemporaries and to posterity; he payed particular attention to those valuable items that he considered most likely to vanish irrecoverably with the passage of time.

The success of this first venture emboldened Moore to undertake a more ambitious project on the revolutionary era. His researches in the newspaper files of The New-York Historical Society had made him vividly aware of the extraordinary qualities of revolutionary journalism—its intellectual profundities, its terse on-the-spot reporting, its literary power, and the quality of its satire and political commentary—as a mirror of the life of that time. In 1856 he signed a contract with Scribner's, hired two copyists, and from that year until 1860 worked upon the preparation of the *Diary of the American Revolution*. This was one of Moore's most successful ventures; we shall return to a more detailed examination of it.

When the Civil War broke out in 1861 Moore joined the Union Army and reached the rank of colonel. Whatever the nature of his military service—and we have as yet no record of this—it did not deflect him from his chosen work; but it provided a further direction and impetus. During the war years and the early Reconstruction period, Moore spent much of his time in Washington, and a great deal of his energy went in recording and chronicling the struggle in which the American people were involved. He collected and edited ten volumes of the *Rebellion Record*, a treasury of reports, letters, anecdotes, and verses illuminating the human aspect of the war in a fashion unequalled by any single subsequent historian.

The *Rebellion Record*, in truth a continuation of the *Diary of the American Revolution*, was based primarily upon contemporary newspapers. Moore collected these from all parts of the country, and he culled from them hundreds of thousands of soldiers' letters which had been written and published in order to bring news of the battles to the people back home. From his examination of these writings Moore derived a profound respect for the common people not only as makers of history, as participants in it, but also as the writers and recorders of it. "As a history of the operations of the armies in the field," he wrote to James Garfield, "these letters are unique and invaluable. With them I can describe the different movements and actions of the war from a hundred different standpoints, and in historical writing they are marvelous. For instance, the story of Burnside's Fredericksburg is told by no less than thirteen hundred and more soldiers who took part in the affair, and not one of them ranking a colonel. As a monument to the educated intelligence of the rank and file of our fighting men they have no parallel."[6]

One of the most interesting offshoots of Moore's work in preparing the *Rebellion Record* was his publication in 1864 of a series of little songbooks devoted to lyrics composed principally by the participants in the struggle on both sides. The verses included by Moore in these songsters were taken from the newspapers or came to him as the result of appeals published in the press or sent to individuals.[7] These songbooks still constitute one of the fundamental sources for the study of the musical heritage of the Civil War.[8]

[6] Letter to James A. Garfield. New York City, May 4, 1874. New-York Historical Society mss. In this letter Moore states that Abraham Lincoln followed his work with great interest and passed on to him Confederate papers, from which he clipped letters. In 1864 Lincoln discussed with Moore a plan to set up a Federal office to process the soldiers' letters and prepare them for filing in the Library of Congress.

[7] Judging by the letters that survive, Moore must have addressed hundreds of appeals to individuals to send on to him songs that were in their possession. The different John Brown songs, which he had collected in this way, numbered over 70. One of them was "printed on a remnant of blue wallpaper. . . ." Letter to Haskell. New York City, July 2, 1874.

[8] The Union songs were published by Putnam in the Red, White and Blue series containing three books: *Songs of the Soldiers, Lyrics of Loyalty,* and *Personal and Political Ballads.* The Confederates were represented by *Rebel Rhymes and Rhapsodies.* This was supplemented by a later work, *Songs and Ballads of the Southern People 1861–5* (New York: Appleton, 1886).

Many other works came from Moore's pen during the sixties. One of the most popular was entitled *Anecdotes, Poetry and Incidents of the Civil War*. Issued by Collier in no less than four printings between 1867 and 1900, it was a one volume condensation of the *Rebellion Record* and the soldiers' songsters. *Women of the War*, issued in 1867 and 1869, a brilliant compilation of material from diaries, journals, correspondence, articles, and interviews, was devoted to the heroic services rendered by women on both sides of the battle lines.

II

In 1869 Frank Moore gave over his historical labors and accepted a post, at a salary of $2,000 per annum, as secretary to Elihu B. Washburne, American ambassador to France. Moore arrived in Paris in May 1869 and remained in Europe until the end of 1873. Quitting the literary profession for four and a half years in Europe was a decision which Moore regretted to the end of his days. Later he would write bitterly of his "wasted life in Paris" and of a senseless adventure into "diplomatic humbug and pretentious flummery."

What prompted Moore to make this decision? The years 1865–68 had been years of disillusion for him. As a Republican he had entertained high hopes, at the end of the war, for the victory of human rights in the South and for the reconstruction of that section on a democratic basis; and, at first, he had believed and hoped that Andrew Johnson would take the necessary steps with compassion, firmness, and tact.[9] "If," he wrote many years later, "the Negroes had been protected by the government in their constitutional rights, they would have possessed the property of the South and been represented by Negro Congressmen and Senators for all the Negro States."[10] But these hopes had been dashed by Johnson's intransigence and rigidity, and by the bitter conflict between

[9] Moore's high hopes in Andrew Johnson were reflected in his edition of *The Speeches of Andrew Johnson, President of the United States* (Boston: Little Brown, 1866).

[10] "Notes and Memoranda," February 13, 1893. New Hampshire Historical Society mss.

Congress and President that culminated in the latter's impeachment in 1868. The war was over, but its aftermath was confusion, and Moore was greatly fatigued.

In March 1869 Elihu B. Washburne, a radical Republican from Illinois, member of the Joint Congressional Committee on Reconstruction, and a staunch supporter of General Grant, was designated Minister to France. Moore spoke and wrote fluent French, and was related to the Minister by marriage. The position, no doubt, was not difficult to secure and the prospect of a period in Europe, with fresh sights and scenes, was tempting.

Moore and his wife Laura arrived in Paris—May 24, 1869 —at a time when the Second French Empire was moving swiftly toward war and disaster. In the four and a half years Moore remained there he witnessed cataclysmic events: the outbreak of the Franco-Prussian conflict on July 15, 1870, the stunning disasters suffered by the French Army at Metz and Sedan in September, the declaration of the Republic in that same month, the siege of Paris and its capitulation in January 1871. Hard upon the horrors of war came a civil struggle of unsurpassed bitterness with the declaration of the Commune in April, its bloody suppression in the summer of 1871, and the continuing arrests, trials and executions of the next few years.

Throughout these convulsions the American Embassy in Paris remained open. Moore's official life was occupied with routine, but his irrepressible historical instincts were still at work. He watched the crowds demonstrating in the streets of Paris and noted carefully in his diary the course of the debates in the *Corps legislatif*.[11] "I am collecting material," he wrote, "for a record of the present war. . . ."[12] This

[11] Moore's journal from this period does not, unfortunately, survive. See the letter of August 9, 1870 to Laura Bailey Moore, in which he reports the debates of the deliberative assembly; and that of August 13 in which he states his intention of sending "pages of the journal" forward to Laura in Switzerland. New-York Historical Society mss.

[12] Letter to John Bartlett. Paris, July 22, 1870. New-York Historical Society mss.

observation was deceptively casual. Moore was not only carrying on his collecting work with a single-minded passion, but
speedily became diverted from materials on the war to original
paintings and engravings with which he planned to illustrate
future books. Unfortunately such collecting proved to be
considerably more expensive in Europe than in America. The
urge to acquire old masters and other art works became almost a mania. The Duplessis portrait of Benjamin Franklin
is a case in point. In his rummagings among Paris bookstores
and artshops Moore came across a dealer who put him in
touch with a family in Nancy who owned the original,
painted from life in 1778. For this portrait Moore paid
$1,160 in gold.[13] According to his own statement, these ac-
quisitions were made in Paris and London; hundreds of pictures and engravings were involved, many of them "originals
of great value and beauty."[14] By Moore's estimate these items
cost him a total of $11,000 in gold—$6,000 for the pictures
and the balance for engravings and other copies.[15]

Such a collection could not be acquired on a secretary's
salary of $2,000 a year. Moore fell into debt and contracted
loans both large and small from his business acquaintances,
his wife's relatives, and his friends. He tried to mend his
fortunes by gambling and other speculations, and fell deeper
into debt. The result was loss of reputation, forced resignation from his position with the Embassy in 1872, and aliena-
tion from his wife and family. Moore seems also to have
lived for some time under the shadow of prospective prosecution for defalcations which are only hinted at in the surviving
correspondence.

[13] Letter to the Librarian, Library of Congress. New York City,
January 30, 1875. New-York Historical Society mss. This painting
now hangs in the Metropolitan Museum of Art in New York City.
A copy is in the possession of The New-York Historical Society. See
frontispiece.
[14] Letter to John Weeks Moore. New York City, June 10, 1874.
New-York Historical Society mss.
[15] Letter to Laura Bailey Moore. New York City, January 17,
1875; to J. B. Burr. New York City, July 8, 1874. New-York Historical Society mss.

In February, 1874 Moore returned to the United States alone, ruined, and in disgrace.[16] The European experience, the disintegration of his personal life, and the revelation of his own weakness and folly had shaken him profoundly. He came back to New York City vowing that he would redeem his name and his honor, or "perish in the attempt."[17] Though there is evidence of occasional backsliding, the story of Moore's life for the next twenty years—until 1894 when he vanishes from our view—was to be one of patient, endless, unremitting scholarly toil; a dour, anonymous, poverty-stricken life dedicated to the single end of liquidating his debts and redeeming his dishonor.[18]

Moore arrived in New York practically penniless: He began to solicit any kind of literary or editorial work that would earn him a living. He soon secured a contract for the publication of an illustrated edition of the Bible, and it was not long before he was working on other books as well. He settled down in a lodging on the corner of 2nd Avenue and 9th Street, close to where the Historical Society was then located. "I am very, very, very busy with my books," he wrote. Before the end of 1874 he had seen through the press not only *The Spirit of the Bible*, but also a collection of the writings of Gabriel Furman on early New York lore

[16] A. J. Wall ("Frank Moore," in the *Dictionary of American Biography*) places the date of Moore's return to the United States as 1872. In actual fact he stayed in Europe for eighteen months after his resignation took effect. There is no evidence in Moore's own writing that the separation from Laura Bailey Moore that occurred at this time was not permanent.

[17] Letter to Laura Bailey Moore. New York City, February 16, 1875. Moore answers his wife's bitter charges that he is "squandering" advances from publishers. New-York Historical Society mss.

[18] "This house today is decorated by pictures the result of my insane folly. . . . How much today I regret these things you will never know. I am to begin life again, separate and apart from the Moore family, and I shall use the lesson of adversity to its full extent. . . . Time will show that I can and shall pay back all my honest obligations." Letter to Laura Bailey Moore. New York City, February 4, 1875. New-York Historical Society mss.

and history, entitled *Antiquities of Long Island*.[19] At the same time Moore set about converting most of his assets—rare books, manuscripts, and paintings—into hard cash. He wrote to his wife:

> I am cleaning up the pictures which are to go to auction. I cannot tell you how much it grieves me to part with them, but it is better that they should go than to be living always in fear and under a cloud. As soon as they are sold and Mr. W[ashburne] gets the money I shall devote all my time day and night to getting a living. . . . If I get enough to meet the demands in Paris I shall truly and sincerely thank God. They are of no more interest to me except as they may bring me in enough to help me back to a place I once occupied.[20]

Moore remitted part of the sums thus realized from sales and advances to his wife in Paris for living expenses and the payment of debts.

Early in 1875 Moore turned back to his earlier work on the Revolution in an attempt both to exploit it and to develop it more fully. In February of that year he approached several

[19] Of the *Spirit of the Bible* Moore wrote: "It is really beautiful, and will show, I pray earnestly, that all my love of art and subsequent misfortunes will not come to naught." Letter to Laura Bailey Moore. New York City, September 3, 1874. New-York Historical Society mss. *The Antiquities of Long Island* was published by J. W. Bouton (1874) and combined an earlier work of Furman's on Brooklyn with an unpublished manuscript that had come into Moore's hands. The *Spirit of the Bible* presents a tantalizing mystery. In 1874 the United States Publishing Company announced a "Pictorial Polyglot Spirit of the Holy Bible," with over 650 illustrations by the most famous artists from Dürer to Fragonard, projected and compiled by Frank Moore; and in 1875 this work was twice advertised in the *Publisher's Weekly*, issues of July 3 and October 23 respectively. Thereafter the book simply disappears from view. We do not know what happened to the engravings which Moore had brought together at so great a cost.

[20] Letter to Laura Bailey Moore. New York City, January 17, 1875. New-York Historical Society mss. The Mr. Washburne referred to here is A. C. Washburne, Elihu's brother, and one of Moore's principal creditors.

publishers with the offer of a two volume, expanded edition of revolutionary songs, to be entitled *Illustrated Ballad History of the American Revolution*; and he signed a contract with J. B. Burr of Hartford, Connecticut, for the issue of a special one-volume centennial edition of the *Diary of the American Revolution*. Both these books, the *Illustrated Ballad History* and the *Diary*, were published in 1876. In Moore's mind the musical and the documentary approach to the study of revolutionary history were inseparably linked. To this linked concept we must now pay more detailed attention.

III

The 1876 edition of the *Diary*, retitled *The Diary of the Revolution*, was a volume of over one thousand pages. The editor's aim, as stated in his preface, was to provide "to the student of this day the same view the readers of the revolutionary period enjoyed—the manners and customs of the people, and the moral and religious, as well as political features of the time." The *Diary* accomplishes this aim by unfolding, day after day and month after month for the period 1775–81, a picture of the revolutionary struggle as conveyed by the newspapers of the time.

In preparing his work Moore was able to draw upon sources of unbelievable variety and extent. The rise of the newspaper in America was an eighteenth-century phenomenon; it reflected the development of a complex urban civilization with a need for communication in the many aspects, commercial, social, cultural, and political, of its everyday life. The first American journal was the *Boston News-Letter* founded in 1704; the next half century saw the establishment of weekly papers in the main urban centers—New York, Philadelphia, Newport, and Charleston, to name the most important. By 1763 some twenty-three newspapers were being published in British America; by 1776 over forty journals had been issued at one or another time in the five principal cities, to say nothing of the numerous sheets issued in a dozen or more coastal communities of lesser importance.

The colonial press was a mirror of American civilization in the eighteenth century, and it remains a primary source for the study of the history of those times. It was a powerful force for the establishment of a common national outlook and psychology: it reflected public opinion, molded it, and promoted a sense of common needs, common interests, and common problems. After 1763 the press was converted to political uses; reflecting a national preoccupation with the developing conflict against England, it articulated popular protest and became a powerful instrument of direct revolutionary action against the Crown. The press played a major agitational role during the Stamp Act crisis; waged a campaign against the Townshend Acts; sounded the hue and cry against the occupation of Boston by British troops in 1868–70; waged warfare against the tea-dumping activities of the East India Company; and rallied the entire country to the aid of Boston when that port was closed in 1774.[21]

From a reading of the newspapers of the revolutionary era one gets a sense of great depth—in the variety of issues covered, the richness of factual reporting, the sophistication of political analysis and commentary, the sheer literary power. Journalism as a vehicle for the furtherance of revolutionary agitation and the transmission of revolutionary ideas attracted the best minds and writers of the time. Vivid descriptive power, merciless ridicule and satire, clarity and pungency of political statement, all these characterized the agitational campaigns of the pre-revolutionary period, 1763–75.[22]

The outbreak of the war in 1775 disrupted the publication of many papers. But they found a way to continue production notwithstanding war and invasion and acute technical problems created by shortages of paper, destruction of presses, and

[21] The role of the press in the pre-revolutionary period is carefully analysed by Arthur M. Schlesinger, Sr., *Prelude to Independence: The Newspaper War on Britain, 1764–76* (New York: Alfred A. Knopf, 1958). The more general significance of the American press as a mirror of colonial civilization is brilliantly conveyed in Carl Bridenbaugh's *Cities in Revolt 1743–76* (New York: Alfred A. Knopf, 1955), a work based primarily upon contemporary newspaper sources.

[22] See the *Boston Evening Post's* series *A Journal of the Times*, made available to the modern student under the title *Boston under Military Rule 1768–9*, compiled by O. M. Dickerson (Boston: Chapman and Grimes, 1936).

dispersal of type. The press, furthermore, assumed new functions arising out of the war crisis. Political analysis and commentary, satiric articles, and debate on controversial issues continued to appear; diplomacy, foreign affairs, and the problems of government also received attention. Military despatches, often of extraordinary vigor and conciseness, became numerous. Biographical sketches of military, naval, and governmental leaders were provided.[23]

For Moore the press was a primary source, a key to the political, social, and spiritual life of the American people during the revolutionary era. Because these writings fulfilled this function, and fulfilled it supremely well, they constituted a literary as well as a historic heritage of the first importance. But the songs created in the struggle were just as fundamental for understanding the mood and temper of the times. These songs not only appeared in the newspapers; they were themselves "singing newspapers," struck off in the form of broadsides, that circulated far and wide among the people in the back country and among the soldiers. They gave unique, special, and passionate utterance to the cause for the sake of which the common people suffered, bled, and died.

These songs claim for America the right of self-determination. They affirm that to determine one's own destiny without outside interference is a sacred right; it is so essential to the survival of the nation that men must be prepared to sacrifice their lives for it. Struggle against tyranny is viewed as the supreme cause to which men and women should dedicate themselves; this is the theme of innumerable songs. In his piece "On Independence," for example, Jonathan Sewall writes:

> Heaven's blessing attending us, no tyrant shall say,
> That Americans ever to such monsters gave way,
> But fighting we'll die in America's cause,
> Before we'll submit to tyrannical laws.

(See p. 128.)

[23] For a list of the principal newspapers appearing during the war years, and upon which Moore mainly relied, see Appendix A, "Principal Sources Used by Moore in the Preparation of the *Diary*," p. 555.

The image of a people prepared to give their lives freely and without hesitation for the cause of independence emerges in one of the most famous of revolutionary ballads, "The British Lamentation." A British dragoon, dying in September, 1776 during the New York campaign, is made to say:

> Like lions roaring for their prey,
> They [the Americans] feared no danger nor dismay:
> True British blood runs through their veins,
> And them with courage yet sustains.
> We saw these bold Columbia's sons
> Spread death and slaughter from their guns,
> Freedom or death! was all their cry,
> They did not seem to fear to die.

(See p. 156.)

These songs express the concept of the Revolution as a popular struggle in which the combined power of a nation in arms would prove superior to the professional troops, mercenaries, and conscripts pitted against them; they reflect a bottomless contempt for the strutting, boasting "butchers," the British generals. In the famous "Junto Song," written on the occasion of the arrival in Boston in May, 1775 of Howe, Clinton, and Burgoyne, the three braggarts trumpet their plans:

> Boston we shall in ashes lay,
>   It is a nest of knaves,
> We'll make them soon for mercy pray,
>   Or send them to their graves,
>   And a-taxing we will go, we'll go,
>   And a-taxing we will go.

(See p. 35.)

Other songs make the same point and develop it. Generals and their mercenaries may harry the country, kill innocent people, spread devastation, savagery, and death. Against all such, the people, fighting for freedom on their own soil, are invincible and will in the end prevail. They will spring up "like grasshoppers" in the path of the invader, block his advance, cut off his supplies, attack his rear. They will be everywhere and nowhere. A brilliant song, combining mockery with a shrewd understanding of irregular warfare, was written by Benjamin Franklin on the occasion of the British retreat from Lexington to Boston in 1775; and it is an apt illustration of the point:

It was not fair to shoot at us from behind trees!
If they had stood in the open, as they ought, before
       our great guns, we should have beat them with ease,
They may fight one another *that* way if they please,
But it is not *regular* to stand, and fight with rascals as these.
(See p. 105.)

Regular troops cannot run away in an occupied zone without losing whatever towns or territory they possess. Irregular troops, fighting on their own soil, must always be on the run if they are to keep the tactical initiative and to preserve their forces. This was explained in one of the most profound songs of the war, "To the Commons." The song, written by an anonymous British author in 1776, soon became popular in America as "The Folks on t'Other Side the Wave."

      For further than your bullets fly
        A common many may run, sirs,
      And wheat will grow beneath a sky
        Where cannot reach a gun, sirs.

      Then what are ships, and swords, and guns,
        And men of bloody mind, sirs,
      While Parthian-like, who conquers runs,
        Who loses—stays behind, sirs.
(See p. 147.)

Song after song dwells on the theme that the highest ideal to which a man may commit himself is struggle for his country's freedom. The most famous song in American history, "Yankee Doodle," is a light-hearted paean of praise to the New England militia and the shy country boys who were its backbone.[24] Again and again writers celebrate the heroism of irregulars who fight day and night on their own soil, in their

[24] For Edward Bangs' lyrics of 1775, see p. 54.

own way, at places of their own choosing. Peter St. John of
Norwalk, Connecticut, put it with defiant bluntness in his
great epic, "American Taxation":

> We never will knock under; O George, we do not fear,
> The rattling of your thunder, the lightning of your spear,
> Though rebels you declare us, we're strangers to dismay,
> Therefore you cannot scare us in North America.
>
> (See p. 337.)

Heroism in these songs is defined as commitment to the
struggle even in the face of great trials. Many beautiful lyrics
exploit this theme. On Nathan Hale:

> The faith of a martyr the tragedy showed,
> As he trod the last stage, as he trod the last stage,
> And Britons will shudder at gallant Hale's blood,
> As his words do presage, as his words do presage.
>
> (See p. 165.)

On John Paul Jones:

> The gunner in a fright to Paul Jones he came,
> "We make water quite fast, our side's in a flame";
> Then brave Jones he cried, in the height of his pride,
> "If we can't do no better boys, sink alongside."
>
> (See p. 394.)

Moore's approach to the Revolution emphasized not only
documentary and literary sources, but also folk music. Yet
the *Diary* as originally offered to the public included only a
small number of songs; the editor had made these plentifully
available in other works easily obtainable. But today the situation is different: *Songs and Ballads of the American Revolution* is a rare and expensive book not readily available to the
public; and its usefulness over the years has been diminished
by the absence of musical notation. To emphasize the nature
of Moore's contribution, the present edition of the *Diary*
unites the literary and the musical aspects; it incorporates the
lyrics and music of some thirty revolutionary songs and ballads. They have been chosen for their literary and artistic
merit, and because they represent with clarity the revolution-

ary tradition reflected in countless other writings and songs of the period. The majority of the lyrics chosen for inclusion here appeared in Moore's original edition of *Songs and Ballads of the American Revolution*. Subsequent research into the sources does little more than underline and reaffirm the integrity and inclusiveness of his original contribution.

This is an important conclusion. Is the same true of Moore's researches in the files of the revolutionary press? Does he gives us a representative selection of materials that may serve as an introduction to both the spirit and the meaning of the original? Does he tamper with the sources?

Moore did not tap the New England newspaper files as fully as he did those of the central states. There were good reasons for this. At a time when photocopying techniques did not exist he managed to copy a staggering amount of material from original sources. These manuscripts had to be reproduced in their entirety by hand; and this had to be done where Moore's copyists were employed and could work under supervision—in New York—where, naturally, New England materials were not so easily available. This limitation was counterbalanced by the fact that for many years the colonial newspapers had been in the habit of copying each other's most valuable material. The great *Journal of the Times*, for example, that pilloried the military occupation of Boston in 1768–9, achieved a nationwide circulation because many other papers copied the installments after they had appeared either in the *New-York Journal* or the *Boston Evening Post*; and the same was true of important despatches during the war years. Thus, through his use of the files of The New-York Historical Society with their fine collection of New York and Pennsylvania papers, Moore also had access to some of the best New England productions.

In the editing of his material, Moore limited himself for the most part to minor changes—correcting spelling, eliminating archaisms, and in some cases summarizing the commentary that gave the circumstances or origin of a given despatch. Most of his material was reproduced word for word from the original, without deletions. Although, too, the Tory press was not as abundant as the Whig, it more than made

up in quality what it lacked in quantity. Moore made sure
that it was fully represented in his book. Indeed, the reader
has to be constantly on the alert to identify the political bias
of the writer of any given despatch. This is not as easy as it
sounds. Not only is there a surprising variety of opinion and
viewpoint among the Whigs, or revolutionaries; some Tory
editors—and the most able of them, James Rivington, is the
best example—included Whig as well as Tory viewpoints in
their pages.

IV

Following the 1876 edition of the *Diary*, a long succession
of books came from Moore's pen, some of them anonymously.
We can follow his life from the journal which he kept and in
which he recorded his inner thoughts, the people that he met,
and the things that he did. These "daily notes and memoranda," as he calls them, covered the period from 1877 to
1894. The notes for some days were of considerable length;
in the last years they were much briefer. There is a wealth of
epigram, revealing a whimsical, imaginative, and restless mind.

Moore shared the alarm of other intellectuals at the growth
of irresponsible wealth and power in the post Civil War
years. "No country," he wrote, "where there are privileged
classes can long exist and be free. Laws must be enacted to
prevent the accumulation of great wealth and consequent
power. . . . Cities must cease to be the toys for rich rascals
to play with, and so must banks."[25] Even more unusual for
that time, there ran through the record of all these years the
thread of a deep, continuing concern for the lot of the
Southern Negro, forgotten and abandoned by the country
that had shed so much blood to effectuate his liberation.
Moore bewailed the burning, lynching, and endless oppression of the Negro masses. He concluded: ". . . they've got
to organize all over the nation to . . . prevent the wicked and
cruel treatment that is daily meted out to them. . . ."[26]

[25] "Notes and memoranda," November 7, 1890. New Hampshire
Historical Society mss.
[26] *Ibid.*, February 13, 1893.

The long, lonely years of labor were broken by an occasional fishing expedition, or a summer's jaunt to New England, or a business trip to Washington. In 1890 Moore was in such financial straits that he moved into a servant's room on West 12th Street. "In an attic am I," he wrote, "with nothing but an opaque skylight to tell me when the sun is up or down or mediumly under a cloud." Wistfully, he recorded the changing seasons, the changing weather, the coming of snow or hail, the scudding clouds, the sun, the patter of rain. "I am homesick," he wrote, "for a quieter and more natural place to live in, away from the righteous creatures who live upon each other quite as much as the bigger fish eat and fatten on the smaller ones."[27]

Thus, some ten years before his death in Massachusetts, in 1904,[28] one of the great scholars and historians of the American nineteenth century vanishes from our view—in a servant's attic where he toils by day, tossing restlessly at night as he listens to the chatter of women's voices in the rooms below, dreaming of the wild woods of New England where a man's soul might be at peace.

Frank Moore was a pioneer in the work of historical conservation, the safeguarding of the literary records which enshrine the American people's traditions, their national and spiritual existence. For him the conservation of the record of our people's life was as important as good soil, pure water, uncontaminated air. Moore battled against the cold indifference to human creativity that casts aside the work of the past, discards and destroys it, and values it as nothing. He was concerned, above all, with the human dimension in American history. His writings, from first to last, breathe a deep love of ordinary men and women, a faith that they can tell their own story well, and that what they experience and achieve must be preserved for the posterity for whose sake they live, battle, and suffer. The meaning of the immense labors of

[27] *Ibid.*, November 7, 1890.
[28] He died August 10, 1904, at the McLean Hospital, Belmont, Massachusetts, of a strangulated hernia. The time, place and cause of death were verified by courtesy of Edward L. Kerr, town clerk of Belmont.

Frank Moore's long life might be aptly summarized in a sentence taught him by his beloved uncle, John Weeks Moore: "Gather up the fragments that remain, that nothing be lost: tradition is a meteor which, if it once fall, can never be rekindled."[29]

The present edition of the *Diary* has been shortened by the elimination of reports or essays that in principle add little or nothing to what the reader already knows—such as news of minor skirmishes and raids, and Whig. and Tory propaganda rhetoric. The two abridged articles are so marked. A number of footnotes in which Moore provided supplementary material have also been eliminated, while others containing new and important information are incorporated in the next within square brackets. The language of the original has not been modernized and follows Moore's edition faithfully. Colloquialisms such as "Jonathan"—a British slang term for a Yankee rebel—should become clear from the context in which they are used. It is hoped that the *Diary* as here presented unfolds the events of the Revolutionary War at a somewhat more rapid pace than the original, but that it does this with the sacrifice of little or any of the writing that is at the heart of this work's usefulness and vitality.

The context will make clear whether the date under which an entry appears tells when the despatch was written or when the events described occurred. The organ in which the despatch was printed, and the date of publication, are given on the right hand side of the page at the end of the entry in question. Most of Moore's sources may be checked easily enough; a few of them remain obscure and cannot be checked. "Clift's Diary" is a case in point: This may well have been a manuscript diary in Moore's own possession that has since vanished along with the rest of his papers. "Upcott" refers to the Upcott collection of revolutionary materials in

[29] From the copyright notice to John Weeks Moore, *Historical, Biographical and Miscellaneous Gatherings Relative to Printers, Printing, Publishing and Editing of Books, Newspapers and Magazines, 1420–1886.* J. W. Moore mss, New Hampshire Historical Society.

The New-York Historical Society. But this citation is no
longer useful to us because the Society's holdings have been
reorganized and enlarged since Moore conducted his researches there.

The songs and ballads reproduced in the present edition
are taken from various sources. A few appeared in the original
editions of the *Diary*; many more are reproduced here from
Songs and Ballads of the American Revolution; some have
been taken from the broadside collections and from oral
sources. The notes that accompany these songs provide cita-
tions so that the sources may be checked. Ford, *Check List*
refers to Worthington C. Ford, *Broadsides and Ballads
Printed in Massachusetts 1639–1800* (Boston: Massachusetts
Historical Society, 1922); *Isaiah Thomas* refers to the same
compiler's check list of broadsides in the Isaiah Thomas Collection of the American Antiquarian Society—*The Isaiah
Thomas Collection of Ballads* (Worcester, Massachusetts:
American Antiquarian Society, 1924). Taken together these
two lists are a valuable guide to the nature and location of
many surviving broadsides either printed or composed during
the revolutionary period. In many cases melodies for these
songs have been provided by the present editor; their prove-
nance is explained in the notes.

The steel engravings of eminent men included in this edition of the *Diary* have been reproduced from a larger number
of illustrations originally brought together by Moore.

Four appendices have been added by the present editor.
A] lists Moore's principal newspaper and other sources, and
provides information about their place and date of publication. B] gives the titles, publishers, and dates of publication
of Moore's principal works. This is neither complete nor
exhaustive; its purpose is primarily to indicate the range and
extent of Moore's contribution to Revolutionary and Civil
War literature. c] is a selective book list of works currently
in print, many of them paperbacks, that provide fundamental
reading on various aspects of the revolutionary epoch. D]
provides special information on the sources for further study
of revolutionary songs and ballads.

In the preparation of the *Diary*, I am indebted to a number of people and institutions. Bill Bonyun first drew my attention to Frank Moore's significance as a folklore pioneer and historian; my son John W. Scott located and tracked down copies of old revolutionary broadsides; James S. Pickering, Assistant Astronomer at the Hayden Planetarium, provided information concerning the eclipse of January 9, 1777; and David C. Mearns, Chief of the Manuscript Division of the Library of Congress, undertook a search for Moore's Civil War scrapbooks. Phillip Flayderman and Daniel Kurland of Washington Square Press gave the project generous encouragement and helped it wisely to completion. The New York and the New Hampshire Historical Societies, the Essex Institute of Salem, Massachusetts, Brown and Columbia Universities, and the American Antiquarian Society all made their resources available to me. Kenneth Nesheim, Assistant Librarian at the Beinecke Rare Book Library of Yale University, and Elizabeth Eisenhart, Librarian of the American Bible Society, labored diligently to track down Moore's *Spirit of the Bible*. My wife Maria assisted with the proof.

John Anthony Scott

New York City
April, 1967

THE DIARY OF THE AMERICAN
REVOLUTION
1775-1781

PREFACE TO THE 1876 EDITION

THE MATERIALS of these volumes are taken from Whig and Tory newspapers, published during the American Revolution, private diaries, and other cotemporaneous writings. They present to the student of this day the same view the readers of the revolutionary period enjoyed—the manners and customs of the people, and the moral and religious, as well as political features of the time.

As far as practicable, the language of the writers has been preserved. For every assertion presented the reader will find an authority which must be his guide in ascertaining its value in an historical point of view; while, at the same time, he must keep in mind the truth that the errors and lampoons of a period belong as much to its history as the facts and flatteries.

Among the newspapers from which the editor has drawn his material, no one requires an especial notice in this place; a history of the periodical writers of the last century would in itself exceed the limits of these volumes. Such a work would prove an interesting and important addition to the literature of America.

In conclusion, the editor acknowledges his obligations for the many favors and facilities extended to him by the various Historical Societies of the United States, most especially to the officers of the New York Historical Society, from whom he has received the most valuable assistance.

New York, July, 1875

1775

JANUARY

January 23

PENNSYLVANIA   Saturday last, after a few days' illness, died at Philadelphia, in the fifty-fourth year of his age, universally lamented, Thomas Lawrence, Esq., Vendue Master, one of the aldermen, and for some time mayor of that city, which offices he filled with unsullied reputation. In short, benevolence marked his character, and virtue in him wore her most amiable dress, being constantly exercised in love towards his family, uprightness in his dealings, sincerity in his friendships, cheerfulness in his conversation, and an earnest desire to promote peace and happiness around him. This day his remains were deposited in the family vault in Christ Church burying-ground, attended by a very large number of respectable citizens. The funeral was conducted agreeable to the resolves of the Continental Congress. ["On the death of any relation or friend, none of us, or any of our families, will go into any further mourning-dress than a black crape or ribbon on the arm or hat, for gentlemen; and a black ribbon and necklace for ladies; and we will discontinue the giving of gloves and scarfs at funerals." *Journals of Congress*, October 20, 1774.]
New York Gazette and Weekly Mercury, January 30

January 28

NEW YORK   Yesterday the house, barn, and barrack of Jacob Van Binschola, of Poughkeepsie, Dutchess County, was burnt to the ground, together with every thing therein con-

1

tained. The villainous action was perpetrated by a Negro fellow belonging to the family, who some time before had been
corrected by his master. Confessing his guilt, he has been
tried and burnt to-day.

New York Gazette and Weekly Mercury, February 13

FEBRUARY

February 16

NEW YORK   On Thursday morning, the 2d instant, the
ship *James*, Captain Watson, arrived at New York from
Glasgow, with a cargo of coals and dry goods, but as she did
not arrive within the time prescribed by the tenth article of
the association of the Continental Congress, a strict watch
was constantly kept, by some of the subcommittee, and a
number of inhabitants, to prevent the landing of any goods,
in a clandestine manner; and the captain was requested to
procure such necessaries as he might stand in need of, and
immediately quit the port. With this request, he seemed
rather unwilling to comply, and was encouraged to hope from
the assurances of a number of ministerial tools, who promised
to support him, that his cargo would be landed; for which
purpose they employed a few vagrants to go on board the
ship, which then lay in the harbor, and bring the colors on
shore, with a view of raising a posse, to assist in landing the
goods; but the banditti that were collected for this purpose
were soon suppressed by the inhabitants, who are for supporting the association, and who began to assemble in great numbers; upon which the captain, conceiving the ship to be in
great danger, sent the mate on shore, requesting assistance
to get her under sail, as the seamen refused to do that duty.
This request being complied with, they immediately got her
under weigh, and fell down about four miles below the city,
where she remained, attended by a boat, with a member of
the committee and some of the townsmen on board, till last

Thursday night (9th), when she was again brought into the harbor, by an officer and a number of men belonging to his Majesty's ship *King Fisher*; which ship it is supposed came down from Turtle Bay expressly for the purpose of protecting her, and intimidating the inhabitants.

As soon as it was known that the ship was coming up again, the people, highly exasperated, began to assemble together in great numbers, and immediately went to the captain's lodgings; seized him, and after conducting him through many of the principal streets, attended by a prodigious concourse of people, he was, without suffering the least hurt or injury, put on board a boat, with some hands to row him, and sent off. His ship then lying at anchor ten miles below the town, he went on board the man-of-war, which lay in the harbor, where his own ship did not arrive until the next morning, when she came to anchor under the cannon of the *King Fisher*. In this situation matters remained until Saturday, when they began to unmoor the ship, intending to get under sail, but were prevented by the lieutenant of the man-of-war, who hailed the ship, and demanded if they had a clearance. Being assured in the negative he ordered them not to unmoor. This obstruction greatly exasperated a number of people that were collected to see her get under sail, who went in quest of the captain of the *King Fisher*, to know by what authority he detained the ship, but they could not meet with him; he was, however, soon after waited upon, by one of the gentlemen to whom the ship was consigned, and on being informed of the lieutenant's conduct, and asked his reasons for detaining her, he replied that he had nothing to do with her, and immediately gave orders to let her pass. Accordingly she got under sail the next morning about ten o'clock, accompanied by a boat, with two of the committee and a number of inhabitants on board; which boat, after taking out the pilot, left her at two o'clock P.M., about a league to the southward of Sandy Hook, with a fresh gale, and at half-past four o'clock she was out of sight.

As every artifice has been used, and a variety of manœuvres put in practice, by a set of ministerial hirelings, to procure the landing of the cargo of this ship, it must give real pleasure to every lover of this country to observe that the good people of New York are determined to support the association of the General Congress at all events.

New-York Journal, February 16

MARYLAND   It appears that the inhabitants of Maryland are all in motion; forming county meetings, choosing committees of observation to carry into effectual execution, without fear, favor, or partiality, the measures recommended by the grand Continental Congress, and forming companies to learn the art military. Anne Arundel County, including the citizens of Annapolis, have resolved that every person who should refuse to contribute to the purchase of arms and ammunition for the use of that county, before the first of this month (Feb.), shall be deemed an enemy to America, and his name published in the *Maryland Gazette*. The General Assembly of New Jersey have approved of the proceedings of the Continental Congress, and instructed their delegates to propose and agree to every reasonable and constitutional measure for the accommodation of the unhappy differences at present subsisting between the mother country and the colonies.

Upcott, IV, 297

NEW YORK   On Friday last, at Messrs. Sharp and Curtenius's furnace, in New York, a cylinder was cast for the steam-engine of the waterworks now in course of erection in that city. This is the first performance of the kind ever attempted in America, and allowed by judges to be extremely well executed.

Rivington's Gazette, February 16

February 18

NEW JERSEY   A few days ago a riot occurred at Elizabethtown in Jersey. The scene opened between twelve and one o'clock, with seizing a poor Staten Islander, for no other crime than because some people of that ever loyal island were supposed to have been ready to assist in landing some goods from Captain Watson's Scotch ship, which lately left New York, and is departed with his cargo for Jamaica, having arrived at New York after the first of February, the day limited by the Congress for the importation of goods. The man's boat was dragged ashore, and his oysters distributed to the hungry vagabonds, who were visibly headed in the centre of the town, by Jonathan Hampton, a Justice of the Peace, a Judge of the county court, and chairman of the committee. Hampton was the man who attempted lately to obstruct the passage of his Majesty's royal regiment of Ireland, over the ferries, and prevented wagons from carrying their baggage; this same Hampton was the man who raised a riot lately in Sussex County, attacked a peddler, and destroyed his property. About four o'clock, when the mob discharged the poor oyster man, they proceeded to abuse all the people in the town who were known to be well affected to the constitution; they erected a gallows, in order more particularly to insult them, and fixed up a liberty pole in the middle of the town. It must be observed, that the worshipful Judge, Jonathan Hampton, was, as usual, completely drunk when the riot commenced. For the honor of the police, it must be recorded, that two of the aldermen, Messrs. Blanchard and Dayton, exerted themselves greatly to suppress those violences, but they were only able to check them. Two of the *Delegates* contributed towards a collection that was made for their ever-staunch friends the *mob*. Mr. Alderman Blanchard ordered the gallows to be demolished, after it had existed two hours; and their deity, the liberty pole, was struck by an order from the committee, without the consent of that exemplary and able guarantee of American freedom, the righteous and immaculate Judge Jonathan Hampton.

This was a glorious day to the sons of licentiousness; and it was also a glorious day to the sons of loyalty; for it has made in Elizabethtown more proselytes to the side of order and government, than all the other endeavors that have been exerted to abate the fever of the times.

Rivington's Gazette, March 2

February 20

MASSACHUSETTS   The Provincial Congress of Massachusetts Bay has resolved: that the great law of self-preservation

calls upon the inhabitants of that colony, immediately to prepare against every attempt that may be made to attack them
by surprise. And, upon serious deliberation, most earnestly
recommended to the militia in general, as well as the detached
part of it in minute-men, that they spare neither time, pains,
nor expenses, at so critical a juncture, in perfecting themselves
forthwith in military discipline; and that skilful instructors be
provided for those companies which are not already provided
therewith. It also recommends to the towns and districts in
that colony, that they encourage such persons as are skilled
in the manufactory of fire-arms and .bayonets, diligently to
apply themselves there for supplying such of the inhabitants
as shall be deficient.

They have since adjourned to the twenty-second of next
month, then to meet at Concord, an inland town, about eighteen miles from Boston.

New York Gazette and Weekly Mercury, February 27

MARCH

March 8

MASSACHUSETTS   A writer in Boston addresses the Provincial Congress of Massachusetts as follows:—

"Your assuming the government of Massachusetts Bay,
makes it unnecessary for me to make any apology for address-
ing you in this public manner, further, than by acquainting
you that it is to represent to you the distresses of some of
those people, who, from a sense of their duty to the King, and
a reverence for his laws, have behaved quietly and peaceably;
and for which reason they have been deprived of their liberty,
abused in their persons, and suffered such barbarous cruelties,
insults, and indignities, besides the loss of their property, by
the hands of lawless mobs and riots, as would have been disgraceful even for savages to have committed. The courts of
justice being shut up in most parts of the province, and the

justices of those courts compelled by armed force, headed by some who are members of your Congress, to refrain from doing their duties, at present it is rendered impracticable for those sufferers to obtain redress, unless it be by your interposition, or the aid of military force, which will be applied for in case this application fails. A particular enumeration of all the instances referred to, is apprehended unnecessary, as many of your members are personally knowing to them, and for the information of any of you who may pretend ignorance of them, the following instances are here mentioned.

"In August last, a mob in Berkshire forced the justices of the Court of Common Pleas from their seats, and shut up the court-house. They also drove David Ingersoll from his house, and damaged the same, and he was obliged to leave his estate; after which his enclosures were laid waste. At Taunton, Daniel Leonard was driven from his house, and bullets fired into it by the mob, and he obliged to take refuge in Boston, for the supposed crime of obeying his Majesty's requisition as one of his council for this province. Colonel Gilbert, of Freetown, a firm friend to government, in August last being at Dartmouth, was attacked at midnight by a mob of about an hundred, but by his bravery, with the assistance of the family where he lodged, they were beaten off. The same night Brigadier Ruggles was also attacked by another party, who were routed after having painted and cut the hair off of one of his horse's mane and tail. Afterwards he had his arms taken from his dwelling-house in Hardwick, all of which are not yet returned. He had at another time a very valuable English horse, which was kept as a stallion, poisoned, his family disturbed, and himself obliged to take refuge in Boston, after having been insulted in his own house, and twice on his way, by a mob. The chief justice of the province in Middleborough, was threatened to be stopped on the highway in going to Boston court, but his firmness and known resolution, supporting government in this as well as many other instances, intimidated the mob from laying hands on him; he was also threatened with opposition in going into court, but the terror of the troops prevented. The whole bench were hissed by a mob as they came out of court.

"In September, Mr. Sewall, his Majesty's Attorney-General for Massachusetts Bay, was obliged to repair to Boston for refuge. His house at Cambridge was attacked by a mob, and his windows were broken, but the mob was beaten off by the gallant behavior and bravery of some young gentlemen of his family. About the same time the Lieutenant-Governor Oliver, president of his Majesty's council, was attacked at Cambridge, by a mob of about four thousand, and was compelled to resign his seat at the board, since which, upon further threats, he has been obliged to leave his estate, and take refuge with his family in Boston.

"At Worcester, a mob of about five thousand collected, prevented the Court of Common Pleas from sitting, (about one thousand of them had fire-arms,) and all drawn up in two files, compelled the judges, sheriffs, and gentlemen of the bar, to pass them with cap in hand, and read their disavowal of holding courts under the new acts of parliament, not less than thirty times in their procession. Daniel Oliver, Esq., of Hardwick, was disarmed by a mob, and has been obliged to take refuge in Boston, to the total loss of his business. Colonel Phips, the very reputable and highly esteemed sheriff of the county of Middlesex, by a large mob was obliged to promise not to serve any processes of courts, and to retire to Boston for protection from further insults. Colonel Saltonstall, the very humane sheriff of the county of Essex, has been obliged to take refuge in Boston, to screen himself from the violence of the mob. The Court of Common Pleas was forbidden to sit at Taunton, by a large mob, with a justice acting as one of their committee. At Middleborough, Peter Oliver, Esq., was obliged to sign a paper, not to execute his office, under the new acts. At Springfield, the Courts of Common Pleas and General Sessions of the Peace, were prevented sitting by a large mob, who kept the justices from entering the courthouse, and obliged them, the sheriff, and gentlemen of the bar, to desist, with their hats off, from holding any courts. Colonel Edson, one of his Majesty's council, has been driven from his house in Bridgewater, and kept from it ever since last August, for being a friend to government, and accepting his Majesty's appointment as counsellor.

"The Courts of General Session of the Peace and inferior Courts of Common Pleas for the County of Plymouth, have been shut up. In August, Colonel Putnam of Worcester, a firm friend to Government, had two fat cows stolen and taken from him, and a very valuable grist-mill burnt, and was obliged to leave a fair estate in Worcester, and retire to Boston, where he has been ever since, for his protesting against riots, &c. Colonel Murray, of Rutland, one of his Majesty's council, has been obliged to leave a large estate in the country, and repair to Boston to save himself from being handled by the mob, and compelled to resign his seat at council board. His house has been attacked, his family put in fear. Colonel Vassall, of Cambridge, from intolerable threats, and insolent treatment by mobs, of his friends and himself, has left his elegant seat there, and retired to Boston, with his amiable family, for protection. John Borland, Esq., is in the same predicament with Colonel Vassall. Honorable John Chandler, Esq., judge of probate, &c., for the county of Worcester, has been obliged to retreat to Boston for protection, and leave his business, and a numerous family of hopeful youths behind him, with great reluctance, and who, before he came away, was ordered by the mob to hold his office till further orders.

"The Plymouth protesters, addressers, and military officers, were compelled by a mob of two thousand, collected from Plymouth and Barnstable counties, to recant and resign their military commissions. Thomas Foster, Esq., an ancient gentleman, was obliged to run into the woods, and had like to have been lost, and the mob, although the justices, with Mr. Foster, were sitting in the town, ransacked his house, and damaged his furniture. He was obnoxious as a friend to government, and for that reason they endeavored to deprive him of his business, and to prevent even his taking the acknowledgment of a deed. Richard Clark, Esq., a consignee of the tea, was obliged to retire from Salem to Boston, as an asylum; and his son Isaac went to Plymouth to collect debts, but in the night was assaulted by a mob and obliged to get out of town at midnight. Jesse Dunbar, of Halifax, in Plymouth County, bought some fat cattle of Mr. Thomas the counsellor, and drove them to Plymouth for sale; one of the oxen being

skinned and hung up, the committee came to him, and finding
he bought it of Mr. Thomas, they put the ox into a cart, and
fixing Dunbar in his belly, carted him four miles, and there
made him pay a dollar, after taking three more cattle and a
horse from him. The Plymouth mob delivered him to the
Kingston mob, which carted him four miles further, and forced
from him another dollar, then delivered him to the Duxbor-
ough mob, who abused him by throwing the tripe in his face,
and endeavoring to cover him with it to the endangering his
life. They then threw dirt at him, and after other abuses
carried him to said Thomas's house, and made him pay another sum of money, and he not taking the beef, they flung it
in the road and quitted him. Daniel Dunbar, of Halifax, an
ensign of militia there, had his colors demanded by the mob,
some of the selectmen being the chief actors. He refused; they
broke into his house, took him out, forced him upon a rail,
and after keeping him for two or three hours in such abuses,
he was forced to give his colors up to save his life.

"A constable of Hardwick, for refusing to pay his collections,
directly contrary to the oath of his office, was bound and confined six and thirty hours, and threatened with being sent to
Simsbury mines. His wife being dangerously ill, he was released
after signing a something which one of the mob had prepared
for him. The mob committee of the county of York, ordered
that no one should hire any of Sir William Pepperell's estates,
buy no wood of him, or pay any debts due to him. In February,
at Plymouth, a number of ladies attempted to divert themselves
at their assembly room, but the mob collected, (the committee having met previous thereto,) and flung stones which broke
the shutters and windows, and endangered their lives. They
were forced to get out of the hall, and were pelted and abused
to their own homes. After this the ladies diverted themselves
by riding out, but were followed by a mob, pelted and abused,
with the most indecent Billingsgate language. These things
happened at the time when some of the people of Plymouth,
in conjunction with the committee men from other towns in
that county, aided and assisted by four dissenting clergymen,
were presenting to General Gage, by their memorial, the

peaceable state they were in before the arrival of a party of
soldiers at Marshfield, in that county.

"The Honorable Israel Williams, Esq., one who was appointed of his Majesty's new council, but had declined the
office through infirmity of body, was taken from his house by
the mob in the night, carried several miles, put into a room
with a fire, the chimney at the top, the doors of the room
closed, and kept there for many hours in the smoke, till his
life was in danger; then he was carried home, after being
forced to sign what they ordered, and a guard placed over
him to prevent his leaving the house.

"To recount the suffering of all from mobs, rioters, and
trespassers, would take more time and paper than can be
spared for that purpose. It is hoped the foregoing will be
sufficient to put you upon the use of proper means and measures for giving relief to all that have been injured by such
unlawful and wicked practices."

Rivington's Gazette, March 9

March 9

MASSACHUSETTS   As the populace of Boston have thought
fit to repeal the tarring and feathering act, the King's troops
have thought fit to revive the said statute; and in consequence
of such a determination, to-day they gave us a specimen of a
royal mob. The soldiers have been encouraged by their officers
to take every method of tricking the unwary. Yesterday, an
honest countryman was inquiring for a firelock, when a soldier
hearing him, said he had one he would sell. Away goes the
ignoramus, and after paying the soldier very honestly for the
gun, (which was only an old one without a lock,) was walking
off when half a dozen seized him and hurried the poor fellow
away under guard, for a breach of the act against trading with
the soldiers. After keeping him in duress all night, this morning, instead of carrying him before a magistrate, who on
complaint would have fined him, (as has been the case in
several instances,) the officers condemned him without a hearing, to be tarred and feathered, which sentence has been
executed.

After stripping him naked and covering him with tar and feathers, they mounted him on a one-horse truck, and surrounding the truck with a guard of twenty soldiers with fixed bayonets, accompanied with all the drums and fifes of the regiment, (forty-seventh,) and a number of officers, Negroes, and sailors, exhibited him as a spectacle through the principal streets of the town. They fixed a label on the man's back, on which was written AMERICAN LIBERTY, OR A SPECIMEN OF DEMOCRACY; and to add to the insult they played Yankee Doodle:—Oh Britain, how art thou fallen! Is it not enough that British troops, who were once the terror of France and Spain, should be made the instruments of butchering thy children! but must they descend also to exploits too infamously dirty for any but the meanest of the mobility to practice? What a wretched figure will the Boston expedition hereafter make in the historic page!

New-York Journal, March 30

March 11

VIRGINIA   This day the "freeholders of Botetourt," in Virginia, instructed their representatives as follows: "We require you to represent us with hearts replete with the most grateful and loyal veneration for the race of Brunswick, for they have been truly our fathers; and at the same time the most dutiful affection for our sovereign, of whose honest heart we cannot entertain any diffidence, but sorry we are to add, that in his councils we can no longer confide. A set of miscreants unworthy to administer the laws of Britain's empire, have been permitted impiously to sway. How unjustly, cruelly, and tyrannically they have invaded our rights we need not now put you in mind.

"We only say, and we assert it with pride, that the subjects of Britain are *one*, and when the honest man of Boston, who has broken no law, has his property wrested from him, the hunter of the Alleghanies must take the alarm, and as a freeman of America, he will fly to the representatives, and thus instruct them: 'Gentlemen, my gun, my tomahawk, my life, I desire you to tender to the honor of my King and country;

but my LIBERTY to range these woods upon the same terms my father has done, is not mine to give up. It was not purchased by me, and purchased it was. It is entailed upon my son, and the tenure is sacred. Watch over it, gentlemen, for to him it must descend unviolated, if my arm can defend it; but if not, if wicked power is permitted to prevail against me, the original purchase was blood, and mine shall seal the surrender.'

"That our countrymen, and the world may know our disposition, we choose that this be published. And we have one request to add, that is, that the SONS OF WORTH AND FREEDOM, who appeared for us at Philadelphia, will accept our most ardent grateful acknowledgments. And we hereby plight them our faith, that we will religiously observe their resolutions, and obey their instructions, in contempt of power and temporary interest; and should the measures they have wisely calculated for our relief fail, *we will stand prepared for every contingency*."

New-York Journal, March 30

March 19

MASSACHUSETTS   Since the army have found the season has passed for nature's forming a bridge from Boston, they become abusive and insulting. They are now finishing their fortifications on the Neck, by picketing each side. Thursday last being recommended by the Provincial Congress to be a day of fasting and prayer, on the morning of that day the society at the west end of Boston were greatly disturbed by a party of officers and soldiers of the fourth or the King's own regiment. When the people were assembling, they brought two marquee tents, and pitched them within ten yards of the meeting-house, then sent for three drums and three fifes, and kept them beating and playing till the service was over.

In the evening of the next day, Colonel Hancock's elegant seat, situated near the common, was attacked by a number of officers, who, with their swords, cut and hacked the fence before his house in a most scandalous manner, and behaved very abusively, by breaking people's windows, and insulting almost every person they met.

Yesterday the Neck guard seized a quantity of musket cartridges with ball, (we suppose through the information of some dirty scoundrel, many of which we now have among us,) and about three thousand pounds of ball, which were being carried into the country. This was private property. The owner applied to the General first, but he absolutely refused to deliver it. They abused the teamster very much, and run a bayonet into his neck. The same evening a number of officers heated with liquor, (as it is said,) with drawn swords ran through the streets, like what they really were, madmen, cutting every one they met. The stage coach just arrived from Providence, passing by, they attacked it, broke the glass, and abused the passengers. The driver being a smart fellow jumped off his seat, caught one of them, Captain G. [Gore], and some blows passed, when the officer retired not much to his credit.

To-day Colonel Hancock was again much insulted by a number of inferior officers and privates, who entered his inclosures, and refused to retire after his requesting them so to do; telling him that his house, stables, &c., would soon be theirs, and then they would do as they pleased. However, on his application to the General, he immediately sent one of his aide-de-camps to the officer of the guard at the bottom of the common, to seize any officer or private who should molest Colonel Hancock, or any inhabitant, in their lawful calling.

Upcott, IV, 301

March 20

MASSACHUSETTS We are constantly agitated by hearing complaints from different persons of the more than savage barbarity of the soldiers in Boston, encouraged and often joined and headed by the officers. They are now become so insolent that it is hardly safe to walk the streets at noonday, and there seems to be no check or control. But they are rather countenanced and encouraged by their superiors, in their lawless outrages. They appear to be a banditti of lawless freebooters, just let loose upon us, for the innocent and laudable purpose of robberies, rapes, and murders; nor can we at present see any prospect of avoiding these calamities, but by a general evacuation of the town. The late news seems to increase their insolence, which was barely tolerable before. The reason is obvious. The common soldiers and their wives have frequently and loudly complained of the fallacy and injustice of the officers, who promised them fine houses, rich plunder, and a thousand other gratifications, which they hoped to be in possession of long before this. These expectations have undoubtedly prevented the desertion of hundreds. But they grow more and more impatient, so that we fear violence will, sooner or later, take place, let what will be the determinations in England, unless some method can be adopted to prevent or restrain them, tantamount to leaving the town, as the people in general do not seem inclined to go out.

Letter from Boston
Newport Mercury, April 3
Pennsylvania Journal, April 12

March 30

MASSACHUSETTS   This morning at daylight, the troops at Boston beat to arms, and five regiments marched out, with Earl Percy at their head. It was supposed they were going to Concord, where the Provincial Congress is now sitting. A quantity of provisions and warlike stores are lodged there. Several expresses were immediately sent away to give notice of their marching. Important consequences were apprehended; but, happily, they only went a few miles out, and then returned. The town and country were alarmed, and many of them got equipped for a march. It has given such uneasiness, that committees from twelve of the near towns have met upon it; and intend sending a petition to the Provincial Congress, representing this affair to them, and desiring they will take up the matter, and remonstrate with the General upon it. The troops went out of the common road, marched over the people's land, where their grain was sown, and through their gardens; broke down their fences, walls, &c., and did other injuries. It is thought such proceedings will bring on bad consequences, if not prevented.

The late conduct of the Regulars in Boston, in tarring and feathering a countryman, headed by one of their colonels, and other officers, and the spirited remonstrance it occasioned from the selectmen of the town of Billerica, to General Gage, has made much talk. The military spirit and resolution prevailing in this province, in support of their liberties and constitution, is astonishing. We hope we shall soon have some good news from home, to prevent any breaking out, which we begin to fear, especially if the troops continue their marchings out. It is said that forty or fifty of the troops were so fatigued by their march, that they could not keep up with their fellow-soldiers, on their return. It is also said they are intending to go out again soon.

Letter from Boston, April 1
Pennsylvania Journal, April 12

MASSACHUSETTS   The following is the remonstrance presented to General Gage:—May it please your Excellency:—We the selectmen of the town of Billerica, beg leave to remonstrate to your Excellency, that on the Eighth of March last, one Thomas Ditson, an inhabitant of said town of Billerica, was tarred and feathered and very much abused by a party of his Majesty's forty-seventh regiment, under the command of Lieut.-Col. Nesbitt. As guardians for said town, and from a regard for the liberties and properties of its inhabitants, we cannot but resent this procedure. Your Excellency must be sensible that this act is a *high infraction* on that personal security which every Englishman is entitled to; and without which his boasted constitution is but a name. It is sufficiently unhappy for us that we find troops quartered among us for the purpose of enforcing obedience to acts of Parliament, in the highest sense iniquitous, cruel, and unjust. It is still more unhappy, if these troops, instead of preserving the character which British troops once had, should pour in additional insult, and be guilty of the most brutal outrages. * * * Lieutenant-Colonel Nesbitt is an officer under your Excellency's command. Of *you*, therefore, we DEMAND satisfaction for the insult committed by him. We think it is in your power. We beg your Excellency that the breach now too wide between Great Britain and this Province, may not by such brutality still be increased. We assure you, sir, it always has been, and still is, our sentiment and prayer, that harmony may be restored, and that we may not be driven to the last distress of nations:— But may it please your Excellency, we must tell you, we are determined, if the innocent inhabitants of our country towns must be interrupted by soldiers, in their lawful intercourse with the town of Boston, and treated with the most brutish ferocity, we shall hereafter use a different style from that of petition and complaint. If the grand bulwarks of our constitution are thus violently torn away, and the powers on earth prove unfriendly to the cause of virtue, liberty, and humanity, we are still happy. We can appeal to Him who judgeth righteously; and to Him we cheerfully leave the event.

New-York Journal, March 30

A New SONG,

To animate and exhort the SONS of LIBERTY to stand for their PROPERTY, &c.

———— • ————

During the colonial period many "broadsides" were struck off by the presses and circulated among the people. These were proclamations, laws, speeches, sermons, funeral odes or other verses printed upon one or both sides of a single sheet of paper. When the revolutionary period arrived, broadsides were put to a new use and became a weapon of propaganda; songwriters hastened to exploit this medium. Some of the finest songs and ballads of the Revolution that survive first appeared as broadsides. "A New Song . . ." is reproduced here from a Boston sheet that made its appearance some time during 1774 or 1775. It is an altogether excellent expression of the popular mood on the threshold of the struggle with Britain. (Harris Collection, Brown University.)

A

New SONG,

To animate and exhort the SONS of

Liberty

To ſtand for their PROPERTY, &c.

ATTEND ye ſons of liberty,
For this my voice is unto thee;
O thou, my friends, AMERICA,
It is with us a darkſome day.

The noon-day's like a darkſome night,
Which dims our pleaſures and delight;
But all theſe darkſome clouds behold,
Shall from before our eyes be roll'd.

Tho' enemies 'gainſt us reſide,
God ſurely will cut off their pride;
New-England planted by his hand,
In ſpite of all it's foes ſhall ſtand.

God is our ſtrength and chief delight,
The Lord upon our ſide ſhall fight:
God has defeated all the foes
That e'er againſt New-England roſe.

It is in GOD we put our truſt,
Our foes he will tread to the duſt;
O! how can they expect to ſtand,
And fight againſt their maker's hand?

O Vanity of Vanities!
What darkneſs is before their eyes!
Our fathers left their native land,
And came here but a little band.

They chang'd the land of their diſtreſs
For this then howling wilderneſs;
They found the land hard to ſubdue,
And their numbers but very few.

And here they found a ſavage crew,
Which they conquer'd with much ado;
Here they did meet with much diſtreſs,
Their blood did paint this wilderneſs.

I think they fairly bought the land
Where now upon their children ſtand;
Then let us ſtand both firm and ſtrong,
And ſee that none doth do us wrong.

Our liberties now let us hold,
Which is in value more than gold;
If we our liberties ſhould looſe,
How could we our religion chooſe?

The croſs we muſt then ſurely ſee,
Which ought to be on Calvary;
Tho' hell and earth ſhould both combine,
Yet w' will not in the leaſt incline.

The more our enemies incloſe,
The ſtronger let us them oppoſe;
We are become a mighty band,
God's church doth firm among us ſtand.

We are peculiar to the Lord,
And ſhall we fear a feeble ſword?
Be ſure the Lord is on our ſide,
And all our wants ſhall be ſupply'd.

He ſendeth food to us from far,
For to ſupport us in our war;
When this people ſhall once ariſe,
Then wo be to their enemies.

They can't environ us around,
Though they may ſpoil our chiefeſt towns,
What ſhall this town compared be
To all this our land and country?

When tories come to us in Grief,
O let us grant them no relief;
Can we for their proſperity
Pray to the Lord that dwells on high.

Tories muſt to deſtruction go,
And popiſh prieſt and friars too;
For theſe are but the devil's crew,
Which God's armies ſhall ſoon ſubdue

To ſhut up yourſelves I you intreat,
To pray while they curſe in the ſtreet;
Let patience all our ſouls poſſeſs,
For God will ſoon end our diſtreſs.

A *New Song, To animate and exhort the Sons of Liberty.* Boston broadside, 1774 or 1775. An excellent expression of the popular mood at the opening of the struggle with Britain. Reproduced from the Harris Collection of Brown University, by permission.

Attend ye sons of liberty,
For this my voice is unto thee;
O thou, my friends, AMERICA,
It is with us a darksome day.

The noon-day's like a darksome night,
Which dims our pleasures and delight;
But all these darksome clouds behold,
Shall from before our eyes be roll'd.

Tho' enemies 'gainst us reside,
God surely will cut off their pride;
New-England planted by his hand,
In spite of all its foes shall stand.

God is our strength and chief delight,
The Lord upon our side shall fight:
God has defeated all the foes
That e'er against New-England rose.

It is in GOD we put our trust,
Our foes he will tread to the dust;
O! how can they expect to stand,
And fight against their maker's hand?

O Vanity of Vanities!
What darkness is before their eyes!
Our fathers left their native land,
And came here but a little band.

They chang'd the land of their distress
For this then howling wilderness;
They found the land hard to subdue,
And their numbers but very few.

And here they found a savage crew,
Which they conquer'd with much ado;
Here they did meet with much distress,
Their blood did paint this wilderness.

I think they fairly bought the land
Where now upon their children stand;
Then let us stand both firm and strong,
And see that none doth do us wrong.

Our liberties now let us hold,
Which is in value more than gold;
If we our liberties should loose,
How could we our religion choose?

The cross we must then surely see,
Which ought to be on Calvary;
Tho' hell and earth should both combine,
Yet we will not in the least incline.

The more our enemies inclose,
The stronger let us them oppose;
We are become a mighty band,
God's church doth firm among us stand.

We are peculiar to the Lord,
And shall we fear a feeble sword?
Be sure the Lord is on our side,
And all our wants shall be supply'd.

He sendeth food to us from far,
For to support us in our war;
When this people shall once arise,
Then wo be to their enemies.

They can't environ us around,
Though they may spoil our chiefest towns,
What shall this town compared be
To all this our land and country?

When Tories come to us in Grief,
O let us grant them no relief;
Can we for their prosperity
Pray to the Lord that dwells on high?

Tories must to destruction go,
And popish priest and fryars too;
For these are but the devil's crew,
Which God's armies shall soon subdue.

To shut up yourselves I you intreat,
To pray while they curse in the street;
Let patience all our souls possess,
For God will soon end our distress.

APRIL

April 3

SOUTH CAROLINA   This day the committee at New York received a letter from the general committee of South Carolina, in which they say: "The present struggle seems to us most glorious and critical. We seem to ourselves to stand upon the very division line between all the blessings of freedom, and the most abject vassalage. The very idea of an earthly power, which shall bind the present and future millions of America, in all cases whatsoever; in the direction of which we are to have no more voice than our oxen, and over which we can have no constitutional control, fills us with horror. To hold not only our liberty and property at will, but our lives also, as well as the lives of all our posterity! To be absolutely dependent for the air in which we breathe, and the water which we drink, upon a set of men at the distance; who, even when they abuse that power, are out of the reach of our vengeance, is a proposal which this colony hears with indignation, and can only submit to when there is no possible remedy. By the late detestable acts of the British Parliament respecting America, all mankind will judge whether that body may be safely entrusted with such a power. We have now appealed to the remaining justice of the nation; we have endeavored to arouse them to a sense of their own dangers; we have appealed to their mercantile interests for our defence. Our hopes of success are not yet damped by any thing but the possibility of disunion among ourselves. We have the pleasure to inform you, that in this colony, the association takes place as effectually as law itself. Sundry vessels from England have been already obliged to return with their merchandise, or have thrown it overboard as common ballast.

"We may assure you of our fixed determination to adhere to the resolutions at all hazards, and that ministerial opposition is here obliged to be silent; we wish for the day when it shall be silenced among you likewise. And whatever noise is made by the friends of arbitrary rule, about the design of those proceedings in your House of Assembly, we cannot, and will not believe that you intend to desert the cause. We feel ourselves bound to you by the closest ties of interest and affection. We consider this season as big with American glory, or with American infamy, and, therefore, most ardently wish you the direction and aid of that Almighty Being, who presides over all.

"We confidently expect to meet you in General Congress at Philadelphia, with hearts full of zeal in our country's cause, and full of mutual confidence in the integrity of each other."

Dunlap's Pennsylvania Packet, April 10

April 7

NORTH CAROLINA   Last Tuesday, [4th,] Governor Martin met the Assembly of North Carolina, at Newbern, and addressed them in a high-flying, abusive, anti-American speech, in which he spoke hard things of all the colonies, congresses, committees, and people on this continent, except those of his own stamp, and begged of his assembly not to approve of sending delegates to the Congress in May. To this the Assembly returned a truly noble answer, and to-day they have passed the following resolution: "That the House do highly approve of the proceedings of the Continental Congress lately held at Philadelphia, and that they are determined, as members of the community in general, that they will strictly adhere to the said resolutions, and will use the influence they have to induce the same observance by every individual of this colony."

New-York Journal, April 27

April 11

NEW YORK   This morning a very respectable number of freeholders and inhabitants of the county of Westchester, assembled at the White Plains, agreeable to notice given, that their sentiments might be known concerning the choice of a committee, to meet other committees in the city of New York, for the purpose of choosing delegates to the next Continental Congress.

The friends to order and government met at the house of Captain Hatfield. Those who were for a committee, put up at another public house in the town. About twelve o'clock, word was brought to the gentlemen at Captain Hatfield's, that the opposite party had already entered upon the business of the day; upon which they immediately walked down to the court-house, although not half of their friends who were expected had yet appeared; where they found the other company collected in a body. The numbers on each side seemed to be nearly equal, and both together might amount to two hundred, or, at most, to two hundred and fifty. The friends to government then declared, that as they had been unlawfully called together, and for an unlawful purpose, they did not intend to contest the matter with them by a poll, which would be tacitly acknowledging the authority that had summoned them, but that they came only with a design to protest against all such disorderly proceedings, and to show their detestation of all unlawful committees and congresses. They then declared their determined resolution to continue steadfast in their allegiance to their gracious and merciful sovereign, King George the Third; to submit to lawful authority, and to abide by and support the only true representatives of the people of the colony, the General Assembly. Then giving three huzzas, they returned to Captain Hatfield's, singing, as they went, with a loyal enthusiasm, the grand and animating song of "God save great George our King, / Long live our noble King," &c. At their return, finding that many of their friends had arrived during their absence, and that many still kept coming in, they proceeded to draw up, and sign a *declaration*, which they seemed to do with as much patriotic zeal as ever warmed the hearts of true and faithful subjects.

The following is the declaration:—"We, the subscribers, freeholders and inhabitants of the county of Westchester, having assembled at the White Plains, in consequence of certain advertisements, do now declare that we met here to express our honest abhorrence of all unlawful congresses and committees, and that we are determined, at the hazard of our lives and properties, to support the King and Constitution, and that we acknowledge no representatives but the General Assembly, to whose wisdom and integrity we submit the guardianship of our rights, liberties, and privileges."—This was signed by a large body of the residents of Westchester County.

Rivington's Gazette, April 20

April 19

MASSACHUSETTS About ten o'clock last night, the troops in Boston were discovered to be in motion in a very secret manner, and it was found they were embarking in boats which they had privately brought to the place in the evening at the lower end of the common. Expresses set off immediately to alarm the country, that they might be on their guard. When they were passing about a mile beyond Lexington, they were stopped by a party of officers who came out of Boston in the afternoon of that day, and were seen lurking in bye-places in the country until after dark. One of the expresses immediately fled, and was pursued a long distance by an officer, who, when he had overtaken him, presented a pistol and cried out, "You're a dead man if you don't stop!" but he kept on until he gained a house, when, stopping suddenly, he was thrown from his horse; and having the presence of mind to call out to the people of the house, "Turn out! turn out! I've got one of them!" the officer immediately retreated as fast as he had pursued. The other express [Paul Revere] after undergoing a strict examination, was allowed to depart.

The body of the troops, in the mean time, under the command of Lieutenant-Colonel Smith, had crossed the river and landed at Phipps' farm. They proceeded with great silence to Lexington, six miles below Concord. A company of militia, numbering about eighty men, had mustered near the meeting-house. Just before sunrise the King's troops came in sight, when the militia began to disperse. The troops then set out upon the road, hallooing and huzzaing, and coming within a few rods of them, the commanding officer cried out in words to this effect, "Disperse, you damned rebels! damn you, disperse!" upon which the troops again huzzaed, and at the same time one or two officers discharged their pistols, which were instantaneously followed by the firing of four or five of the soldiers, and then there seemed to be a general discharge from the whole. It is to be noticed, they fired upon the militia as they were dispersing agreeably to their command, and that they did not even return the fire. Eight of our men were killed, and nine wounded. The troops then laughed, and damned the Yankees, and said they could not bear the smell of gunpowder.

Soon after this action, the troops renewed their march to Concord, where they divided into parties, and went directly to the several places where the province stores were deposited. Each party was supposed to have a Tory pilot. One body went into the jail yard, and spiked and otherwise damaged the cannon belonging to the province, and broke and set fire to the carriages. They then entered a store and rolled out about a hundred barrels of flour, which they unheaded, and emptied about forty into the river. Some took possession of the town-house, which was soon after discovered to be on fire, but which was extinguished without much damage. Another party took possession of the North Bridge. About one hundred and fifty of the militia, who had mustered upon the alarm, coming towards the bridge, were fired upon by the troops, and two were killed upon the spot. Thus did the troops of Britain's King fire FIRST at two several times upon his loyal American subjects, and put a period to ten lives before one gun was fired upon them! Our people THEN returned the fire, and obliged the troops to retreat, who were soon joined by their other parties, but finding they were still pursued, the whole body moved back to Lexington, both troops and militia firing as they went.

During this time an express was sent to General Gage, who despatched a reinforcement under the command of Earl Percy, with two field-pieces. Upon the arrival of this reinforcement at Lexington, just as the retreating party had reached there, they made a stand, picking up their dead, took all the carriages they could find, and put their wounded thereon. Others of them—to their eternal disgrace be it spoken—were robbing and setting houses on fire, and discharging their cannon at the meeting-house.

While this was transacting a party of the militia at Menotomy, attacked a party of twelve of the enemy, who were carrying stores and provisions, killed one of them and took possession of their arms and stores, without any loss.

The troops having halted about an hour at Lexington, found it necessary to make a second retreat, carrying with them many of their dead and wounded. This they continued from Lexington to Charlestown, with great precipitation, the militia closely following them, firing till they reached Charlestown Neck, where they arrived a little after sunset. Passing over the Neck the enemy proceeded up Bunker Hill and encamped for the night.

Pennsylvania Journal, May 24

The Irishman's Epistle

———————•—•———————

This ballad celebrates the British troops' disastrous retreat from Concord, April 19, 1775, and records the beginning of the siege of Boston. The song became popular as a broadside, and also found its way into the newspapers. The jig tune to which the lyrics are here set—"The Irish Washerwoman"—was provided by Bill Bonyun. (Moore, Songs and Ballads, 92–4.)

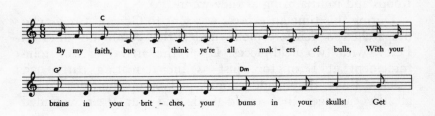

By my faith, but I think ye're all mak-ers of bulls, With your brains in your brit-ches, your bums in your skulls! Get

home with your mus-kets and put up your swords, And
look in your books for the mean-ing of words. You
see now, my hon-eys, how much you're mis-tak-en, For
Con-cord by dis-cord can nev-er be tak-en.

How brave you went out with your muskets all bright,
And thought to be-frighten the folk with the sight;
But when you got there how they powdered your pums
And all the way home how they peppered your bums.
And is it not, honeys, a comical crack
To be proud in the face and shot in the back?

With all of your talkin' and all of your wordin',
And all of your shoutin' and marchin' and swordin',
How come ye to think now they didn't know how
To be after their firelocks as smartly as you?
You see now, my honeys, 'tis nothing at all,
But to pull at the trigger and pop goes the ball!

And what have you got now for all your designin',
But a town without vittles to sit down and dine in,
And stare at the floor and scratch at your noodles,
And sing how the Yankees have beaten the Doodles.
I'm sure if you're wise, you'll make peace for a dinner,
For fighting and fasting will soon make you thinner.

April 20

MASSACHUSETTS   The first stand made by the country
in the late engagement was with only two hundred men at
Concord Bridge, which the soldiers were endeavoring to pull
up. The soldiers gave the first fire, and killed three or four.
It was returned with vigor by the country people, and the

Regulars began soon to retire. The country people immediately lined the roads, which are secured with stone walls, and their numbers hourly increasing, they annoyed the Regulars exceedingly, allowing them to halt but two or three times, and then in open plains for a few minutes.

A considerable body of provincials formed an ambuscade near Cambridge for the troops on their return; but the bridge having been destroyed by the first brigade in their march out, the troops took their route through Charlestown, and by that means avoided a total overthrow. The number of the Regulars when the two brigades joined, is said to have been at least eighteen hundred. It does not appear that they were attacked by more than six hundred provincials until they got near to Charlestown, when a very strong reinforcement from the towns of Marblehead and Salem fell in with them, and gave them two severe fires. This quickened their pace to Bunker Hill, where they took refuge, formed in order, and remained until reinforced by the third brigade sent over from Boston to secure their retreat. This was effected without further loss.

A gentleman, who mixed with the soldiers at Charlestown Ferry, says he saw at least two officers and soldiers brought over wounded in an hour. It is impossible at this time to ascertain the number of the killed and wounded on either side. A young gentleman who was within twelve miles of the field of battle informs us that the country had buried one hundred and ninety soldiers, and it is supposed a great number must have been carried off and burnt on Bunker Hill by their comrades. General Haldiman and Lord Percy are both returned safe, having been enclosed on all sides by their soldiers, during the retreat. Mr. Paul Revere, who left Boston to acquaint Messrs. Hancock and Adams of the design against them, was taken prisoner, but got clear again by a stratagem. Colonel Murray's son, who conducted the first brigade to Concord, is a prisoner, and not killed as reported. Upon the whole, Lord North's troops have had a severe drubbing; and when we consider the disparity of numbers and discipline, we have reason to acknowledge the interposition of Heaven on that memorable day.

Dunlap's Pennsylvania Packet, May 1

April 24

MASSACHUSETTS   The communication between Boston and the country is entirely stopped up, and not a soul permitted to go in or out without a pass. This day the Governor has disarmed all the inhabitants, after giving them his word and honor that the soldiers should not molest nor plunder them. Cambridge is the head-quarters of the provincials, and they are commanded by General Putnam. They are entrenching themselves at Roxbury, and erecting batteries to play on the lines.

Letter from Boston
New York Gazette and Weekly Mercury, May 1

April 29

NEW YORK   The following association was set on foot in New York to-day, and signed by above one thousand of the principal inhabitants. It is to be transmitted through all the counties in the province, where, we make no doubt, it will be signed by all ranks of people:

"Persuaded that the salvation of the rights and liberties of America, depends, under God, on the firm union of its inhabitants, in a vigorous prosecution of the measures necessary for its safety, and convinced of the necessity of preventing the anarchy and confusion which attend a dissolution of the powers of government; we, the freemen, freeholders, and inhabitants of the city and county of New York, being greatly alarmed at the avowed design of the ministry to raise a revenue in America, and shocked by the bloody scene now acting in the Massachusetts Bay, do, in the most solemn manner, resolve never to become slaves; and do associate under all the ties of religion, honor, and love to our country, to adopt and endeavor to carry into execution, whatever measures may be recommended by the Continental Congress, or resolved upon by our provincial convention, for the purpose of preserving our constitution and opposing the execution of several arbitrary and oppressive acts of the British Parliament, until a reconciliation between Great Britain and America, on constitutional principles, (which we most ardently desire,) can be obtained; and that we will, in all things, follow the advice of our general committee, respecting the purposes aforesaid, the preservation of peace and good order, and the safety of individuals and private property."

Rivington's Gazette, May 4

MAY

May 6

NEW YORK   This afternoon, arrived at New York from the eastward, on their way for Philadelphia, to attend the Continental Congress, the Hon. John Hancock and Thomas Cushing, Esqs.; Samuel Adams and Robert Treat Paine, Esqs., delegates for the province of Massachusetts Bay; and the Hon. Eliphalet Dyer, Roger Sherman, Esq., and Silas Deane, Esq., delegates for the colony of Connecticut. They were met a few miles out of town by a great number of principal gentlemen of that place, in carriages and on horseback, and escorted into the city by near a thousand men under arms. The roads were lined with a greater number of people than were ever known on any occasion before. Their arrival was announced by the ringing of bells, and other demonstrations of joy. They have double sentries placed at the doors of their lodging.

Rivington's Gazette, May 11

VIRGINIA   The first express with the news of the Battle of Lexington reached Williamsburg on the morning of the twenty-ninth of April. The express leaving Watertown on the morning of the battle, passed through Worcester, Mass., Brookline, Norwich, New London, Lyme, Saybrook, Killingworth, East Guilford, Guilford, Branford, and New Haven, and arrived at Fairfield, (on the 22d.) It arrived at New York on Sunday, (23d,) and was immediately forwarded to Philadelphia, by Isaac Low, chairman of the New York Committee, and reached that place at four o'clock in the afternoon of the next day, (24th.) On the arrival of the news at Baltimore, the inhabitants seized upon the Provincial magazine, containing fifteen hundred stands of arms.

Pennsylvania Journal, April 24
Virginia Gazette, April 29
New-York Journal, June 1

VIRGINIA   Yesterday there was a meeting at Williamsburg, Virginia, of the committee and part of the militia of King William County; when the contents of the second express from the northward was communicated. It had such an effect on the minds of the people, that near two hundred pounds was immediately subscribed for the use of our brethren now fighting in the common cause. Most of the principal gentlemen subscribed ten pounds each, and as not half the country were present, there is no doubt it will be nearly doubled.

Virginia Gazette, May 6

May 9

PENNSYLVANIA   The committee of Bucks County, Pennsylvania, met yesterday and recommended the people to associate into companies, and learn the military exercise of arms. Some townships have already begun, and many others, animated with the same zeal for the welfare of their country, readily fall in with the plan, a knowledge of which, we have great reason to fear, we shall be soon called upon to give a proof of. The unanimity, prudence, spirit and firmness, which appeared in the deliberations of yesterday, do honor to Bucks County, and will, we hope, in some measure, wipe off those aspersions they too deservedly lay under. A large number of the inhabitants assembled, and the resolves of the day being made public, testified their highest approbation of the conduct of the committee, and unanimously voted them the thanks of the county. A disciple of that species of creatures called *Tories* being formally introduced to a tar-barrel, of which he was repeatedly pressed to smell, thought prudent to take leave abruptly, lest a more intimate acquaintance with it should take place.

Dunlap's Pennsylvania Packet, May 15

May 10

PENNSYLVANIA   To-day the eastern delegates arrived at
Philadelphia. They were met about six miles out by the
officers of all the companies in the city, and by many other
gentlemen on horseback, in all amounting to five hundred.
When they came within two miles of the city they were met
by the company of riflemen, and a company of infantry, with
a band of music, who conducted them through the most
public streets of the city to their lodgings, amidst the acclamations of near fifteen thousand spectators.

Virginia Gazette, May 27

MASSACHUSETTS   The proceedings of April nineteenth
have united the colonies and continent, and brought in New
York to act as vigorously as any other place whatsoever, and
has raised an army in an instant, which are lodged in the several houses of the towns round Boston, till their tents are
finished, which will be soon. All that is attended to, besides
ploughing and planting, is making ready for fighting. The
non-importations and non-exportations will now take place
from necessity, and traffic give place to war. We have a fine
spring, prospects of great plenty; there was scarce ever known
such a good fall of lambs; we are in no danger of starving,
through the cruel acts against the New England governments;
and the men who had been used to fishery, a hardy generation
of people, Lord North has undesignedly kept in the country
to give strength to our military operations, and to assist as
occasion may require. Thanks to a superior wisdom for his
blunders. The General is expecting reinforcements, but few
have arrived as yet, the winds, contrary to the common run
this season, instead of being easterly, have been mostly the
reverse. When the reinforcement arrives, and is recovered of
the voyage, the General will be obliged in honor to attempt
dislodging the people, and penetrating the country. Both
soldiers and inhabitants are in want of fresh provisions, and
will be like to suffer much, should the provincial army be able
to keep the town shut up on all sides, excepting by water, as
at present.   *New York Gazette and Weekly Mercury, June 19*

May 17

NEW YORK   This evening arrived at Philadelphia, John Brown, Esq., from Ticonderoga, express to the General Congress, from whom we learn that on the beginning of this instant, a company of about fifty men from Connecticut, and the western part of Massachusetts, joined by upwards of one hundred from Bennington, in New York government, and the adjacent towns, proceeded to the eastern side of Lake Champlain, and on the night before the tenth current, crossed the lake with eighty-five men, not being able to obtain craft to transport the rest, and about day-break invested the fort, whose gate, contrary to expectation, they found shut, but the wicker open, through which, with the Indian war-whoop, all that could, entered one by one, others scaling the wall on both sides of the gate, and instantly secured and disarmed the sentries, and pressed into the parade, where they formed the hollow square; but immediately quitting that order, they rushed into the several barracks on three sides of the fort, and seized on the garrison, consisting of two officers, and upwards of forty privates, whom they brought out, disarmed, put under guard, and have since sent prisoners to Hartford in Connecticut. All this was performed in about ten minutes, without the loss of life, or a drop of blood on our side, and but very little on that of the King's troops.

In the fort were found about thirty barrels of flour, a few barrels of pork, seventy odd chests of leaden ball, computed at three hundred tons, about ten barrels of powder in bad condition, near two hundred pieces of ordnances of all sizes, from eighteen-pounders downwards, at Ticonderoga and Crown Point, which last place, being held only by a corporal and eight men, falls of course into our hands.

By this sudden expedition, planned by some principal persons in the four neighboring colonies, that important pass is now in the hands of the Americans, where, we trust, the wisdom of the grand Continental Congress will take effectual measures to secure it, as it may be depended on, that administration means to form an army in Canada, composed of

British Regulars, French, and Indians, to attack the colonies on that side.
                              Pennsylvania Journal, May 24

May 21

MASSACHUSETTS   A correspondent writing from Boston, says:— "As to the inhabitants removing, they are suffered to go out under certain restrictions. This liberty was obtained after many town-meetings, and several conferences between their committee and General Gage. The terms mutually agreed to were: 'That the inhabitants should deliver up all their arms to the selectmen.' This was generally done, though it took up some days. On this condition the inhabitants were to have had liberty to move out of town, with their effects, and during this to have free egress and regress. But mark the event. The arms being delivered, orders were issued by the general, that those who inclined to remove, must give in their names to the selectmen, to be by them returned to the military town major, who was then to write a pass for the person or family applying, to go through the lines or over the ferry. But all merchandise was forbid; after a while, all provisions were forbid; and now, all merchandise, provisions, and medicine. Guards are appointed to examine all trunks, boxes, beds, and every thing else to be carried out; these have proceeded to such extremities, as to take from the poor people a single loaf of bread and half a pound of chocolate; so that no one is allowed to carry out a mouthful of provisions; but all is submitted to quietly. The anxiety indeed is so great to get out of town, that even were we obliged to go naked, it would not hinder us. But there are so many obstructions thrown in the way, that I do not think those who are most anxious, will be all out in less than two or three months. Vastly different from what was expected; for the general at first proposed, unasked, to procure the admiral's boats to assist the inhabitants in the transportation of their effects, which is not done, and there are but two ferry boats allowed to cross. They have their designs in this, which you may easily guess at. We suffer much for want of fresh meat. The transports, with the marines, are all arrived."
                              Pennsylvania Journal, June 7

May 25

MASSACHUSETTS   The man-of-war *Cerberus* arrived at Boston, with the three generals Howe, Clinton, and Burgoyne, together with about seven hundred marines and two hundred drafts.

New-York Journal, June 8

A Junto Song

Fish and Tea

———•———

In 1774 the Port of Boston had been closed as a measure of retaliation for the tea party of December 1773. Colonial resistance stiffened. Britain began to dispatch military reinforcements to subdue the rebellion. On May 25, 1775, three generals, the "junto" of William Howe, Henry Clinton, and John Burgoyne, arrived on the Cerberus to take charge of operations.

These songs reflect the immediate popular reaction to this ominous news. "A Junto Song" is an example of revolutionary satiric verse at its best. It expresses a bottomless contempt for the strutting, boasting militarists who could only offer the American people savagery and death. The form and melody of the composition were borrowed from a traditional Scots song, "A-begging we will go." (The New-York Journal, September 7, 1775, probably copied from a Boston broadside; Moore, Diary, 134.)

"Fish and Tea" attacks oppression, the Coercive Acts of 1774, and the Newfoundland Fisheries Act of March 1775 which closed those fisheries to New England seamen. The Earl of Chatham (William Pitt), Lord Camden (Chief Justice of the Court of Common Pleas), Colonel Isaac Barre, Edmund Burke, and John Booth Wilkes were all members of Parliament who had opposed taxation of the colonists. The melody, "Chevy Chase," is one of the old stock tunes. (Moore, Songs and Ballads, 106–8; slightly abridged.)

A Junto Song

'Tis mon-ey makes the mem-ber vote And sanc-ti-fies our ways; It makes the pa-triot turn his coat, And mon-ey— we must raise. And a-tax-ing we will go, we'll go, And a-tax-ing we will go.

More taxes we must sure impose,
　To raise the civil list;
Also pay our ayes and noes,
　And make opposers hist.

　　And a-taxing we will go, etc.

One single thing untaxed at home,
　Old England could not show,
For money we abroad did roam,
　And thought to tax the *new*.

　　And a-taxing we will go, etc.

The power supreme of Parliament,
　Our purpose did assist,
And taxing laws abroad were sent,
　Which rebels do resist.

　　And a-taxing we will go, etc.

Shall we not make the rascals bend
　To Britain's supreme power?
The sword shall we not to them send,
　And leaden balls a shower?

　　And a-taxing we will go, etc.

Boston we shall in ashes lay,
　It is a nest of knaves:

We'll make them soon for mercy pray,
   Or send them to their graves.

      And a-taxing we will go, etc.

But second thoughts are ever best,
   And lest our force should fail,
What fraud can do, we'll make a test,
   And see what bribes avail.

      And a-taxing we will go, etc.

Each colony, we will propose,
   Shall raise an ample sum;
Which well applied, under the rose,
   May bribe them—as at home.

      And a-taxing we will go, etc.

We'll force and fraud in one unite,
   To bring them to our hands;
Then lay a tax on the sun's light,
   And king's tax on their lands.

      And a-taxing we will go, etc.

Fish and Tea

What a court hath old Eng - land of fol - ly and sin, Spite of
Chat - ham and Cam - den, Barre, Burke, Wilkes and Glynn! Not con -
tent with the game act, they tax fish and sea, And A - mer - i - ca drench with hot
wa - ter and tea. Der - ry down, down, down der - ry down.

But if the wise council of England doth think,
They may be enslaved by the power of drink,
They're right to enforce it; but then, do you see?
The Colonies, too, may refuse and be free.

       Derry down, down, down derry down.

There's no knowing where this oppression will stop;
Some say—there's no cure but a capital chop;
And that I believe's each American's wish,
Since you've drenched 'em with tea, and depriv'd 'em of fish.

       Derry down, down, down derry down.

The birds of the air, and the fish of the sea,
By the gods, for poor Dan Adam's use were made free,
Till a man with more power, than old Moses would wish,
Said, "Ye wretches, ye shan't touch a fowl or a fish!"

       Derry down, down, down derry down.

Three Generals these mandates have borne 'cross the sea,
To deprive 'em of fish and to make 'em drink tea;
In turn, sure, these freemen will boldly agree,
To give 'em a dance upon Liberty Tree.

       Derry down, down, down derry down.

Then *freedom*'s the word, both at home and abroad,
And [away] every scabbard that hides a good sword!
Our forefathers gave us this freedom in hand,
And we'll die in defence of the rights of the land.

       Derry down, down, down derry down.

JUNE

June 1

NEW YORK   The synod of New York and Philadelphia, at
their late meeting in the former city, appointed the last Thurs-

day in June to be observed by all the congregations under their care, as a day of fasting and prayer, on account of the alarming state of our public affairs. Should the Continental Congress appoint a fast, the synod have directed that to be observed in preference to the day appointed by themselves, provided that it is not more than four weeks distant from the last Thursday of June; if at a greater distance, they have ordered both days to be kept. They also recommend to all the congregations in their charge, to spend the afternoon of the last Thursday in every month in public prayer, during the continuance of our present troubles.

New-York Journal, June 1

NEW JERSEY   The martial spirit which prevails among the inhabitants of Somerset County, in New Jersey, truly merits the attention of the public. We have certain intelligence that they are forming themselves into companies, and daily exercising, to become complete masters of the military discipline; and particularly, that the township of Bridgewater, in said county, met at Rariton, the sixth instant, and chose Mr. Abraham Ten Eyck, captain, under whose command eighty-five volunteers immediately enlisted, to be in readiness at an hour's warning, to march for the assistance of any neighboring colony, on any emergency. Their pay and other necessaries are provided by said township. The other counties and townships, it is hoped, will follow their example, as it may be necessary to repel force by force, in order to secure our national rights and privileges.

Rivington's Gazette, June 1

June 4

VIRGINIA   Yesterday morning a detachment of cavalry from the Williamsburg volunteers, in their uniforms, well mounted and equipped, with a wagon containing their baggage and provisions, set out in a regular military procession, to meet the Hon. Peyton Randolph, Esq., late president of the Grand Continental Congress, on the way from Philadelphia, his presence being requisite at the general assembly now sitting. To-day about noon, the troop of horse met that gentleman at Ruffin's ferry, accompanied by Colonel Carter Braxton, and escorted them to Williamsburg, after having been joined by a company of infantry, who marched out the distance of two miles for the same purpose. They arrived about sunset, and were attended to the hon. gentleman's house by the whole body of cavalry and infantry, whose very martial appearance gave great satisfaction to the spectators. The bells began to ring as our worthy delegate entered the city, and the unfeigned joy of the inhabitants, on this occasion, was visible in every countenance; there were illuminations in the evening, and the volunteers, with many other respectable gentlemen, assembled at the Raleigh, spent an hour or two in harmony and cheerfulness, and drank several patriotic toasts.

Dunlap's Pennsylvania Packet, June 19

June 12

MASSACHUSETTS   To-day General Gage has issued a proclamation, offering pardon in the King's name to all those, excepting Samuel Adams and John Hancock, who will forthwith lay down their arms, and return to their usual occupations. Those who do not accept the mercy he offers, and who give protection to those gentlemen, or assist them in any way, are to be treated as rebels and traitors. Martial law is also declared, "for so long a time as the present unhappy occasion shall necessarily require." A correspondent says:—"The proclamation is replete with consummate impudence, the most abominable lies, and stuffed with daring expressions of tyranny as well as rebellion against the established constitutional authority both of Great Britain and of the American States."

Pennsylvania Journal, June 28

June 14

NEW YORK   A few days ago returned to New York from the eastward, Mr. William Goddard, who has been indefatigable in soliciting the establishment of post-offices on constitutional principles, in which he has at last succeeded. The matter has been taken up by the committees, provincial Congresses, or assemblies, in the colonies of New Hampshire, Massachusetts Bay, Rhode Island, and Connecticut, throughout which, offices, postmasters, riders, and rates of postage have been established and are to be laid before the Continental Congress, there to be approved or altered as shall be thought expedient. It is hoped New York and the other governments will adopt similar measures. The rates of postage have been continued as before.

New-York Journal, June 15

June 17

MASSACHUSETTS   Last night a detachment from the camp at Cambridge, marched to Charlestown, and there took possession of Breed's Hill, about half a mile from the ferry. Their intrenching tools not coming up in season, it was twelve o'clock before they began their work. At daylight this morning they were discovered from Boston, when the men-of-war at the ferry, the battery from Cop's Hill, and the floating batteries, kept up a continual cannonading and bombarding, which fortunately did but little execution, although their intrenchments were very far from being completed. This continued till about two o'clock, when a large army, under the command of General Howe, landed in Charlestown, and after plundering it of all its valuable effects, set fire to it in ten different places. Then, dividing the army, part of it marched up in the front of the provincial intrenchment and began an attack at long shot; the other part marched round the town of Charlestown under cover of the smoke occasioned by the fire of the town. The provincial sentries discovered the Regulars marching upon their left wing, and gave notice to the Connecticut forces posted there. Captain Knowlton, of Ashford, with four hundred of said forces, immediately repaired to, and pulled up, a post and rail fence, and carrying the posts and rails to another fence, put them together for a breastwork. He then gave orders to the men not to fire until the enemy were got within fifteen rods, and then not till the word was given. The word being given, the Regulars fell surprisingly; it was thought by spectators who stood at a distance that the provincials did great execution.

The action continued about two hours, when the Regulars
on the right wing were put into confusion and gave way. The
Connecticut troops closely pursued them, and were on the
point of pushing their bayonets, when orders were received
from General Pomeroy, for those who had been in action for
two hours to fall back, and their places to be supplied by fresh
troops. These orders being mistaken for a direction to retreat,
the troops on the right wing began a general retreat, which
was handed to the left, the principal place of action, where
Captains Knowlton, Chester, Clark, and Putnam, had forced
the Regulars to give way, and being warmly pursuing them,
were, with difficulty, persuaded to retire; but the right wing
by mistaking the orders having already retreated, the left, to
avoid being encircled, were obliged to retreat with the main
body. They retreated with precipitation across the causeway to
Winter's Hill, in which retreat they were exposed to the fire
of the enemy from their shipping and floating batteries.

The provincials sustained their principal loss in passing the
causeway. The Regulars pursued the provincials to Winter's
Hill, where the latter being reinforced by General Putnam,
renewed the battle, repulsed the Regulars with great slaughter,
and pursued them till they got under cover of their cannon on
the shipping. The Regulars then returned to Bunker Hill, and
the provincials to Winter's Hill, where they are now intrenching and erecting batteries.

In this action fell our worthy and much lamented friend,
Doctor Warren, with as much glory as Wolfe, after performing many feats of bravery, and exhibiting a coolness and conduct which did honor to the judgment of his country in
appointing him a few days before one of our major generals.

The number of Regulars which first attacked the provincials,
was not less than two thousand. The number of the provincials was only fifteen hundred, who, it is supposed would soon
have gained a complete victory had it not been for the unhappy mistake already mentioned. The Regulars were afterwards reinforced with a thousand men. It is uncertain how
great a number of them were killed or wounded, but all agree
that their loss is more than one thousand. General Howe says,

"you may talk of your Mindens and Fontenoys, but I never saw nor heard of such a carnage in so short a time."

Dunlap's Pennsylvania Packet, June 26
New York Gazette and Weekly Mercury, July 3

MASSACHUSETTS Another account of this battle is given by a gentleman in Providence, Rhode Island, to his friend in New York, as follows:—"On the evening of the 16th, Col. Putnam took possession of Bunker Hill with about two thousand men, and began an intrenchment, which they had made some progress in. At eight in the morning, a party of Regulars landed at Charlestown, and fired the town in divers places. Under cover of the smoke, a body of about five thousand men marched up to our intrenchments, and made a furious and sudden attack; they were driven back three times; and when they were making the third attack, one of our people imprudently spoke aloud that their powder was all gone, which being heard by some of the regular officers, they encouraged their men to march up to the trenches with fixed bayonets, and entered them; on which our people were ordered to retreat, which they did with all speed, till they got out of musket-shot. They then formed, but were not pursued. In the mean time six men-of-war and four floating batteries were brought up, and kept up a continual fire on the causeway that leads on to Charlestown. Our people retreated through the fire, but not without the loss of many of the men. The brave Doctor Warren is among the killed, and Colonel Gardner is wounded. We left six field-pieces on the hill. Our people are now intrenched on Pleasant Hill, within cannon shot of Bunker Hill. The loss of the King's troops must be very considerable; the exact number we cannot tell. Among the slain is Major Pitcairn. If our people had been supplied with ammunition they would have held possession most certainly. Our people are in high spirits, and are very earnest to put this matter on another trial."

Rivington's Gazette, June 29

Poem, On the Bloody engagement Fought on Bunker's Hill

Battle of Bunker Hill

Bunker Hill was taken by the British on June 17, 1775. But it was a moral victory for the colonists. Many songs were written to commemorate the battle. The artless poem reproduced here from the pen of Elisha Rich is perhaps one of the best. Nathaniel Coverly, Sr., of Boston issued it as a broadside in 1775. (Reproduced by courtesy of The New-York Historical Society, New York City. Ford, Check List, 1922.)

A British version of the battle was issued in at least three different editions by colonial presses in Boston and Providence. One of these bore the subtitle "composed by the British Butchers, after the Fight at Bunker-Hill on the 17th of June 1775." A Providence, R.I., edition substituted the following anti-British ending:

> *Bad luck to him [Howe] by land and sea,*
> > *For he's despised by many,*
> *The name of Bunker Hill he dreads*
> *Where he was flog'd most plainly.*
> *And now my song is at an end,*
> > *And to conclude my ditty*
> *'Tis only Britons ignorant*
> *[And only them I pity.]*
> *As for our KING and WM. HOWE,*
> > *And Gen. GAGE if they're taken,*
> *The Yankees will hang their heads up high*
> *On that fine hill call'd Beacon.*

We reproduce below an abridgment of the original British text. A facsimile copy of the Providence broadside with its anti-British emendations appears on page 48. (Ford, Check List, 1930–1934; Isaiah Thomas, 15.)

POEM

On the Bloody engagement that was Fought on BUNKER'S HILL in Charlestown NEW-ENGLAND, on the 17th of JUNE, 1775: Together with some Remarks of the Cruelty and Barbarity of the BRITISH Troops, by Destroying the above mention'd Town by FIRE, by which a Number of Distresed Inhabitants were forced to Flee from the Flames, to seek Relief and Shelter among their Sympathizing Brethren in the neighbouring TOWNS.

By ELISHA RICH, Minister of the Gospel.

I.

AMERICANS pray lend an Ear
And you a solemn Tale shall hear
'Twas on the seventeenth of JUNE
Men were cut down all in their bloom.

II.

GOD grant it's memory may lye
A witness against TYRANNY,
Also against NEW ENGLAND'S sin
Which hath let cruel TYRANTS in.

III.

[Indecipherable]

IV.

Last JUNE, upon the seventeenth day,
These Troops for CHARLESTOWN made their way,
For to resist our SOLDIERS there,
Who a strong FORT preparing were.

V.

The SHIPS OF WAR had gather'd round,
To make our Soldiers quit the ground.
And tho' some Men by them were slain,
Yet still their courage they retain.

VI.

But when these Troops had landed there,
Our Men to fight them did prepare,
And when our Men shot their first round,
Many BRITAINS gasped on the ground.

VII.

They Fought like brave MEN on both sides,
And many a valiant HERO dy'd,
The Earth was soaked with their blood,
And wounded wallow'd in the Flood.

VIII.

So warm a Fight is seldom known,
Men were cut down like Grass that's mown,
And some say Gage who did them 'spie,
Said we that ground too dear shall buy.

IX.

Our Men that fought, they were but few,
Their POWDER being spent, withdrew,
And left the ground unto their foe,
And back again were forc'd to go.

X.

Tho' BRITISH TROOPS the ground did gain,
Yet many more of them were slain,
The best intelligence doth tell,
One THOUSAND and near FIFTY fell.

XI.

'Tis thought they lost five to our one,
Altho' our Men were forc'd to run
They bought the victory so dear
It did not much increase our fear.

XX.

Let's view the rod that GOD hath sent,
And for our many sins relent,
So that God's wrath again may cease
And may restore our land to peace.

XXI.

That TYRANTS may no more arise
And brand their swords with haughty eyes,
May Heaven cause their pride to cease,
That so Christ's Kingdom may encrease.

XXII.

May God bring on the happy day
When carnal swords no more shall slay,
And CHRIST as Prince of peace shall reign,
And War be learnt no more again.

Battle of Bunker Hill

It was on the seventeenth—by break of day,
　The Yankees did surprise us,
With their strong works they had thrown up,
　To burn the town and drive us.
But soon we had an order came,
　An order to defeat them,
Like rebels stout, they stood it out,
　And thought we ne'er could beat them.
About the hour of twelve that day,
　An order came for marching,
With three good flints and sixty rounds,
　Each man hop'd to discharge them.

Battle of Bunker Hill.

IT was on the seventeenth by break of day,
  The Yankees did surpize us,
With their strong works they had thrown up
  To burn the town and drive us.
But soon we had an order came,
  An order to defeat them,
Like rebels stout, they stood it out,
  And thought we ne'er could beat them.
About the hour of twelve that day,
  An order came for marching,
With three good flints and sixty rounds,
  Each man hop'd to discharge them,
We marched down to the long wharf,
  Where boats were ready waiting,
With expedition we embark'd,
  Our ships kept cannonading,
And when our boats all filled were,
  With officers and soldiers,
With as good troops as England had
  To oppose, who dare controle us.
And when our boats all filled were,
And when our boats all filled were,
  We row'd in line of battle,
Where showers of ball like hail did fly,
  Our cannon loud did rattle.
There was Cop's hill battery near Charlestown
  Our twenty-fours they played,
And the three frigates in the stream,
  That very well behaved.
The Glasgow frigate clear'd the shore,
  All at the time of landing,
With her grape shot and cannon balls,
  No Yankees e'er could stand them.
And when we landed on the shore,
  We draw'd up altogether,
The Yankees they'd all man'd their works,
  And thought we'd ne'er come thither.
But soon they did perceive brave Howe,
  Brave Howe, our bold commander,
With grenadiers, and infantry,
  We made them to surrender.
Brave William Howe on our right wing
  Cry'd, boys fight on like thunder ;
You soon will see the rebels flee,
  With great amaze and wonder.
Now some lay bleeding on the ground,
  And some fell fast a running,
O'er hills and dales and mountains high,

Crying zounds ! brave Howe's a coming.
Brave Howe is so considerate,
  As to guard against all dangers
He allow'd each half a gill this day—
  To rum we are no strangers !
They began to play on our left wing.
  Where Pigot he commanded,
But we return'd it back again,
  With courage most undaunted.
To our grape shot and musket balls,
  To which they were but strangers,
They thought to come with sword in hand
  But soon they found their danger.
And when the works were got into,
  And put them to the flight, sir,
They pepper'd us poor British elves,
  And show'd us they could fight sir.
And when their works we got into
  With some hard knocks and danger,
Their works we found both firm and strong,
  Too strong for British Rangers.
But as for our Artillery,
  They all gave way and run,
For while their ammunition held,
  They gave us Yankee fun
But our commander he got broke,
  For his misconduct sure, sir,
The shot he sent for twelve pound guns,
  Were made for twenty-fours, sir.
There's some in Boston pleas'd to say,
  As we the field were taking,
We went to kill their countrymen,
  While they their hay were making
For such stout whigs I never saw,
  To hang them all I'd rather,
By making hay with musket balls,
  Lord Howe cursedly did bother !
Bad luck to him by land and sea,
  For he's despis'd by many,
The name of Bunker Hill he dreads,
  Where he was flog'd most plainly.
And now my song is at an end,
  And to conclude my ditty,
'Tis only Britons ignorant
  As for our KING and WM. HOWE,
  And Gen GAGE, if they're taken,
The Yankees will hang their heads up high
  On that fine hill call'd Bacon.

Battle of Bunker Hill. Providence, R. I., broadside. Note the advertisement in the center of the ballad sheet for wholesale rates of two hundred other broadsides available for circulation. Reproduced by courtesy of The New-York Historical Society, New York City.

We marched down to the long-wharf,
   Where boats were ready waiting,
With expedition we embark'd,
   Our ships kept cannonading,
And when our boats all filled were,
   With officers and soldiers,
With as good troops as England had
   To oppose—who dar'd controul us.
And when our boats all filled were,
   We row'd in line of battle,
Where showers of ball like hail did fly,
   Our cannon loud did rattle.
There was Cop's hill battery near Charlestown,
   Our twenty-fours they play'd,
And the three frigates in the stream,
   That very well behav'd.
The *Glasgow* frigate clear'd the shore,
   All at the time of landing,
With her grape shot and cannon balls,
   No Yankees e'er could stand them,
And when we landed on the shore,
   We draw'd up all together,
The Yankees they'd all man'd their works
   And thought we'd ne'er come thither.
But soon they did perceive brave Howe,
   Brave Howe our bold commander,
With grenadiers, and infantry,
   We made them to surrender,
Brave William Howe on our right wing,
   Cry'd boys fight on like thunder;
You soon will see the rebels flee,
   With great amaze and wonder.
Now some lay bleeding on the ground,
   And some full fast a running,
O'er hills and dales and mountains high,
   Crying zounds, brave Howe's a coming.
They began to play on our left wing,
   Where Pigot he commanded,
But we return'd it back again,
   With courage most undaunted,

To our grape shot and musket balls,
  To which they were but strangers
They thought to come with sword in hand,
  But soon they found their danger.
And when the works we got into,
  And put them to the flight, sir,
Some of them did hide themselves,
  And others died of fright, sir,
And when their works we'd got into,
  Without great fear or danger,
The work they'd made was firm and strong,
  The Yankees are great strangers.
But as for our Artillery,
  They all behaved dinty,
For while our ammunition held,
  We gave it to them plenty.
But our conductor he got broke,
  For his misconduct, sure, sir,
The shot he sent for twelve pound guns,
  Were made for twenty-fours, sir,
There's some in Boston pleas'd to say,
  As we the field were taking,
We went to kill their countrymen,
  While they their hay were making.
For such stout whigs I never saw,
  To hang them all I'd rather,
For making hay with musket balls
  And buck-shot mix'd together.
Brave Howe is so considerate,
  As to prevent all danger,
He allows us half-a-pint-a-day,
  To rum we are no strangers,
Long may he live by land and sea,
  For he's belov'd by many,
The name of Howe the Yankees dread,
  We see it very plainly.
And now my song is at an end,
  And to conclude my ditty,
It is the poor and ignorant
  And only them I pity:

As for their king John Hancock,
    And Adams if they're taken,
    There heads for signs shall hang up high,
Upon that hill call'd Beacon.

June 20

PENNSYLVANIA   This morning the three battalions of Philadelphia, and the liberties, together with the artillery company, a troop of lighthorse, several companies of light infantry, rangers, and riflemen, in the whole about two thousand, marched out to the commons, and having joined in brigade, were reviewed by General Washington, who is appointed Commander-in-chief of all the North American forces by the honorable Continental Congress. They went through the manual exercise, firings, and manœuvres with great dexterity and exactness.

This evening Thomas Jefferson, Esq., arrived here from Virginia, to attend the Congress, agreeable to his election, in the room of the Hon. Peyton Randolph, Esq. He is attended by Doctor M'Clurg.

Rivington's Gazette, June 29

June 24

PENNSYLVANIA   Yesterday morning General Washington and General Lee set off from Philadelphia to take command of the American army at Massachusetts Bay. They were accompanied a few miles from town by the troop of lighthorse, and by all the officers of the city militia on horseback. They parted with our celebrated commanders, expressing the most ardent wishes for their success over the enemies of our liberty and country.

Major Thomas Mifflin is appointed aide-de-camp to General Washington, and accompanies the general to the camp near Boston. The active and successful part which this gentleman has taken in the civil and military affairs of the province of Pennsylvania, has endeared him so much to his fellow-citizens that few men have ever left us more universally beloved or regretted.

Rivington's Gazette, June 29

June 25

NEW YORK   This afternoon at four o'clock, General
Washington, attended by Generals Lee and Schuyler, and the
lighthorse of Philadelphia, on the way for the American camp
at Cambridge, landed at Colonel Lispenard's seat, about a
mile above New York, from whence they were conducted into
the city, by nine companies of foot, in their uniforms, and a
greater number of the principal inhabitants of that city than
ever appeared on any occasion before.

Pennsylvania Journal, June 28

June 27

NEW YORK   Yesterday afternoon General Washington
with his suite, attended by the several New York militia companies, a troop of gentlemen of the Philadelphia lighthorse,
commanded by Captain Markoe, and a number of the inhabitants of New York, set out for the provincial camp at
Cambridge, near Boston. Last night he rested at King's
Bridge, and this morning proceeded on his journey.

Before the general's departure, the Provincial Congress of
New York presented him with an address, in which, after expressing their gratification at his appointment, they say:—
"In you, sir, and in the worthy generals under your command,
we have the most flattering hopes of success in the glorious
struggle for American liberty, and the fullest assurances, that,
whenever this important contest shall be decided by that
fondest wish of every American soul, an accommodation with
our mother country, you will cheerfully resign the important
deposit committed into your hands, and reassume the character of our worthiest citizen."

The general, after declaring his gratitude for the regard
shown him, added, "May your warmest wishes be realized in
the success of America at this important and interesting
period, and be assured that every exertion of my worthy col-
leagues and myself, will be equally extended to the re-establishment of peace and harmony between the mother country
and these colonies. As to the fatal but necessary operations of

war, when we assumed the soldier, we did not lay aside the citizen, and we shall most sincerely rejoice with you in that happy hour, when the establishment of American liberty, on the most firm and solid foundations, shall enable us to return to our private stations in the bosom of a free, peaceful, and happy country."

Pennsylvania Journal, July 5

JULY

July 3

A writer in London says:—"Though the American soldiery perhaps may not be so regularly disciplined as the King's troops, yet it must be considered that there is a very material difference between a man who fights for his natural liberty, and the man who only fights because he is paid for it. The former defends himself in a just cause; the latter is the mere dupe of power. The former is animated by the zeal of his attachments to the public weal; the latter has no attachments at all, except to his pay for slaughter and bloodshed."

New York Gazette and Weekly Mercury, July 3

None of the men who have been raised by the several colonies, are, in future, to be distinguished as the troops of any particular colony, but as the forces of "THE UNITED COLONIES OF NORTH AMERICA," into whose joint service they have been taken by the Continental Congress, and are to be paid and supported accordingly.

Letter from Dr. Leonard to John Murray. Winslow

The Yankees Return from Camp
(Yankee Doodle)

———•◆•———

"Yankee Doodle," the most famous song in American history, is a light-hearted paean of praise to the New England militia and to the shy country boys who were its backbone. The words and music were first published in England in 1775 under the title "YANKEE DOODLE, or (as now Christened by the Saints of New England) THE LEXINGTON MARCH n.b. The Words to be Sung thro' the Nose, and in the West Country drawl and dialect." The lyrics certainly, and the melody probably, were of colonial origin. For a while the song was popular with British troops, for it mocked the cowardice of the colonial militia; but after Bunker Hill the Americans reclaimed their ballad. The lyric was reworked by Edward Bangs, a Harvard sophomore, and enjoyed an immense popularity during the Revolutionary War under the title "The Yankees Return from Camp." Many different early broadside issues survive. Reproduced here are the lyrics of a Boston broadside, circa 1810. (S. Foster Damon, Yankee Doodle.)

Father and I went down to camp,
    Along with Captain Gooding,
There we see the men and boys
    As thick as hasty pudding.

    Yankee doodle, keep it up,
        Yankee doodle, dandy;
    Mind the music and the step,
        And with the girls be handy.

And there we see a thousand men,
    As rich as 'Squire David;
And what they wasted every day,
    I wish it could be saved.

    Yankee doodle, etc.

The 'lasses they eat every day,
  Would keep an house a winter;
They have as much that I'll be bound
  They eat it when they're amind to.

    Yankee doodle, etc.

And there we see a swamping gun,
  Large as a log of maple,
Upon a deuced little cart,
  A load for father's cattle.

    Yankee doodle, etc.

And every time they shoot it off,
  It takes a horn of powder;
It makes a noise like father's gun,
  Only a nation louder.

    Yankee doodle, etc.

I went as nigh to one myself,
  As 'Siah's underpining;
And father went as nigh again,
  I thought the deuce was in him.

    Yankee doodle, etc.

Cousin Simon grew so bold,
  I thought he would have cock'd it:
It scar'd me so, I shrink'd it off,
  And hung by father's pocket.

    Yankee doodle, etc.

And Captain Davis had a gun,
  He kind of clap'd his hand on't,
And struck a crooked stabbing iron
  Upon the little end on't.

    Yankee doodle, etc.

And there I see a pumpkin shell
  As big as mother's bason,

THE YANKEES

RETURN FROM CAMP.

FATHER and I went down to camp,
    Along with captain Gooding,
There we see the men and boys,
    As thick as hasty pudding.
    Yankey doodle, keep it up,
      Yankey doodle, dandy ;
CHORUS. *Mind the music and the step,*
      And with the girls be handy.

And there we see a thousand men,
    As rich as 'Squire David ;
And what they wasted every day,
    I wish it could be saved.
        Yankey doodle, &c.

The 'lasses they eat every day,
    Would keep an house a winter ;
They have as much that I'll be bound
    They eat it when they're amind to.
        Yankey doodle, &c.

And there we see a swamping gun,
    Large as a log of maple,
Upon a deuced little cart,
    A load for father's cattle.
        Yankey doodle, &c.

And every time they shoot it off,
    It takes a horn of powder ;
It makes a noise like father's gun,
    Only a nation louder.
        Yankey doodle, &c.

I went as nigh to one myself,
    As 'Siah's underpining ;
And father went as nigh again,
    I thought the deuce was in him.
        Yankey doodle, &c.

Cousin Simon grew so bold,
    I thought he would have cock'd it :
It scar'd me so, I shrink'd it off,
    And hung by father's pocket.
        Yankey doodle, &c.

And Captain Davis had a gun,
    He kind of clap'd his hand on't,

And struck a crooked stabbing iron
    Upon the little end on't.
        Yankey doodle, &c.

And there I see a pumpkin shell
    As big as mother's bason,
And every time they touch'd it off,
    They scamper'd like the nation.
        Yankey doodle, &c.

I see a little barrel too,
    The heads were made of leather,
They knock'd upon't with little clubs,
    And call'd the folks together.
        Yankey doodle, &c.

And there was Captain Washington,
    And gentlefolks about him,
They say he's grown so tarnal proud,
    He will not ride without 'em.
        Yankey doodle, &c.

He got him on his meeting clothes,
    Upon a slapping stallion,
He set the world along in rows,
    In hundred and in millions.
        Yankey doodle, &c.

The flaming ribbons in their hats,
    They look'd so taring fine, ah,
I wanted pockily to get,
    To give to my Jemimah.
        Yankey doodle, &c.

I see another snarl of men
    A digging graves, they told me,
So tarnal long, so tarnal deep,
    They 'tended they should hold me.
        Yankee doodle, &c.

It scar'd me so, I hook'd it off,
    Nor stopt, as I remember,
Nor turn'd about till I got home,
    Lock'd up in mother's chamber.
        Yankey doodle, &c.

N. Coverly, jr. Printer, *Milk-Street, Boston.*

And every time they touch'd it off,
  They scamper'd like the nation.

    Yankee doodle, etc.

I see a little barrel too,
  The heads were made of leather,
They knock'd upon't with little clubs,
  And call'd the folks together.

    Yankee doodle, etc.

And there was Captain Washington,
  And gentlefolks about him,
They say he's grown so tarnal proud,
  He will not ride without 'em.

    Yankee doodle, etc.

He got him on his meeting clothes,
  Upon a slapping stallion,
He set the world along in rows,
  In hundreds and in millions.

    Yankee doodle, etc.

The flaming ribbons in their hats,
  They look'd so taring fine, ah,
I wanted pockily to get,
  To give to my Jemimah.

    Yankee doodle, etc.

I see another snarl of men
  A-digging graves, they told me,
So tarnal long, so tarnal deep,
  They 'tended they should hold me.

    Yankee doodle, etc.

It scar'd me so, I hook'd it off,
  Nor stopt, as I remember,
Nor turn'd about till I got home,
  Lock'd up in mother's chamber.

    Yankee doodle, etc.

July 10

MASSACHUSETTS   A gentleman who came out of Boston to-day, says the inhabitants have been numbered, and amount to six thousand five hundred and seventy-three. The soldiers number, women and children, thirteen thousand six hundred. Three hundred Tories are chosen to patrol the streets; forty-nine at night. It is very sickly there; from ten to thirty funerals in a day, and no bells allowed to toll; Master Lovell has been taken up and put in jail, in consequence of some letters found in Dr. Warren's pockets.

Pennsylvania Journal, July 26

July 16

MASSACHUSETTS   As to intelligence from Boston, it is seldom we are able to collect any that may be relied on; and to repeat the vague flying rumors would be endless. We heard yesterday by one Mr. Rolston, a goldsmith, who got out from Boston in a fishing schooner, that the distress of the troops increases fast, their beef is spent, their malt and cider all gone; all the fresh provisions they can procure, they are obliged to give to the sick and wounded; that thirteen of the provincials who were in jail, and were wounded at Charles-town, are dead; that no man dared to be seen talking to his friend in the street; that they are obliged to be within every evening at ten o'clock according to martial law, nor can any inhabitant walk the streets after that time without a pass from Gage; that Gage has ordered all the molasses to be distilled into rum for the soldiers; that he has taken away all licenses for selling of liquors, and given them to his creatures; that he has issued an order that no one else shall sell under a penalty of ten pounds; that the spirit which prevails among the soldiers is that of malice and revenge; that there is no true courage to be observed among them; that their duty is hard, always holding themselves in readiness for an attack, which they are in continual fear of; that Doctor Eliot was not on board of a man-of-war as was reported; Mr. Lovel, with many others, is certainly in jail; that last week a poor milch cow was killed in town and sold for a shilling sterling a pound; that the transports from Ireland and New York arrived last week, but every additional man adds to their distress.

Pennsylvania Journal, August 2

July 19

CONNECTICUT Wednesday evening last, a number of ladies and gentlemen collected at a place called East Farms, in Connecticut, where they had a needless entertainment, and made themselves extremely merry with a good glass of wine. Such entertainments and diversions can hardly be justified upon any occasion; but at such a day as this, when every thing around us has a threatening aspect, they ought to be discountenanced, and every good man should use his influence to suppress them. And are not such diversions and entertainments a violation of the eighth article of the Association of the Continental Congress? And is it not expected that the Committee of Inspection will examine into such matters, and if they find any persons guilty of violating said Association, that they treat them according as the rules of it prescribe?

Barber's Historical Collections of Connecticut, 175

July 21

NEW YORK Yesterday, agreeably to the recommendation of the delegates in the hon. Continental Congress, was observed with the utmost solemnity, by fasting, abstinence, and devotion. In all the churches in New York were large congregations, and excellent discourses, delivered from the several pulpits, expressive of the truly calamitous situation of this unhappy continent.

New York Gazette and Weekly Mercury, July 24

AUGUST

August 7

PENNSYLVANIA   On Friday evening last, [4th,] arrived at
Lancaster, Pennsylvania, on their way to the American camp,
Captain Cresap's company of riflemen, consisting of one hundred and thirty active, brave young fellows; many of whom
have been in the late expedition under Lord Dunmore, against
the Indians. They bear in their bodies visible marks of their
prowess, and show scars and wounds which would do honor to
Homer's *Iliad*. They show you, to use the poet's words:—

"Where the gor'd battle bled at every vein!"

One of these warriors, in particular, shows the cicatrices of
four bullet holes through his body. These men have been
bred in the woods to hardships and dangers from their infancy. They appear as if they were entirely unacquainted with,
and had never felt the passion of fear. With their rifles in
their hands, they assume a kind of omnipotence over their
enemies. One cannot much wonder at this, when we mention a fact which can be fully attested by several of the reputable persons who were eye-witnesses of it. Two brothers in
the company took a piece of board five inches broad and
seven inches long, with a bit of white paper, about the size
of a dollar, nailed in the centre, and while one of them supported this board perpendicularly between his knees, the
other, at the distance of upwards of sixty yards, and without
any kind of rest, shot eight bullets through it successively,
and spared a brother's thigh! Another of the company held a
barrel stave perpendicularly in his hands with one edge close
to his side, while one of his comrades, at the same distance,
and in the manner before mentioned, shot several bullets
through it, without any apprehension of danger on either
side. The spectators appearing to be amazed at these feats,

were told that there were upwards of fifty persons in the same
company could do the same thing; that there was not one
who could not plug nineteen bullets out of twenty, as they
termed it, within an inch of the head of a tenpenny nail. In
short, to evince the confidence they possessed in their dexterity at these kinds of arms, some of them proposed to stand
with apples on their heads, while others at the same distance,
undertook to shoot them off; but the people who saw the
other experiments declined to be witnesses of this. At night
a great fire was kindled around a pole planted in the Court
House Square, where the company, with the captain at their
head, all naked to the waist, and painted like savages, (except
the captain, who was in an Indian shirt,) indulged a vast
concourse of people with a perfect exhibition of a war-dance,
and all the manœuvres of Indians, holding council, going to
war, circumventing their enemies by defiles, ambuscades, attacking, scalping, &c. It is said by those who are judges, that
no representation could possibly come nearer the original.
The captain's expertness and agility, in particular, in these
experiments astonished every beholder. This morning they
will set out on their march for Cambridge.

Pennsylvania Journal, August 23
Virginia Gazette, September 9

August 9

PENNSYLVANIA   This morning the following appeal was
posted in the city of Philadelphia:—"To the SPINNERS in
this city, the suburbs, and country:—Your services are now
wanted to promote the AMERICAN MANUFACTORY, at the
corner of Market and Ninth streets, where cotton, wool, flax,
&c., are delivered out; strangers, who apply, are desired to
bring a few lines, by way of recommendation, from some
respectable person in their neighborhood.

"One distinguishing characteristic of an excellent woman,
as given by the wisest of men is, 'That she seeketh wool and
flax, and worketh willingly with her hands to the spindle, and
her hands holdeth the distaff.' In this time of public distress,
you have now, each of you, an opportunity not only to help

to sustain your families, but likewise to cast your mite into the treasury of the public good. The most feeble effort to help to save the state from ruin, when it is all you can do, is as the widow's mite, entitled to the same reward as they who, of their abundant abilities, have cast in much."

Pennsylvania Journal, August 9

MASSACHUSETTS   The riflemen from York County [Pennsylvania] have annoyed the Regulars very much. By a gentleman who left Boston yesterday, we hear that Captains Percival and Sabine, of the marines, Captain Johnson of the royal Irish, and Captain Le Moine. of the Train, were killed on Monday. Captain Chetwyn, son of Lord Chetwyn, is mortally wounded. The number of privates killed this week we have not heard. The Regulars have thrown up a breastwork across the neck at the foot of Bunker Hill, to secure their sentries and advanced guards. Yesterday Captain Morgan arrived from Virginia with his company of riflemen; but they are grown so terrible to the mercenaries, that nothing is to be seen from their breastworks but a hat. General Gage has built thirteen boats, which will carry sixty men each, and they have been several days practising the men to row them about in Boston harbor, from which we may suppose some party is to be made by water.

Letter from Cambridge, August 9
Pennsylvania Journal, August 16

August 14

MASSACHUSETTS   This day being the anniversary of the ever memorable 14th of August, 1765, when an opposition to the ministerial plan to enslave the Americans was first made, it was celebrated by the field-officers of the sixth brigade, under the command of Colonel James Frye, at the house of Jonathan Hastings, Esq., in Cambridge, Massachusetts, where the following toasts were drank, viz.:

1. The Continental Congress. 2. Success to our undertakings. 3. The memorable 14th of August, 1765. 4. May American valor ever prove invincible to the attempt of ministerial tyranny to oppress them. 5. The twelve united colonies.

6. All our friends in Great Britain. 7. Liberty without licentiousness. 8. A speedy and happy conclusion to the present unhappy disputes. 9. The 19th of April, 1775. 10. A speedy entrance, possession, and opening of the town of Boston. 11. The President of the Continental Congress. 12. General Washington, and the other general officers of the American army. 13. A speedy export to all the enemies of America, without any drawback. 14. Immortal honor to that patriot and hero, Doctor Joseph Warren, and the brave American troops, who fought the battle at Charlestown, on the 17th of June, 1775.

New York Gazette and Weekly Mercury, August 28

August 21

MASSACHUSETTS   Captain Ross, with his company of riflemen and the stores, arrived at Cambridge on Friday last, [18th.]. There has not a random shot of a rifleman done any execution lately, worth mentioning. A letter from a selectman in Boston to his son in our camp, advises him to quit it, as there was to be some very important stroke made in a few days; we do not pay much regard to it, as it is very improbable he should know any thing of what they intend. Our lines are so strong we have nothing to fear but a surprise. There have been letters passing between the Generals Washington and Gage, on his treatment of our officers who are in jail in Boston. Our letter was in very mild terms, carefully avoiding any epithets that might be deemed unpolite. Gage's answer was in a different strain, directed to "George Washington, Esq.," calling us rebels and usurpers, and what not, affecting great clemency in having forborne to hang our prisoners. General Washington gave him a suitable reply; and so it stands:—We broke a Colonel Gerish yesterday, for cowardice on Bunker Hill, the 17th of June.

Letter from Cambridge, August 21
New York Gazette and Weekly Mercury, September 11

August 28

NEW YORK   The Provincial Congress of New York having resolved that the cannon should be removed from the battery in the city, a number of the citizens collected for that purpose last Wednesday evening, [23rd;] and part of the provincial artillery, under the command of Captain John Lamb, were posted on the battery to prevent the landing of any party from the *Asia* man-of-war, to annoy them while at work. When they marched down, which was about eleven o'clock, they observed one of the above ship's barges lying at some distance from the shore, where she continued upwards of an hour; then she got under sail, and fired a musket at the men that were posted on the Battery. This was immediately returned by a smart fire of musketry from the artillery, and a few of the Independent light infantry belonging to Colonel Lasher's battalion, that were likewise posted there for the above purpose. Soon after this the *Asia* fired three cannon, when the drums beat to arms, which alarmed the inhabitants. When they had assembled she began a heavy and smart fire, of nine, eighteen, and twenty-four-pounders, and some grapeshot, succeeded by a discharge of musketry from the marines, but without doing any other mischief than damaging the upper part of several houses near the fort and Whitehall, and wounding three men. Notwithstanding the fire from the *Asia*, the citizens effected their purpose, and carried off twenty-one pieces of cannon, being all that were mounted on carriages. Since this disturbance the women and children have been continually moving out of town, with their most valuable effects.

New York Gazette and Weekly Mercury, August 28

SEPTEMBER

September 5

ENGLAND   The following remarkable piece was distributed in a handbill, through the city of London, last July:

Lieutenant-General Bastwick's beating orders for free American Volunteers:—"All gentlemen volunteers, natives of Great Britain, friends to the liberty of America, who are willing to serve their sovereign by saving their country, and to succor and support their injured brethren, inhabitants and possessors of the great Western Hemisphere, suffering by the murderous orders of an unoffended but implacable man, have now the singular honor paid them of being solicited to stand forward in a cause, where their own character, their conscience, and even their interests should urge them to the most conspicuous exertions. Let all such, of all sizes from three feet nine to six feet three, and the shorter the better, who can feel no wounds but the wounds of the constitution, who bleed already at every pore for the distresses of the oppressed Americans, whose lungs are panting for the fame they are going to enjoy by relieving them, whose hearts lie in the right places, and are ready to burst within their breasts, for want of vent to the vengeance they wish to take. Let all such repair to the Castle and Falcon Inn, Aldergate street, where they will be honorably entertained by Lieutenant-General Jedediah Bastwick, and may enter into present pay and quarters. Entrance money, fifty acres of land in the Alleghany Mountains, or their value payable at the Royal Exchange. Bringers will be proportionally rewarded. No persons well and alive will be refused. A fine fifty gun ship lies ready at the Nore, to waft the brave adventurers in military heroism to the real scenes of action in America, to the scenes of glory, victory, and triumph. Now is your time for making your fortunes. Who is there afflicted whom I will not relieve?

The ends of the world are come upon us, and we shall soon possess them for our own. The completion of the scripture is at hand. 'Come unto me, all ye that are heavy laden, and I will relieve you.' Your armor is but light. A rifle barrel, or a tomahawk, is all you have to bear; and you have now your choice of joining with myriads of brave partakers in the same glorious warfare, by entering into one of the following regiments: Ticonderoga Pioneers, Schenectady Scalpers, Mohawks, Missalago Hatchetmen, Ohio Scouts, Massachusetts Minute Men, Scarondarona Split Shirts, Lake Champlain Pikes, Lake Ontario Jacks, Concord Riflemen, or the General's own Regiment of Alleghany Mountaineers. GOD SAVE AMERICA!"

Constitutional Gazette, September 23

America is determined and unanimous, a very few Tories excepted, who will probably soon export themselves. Britain, at the expense of three millions, has killed one hundred and fifty Yankees this campaign, which is twenty thousand pounds a head, and on Bunker Hill she gained a mile of ground, half of which she has since lost by not having post on Ploughed Hill; during the same time sixty thousand children have been born in America. From this data ——'s excellent mathematical head will easily calculate the time and expense requisite to kill us all, and conquer our whole territory.

Clift's Diary

September 15

MASSACHUSETTS   An officer in Boston, writes thus to his father in London: "Why should I complain of hard fate? General Gage and his family have for this month past, lived upon salt provisions. Last Saturday, General Putnam in the true style of military complaisance, which abolishes all personal resentment and smooths the horrors of war when discipline will permit, sent a present to the General's lady of a fine fresh quarter of veal, which was very acceptable, and received the return of a very polite card of thanks."

Constitutional Gazette, September 16

September 18

We are much astonished at the behavior of some of those captains of men-of-war, who are stationed upon our coasts. They seem greedily to anticipate the horror of blood shedding; and although war is not yet proclaimed, nor any hostilities ordered by Parliament against the colonies in general, yet confiding in their strength, they daringly assault our towns, and destroy lives upon the least provocation whatever.

When Porto Bello was restored to the Spaniards, it was agreed that the English should have a free trade there; before some of the people of the town destroyed one of the English vessels there in the night, and murdered the men on board her. When this was known, ships were sent to demand satisfaction, which was refused. Orders were then given to beat down the town. The commander in that service sent a boat on shore to inform the inhabitants of his business, and desire the women and children to remove out of the city. He allowed them a whole day for the purpose—sent ashore again to see if it was done, and then battered down only some of the houses, and a church or two, and that in the day time. Such was the true old British spirit, even when dealing with Spaniards and executing positive orders! How different from this is the conduct of those inhuman commanders now upon our coasts! How detestable their character! A Wallace and an Ayscough disgraced humanity and brought reproach upon the British Navy by wantonly employing it to terrify women and children. But the conduct of a Vandeput is more surprising and cruel than even theirs. They only threatened—he actually fired upon a defenceless town, and his previous preparations showed that he was not actuated by a sense of duty, but by the cold-blooded barbarity of an assassin. He acknowledges in his first letter that he was informed of the design of taking away the cannon from the battery; why then did he not, by a letter to the magistrates, let the city know he esteemed it his duty to defend those guns? In that case the town, apprised of his determination, might have thought it more prudent to desist than to provoke him. But upon his own principle of protecting the battery, what right had he to elevate his guns, and fire heavy balls at random upon the city, a great part of whose inhabitants must consist of children and women. Surely the blood of innocents will rise in judgment against him. It was not owing to his wishes or endeavors, but only to the goodness of Almighty God, that hundreds of men, totally ignorant of what was doing at the battery, were not murdered. O! had this happened in the days of good old King George, that father of his people, it would have cost Vandeput not only his character and his ship, but his head would atone for his horrid barbarity.

Letter from Annapolis, Maryland
Constitutional Gazette, September 20

September 20

VIRGINIA   A system of justice similar to that adopted against the devoted town of Boston, is likely to be established in Virginia, by the renowned commander [Squires] of the fleet there. He has in the course of this week, as a reprisal for the loss of a tender, seized every vessel belonging to Hampton that came within his reach, and thereby rendered himself the terror of all the small craft and fishing boats in this river, especially the latter, having brought some of them under his stern, by a discharge of his cannon at them. He has likewise seized a vessel belonging to the eastern shore, and having honored the passengers so far with his notice, as to receive them on board his own vessel, took the liberty of sending one of their horses as a present to Lord Dunmore. This act of generosity, we doubt not, will gain him considerable interest with his lordship, it being an instance of his industry in distressing a people, who have of late become obnoxious to his excellency for their spirited behavior. We hope that those who have lived under and enjoyed the blessings of the British Constitution, will not continue tame spectators of such flagrant violations of its most salutary laws in defence of private property. The crimes daily committed by this plunderer, we would not willingly brand with the odious name of piracy, but we are confident they come under those offences to which the English laws have denied the benefit of clergy.

Virginia Gazette, September 23

September 30

VIRGINIA   This afternoon, between two and three o'clock, an officer at the head of a party of marines and sailors landed at the County Wharf, in Norfolk, in Virginia, under cover of the men-of-war, who made every appearance of firing on the town, should the party be molested, and marched up the main street to Mr. Holt's printing-office, from whence they carried off the types, and sundry other printing implements, with two of the workmen, and, after getting to the water-side with their booty, gave three cheers, in which they were joined by a crowd of rascally Negroes. A few spirited gentlemen in Norfolk, justly incensed at so flagrant a breach of good order and the constitution, and highly resenting the conduct of Lord Dunmore and the navy gentry, who have now commenced to be downright pirates and banditti, ordered the drums to beat to arms, but were joined by very few; so that it appears Norfolk is, at present, a very insecure place for the life or property of any individual, and is consequently deserted daily by numbers of the inhabitants, with their effects.

Lord Dunmore is exceedingly offended with the Virginia printers, for presuming to furnish the public with a faithful relation of occurrences, and now and then, making a few strictures upon his lordship's own conduct, as well as that of some of his delightful associates, such as Dicky Squire and little white-headed Montagu. Some of their actions have certainly deserved the severest reprehension, to say no more; for which the printers appeal to the whole world, even Freddy North himself, and the immaculate Johnny Bute. It seems his lordship has it much at heart to destroy every channel of public intelligence that is inimical to his designs upon the liberties of this country, alleging that they poison the minds of the people; or, in other words, lay open to them the tyrannical designs of a wicked ministry, which hath been supported in character by most of their slavish dependents. It is to be hoped, however, that neither his lordship, nor any other person, however dignified, will have it in his power to succeed in so diabolical a scheme, only fit to be accomplished among Turks, and never could have been devised but by a person of the most unfriendly principles to the liberties of mankind.

Virginia Gazette, October 7
Constitutional Gazette, October 21

The following is said to be the plan which will be put in execution for reducing America:—Ten thousand Hanoverians are to be taken into British pay, the expenses to be defrayed out of duties to be laid by parliament, and levied in America. This body of men is to be stationed in several parts of that continent, and to be kept on foot in peace as well as in war. Fortresses are to be built in the provinces of New England, New York, Pennsylvania, and Virginia, in which those foreign mercenaries are to be stationed, and accommodated with barracks, firing, etc., at the expense of the several colonies in which they shall happen to be quartered. Besides this, a fleet of five ships of the line and twenty frigates are always to be stationed in that service, both to prevent smuggling, and, in case of any disturbance, to be ready to co-operate in reducing the rebellious or disaffected to obedience. Every Hanoverian soldier, who shall have served seven years with the approbation of his superior officer or officers, shall have a portion of ground, not more than fifty nor less than twenty acres, rent free, forever. The expense of raising a proper habitation, furnishing same, purchasing implements of husbandry, etc., to be defrayed by the colony in which he shall be then resident. The whole expense of recruiting to be provided for in like manner—that is to say, fifty pounds for every soldier, and one hundred for every trooper, rating his horse at fifty and himself at as much more. This mercenary army is to consist of thirty battalions of infantry, of five hundred men each, and four regiments of cavalry; twenty battalions and two regiments of which are always to be stationed in the four New England provinces, and the remaining ten battalions and two regiments at New York, Philadelphia, and Williamsburg in Virginia, and their neighborhoods. On the whole, as the Germans are known to be a very prolific people, it is supposed that by the beginning of the year 1800, there will be no less than a million of that nation, including their offspring, within the four New England provinces alone.

Constitutional Gazette, September 30

OCTOBER

October 2

NEW HAMPSHIRE   This evening arrived in the Piscataqua River a ship from England intended for Boston. It appears that yesterday she was in company with the *Raven* man-of-war, bound to the same place, but parted with her in the night. Meeting a fisherman at the eastward of Cape Ann, the captain inquired the course to Boston. The honest fisherman, pointing towards the Piscataqua, said, "There is Boston." The crew shaped their course accordingly, and soon found themselves under the guns of a battery lately erected by the people of New Hampshire. The commander of the battery, with a number of men, very humanely went on board to pilot the ship up to Portsmouth. "I cannot go there," said the captain of the ship, "I am bound to Boston." "But you must," replied the other. Then he ordered her to get under way, and soon carried her safe alongside a wharf, where she is taken proper care of. She has been out eleven weeks from Bristol, in England, and has on board eighteen hundred barrels, and four hundred half barrels, of flour, intended for the use of the besieged army in Boston.

New-York Journal, October 12

October 4

A correspondent at London says, "It is under consideration to form a parliament, or general council, for all the provinces in America, something similar to that of Ireland; the governors and some particular officers to form an upper house."—With due thanks to our aged mother, now debilitated in her mental faculties, for her solicitude in forming a government for us, we would desire her to spare herself that trouble. We, being now of age to manage our own business, shall take care to form a government for ourselves, in which we want no one to interpose, though we shall always have a dutiful regard to our mother, desire to be upon good terms with her, and render her all the help that is consistent with the necessary care of our freedom and interest—which is as much as any reasonable, affectionate mother can expect or desire.

New-York Journal, October 5

October 8

RHODE ISLAND   Yesterday afternoon appeared in sight of Bristol harbor a very formidable fleet, consisting of sixteen sail, viz.: three men-of-war, one bomb ketch, and other armed vessels, all of which, excepting the *Glasgow*, which ran ashore at Papaquash point, drew up in a line of battle from one end of the town to the other. Soon after they had moored, a barge came from the *Rose* to the head of a wharf, with the lieutenant, who asked if there were any gentlemen on the wharf? William Bradford being present, answered yes; whereupon the lieutenant informed him Captain Wallace had a demand to make on the town, and desired that two or three of the principal men, or magistrates, of the town, would go on board his ship, within an hour, and hear his proposals; otherwise hostilities would be commenced against the town. The above gentleman replied, as a magistrate, that, in his opinion, Captain Wallace was under a greater obligation to come ashore and make his demands known to the town, than for the magistrates to go on board his ship to hear them; and added, that if Captain Wallace would come to the head of the wharf the next morning, he should be treated as a gentleman, and the town would consider of his demands. With this answer the lieutenant returned on board the *Rose*. The inhabitants being made acquainted with the above association, repaired to the wharf and waited with the utmost impatience for a reply from Captain Wallace, till an hour had expired, when the whole fleet began a most heavy cannonading, and the bomb vessel to bombard and heave shells and carcases into the town; which continued, without intermission an hour and a half.

In the mean time, Colonel Potter, in the hottest of the fire, went upon the head of the wharf, hailed the *Rose*, went on board, and requested a cessation of hostilities, till the inhabitants might choose a committee to go on board and treat with Captain Wallace; which request was complied with; and six hours were allowed for the above purpose. Colonel Potter returned and made a report to the committee of inspection, who chose a select committee to hear Captain Wallace's demands, which, after they had gone on board, Captain Wallace informed them were a supply of two hundred sheep and thirty fat cattle. This demand, the committee replied, it was impossible to comply with; for the country people had been in and driven off their stock, saving a few sheep and some milch cows.

After some hours had expired, during the negotiation, without coming to any agreement, Captain Wallace told them: "I have this one proposal to make: if you will promise to supply me with forty sheep, at or before twelve o'clock, I will assure you that another gun shall not be discharged." The committee, seeing themselves reduced to the distressing alternative, either to supply their most inveterate enemy with provisions, or to devote to the flames the town, with all the goods, besides near one hundred sick persons, who could not be removed without the utmost hazard of their lives; I say, seeing themselves reduced to this dreadful dilemma of two evils, reluctantly chose the least, by agreeing to supply them with forty sheep at the time appointed, which was punctually performed.

The Reverend Mr. John Burt, having been confined to his house by the camp distemper, when the cannonading began, left his habitation to seek some place of safety, and to-day was found dead in a neighboring field. It is conjectured that, being overcome with fear and fatigue, he fell down and was unable to raise himself up, and so expired. A child of Captain Timothy Ingraham, having been removed in the rain, is also dead.

What equally challenges our admiration and gratitude to God is, that no more lives were lost, or persons hurt, by such an incessant and hot fire; the streets being full of men, women, and children, the whole time. The shrieks of the women, the cries of the children, and groans of the sick, would have extorted a tear from even the eye of a Nero.

Letter from Bristol, Rhode Island
New York Gazette and Weekly Mercury, October 23

October 19

NEW YORK   Yesterday, at New York, departed this life, of a fever, Michael Cresap, Esq., eldest son of Colonel Thomas Cresap, of Potomac, in Virginia, in the twenty-eighth year of his age. He was captain of a rifle company now in the Continental army before Boston. He served as a captain under the command of Lord Dunmore, in the late expedition against the Indians, in which he eminently distinguished himself, by his prudence, firmness, and intrepidity, as a brave officer; and in the present contest between the parent state and the colonies, gave proofs of his attachment to the rights and liberties of his country. He has left a widow and four children to deplore the loss of a husband and a father; and by his death his country is deprived of a worthy and esteemed citizen. To-day he was interred at Trinity Church. His funeral was attended from his lodgings by the independent companies of militia, and the most respectable inhabitants, through the principal streets to the church. The grenadiers of the first battalion fired three volleys over his grave. The whole was conducted with great decency, and in military form.

Constitutional Gazette, October 23
Rivington's Gazette, October 26

October 28

VIRGINIA   After Lord Dunmore, with his troops and navy, had been for several weeks seizing the persons and property of his Majesty's peaceable subjects in Virginia, on Wednesday night last [25th] a party from an armed tender landed near Hampton, and took away a valuable Negro man slave and a sail from the owner; next morning there appeared off the mouth of Hampton River a large armed schooner, a sloop, and three tenders, with soldiers on board, and a message was received at Hampton from Captain Squires, on board the schooner, that he would that day land and burn the town; on which a company of Regulars and a company of minute men, who had been placed there in consequence of former threats denounced against that place, made the best disposition to prevent their landing, aided by a body of militia who were suddenly called together on the occasion. The enemy accordingly attempted to land, but were retarded by some boats sunk across the channel for that purpose; upon this they fired several small cannon at the provincials, without any effect, who, in return, discharged their small arms so effectually, as to make the enemy move off, with the loss of several men, as it is believed; but they had, in the mean time, burnt down a house belonging to a Mr. Cooper, on that river.

On intelligence of this reaching Williamsburg, about nine at night, a company of riflemen were despatched to the aid of Hampton, and the colonel of the second regiment sent to take the command of the whole; who with the company, arrived about eight o'clock next morning. The enemy had, in the night, cut through the sunken boats and made a passage for their vessels, which were drawn up close to the town, and began to fire upon it soon after the arrival of the party from Williamsburg; but as soon as our men were so disposed as to give them a few shot, they went off so hastily that our people took a small tender with five white men, a woman, and two slaves, six swivels, seven muskets, some small arms and other things, a sword, pistols, and several papers belonging to a

Lieutenant Wright, who made his escape by jumping over-board and swimming away, with Mr. King's Negro man. They are on shore, and a pursuit, it is hoped, may overtake them. There were in the vessel two men mortally wounded; one is since dead and the other near his end; besides which, nine men were seen to be thrown overboard from one of the vessels. We had not a man even wounded. The vessels went over to Norfolk, and the whole force from thence is intending to visit Hampton to-day. If they come, we hope our brave troops will be prepared for them.

Rivington's Gazette, November 9

NOVEMBER

November 1

MASSACHUSETTS   Nearly all the people belonging to Cape Ann, in Massachusetts, have evacuated the town, and have proceeded so far in removing their effects, as to take away the glass windows from the meeting-house and many of the dwelling-houses. Lieutenant-colonel Mason, of the artillery, has been down from Cambridge to give directions in fortify-ing the harbor, where two batteries are already erected, and other measures taken for giving the enemy a proper reception.

New England Chronicle, November 2

November 7

NEW HAMPSHIRE   The province of New Hampshire has asked advice of the Congress relative to assuming government. The Congress advised the Provincial Convention to grant war-rants for a free and full election of representatives of the colony, who, if they think it necessary, are to choose such a form of government as they, in their judgment, shall think will best promote the happiness of the people, and preserve peace and good order during the present dispute with Great Britain.

The same advice was given to South Carolina, and in a few months we hope every colony will be perfectly free.

Letter from Philadelphia
Constitutional Gazette, December 6

VIRGINIA   This day Lord Dunmore issued the following proclamation, from his retreat on board the war-ship *William*, now at anchor off Norfolk, Virginia. It at once shows the baseness of his heart, his malice and treachery against the people who were once under his government, and his officious violation of all law, justice, and humanity; not to mention his arrogating to himself a power which neither he can assume, nor any power upon earth invest him with.

"A PROCLAMATION:—As I have ever entertained hopes that an accommodation might have taken place between Great Britain and this colony, without being compelled, by my duty, to this most disagreeable, but now absolutely necessary step; rendered so by a body of armed men, unlawfully assembled, firing upon his Majesty's tenders; and the formation of an army, and that army now on their way to attack his Majesty's troops and destroy the well-disposed subjects of this country. To defeat such treasonable purposes, and that all such traitors and their abettors may be brought to justice, and that the peace and good order of this colony may be again restored, which the ordinary course of the civil law is unable to effect; I have thought fit to issue this, my proclamation, hereby declaring, that until the aforesaid good purposes can be obtained, I do, in virtue of the power and authority to me given by his Majesty, determine to execute martial law, and cause the same to be executed throughout this colony; and to the end that peace and good order may the sooner be restored, I do require every person capable of bearing arms to resort to his Majesty's STANDARD, or be looked upon as a traitor to his crown and government, and thereby become liable to the penalty the law inflicts upon such offences, such as forfeiture of life, confiscation of lands, etc., etc. And I do hereby further declare all indentured servants, Negroes, or others, appertaining to rebels, FREE, that are willing and able to bear arms; they joining his Majesty's troops, as soon as may be, for the purpose of reducing this colony to a proper sense of their duty to his Majesty's crown and dignity. I do further order and require, all his Majesty's liege subjects to retain their quit rents, or any other taxes due, or that may become due, in their own custody, till such time as peace be again restored to this at present most unhappy country, or demanded of them, for their former salutary purposes, by officers properly authorized to receive the same."

Pennsylvania Journal, December 6

It is necessary, for the welfare of two sorts of people, that the appearance of this proclamation should be attended with some comment. Such as have mixed much in society, and have had opportunities of hearing the subject of the present unnatural contest discussed, will be but little startled at the appellation of *rebel*, because they will know it is not merited. But others there may be, whose circumstances may, in a great measure, have excluded them from the knowledge of public matters, who may be sincerely attached to the interest of their country, and who may yet be frightened to act against it, from the dread of incurring a guilt which, by all good men, is justly abhorred. To these, it may be proper to address a few remarks upon this proclamation; and, as a part of it respects the Negroes, and seems to offer something very flattering and desirable to them, it may be doing them, as well as the country, a service, to give them a just view of what they are to expect, should they be so weak and wicked as to comply with what Lord Dunmore requires. Those, then, who are afraid of being styled *rebels*, we would beg to consider, that although Lord Dunmore, in this proclamation, insidiously mentions his having till now entertained hopes of an accommodation, yet the whole tenor of his conduct, for many months past, has had the most direct and strongest tendency to widen the unhappy breach, and render a reconciliation more difficult. For what other purpose did he write his false and inflammatory letters to the ministers of state? Why did he, under cover of the night, take from us our powder, and render useless the arms of our public magazine? Why did he secretly and treacherously lay snares for the lives of our unwary brethren; snares that had likely to have proved but too effectual? Why did he, under idle pretences, withdraw himself from the seat of government, where alone he could, had he been willing, have done essential service to our country? Why, by his authority, have continual depredations been since made upon such of our countrymen as are situated within the reach of ships-of-war and tenders? Why have our towns been attacked, and houses destroyed? Why have the persons of many of our most respectable brethren been seized upon, torn from all their connections, and confined on board of ships? Was all this to bring about a reconciliation? Judge for yourselves, whether the injuring of our persons and properties be the readiest way to gain our affections. After insulting our persons, he now presumes to insult our understandings also. Do not believe his words, when his actions so directly contradict them. If he wished for an accommodation; if he had a desire to restore peace and order, as he professes, it was to be upon terms that would have been disgraceful, and, in the end, destructive of every thing dear and valuable.

Consider, again, the many attempts that have been made to enslave us. Nature gave us equal privileges with the people of Great Britain: we are equally, with them, entitled to the disposal of our own property; and we have never resigned to them those rights, which we derived from nature. But they have endeavored, unjustly, to rob us of them. They have made acts of parliament, in which we in no manner concurred, which dispose of our property; acts which abridge us of liberties we once enjoyed, and which impose burdens and restraints upon us too heavy to be borne. Had we immediately taken up arms to assert our rights, and to prevent the exercise of unlawful power, though our cause would have been just, yet our conduct would have been precipitate, and, so far, blamable. We might then, with some shadow of justice, have been charged with *rebellion*, or a disposition to rebel. But this was not the way we behaved. We petitioned once and again, in the most dutiful manner; we hoped the righteousness of our cause would appear, that our complaints would be heard and attended to; we wished to avoid the horrors of a civil war, and so long proceeded in this fruitless track, that our not adopting a more vigorous opposition seemed rather to proceed from a spirit of meanness and fear than of peace and loyalty; and all that we gained was, to be more grievously oppressed. At length we resolved to withhold our commerce from Great Britain, and, by thus affecting her interest, oblige her to redress our grievances. But in this also we have been disappointed. Our associations have been deemed unlawful combinations, and opposition to government. We have been entirely deprived of our trade to foreign countries, and even amongst ourselves, and fleets and armies have been sent to reduce us to a compliance with the unjust and arbitrary demands of the British minister and corrupt parliament. Reduced to such circumstances, to what could we have recourse but to arms? Every other expedient having been tried and found ineffectual, this alone was left, and this we have, at last, unwillingly adopted. If it be *rebellion* to take up arms in such a cause as this, rebellion, then, is not only justifiable, but an honorable thing.

But let us not be deceived with empty sounds. They who call us rebels cannot make us so. Rebellion is open, and avows opposition to lawful authority; but it is usurped and arbitrary power which we have determined to oppose. Societies are formed and magistrates appointed, that men may the better enjoy the blessings of life. Some of the rights which they have derived from nature they part with, that they may the more peaceably and safely possess the rest. To preserve the rights they have reserved, is the duty of every member of society; and to deprive a people of these is *treason, is rebellion against the state.* If this doctrine, then, be right, which no one, we believe, will venture to deny, we are dutiful members of society; and the persons who endeavor to rob us of our rights, *they are the rebels,—rebels to their country and to the rights of human nature.* We are acting the part of loyal subjects, of faithful members of the community, when we stand forth in opposition to the arbitrary and oppressive acts of any man, or set of men. Resort not, then, to the standard which Lord Dunmore has set up; and, if any of you have been so mistaken in your duty as to join him, fly from his camp as an infected place, and speedily rejoin your virtuous, suffering countrymen; for be you well assured, that the time will come when these invaders of the rights of human kind will suffer the punishment due to their crimes; and when the insulted and oppressed Americans will, if they preserve their virtue, triumph over all their enemies.

The second class of people, for whose sake a few remarks upon this proclamation seem necessary, is the Negroes. They have been flattered with their freedom, if they be able to bear arms, and will speedily join Lord Dunmore's troops. To none, then, is freedom promised, but to such as are able to do Lord Dunmore service. The aged, the infirm, the women and children, are still to remain the property of their masters; masters who will be provoked to severity, should part of their slaves desert them. Lord Dunmore's declaration, therefore, is a cruel declaration to the Negroes. He does not even pretend to make it out of any tenderness for them, but solely on his own account; and, should it meet with success, it leaves by far the greater number at the mercy of an enraged and injured people. But should there be any among the Negroes weak enough to believe that Dunmore intends to do them a kindness, and wicked enough to provoke the fury of the Americans against their defenceless fathers and mothers, their wives, their women and children, let them only consider the difficulties of effecting their escape, and what they must expect to suffer if they fall into the hands of the Americans. Let them farther consider what must be their fate, should the English prove conquerors in this dispute. If we can judge of the future from the past, it will not be much mended. Long have the Americans, moved by compassion, and actuated by sound policy, endeavored to stop the progress of slavery. Our assemblies have repeatedly passed acts laying heavy duties upon imported Negroes, by which they meant altogether to prevent the horrid traffic; but their humane intentions have been as often frustrated by the cruelty and covetousness of a set of English merchants, who prevailed upon the King to repeal our kind and merciful acts, little indeed to the credit of his human-ity. Can it then be supposed that the Negroes will be better used by the English, who have always encouraged and upheld this slavery, than by their present masters, who pity their condition, who wish, in general, to make it as easy and comfortable as possible, and who would willingly, were it in their power, or were they permitted, not only prevent any more Negroes from losing their freedom, but restore it to such as have already unhappily lost it?

No; these ends of Lord Dunmore and his party being answered, they will either give up the offending Negroes to the rigor of the laws they have broken, or sell them in the West Indies, where every year they sell many thousands of their miserable brethren, to perish either by the inclemency of the weather, or the cruelty of barbarous masters. Be not then, ye Negroes, tempted by this proclamation to ruin yourselves. We have given you a faithful view of what you are to expect; and declare, before God, in doing it, we have considered your welfare as well as that of the country. Whether you will profit by the advice, we cannot tell; but this we know, that whether we suffer or not, if you desert us, *you* most certainly will.

Virginia Gazette, November 25

November 9

SOUTH CAROLINA   In South Carolina they have two thousand men in actual pay, and five hundred horse on the frontiers. Colonel Gadsden, commander-in-chief, and Colonel Isaac Huger, second colonel, first regiment. Second regiment, Colonel Moultrie, Isaac Mott, lieutenant-colonel, late of the Royal Americans. Fort Johnson fortified, and garrisoned with four hundred and fifty men. Mount Pleasant fortified with four cannon, two hundred men stationed to prevent the shipping taking water. No provisions allowed the King's ships. Two schooners fitted out, mounting fourteen and twelve guns, and full manned as cruisers. The three forts in Charleston and the first bastion, fortified with cannon. An intrenchment, about four miles from town, laid out; tools made and men ready to begin the intrenchment when the express came away. Women and children almost all moved out of town, and barracks built for them in the country. They have twenty tons of powder, and the quantity daily increasing. Two thousand men in uniforms, blue faced with red. Light horse, five hundred, blue faced with white, and well furnished. The militia in the country in fine order; drill sergeants having been sent among them many months past. The regulators in the back country, who were under oath, have entered into a treaty to remain neuter; Thomas Fletcher and Patrick Cunningham, their chiefs, are now in Charleston. The people are under no apprehensions from their Negroes. The Honorable William Henry Drayton, the worthy judge of the superior court, has made a treaty with the Cherokees to assist the inhabitants in case of necessity.

Rivington's Gazette, November 9

November 10

MASSACHUSETTS   Yesterday a party of Regulars from Boston, amounting to four or five hundred men, embarked in a number of barges from Charlestown Point, about one o'clock, P.M., when the tide was at a high flood, and landed upon Lechmere's Point, under cover of a man-of-war and a floating battery, where they seized a sentinel who was drunk and asleep upon his post. The other sentinels fired upon them, and then gave the alarm to the camp upon Prospect Hill. Lechmere's Point is a piece of high land surrounded by marsh, and when the tide is up is entirely an island. This circumstance the Regulars knew, and intended to take advantage of it. Their purpose was to steal the sheep and cattle that were feeding there. They effected a landing without opposition (as indeed there were none at that time on the ground to oppose them), and began to drive the cattle to their boats. His Excellency [Gen. Washington] ordered Colonel Thompson and his regiment of Pennsylvania riflemen to turn out immediately, and they obeyed with cheerfulness. Colonel Thompson and Colonel Mifflin headed them, and passed the morass up to their breasts in water. When they were all over and formed under cover of a hill, they marched forward. Colonel Thompson gave the Indian yell, which was re-echoed back from the whole regiment, who immediately rushed out from their ambuscade, and poured in whole volleys upon the Regulars, who returned the fire in great confusion, and retreated with the greatest precipitation on board their boats, firing at random upon our men, who kept up a heavy fire upon them, notwithstanding the constant blaze from the man-of-war, floating battery, and boats, which latter mounted six patteraroes, or swivels, each. The event of the skirmish is yet uncertain: doubtless they must have lost a number of men, as our shot were well planted. We fired a few shot at them from Prospect Hill, and a field-piece, we had planted for the purpose, in the valley below. Some of our men are badly wounded, but we hear of none of them who were killed. When the enemy saw they were likely to be prevented in accomplishing their purpose, with a villanous malice, characteristic of the tools of despotism, they stabbed the poor dumb cattle. During the engagement twenty-two large ships hove in sight, with troops from England and Ireland.

Rivington's Gazette, November 23

MASSACHUSETTS   This day three dead bodies have floated along shore, supposed to be drowned by the sinking of a barge, which our field-pieces stove. The enemy had cannon placed at the water's edge, along Charlestown Point, which, together with the large artillery from Bunker Hill, made an incessant roar, with grape-shot, chain-shot, &c., but to no purpose. The riflemen drove them like a herd of swine down a steep place, where some of them were killed, drowned, or scared to death, in sight of their brethren in iniquity, who covered the tops of Fort Beacon and Bunker Hill to view the noble exploit of cow-stealing. The general has since ordered all the stock to be driven off the peninsula of Dorchester.

Letter from Roxbury, Massachusetts
Pennsylvania Journal, November 29

November 17

VIRGINIA   Colonel [Patrick] Henry received an express yesterday morning, at Williamsburg, Virginia, with the following intelligence, viz.: that Lord Dunmore having received advice that about two hundred of the militia [of Princess Anne County] were on their march to join the troops destined for the protection of the lower parts of the country, marched from Norfolk last Tuesday, about one o'clock in the afternoon, with about three hundred and fifty men, consisting of Regular soldiers, sailors, runaway Negroes, and Tories, to intercept them; who, not having the last intelligence of his lordship's approach, were obliged to engage under every disadvantage, both as to the enemy's superiority in point of numbers, and the situation of the ground, being hemmed in by a fence. Our people fought a considerable time, and it is thought did great execution; but were at last overpowered, and forced to retreat, with the loss of Mr. John Ackiss, in the minute service, killed on the spot; and Colonel Joseph Hutchings, and one Mr. Williams wounded, who were taken prisoners with seven others. The public, no doubt, will be exceedingly incensed, on finding that Lord Dunmore has taken into his service the very scum of the country, to assist him in his diabolical schemes, against the good people of this government, all well attached to his Majesty, but mortal enemies to his infamous ministry and their subordinate tools; but it is to be hoped his sphere of mischief will soon be circumscribed within narrow bounds, as Colonel Woodford, with about eight hundred as brave troops as the world can produce, are now on their march to Norfolk; and, should his lordship incline to give them battle, we have not the smallest doubt they will give a very satisfactory account of him.

New York Gazette and Weekly Mercury, December 4

DECEMBER

December 6

NEW JERSEY   At Quibbletown, New Jersey, Thomas Randolph, cooper, who had publicly proved himself an enemy to his country, by reviling and using his utmost endeavors to oppose the proceedings of the continental and provincial conventions, in defence of their rights and liberties; and being judged a person not of consequence enough for a severer punishment, was ordered to be stripped naked, well coated with tar and feathers, and carried in a wagon publicly around the town—which punishment was accordingly inflicted. As soon as he became duly sensible of his offence, for which he earnestly begged pardon, and promised to atone, as far as he was able, by a contrary behavior for the future, he was released and suffered to return to his house, in less than half an hour. The whole was conducted with that regularity and decorum that ought to be observed in all public punishments.

New-York Journal, December 28

NEW YORK   Some time ago some boys in the Queen's County, Long Island, having caught several *cats*, went to the plain, with their dogs, to have the pleasure of hunting them. A cat being let out of the bag was pursued by the dogs; and the lads, who were on horseback, followed in full chase. The cat led them towards Hempstead, and just at that instant they were seen by an assembly man, whose imagination converted them into Yankees. He set off immediately post haste to alarm the people, who had for some time dreaded a visit from their friends in New England, and a great part of the country were thrown into the utmost consternation. Some betook themselves to flight for safety; others thought to shelter in recluse and solitary places, and waiting trembling in retirement, until they found their property remained unhurt, when they returned home, and were informed that all the confusion was occasioned by a few boys hunting some cats. A justice of the peace was absent from home three days on this occasion.

Constitutional Gazette, December 30

December 9

VIRGINIA   This morning, after reveille beating, two or three great guns and some muskets were discharged from the enemy's fort near Great Bridge, which, as it was not an unusual thing, was little regarded by Colonel Woodford [Commander of the Virginia Militia]. However, soon after he heard a call to the soldiers to stand to their arms; upon which, with all expedition, he made the proper disposition to receive the enemy.

[As the scene of action is but little known to the generality of people, it may be necessary to give some description of it, that the relation may be more clear and satisfactory. The Great Bridge is built over what is called the southern branch of Elizabeth River, twelve miles above Norfolk. The land on each side is marshy to a considerable distance from the river, except at the two extremities of the bridge, where are two pieces of firm land, which may not improperly be called islands, being surrounded entirely by water and marsh, and joined to the mainland by causeways. On the little piece of firm ground on the farther or Norfolk side, Lord Dunmore had erected his fort in such a manner that his cannon commanded the causeway on his own side, and the bridge between him and us, with the marshes around him. The island on this side of the river contained six or seven houses, some of which were burnt down (the nearest to the bridge) by the enemy, after the arrival of our troops; in the others, adjoining the causeway on each side, were stationed a guard every night by Colonel Woodford, but withdrawn before day, as they might not be exposed to the fire of the enemy's fort in recrossing the causeway to our camp, this causeway being also commanded by their cannon. The causeway on our side was in length, about one hundred and sixty yards, and on the hither extremity our breastwork was thrown up. From the breastwork ran a street, gradually ascending, about the length of four hundred yards, to a church, where our main body was encamped. *Pinkney's Virginia Gazette*, December 20.]

In the mean time the enemy had crossed the bridge, fired the remaining houses on the island, and some large piles of shingles, and attacked our guard in the breastwork. Our men returned the fire, and threw them into some confusion, but they were instantly rallied by Captain Fordyce, and advanced along the causeway with great resolution, keeping up a constant and heavy fire as they approached. Two field-pieces, which had been brought across the bridge and planted on the edge of the island, facing the left of our breastwork, played briskly at the same time upon us. Lieut. Travis, who commanded in the breastwork, ordered his men to reserve their fire till the enemy came within the distance of fifty yards, and then they gave it to them with terrible execution. The brave Fordyce exerted himself to keep up their spirits, reminded them of their ancient glory, and, waving his hat over his head, encouragingly told them the day was their own. Thus pressing forward he fell within fifteen steps of the breastwork. His wounds were many, and his death would have been that of a hero, had he met it in a better cause. The progress of the enemy was now at an end; they retreated over the causeway with precipitation, and were dreadfully galled in the rear. Hitherto on our side only the guard, consisting of twenty-five and some others, upon the whole not amounting to more than ninety, had been engaged. Only the Regulars of the 14th regiment, in number one hundred and twenty, had advanced upon the causeway, and about two hundred and thirty Tories and Negroes had, after crossing the bridge, continued upon the island. The Regulars, after retreating along the causeway, were again rallied by Captain Leslie, and the two field-pieces continued to play upon our men. It was at this time that Colonel Woodford was advancing down the street to the breastwork with the main body, and against him was now directed the whole fire of the enemy. Never were cannon better served; but yet, in the face of them and the musketry which kept up a continual blaze, our men marched on with the utmost intrepidity. Colonel Stevens, of the Culpeper battalion, was sent around to the left to flank the enemy, which was done with such activity and spirit that a rout immediately ensued.

The enemy fled into their fort, leaving behind them the two field-pieces, which, however, they took care to spike up with nails. Many were killed and wounded in the flight, but Colonel Woodford very prudently restrained his troops from urging their pursuit too far. From the beginning of the attack till the repulse from the breastwork might be about fourteen or fifteen minutes; till the total defeat, upwards of half an hour. It is said that some of the enemy preferred death to captivity, from a fear of being scalped, which Lord Dunmore inhumanly told them would be their fate should they be taken alive. Thirty-one killed and wounded fell into our hands, and the number borne off was much greater. Through the whole of the engagement every officer and soldier behaved with the greatest courage and calmness. The conduct of our sentinels we cannot pass over in silence. Before they quited their stations, they fired at least three rounds as the enemy were crossing the bridge, and one of them, who was posted behind some shingles, kept his ground till he had fired eight times; and after receiving a whole platoon, made his escape over the causeway into our breastwork.

The scene was closed with as much humanity as it had been conducted with bravery. The work of death being over, every one's attention was directed to the succor of the unhappy sufferers, and it is an undoubted fact that Captain Leslie was so affected with the tenderness of our troops towards those who were yet capable of assistance, that he gave signs from the fort of his thankfulness for it. What is not to be paralleled in history, and will scarcely appear credible, except to such as acknowledge a Providence over human affairs, this victory was gained at the expense of no more than a slight wound in a soldier's hand; and one circumstance which renders it still more amazing is, that the field-pieces raked the whole length of the street, and absolutely threw double-headed shot as far as the church; and afterwards, as our troops approached, cannonaded them heavily with grape-shot.

Pennsylvania Evening Post, January 6

December 31

CANADA   The Americans have made an unsuccessful attack upon the town of Quebec. General [Richard] Montgomery[1] finding his cannon too light to effect a breach, and

---

[1] RICHARD MONTGOMERY was born in the north of Ireland, in the year 1737. He entered the English army, and was with General Wolfe at Quebec in 1759. Quitting the army in 1772, he settled in America, where he married a daughter of R. R. Livingston. On the commencement of the difficulties between the colonies and Great Britain, he warmly espoused the cause of the colonists, and, in the fall of 1775, was connected with General Schuyler in the command of the expedition against Canada. In October, owing to the indisposition of General Schuyler, the chief command of the army devolved upon Montgomery.

that the enemy would not hearken to terms of capitulation,
formed a design of carrying the town by escalade. In this he
was encouraged by the extensiveness of the works, and the
weakness of the garrison. When every thing was prepared,
while he was awaiting the opportunity of a snow-storm to
carry his design into execution, several of his men deserted
to the enemy. His plan, at first, was to have attacked the upper
and lower town at the same time, depending principally for
success upon the upper town. But discovering, from the
motions of the enemy, that they were apprised of his design,
he altered his plan, and, having divided his small army into
four detachments, ordered two feints to be made against the
upper town, one by Colonel [Henry] Livingston at the head
of the Canadians, against St. John's gate, the other by Captain Brown, at the head of a small detachment, against Cape
Diamond, reserving to himself and Colonel [Benedict] Arnold,
the two principal attacks against the lower town.

At five o'clock this morning, the hour appointed for the
attack, the general, at the head of the New York troops,
advanced against the lower town. Being obliged to take a
circuit, the signal for the attack was given and the garrison
alarmed before he reached the place. However, pressing on,
he passed the first barrier, and was just opening the attempt
on the second, when, by the first fire from the enemy, he was
unfortunately killed, together with his aide-de-camp, Captain
J. McPherson, Captain Cheesman, and two or three more.
This so dispirited the men, that Colonel Campbell, on whom
the command devolved, found himself under the disagreeable
necessity of drawing them off.

The progress of his troops from Ticonderoga to the redoubts before
Quebec, was marked with bravery and success. They took Chamblee
on the 18th of October, St. John's on the 3d of November, and on the
12th he led them into Montreal. In December, he joined General
Arnold, who had come from the camp at Cambridge, through the
wilderness of Maine, and they together marched to Quebec.

Every mark of distinction was shown to the corpse of General Montgomery, who was interred in Quebec on the 2nd of January, 1776. In
1818, his body was removed, in accordance with an act of the New
York Legislature, and re-interred at St. Paul's church-yard, in New
York city. [Frank Moore]

In the meanwhile Colonel Arnold, at the head of about three hundred and fifty of those brave troops, (who with unparalleled fatigue had penetrated Canada under his command,) and Captain Lamb's company of artillery, had passed through St. Roques' gate, and approached near a two-gun battery, picketed in, without being discovered. This he attacked, and though it was well defended for about an hour, carried it, with the loss of a number of men. In this attack, Colonel Arnold had the misfortune to have his leg splintered by a shot, and was obliged to be carried to the hospital. After gaining the battery, his detachment passed on to a second barrier, which they took possession of. By this time the enemy, relieved from the other attack, by our troops being drawn off, directed their whole force against his detachment, and a party sallying out from Palace gate, attacked them in the rear. These brave men sustained the whole force of the garrison for three hours, but finding themselves hemmed in, and no hopes of relief, they were obliged to yield to numbers, and the advantageous situation the garrison had over them.

After this unfortunate repulse, the remainder of the army retired about eight miles from the city, where they have posted themselves advantageously, and are continuing the blockade, waiting for the reinforcements which are now on their march to join them.

New York Packet, February 1, 1776

A Song on the Brave General
MONTGOMERY
Who Fell Within the Walls of Quebec
Dec. 31, 1775,
in attempting to storm that city

———•·•———

In the summer of 1775 the Americans mounted an invasion of Canada. It was one of the most heroic and ill-fated ventures of the entire war. The climax came when the two attacking forces under the command of Richard Montgomery and Benedict Arnold stormed the fortress of Quebec on December 31. Montgomery lost his life during the assault; the remnants of the American troops, who had suffered inconceivable hardships during their northward march, were obliged to surrender. The verses reproduced here are taken from a 1776 broadside issued in Danvers, Massachusetts. For melody, see "The Battle of Trenton," p. 188, below. (Essex Institute, Salem, Massachusetts. Reproduced by permission.)

———

Come Soldiers all in chorus join,
To pay the tribute at the shrine
    Of brave Montgomery,
Which to the memory is due
Of him who fought and died that you
    Might live and yet be free.

With cheerful and undaunted mind,
Domestic happiness resigned,
    He with a chosen band
Through deserts wild, with fixed intent,
Canada for to conquer went,
    Or perish sword in hand.

Six weeks before St. John's they lay,
While cannon on them constant play,
    On cold and marshy ground;

When Prescott forced at length to yield,
Aloud proclaimed it in the field,
    Virtue a friend had found.

To Montreal he winged his way,
Which seemed impatient to obey
    And opened wide its gates,
Convinced no force could e'er repel
Troops who had just behaved so well,
    Under so hard a fate.

With scarce one third part of his force
Then to Quebec he bent his course,
    That grave of heroes slain;
The pride of France the great Montcalm,
And Wolfe, the strength of Britain's arm,
    Both fell on Abraham's plain.

Having no less of fame required,
There too Montgomery expired
    With Cheeseman by his side.
Carleton, 'tis said, his corpse conveyed
To earth in all the grand parade,
    Of military pride.

1776

JANUARY

January 2

VIRGINIA   Yesterday, at about quarter after three o'clock, the British fleet lying off Norfolk, Virginia, commenced a cannonade against that town, from upwards of one hundred pieces of cannon, and continued till nearly ten o'clock at night, without intermission. It then abated a little, and continued till two this morning. Under cover of their guns, the Regulars landed and set fire to the town in several places near the water, though our men strove all in their power to prevent them. The houses being chiefly of wood, took fire immediately, and the fire spread with amazing rapidity. It is now become general, and the whole town will probably be consumed in a day or two. Expecting that the fire would throw the Americans into confusion, the enemy frequently landed, but were every time repulsed. The burning of the town has made several avenues through which the enemy may now fire with greater effect. The tide is now rising, and we expect, at high water, another cannonade. May it be as ineffectual as the last, for we have not one man killed, and but a few wounded.

Pennsylvania Evening Post, January 16
New York Packet, January 25

VIRGINIA   We hope our countrymen will not be at all dispirited at the destruction of Norfolk, but rather rejoice that half the mischief our enemies can do us is done already. They have destroyed one of the first towns in America, and the only one (except two or three) in Virginia, which carried on any thing like a trade. We are only sharing part of the sufferings of our American brethren, and can now glory in having received one of the keenest strokes of the enemy, without flinching. They have done their worst, and to no other purpose than to harden our soldiers, and teach them to bear without dismay, all the most formidable operations of a war carried on by a powerful and cruel enemy; to no other purpose than to give the world specimens of British cruelty and American fortitude, unless it be to force us to lay aside that childish fondness for Britain, and that foolish, tame dependence on her. We had borne so long with the oppressions of an ungenerous restriction of our trade—of a restriction, in some instances, which seemed calculated merely as badges of our subjection, and had been contented so long with barely refusing to purchase commodities which they had taxed for the purpose of raising a revenue in America, that our patience and moderation served but to encourage them to proceed to greater lengths. To greater lengths they have proceeded, as far as the proudest tyrant's lust of despotism, stimulated by cruelty, a rancorous malice, and an infernal spirit of revenge, could hurry them. How sunk is Britain! Could not Britons venture to wage war with America till they were told that Americans were cowards—till they had disarmed them, or had, as they thought, put it out of their power to procure arms; nor even then without the assistance of Roman Catholics and Indians, and endeavoring to raise amongst us a domestic enemy? Was this like a brave and generous nation? If they were lost to all the feelings of Britons, for men contending for the support of the British constitution, if they were determined to conquer America, why did they not attempt it like Britons? Why meanly run about to the different powers of Europe, entreating them not to assist us? Why make use of every base and inhuman stratagem, and wage a savage war unknown amongst civilized nations? Surely who ever has heard of Carleton's, Connolly's, and Dunmore's plots against us, cannot but allow that they must have been authorized by a higher power; and whoever believes this cannot but wish to be instantly and forever removed from under such a power, and to be guarded most effectually against it. Most freely would we cut the gordian knot which has hitherto so firmly bound us to Britain, and call on France and Spain for assistance against an enemy who seem bent on our destruction, but who, blessed be the God of Hosts, have been baffled in most of their attempts against us, been chastised in all, and have made many attacks against us without being able to kill a single man.

"An American," Virginia Gazette, January 5

January 8

MASSACHUSETTS   This evening, Major Knowlton was despatched with a hundred men, to make an incursion into Charlestown. He crossed the mill dam, which lies between Cobble Hill and Bunker Hill, about nine o'clock, and immediately proceeded down the street, on the westerly side of Bunker Hill. A part of the men, under the command of Captain Keyes, at the same time were ordered to take post on the east side of the street, just under the hill, in order to intercept any person who might escape from the houses in the street, some of which were occupied by the enemy. These houses, which are a little without the compact part of the town, the enemy suffered to remain, in June last, for their own convenience.

They were now surrounded and set fire to by our men. In one of them they found six soldiers, and one woman, all of whom, except one refractory fellow who was killed, were brought off. In another of the houses, according to the information of the prisoners, lived seventeen of the enemy's carpenters. The woman says she went to this house in order to borrow something, just before our men arrived; but seeing no light, and not being able to get into that part of the house where they kept, she concluded they were all asleep. As it is very certain no one escaped from the house, and as our men set the building on fire very suddenly, it is thought the whole seventeen perished in the flames. We burnt ten houses, and brought off six or seven muskets. Three or four houses are still standing. The whole was performed in less than an hour, without the loss of a single man, either killed or wounded. The Regulars in the fort on Bunker Hill did not act with that regularity which those gentlemen who labor hard to show the superiority of red coats over brown coats, would persuade us that Regulars always do; for they kept a hot and close fire on absolutely nothing at all: that is, they fired without an object. Our people calmly executed their purpose, laughed in security, and in security returned to their camp.

Pennsylvania Evening Post, January 23 and 30

MASSACHUSETTS   Another account of Major Knowlton's expedition is given by an officer in the King's army:—On the 8th instant, between eight and nine o'clock at night, we were alarmed by some of the enemy, who came over a small neck of land by a mill upon Charlestown side, and came into some houses that were not destroyed on the 17th of June, where they surprised and took one sergeant and three private men prisoners, who belonged to a wooding party, after which they set fire to the houses, and retreated under a heavy fire of cannon and musketry from one of our redoubts. Among the rest they had got a stout fellow of ours (a grenadier) prisoner, who pretended to be lame, and could walk but slowly, upon which they made him deliver up his arms; and the rebel captain who commanded the party told his men to retreat, saying, "I swear I will take this serpent of a Regular under my charge;" but upon his going over the neck of land, the grenadier struck the captain a severe blow on his face with his fist, took him up in his arms, pitched him headlong into the mud, and then ran off. But what is most extraordinary, a new farce was that night to have been acted at Boston, called The Blockade of Boston; the play was just ended and the curtain going to be drawn up for the farce, when the actors heard from without that an attack was made on the heights of Charlestown, upon which one of them came in, dressed in the character of a Yankee sergeant (which character he was to play) desired silence, and informed the audience the alarm guns were fired; that the rebels had attacked the town, and were at it tooth and nail over at Charlestown. The audience thinking this was the opening of the new piece, clapped prodigiously; but soon finding their mistake, a general scene of confusion ensued. They immediately hurried out of the house to their alarm posts; some skipping over the orchestra, trampling on the fiddles, and every one making his most speedy retreat. The actors (who were all officers) calling out for water to wash the smut and paint from off their faces; women fainting, and, in short, the whole house was nothing but one scene of confusion, terror, and tumult. I was upon guard at the advance lines before the town of Roxbury, and we expected a general attack that night, but the rebels were not so forward, for in a few hours every thing was quiet.

Letter from Boston
Middlesex Journal, February 27

FEBRUARY

February 6

VIRGINIA   The Virginia forces, under Colonel Howe, abandoned Norfolk this morning, after removing the poor inhabitants, with such effects as they could carry along with them, and demolishing the intrenchments, which Lord Dunmore threw up a little before he fled on board the fleet, now lying before that place. What few houses remained after the late bombardment were likewise destroyed, after being valued, to prevent the enemy's taking shelter in them. Thus, in the course of five weeks, has a town which contained upward of six thousand inhabitants, many of them in affluent circumstances, a place that carried on an extensive trade and commerce, consequently affording bread to many thousands, been reduced to ashes, and become desolate, through the wicked and cruel machinations of Lord North and the junto, aided by their faithful servants, my Lord Dunmore, with his motley army, and the renowned Captain Bellew, commodore of his Britannic Majesty's fleet in Virginia, and his generous and valiant crew. Truly may it be now said, "Never can true reconcilement grow / Where wounds of deadly hate have pierc'd so deep." The troops are now stationed at Kemp's Landing, the Great Bridge, and in and about Suffolk.

Constitutional Gazette, February 28

February 10

Some people among us seem alarmed at the *name of Independence*, while they support measures and propose plans that comprehend all the *spirit* of it. Have we not made laws, created courts of judicature, established magistrates, made money, levied war, and regulated commerce, not only without his Majesty's intervention, but absolutely against his will? Are we not as criminal in the eye of Britain for what we have done as for what we can yet do? If we institute any government at all, for heaven's sake let it be the best we can. We shall be as certainly hanged for a bad as a good one, for they will allow nothing for the waverings of filial tenderness. It will all be placed to the account of blundering ignorance. If, therefore, we incur the danger, let us not decline the reward. In every other instance, *Independence* raises an idea in the mind that the heart grasps at with avidity, and a feeling soul never fails to be stricken and depressed with the very sound of dependence. If in a private family the children, instead of being so educated as to take upon them the functions of good citizens, should be brought to years of maturity under the apparel, food and discipline of infancy, what laws, natural or civil, would acquit the parents of the child of infamy and criminality? A set of great lounging infants tied to mamma's apron at two-and-twenty, with long bibs and pap-spoons, would put a Sybarite to the blush.

Now, as every moral virtue or vice is vastly enhanced when considered in relation to a community as well as individuals, I insist upon it that he who would keep a community in a state of infantile dependence, when it became a fit member of the great republic of the world, would be vastly more criminal and infamous than the imaginary family mentioned before. Whenever I have been an advocate for dependence, I have felt a conscious want of public virtue. I own it arises

from laziness in me. I was willing to brush through life as I
began it, and to leave the rooting out the thorns and thistles,
as well as the harvest of the laurels, to posterity, and this, I
think, was the case of most of us; but now that we have gone
through the rough work, to desert the glorious prospect it
opens to us, would be heretical, damnable, and abominable,
even to a sensible Pope. It is a duty of much moment to us
as men, and of the last degree of magnitude as citizens, to
maintain, at every risk, a perfect independence of every thing
but good sense, good morals, good laws, good government, and
our good Creator.

Letter from a member of the Virginia Convention
New York Packet, April 3

February 16

PENNSYLVANIA   This evening, Captain Souder arrived
at Philadelphia from Grenada. On his passage, he spoke a
vessel from Cork, the master of which informed him that
twenty-five transports, with four thousand troops on board,
had sailed from Cork for America. Captain Souder says, that
before he left Grenada, a London paper of the thirtieth of
last November arrived there, in which was a list of the thirty-
nine commissioners appointed to *treat with the Congress*,
among whom were Lord Howe and Governor Johnston.

Pennsylvania Evening Post, February 17

February 27

The pamphlet entitled "Common Sense" [by Thomas Paine:
published January 9] is indeed a wonderful production. It is
completely calculated for the meridian of North America.—
The author introduces a new system of politics, as widely different from the old, as the Copernican system is from the
Ptolemaic. The blood wantonly spilt by the British troops at
Lexington, gave birth to this extraordinary performance, which
contains as surprising a discovery in politics as the works of
Sir Isaac Newton do in philosophy. This animated piece dis-
pels, with irresistible energy, the prejudice of the mind against
the doctrine of independence, and pours in upon it such an

inundation of light and truth, as will produce an instantaneous and marvellous change in the temper—in the views and feelings of an American. The ineffable delight with which it is perused, and its doctrines imbibed, is a demonstration that the seeds of independence, though imported with the troops from Britain, will grow surprisingly with proper cultivation in the fields of America. The mind indeed exults at the thought of a final separation from Great Britain, whilst all its prejudices and enchanting prospects in favor of a reconciliation, like the morning cloud, are chased away by the heat and influence of this rising luminary, and although the ties of affection and other considerations have formerly bound this country in a threefold cord to Great. Britain, yet the connexion will be dissolved, and the gordion knot be cut. "For the blood of the slain, the voice of weeping nature cries it is time to part."

Constitutional Gazette, February 24

NORTH CAROLINA   This morning, the North Carolina minute-men and militia, under the command of Brigadier-General James Moore, had an engagement with the Tories, at Widow Moore's Creek bridge. At the break of day, an alarm gun was fired, immediately after which, scarcely leaving the Americans a moment to prepare, the Tory army, with Captain McCloud at their head, made their attack on Colonels Caswell and Lillington, posted near the bridge, and finding a small intrenchment vacant, concluded that the Americans had abandoned their post. With this supposition, they advanced in a most furious manner over the bridge. Colonel Caswell had very wisely ordered the planks to be taken up, so that in passing they met with many difficulties. On reaching a point within thirty paces of the breastworks, they were received with a very heavy fire, which did great execution. Captains McCloud and Campbell were instantly killed, the former having nine bullets and twenty-four swan shot through and into his body. The insurgents retreated with the greatest precipitation, leaving behind them some of their wagons, &c. They cut their horses out of the wagons, and mounted three upon a horse. Many of them fell into the creek and were drowned. Tom Rutherford ran like a lusty fellow:—both he and Felix Keenan were in arms against the Carolinians, and they by this time are prisoners, as is Lieutenant-Colonel Cotton, who ran at the first fire. The battle lasted three minutes. Twenty-eight of the Tories, besides the two captains, are killed or mortally wounded, and between twenty and thirty taken prisoners, among whom is his Excellency General Donald McDonald. This, we think, will effectually put a stop to Toryism in North Carolina.

Pennsylvania Evening Post, March 23
New York Packet, March 28

MARCH

March 9

MASSACHUSETTS　　　Last Saturday night, [2nd,] the artillery at the fortresses of Cobble Hill and Lechmere's Point, below Cambridge, and at Lamb's dam in Roxbury, bombarded and cannonaded the town. The following night, the same was continued with great briskness; and the whole of Monday night, the artillery from all the above fortresses played incessantly. The shot and shells were heard to make a great crashing in the town, but we have not learnt any of the particulars of the execution done thereby. The Regulars returned the fire from their batteries at West Boston, and from their lines on the Neck, very vigorously. They threw many shells into the battery at Lechmere's Point, one into the fort on Prospect Hill, and one or two as far as fort "number two," within a quarter of a mile of the College.

The grand object of the Americans was to draw off the attention of the British from Dorchester Heights, until they could take possession of that position on Monday night. This was accomplished by three thousand men, under General Thomas. The men worked with such alertness, that by morning they were in a condition to sustain any attack of the enemy. On Tuesday, the whole army were assembled at their proper posts, to act as circumstances required. It was expected and hoped that General Howe would send out such a force as he thought competent, to dislodge the Americans from Dorchester Hill; that being the case, they were prepared to push into Boston, from Cambridge, with four thousand men. We are since informed that Lord Percy was detached, with three thousand men in transports, to the castle, in order to land on Wednesday from that quarter. On Tuesday night there was such a high gale of wind, which continued part of next day, that, glad of a plea for not attacking, they returned to Boston, and have been busy ever since, in carrying off their best effects from Boston on board their ships; and by their movements, which we can plainly discover, they are now busy in dismantling their fortifications and in getting ready to go off. This is confirmed by the captain of one of their transport vessels, who escaped from them the night before last, with all his crew. He says, on Tuesday morning, our works being discovered from the shipping, the Admiral immediately sent word of it to General Howe, informing him at the same time, that unless he could dispossess the Americans of that post, there was no safety for the fleet, and he should immediately fall down to Narraganset Road. We longed for nothing so much as their coming, but they are too prudent. It is reduced to the greatest moral certainty, that they are now preparing with all despatch, to abandon the town. This does not slacken, but rather increases the ardor of our troops to push on their works on Dorchester Hill, so that by the middle of the week, we may expect to have constructed such a battery there, as will command both the town and shipping, and if they don't leave it before, will oblige them to hasten their departure, and, we hope, compel them to abandon many valuable articles they wish to take off with them.

Pennsylvania Journal, March 20

March 14

MASSACHUSETTS   The common topic of conversation, since last Friday, has been the evacuation of the town of Boston by King George's plundering, murdering army, under

General Howe. On that day, a paper was brought out by a flag of truce, to which was affixed the names of sundry inhabitants, among which were some of the selectmen, advising that they were permitted by General Howe, in behalf of the town, to notify our army, that if the firing into the place was discontinued, the British troops would leave the same in three or four days, without destroying it. Though the enemy might really be preparing to leave the town, this paper was thought worthy of little attention, as being nothing more than a mere finesse, to induce a relaxation in our proceedings. Sundry persons, since the above paper came out, have escaped from the town, and inform that the enemy are very busy in shipping their effects on board the transports, and that there is great appearance of their going off very speedily. Yesterday it was reported that they were plundering the town, breaking and destroying every thing they cannot carry away.

Constitutional Gazette, March 23

The ministry have boasted much of their *regular*, their *disciplined* troops, which they fancied capable of beating all the *irregulars* in the world. One would wonder how men of any attention to what has passed, could deceive themselves into such an opinion, when so many FACTS within the memory of men not very old, evince the contrary.

The following *Yankee* song gives us a pretty little collection of those facts, and is printed for the encouragement of our militia; for though it is not safe for men too much to despise their enemies, it is of use that they should have a good opinion of themselves, if just, when compared with those they are to fight with.

If we search for the cause of this superior bravery in the *people* of a country, compared with what are called *regular troops*, it may be found in these particulars: that the men who compose a European regular army, are generally such as have neither property nor families to fight for, and who have no principle, either of honor, religion, public spirit, regard for liberty, or love of country, to animate them. They are therefore only pressed on to fight by their officers, and had rather be anywhere else than in a battle. Discipline only gives the officers the power of actuating them; and superior discipline may make them superior to other troops of the same kind not so well disciplined. Thus discipline seems to supply, in some degree, the defect of principle. But men equally armed, and animated by principle, though without discipline, are always superior to them when only equal in numbers; and when principle and discipline are united on the same side, as in our present militia, treble the number of mere unprincipled mercenaries, such as the regular armies commonly consist of, are no match for such a militia.

Let us, however, not be presumptuously careless in our military operations, but mix caution with courage, and take every prudent measure to guard against the attempts of our enemies; it being as advantageous to defeat their designs as their forces.

Pennsylvania Evening Post, March 30

The King's Own Regulars

In a hostile country, amid a hostile people, an invading army is like a ship on the ocean: it must pass through without the power to leave a permanent trace of its passage. This witty and satirical poem is an apt illustration; it combines mockery with a shrewd understanding of the nature of irregular warfare. Written by Benjamin Franklin after the British retreat from Lexington, it was published in the Pennsylvania Evening Post, March 30, 1776—*evidently as a parting thrust at the British as they sailed away from Boston. "Monongahela" in verse three is a reference to Braddock's defeat before Fort Duquesne in 1755. Colonials believed that death and disaster had attended that expedition because Braddock deployed his troops in European fashion and refused to heed Washington's advice to disperse his forces. (Moore, Diary, 214–6; abridged.)*

Since you all will have singing, and won't be said nay,
I cannot refuse, when you so beg and pray;
So I'll sing you a song,—as a body may say,
'Tis of the King's Regulars, who ne'er ran away.
   O! the old soldiers of the King, and the King's own Regulars.

No troops perform better than we at reviews,
We march and we wheel, and whatever you choose,
George would see how we fight, and we never refuse,
There we all fight with courage—you may see 't in the news.

To Monongahela, with fifes and with drums,
We marched in fine order, with cannon and bombs;
That great expedition cost infinite sums,
But a few irregulars cut us all into crumbs.

It was not fair to shoot at us from behind trees,
If they had stood open, as they ought, before our great guns,
   we should have beat them with ease,
They may fight with one another that way if they please,
But it is not *regular* to stand, and fight with such rascals as
   these.

Grown proud at reviews, great George had no rest,
Each grandsire, he had heard, a rebellion suppressed,
He wish'd a rebellion, looked round and saw none,
So resolved a rebellion to make—of his own.

Our general with his council of war did advise
How at Lexington we might the Yankees surprise;
We march'd—and re-march'd—all surprise—at being beat;
And so our wise general's plan of *surprise*—was complete.

For fifteen miles, they follow'd and pelted us, we scarce had
   time to pull a trigger;
But did you ever know a retreat performed with more vigor?
For we did it in two hours, which saved us from perdition;
'Twas not in *going out*, but in *returning*, consisted our
   EXPEDITION.

Says our general, "We were forced to take to our *arms* in our
   own defence,
(For *arms* read *legs*, and it will be both truth and sense,)

Lord Percy, (says he,) I must say something of him in civility,
And that is—'I can never enough praise him for his great—
    agility.' "

Of their firing from behind fences, he makes a great pother;
Every fence has two sides, they made use of one, and we only
    forgot to use the other;
That we turned our backs and ran away so fast; don't let that
    disgrace us,
'Twas only to make good what Sandwich said, that the
    Yankees—could not face us.

As they could not get before us, how could they look us in the
    face?
We took care they shouldn't, by scampering away apace.
That they had not much to brag of, is a very plain case;
For if they beat us in the fight, we beat them in the race.

March 17

MASSACHUSETTS   This morning the British army in
Boston, under General Howe, consisting of upwards of seven
thousand men, after suffering an ignominious blockade for
many months past, disgracefully quitted all their strongholds
in Boston and Charlestown, fled from before the army of
the United Colonies, and took refuge on board their ships.
The most material particulars of this signal event are as follows:
    About nine o'clock, a body of the Regulars were seen
to march from Bunker Hill, and, at the same time, a very
great number of boats, filled with troops, put off from Boston,
and made for the shipping, which lay chiefly below the castle.
On the discovery of these movements, the continental army
paraded; several regiments embarked in boats and proceeded
down the river from Cambridge. About the same time two
men were sent to Bunker Hill, in order to make discoveries.
They proceeded accordingly, and, when arrived, making a
signal that the fort was evacuated, a detachment was immediately sent down from the army to take possession of it. The
troops on the river, which were commanded by General Put-

nam, landed at Sewall's Point, where they received intelligence that all the British troops had left Boston, on which a detachment was sent to take possession of the town, while the main body returned up the river. About the same time, General Ward, attended by about five hundred troops from Roxbury, under the command of Colonel Ebenezer Learned, who embarked and opened the gates, entered the town on that quarter, Ensign Richards carrying the standard.

The command of the whole being then given to General Putnam, he proceeded to take possession of all the important posts, and thereby became possessed, in the name of the Thirteen United Colonies of North America, of all the fortresses in that large and once populous and flourishing metropolis, which the flower of the British army, headed by an experienced general, and supported by a formidable fleet of men-of-war, had, but an hour before, evacuated in the most precipitate and cowardly manner. God grant that the late worthy inhabitants, now scattered abroad, may speedily reoccupy their respective dwellings, and never more be disturbed by the cruel hand of tyranny; and may the air of that capital be never again contaminated by the foul breath of Toryism.

The joy of our friends in Boston, on seeing the victorious and gallant troops of their country enter the town almost at the heels of their barbarous oppressors, was inexpressibly great. The mutual congratulations and tender embraces which soon afterwards took place, between those of the nearest connections in life, for a long time cruelly rent asunder by the tyranny of our implacable enemies, surpasses description. From such a set of beings, the preservation of property was not expected. And it was found that a great part of the evacuated houses had been pillaged, the furniture broken and destroyed, and many of the buildings greatly damaged. It is worthy of notice, however, that the buildings belonging to the honorable John Hancock, Esq., particularly his elegant mansion house, are left in good order. All the linen and woollen goods, except some that may be secreted, are carried off, and all the salt and molasses is destroyed. The Regulars have also destroyed great quantities of effects belonging to themselves, which they could not carry away, such as gun carriages and other carriages of various kinds, house furniture, &c., together with a quantity of flour and hay. All their forts, batteries, redoubts, and breastworks remain entire and complete. They have left many of their heaviest cannon mounted on carriages, and several of them charged, all of which are either spiked, or have a trunnion beaten off. They have also left several of their largest mortars; quantities of cannon shot, shells, numbers of small arms, and other instruments of war, have been found, thrown off the wharves, concealed in vaults or broken in pieces. In the fort on Bunker Hill, several hundred good blankets were found. It is said about fifteen or twenty of the King's horses have also been taken up in the town; and it is thought that about the same number of Tories remain behind.

We are told that the Tories were thunder-struck when orders were issued for evacuating the town, after being many hundred times assured, that such reinforcements would be sent, as to enable the King's troops to ravage the country at pleasure. Thus are many of those deluded creatures, those vile traitors to their country, obliged at last, in their turn, to abandon their once delightful habitations, and go they know not where. Many of them, it is said, considered themselves as undone, and seemed, at times, inclined to throw themselves on the mercy of their offended country, rather than leave it. One or more of them, it is reported, have been left to end their lives by the unnatural act of suicide.

The British, previous to their going off, scattered great numbers of crows' feet on Boston Neck, and in the streets, in order to retard our troops in case of a pursuit; and with such silence and precaution did they embark, that a great part of the inhabitants did not know it until after they were gone.

To the wisdom, firmness, intrepidity and military abilities of our amiable and beloved general, his Excellency George Washington, Esq., to the assiduity, skill, and bravery of the other worthy generals and officers of the army, and to the hardiness and gallantry of the soldiery, is to be ascribed, under God, the glory and success of our arms, in driving from one of the strongest holds in America, so considerable a part of the British army as that which last week occupied Boston.

This afternoon, a few hours after the British retreated, the Reverend Mr. Leonard preached at Cambridge an excellent sermon, in the audience of his Excellency the General, and others of distinction, well adapted to the interesting event of the day, from Exodus xiv. 25: "And took off their chariot wheels, that they drave them heavily; so that the Egyptians said, Let us flee from the face of Israel, for the Lord fighteth for them against the Egyptians."

Pennsylvania Evening Post, March 30

———•———

APRIL

April 20

A writer gives the following reasons for a declaration of the independence of the American colonies:—1. The colonies will be delivered from two governments directly opposed to each other. 2. The colonies will be delivered from the disorders which arise from the unlimited, undescribed, and sometimes arbitrary power of conventions, committees of safety, and committees of inspection. 3. A criminal correspondence with the enemies of this country will be prevented, or punished, under the articles of high treason. 4. The colonies will be delivered from the danger of crown officers, whose apparent interest it will always be to remain inactive, or to cooperate with the enemies of America. 5. The British constitution may be immediately restored to each colony, with the great and necessary improvements of a governor and council chosen by the people. 6. France will immediately attack Britain in the most defenceless parts of her empire, and thus draw off her fleets and armies from our coasts. 7. All the powers of Europe will conceive such ideas of our union, love of freedom and military resources, that they will not be tempted to accept of a share in us, upon the condition of conquering us.

Pennsylvania Evening Post, April 20

This is not a time to trifle. Men who know they deserve nothing from their country, and whose hope is on the arm that hath sought to enslave ye, may hold out to you, as Cato hath done, the false light of reconciliation. There is no such thing. 'Tis gone! 'Tis past! The grave hath parted us—and death, in the persons of the slain, hath cut the thread of life between Britain and America. Conquest, and not reconciliation, is the plan of Britain. But admitting even the last hope of the Tories to happen, which is, that our enemies after a long succession of losses, wearied and disabled, should despairingly throw down their arms and propose a reunion. In that case, what is to be done? Are defeated and disappointed tyrants to be considered like mistaken and converted friends? Or would it be right to receive those for governors, who, had they been conquerors, would have hung us up for traitors? Certainly not. Reject the offer then, and propose another; which is, we will make peace with you as with enemies, but we will never reunite with you as friends. This effected, and ye secure to yourselves the pleasing prospect of an eternal peace. America, remote from all the wrangling world, may live at ease. Bounded by the ocean, and backed by the wilderness, who hath she to fear but her God?

Be not deceived. It is not a little that is at stake. Reconciliation will not now go down, even if it were offered. 'Tis a dangerous question, for the eyes of all men begin to open. There is now no secret in the matter; there ought to be none. It is a case that concerns every man, and every man ought to lay it to heart. He that *is* here, and he that was *born* here, are alike concerned. It is needless, too, to split the business into a thousand parts, and perplex it with endless and fruitless investigations. This unparalleled contention of nations is not to be settled like a school boy's task of pounds, shillings, pence, and fractions. The first and great question, and that which involves every other in it, and from which every other will flow, is *happiness*. Can this continent be happy under the government of Great Britain, or not? Secondly. Can she be happy under a government of our own? To live beneath the authority of those whom we cannot love, is misery, slavery, or what name you please. In that case there will never be

peace. Security will be a thing unknown, because a treacherous friend in power is the most dangerous of enemies. The
answer to the second question—can America be happy under
a government of her own, is short and simple, viz.: As happy
as she pleases; she hath a blank sheet to write upon. Put it
not off too long.

Painful as the task of speaking truth must sometimes be,
yet we cannot avoid giving the following hint, because much,
nay, almost every thing, depends upon it; and that is, a
thorough knowledge of the persons whom we trust. It is the
duty of the public, at this time, to scrutinize closely into the
conduct of their committee members, members of assembly,
and delegates in Congress, to know what they do and their
motives for so doing. Without doing this we shall never know
who to confide in, but shall constantly mistake friends for
enemies, and enemies for friends, till in the confusion of
persons we sacrifice the cause.

"The Forrester," Pennsylvania Journal, April 24

MAY

May 16

PENNSYLVANIA   The Committee of Safety in Philadelphia having already made known to the inhabitants of that
city, the pressing occasion there is for a large quantity of
LEAD, to be employed in the defence of this country, and
requested them to spare for the public use the various species
of leaden weights in their respective families; they have, as
the most expeditious and easy method of procuring such
LEAD, appointed Thomas Nevill, Frazer Kinsley, William
Colliday, and John Darcy to go round the city and receive it
at the several houses, they paying at the rate of sixpence per
pound as formerly specified, it being understood that clock
weights are not at present comprehended among them, as
the iron weights to replace them are not yet made.

It is expected that every virtuous citizen will immediately and cheerfully comply with this requisition, but if any persons should be so lost to all sense of the public good as to refuse, a list of their names is directed to be returned to the committee.

Pennsylvania Evening Post, May 18

VIRGINIA   Yesterday is rendered memorable by a unanimous resolution of the Virginia Convention, now sitting at Williamsburg, to instruct their delegates in the Continental Congress to move for a declaration of independence and freedom. It is the result of the most mature deliberation, and we hope will be speedily ratified by the Congress. Let the DOUBTERS read it:—["Forasmuch as all the endeavors of the United Colonies, by the most decent representations and petitions to the King and Parliament of Great Britain, to restore peace and security to America under the British government, and a reunion with that people upon just and liberal terms instead of a redress of grievances, have produced, from an imperious and vindictive administration, increased insult, oppression, and a vigorous attempt to effect our total destruction. By a late act, all these colonies are declared to be in rebellion, and out of the protection of the British crown, our properties subjected to confiscation, our people, when captivated, compelled to join in the murder and plunder of their relations and countrymen, and all former rapine and oppression of Americans declared legal and just. Fleets and armies are raised, and the aid of foreign troops engaged to assist these destructive purposes. The King's representative in this colony hath not only withheld all the powers of government from operating for our safety, but, having retired on board an armed ship, is carrying on a piratical and savage war against us, tempting our slaves, by every artifice, to resort to him, and training and employing them against their masters. In this state of extreme danger, we have no alternative left but an abject submission to the will of those overbearing tyrants, or a total separation from the crown and government of Great Britain, uniting and exerting the strength of all America for defence, and forming alliances with foreign powers for commerce and aid in war. Wherefore, appealing to the Searcher of Hearts for the sincerity of former declarations, expressing our desire to preserve the connection with that nation, and that we are driven from that inclination by their wicked councils, and the eternal laws of self-preservation.

"*Resolved unanimously*, That the delegates appointed to represent this colony in General Congress, be instructed to propose to that respectable body, TO DECLARE THE UNITED COLONIES FREE AND INDEPENDENT STATES, absolved from all allegiance to or dependence upon the crown or Parliament of Great Britain; and that they give the assent of this colony to such declaration, and to whatever measures may be thought proper and necessary by the Congress, for forming foreign alliances, and a CONFEDERATION OF THE COLONIES, at such time, and in the manner as to them shall seem best. Provided, that the power of forming government for, and the regulations of the internal concerns of each colony, be left to the respective colonial legislatures.

"*Resolved unanimously*, That a committee be appointed to prepare a declaration of rights, and such a plan of government as will be most likely to maintain peace and order in this colony, and secure substantial and equal liberty to the people."

The procuring of foreign assistance was the immediate object of this resolution, as the alternative of separation or submission was the assigned ground of it. But a political connection on any terms, with a people who have exerted against us every species of barbarity and insult, would have had few advocates.

In consequence of the resolution, universally regarded as the only path which will lead to safety and prosperity, some gentlemen made a handsome collection for the purpose of treating the soldiery, who to-day were paraded in Waller's grove, before Brigadier-General Lewis, attended by the gentlemen of the Committee of Safety, the members of the general convention, the inhabitants of the city, and others. The resolution being read aloud to the army, the following toasts were given, each of them accompanied by a discharge of the artillery and small arms, and the acclamations of all present:—

1. The American Independent States. 2. The grand Congress

of the United States, and their respective Legislatures. 3. General Washington, and victory to the American arms.

The union flag of the American states waved upon the capitol during the whole of this ceremony, which, being ended, the soldiers partook of the refreshment prepared for them by the affection of their countrymen, and the evening concluded with illuminations, and other demonstrations of joy. Every one seems pleased that the domination of Great Britain is now at an end, so wickedly and tyrannically has it been exercised for these twelve or thirteen years past, notwithstanding our repeated prayers and remonstrances for redress. *Pennsylvania Journal,* May 29.]

Clift's Diary

JUNE

June 1

Notwithstanding the savage treatment we have met with from the King of Britain, and the impossibility of the colonies being ever happy under his government again, according to the usual operation of natural and moral causes, yet we still find some people wishing to be dependent once more upon the crown of Britain. I have too good an opinion of the human understanding, to suppose that there is a man in America who believes that we ever shall be happy again in our old connection with that crown. I, therefore, beg leave to oblige the advocates for dependence to speak for themselves in the following order:—

1. I shall lose my office. 2. I shall lose the honor of being related to men in office. 3. I shall lose the rent of my houses for a year or two. 4. We shall have no more rum, sugar, tea nor coffee, in this country, except at a most exorbitant price. 5. We shall have no more gauze or fine muslins imported among us. 6. The New England men will turn Goths and Vandals, and overrun all the Southern Colonies. *N.B.*—It is

the fashion with the people who make this objection to independence, to despise the courage and discipline of the New England troops, and to complain that they are unwilling to fight out of their own colonies. 7. The church will have no king for a head. 8. The Presbyterians will have a share of power in this country. N. B.—These people have been remarked, ever since the commencement of our disputes with Great Britain, to prefer a Quaker or an Episcopalian, to one of their own body, where he was equally hearty in the cause of liberty. 9. I shall lose my chance of a large tract of land in a new purchase. 10. I shall want the support of the first officers of government, to protect me in my insolence, injustice, and villany. 11. The common people will have too much power in their hands. N. B.—The common people are composed of tradesmen and farmers, and include nine-tenths of the people of America.

Finally.—Sooner than submit to the chance of these probable evils, we will have our towns burnt, our country desolated, and our fathers, brothers, and children butchered by English, Scotch, and Irishmen; by Hanoverians, Hessians, Brunswickers, Waldeckers, Canadians, Indians, and Negroes. And, after all, such of us as survive these calamities, will submit to such terms of slavery as King George and his Parliament may impose upon us.

Pennsylvania Evening Post, June 1

June 10

PENNSYLVANIA   Today, the grand question of Independency was proposed to the first, second, fourth, and fifth battalions of associators of Philadelphia and suburbs; consisting of about two thousand officers and men. Against it, in the first battalions, four officers and twenty three privates—second, two privates—fourth and fifth unanimous for independence.

The lieutenant of the third battalion refusing to put the question, gave great umbrage to the men, one of whom replied to him in a genteel spirited manner.

"How our delegates in Congress may act," says a Pennsylvanian, "we know not, though we have a right to know, and intend to promote an inquiry for that purpose."—Take heed, Tories; you are at your last gasp! You have had many warnings, and many kind invitations!

Pennsylvania Evening Post, June 11

June 18

NEW YORK   This afternoon, the Provincial Congress of New York gave an elegant entertainment to General Washington and his suite; the general and staff officers, and the commanding officer of the different regiments in and near the city. Many patriotic toasts were offered and drank with the greatest pleasure and decency. After the toasts, little Phil, of the Guard, was brought in to sing H—'s new campaign song, and was joined by all the under officers, who seemed much animated by the accompanying of Clute's drumsticks and Aaron's fife. Our good General Putnam got sick and went to his quarters before dinner was over, and we missed him a marvel, as there is not a chap in the camp who can lead him in the *Maggie Lauder* song.

Mss. letter from Captain Caleb Gibbs,
of Washington's Guard, to his "Dear Penelope"

June 24

NEW YORK   Since Friday last, a most barbarous and infernal plot has been discovered among the Tories in New York. Two of General Washington's guards are concerned, a third whom they tempted to join them made the first discovery. The general report of their design is as follows: upon the arrival of the British troops, they were to murder all the staff officers, blow up the magazines, and secure the passes of the town. Gilbert Forbes, a gunsmith, in the Broadway, was taken between two and three o'clock on Saturday morning, and carried before our Congress, who were then sitting. He refused to make any discovery, upon which he was sent to jail. The Reverend Mr. Livingston went to see him early in the morning, and told him he was very sorry to find he had been concerned, that his time was very short, not having above three days to live, and advised him to prepare himself. This

had the desired effect; and he requested to be carried before the Congress again, promising to discover all he knew. Several have been since taken, between twenty and thirty, among them the mayor [David Matthews]. They are all now in confinement. Their party, it is said, consisted of about five hundred.

A further account in the same paper says:—"Yesterday [Friday,] the mayor was examined twice, and returned prisoner under a strong guard. We have now thirty-four prisoners, and many more it is expected will be taken up. A party of our men went over to Long Island, Saturday last, to take up some of the Tories; they returned yesterday, and brought to town one Downing, who is charged with being in the hellish plot. They took six more prisoners and put them in Jamaica jail, on Long Island. The Tories made some resistance, and fired on our men in the woods; our people returned the fire, wounding one man mortally; they then called for quarter. This morning a party of three hundred men is ordered, but on what business is not known. The mayor acknowledges he paid Mr. Forbes, the gunsmith, who is one of the gang now in irons, £140, by order of Governor Tryon. Yesterday the general's housekeeper was taken up; it is said she is concerned."

Pennsylvania Journal, June 26

June 28

NEW YORK   This forenoon, was executed in a field between the Colonels M'Dougall and Huntington's camp, near the Bowry-lane, New York, in the presence of near twenty thousand spectators, a soldier belonging to his Excellency General Washington's guards, for mutiny and conspiracy; being one of those who formed, and was soon to have put in execution, that horrid plot of assassinating the staff officers, blowing up the magazines and securing the passes of the town, on the arrival of the hungry ministerial myrmidons. It is hoped the remainder of those miscreants, now in our possession, will meet with a punishment adequate to their crimes.

Pennsylvania Evening Post, July 2

June 29

SOUTH CAROLINA   Our boys have pretty well thrashed
Sir Peter Parker and all his forces. Yesterday morning, an attack was commenced by one of the small vessels of the British
fleet, on the fort at Sullivan's Island, and, notwithstanding
our small number, a part of which was engaged in watching
Clinton and Cornwallis, at the other (east) end of the island,
we sustained it with the most complete success.

Clift's Diary

SOUTH CAROLINA   A writer on board the fleet gives the
following account of this action: "The signal for attacking
was made by Sir Peter Parker, on the twenty-seventh of June,
but the wind coming suddenly to the northward, the ships
were obliged again to anchor. The troops had been encamped
on Long Island since the fifteenth, and it was intended that
General Clinton should pass the neck that divides Long Island
from Sullivan's Island, and attack by land, while Sir Peter
Parker attacked by sea. General Lee had made such a disposition of masked batteries, troops, &c., that it is the opinion
of all the officers of the army whom I have heard mention this
circumstance, that if our troops had attacked, they must have
been cut off; but this assertion does not satisfy the navy, for
they certainly expected great assistance from the army.

"On the morning of the twenty-eighth, the wind proved
favorable, and it was a clear, fine day, but very sultry. The
Thunder Bomb began the attack at half-past eleven, by throwing shells, while the ships were advancing. The ships that
advanced to attack the battery were the *Bristol* and *Experiment*, two fifty-gun ships, the *Solebay*, *Active*, *Actæon*, and
Syren of twenty-eight guns, the *Sphynx* of twenty, and the
Friendship, an armed ship of twenty-eight guns. With this
force what might not have been expected? Unfortunately, the
Bomb was placed at such a distance, that she was not of the
least service. This, Colonel James, the principal engineer,
immediately perceived; to remedy which inconvenience, an
additional quantity of powder was added to each mortar: the

consequence was the breaking down the beds, and totally disabling her for the rest of the day.

"The *Bristol* and *Experiment* suffered most incredibly: the former very early had the spring of her cable shot away, and, as she lay end on to the battery, was raked fore and aft; she lost upward of one hundred men, killed and wounded. Captain Morris, who commanded her, lost his arm. Perhaps an instance of such slaughter cannot be produced. Twice the quarter-deck was cleared of every person except Sir Peter, and he was slightly wounded; she had nine thirty-two pounders in her mainmast, which is so much damaged as to be obliged to be shortened; the mizzen had seven thirty-two pounders, and was obliged, being much shattered, to be entirely cut away. It is impossible to pretend to describe what the shipping suffered. Captain Scott, of the *Experiment*, lost his right arm, and the ship suffered exceedingly; she had much the same number killed and wounded as the *Bristol*. Our situation was rendered very disagreeable, by the *Actæon*, *Syren*, and *Sphynx* running foul of each other, and getting on shore on the middle ground. The *Sphynx* disengaged herself by cutting away her bowsprit; and as it was not yet flood tide, she and the *Syren* fortunately warped off. The *Actæon* was burnt next morning by Captain Atkins, to prevent her falling into the hands of the Provincials.

"Our ships, after lying nine hours before the battery, were obliged to retire with great loss. The Provincials reserved their fire until the shipping were advanced within point blank shot. Their artillery was surprisingly well served, it is said, under the command of a Mr. Masson and De Brahm. It was slow, but decisive indeed. They were very cool, and took great care not to fire except their guns were exceedingly well directed: but there was a time when the battery appeared to be silenced for more than an hour. The navy say, had the troops been ready to land at this time, they could have taken possession; how that is, I will not pretend to say. I will rather suppose it; but the fire became exceedingly severe when it was renewed again, and did amazing execution, after the battery had been supposed to have been silenced. This will not be believed when it is first reported in England. I can scarcely

believe what I saw on that day; a day to me one of the most
distressing of my life. The navy, on this occasion, have behaved with their usual coolness and intrepidity. One would
have imagined that no battery could have resisted their incessant fire."

Middlesex Journal, September 14

Sir Peter Parker

*Composed early in 1777, this ballad was immensely popular
throughout the States. It appeared in the contemporary prints under
the title, "A New War Song, by Sir Peter Parker." It burlesques
Clinton and Parker's comic-opera exploits against Sullivan's Island
and Fort Moultrie with devastating wit; it is, in addition, a remarkably accurate summary of the principal events of that ill-fated am-
phibian expedition. (Moore, Songs and Ballads, 135–7.)*

My lords, with your leave, An ac-count I will give That de-serves to be writ-ten in
me-tre.___ For the reb-els and I Have been pret-ty nigh, Faith,
al-most too nigh for Sir Pe-ter!___ Ti-mi-al-der-ry-o, Ti-mi-
al-der-ry-day, Faith, al-most too nigh for Sir Pe-ter!___

With much labor and toil
Unto Sullivan's Isle,
I came firm as Falstaff or Pistol;
But the Yankees, God rot 'em,
I could not get at 'em;
They most terribly mauled my poor *Bristol.*

    Timialderry O, etc.

Bold Clinton by land
Did quietly stand,
While I made a thundering clatter.
But the channel was deep,
So he only could peep
And not venture over the water.

    Timialderry O, etc.

Devil take 'em, their shot
Came so swift and so hot,
And the cowardly dogs stood so stiff, sirs!
That I put ship about
And was glad to get out
Or they would not have left me a skiff, sirs!

    Timialderry O, etc.

Now, bold as a Turk,
I proceed to New York,
Where with Clinton and Howe you may find me.
I've the wind in my tail, and am hoisting sail,
To leave Sullivan's Island behind me.

    Timialderry O, etc.

But, my lords, do not fear,
For before the next year,
Although a small island could fret us,
The continent whole,
We shall take, by my soul,
If the cowardly Yankees will let us.

    Timialderry O, etc.

JULY

July 4

This day, "after much deliberation, the Congress has adopted Independency, for the following reasons:"

WHEN in the course of human events, it becomes necessary for one people to dissolve the political bands which have connected them with another, and to assume among the powers of the earth, the separate and equal station to which the laws of nature and of Nature's God entitle them, a decent respect to the opinions of mankind requires that they should declare the causes which impel them to the separation.

We hold these truths to be self-evident, that all men are created equal, that they are endowed by their Creator with certain unalienable rights, that among these are life, liberty, and the pursuit of happiness.—That to secure these rights governments are instituted among men, deriving their just powers from the consent of the governed, that whenever any form of government becomes destructive of these ends, it is the right of the people to alter or to abolish it, and to institute new government, laying its foundation on such principles, and organizing its powers in such form, as to them shall seem most likely to effect their safety and happiness. Prudence, indeed, will dictate that governments long established, should not be changed for light and transient causes; and accordingly, all experience hath shown, that mankind are more disposed to suffer, while evils are sufferable, than to right themselves by abolishing the form to which they are accustomed. But when a long train of abuses and usurpations, pursuing invariably the same object, evinces a design to reduce them under absolute despotism, it is their right, it is their duty, to throw off such government, and to provide new guards for their future security. Such has been the patient sufferance of these colonies; and such is now the necessity which constrains them to alter their former systems of government. The history of the present King of Great Britain is a history of repeated injuries and usurpations, all having in direct object the establishment of an absolute tyranny over these states. To prove this let facts be submitted to a candid world.

He has refused his assent to laws, the most wholesome and necessary for the public good.

He has forbidden his governors to pass laws of immediate and pressing importance, unless suspended in their operation till his assent should be obtained, and when so suspended, he has utterly neglected to attend to them.

He has refused to pass other laws for the accommodation of large districts of people, unless those people would relinquish the right of representation in the legislature, a right inestimable to them and formidable to tyrants only.

He has called together legislative bodies at places unusual, uncomfortable, and distant from the depository of their public records, for the sole purpose of fatiguing them into compliance with his measures.

He has dissolved representative houses repeatedly, for opposing with a manly firmness his invasions on the rights of the people.

He has refused for a long time, after such dissolutions, to cause others to be elected; whereby the legislative powers, incapable of annihilation, have returned to the people at large for their exercise; the state remaining in the mean time exposed to all the dangers of invasions from without, and convulsions within.

He has endeavored to prevent the population of these states; for that purpose obstructing the laws for naturalization of foreigners, refusing to pass others to encourage their migrations hither, and raising the conditions of new appropriations of lands.

He has obstructed the administrations of justice, by refusing his assent to laws for establishing judiciary powers.

He has made judges dependent on his will alone, for the tenure of their offices, and the amount and payment of their salaries.

He has erected a multitude of new offices, and sent hither

swarms of officers to harass our people, and eat out their substance.

He has kept among us, in times of peace, standing armies without the consent of our legislatures.

He has affected to render the military independent of, and superior to the civil power.

He has combined with others to subject us to a jurisdiction foreign to our constitution, and unacknowledged by our laws; giving his assent to their acts of pretended legislation.

For quartering large bodies of armed troops among us.

For protecting them, by a mock trial, from punishment for any murders which they should commit on the inhabitants of these states.

For cutting off our trade with all parts of the world.

For imposing taxes on us without our consent.

For depriving us, in many cases, of the benefits of trial by jury.

For transporting us beyond seas to be tried for pretended offences.

For abolishing the free system of English laws in a neighboring province, establishing therein an arbitrary government, and enlarging its boundaries, so as to render it at once an example and fit instrument for introducing the same absolute rule into these colonies.

For taking away our charters, abolishing our most valuable laws, and altering fundamentally the forms of our governments.

For suspending our own legislatures, and declaring themselves invested with power to legislate for us in all cases whatsoever.

He has abdicated government here, by declaring us out of his protection and waging war against us.

He has plundered our seas, ravaged our coasts, burnt our towns, and destroyed the lives of our people.

He is, at this time, transporting large armies of foreign mercenaries to complete the works of death, desolation, and tyranny, already begun with circumstances of cruelty and perfidy, scarcely paralleled in the most barbarous ages, and totally unworthy the head of a civilized nation.

He has constrained our fellow-citizens, taken captive on the high seas, to bear arms against their country, to become the executioners of their friends and brethren, or to fall themselves by their hands.

He has excited domestic insurrections amongst us, and has endeavored to bring on the inhabitants of our frontiers, the merciless Indian savages, whose known rule of warfare is an undistinguished destruction of all ages, sexes, and conditions.

In every stage of these oppressions we have petitioned for redress in the most humble terms. Our repeated petitions have been answered only by repeated injury. A prince, whose character is thus marked by every act which may define a tyrant, is unfit to be the ruler of a free people.

Nor have we been wanting in attentions to our British brethren. We have warned them from time to time of attempts by their legislature to extend an unwarrantable jurisdiction over us. We have reminded them of circumstances of our emigration and settlement here. We have appealed to their native justice and magnanimity, and we have conjured them by the ties of our common kindred to disavow these usurpations, which would inevitably interrupt our connections and correspondence. They too have been deaf to the voice of justice and of consanguinity. We must, therefore, acquiesce in the necessity which denounces our separation, and hold them, as we hold the rest of mankind, enemies in war, in peace, friends.

We, therefore, the representatives of the United States of America, in general congress assembled, appealing to the Supreme Judge of the world for the rectitude of our intentions, do, in the name, and by the authority of the good people of these colonies, solemnly publish and declare, that these UNITED COLONIES are, and of right ought to be, FREE AND INDEPENDENT STATES; that they are absolved from all allegiance to the British crown, and that all political connection between them and the state of Great Britain, is and ought to be totally dissolved; and that as Free and Independent States, they have full power to levy war, conclude peace, contract alliances, establish commerce, and to do all other acts and things which Independent States may of right do. And for the support of this declaration, with a firm reliance on the protection of Divine Providence, we mutually pledge to each other our lives, our fortunes, and our sacred honor.

Pennsylvania Journal, July 10

On Independence

First published in Benjamin Dearborn's Freeman's Journal, *August 17, 1776, this song is an expressive commentary on the popular reaction in New Hampshire to the news of the Declaration of Independence. (Moore, Diary, 276–7.)*

Come all you brave soldiers, both valiant and free,
It's for independence we all now agree;
Let us gird on our swords, and prepare to defend
Our liberty, property, ourselves, and our friends.

In a cause that's so righteous, come let us agree,
And from hostile invaders set America free.
The cause is so glorious we need not to fear,
But from merciless tyrants we'll set ourselves clear.

Heaven's blessing attending us, no tyrant shall say
That Americans e'er to such monsters gave way,
But fighting we'll die in Americas' cause,
Before we'll submit to tyrannical laws.

George the Third of Great Britain, no more shall he reign,
With unlimited sway o'er these free states again;
Lord North, nor old Bute, nor none of their clan,
Shall ever be honor'd by an American.

May heaven's blessings descend on our United States,
And grant that the union may never abate,
May love, peace, and harmony ever be found,
For to go hand in hand America round.

Upon our grand Congress, may heaven bestow
Both wisdom and skill our good to pursue,
On heaven alone, dependent we'll be,
But from all earthly tyrants we mean to be free.

Unto our brave generals may heaven give skill,
Our armies to guide and the sword for to wield;
May their hands taught to war and their fingers to fight,
Be able to put British armies to flight.

And now brave Americans, since it is so,
That we are independent we'll have them to know,
That united we are, and united we'll be,
And from all British tyrants we'll try to keep free.

May heaven smile on us in all our endeavors,
Safe guard our seaports, our towns, and our rivers,
Keep us from invaders by land and by sea,
And from all who'd deprive us of our liberty.

July 5

CONNECTICUT   Married, a short time since, in Mansfield,
Connecticut, Mr. Luke Flint, of Windham, to Miss Mary
Slate, daughter of Mr. Ezekiel Slate,—an agreeable and happy
pair. What deserves the public notice, and may serve to encourage the manufacturers of this country, is, that the entertainment, though served up with good wine, and other spirituous
liquors, was the production of their fields and fruit gardens,
assisted alone by a neighboring grove of spontaneous maples.

The bride and two of her sisters appeared in very genteel-like gowns, and others of the family in handsome apparel,
with sundry silk handkerchiefs, &c., entirely of their own
manufacture.

Connecticut Gazette, July 11, 18

Titles are the offspring of monarchical and arbitrary governments. While the object of the present war with Great Britain was *reconciliation*, the title of excellency, honorable, &c., were submitted to by the people of America; but since the Declaration of Independence, the colonies have divorced monarchy forever, and become free, independent states. It becomes then necessary to adopt the simple language of free governments.

The Roman Senate in the height of its glory and happiness had no other title than *Senatus populus que Romanus*, that is, the senate and people of Rome. Scipio was addressed by the name of Scipio, at the head of his army. Aristides was called Aristides, in the councils and public streets of Athens. Let us leave the titles of excellency and honorable to the abandoned servants of a tyrant King,—the King of England, while we satisfy ourselves with beholding our senators, governors, and generals rich in real excellence and honor.

Pennsylvania Evening Post, July 13

July 8

PENNSYLVANIA   At twelve o'clock to-day, the Committees of Safety and Inspection of Philadelphia, went in procession to the State House, where the Declaration of the Independency of the United States of America was read to a very large number of the inhabitants of the city and county, and was received with general applause and heartfelt satisfaction. And, in the evening, our late King's coat-of-arms was brought from the hall in the State House, where the said King's courts were formerly held, and burned amidst the acclamations of a crowd of spectators.

Constitutional Gazette, July 17

PENNSYLVANIA   The Declaration was received at Easton, in Pennsylvania, and proclaimed in the following order:— The Colonel and all the other field officers of the first battalion repaired to the court-house, the light infantry company marching there with their drums beating, fifes playing, and the standard, (the device for which is the thirteen United Colonies,) which was ordered to be displayed. After that the

Declaration was read aloud to a great number of spectators, who gave their hearty assent with three loud huzzas, and cried out, "May God long preserve and unite the FREE and INDEPENDENT States of America."

Pennsylvania Evening Post, July 11

NEW JERSEY   At Trenton, New Jersey, the Declaration was this day proclaimed, together with the new constitution of the colony, lately established, and the resolve of the Provincial Congress for continuing the administration of justice during the interim. The members of the Provincial Congress, the gentlemen of the committee, the officers and privates of the militia under arms, and a large concourse of the inhabitants, attended on this great and solemn occasion. The Declaration and other proceedings were received with loud acclamations.

The people now are convinced of what we ought long since to have known, that our enemies have left us no middle way between perfect freedom and abject slavery. In the field, we trust, as well as in council, the inhabitants of New Jersey will be found ever ready to support the freedom and independence of America.

Pennsylvania Journal, July 17

July 9

NEW JERSEY   This evening Nassau Hall, at Princeton, in New Jersey, was grandly illuminated, and INDEPENDENCY proclaimed under a triple volley of musketry, and a universal acclamation for the prosperity of the United States. The ceremony was conducted with the greatest decorum.

Letter from Princeton
Pennsylvania Evening Post, July 13

July 10

NEW YORK   This afternoon the Declaration of Independence was read at the head of each brigade of the Continental army, posted at and in the vicinity of New York. It was received everywhere with loud huzzas, and the utmost demonstrations of joy; and to-night the equestrian statue of George III, which Tory pride and folly raised in the year 1770, has, by the Sons of Freedom, been laid prostrate in the dirt—the just desert of an ungrateful tyrant! The lead wherewith the monument was made is to be run into bullets, to assimilate with the brains of our infatuated adversaries, who, to gain a pepper-corn, have lost an empire. A gentleman who was present at this ominous fall of leaden majesty, looking back to the original's hopeful beginning, pertinently exclaimed, in the language of the Angel to Lucifer, "If thou be'st he! But ah, how fallen! how changed!"

A few hours before the Declaration was read, the light dragoon regiment of Connecticut troops arrived in the city, and paraded on horseback through the streets, making a noble and martial appearance. Nothing could be more agreeable or animating to all the true friends of their country, than the sight of this corps, which is composed of the substantial yeomanry of a virtuous sister state. Some of them assisted, in their present uniforms, at the first reduction of Louisburg, and their "lank, lean cheeks and war-torn coats," are viewed with more veneration by their *honest* countrymen, than if they were glittering nabobs from India, or bashaws with nine tails.

Pennsylvania Journal, July 17

July 18

NEW YORK   On the 18th of July, by order of the Convention of the State of New York, the Declaration of the Independency of the United States of America was read at the State House in New York, to a numerous and respectable body of the freeholders and principal inhabitants of the city and county, and was received with general applause and heartfelt satisfaction; and, at the same time, our late King's coat of arms was brought from the City Hall, where his courts were commonly held, and burned, amidst the acclamations of thousands of spectators.

MASSACHUSETTS   The same day, the Declaration was proclaimed from the State House, in Boston, Mass., amidst the acclamations of thousands, who assembled on the occasion.

Pennsylvania Journal, July 24
Pennsylvania Evening Post, August 3

July 20

NEW YORK   This day, Lieutenant-Colonel Patterson, of the British army, came to New York, from Lord Howe's fleet, and landed near the main battery. He passed through a file of the Life Guards of General Washington, and had a private conference with him, at Colonel Knox's, for near half an hour.

After usual compliments, in which, as well as through the whole conversation, Colonel Patterson addressed General Washington by the title of Excellency, he entered upon the business by saying, that General Howe much regretted the difficulties which had arisen, respecting the address of the letters to General Washington, and that it was deemed consistent with propriety, and founded upon precedents of the like nature by ambassadors and plenipotentiaries where disputes or difficulties of rank had arisen. He also said that General Washington might recollect he had, last summer, addressed a letter to General Howe, *To the Hon. William Howe, Esq.;* that Lord Howe and General Howe did not mean to derogate from the respect or rank of General Washington; that they held his person and character in the highest esteem, and that the direction, with the addition of &c., &c., &c., implied every thing that ought to follow. He then produced a letter, which he did not directly offer to General Washington, but observing that it was the same letter which had been sent, with a superscription To George Washington, &c., &c., &c., he laid it on the table. The general declined the letter, and said, that a letter directed to a person in a public character, should have some description or indication of it, otherwise it would appear a mere private letter; that it was true the &c., &c., &c., implied every thing, and they also implied any thing; that the letter to General Howe alluded to, was an answer to one received under a like address from him, which the officer on duty having taken, he did not think proper to return, but answered it in the same mode of address. He then said he should absolutely decline any letters directed to him as a private person, when it related to his public station.

Colonel Patterson then remarked, that General Howe would not urge his delicacy further, and repeated his assertions, that no failure of respect was intended. He then said that he would endeavor, as well as he could, to recollect General Howe's sentiments on the letter and resolves of Congress, sent him a few days before, respecting the treatment of our prisoners in Canada. "That the affairs of Canada were in another department, not subject to the control of General Howe, but that he and Lord Howe utterly disapproved of every infringement of the rights of humanity."

Colonel Patterson then took a paper out of his pocket, and, after looking it over, said he had expressed nearly the words. General Washington then said that he had also forwarded a copy of the resolve to General Burgoyne.

To which Colonel Patterson replied, he did not doubt a proper attention would be paid to it, and that he (General Washington) was sensible that cruelty was not the characteristic of the British nation. Colonel Patterson then proceeded to say he had it in charge to mention the case of General Prescott, who they were informed was treated with such rigor, that under his age and infirmities, fatal consequences might be apprehended.

General Washington replied that General Prescott's treatment had not fallen under his notice; that all persons under his particular direction he had treated with kindness, and their situation was made as easy as possible; that he did not know where General Prescott was, but believed his treatment very different from their information. General Washington then mentioned the case of Colonel Allen, and the officers who had been confined in Boston jail. As to the first, Colonel Patterson answered, that General Howe had no knowledge of it but by information from General Washington, and that the Canada department was not under his direction or control;

that as to the other prisoners at Boston, whenever the state of the army at Boston admitted it, they were treated with humanity and even indulgence; that he asserted this upon his honor, and should be happy in an opportunity to prove it.

General Washington then observed, that the conduct of several of the officers would well have warranted a different treatment from what they had received; some having refused to give any parole, and others having broken it when given, by escaping or endeavoring so to do. Colonel Patterson answered, that as to the first they misunderstood the matter very much, and seemed to have mistook the line of propriety exceedingly; and as to the latter, General Howe utterly disapproved and condemned their conduct.

That if a remonstrance was made, such violations of good faith would be severely punished; but that he hoped General Washington was too just to draw public inferences from the misbehavior of some private individuals; that bad men were to be found in every class and society; that such behavior was considered as a dishonor to the British army. Colonel Patterson then proceeded to say that the goodness and benevolence of the King had induced him to appoint Lord Howe and General Howe his commissioners to accommodate the unhappy dispute; that they had great powers, and would derive the greatest pleasure from effecting an accommodation; and that he (Colonel Patterson) wished to have this visit considered as making the first advances to this desirable object. General Washington replied he was not vested with any powers on this subject, by those from whom he derived his authority and power. But from what had appeared or transpired on this head, Lord Howe and General Howe were only to grant pardons; that those who had committed no fault wanted no pardon; that we were only defending what we deemed our indisputable right. Colonel Patterson said that would open a very wide field for argument. He then expressed his apprehensions that an adherence to forms was likely to obstruct business of the greatest moment and concern.

He then observed, that a proposal had been formally made of exchanging Governor Skene for Mr. Lovell; that he now had authority to accede to that proposal. General Washington replied, that the proposition had been made by the direction of Congress, and having been then rejected, he could not now renew the business, or give any answer, till he had previously communicated it to them.

Colonel Patterson behaved with the greatest attention and politeness during the whole business, and expressed strong acknowledgments that the usual ceremony of blinding his eyes had been dispensed with. At the breaking up of the conference, General Washington strongly invited him to partake of a small collation provided for him, which he politely declined, alleging his late business, and an impatience to return to General Howe, though he had not executed his commission so amply as he wished. Finding he did not propose staying, he was introduced to the general officers, after which he took his leave, and was safely conducted to his own boat, which waited for him about four miles distant from the city.

Pennsylvania Journal, July 31

July 22

RHODE ISLAND   Day before yesterday, the honorable the General Assembly of Rhode Island, being then sitting at the state house in Newport, at twelve o'clock, the brigade stationed there, under the command of Colonels William Richmond and Christopher Lippitt, marched from head-quarters, and drew up in two columns, on each side the parade, before the state house door. His honor the Governor and the members of the Assembly then marched through and received the compliments of the brigade; after which the secretary, at the head of the company, read a resolve of the assembly, concurring with the Congress in the Declaration of Independence. The Declaration was then read; next thirteen cannon were discharged at Fort Liberty, and then the brigade drew up and fired in thirteen divisions, from east to west, agreeable to the number and situation of the United States. The Declaration was received with joy and applause by all ranks, and the whole was conducted with great solemnity and decorum.

Pennsylvania Evening Post, August 1

July 30

RHODE ISLAND   The representatives of the State of Rhode Island and Providence plantations have passed a resolve, That if any person within that state shall, under pretence of preaching or praying, or in any other way or manner whatever, acknowledge or declare their late King to be their rightful lord or sovereign, or shall pray for the success of his arms, or that he may vanquish or overcome all his enemies, shall be deemed guilty of high misdemeanor, and therefore be presented by the grand jury of the county, where the offence shall be committed, to the superior court of the same county; and upon conviction thereof, shall forfeit and pay, as a fine, to and for the use of that state, the sum of one hundred thousand pounds lawful money, and pay all costs of prosecution, and shall stand committed to gaol until the same be satisfied.

Constitutional Gazette, July 31

AUGUST

August 7

NEW HAMPSHIRE   This day was carried into Portsmouth, New Hampshire, by the *Hancock* privateer, which sailed from Philadelphia, a large three-decked ship, named the *Reward*, of between five and six hundred tons burden. She was a twenty-gun ship last war, in the service of the British King. She was from Tortola, bound to London, and had on board between ten and eleven hundred hogsheads of sugar, eighty-six hogsheads of rum, twelve bales of cotton, and nine cannon, some of them brass. There were on board the ship a number of turtles, directed to Lord North, with his name cut in the shell, the best of which Captain Wingate Newman, master of the privateer, is determined to send to the Honorable John Hancock.

Pennsylvania Evening Post, August 20

NEW JERSEY   The committee of inspection for the county of Cumberland, in the State of New Jersey, the officers of the militia, and a great number of other inhabitants, having met at Bridgetown, went in procession to the court-house, where the declaration of independency, the constitution of New Jersey, and treason ordinance, were publicly read, and unanimously approved of. These were followed with a spirited address by Doctor Elmer, chairman of the committee, after which the peace officers' staves, on which were depicted the King's coat-of-arms, with other ensigns of royalty, were burnt in the street. The whole was conducted with the greatest decency and regularity.

The following is the substance of the before mentioned address: "Gentlemen of the Committee, Officers of the Militia, and Gentlemen Spectators:—From what has now been read, you see the long wished for, but much dreaded period has arrived, in which the connection between Great Britain and America is totally dissolved, and these colonies declared free and independent states. As this is an event of the greatest importance, it must afford satisfaction to every intelligent person to reflect that it was brought about by unavoidable necessity on our part, and has been conducted with a prudence and moderation becoming the wisest and best of men.

"With the independency of the American States, a new era in politics has commenced. Every consideration respecting the propriety or impropriety of a separation from Britain, is now entirely out of the question; and we have now no more to do with the King and people of England, than we have with the King and people of France or Spain. No people under heaven were ever favored with a fairer opportunity of laying a sure foundation for future grandeur and happiness than we. The plan of government established in most states and kingdoms of the world, has been the effect of chance or necessity; ours of sober reason and cool deliberation. Our future happiness or misery, therefore, as a people, will depend entirely upon ourselves. If actuated by principles of virtue and genuine patriotism, we make the welfare of our country the sole aim of all our actions; if we intrust none but persons of ability and integrity with the management of our public affairs; if we carefully guard against corruption and undue influence in the several departments of government; if we are steady and zealous in putting the laws in strict execution, the spirit and principles of our new constitution, which we have just now heard read, may be preserved for a long time: but if faction and party spirit, the destruction of popular governments, take place, anarchy and confusion will soon ensue, and we shall either fall an easy prey to a foreign enemy, or some factious and aspiring demagogue possessed of popular talents and shining qualities. A Julius Cæsar, or an Oliver Cromwell, will spring up among ourselves, who, taking advantage of our political animosities, will lay violent hands on the government, and sacrifice the liberties of his country to his own ambitious and domineering humor. God grant that neither of these may ever be the unhappy fate of this, or any of the United States! To prevent which, while we are striving to defend ourselves against the unjust encroachments of a foreign and unnatural enemy, let us not neglect to keep strict and jealous eye over our internal police and constitution. Let the fate of *Greece, Rome, Carthage,* and *Great Britain,* warn us of our danger; and the loss of liberty in all those states, for want of timely guarding against the introduction of tyranny and usurpation, be a standing admonition to us, to avoid the rock on which they have all shipwrecked.

"Let us, as honest citizens and sincere lovers of our country, exert ourselves in the defence of our state, and in support of our new constitution; but, while we strive to vindicate the glorious cause of liberty, on the one hand, let us on the other hand, carefully guard against running into the contrary extreme of disorder and licentiousness.

"In our present situation, engaged in a bloody and dangerous war with the power of Great Britain, for the defence of our lives, our liberties, our property, and every thing that is dear and valuable; every member of this state, who enjoys the benefits of its civil government, is absolutely bound, by the immutable law of self-preservation, the laws of God and of society, to assist in protecting and defending it. This is so plain and self-evident a proposition, that I am persuaded every person here present makes it the rule of his conduct on all occasions; and consequently, in a time of such imminent danger, will be extremely careful, at our ensuing election, not to trust any one with the management of our public affairs, who has not, by his vigilance and activity in the cause of liberty, proved himself to be a true friend to his country. The success, gentlemen, of our present glorious struggle wholly depends upon this single circumstance. For, though the situation and extent of the United States of America, and our numberless internal resources, are sufficient to enable us to bid defiance to all Europe; yet should we be so careless about our own safety, as to intrust the affairs of our state, while the bayonet is pointed at our breasts, to persons whose conduct discovers them to be enemies to their country, or whose religious principles will not suffer them to lift a hand for our defence, our ruin will inevitably follow.

"As it is impossible for any one, possessed of the spirit of a man, who is a friend to the United States, and whose conscience does not furnish him with an excuse, to stand by, an idle spectator, while his country is struggling and bleeding in her own necessary defence; all such inactive persons ought, therefore, to be shunned as enemies or despised as cowards. And as I have reason to believe that many who plead conscience as an excuse, are sincere in their pretensions; and as every man's conscience ought to be free from compulsion, this single consideration should restrain us from forcing such into any of the departments of government. For to put such persons, at this time, in places of public trust, is actually to deprive them of liberty of conscience; for we thereby compel them either to betray the trust reposed in them, or to act contrary to the dictates of their own consciences. A dilemma in which, act as they will, their conduct must be criminal. Besides, if we consulted only our own safety, it is plain, that to intrust the affairs of our government, at this juncture, to such people, is as dangerous as to intrust the management of a ship in a violent storm, to an infant, or an idiot.

"As a friend to my country and a lover of liberty, I thought it my duty to address you on this occasion, and having now, as a faithful member of society, discharged my duty, I shall leave you to the exercise of your own judgment and conclude with a request, that you would conduct yourselves this day in such a manner as to convince the public that your abhorrence of the cruel and bloody *Nero* of Britain, and his despicable minions of tyranny and oppression, arises, not from the mere impulse of blind passion and prejudice, but from sober reason and reflection; and while we rejoice in being formally emancipated from our haughty and imperious *Task-masters*, let us remember, that the final termination of this grand event is not likely to be brought about without shedding the blood of many of our dear friends and countrymen."

Pennsylvania Journal, August 28

August 10

GEORGIA   At Savannah, in Georgia, a declaration being received from the honorable John Hancock, Esq., by which it appeared that the Continental Congress, in the name and by the authority of their constituents, had declared that the United Colonies of North America are, and of right ought to be, FREE AND INDEPENDENT STATES, and absolved from all allegiance to the British crown, his Excellency the President, and the honorable the council, met in the council chamber and read the Declaration.

They then proceeded to the square before the assembly house, and read it to a great concourse of people, when the grenadier and light infantry companies fired a general volley. After this they proceeded in the following procession to the liberty pole: The grenadiers in front; the provost-marshal, on horseback, with his sword drawn; the secretary, with the Declaration; his Excellency the President; the honorable the council, and the gentlemen attending; then the light infantry and the rest of the militia of the town and district of Savannah.

At the liberty-pole they were met by the Georgia battalion, who, after the reading of the Declaration, discharged their field-pieces, and fired in platoons. Upon this they proceeded to the battery, at the trustee's gardens, where the Declaration was read for the last time, and the cannon of the battery discharged.

His Excellency and council, Colonel Lachlan McIntosh, and other gentlemen, with the militia, dined under the cedar trees, and cheerfully drank to the UNITED, FREE, AND INDEPENDENT States of America. In the evening the town was illuminated, and there was exhibited a very solemn funeral procession, attended by the grenadier and light infantry companies, and other militia, with their drums muffled, and fifes, and a greater number of people than ever appeared on any occasion before, in that province, when George the Third was interred before the court-house in the following manner:

"Forasmuch as George the Third, of Great Britain, hath most flagrantly violated his coronation oath, and trampled on the constitution of our country, and the sacred rights of mankind: we, therefore, commit his political existence to the ground—corruption to corruption—tyranny to the grave— and oppression to eternal infamy, in sure and certain hope that he will never obtain a resurrection, to rule again over these United States of America. But, my friends and fellow-citizens, let us not be sorry, as men without hope, for *Tyrants* that thus depart—rather let us remember that America is free and independent; that she is, and will be, with the blessing of the Almighty, GREAT among the nations of the earth. Let this encourage us in well-doing, to fight for our rights and privileges, for our wives and children, for all that is near and dear unto us. May God give us his blessing, and let all the people say AMEN."

Connecticut Gazette and Universal Intelligencer
Pennsylvania Evening Post, October 8

August 22

NEW YORK   This night we have reason to expect the grand attack from our barbarian enemies; the reasons why, follow: The night before last, a lad went over to Staten Island, supped there with a friend, and got safe back again undiscovered. Soon after he went to General Washington, and upon good authority reported, that the English army, amounting to fifteen or twenty thousand, had embarked and were in readiness for an engagement; that seven ships of the line, and a number of other vessels of war, were to surround this city and cover their landing; that the Hessians, being fifteen thousand, were to remain on the island and attack Perth Amboy, Elizabethtown Point, and Bergen, while the main body were doing their best at New York; that the Highlanders expected America was already conquered, and that they were only to come over and settle on our lands, for which reason they had brought their churns, ploughs, &c.; being deceived, they had refused fighting, upon which account General Howe had shot one, hung five or six, and flogged many.

Last evening, in a violent thunder storm, Mr. —— (a very intelligent person) ventured over. He brings much the same account as the above lad, with this addition:—that all the horses on the island were by Howe's orders killed, barrelled up, and put on board—the wretches thinking they could get no landing at New York, and of consequence be soon out of provision; that the Tories were used cruelly, and with the Highlanders were compelled to go on board the ships to fight in the character of common soldiers against us. The British army are prodigiously incensed against the Tories, and curse them as the instruments of the war now raging. Mr. —— further informs, that last night the fleet was to come up, but the thunder storm prevented. The truth of this appears, from the circumstance of about three thousand red coats landing at ten o'clock this morning on Long Island, where by this time it is supposed our people are hard at it. There is an abundance of smoke to-day on Long Island, our folks having set fire to stacks of hay, &c., to prevent the enemy's being benefited in case they get any advantage against us. All the troops in New York are in high spirits, and have been under arms most of the day, as the fleet have been in motion, and are now, as is generally thought, only waiting for a change of tide. Forty-eight hours or less, will determine it as to New York, one way or the other.

The thunder storm of last evening was one of the most dreadful we ever witnessed; it lasted from seven to ten o'clock. Several claps struck in and about New York. Many houses were damaged, and several lives lost. Three officers, a captain and two lieutenants, belonging to Colonel M'Dougal's regiment, were struck instantly dead. The points of their swords, for several inches, were melted, with a few silver dollars they had in their pockets; they (the persons) were seemingly roasted. A dog in the same tent was also killed, and a soldier near it struck blind, deaf, and dumb. One in the main street was killed, as likewise ten on Long Island. Two or three were much burnt, and greatly hurt. When God speaks, who can but fear?

Pennsylvania Journal, August 28

August 26

NEW YORK   Tuesday last [20th,] a number of ships with troops on board, sailed from Staten Island out of the Narrows; next day they were followed by many more, and about ten o'clock Thursday morning, about ten thousand men landed between New Utrecht and Gravesend, on Long Island. Friday, a party of them came and took possession of Flatbush, which immediately brought on a very hot fire from the Americans, who are advantageously posted in the woods, and on every eminence round that place.

The advanced party of the Regulars are encamped a little to the north-west of Flatbush Church, and have a battery somewhat to the westward of Mr. Jeremiah Vanderbilt's, from whence they continue to fire briskly on our people, who often approach and discharge their rifles within two hundred yards of their works. We have had only four men wounded since the enemy landed, but we were certain many of them fell; and a Hessian was killed last Friday. Several dollars were found in his pocket, and he had an excellent rifle. Many of the Regulars are in rifle dresses.

Freeman's Journal, September 7

August 30

NEW YORK   About twelve o'clock last Monday night, (26th,) we were alarmed by the return of some of our scouting parties, who advised us that the English were in motion, and coming up the island, with several field-pieces. It was generally thought not to be the main body, but only a detachment, with a view to possess themselves of some advantageous heights. On which near three thousand men were ordered out, consisting chiefly of the Pennsylvania and Maryland troops, to attack them on their march. About sunrise the next morning, (27th,) we came up with a very large body of them.

The Delaware and Maryland battalions made one party. Colonel Atlee with his battalion, a little before us, had taken post in an orchard and behind a barn; and, on the approach of the enemy, he gave them a very severe fire, which he bravely kept up for a considerable time, until they were near surrounding him, when he retreated to the woods. The enemy then advanced to us, upon which Lord Stirling, who commanded, drew us up in a line, and offered them battle in the true English taste. The British army then advanced within about three hundred yards of us, and began a very heavy fire from their cannon and mortars, for both the balls and shells flew very fast, now and then taking off a head. Our men stood it amazingly well—not even one of them showed a disposition to shrink.

Our orders were not to fire until the enemy came within fifty yards of us; but when they perceived we stood their fire so coolly and resolutely, they declined coming any nearer, although treble our number. In this situation we stood from sunrise till twelve o'clock, the enemy firing upon us the chief part of the time, when the main body of their army, by a route we never dreamed of, had entirely surrounded us and drove within the lines, or scattered in the woods all our men except the Delaware and Maryland battalions, who were standing at bay with double their number. Thus situated, we were ordered to attempt a retreat, by fighting our way through the enemy, who had posted themselves, and nearly filled every field and road between us and our lines. We had not retreated a quarter of a mile before we were fired upon by an advanced part of the enemy, and those upon our rear were playing upon us with their artillery. Our men fought with more than Roman virtue, and would have stood until they were shot down to a man. We forced the advanced party,

which first attacked us, to give way, through which opening
we got a passage down to the side of a marsh, seldom before
waded over, which we passed, and then swam a narrow river,
all the time exposed to the fire of the enemy. The companies
commanded by Captains Ramsey and Scott were in the front,
and sustained the first fire of the enemy, when hardly a man
fell.

The whole of the right wing of our battalion, thinking it
impossible to march through the marsh, attempted to force
their way through the woods, where they were almost to a
man killed or taken. The Maryland battalion has lost two
hundred and fifty-nine men, amongst whom are twelve officers. Captains Veazey and Bowey, the first certainly killed;
Lieutenants Butler, Sterret, Dent, Courley, Muse, Prawl, Ensigns Coats and Fernandes; who of them are killed or who
prisoners, is yet uncertain. Many of the officers lost their
swords and guns. We have since entirely abandoned Long
Island, bringing off all our military stores.

Generals Sullivan and Stirling are both prisoners; Colonels
Atlee, Miles, and Piper, are also taken. There are about a
thousand men missing in all; we took a few prisoners. By a
lieutenant we took, we understand they had about twenty-
three thousand men on the island that morning. Most of our
generals were on a high hill in our lines, viewing us with
glasses. When we began our retreat, they could see the
enemy we had to pass through, though we could not. Many
of them thought we would surrender in a body, without firing.
When we began the attack General Washington wrung his
hands, and cried out, "Good God, what brave fellows I must
this day lose." Major Guest commanded the Maryland battalion, the colonel and lieutenant-colonel being both at York;
Captains Adams and Lucas were sick. The major, Captain
Ramsey, and Lieutenant Plunket, were foremost, and within
forty yards of the enemy's muzzles, when they were fired
upon by the enemy, who were chiefly under cover of an
orchard, save a few that showed themselves and pretended to
give up, clubbing their firelocks until we came within that
distance, when they immediately presented and blazed in our
faces. They entirely overshot us, and killed some men away

in the rear. I had the satisfaction of dropping one of them the first fire I made; I was so near that I could not miss. I discharged my rifle seven times that day as deliberately as ever I did at a mark, and with as little perturbation.

Letter from New York, September 1
Freeman's Journal, September 28

The Folks on t'Other Side the Wave

This song was written in England in 1776 for the Middlesex Journal, *and subsequently published as a broadside. It makes an accurate appraisal of the nature of the war that Britain would be forced to fight in the wilderness, warns the House of Commons to reconsider its policy, and urges the recall of troops and ships from America. No melody was provided by the original author; in such cases singers fell back upon one of several stock tunes that might fit. The "stock" given here was provided by Bill Bonyun. The melody is based upon an old sea shanty and fits the verse very well; the refrain is also appropriate. (Moore, Songs and Ballads, 141–3; abridged.)*

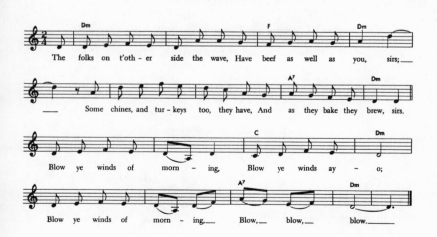

The folks on t'oth-er side the wave, Have beef as well as you, sirs;___
___ Some chines, and tur-keys too, they have, And as they bake they brew, sirs.
Blow ye winds of morn - ing, Blow ye winds ay - o;
Blow ye winds of morn - ing,___ Blow,___ blow,___ blow.___

What, tho' your cannon raze their towns,
　And tumble down their houses,
They'll fight like devils, blood and bones,
　For children and for spouses.

　　Blow ye winds of morning, etc.

Another truth—nay, 'tis no boast,
　Nor yet the lie o' the day, sirs;
The saints on Massachusetts coast,
　Gain if they run away, sirs.

　　Blow ye winds of morning, etc.

For further than your bullets fly,
　A common man may run, sirs,
And wheat will grow beneath a sky,
　Where cannot reach a gun, sirs.

　　Blow ye winds of morning, etc.

Then what are ships, and swords, and guns,
　And men of bloody mind, sirs,
While, Parthian-like, who conquers runs,
　Who loses, stays behind, sirs.

　　Blow ye winds of morning, etc.

Recall your ships, your troops recall,
　Let friends each other nourish,
So shall old England rule the ball,
　And George and freedom flourish.

　　Blow ye winds of morning, etc.

———•—•———

SEPTEMBER

September 3

NEW YORK　General Howe gives the following account of
the late action on Long Island:—On the twenty-second of

last month, in the morning, the British, with Colonel Donop's corps of Chasseurs and Hessian grenadiers, disembarked near Utrecht on Long Island, without opposition, the whole being landed with forty pieces of cannon, in two hours and a half, under the direction of Commodore Hotham, Lieutenant-General Clinton commanding the first division of the troops.

The enemy had only small parties upon the coast, who, upon the approach of the boats, retired to the woody heights commanding a principal pass on the road from Flatbush to their works at Brooklyn. Lord Cornwallis was immediately detached to Flatbush with the reserve, two battalions of light infantry, and Colonel Donop's corps, with six field-pieces, having orders not to risk an attack upon the pass, if he should find it occupied; which proving to be the case, his lordship took post in the village, and the army extended from the ferry at the Narrows, through Utrecht and Gravesend, to the village of Flatland.

On the twenty-fifth, Lieutenant-General de Heister, with two brigades of Hessians from Staten Island, joined the army, leaving one brigade of his troops, a detachment of the 14th regiment from Virginia, some convalescents and recruits, under the command of Lieutenant-Colonel Dalrymple, for the security of that island.

On the twenty-sixth, Lieutenant-General de Heister took post at Flatbush, and in the evening Lord Cornwallis, with the British, drew off to Flatland. About nine o'clock, the same night, the van of the army, commanded by Lieutenant-General Clinton, consisting of light dragoons and brigade of light infantry, the reserve under the command of Lord Cornwallis, excepting the 42d regiment, which was posted to the left of the Hessians, the first brigade, and the 71st regiment, with fourteen field-pieces, began to move from Flatland across the country through the new lots, to seize a pass in the heights, extending from east to west along the middle of the island, and about three miles from Bedford, on the road to Jamaica, in order to turn the enemy's left, posted at Flatbush.

General Clinton being arrived within half a mile of the pass, about two hours before daybreak, halted and settled his dispositions for the attack. One of his patrols, falling in with a patrol of the enemy's officers, took them, and the general learning from their information that the rebels had not occupied the pass, detached a battalion of light infantry to secure it, and, advancing with his corps, upon the first appearance of day, possessed himself of the heights, with such a disposition as must have insured success, had he found the enemy in force to oppose him.

The main body of the army, consisting of the guards, 2d, 3d, and 5th brigades, with ten field-pieces, led by Lord Percy, marched soon after General Clinton, and halted an hour before day in his rear. This column (the country not admitting of two columns of march) was followed by the 49th regiment, with four medium twelve-pounders, and the baggage closed the rear with a separate guard.

As soon as these corps had passed the heights, they halted for the soldiers to take a little refreshment, after which the march was continued, and about half an hour past eight o'clock, having got to Bedford, in the rear of the enemy's left, the attack was commenced by the light infantry and light dragoons upon large bodies of the rebels having cannon, who were quitting the wood heights before mentioned, to return to their lines, upon discovering the march of the army. Instead of which, they were driven back, and the army still moving on to gain the enemy's rear, the grenadiers and 32d regiment being in front of the column, soon approached within musket-shot of the enemy's lines at Brooklyn, from whence these battalions, without regarding the fire of cannon and small arms upon them, pursued numbers of the rebels that were retiring from the heights so close to their principal redoubt, and with such eagerness to attack it by storm, that it required repeated orders to prevail upon them to desist from the attempt. Had they been permitted to go on, it is my opinion they would have carried the redoubt; but as it was apparent the lines must have been ours at a very cheap rate, by regular approaches, I would not risk the loss that might have been sustained in the assault, and ordered them back to a hollow way, in the front of the works, out of the reach of musketry.

Lieutenant-General de Heister began soon after daybreak

to cannonade the enemy in his front, and, upon the approach of our right, ordered Colonel Donop's corps to advance to the attack of the hill, following himself at the head of the brigades. The light infantry, about that time, having been reinforced by the light company, the grenadier company, and two other companies of the guards, who joined them with the greatest activity and spirit, had taken three pieces of cannon, and were warmly engaged with very superior numbers in the woods, when, on the Hessians advancing, the enemy gave way, and was entirely routed in that quarter.

On the left, Major-General Grant, having the fourth and sixth brigades, the 42d regiment, and two companies of the New York Provincials, raised by Governor Tryon in the spring, advanced along the coast with ten pieces of cannon, to divert the enemy's attention from their left. About midnight, he fell in with their advanced parties, and at daybreak with a large corps, having cannon and advantageously posted, with whom there was skirmishing, and a cannonade for some hours, until by the firing at Brooklyn, the rebels, suspecting their retreat would be cut off, made a movement to their right, in order to secure it across a swamp and creek, that covered the right of their works; but being met in their way by a party of 2d grenadiers, who were soon after supported by the 71st regiment, and General Grant's left coming up, they suffered considerably. Numbers of them, however, did get into the morass, where many were suffocated or drowned.

The force of the enemy detached from the lines where General Putnam commanded, was not less, from the best accounts I have had, than ten thousand men, who were under the orders of Major-General Sullivan, Brigadier-Generals Lord Stirling and Woodhull. Their loss is computed to be about thirty-three hundred killed, wounded, prisoners, and drowned, with five field-pieces and one howitzer taken.

On the part of the King's troops, five officers, and fifty-six non-commissioned officers and rank and file are killed; twelve officers, and two hundred and forty-five non-commissioned officers and rank and file are wounded; one officer and twenty grenadiers of the marines taken, by mistaking the enemy for the Hessians.

The Hessians had two privates killed, three officers, and twenty-three rank and file wounded. The wounds are in general very slight. Lieutenant-Colonel Monckton is shot through the body, but there are the greatest hopes of his recovery.

The behavior of both officers and soldiers, British and Hessians, was highly to their honor. More determined courage and steadiness in troops have never been experienced, or a greater ardor to distinguish themselves, as all those who had opportunity amply evinced by their actions.

In the evening of the 27th, the army encamped in front of the enemy's works. On the 28th, at night, broke ground six hundred yards distant from a redoubt upon their left, and on the 29th, at night, the rebels evacuated their intrenchments, and Red Hook, with the utmost silence, and quitted Governor's Island the following evening, leaving their cannon and a quantity of stores, in all their works. At daybreak on the 30th, their flight was discovered; the pickets of the line took possession, and those most advanced reached the shore opposite to New York, as their rear guard was going over, and fired some shot among them.

The enemy is still in possession of the town and island of New York, in force, and making demonstration to oppose us in their works on both sides of King's Bridge.

The inhabitants of Long Island, many of whom had been forced into rebellion, have all submitted, and are ready to take the oaths of allegiance.

Letter from General Howe to Lord George Germaine
Upcott, IV, 401

September 6

NEW YORK   A meeting of a large body of the inhabitants of Long Island, New York, was held, at which the following speech was delivered by an American recruiting officer in the Provincials, now raising for his Majesty's service, by order of his Excellency General Howe:—

GENTLEMEN, FRIENDS, AND COUNTRYMEN:—Being appointed by his Excellency General Howe to raise a corps of Provincials for his Majesty's service, I readily engage in the attempt from principle, and in consequence of the fullest conviction that there are yet very many among us who still retain the most unshaken loyalty to our gracious sovereign, and zealous attachment to the blessings of the British constitution; who have long been anxious to wipe away from our country the reproach of a supposed universal revolt and disaffection of the Americans; and who are prompted as well by inclination, as by a sense of duty, to embrace the earliest opportunity of testifying by their conduct a continuance of their allegiance to his Majesty King George the Third, and a willing acknowledgment of the necessary and constitutional supremacy of the British legislature over the whole empire.

It is irksome to censure any collective bodies of our countrymen—we wish their conduct had been less culpable. I am confident we all hope that the sword of justice may be directed by the hand of compassion—that the guilty may be reclaimed, and that the deluded may be received with tenderness and mercy. But, gentlemen, now is the time to exert our endeavors if we wish to rescue ourselves from the evils of Republican tyranny, or our country from ruin. The misrule and persecutions of committees, conventions, and Congresses are no longer to be endured; they have become insupportable—they are too enormous for description. There are none of us but what have already either seen or felt the cruelty and oppression of their Republican despotism. Without effecting one salutary purpose, those self-created bodies have violated all the sacred ties of civil society, prostrated all law and government, and arbitrarily usurped an absolute control over the natural rights, the reason, and the consciences of their fellow-subjects. Instead of supporting constitutional liberty, and redressing public grievances, the special purposes of their original associations, they have denied their fellow-citizens the greatest and most valuable of all possible privileges: those of personal liberty, and freedom of speech. Instead of endeavoring, by dutiful representations in a constitutional method, for a reconciliation with the parent state, and thereby restoring to us the innumerable benefits and advantages of the former happy union between Great Britain and the colonies, they have most unjustifiably and perversely erected the standard of independency.

This is not all. They have increased and multiplied the distresses of poverty and want among our poor. They have, moreover, deliberately involved their country in all the turbulence of faction, in all the evils of anarchy and licentiousness; and to complete the transcendent enormity of their crimes against the interest and prosperity of America, as well as the state to which we are united by the ties of nature, and bound by every civil, moral, and political obligation, they have disregarded the liberal and benevolent declaration of his Majesty's commissioners of peace, and with the most obdurate and unfeeling dispositions for the distresses of their countrymen, obstinately and wickedly precipitated the whole British continent of America into all the guilt of rebellion, and all the horrors and calamities of a civil war. In a few words, gentlemen, they have deluded the populace, they have betrayed their trust, they have forfeited the confidence of the public, they have ruined our country. Not to oppose them and their measures, were criminal. Not to join and assist the King's forces at this time would be at once unwise, unmanly, and ungrateful. And, gentlemen and countrymen, permit me to add, that the repeated assurances which have been given by the friends of government and good order, of their readiness to enter into his Majesty's service, leave me no room to doubt of the most immediate and honorable success. Your loyalty to your King, your duty to your country, your regard for your wives and children, the cause of violated justice and of injured majesty, all call aloud for your strenuous aid and united endeavors in assisting the royal army and navy in re-establishing the authority of his Majesty's government in the colonies, and with it a return to America of those happier days we all have seen, when the voice of peace and plenty was heard in our land, and we experienced, under the protection and benignity of the British State, the tranquil enjoyment of such constitutional and established liberties and privileges as were equal to our wishes, and known only to British subjects.   *New York Gazette and Weekly Mercury*
(Serle edition), October 14

September 7

The following letter to Lord Viscount Howe, commander-in-chief of his Britannic Majesty's forces in North America, is published in the paper of to-day:—My Lord: I am told there is great exultation among the English and mercenary troops under your lordship's command, on account of the late victory they obtained with an army of ten thousand men, (having a large train of artillery and many light horse to assist them in the work,) over three thousand Americans, having neither artillery nor horse to oppose their enemies with. Your army was commanded by a great many generals, colonels, &c., which, by superior cunning or generalship, had inclosed this handful of Americans, in full confidence of taking captive all that they spared alive; but the courage of these men baffled your hopes, who after laying great numbers of their enemies dead, that opposed their retreat, more than two-thirds reached their own lines in safety; therefore, we think you have no cause to exult.

My Lord, I assure you the Americans are not in the least dispirited at this unequal defeat; but, on the contrary, are much exasperated that you should act so cowardly in attacking three thousand men badly provided, with at least ten thousand of your veteran English troops, accompanied by thousands of orang-outang murdering brutes. The Americans wish for an opportunity to fight the invaders of their once happy land, on an equal footing, and let the fate of America rest on the issue of this conflict.

The mode we would propose is as follows, and which we are anxious for your lordship to adopt; and, it being equitable, and your lordship being famed for generosity of sentiment, we have no doubt of succeeding to your wish. Let your lordship select ten thousand of your best troops and officers, with your lordship at their head; draw them up on the extensive plains of Long Island, where you will have every opportunity of displaying your great abilities. Arrange them in whatever manner you please; then let an equal number of Americans form themselves in battalia, and let each army be provided in all respects equal, with trains of artillery, and all other offensive weapons; then, on a given signal, begin the attack, and leave the issue to the God of armies. This is what the Americans have requested me to propose to Lord Howe; and the sooner he agrees to the proposal the better.

"Fair battle," Pennsylvania Evening Post, September 7

September 16

NEW YORK   Yesterday morning, about eleven o'clock, the British troops, under cover of a tremendous fire from eight or ten ships-of-war, effected a landing near Mr. Stuyvesant's house in the Bowery, and in a few hours after took possession of the city of New York. About the same time, the *Asia* man-of-war and two other ships proceeded up the North River, but were very roughly handled by the American battery at Powle's Hook. This morning, at daylight, the *Asia* came down much faster than she went up, she and her consorts having narrowly escaped destruction by four of our fire ships that run in among them.

Freeman's Journal, October 5

The British Lamentation

———•·•———

This ballad, one of the classic broadsides of the American Revolution, is evidently a composition dating from 1776 or 1777; more than likely, it originated in an incident that actually occurred upon the battlefield. The story summarizes the experiences of a British soldier from the time that he was sent overseas in 1774 to his death shortly after the invasion of Manhattan in September 1776. We may think of it as propaganda of the most effective type. It is filled with a sense of compassion for a British soldier sent away from home to die uselessly in a cause that is not his own; it portrays Americans as heroes who rise up "like grasshoppers" to defend their land and who show a contempt of death in the struggle for liberty. At least two broadside issues survive, differing from each other in minor detail. The version reproduced here is one that comes to us from oral tradition; it was learned quite recently by Frank Warner from the lips of John Galusha of Minerva, N.Y., who died in 1950. Minor gaps in this version have been rounded out from a study of the broadsides. The fine melody, with its mood of haunting sadness, is transcribed from the singing of Frank Warner. (Frank Warner, by permission. Ford, Check List, 2993, 2994; Isaiah Thomas, 30.)

Come all you good peo-ple, wher-ev-er you be, Who walk on the land__ or__ sail by the sea; Come lis-ten to the words of a dy-ing man, I think that__ you'll__ re - mem-ber them. 'Twas on De-cem-ber the six-teenth day__ That we set sail for A-mer-i-ca; Our drums did beat and trum-pets sound And un-to__ Bos-ton__ we__ were bound.

And when to Boston we did come
We thought by the aid of our British guns
To drive the rebels from that place
And fill their hearts with sore disgrace.

But to our sad and sore surprise,
We saw men like grasshoppers rise:
They fought like heroes much enraged
Which surely frightened General Gage.

Like lions roaring for their prey
They feared no danger nor dismay;
True British blood runs through their veins
And them with courage yet sustains.

THE BRITISH LAMENTATION,

TOGETHER WITH

GREEN ON THE CAPE,

OR THE IRISH HERO.

TWAS on that dark and dismal day,
When we set sail for America ;
'Twas on that fourteenth day of May,
When we set sail for America.

'Twas on that dark and dismal time,
When we set sail for the northern clime ;
Where drums do beat and trumpets sound
And unto Boston we were bound.

And when to Boston we did come,
We thought by our British drums
To drive those rebels from that place,
And fill their hearts with sore disgrace.

But to our sorrow and surprize,
We saw them like grasshoppers rise,
They fight like heroes much enrag'd,
Which did affright old general Gage.

Like lions roaring for their prey,
They fear no danger nor dismay ;
Bold British blood runs thro' their veins,
But still with courage they sustain.

We saw those bold Columbian sons,
Spread death and slaughter from their guns,
Freedom or death ! these heroes cry,
I'm sure they're not afraid to die.

We sail'd to York, as you've been told,
There the loss of many a Briton bold,
For to make those rebels own their king,
And daily tribute to him bring.

In York was many traitors found,
They said that they could win the ground,
They said that they could win the day,
There was no danger they did say.

New-York it was a garden place,
They said they could in a short space,
Pull down your towns, lay waste your lands
In spite of all your Boston bands.

A garden place it was indeed,
And in it grows a bitter weed,
Which will pull down our highest hopes,
And sorely wound our British troops,

'Tis now September, the seventeenth day,
I wish I'd ne'er come to America,
Full fifteen thousand has been slain,
Bold British heroes every one.

Now I receiv'd my mortal wound,
I bid adieu to old England's ground ;
My wife and children mourn for me,
But never more can they me see.

Fight on, fight on American boys, .
Fear not old England's thund'ring noise ;
Maintain your cause from year to year,
God's on your side, you need not fear.

Green on the Cape.

I'M a lad that's forc'd to travel from my native land,
By a note that's sworn against me, my country I can't stand,
It's from all danger I made my escape ;
With my national colors, I wore green on my cape,
    I wore green on my cape,
 Chorus. I wore green on my cape,
    With my national colours,
    I wore green on my cape.
I went down to Belfast, that seaport so gay,
For to let my friends know that no longer I could stay,
And like a bold ensign I past the baron gate,
With my national colours I wore green on my cape.
There I met with a captain, and he bargain'd with me cheap,
And he told me his ship's company wore green on their cape,
They wore green on their cape, they wore green on their cape,
And he told me his ship's company wore green on their cape.
With a prosperous gale we sail'd away to France,
And so happy was I to meet with such a chance,
To meet with such a chance to make my escape,
With my national colours I wore green on my cape.
And when I got to Paris, there I walked up and down,
I met with Dukes and Lords and men of great reknown,
They took me by the hand, saying how made you your escape,
For they knew that I was united by the green on my cape.
There I met with Bonaparte, and he took me by the hand,
Saying how is old Ireland, and how does it stand ?
It is a poor distressed place as ever yet was seen,
For they hang both men and women for wearing the green.
Cheer up my lively lad you have friends in this town,
We will send a fleet over to pull the orange down,
To pull the orange down, and it plainly shall be seen,
There is nothing like the Irish lads for wearing the green,
    For wearing the green,
    For wearing the green,
 Chorus. There is nothing like the Irish lads,
    For wearing the green.

The British Lamentation; together with Green on the Cape, or The Irish Hero. This broadside version, issued by Nathaniel Coverly, Jr., of Boston some time after 1800, is testimony of the continuing popularity of the song after the end of the Revolution. Reproduced from the Isaiah Thomas Collection of Broadside Ballads by permission of the American Antiquarian Society, Worcester, Massachusetts.

We saw those bold Columbia sons,
Spread death and slaughter from their guns,
Freedom or death! was all their cry,
They did not seem to fear to die.

We sailed to York, as you've been told
With the loss of many a Briton bold,
For to make those rebels own our King,
And daily tribute to him bring.

They said it was a garden place,
And that our armies could, with ease,
Pull down their towns, lay waste their lands,
In spite of all their boasted bands.

A garden place it was indeed,
And in it grew many a bitter weed,
Which did pull down our highest hopes
And sorely wound the British troops.

'Tis now September the seventeenth day,
I wish I'd ne'er come to America,
Full fifteen hundred has been slain
Bold British heroes every one.

Now I've received my deathly wound,
I bid farewell to England's ground;
My wife and children will mourn for me,
Whilst I lie cold in America.

Fight on, America's noble sons,
Fear not Brittania's thundering guns,
Maintain your rights from year to year,
God's on your side, you need not fear.

September 22

NEW YORK   Yesterday there was a terrible fire in New York. It broke out first at the most southerly part of the city, near Whitehall, and was discovered between twelve and one o'clock in the morning, the wind blowing very fresh from the south, and the weather exceeding dry. The rebel army having carried off all the bells of the city, the alarm could not be speedily communicated, and very few of the citizens were in town, most of them being driven out by the calamities of war, and several, of the first rank, sent prisoners to New England and other distant parts. A few minutes after the fire was discovered at Whitehall, it was observed to break out in five or six other places, at a considerable distance.

In this dreadful situation, when the whole city was threatened with destruction, Major-General Robertson, who had the chief command, sent immediately for two regiments that were encamped near the city, placed guards in several streets, and took every other precaution that was practicable to ward off the impending ruin. Lord Howe ordered the boats of the fleet to be manned, and after landing a large number of officers and seamen to assist us, the boats were stationed on each side of the city in the North and East Rivers, and the lines near the royal army were extended across the island, as it manifestly appeared the city was designedly set on fire.

The fire raged with inconceivable violence, and in its destructive progress swept away all the buildings between Broad street and the North River, almost as high as the City Hall; and from thence, all the houses between Broadway and the North River, as far as King's College, a few only excepted. Long before the main fire reached Trinity Church, that large, ancient, and venerable edifice was in flames, which baffled every effort to suppress them. The steeple, which was one hundred and forty feet high, the upper part wood, and placed on an elevated situation, resembled a vast pyramid of fire, exhibiting a most grand and awful spectacle. Several women and children perished in the fire. Their shrieks, joined to the roaring of the flames, the crush of falling houses, and the widespread ruin which everywhere appeared, formed a scene of horror great beyond description, which was still heightened by the darkness of the night. Besides Trinity Church, the rector's house, the charity school, the old Lutheran Church, and many other fine buildings, were consumed. St. Paul's Church and King's College were directly in the line of fire, but saved with very great difficulty. After raging about ten hours, the fire was extinguished between ten and eleven o'clock this morning.

During this complicated scene of devastation and distress, at which the most savage heart might relent, several persons were discovered with large bundles of matches, dipped in melted rosin and brimstone, attempting to set fire to the houses. A New England man, who had a captain's commission under the Continental Congress, and in their service, was seized, having these dreadful implements of ruin. On being searched, the sum of five hundred pounds was found upon him. General Robertson rescued two of these incendiaries from the enraged populace, (who had otherwise consigned them to the flames,) and reserved them for the hand of deliberate justice. One White, a carpenter, was observed to cut the leather buckets which conveyed water; he also wounded, with a cutlass, a woman who was very active in handing water. This provoked the spectators to such a degree, that they instantly hung him up. One of those villains set fire to the college and was seized; many others were detected in the like crime and secured.

The officers of the army and navy, the seamen and soldiers, greatly exerted themselves, often with the utmost hazard to themselves, and showed all that alertness and activity for which they are justly celebrated on such occasions. To their vigorous efforts in pulling down such wooden buildings as would conduct the fire, it is owing, under Providence, that the whole city was not consumed; for the number of inhabitants was small, and the pumps and fire-engines were very much out of order. This last circumstance, together with the removal of our bells, the time and place of the fire's breaking out, when the wind was south, the city being set on fire in so many different places nearly at the same time, so many incendiaries being caught in the very act of setting fire to houses; these, to mention no other particulars, clearly evince, beyond the possibility of a doubt, that this diabolical affair was the result of a preconcerted, deliberate scheme. Thus, the persons who called themselves our friends and protectors, were the perpetrators of this atrocious deed, which in guilt and villany, is not inferior to the Gun-powder Plot; whilst those who were held up as our enemies were the people who gallantly stepped forth, at the risk of their lives, to snatch us from destruction. Our distress was very great before, but this disaster has increased it tenfold. Many hundreds of families have lost their all, and are reduced from a state of affluence to the lowest ebb of want and wretchedness—destitute of shelter, food, and clothing.

Surely "there must be some chosen curse—some secret thunder in the stores of heaven, red with uncommon wrath to blast" the miscreants who thus wantonly sport with the lives, property, and happiness of their fellow-creatures, and unfeelingly doom them to inevitable ruin.

> *New York Gazette and Weekly Mercury*
> *(Serle edition), September 30, 1776*
> *Freeman's Journal, January 7, 1777*

NEW YORK   Mr. David Grim, a merchant in New York, who saw the conflagration, has left the following account of it:—It commenced in a small wooden house, on the wharf, near Whitehall slip, which was then occupied by a number of men and women of a bad character. The fire began late at night. There being but a few inhabitants in the city, in a short time it raged tremendously. It burned all the houses on the east side of Whitehall slip, and the west side of Broad street to Beaver street. A providential and happy circumstance occurred at this time; the wind was then southwesterly. About two o'clock in the morning the wind veered to the southeast; this carried the flames of the fire to the northwestward, and burned both sides of Beaver street to the east side of Broadway, then crossed Broadway to Beaver lane, and burning all the houses on both sides of Broadway, with some few houses in New street to Rector street, and to John Harrison's, Esq., three-story brick house, which house stopped the fire on the east side of Broadway; from thence it continued burning all the houses in Lumber street, and those in the rear of the houses on the west side of Broadway to St. Paul's Church, then continued burning the houses on both sides of Partition street, and all the houses in the rear (again) of the west side of Broadway to the North River. The fire did not stop until it got into Mortkile street, now Barclay street. The college yard and the vacant ground in the rear of the same, put an end to this awful and tremendous fire. Trinity Church being burned, was occasioned by the flakes of fire that fell on the south side of the roof. The southerly wind fanned those flakes of fire in a short time to an amazing blaze, and it soon became out of human power to extinguish the same; the roof of this noble edifice being so steep that no person could go on it. St. Paul's Church was in the like perilous situation. The roof being flat, with a balustrade on the eaves, a number of citizens went on the same, and extinguished the flakes of fire as they fell on the roof. Thus happily was this beautiful church saved from the destruction of this dreadful fire, which threatened the ruin thereof and that of the whole city. The Lutheran Church being contiguous to the houses adjoining the same fire, it was impossible to save it from destruction. This fire was so furious and violently hot, that no person could go near it, and there were no fire engines to be had, at that time, in the city.

Barber's Historical Collection of the State of New York, 303

NEW YORK   This day, one [Nathan] Hale, in New York, on suspicion of being a spy was taken up and dragged without ceremony to the execution post, and hung up. General Washington has since sent in a flag, supposed to be on that account.

No source

The subjoined account was published some time after his execution.—

Samuel Hale, late of Portsmouth, in New Hampshire, after his elopement from thence, visited an uncle in Connecticut, where he was hospitably entertained; but as his uncle was a Whig, and had a son, a young gentleman of a liberal education and most amiable disposition, who strongly felt for his bleeding country, and being very active in the military way, was urged and prevailed upon to take a commission in the Continental army; consequently Samuel was obliged to conduct with caution, and counterfeit, as well as he could, a whiggish phiz while he tarried, which, however, was but a short time, before he made his escape to General Howe in

New York. Some time after this, Captain Hale, at the request
of the general, went into New York in disguise, and having
nearly accomplished his designs, whom should he meet but
his aforesaid cousin Samuel, whom he attempted to shun,
but Sam knew him too well. Captain Hale soon found he was
advertised, and so particularly described that he could not
get through Long Island; he therefore attempted to escape
by the way of King's Bridge, and so far succeeded as to get
to the outer guard, where he was suspected, apprehended,
carried back and tried, and yet would have been acquitted
had not his affectionate and grateful cousin Samuel appeared
and made oath, that he was a captain in the Continental
army, and that he was in there as a spy; in consequence of
which he was immediately hung up. However, at the gallows
he made a sensible and spirited speech, among other things
told them they were shedding the blood of the innocent, and
that if he had ten thousand lives, he would lay them all down,
if called to it, in defence of this injured, bleeding country.

The Printers throughout the continent are desired to exhibit this tragical scene to the public, that they may see what
mercy they are to expect if they fall into the hands of Tories.

Freeman's Journal, February 18, 1777

September 29

SOUTH CAROLINA   Since the victory at Charleston, the
inhabitants of the southern colonies are more unanimous and
spirited in support of the cause of American Independence
than they were before. A very artful speech made at Philadelphia by Samuel Adams (who is esteemed by all as one of
the most subtle men in the Congress) to a very numerous
body of the citizens, militia, &c., has almost irritated them to
madness against Great Britain, and made them resolve to
conquer or die in the cause they have espoused.

Upcott, IV, 397

Nathan Hale

This beautiful lament for the fallen patriot appears in Moore,
Songs and Ballads, 131–3, without any indication as to its source or
authorship. The version given here is slightly abridged; the melody
provided by Bill Bonyun is an adaptation of one used in a later
Nathan Hale ballad.

The breez – es went stead – i – ly through the tall pines, A –
say – ing "oh hush!" a – say – ing "oh hush!" As stil – ly stole by a bold
le – gion of horse, For Hale in the bush, for Hale in the bush.

Cooling shades of the night were coming apace,
     The tattoo had beat; the tattoo had beat.
The noble one sprang from his dark lurking place,
     To make his retreat; to make his retreat.

He warily trod on the dry rustling leaves,
     As he pass'd through the wood; as he pass'd through the
          wood;
And silently gained his rude launch on the shore,
     As she played with the flood; as she played with the flood.

The guards of the camp, on that dark, dreary night,
     Had a murderous will; had a murderous will.

They took him and bore him afar from the shore,
    To a hut on the hill; to a hut on the hill.

An ominous owl with his solemn bass voice,
    Sat moaning hard by; sat moaning hard by.
"The tyrant's proud minions most gladly rejoice,
    For he must soon die; for he must soon die."

They took him and bound him and bore him away,
    Down the hill's grassy side; down the hill's grassy side;
'Twas there the base hirelings in royal array,
    His cause did deride; his cause did deride.

The faith of a martyr, the tragedy showed,
    As he trod the last stage; as he trod the last stage.
And Britons will shudder at gallant Hale's blood,
    As his words do presage; as his words do presage.

OCTOBER

October 1

ENGLAND   A writer in the *London Gazette*, in a letter to the Lord Mayor, says:—I was last week on board the American privateer called the *Yankee*, commanded by Captain Johnson, and lately brought into this port by Captain Ross, who commanded one of the West India sugar ships, taken by the privateer in July last; and, as an Englishman, I earnestly wish your lordship, who is so happily placed at the head of this great city, (justly famed for its great humanity even to its enemies,) would be pleased to go likewise, or send proper persons, to see the truly shocking, and I may say, barbarous and miserable condition of the unfortunate American prisoners, who, however criminal they may be thought to have been, are deserving of pity, and entitled to common humanity.

They are twenty-five in number, and all inhumanly shut close down, like wild beasts, in a small, stinking apartment, in the hold of a sloop, about seventy tons burden, without a breath of air, in this sultry season, but what they receive through a small grating overhead, the openings in which are not more than two inches square in any part, and through which the sun beats intensely hot all day, only two or three being permitted to come on the deck at a time; and then they are exposed in the open sun, which is reflected from the decks and water like a burning glass.

I do not at all exaggerate, my lord; I speak the truth; and the resemblance that this barbarity bears to the memorable black hole at Calcutta, as a gentleman present on Saturday observed, strikes every one at the sight. All England ought to know that the same game is now acting upon the Thames on board this privateer, that all the world cried out against, and shuddered at the mention of in India, some years ago, as practised on Captain Hollowell, and other of the King's good subjects.

The putrid steams issuing from the hold are so hot and offensive, that one cannot, without the utmost danger, breathe over it, and I should not be at all surprised, if it should cause a plague to spread. The miserable wretches below look like persons in a hot bath, panting, sweating, and fainting for want of air; and the surgeon declares, that they must all soon perish in that situation, especially as they are almost all in a sickly state with bilious disorders.

The captain and surgeon, it is true, have the liberty of the cabin, (if it deserves the name of a cabin,) and make no complaints on their own account. They are both sensible, and well-behaved young men, and can give a very good account of themselves, having no signs of fear, and being supported by a consciousness of the justice of their cause. They are men of character, of good families in New England, and highly respected in their different occupations; but being stripped of their *all* by the burning of towns and other destructive measures of the present unnatural war, were forced to take the disagreeable method of making reprisals to maintain themselves and their children, rather than starve.

Numbers of gentlemen, and friends of government, who were on board at the same time, will confirm the truth of this my representation, being very sensibly touched themselves at the horrid sight.

English prisoners, taken by the Americans, have been treated with the most remarkable tenderness and generosity, as numbers who are safely returned to England most freely confess, to the honor of our brethren in the colonies. And it is a fact, which can be well attested in London, that this very surgeon on board the privateer, after the Battle of Lexington, April nineteenth, 1775, for many days voluntarily and generously, without fee or reward, employed himself in dressing the King's wounded soldiers, who but an hour before would have shot him if they could have come at him, and in making a collection for their refreshment, of wine, linen, money, &c., in the town where he lived. This is a real fact, of which the most ample testimony may be had.

The capture of the privateer was solely owing to the ill-judged lenity and brotherly kindness of Captain Johnson, who not considering his English prisoners in the same light that he would Frenchmen or Spaniards, put them under no sort of confinement, but permitted them to walk the decks as freely as his own people, at all times. Taking advantage of this indulgence, the prisoners one day watching their opportunity, when most of the privateer's people were below and asleep, shut down the hatches, and making all fast, had immediate possession of the vessel without using any force.

I shall conclude with saying, that though this letter is addressed to your lordship, I hope that all who may read it, and have any influence, will do all in their power to gain the necessary relief; and it is humbly apprehended, that the well disposed, who are blessed with affluence, could not better bestow their bounty than upon those poor objects. Vegetables and ripe fruits of all kinds, with porter, &c., must be very useful, as well as the means to procure other necessaries. The privateer lies opposite to Ratcliffe Cross, a mile and a half below the Tower, and by asking for Captain Johnson, admittance may be obtained.

"Humanitas," Pennsylvania Journal, November 6

October 8

NEW YORK   So vast a fleet was never before seen together in the port of New York, or perhaps in all America. The ships are stationed up the East River or Sound, as far as Turtle Bay, and near the town. The multitude of masts carries the appearance of a wood. Some are moored up the North River, others in the bay between Red and Yellow Hook; others, again, off Staten Island, and several off Powle's Hook, and towards the kills. The men-of-war are moored chiefly up New York Sound, and make, with the other ships, a very magnificent and formidable appearance. Five men-of-war have been detached from the squadron into the North River, above Greenwich, probably to assist the operations of the army against the rebels, who still remain on the northern extremity of the island, and on the heights above King's Bridge.

The savage burning of the city by the New England incendiaries will be a lasting monument of inveterate malice against the trade and prosperity of this colony, as well as rooted disaffection to British law and government. They had long threatened the performance of this villanous deed; and this is the best return that the people of property in this city, who have espoused their cause, are to expect for their heedless credulity.

see Freeman's Journal, October 29

October 14

It has been observed that the British power, in the beginning of a war, generally makes but feeble, and oftentimes unsuccessful exertions; but that in the prosecution of hostilities, her force gradually increasing, like a gathered torrent, becomes almost irresistible. The last war is a striking evidence of the truth of this observation; and we have seen since the commencement of these troubles, the same line of conduct pursued towards these colonies. The first force sent out was small, and employed with apparent reluctance—we might have said, sent out with a wish that they might not be employed at all. This, instead of being imputed to its proper motive, was construed into the weakness and (who could have thought it!) into the timidity of Britain. Our country-men at home were stigmatized as cowards, while their brave hearts only abhorred the idea of fighting against those who claimed the title of brethren and friends. Nothing but re-peated insults and menaces against their King, their country, and themselves, could have induced a persuasion in the army, that the leaders of the sedition seriously meant nothing else than to become rebels and enemies. At last the British lion is roused. We have seen, in the course of a summer, a powerful army cross over the Atlantic, under the conduct of a gallant fleet. We have heard of other considerable armaments arriv-ing safely elsewhere upon this continent; and we have no reason to doubt but that, if it were possible these should fail, greater and greater would be sent out to reduce this country to its indefeasible allegiance and duty. To all this there are only to be opposed the *wisdom* of a Congress consisting of men either of new and doubtful characters, or of none at all; a wretched paper currency which will only eat up the property of the continent without adding an atom to it; and a vagabond army of ragamuffins, with paper pay, bad clothes, and worse spirits. Is it reasonable to think that such a cause, with such supporters, will ever be able to maintain itself against veteran battalions of brave and loyal Britons, contending for British honor and constitutional liberty? Is it not strange that a peo-ple in such circumstances should be persuaded to reject all overtures of reconciliation, by the machinations of an artful and ambitious Congress? It can only be accounted for by the old adage, *Quos Deus vult perdere prius dementat.*

New York Gazette and Weekly Mercury
(Serle edition), October 14

October 23

By the favor of Providence we have reached that political point (which the wise have long seen to be the only founda-tion of safety)—*Independence;* our work is now plain before us—to persevere to the end in supporting the Declaration we have made to the world. To do this, every consideration urges us; to retreat is death—is slavery, calamities of every name, and all the gloomy horrors of the most odious and execrable tyranny. Before us is all the glory of *Freedom*, pregnant with every felicity our wishes can grasp, or human nature enjoy. If we continue our exertions with that wisdom and magnanimity with which we began, *Liberty* will soon triumph, wealth flow in through ten thousand channels, and America become the glory of all lands. Tyranny is now exerting her utmost power, and if resisted a little longer, George, and all his murderers, must bid adieu to America forever; then we shall have the double happiness and honor of subduing the tyrants, and enjoying liberty; the expense and dangers it has cost us will sweeten the blessing. If we have not suffered enough yet to make us duly prize the inestimable jewel, let us patiently bear what is yet to come. But if we continue in the ways of well-doing, we shall certainly succeed; for unerring wisdom has told us, "if we trust in the Lord and do good, we shall dwell in the land and be fed;" therefore we have nothing to do but to be faithful to God and our country, and the blessings we contend for will be the portion of us and our children.

The price of liberty is not to be gained in a day, nor bought with a small price, but is the reward of long labor and unremitting exertions; and a people are commonly made to realize their dependence on Heaven for so great a favor, before they are crowned with complete success. The poor Dutch provinces were oppressed by a Spanish tyrant, like George of Britain, and they (although poor and small in number, compared with the States of America) resisted the tyrant who had at his command a great and rich nation, and after a bloody contest of many years, gloriously triumphed in the complete freedom of their country. During the conflict, they were sometimes reduced to such extreme difficulties as would have sunk any but free minds into absolute despair; but they were blessed with a succession of heroes and statesmen, who wisely preferred liberty to every thing else; and persevered through a long series of the severest calamities of every kind, with undiminished fervor in the glorious cause, until they arrived at the blissful period of Independent States, and remain to this day a glorious monument of the supereminent virtue and valor of freemen.

Let us imitate this bright example. With them we shall shine in the history of mankind, until the heavens are no more. The blood and treasure it may cost, will heighten the value of liberty, and brighten the future days of peace and glory, when we or posterity shall recount the noble exertions, and amazing intrepidity of those who were honored by Heaven as the instruments of saving this great people from infernal tyranny. It will add to the joys of prosperity, and sweeten the sacred triumphs of freemen, when encircled with the charms of peace, to look back upon the trying scenes of the present time, and review the difficulties surmounted through a series of conflicts, while each moment was big with importance, and the fate of thousands hung upon every hour.

Addressed to the Independent Sons of America
New Hampshire Gazette, November 26

NOVEMBER

November 1

NEW YORK   Last Monday [October 28th] we [the Americans at White Plains] received intelligence that the enemy, with their whole body, were advancing towards us. The army were immediately alarmed, and part of General Wadsworth's brigade, with some other regiments under the command of General Spencer, consisting in the whole of five or six hundred men, were sent out as an advance party, to skirmish with the enemy, and harass them in their march. We marched on to a hill about one mile and a half from our lines, with an artillery company and two field-pieces, and placed ourselves behind walls and fences, in the best manner we could, to give the enemy trouble. About half after nine o'clock, our advance parties all came in, retreating before the enemy; and the light parties of the enemy, with their advanced guard, consisting of two or three thousand, came in sight, and marched on briskly towards us, keeping the high grounds; and the light horse pranced on a little in the rear, making a very martial appearance. As our light parties came on to the hills and discovered where we were, the enemy began to cannonade us, and to fling shells from their hobits and small mortars. Their light parties soon came on, and we firing upon them from the walls and fences, broke and scattered them at once; but they would run from our front and get round upon our wings to flank us, and as soon as our fire discovered where we were, the enemy's artillery would at once begin to play upon us in the most furious manner. We kept the walls until the enemy were just ready to surround us, and then we would retreat from one wall and hill to another, and maintain our ground there in the same manner, till numbers were just ready to surround us. Once the Hessian grenadiers came up in front of Colonel Douglass's regiment, and we fired a general volley upon them, at about twenty rods distance, and scattered them like leaves in a whirlwind; and they ran off so far that some of the regiment ran out to the ground where they were when we fired upon them, and brought off their arms and accoutrements, and rum, that the men who fell had with them, which we had time to drink round with before they came on again. They formed at a distance, and waited until their artillery and main body came on, when they advanced in solid columns upon us, and were gathering all around us, ten to our one. Colonel Douglass's and Silliman's regiments fired four or five times on them, as they were advancing, and then retreated, but not until the enemy began to fire on their flanks. Colonels Silliman, Douglass, and Arnold behaved nobly, and the men gained much applause. Colonels Webb's, Silliman's, and Douglass's regiments had the principal share in the action. Colonel Webb had four killed, and eight or ten wounded; Colonel Silliman lost six, and had ten or twelve wounded; Colonel Douglass had three killed, and six wounded. Colonels Brooks's, Smallwood's, and Ritzma's regiments, who were drawn up on the hill near the lines, suffered considerably. Our loss in the

Engraved by Geo.E.Perine.N.Y.

Israel Putnam

whole may be seventy or eighty killed or wounded. It is said by all the deserters and captains, who agree in their stories, that the enemy had about three hundred killed and wounded.

The scene was grand and solemn; all the adjacent hills smoked as though on fire, and bellowed and trembled with a perpetual cannonade and fire of field-pieces, hobits, and mortars. The air groaned with streams of cannon and musket shot; the hills smoked and echoed terribly with the bursting of shells; the fences and walls were knocked down and torn to pieces, and men's legs, arms, and bodies, mangled with cannon and grape-shot all around us: I was in the action, and under as good advantages as any one man, perhaps, to observe all that passed, and write these particulars of the action from my own observation.

No general action was designed on our part, and I believe one thousand men were never, at one time, engaged with the enemy. They came on to the hills opposite our lines, and halted; and after cannonading part of the lines a short time, they became very still and quiet.

Yesterday, (October 31st,) it was observed that they had near finished four or five batteries which they had erected against us; and as our ground, near the centre of the town at White Plains, was not good, being overlooked by neighboring hills, the generals, last night, drew off most of the troops from the lines there, and this morning the guards and sentries burned the town and forage all around it, and came off about nine o'clock.

We carried off all our stores, and planted our artillery on the hills about a mile and a half back of the centre of the town. The enemy advanced, this forenoon, on to the ground we left, but as soon as they came over the hill, we saluted them with our cannon and field-pieces, and they advanced no further. Their main body now lies over against us, and they have formed no lines across the country, as yet, below us. Their light horse may possibly scour across as far as the river, but how that is we cannot determine. All things seem to be quiet at Fort Washington.

Pennsylvania Evening Post, November 14

November 3

There is a general curiosity in mankind to inquire into the character of those who arrive at stations of high trust and dignity. In the dreadful times of public commotion and civil discord, this laudable passion is most strongly excited. To satisfy this in part, an old friend of General Putnam's gives the following authentic account of that officer:

The general's paternal state consisted of a small farm in the colony of Connecticut, by the diligent cultivation of which, he supported himself till he entered the colony's service, during the late French war in America. The stories that have been repeatedly told, of his being a blacksmith and carpenter, are the contradictory effusions of ignorance and falsehood. When very young, he gave a proof of early courage, in following a wolf, that had plundered the sheep-fold, into its den, creeping on his hands and knees, where, discovering it by the brightness of its own eyes, he destroyed it. This is not a very important fact, but it is a real one, well known to the people of Pomfret.

When a major of the Rangers, in the year 1758, leading the van of a scouting party, he was overpowered and taken by a body of five hundred Indians and Canadians. During the latter part of the engagement; he was tied to a tree, and exposed to the fire of his own men. At last the enemy being forced to retreat, an Indian, in passing, struck him with the butt end of his musket, intending to kill him, but happened only to break one of his jaw-bones; immediately after a Canadian came up, cut the straps that fastened him to the tree, and led him off. He was carried to Ticonderoga, and soon after exchanged. A romantic account of this skirmish was given in the public prints some months ago, in which it was said that he had received a multitude of wounds, beside being scalped. All this is fiction; the blow above mentioned was the only one he received in that action.

In the colony service he considerably increased his estate. He has now a large, well-cultivated farm, and generally represents the town of Pomfret, in the colony assembly.

When the discontents in New England rose very high, in 1775, he was very much caressed by the American party; and, on a false rumor spreading through the country, of the King's troops having massacred five hundred inhabitants of Boston, he headed a large party of volunteers, in Connecticut, and marched to the relief of Boston, but soon returned home, on that intelligence being contradicted.

After the action at Concord, in April, 1775, he joined the Massachusetts troops, commanded by Warren. He was then a colonel in rank. On June seventeenth, at one o'clock in the morning, they took possession of Bunker Hill, opposite to Boston, where in a few hours they threw up a redoubt and in-trenchment. When he saw the British troops embarking to attack them, he advised Warren, who commanded in chief, to retreat, and founded his opinion on the following reasons:— "That he had often served with the King's troops; that al-though one-half or two-thirds of them should be killed, yet those that remained would certainly storm their works; that the moment the intrenchment was mounted, his countrymen, whom he knew very well, would run; for though they would fight as long as any troops whatever, while under cover, yet they would never stand an open engagement, and the push of the bayonet; that the spirit of veteran troops ought not to be expected from them, who were raw men, badly disciplined, and badly armed; that it would be highly injudicious to put them, at first, to so severe a trial, as the check they would in all probability receive, would tend greatly to dishearten them, and have a very bad effect on all their future operations."

This salutary advice was rejected by Warren, who was very opinionated, addicted to liquor, and in haste to distinguish himself, this being the very first morning of his apprenticeship in the art of war. He replied, "That they had been branded as cowards, but would show the military they could fight as well as themselves," and ordered the colonel to return to Cambridge, and bring on the rest of the men. Putnam obeyed. On the march back, his men followed him with spirit enough till they reached the fort of Bunker Hill, when the heavy firing, it being then the heat of the engagement, made them shrink. (This he has often mentioned when speaking of that day's service.) Whilst he was laboring fruitlessly in this manner, the King's troops stormed the redoubt, and he was instantly joined by the fugitives; upon which they all retreated over the neck as fast as possible. The colonel had frequently given it as his opinion that if but five hundred men had pursued them, he could not have kept one man at Cambridge. But no pursuit being made, he took post there; and as they heard from Boston that very night what dreadful havoc they had made amongst the King's troops, the men immediately recovered their spirits. So much does success in war depend on the improvement of a single moment.

The colonel was now promoted to the rank of major-general, but his commission was hardly delivered to him, when it was debated, in the General Congress, to supersede him, and give his rank to Mr. Thomas, a favorite of General Washington. He was only saved from this insult by the necessity they had for his services. During the summer and autumn, 1775, whilst Boston was blockaded, he was by far the most popular officer in the American camp; he was the first to take up the spade and the mattock, and to join the common men in all the fatigues of the day, which very naturally endeared him to them. His popularity, however, suffered a great shock, towards the latter end of the same year; for, at the request of the General Congress and the Commander-in-chief, attempting to persuade the men, whose time of service was nearly expired, to continue in arms four months longer, till another army could be embodied, he raised a general clamor against himself. The men went off precisely at their time, and exclaimed against him over all the country, as an enemy to liberty. By this defection, in the space of six weeks in the middle of winter, there were not more than seven thousand men in the extensive lines round Boston. If General Howe had had good intelligence, he might have cleared the whole environs of that town in less than twenty-four hours; for such a small body of troops were very insufficient to defend a line of intrenchments and redoubts, that extended at least twelve or fourteen miles, from Mystic River all round the head of the Bay to Dorchester Point. Another raw army was at last drawn together, which made some semblance of attacking Boston, on which General

Howe left it. Since the war has been moved into the territory of New York, we find General Putnam commanding in the lines, at the battle of Brooklyn. It is not surprising that new levies should be beat by veterans. After the defeat, the desertion of their lines was a wise measure, as their retreat might have been cut off by ships of war posted in the East River.

There is no doubt but General Putnam wishes as sincerely for peace as any man on either side of the question; yet there is no man in either army will do his duty with greater bravery in the field. He never was a favorer of American Independency. As to his person, he is middle size, very strongly made, no fat, all bones and muscles; he has a lisp in his speech, and is now upwards of sixty years of age.

Middlesex Journal, December 21

November 9

NEW YORK   Hitherto the achievements of our little army on York Island have been extremely fortunate. The genius that presides there seems to be of the enterprising kind. Last campaign it was thought a matter of great hardihood and praise to burn the enemy's guard house at Roxbury, on Boston Neck, and a few houses in Charlestown, under cover of the night; but here such exploits are conducted in open day.

This morning, we found the enemy once more in possession of the rock from whence we had routed them yesterday. About eighty men, under the command of Colonel Penrose, of Philadelphia, and Major Hubley, (late an officer at the northward,) resolved to dislodge them a second time. As the men were in high spirits, and the barn and dwelling-house which the guard occupied at but a small distance, the colonel proposed storming them. We soon regained the rock, and, with surprising rapidity, the houses, notwithstanding an incessant fire from the enemy's artillery, main guard, and a small redoubt in an orchard adjoining the guard, that commanded the road. The Hessians were soon obliged to abandon their posts. We killed on the spot about ten, and the rest either escaped or were burned in the houses, which some of our men, without orders, immediately fired.

It is something remarkable that on our side we had only one man wounded. Perhaps the sally was so unexpected as to have entirely disconcerted and confused the enemy. As it is, no men ever behaved more resolutely or bravely than ours.

Pennsylvania Evening Post, November 21

November 13

NEW YORK   Yesterday the British decamped from Dobb's Ferry, and marched as far as Phillip's manor, (five miles from King's Bridge,) where they halted and pitched their tents. They seem to be bending their course towards York Island, and it is apprehended they mean to attack Fort Washington. Yesterday we reinforced the garrison at that place with five hundred men, and we hope it is very tenable. Deserters inform us that they are resolved to take it this campaign, if they are obliged to invest it with their whole army. The three ships which went up the North River a few days ago, have fallen down within three miles of Fort Lee, and will push by the first fair wind.

Pennsylvania Journal, November 20

November 16

NEW YORK   About two o'clock this afternoon a large body of British troops from New York, with a body of Hessians from King's Bridge, made an attack upon the American lines at that place. At the same time, a number of boats from the shipping came up Harlem River, and landed a party of men, who advanced forward with an intention to cut off our retreat, which in part they effected; but a part of our men taking advantage of a hill, got safe to the fort; the other part, being almost surrounded, were obliged to fight their way through the enemy, by which means the heaviest fire from our troops was directed against the Hessians, who were beat back, and obliged to be reinforced there several times by large detachments from their main body. In this manner our small army, under the command of Colonel Magaw, retreated, sustaining with unexampled resolution a continual fire of the cannon, field-pieces, and musketry of more than five to one in number, till they reached Fort Washington, when the engagement ceased. Soon after the engagement ended, the enemy made a demand of the fort, and Colonel Magaw finding it impossible to defend it, surrendered the same to the enemy about sunset.

The number of our men who were killed in the above engagement is uncertain, but the whole loss in killed and taken prisoners, is upwards of two thousand. What loss the enemy sustained is likewise uncertain, but if we may believe the account given by a deserter who came to head-quarters since the engagement, the Hessians had between four and five thousand men killed on the spot.

Master James Lovel, of Boston, who has been a prisoner more than eighteen months, is now on his way from New York to Boston, having been exchanged for Governor Skeene, who was some time held a prisoner in Hartford.

We hear Colonel Ethan Allen is now on board a ship at New York; that he has been treated since his being taken a prisoner with the utmost barbarity, till lately, but the rigor of his oppressors has been a little softened, and he is now treated according to his rank; and we hope an exchange will soon take place, when he may again return into the bosom of his grateful country.

Freeman's Journal, December 3

November 18

NEW YORK   By a person lately from the American camp, a gentleman of undoubted veracity, who was prisoner and enlarged by General Howe, we are informed that the enemy lost before the lines of Fort Washington, seventeen hundred killed on the field, and ninety-six wagon loads of wounded, the most mortally; that our people behaved with the greatest intrepidity and resolution; that our loss was about three hundred killed and wounded.—This account may be depended on, as it came from divers of the British officers, with whom the gentleman was intimately acquainted.

The attack did not commence at the lines at Harlem, as

has been reported, that post being at least six miles distant from Fort Washington, but at the outlines north of the fort, distant about a quarter of a mile; that the Hessians made the attack, and marched within point blank pistol shot of the lines, where they were kept at least two hours, and were, by the intrepidity and well-placed fire of our people, cut down in whole ranks. The brave Americans kept their post until a heavy column of British troops appeared in their rear; the lines there being entirely open, obliged them to retreat and endeavor to gain the fort; but the British troops being nearer the fort, cut off and obliged a considerable part to surrender prisoners. The fort was immediately summoned, but the commanding officer first pleaded for a term of five days; that being refused, plead for the honors of war, which was also denied, and the garrison was informed that unless they surrendered at discretion, the fort would be immediately invested, and they must abide the consequence. A council of war was immediately held, and it was decided that, as they had not any water, nor could get any at the places from which the garrison had been supplied with the article, they being in possession of the enemy, and that the fort was not capable of defence, agreed to surrender it and themselves at discretion. The commanding officer of the fort is a gentleman of great courage, and would have defended it as long as a single soldier remained to support it, had it been capable of defence. The highest honors are due to him, his gallant officers, and the brave soldiers who were under his command.

Freeman's Journal, December 10

November 21

NEW YORK   Yesterday, a party of the British army landed near Dobb's Ferry, and soon after took possession of Fort Lee. On the appearance of our troops, the rebels fled like scared rabbits, and in a few moments after we reached the hill near their intrenchments, not a rascal of them could be seen. They have left some poor pork, a few greasy proclamations, and some of that scoundrel Common Sense man's letters, which we can read at our leisure, now that we have got one of the "impregnable redoubts" of Mr. Washington's to quarter in.

Markoe to Oswald

PENNSYLVANIA   There is very good intelligence that the British intend to make a push for Philadelphia. We hear part of their force is embarked, either to go up the Delaware, and make their attacks on both sides at once, or else to amuse the Southern States, and prevent their sending any assistance to Philadelphia. We have not force enough to oppose their march by land. We look to New Jersey and Pennsylvania for their militia, and on their spirit depends the preservation of America. If in this hour of adversity they shrink from danger, they deserve to be slaves indeed! If the freedom that success will insure us, if the misery that awaits our subjection, will not rouse them, why let them sleep till they awake in bondage.

Pennsylvania Journal, November 27

DECEMBER

December 1

NEW JERSEY   Since the rebels abandoned Fort Lee, they have been hurrying through the Jerseys, closely followed by Cornwallis and his *magic lights*. The arch-rebel Washington is now at Brunswick, but how long he will remain the devil only knows, (for the Lord won't have any thing to do with him.) Yesterday we heard that our friends were coming on, and, in that event, we shall soon lose the company of the Congress *tatter de mallions*, which certainly most of the people here (Brunswick) do not feel sorry for.

Carver

December 2

NEW JERSEY   Yesterday, on the appearance of the enemy at Brunswick, General Washington ordered a retreat to

Princeton, where we arrived early this morning. We are in a terrible situation, with the enemy close upon us, and whole regiments of Marylanders and Jerseymen leaving us. Tomorrow we go to Trenton, where the general is determined to make a stand.

Clift's Diary

December 12

NEW JERSEY   Since last Sunday, [8th,] we have all been at the laboring oar, from the generals to the privates. Early in that day we heard that Cornwallis was coming in three different ways. Knowing our weak situation, he made a forced march to come up with us, and was within two miles of Princeton, when Lord Stirling began his retreat with two brigades. Boats from every quarter were collected, and our stores, together with the troops remaining at Trenton, were immediately conveyed over the Delaware. On Sunday morning, having every thing over, we crossed the Delaware, and took our quarters about half a mile from the river. About eleven o'clock the enemy came marching down with all the pomp of war, in great expectation of getting boats, and immediately pursuing; but of this we took proper care, by destroying every boat, shallop, &c., we could lay our hands on. They made forced marches up and down the river, in pursuit of boats, but in vain. This is Thursday; the enemy are much scattered, some in Trenton, directly opposite; from that on their left to Bordentown and Burlington, on the river banks. They are at least twelve thousand strong, determined for Philadelphia, for which purpose they are transporting flat-bottomed boats from Brunswick to Trenton by land.

Letter from Trenton Falls, New Jersey
Freeman's Journal, December 31

December 13

NEW JERSEY   This morning, about eleven o'clock, General Lee was taken prisoner at Baskenridge, in New Jersey, by Colonel Harcourt with a party of light horse. The sentry placed at the door of the house at which General Lee was stopping, saw the troopers coming on the run, and at first supposed them to be ours; but soon perceived his mistake by their swords, which are more crooked than ours. His piece not being loaded, he charged; they rode up to him and said, "Don't shoot; if you fire we will blow your brains out." General Lee cries out, "for God's sake, what shall I do?" The lady of the house took him up stairs, in order to hide him between the chimney and the breastwork over the fire-place, but he could not, the place being so small. The enemy at this time firing in at the windows, the captain gave orders to set fire to the house. The general seeing no way of escaping, sent down he would resign himself. They fired three times at the messenger, but missed him. The general came down without his hat or outside coat, and said, "I hope you will use me as a gentleman; let me get my hat and coat." The captain said, "General Lee, I know you well; I know you are a gentleman; you shall be used as such. I know you too well to suffer you to go for your hat and coat," and ordered him to mount. Upon which they went off, carrying with them the general and a Frenchman, left the baggage, wounded one of the aide-de-camps, and one or two of the guard. There were but thirteen men with the general. He was about four miles from his division, and a mile out of the road.

Intelligence of General Lee's unguarded situation was given to the enemy last night, by an inhabitant of Baskenridge, personally known to the general, and who had made great pretensions of friendship for the American cause, though at heart the greatest villain that ever existed. This Judas rode all the preceding night to carry the intelligence, and served as a pilot to conduct the enemy, and came personally with them to the house where the general was taken.

The enemy showed an ungenerous, nay, boyish triumph, after they had got him secure at Brunswick, by making his horse drunk, while they toasted their King till they were in the same condition. A band or two of music played all night to proclaim their joy for this important acquisition. They say we cannot now stand another campaign. Mistaken fools! to think the fate of America depended on one man. They will find ere long that it has no other effect than to urge us on to a noble revenge.

Freeman's Journal, December 31, 1776;
January 14, 21, 1777

December 26

NEW JERSEY   General Washington, finding it absolutely necessary to rouse the spirits of the army, which have been sorely depressed by the long series of disasters which have attended us for almost the whole of this month, resolved to attempt surprising a considerable body of Hessians, quartered at Trenton, consisting of about nineteen hundred, and a detachment of British light horse. The plan was as spiritedly executed as it was judiciously concerted, and terminated in fully answering the warmest expectations of its projectors. Yesterday morning, orders were given for a large part of the army to have three days' provisions ready cooked, and forty rounds a man, and to be ready to march by three o'clock in the afternoon; accordingly the farthest brigades marched by two o'clock. About eleven o'clock at night it began snowing, and continued so until daybreak, when a most violent northeast storm came on, of snow, rain, and hail together.

Early, the American army, which did not exceed twenty-four hundred men, crossed the Delaware with several companies of artillery, and thirteen field-pieces, and formed in two divisions; one commanded by General Greene, the other by General Sullivan, and the whole by General Washington. The attack began about seven o'clock by the van guard of Sullivan's division, who attacked the Hessians' advanced guard, about a mile from the town. These they soon drove, when the whole pushed with the utmost vigor for the town, which they immediately entered. General Greene's division attacked the town on the other side at the same time. The Hessians did as much as could be expected from people so surprised, but the impetuosity of our men was irresistible; fifteen minutes decided the action, and the enemy threw down their arms and surrendered prisoners of war. They consisted of three regiments of grenadiers and fusileers, and were equal to any troops the Prince of Hesse could boast of. The troop of British dragoons, without waiting to be charged, scampered off with the utmost expedition. Could the brigade under Colonel Ewing have landed below the town, as was intended, the light horse must inevitably have been taken, as well as a considerable number of the Hessians who got off; but the violence of the wind was such, and the quantity of ice so great, that he found it impossible to cross. Our success, though not complete, was great. The men behaved with the utmost bravery. Finding that their guns did not generally go off, owing to their having been exposed to the snow and rain for six hours, they charged bayonets, and, with three cheers, rushed like bloodhounds upon the Hessians, who, astonished at their fury, fled or threw down their arms; and it was owing to the ardor of the attack that so little blood was shed.

The army returned the same day, and, notwithstanding a continual pelting for twelve hours, of a most violent rain, hail, and snow-storm, we had only two men frozen to death. Luckily they found some hogsheads of rum at Trenton, large draughts of which alone preserved the lives of many. The soldiers behaved exceedingly well with respect to plundering, considering they were animated by revenge for past insults, exasperated by the injuries done their messmates taken at Fort Washington, and animated by every incentive that could work upon the license of a successful army. The general gave the Hessians all their baggage, and they have since gone to the western counties of Pennsylvania, with their packs unsearched. They were amazed at the generosity of the general, so opposite to their own conduct, and called him a very good rebel.

The enemy who lay at Bordentown soon had the alarm, which was communicated to all the parties along the river, who, after remaining under arms the whole day, in the evening marched off, leaving us to take possession of Bordentown, Mount Holly, and Burlington.

Freeman's Journal, January 21, 1777

The Battle of Trenton

This stirring lyric accurately summarizes and vividly commemorates a battle that proved to be a turning point in the military fortunes of the Revolution. The melody is a variant of "The Three Ravens," an English ballad that dates back to late medieval times. (Moore, Songs and Ballads, 150–2.)

On Christ - mas day in sev - en - ty - six, Our rag - ged troops with bay - o - nets fixed For Tren - ton marched a - way. The Del - a - ware see! the boat be - low! The light ob - scured by hail and snow: But no signs of dis - may.

Our object was the Hessian band,
That dared invade fair freedom's land,
And quarter in that place.
Great Washington he led us on,
Whose streaming flag in storm or sun,
Had never known disgrace.

In silent march we passed the night,
Each soldier panting for the fight,
Though quite benumbed with frost.
Greene, on the left, at six began,
The right was led by Sullivan,
Who never a moment lost.

Their pickets stormed, the alarm was spread,
That rebels risen from the dead,
Were marching into town.
Some scampered here, some scampered there,
And some for action did prepare,
But soon their arms laid down.

Now, brothers of the patriot bands,
Let's sing deliverance from the hands
Of arbitrary sway.
And as our life is but a span,
Let's touch the tankard while we can,
In memory of that day.

———◆•◆———

1777

JANUARY

January 1

His Majesty intends to open this year's campaign with ninety thousand Hessians, Tories, Negroes, Japanese, Moors, Esquimaux, Persian archers, Laplanders, Feejee Islanders, and light horse. With this terrific and horrendous armament, in conjunction with a most tremendous and irresistible fleet, he is resolved to terminate this unnatural war the next summer, as it will be impossible for the rebels to bring an equal number in the field. His Majesty has also the strongest assurances that France will co-operate with him in humbling his seditious subjects; and as his admiral and general are still extending the arms of mercy for the gracious reception of those who will yet return to their duty and allegiance, for Heaven's sake, ye poor, deluded, misguided, bewildered, cajoled, and bamboozled Whigs! ye dumbfounded, infatuated, back-bestridden, nose-led-about, priest-ridden, demagogue-beshackled, and Congress-becrafted independents, fly, fly, oh fly, for protection to the royal standard, or ye will be swept from the face of the earth with the besom of destruction, and cannonaded in a moment into nullities and nonentities, and no mortal can tell into what other kind of quiddities and quoddities.

Letter from London
Freeman's Journal, March 22

January 7

NEW JERSEY   On the second instant, intelligence was received by express, that the enemy's army was advancing from Princeton towards Trenton, where the main body of the Americans were stationed. Two brigades under Brigadier-Generals Stephen and Fermoy, had been detached several days before, from the main body, to Maidenhead, and were ordered to skirmish with the enemy during their march, and to retreat to Trenton, as occasion should require. A body of men under command of Colonel Hand, were also ordered to meet the enemy, by which means their march was so much retarded as to give ample time for our forces to form, and prepare to give them a warm reception upon their arrival. Two field-pieces, planted upon a hill, at a small distance above the town, were managed with great advantage, and did considerable execution for some time; after which they were ordered to retire to the station occupied by our forces on the south side of the bridge, over the little river which divides the town into two parts, and opens at right angles into the Delaware. In their way through the town, the enemy suffered much by an incessant fire of musketry from behind the houses and barns. Their army had now arrived at the northern side of the bridge, whilst our army were drawn up, in order of battle, on the southern side. Our cannon played very briskly from this eminence, and were returned as briskly by the enemy. In a few minutes after the cannonade began, a very heavy discharge of musketry ensued, and continued for ten or fifteen minutes. During this action, a party of men were detached from our right wing, to secure a part of the river, which, it was imagined, from the motions of the enemy, they intended to ford. This detachment arrived at the pass very opportunely, and effected their purpose; after this the enemy made a feeble and unsupported attempt to pass the bridge, but this likewise proved abortive. It was now near six o'clock in the evening, and night coming on, closed the engagement. Our fires were built in due season, and were very numerous; and whilst the enemy were amused by these appearances, and preparing for a general attack the ensuing day, our army marched, at about one in the morning, from Trenton, on the south side of the creek, to Princeton. When they arrived near the hill, about one mile from the town, they found a body of the enemy formed upon it, and ready to receive them; upon which a spirited attack was made, both with field-pieces and musketry, and, after an obstinate resistance, and losing a considerable number of their men upon the field, those of them who could not make their escape, surrendered prisoners of war. We immediately marched on to the centre of the town, and there took another party of the enemy near the college. After tarrying a very short time in the town, General Washington marched his army from thence, towards Rocky Hill, and they are now near Morristown, in high spirits, and in expectation of a junction with the rest of our forces, sufficiently seasonable to make a general attack upon the enemy, and prevent, at least, a considerable part of them from reaching their asylum in New York. It is difficult precisely to ascertain the loss we have sustained in the two engagements, but we think we have lost about forty men killed, and had near double the number wounded. In the list of the former are the brave Colonel Hazlet, Captain Shippen, and Captain Neal, who fell in the engagement upon the hill near Princeton; amongst the latter was Brigadier-General Mercer, who received seven wounds—five in his body, and two in his head, and was much bruised by the breech of a musket, of which bruises he soon after died. The loss sustained by the enemy was much greater than ours, as was easily discovered by viewing the dead upon the field, after the action. We have near a hundred of their wounded prisoners in the town, which, together with those who surrendered, and were taken in small parties endeavoring to make their escape, amount nearly to the number of four hundred, chiefly British troops. Six brass pieces of cannon have fallen into our hands, a quantity of ammunition, and several wagons of baggage. A Captain Leslie was found amongst the dead of the enemy, and was this day buried with the honors of war. A number of other officers were also found on the field, but they were not known, and were buried with the other dead. According to information from the inhabitants of Princeton, the number which marched out of it to attack our army, amounted to seven thousand men, under command of General Cornwallis. This body, as soon as they discovered that they were out-generaled by the march of General Washington, being much chagrined at their disappointment, (as it seems they intended to have cut our army to pieces, crossed the Delaware, and have marched immediately, without any further delay, to Philadelphia,) pushed with the greatest precipitation towards Princeton, where they arrived about an hour after General Washington had left it; and imagining he would endeavor to take Brunswick in the same manner, proceeded directly for that place. Our soldiers were much fatigued, the greatest part of them having been deprived of their rest the two preceding nights; otherwise we might, perhaps, have possessed ourselves of Brunswick. The enemy appear to be preparing to decamp and retire to New York, as they are much disgusted with their late treatment in New Jersey, and have a great inclination to rest themselves a little in some secure winter-quarters.

Pennsylvania Journal, February 5

January 9

NEW JERSEY   The enemy have abandoned Elizabethtown. Our people have entered it and taken thirty Waldeckers and fifty Highlanders, and about thirty baggage wagons fully loaded. The enemy who had all the Jerseys, are now only in possession of Amboy and Brunswick. This is a great reverse in the course of a fortnight, to the British power. Whether they mean to collect their whole force at Brunswick, and give us battle, or whether they mean to push for Staten Island, and abandon the Jerseys entirely, is matter of doubt. We shall make a move towards them to-day, with a view to avail ourselves of circumstances. The enemy appear to be panic-struck in the extreme. God prospers our arms in an extraordinary manner. There is to be an eclipse of the sun to-day; we mean, if possible, to attack the Germans as soon as it begins, and take the advantage of their ignorant superstition. [On January 9, 1777, there was an annular eclipse of the sun, which began at sunrise in what is now Utah and crossed New Mexico and part of Texas. *Ed.*]

Letter from Morristown, New Jersey
Freeman's Journal, January 28

January 19

NEW YORK   General Howe has discharged all the privates, who were prisoners in New York; one-half he sent to
the world of spirits for want of food—the other he hath sent
to warn their countrymen of the danger of falling into his
hands, and to convince them by ocular demonstration, that
it is infinitely better to be slain in battle, than to be taken
prisoners by British brutes, whose tender mercies are cruelties.

The following account of the sufferings of these unfortunate
men was obtained from the prisoners themselves:—As soon
as they were taken they were robbed of all their baggage, of
whatever money they had, though it were of paper, and could
be of no advantage to the enemy, of their silver shoe-buckles,
and knee-buckles, &c., and many were stripped almost naked
of their clothes. Especially those who had good clothes, were
stripped at once, being told that *such clothes were too good
for rebels*. Thus deprived of their clothes and baggage they
were unable to shift even their linen, and were obliged to
wear the same shirts for even three or four months together,
whereby they became extremely nasty; and this of itself was
sufficient to bring on them many mortal diseases.

After they were taken, they were in the first place put on
board the ships and thrust down into the hold, where not a
breath of fresh air could be obtained and they were nearly
suffocated for want of air. Particularly some who were taken
at Fort Washington, were first in this manner thrust down
into the holds of vessels in such numbers, that even in the
cold season of November they could scarcely bear any clothes
on them, being kept in a constant sweat. Yet these same
persons, after lying in this situation awhile, till the pores of
their bodies were as perfectly opened as possible, were of a
sudden taken out and put into some of the churches in New
York; without covering or a spark of fire, where they suffered
as much by the cold as they did by the sweating stagnation
of the air in the other situation; and the consequence was,
that they took such colds as brought on the most fatal diseases, and swept them off almost beyond conception.

Besides these things, they suffered extremely for want of

provisions. The commissary pretended to allow half a pound of bread and four ounces of pork per day; but of this pittance they were much cut short. What was given them for three days was not enough for one day; and in some instances, they went for three days without a single mouthful of food of any sort. They were pinched to that degree, that some on board the ships would pick up and eat the salt which happened to be scattered there; others gathered up the bran which the light horse wasted, and ate it, mixed with dirt and filth as it was. Nor was this all, both the bread and pork which they did allow them was extremely bad. For the bread, some of it was made out of the bran which they brought over to feed their light horse, and the rest of it was so muddy and the pork so damnified, being so soaked in bilge water in the transportation from Europe, that they were not fit to be eaten by human creatures; and when they were eaten, were very unwholesome. Such bread and pork as they would not pretend to give their own countrymen, they gave to our poor sick, dying prisoners.

Nor were they in this doleful condition allowed a sufficiency of water. One would have thought that water was so cheap and plentiful an element, that they would not have grudged them that. But there are, it seems, no bounds to their cruelty. The water allowed them was so brackish and withal nasty, that they could not drink it, till reduced to extremity. Nor did they let them have a sufficiency even of such water as this.

When winter came on, our people suffered extremely for want of fire and clothes to keep them warm. They were confined in churches where there were no fireplaces, that they could make fires even if they had wood. But wood was only allowed them for cooking their pittance of victuals; and for that purpose very sparingly. They had none to keep them warm even in the extremest of weather, although they were almost naked, and the few clothes that were left upon them were their summer clothes. Nor had they a single blanket or any bedding, not even straw, allowed them till a little before Christmas.

At the time those were taken on Long Island, a considerable part of them were sick of the dysentery, and with this distemper on them were first crowded on board the ships, afterwards in the churches in New York, three, four, or five hundred together without any blankets, or any thing for even the sick to lie upon, but the bare floors or pavements. In this situation that contagious distemper soon communicated from the sick to the well, who would probably have remained so, had they not in this manner been thrust in together without regard to sick or well, or to the sultry, unwholesome season, it being then the heat of summer. Of this distemper numbers died daily, and many others, by their confinement and the sultry season, contracted fevers and died of them. During their sickness, with these and other diseases, they had no medicines, nothing soothing or comfortable for sick people, and were not so much as visited by the physician by the month together.

Nor ought we to omit the insults which the humane Britons offered to our people, nor the artifices which they used to enlist them in their service and fight against their country. It seems that one end of their starving our people was to bring them, by dint of necessity, to turn rebels to their own country, their own consciences, and their God. For while thus famishing they would come and say to them, "This is the just punishment of your rebellion. Nay, you are treated too well for rebels; you have not received half you deserve or half you shall receive. But if you will enlist into his Majesty's service, you shall have victuals and clothes enough."

As to insults, the British officers, besides continually curs-ing and swearing at them as rebels, often threatened to hang them all; and on a particular time, ordered a number, each man to choose his halter out of a parcel offered, wherewith to be hanged; and even went so far as to cause a gallows to be erected before the prison, as if they were immediately to be executed. They further threatened to send them all into the East Indies, and sell them there for slaves. In these, and num-berless other ways, did the British officers seem to rack their inventions to insult, terrify, and vex the poor prisoners. The meanest upstart officers among them would insult and abuse our colonels and chief officers.

In this situation, without clothes, without victuals or drink, and even water, or with those which were base and unwholesome, without fire, a number of them sick, first with a contagious and nauseous distemper; these, with others, crowded by hundreds into close confinement, at the most unwholesome season of the year, and continued there for four months without blankets, bedding, or straw; without linen to shift, or clothes to cover their bodies. No wonder they all became sickly, and having at the same time no medicine, no help of physicians, nothing to refresh or support nature, died by scores in a night; and those who were so far gone as to be unable to help themselves, lay uncared for, till death, more kind than Britons, put an end to their misery.

By these means, and in this way, fifteen hundred brave Americans, who had nobly gone forth in defence of their injured, oppressed country, but whom the chance of war had cast into the hands of our enemies, died in New York, many of whom were very amiable, promising youths, of good families—the very flower of our land. And of those who lived to come out of prison, the greater part, as far as I can learn, are dead and dying. Their constitutions are broken, the stamina of nature worn out, they cannot recover—they die. Even the few that might have survived, are dying of the small-pox. For it seems that our enemies determined that even these, whom a good constitution and a kind Providence had carried through unexampled sufferings, should not at last escape death, just before their release from imprisonment infected them with that fatal distemper.

To these circumstances we subjoin the manner in which they buried those of our people who died. They dragged them out of their prisons by one leg or one arm, piled them up without doors, there let them lie till a sufficient number were dead to make a cart load; then loaded them up in a cart, drove the cart thus loaded out to the ditches made by our people when fortifying New York; there they would tip the cart, tumble the corpses together into the ditch, and afterwards slightly cover them with earth.

Freeman's Journal, February 18

January 24

At a crisis when America is invaded by one of the most powerful fleets and armies that ever the world beheld arrayed in
order of battle; when the hand of tyranny is uplifted to fell
the glorious plant of liberty, which our ancestors have cher-
ished from the earliest ages as the tree-of-life; when war, with
all its horrors, is invading this once happy land, and every
sacred right is at stake; when every filial and affectionate sentiment should engage us to step forth in support of those who
have been the guardians of our tender years, or the sweet
companions of our halcyon days, must not that soul be frozen
even to apathy that is not roused by such important and irresistible impulses! Our country, our lives, our liberties, our
parents, our children, and our wives, &c., are the sacred
pledges for which we are now contending. We stand on the
brink of a precipice, from which we cannot advance without
the noblest exertions of virtue, unanimity, and fortitude. A
single false step may precipitate us from the enjoyment of the
inestimable blessings of liberty, peace, and independence, to
the abyss of slavery and woe. But, on the contrary, whilst we
are animated by the glorious cause we are engaged in; whilst we
with cheerfulness embark in the defence of the most valuable
of sublunary blessings; whilst we are united in our sentiment,
vigilant in our duty, and active in our operations, we need
not dread the thunder of cannon, nor tremble at the names
of heroes arrayed in all the splendor of a corrupt court, or
crowned with the faded laurels which have been plucked by
the hand of tyranny.

Such, my countrymen, is the present state of America; such
the consequence of slumbering in the arms of peace, whilst
your enemy is at your gates; and such the glorious reward of
those who nobly stand forth and oppose the progress of a
mercenary army, more venal than a court favorite, more
savage than a band of Tartars, and more spiritless than the
sorry, sooty sons of Afric, when opposed by men animated by
liberty and the sacred love of their country.

Should any one among you require the force of example to

animate you on this glorious occasion, let him turn his eyes to that bright luminary of war, in whose character the conduct of Emillus, the coolness of a Fabius, the intrepidity of a Hannibal, and the indefatigable ardor and military skill of a Cæsar, are united. Let not the name of Brutus or Camillus be remembered whilst that of Washington is to be found in the annals of America. Great in the cabinet as in war, he shines with unrivalled splendor in every department of life; and whilst his abilities as a statesman and a general excite our wonder, his disinterested patriotism and domestic virtues command universal veneration. When sent out by Governor Dinwiddie to order the French to desist from their encroachments on Virginia, view him in the early period of life, traversing in the service of his country the dreadful wilds of America, through nations of savages, with no other attendant but an interpreter. Behold him at the head of a handful of his gallant countrymen, engaged for many hours with more than treble the number of French, at the Meadows, where the fire first ceased on the side of the enemy, who previously proposed a parley; and though surrounded by numbers, yet, a stranger to the impulses of fear, he capitulated on the terms of retiring with the honors of war. Follow him to that tremendous scene which struck a universal panic in the bravest of the British troops, when, as aide-de-camp to the intrepid Braddock, amidst the dreadful carnage of that day, he was engaged in giving out the orders of that unfortunate general with a coolness that marked the hero, and at length brought him off the field of battle, after he had received his mortal wound.

Again, behold him exchanging the din of arms for the calmer scenes of life, still active in the service of his country in the senate, until the impeding storm, which is now bursting on America, called him forth as the guardian protector of his country. Behold him abandoning the delights of peace, the enjoyment of affluence, and the pleasures of domestic felicity, and entering with ardor upon a military life again. Let imagination paint him at the head of a few raw, undisciplined troops, destitute of arms and ammunition, besieging an army of veterans supported by a powerful navy;

consider with what unparalleled fortitude he withstood the difficulties that surrounded him on every side; behold him embracing the earliest opportunities of driving the enemy from their advantageous post, and obliging them to abandon the long persecuted town of Boston. Again, survey the plains of Long Island, whither he flew like a guardian angel to protect and bring off his brave troops, surrounded on every side by a host of foes, and with a conduct unparalleled in history, secured their retreat across a river of which the enemy's ships were in full possession. Surely Heaven interposed in behalf of America on that day, by permitting such numbers to escape with glory from such a superior force! Behold his glorious struggles on the heights of Harlem, and at the White Plains, counteracting the best concerted plans of the ablest generals of the age; in thought attend him, (if thought does not lag behind,) when, as it were, he bounded from the White Plains to the Jersey shore, covering the retreat of his men from Fort Lee, and throwing himself with them before the enemy, and with the scattered remains of his disbanded army, now amounting to only three thousand men, checking at every step the progress of the British army, and often halting to offer battle to numbers vastly superior to his own.

Gracious Heaven! can any Virginian—his countrymen, or can any American who regards him as the saviour of the States, reflect on his situation at that juncture without horror? Would he not rather share his fortunes for the rest of the war, than hazard the salvation of his country by a short enlistment, at the end of which his general might be left without an army to support him? Yet, even in such a situation, his calmness and intrepidity never forsook him, but he appeared still greater in proportion to the dangers that surrounded him. At length, when the enemy flattered themselves with the pleasing expectations of a speedy accomplishment of their darling wish, we behold him by *coup de main* dissipating the fears of his country, and striking terror into troops who, the day before, conceived themselves on the eve of a triumph. Whilst each effeminate son of peace was revelling in luxury, his active mind was employed in preparing for scenes equally glorious to himself, and terrible to his enemies. Success attended this matchless enterprise, and Philadelphia, with the rest of America, hailed him her deliverer and guardian genius.

Such, my countrymen, is the general who directs the military operations of America; such the glorious leader of her armies; such the hero whose bright example should fire every generous heart to enlist in the service of his country. Let it not be said you are callous to the impressions of such noble considerations, but, by following his glorious example, show yourselves worthy of possessing that inestimable jewel, Liberty, and reflect that you have nothing to dread whilst you are engaged in so glorious a cause, and blessed with a Washington for a leader.

Freeman's Journal, April 12

January 25

The following proclamation was this day published by the Lord Protector, Mr. George Washington:

"Whereas several persons, inhabitants of the United States of America, influenced by inimical motives, intimidated by the threats of the enemy, or deluded by a proclamation issued the 30th of November last, by Lord and General Howe, styled the King's Commissioners for granting pardons, &c., (now at open war, and invading these States,) have been so lost to the interest and welfare of their country, as to repair to the enemy, sign a declaration of fidelity, and in some instances have been compelled to take the oaths of allegiance, and engage not to take up arms, or encourage others so to do, against the King of Great Britain: And whereas it has become necessary to distinguish between the friends of America and those of Great Britain, inhabitants of these States, and that every man who receives protection from, and is a subject of any state, (not being conscientiously scrupulous against bearing arms,) should stand ready to defend the same against hostile invasion: I do, therefore, in behalf of the United States, by virtue of the powers committed to me by Congress, hereby strictly command and require every person, having subscribed such declaration, taken such oaths, and accepted such protection and certificate, to repair to head-quarters, or to the quarters of the nearest general officer of the Continental army or militia, (until further provision can be made by civil authority,) and there deliver up such pro-tection, certificate, and passports, and take the oath of alle-giance to the United States of America; nevertheless, hereby granting full liberty to all such as prefer the interest and pro-tection of Great Britain to the freedom and happiness of their country, forthwith to withdraw themselves and families within the enemy's lines. And I do hereby declare, that all and every person who may neglect or refuse to comply with this order, within thirty days from the date hereof, will be deemed adherents to the King of Great Britain, and treated as common enemies of these American States."

'Tis hardly possible to read over this miserable proclama-tion without pity and astonishment. That Mr. Washington, who *once* was esteemed a gentleman, should forfeit that character by becoming the tool of an impracticable ambition, is a matter of commiseration; but, that he should be so con-taminated by the vice of his associates as to lose all regard to the common forms of morality, all dignity of sentiment, and decency of conduct, was not to have been expected from a man who owned the least pride, or felt the least conscious-ness of virtue. His desperate situation may be his apology, but it cannot be his excuse. He might have been mistaken in respect to his notions of civil polity; but he could not have been deceived in those actions and ideas of moral turpi-tude, which is the disgrace of human nature. 'Tis an old and true observation, *Magistratus indicat Virum*, "the Ruler shows the Man;" and we have now nothing more to learn of this famous Mr. Washington.

He has the boldness to declare, that there are "some in-stances" of persons who "have been compelled to take the oath of allegiance." This is an absolute falsehood in fact, and he knew it was a falsehood; he knew such conduct was re-pugnant to the genius and spirit of the British nation, or he would have produced one instance to confirm his assertion. The bravery of Britons, which sooner or later will make him tremble, disdains any but voluntary professions of allegiance, and above all things, despises the dastardly subterfuges of falsehood and slander.

The next material circumstance in this Proclamation, is sufficient to make an honest man shudder. It may be styled, a Proclamation for the encouragement of Perjury. Mr. Washington "strictly commands and requires every person," who has taken a solemn oath of Allegiance to the King, and called God to witness the truth and sincerity of it, to repair to him or his officers, and take another solemn oath, and call God to witness the sincerity and truth of his adherence to the cause of rebellion. Such an impious disregard, such a flagrant violation of all that is serious and sacred among men, has rarely been seen in any age, country, or profession.

For the honor of human nature, it may be said, that it was left for rebels to their King and destroyers of their country, to give a public sanction to *Wilful Perjury*.

'Tis no wonder that a principle of this kind should be attended with a suitable practice. Mr. Washington grants by this proclamation "full liberty" to all such as prefer the protection of Great Britain to his own, "forthwith to withdraw themselves and families within the enemy's lines." This is only a trap to discover those who are not affected to the rebellion; and even this mean idea has been followed by a conduct of which a common Turk would have been ashamed. Doctor Brown, of Newark, in the Jerseys, relying not merely upon Mr. Washington's word as a gentleman, but upon his public faith pledged in the foregoing paper as a public man, immediately wrote to him, desiring leave to withdraw himself and family to New York, pursuant to his proclamation. Instead of complying with the Doctor's wishes, he sent a party of his rebels to drag him away to Morristown. He is now confined there in jail, his family is almost distracted, and all his property seized. So much for the public faith of Mr. Washington!

He seems indebted for the last cruel idea of his Proclamation to the worthy author of "Common Sense," and the "American Crisis." This gentleman is for seizing all the property of people who refuse to join in his measures, for the

sake of the spoil; and has the confidence to declare, that such
a seizure would enable his rebellious adherents to carry on
the war for two years longer. 'Tis to be hoped, for the honor
and safety of America, that the good people of this country
will give an exact account of him and some of his associates
in half the time. It is every man's interest, who has any thing
to lose, to take care of a person who has the impudence to
profess himself a public robber and destroyer, and can call
this unheard of cruelty and devastation by the name of "soft
resentment." However, if men who can encourage perjury by
proclamation, and plunge thousands of families into irre-
trievable ruin, only for the purpose of answering their dark
ambition; if men who can have the consummate boldness to
break their public faith, and, calling the gentle government
of Britain, tyranny, can become the most insolent and out-
rageous tyrants themselves; if such can possibly arrive at the
rule of this once happy country, it will be the interest of
every one who loves the enjoyment of liberty more than the
sound, to retire from America as speedily as he can. In such
an event, (which, however, is not likely to happen,) he would
escape the anarchy, riot, and bloodshed, which these "unprincipled impostors" sooner or later would spread over the
land, and which would then become the vengeance of Providence itself on this most ungrateful and unnatural rebellion.

New York Gazette and Weekly Mercury, February 10

———•———

FEBRUARY

February 6

A correspondent thinks the following new catechism will
amply repay an attentive perusal:

What is war?—It is the curse of mankind, the mother of
pestilence and famine, and the undistinguishing destroyer of
the human species.

How is war divided?—Into offensive and defensive.

What is the chief end of offensive war?—Sometimes it is to regain by the sword what had been unjustly taken away from the rightful possessor; but, for the most part, it is to gratify the ambition of a tyrannic prince, by subjecting to his arbitrary will a people whom God had created free, and giving their hard-earned possessions to support him in luxury, idleness, and sensuality.

Are there any instances of such princes?—Yes, many, both in ancient and modern times. History is filled with the wicked lives and miserable deaths of tyrants. The present King of Great Britain, whose history is not yet completed, is a living example of such a prince. He carried an offensive war into the East Indies, and deprived many thousands of those innocent people of their lives and properties, that he might snuff the spices of the east, and repose his sluggard limbs on the sofa of a nabob. He is now carrying an offensive war into America, without one specious plea for so doing, most wickedly aiming at the absolute disposal of that extensive country and all its numerous inhabitants; for this purpose he has spread desolation and death through their peaceful habitations, pursuing his iniquitous designs with every aggravated species of obstinacy, cruelty, and horror.

What may be said of such a prince?—That he looks upon mankind as created only for his use, and makes their misery his support; that the spirits of thousands, who have fallen a sacrifice to his ambition, cluster around the polished points of his imperial crown, and daily cry aloud to Heaven for justice; that his throne is built of the bones of his fellow creatures, and rests on the skulls of the slain; that his unhallowed feasts are sprinkled with human blood, and that the groans of widows and orphans attend him with innumerable curses at every rising sun.

What will be the probable end of such a prince?—That history will do justice to his memory, in spite of all the fawning sycophants of his court, and hand his name to posterity with infamy and detestation; that whilst his royal carcass fattens the common worms of the earth, his miserable soul shall give an account to God for the wanton slaughter of his creatures, whose blood will most assuredly be required at his hands; and that the vaults of hell shall ring with *Hail, thou great destroyer of the human species!*

What is a defensive war?—It is the taking up arms to resist tyrannic power, and bravely suffering present hardships, and encountering present dangers, to secure lasting liberty, property, and life to future generations.

Is a defensive war justifiable in a religious view?—The foundation of war is laid in the wickedness of mankind. Were all men virtuous, just, and good, there would be no contention, or cause of contention, amongst them; but as the case is far otherwise, war is become absolutely necessary, as many other things are which are only the product of the weaknesses or iniquity of men. Even the invaluable blessings of a constitutional government would be unnecessary incumbrances, were there no open violence or secret treachery to be guarded against. God has given to man wit to contrive, power to execute, and freedom of will to direct his conduct. It cannot be, therefore, but that some will abuse these great privileges, and exert these powers to the ruin of others. The oppressed will then have no way to screen themselves from injury but by executing the same powers in their defence, and it is their duty so to do. If it were otherwise, a few miscreants would tyrannize over the rest of mankind, and make them abject slaves of oppression and pensioners of their will. Thus it is that a just defensive war is not only necessary, but an indispensable duty, and consistent with religion, accommodated as it must be to our present imperfect state of existence.

Is it upon these principles that the people of America are now resisting the arms of England, and opposing force by force?—Strictly so. The Americans had nothing in view but to live peaceably and dutifully in a constitutional submission to Great Britain. They suffered patiently, for a long time, many unjust encroachments of power, being loath to offend their rulers by a too strict attention to every right, till at last the designs of the court became too evident to be mistaken, and they were pushed to the distressing necessity of choosing one of two evils, viz., either to enlist themselves and their unborn posterity the avowed unconditional slaves of a corrupt and wicked administration, or to brave the horrors of war in a noble contest for liberty and life. They have wisely determined on the latter; and after solemnly appealing to God and the world for the justice of their cause, they are prosecuting the war under the favor of Heaven, and with the most promising hopes of success. Supported by the equity of their principles, they have surmounted the greatest difficulties, and exhibited instances of bravery not exceeded by the heroes of antiquity—and may Heaven prosper their virtuous undertaking.

But it has often been said that America is in a state of rebellion: tell me, therefore, what is rebellion?—It is when a great number of people, headed by one or more factious leaders, aim at deposing their lawful prince, without any just cause of complaint against him, in order to place another on his throne.

Is this the case of America?—By no means. They have repeatedly declared, with all sincerity, that they were ever ready to support, with their lives and fortunes, the present King of Great Britain on the throne of his ancestors, and only requested in return the enjoyment of those inestimable rights which the British Constitution confirms to all its subjects, and without which the boasted freedom of that constitution is but a solemn mockery, and an empty name.

To whom has the British court committed the conduct of the present war?—To Lord and General Howe.

Who are these gentlemen?—They are the brothers of a Colonel [George] Howe,[1] who fought bravely by the side of

[1] Lord Viscount George Howe was the eldest son of Sir E. Scrope, second Lord Viscount in Ireland. He arrived at Halifax in the summer of 1757, having under his command five thousand British troops, who had been despatched from England to assist in the expedition against the French. In the next year he was with Abercrombie at the renowned attack on Ticonderoga, and at the first fire of the French, who were posted in the woods a short distance westward of the fort, he fell mortally wounded. "In him the soul of the army seemed to expire." His kindly disposition, bravery, and many virtues, endeared him to the soldiers; and Massachusetts, as a "proof of her love and esteem for his gallantry and daring," erected a monument to his memory in Westminster Abbey. At the time of his death he was thirty-three years of age. [Frank Moore]

the Americans in a former war, and fell in battle; who, by his amiable character, endeared himself to those people so much, that they lamented his fate with unfeigned sorrow, and erected, at their own expense, a costly monument to his memory. But these gentlemen, with unrelenting hearts and sacrilegious hands, have defiled their brother's monument with the blood of those whose affection reared it to his honor, and plunged their murderous weapons into bosoms glowing with love and esteem for their mother's son.

What progress have the English made in subduing America? —Very little. They got possession of Boston by the tacit consent of its inhabitants, but could not hold it long. They were but tenants at will, strictly speaking, for their landlords turned them out without any warning, and distrained upon certain military stores, &c., although they had sat there at a rent of about five hundred pounds per day.

What did they next?—They took Staten Island, where there was nothing to oppose them, and a part of Long Island, by an exertion of almost their whole force against a small part of the American army, and then ferried themselves over to the city of New York; from thence they crept into the Jerseys, and taking advantage of a critical period, when the American army was disbanded by the terms of enlistment, and before a new force could be raised, they heroically advanced to the banks of the Delaware, well knowing there was nothing to oppose their progress. On the banks of the Delaware they set them down, settled, as they thought, for the winter season, and plundered the adjacent country. In the mean time these extraordinary conductors of the war published a wonderful and gracious proclamation, offering such protection as they could afford to all those who would accept of it, upon the easy terms of absolute, unconditional submission. But the Americans, whose resources are endless, soon found a spirited militia to supply the place of the disbanded troops until a new army could be raised. This militia crossed the Delaware in a snow storm at midnight, and after marching ten miles, very uncivilly attacked the enemy before they had breakfasted, and drove them from the banks of the Delaware in the utmost consternation, and with a loss of twelve hundred men. The

American army then recrossed the Delaware and suffered the enemy to return to their post, where they anxiously waited the arrival of an expected reinforcement. But the American general, by a stroke of policy above their comprehension, once more passed the river with his army, and kindled a few fires in the night near their station; and whilst they were foolishly gazing at the beauty of the curling flames, he marched on, attacked, routed, and entirely defeated the said reinforcement. The shattered remains of General Howe's army are now close confined in Brunswick, where they are doing penance on salt meat and musty biscuit.

Where are injustice, obstinacy, and folly united in one character in an eminent degree?—In George the Third. He is unjust, because he endeavors to gain by force what is denied him by the laws of the realm over which he presides, in direct violation of his coronation oath, and pursues his unconstitutional claims to the effusion of human blood; he is obstinate, because he refuses to hear the humble petitions and modest reasonings of an oppressed people, and will not yield to the forcible convictions of truth; and his folly is conspicuous in quarrelling with a people who loved and honored him, who were the chief supporters of his crown and dignity, and a never-failing source of increasing wealth.

Pennsylvania Journal, February 19

MARCH

March 4

PENNSYLVANIA   Ran away from Isaac Harris, living in Pittsgrove, Salem County, Pennsylvania, an English servant man, named William Blackmore; about twenty-two years of age; five feet five, or six feet high; light complexion, light straight hair; a very clumsy fellow, turns the toe of his right foot very much out in his walk; very much addicted to swearing and getting drunk; he has run away several times, and has an iron collar round his neck, marked I. H. and W. B., which he wears under his shirt, but may be easily discovered. Had on, when he went away, a brown cloth coat with blue sleeves, a light colored cloth jacket, leather breeches, and blue stockings. All recruiting officers are requested not to enlist him. He will endeavor to get to the ministerial army if he has opportunity, as he is a great Tory. Whosoever takes up and secures the said servant in any gaol so that his master may have him again, shall receive six dollars and reasonable charges paid if brought home.

Pennsylvania Journal, March 12

March 8

PENNSYLVANIA   This day, between the hours of twelve and one o'clock, Brint Debadee, a soldier belonging to the tenth Pennsylvania regiment, was shot upon the commons in Philadelphia, pursuant to the sentence of a general court-martial. This unhappy man was in his twenty-fourth year, in the vigor of life, and it is hoped his untimely and dreadful end will be a warning to others, who, when they desert, not only defraud their officer and abuse their country, but are also guilty of the dreadful and heinous crime of perjury. Of his past misconduct he appeared very sensible, and behaved in his last moments with great resignation and calmness, declaring that he sincerely forgave all his enemies, and hoped that his example would be serviceable to some of his thoughtless brother soldiers. He was attended by the Rev. Mr. Coombe, and the Rev. Mr. Rogers. The last gentleman, being a chaplain in the service, delivered to the soldiers present a pathetic address, suitable to the melancholy occasion.

Pennsylvania Evening Post, March 8

March 9

NEW JERSEY   Yesterday, the British, supposed to be about three thousand, came out from Amboy, and posted themselves on Punk Hill. They brought artillery and a number of wagons, as if to forage, though there were none left in that neighborhood worth notice. General Maxwell, with the troops under his command, was on a rising ground to the northward, in plain view, though at a good distance. The enemy were too well situated to be attacked. Maxwell sent a party to the left to amuse them, while his real design was to the right, on the heights towards Bonamtown. He sent a strong party that way to examine their lines, if they had any, and to fall in near the end of them, that he might fall on their flank; this was performed by part of Colonel Potter's battalion of Pennsylvania militia, and part of Colonel Thacher's New England troops. Colonel Cook, of the Pennsylvanians, had been ordered from Matuchin to come down on Carman's Hill, and keep along the heights till he met the enemy. About half a mile lower down, between Carman's Hill, and Woodbridge, the two parties being joined, met a strong advanced party of the enemy. On the first firing, Colonel Martin and Lieutenant-Colonel Lindley were sent to support them; they all behaved well and kept their ground till they were supported from the main body, which immediately marched that way. The enemy also sent out a reinforcement, but on another regiment of Americans being sent on the left to cut them off from their main body, the party gave way in great confusion, and the flame catching their main body, all went together. Our people pursued them and took a prisoner and a baggage wagon close in their rear, a good way down in the plain ground. Bonamtown lay too near on the right, and a plain, open ground towards Amboy, to pursue far. They left four dead on the field, and we took three prisoners. By the quantity they carried off in sleds and wagons, it is supposed they had near twenty killed, and twice that number wounded.

General Maxwell says that by a soldier taken prisoner, he learns that General Howe was at Bonamtown during the engagement, till he saw his troops make the best of their way home, when he thought it was time for him to go.

Letter from Haddonfield, New Jersey
Pennsylvania Journal, March 19

APRIL

April 14

NEW JERSEY   Day before yesterday, General Lord Cornwallis, Generals Grant and Matthews, with the first battalion
of grenadiers, one battalion of light infantry, a detachment of
the guards, the light horse, two battalions of Hessians, and
the Jagers, commanded by Colonel Donop, marched from
New Brunswick, in New Jersey, between eight and nine
o'clock at night, in order to surprise a large body of the rebels
stationed at Boundbrook, seven miles distance from that city,
commanded by a General Lincoln. The expedition was conducted with so much secrecy that scarce any of the inhabitants
knew of the departure of the troops till Sunday morning. They
avoided the roads, and got close to the rebel intrenchments
before day; heard the sentinels cry "All's well," and were
ordered to lie on their arms till the rebels should fire their
morning gun. The order being given for the attack, their
troops rushed on with their usual intrepidity, and put the
rebels to flight, killed upwards of one hundred, took seventy-
three prisoners, (among whom was one of Lincoln's aide-de-
camps, one captain, one lieutenant, and a man in irons,
sentenced by the rebels to be shot,) three brass cannon, a
quantity of arms, two wagons loaded with ammunition, a
number of horses, one hundred and twenty head of cattle,
sheep, hogs, &c., besides destroying three hundred barrels of
flour, several hogsheads of whiskey and New England rum,
with sundry other articles that the flourishing States cannot
very well spare. The troops returned on Sunday forenoon, and
the rebels crawled back to Boundbrook on their departure.
Our loss was one man killed, and two Jagers wounded.

Many of the friends of government availed themselves of
the confusion the rebels were thrown in by the above disaster,
and came into Brunswick with the troops; several of the rebels
embraced the same opportunity, and brought in their arms.

It is said that the rebel general had not time to collect his clothes, his safety requiring his utmost dexterity and swiftness. The prisoners were brought to New York to-day, and are lodged in gaol with their wretched brethren.

Upcott, V, 19

The late proclamation, issued by Sir William Howe, we hear has been read to the several corps in the rebel army, by their respective leaders, who strove to show them that the design of it was to lead them to bondage and destruction, to alienate them from their allegiance to Messieurs *John Hancock, Samuel Adams,* and the other members of the Congress, and to bring them out of their present state of happiness and freedom. Many and wonderful were the speeches made upon this occasion, all founded upon an evident fear lest their poor deluded followers should see and think for themselves. Their fear seems to have been just; for many, in following their own senses, have quitted the desperate and wicked cause they have been engaged in, and have brought in (some of them at least) two or three muskets apiece, for which they have been handsomely paid in *silver* dollars. Some whole companies have come in, and particularly from the northward. A party of them who came up a few days since from Amboy, in order to join the royal provincials, were astonished to see any ships in New York harbor, as it had been industriously reported among the rebels that they were all sailed for England, and that the troops were to quit the colonies as soon as fresh ships could arrive to carry them home. A very few weeks will convict these impostors of their numberless falsehoods.

Several men-of-war, and above one hundred transports, are stationed in the North River. The East River is crowded with merchantmen, prize-vessels, and ships of all sorts.

A correspondent remarks, that whilst most of the other seaport towns and colonies groan under the dearness of provisions, and the common necessaries of life, New York is supplied, at very little more than the usual rate in this season of the year, with every species of food and all kinds of clothing and dry goods.

The Philadelphia newspapers are stuffed with continual false accounts of skirmishes and other exploits of their ragamuffins in the Jerseys, in which they always obtain most wonderful and "never-to-be-heard-of-victories." The following may serve for a specimen, taken from the *Pennsylvania Journal* of the second of April. In a skirmish, which is stated to have happened near Quibbletown on the twenty-fourth of March, they say the British "must have lost some men, as they were seen carrying them off in the time of action, which happened within half a mile of their breastworks. We had two rifles broke, but not a man hurt in this skirmish; an evident proof, that Providence shields the just and brave, (they mean themselves,) for we forced them from an advantageous wood, where they were posted behind trees and our people entirely exposed in an open field. The troops that were engaged with ours were British and not Hessian. Our whole party did not exceed one hundred and thirty, and the enemy not less than three hundred men." What opinion must these people have of their followers, when they suppose them capable of believing such enormous falsehoods as these?

Some days ago, the daughter of Mr. Jonathan Kniffin, of Rye, in Connecticut, was murdered by a party of rebels near or upon Budd's Neck. She was carrying some clothes to her father in company of two men who had the charge of a herd of cattle. They were fired upon by the rebels from behind a stone wall. The poor young woman received a ball in her head, of which she instantly died. The men escaped unhurt. They plundered her dead body of its clothes, cut one of her fingers almost off in order to take a ring, and left the corpse most indecently exposed in the highway. Such are the advocates of this cursed rebellion! Yet the officer (so called) who commanded the party, and who is said to be a colonel among the rebels, gloried in the exploit, and swore it was better to kill one woman than two men; adding, moreover, that he would put both man and woman to death, who should presume to cultivate their farms or their gardens in the neighborhood of Rye this spring.

New York Gazette and Weekly Mercury, April 14

PENNSYLVANIA   Three men-of-war have sailed up the Delaware, and anchored off Reedy Island. This has thrown all the rebellious part of Philadelphia, with the congress at their head, into the utmost perturbation. Handbills have been distributed to implore the people to assemble in arms against the troops of their sovereign, but it won't do. The people begin to see the baseness and villany of their leaders, and think it high time to take care of themselves. Some of the New England and other people who do not belong to the province, have attempted to burn the city, and actually did set it on fire in two places. This has induced the Quakers and other inhabitants to mount guard every night for the preservation of their property from destruction by these lawless incendiaries.

New York Gazette and Weekly Mercury, April 21

April 18

The committee appointed by Congress some time ago to inquire into the conduct of the British troops in their different marches through New York and New Jersey, have to-day reported:—That in every place where the enemy has been, there are heavy complaints of oppression, injury, and insult, suffered by the inhabitants, from officers, soldiers, and Americans disaffected to their country's cause.

The committee found these complaints so greatly diversified, that as it was impossible to enumerate them, so it appeared exceedingly difficult to give a distinct and comprehensive view of them, or such an account as would not appear extremely defective when read by unhappy sufferers or the country in general. In order, however, in some degree to answer the design of their appointment, they determined to divide the object of their inquiry into the following parts, and briefly state what they found to be the truth upon each.

First:—*The wanton and oppressive devastation of the country, and destruction of property.*

The whole track of the British army is marked with desolation, and a wanton destruction of property, particularly through Westchester County, in the State of New York, the towns of Newark, Elizabethtown, Woodbridge, Brunswick, Kingston, Princeton, and Trenton, in New Jersey. The fences destroyed, houses deserted, pulled in pieces or consumed by fire, and the

general face of waste and devastation spread over a rich and
once well-cultivated and well-inhabited country, would affect
the most unfeeling with compassion for the unhappy sufferers,
and with indignation and resentment against the barbarous
ravagers.

It deserves notice, that though there are many instances of
rage and vengeance against particular persons, yet the destruction was very general and often undistinguished; those who
submitted and took protections, and some who were known to
favor them, having frequently suffered in the common ruin.
Places and things which from their public nature and general
utility should have been spared by civilized people, have been
destroyed or plundered, or both. But above all, places of
worship, ministers, and other religious persons of some particular Protestant denominations, seem to have been treated
with the most rancorous hatred, and at the same time with
the highest contempt.

Second:—*The inhuman treatment of those who were so
unfortunate as to become prisoners.*

The prisoners, instead of that humane treatment which
those taken by the United States experienced, were in general
treated with the greatest barbarity. Many of them were kept
near four days without food altogether. When they received
a supply, it was insufficient in quantity, and often of the worst
kind. They suffered the utmost distress from cold, nakedness,
and close confinement. Freemen and men of substance suffered all that a generous mind could suffer from the contempt
and mockery of British and foreign mercenaries. Multitudes
died in prison. When they were sent out, several died in being
carried from the boats on shore, or upon the road attempting
to go home. The committee, in the course of their inquiry,
learned that sometimes the common soldiers expressed sym-
pathy with the prisoners, and the foreigners more than the
English. But this was seldom or never the case with the
officers; nor have they been able to hear of any charitable
assistance given them by the inhabitants who remained in or
resorted to the city of New York, which neglect, if universal,
they believe was never known to happen in any similar case
in a Christian country.

Third:—*The savage butchery of those who had submitted,
and were incapable of resistance.*

The committee found it to be the general opinion of the
people in the neighborhood of Trenton and Princeton, that
the British, the day before the battle of Princeton, had determined to give no quarter. They did not, however, obtain any
clear proof that there were general orders for that purpose,
but the treatment of several particular persons at and since
that time, has been of the most shocking kind, and gives too
much countenance to the supposition. Officers wounded and
disabled, some of them of the first rank, were barbarously
mangled or put to death. A minister of the gospel, who neither
was nor had been in arms, was massacred in cold blood at
Trenton, though humbly supplicating for mercy.

Fourth:—*The lust and brutality of the soldiers in abusing
women.*

The committee had authentic information of many instances of the most indecent treatment and actual ravishment
of married and single women; but such is the nature of that
most irreparable injury, that the persons suffering it, though
perfectly innocent, look upon it as a kind of reproach to have
the facts related, and their names known. Some complaints
were made to the commanding officers on this subject, and
one affidavit made before a justice of the peace, but the committee could not learn that any satisfaction was ever given, or
punishment inflicted, except that one soldier in Pennington
was kept in custody for part of a day.

On the whole, the committee are sorry to say that the cry
of barbarity and cruelty is but too well founded; and as in
conversation those who are cool to the American cause, have
nothing to oppose to the facts but their being incredible and
not like what they are pleased to style the generosity and
clemency of the English nation, the committee beg leave to
observe one of the circumstances most frequently occurring in
the inquiry, was the opprobrious, disdainful names given to
the Americans. These do not need any proof, as they occur so
frequently in the newspapers printed under their direction,
and in the intercepted letters of those who are officers, and call
themselves gentlemen. It is easy, therefore, to see what must

be the conduct of a soldiery greedy of prey, towards a people whom they have been taught to look upon, not as freemen defending their rights on principle, but as desperadoes and profligates, who have risen up against law and order in general, and wish the subversion of society itself. This is the most charitable and candid manner in which the committee can account for the melancholy truths which they have been obliged to report. Indeed, the same deluding principle seems to govern persons and bodies of the highest rank in Britain; for it is worthy of notice that not pamphleteers only, but King and Parliament, constantly call those acts *lenity,* which on their first publication filled this whole continent with resentment and horror.

Pennsylvania Evening Post, April 24

MAY

May 8

A correspondent has offered the following query and remarks to General Howe:—"If with thirty thousand men you conquered two towns and one village in *one* year, how many years will it be before you will be able to conquer and occupy all the towns and villages on the continent of America?"

It is incumbent upon your excellency to answer this question immediately, in order that the few recruits whom you have enlisted by your late proclamation, in which you have offered them the forfeited property of the Whigs, may know *exactly* how many *hundred years* they must wait before you eject the Whigs, and give them the peaceable possession of their estates.

Oh, fie, Sir William; fie, for shame! Such proclamations become a general at the head of a powerful and victorious army, and a whole country *almost* prostrate at his feet, and not the poor, contemptible chief of a vanquished, blockaded, half-starved, half-naked, half-rotten, half-paid, mongrel banditti, composed of the sweepings of the jails of Britain, Ireland, Germany, and America. Oh, fie; Sir William! Blush, blush for your proclamation!

> Carleton, Burgoyne, Howe,
> Bow——Wow——Wow!
> "*A Tar*," *Pennsylvania Evening Post, May 8*

May 29

General G——y, from Amboy, to-day, says the *rebels* in Philadelphia are very unsettled in their minds, and are mostly friendly to government, although their situation prevents their acting so. In the evening before the meeting at the state house on the tenth instant, a gentleman who reached Amboy a short time before G——y left, passing the hour at Mrs. D——'s, where a cheerful party of *out-of-door-rebels* had met, amused himself in preparing the following advisory petition to the Congress, which was highly applauded, and forthwith voted to be sent to old Thomson:

LOW AND LOUSY BEGGARS, REBEL TAILORS, LAWYERS, PIMPS, PARSONS, AND COBBLERS:—Since by your machinations you have led us into difficulty with our just and gracious King George the Third, and now have left us at the mercy of a worse than lord protector, we humbly *veouw* we will see you all to the devil before we'll continue our allegiance to you or your pious Connecticutian tricks, either by love, labor, or lying; for which last we are in constant expectation of a judgment. And we further advise and declare, that if you don't "disband, and at once return to the peaceful employments" discerning nature hath pointed out for you, (you, W., to your ink and horn book; you, A., to your cheating; you, H., to your goose, and you, D., to your wax,) you must expect to receive unseasonable things at unseasonable hours.

We have been misled by the knaves among you, bewrayed by the dirtiest of you, and soporated by the stupidity of all of you, until we know not where to go, are unclean, and are become mere tools in your hands, and without the least spark of the ancient freedom of Britons. Therefore, beware!

Get home! Get out of debt, and make your wives happy, and leave the affairs of kingdoms to those your God has placed over you.

Smythe's Journal, 61

JUNE

June 2

NEW JERSEY   The American republicans, like the rebels of all ages, from their *justice, peaceloving, and mercy,* pretend to have the especial favors of God, and none of the devil's, on their side, and for this reason we rarely see a proclamation from the rebel camp, without a pious sentence bringing up the rear. The late orders given by the head rebel at Morristown, in the Jerseys, a copy of which is printed in all the rebel prints, is a greater illustration of this Yankee piety than any yet come out. In it Mr. Washington forbids card playing under the penalty of a court-martial, ostensibly for the reason that it is wicked and brings a disgrace on the officers, but in reality to enlist the parsons and other old women stronger in the cause of rebellion.

Old De Heister used to say, "Isht dakes de veek to fool der Deutsche, isht dakes de day to fool de Anglees, isht dakes der tyfel to fool de rebel, but *all* together couldn't fool de Lord." So it is with Mr. Washington:—However easily he may bait old Witherspoon, Billy Livingston, Jacky Jay, and some of the other pious ones, who are hanging on the rear of his *moral* forces; when the time comes, he'll find he can't "fool the Lord" with pretended piety or Presbyterian general orders.

Carver, 113

The following are the orders referred to:

HEAD-QUARTERS, MORRISTOWN, [N.J.], May 8, 1777.

GENERAL ORDERS:—As few vices are attended with more pernicious consequences in civil life, so there are none more fatal in a military one than that of gaming, which often brings disgrace and ruin upon officers, and injury and punishment upon the soldiery. And reports prevailing, which it is to be feared are too well founded, that this destructive vice has spread its baneful influence in the army, and in a peculiar manner, to the prejudice of the recruiting service, the Commander-in-chief, in the most pointed and explicit terms, forbids all officers and soldiers playing at cards, dice, or at any games, except those of exercise or diversion, it being impossible, if the practice be allowed at all, to discriminate between innocent play for amusement and criminal gaming for pecuniary and sordid purposes.

Pennsylvania Evening Post, May 13

June 30

NEW JERSEY   On Sunday morning, the 22d, the British left Brunswick, in Jersey, apparently with an intention to embark; they gave out that they were going to Philadelphia by water, but their real design was to draw General Washington from the mountains above Quibbletown, and force a general engagement. Their policy, however, was not an overmatch for our prudence. Light parties harassed him, but not in such numbers as to produce any considerable action. Great part of our army, however, had left the mountains, and General Lord Stirling was posted at the short hills with about one thousand men.

On Thursday morning, General Howe having reinforced his army with all the marines that could be spared, began his march towards the American camp. By accounts of deserters and others, his numbers were from twelve to fourteen thousand. He met with Lord Stirling's party early in the morning; a smart engagement ensued, and the Americans stood their ground manfully for a considerable time; but the amazing superiority of numbers obliged them to retreat; and, the enemy having flanked them, they lost two pieces of cannon with a number of men. No return having yet been made, the exact number of killed, &c., cannot be ascertained. The British continued near the place of engagement that day, and are now at Westfield. The Americans are encamped in the old spot, only large bodies are posted at all the passes, and in some advantageous places below the mountains. It is suspected that the enemy would force our camp if possible; but to attack us in the mountains is a thing devoutly to be wished for by every one that desires to see the destruction of the British army.

We must not omit to mention a little affair that happened in the engagement. The fire growing hot, and our men beginning to retreat, a British officer singly rode up to a cannon that was playing on the enemy, and with his pistols and hanger forced every man from it; then seeing Lord Stirling, he cried, "Come here, you damned rebel; and I will do for you." Lord Stirling answered him by directing the fire of four marksmen upon him, which presently silenced the hardy fool by killing him on the spot. Our men recovered the field-piece, which their want of small arms obliged them to abandon.

Pennsylvania Journal, July 2

JULY

July 1

NEW YORK   The movements of the American army in the north, since the commencement of the war, have been, with one or two exceptions, but a series of disgraceful defeats, or more disgraceful retreats. The only satisfaction those who have been taken have enjoyed, is the kind treatment of General Carleton, who has lately been deprived of his commission for his *kindness* to rebels; while the reward of those of us who have managed to escape, has been the hardest of poor fare, and a continual suffering, the usual attendant upon bad generalship and still worse internal mismanagement. * * * * We are now at Ticonderoga, and to-day General Burgoyne, whose army has been hovering around us and in sight for the few days past, has put forth a pompous proclamation, which is probably intended to frighten us into desertion or a surrender.

Letter from John Hawk to his wife
Ticonderoga, July 1

It is as follows:

By John Burgoyne, Esq., Lieutenant-General of his Majesty's armies in America, Colonel of the Queen's regiment of light dragoons, Governor of Fort William, in North Britain, one of the Representatives of the Commons of Great Britain in Parliament, and commanding an army and fleet employed on an expedition from Canada, &c., &c., &c.

The forces entrusted to my command are designed to act in concert, and upon a common principle, with the numerous armies and fleets which already display in every quarter of America, the power, the justice, and, when properly sought, the mercy of the King.

The cause in which the British arms are thus exerted, applies to the most affecting interests of the human heart; and the military servants of the crown, at first called forth for the sole purpose of restoring the rights of the constitution, now combine with love of their country, and duty to their sovereign, the other extensive incitements which spring from a due sense of the general privileges of mankind. To the eyes and ears of the temperate part of the public, and to the breasts of suffering thousands in the provinces, be the melancholy appeal, whether the present unnatural rebellion has not been made a foundation for the completest system of tyranny that ever God, in his displeasure, suffered for a time to be exercised over a froward and stubborn generation.

Arbitrary imprisonment, confiscation of property, persecution and torture, unprecedented in the inquisitions of the Romish church, are among the palpable enormities that verify the affirmative. These are inflicted by assemblies and committees, who dare to profess themselves friends to liberty, upon the most quiet subjects, without distinction of age or sex, for the sole crime, often for the sole suspicion, of having adhered in principle to the government under which they were born, and to which, by every tie, divine and human, they owe allegiance. To consummate these shocking proceedings, the profanation of religion is added to the most profligate prostitution of common reason; the consciences of men are set at naught; and multitudes are compelled not only to bear arms, but also to swear subjection to an usurpation they abhor.

Animated by these considerations; at the head of troops in the full powers of health, discipline, and valor; determined to strike where necessary, and anxious to spare where possible, I, by these presents, invite and exhort all persons, in all places where the progress of this army may point, and by the blessing of God I will extend it far, to maintain such a conduct as may justify me in protecting their lands, habitations, and families.

The intention of this address is to hold forth security, not depredation to the country. To those whom spirit and principle may induce to partake of the glorious task of redeeming their countrymen from dungeons, and re-establishing the blessings of legal government, I offer encouragement and employment; and upon the first intelligence of their associations, I will find means to assist their undertakings. The domestic, the industrious, the infirm, and even the timid inhabitants, I am desirous to protect, provided they remain quietly at their houses; that they do not suffer their cattle to be removed, nor their corn or forage to be secreted or destroyed; that they do not break up their bridges or roads; nor by any other act, directly or indirectly, endeavor to obstruct the operations of the King's troops, or supply or assist those of the enemy. Every species of provision brought to my camp, will be paid for at an equitable rate, and in solid coin.

In consciousness of Christianity, my royal master's clemency, and the honor of soldiership, I have dwelt upon this invitation, and wished for more persuasive terms to give it impression; and let not people be led to disregard it, by considering their distance from the immediate situation of my camp. I have but to give stretch to the Indian forces under my direction, and they amount to thousands, to overtake the hardened enemies of Great Britain and America; I consider them the same wherever they may lurk.

If, notwithstanding these endeavors, and sincere inclinations to effect them, the frenzy of hostility should remain, I trust I shall stand acquitted in the eyes of God and men in denouncing and executing the vengeance of the State against the wilful outcasts. The messengers of justice and of wrath await them in the field; and devastation, famine, and every concomitant horror that a reluctant but indispensable prosecution of military duty must occasion, will bar the way to their return.

Pennsylvania Evening Post, August 21

July 2

The following answer to Burgoyne's proclamation was written by a young officer, and designed for the soldiers in the American army:

To John Burgoyne, Esquire, Lieutenant-General of his Majesty's armies in America, Colonel of the Queen's regiment of light dragoons, Governor of Fort William in North Britain, one of the Representatives of the Commons of Great Britain, and commanding an army and fleet employed on an expedition from Canada, &c., &c., &c.

MOST HIGH, MOST MIGHTY, MOST PUISSANT, AND SUBLIME GENERAL.

When the forces under your command arrived at Quebec, in order *to act in concert and upon a common principle with the numerous fleets and armies which already display in every quarter of America the justice and mercy of your King,* we, the reptiles of America, were struck with unusual trepidation and astonishment. But what words can express the plenitude of our horror when the *Colonel of the Queen's regiment of light dragoons* advanced towards Ticonderoga. The mountains shook before thee, and the trees of the forest bowed their lofty heads; the vast lakes of the north were chilled at thy presence, and the mighty cataracts stopped their tremendous career, and were suspended in awe at thy approach. Judge, then, *oh ineffable Governor of Fort William in North Britain*, what must have been the terror, dismay, and despair that overspread this paltry continent of America, and us its wretched inhabitants. Dark and dreary, indeed, was the prospect before us, till, like the sun in the horizon, your most gracious, sublime, and irresistible proclamation opened the doors of mercy, and snatched us, as it were, from the jaws of annihilation.

We foolishly thought, blind as we were, that your gracious master's fleets and armies were come to destroy us and our liberties; but we are happy in hearing from you (and who can doubt what you assert?) that they were *called forth for the sole purpose of restoring the rights of the constitution to a froward and stubborn generation.*

And is it for this, oh sublime *lieutenant-general*, that you have given yourself the trouble to cross the wide Atlantic, and with incredible fatigue traverse uncultivated wilds? And we ungratefully refuse the proffered blessing? To restore the rights of the constitution you have called together an amiable host of savages, and turned them loose to scalp our women and children, and lay our country waste—this they have performed with their usual skill and clemency, and we yet remain insensible of the benefit, and unthankful for so much goodness!

Our Congress have declared Independence, and our Assemblies, as your highness justly observes, have most *wickedly* imprisoned the avowed friends of that power with which they are at war, and most PROFANELY compelled those, whose consciences will not permit them to fight, to pay some small part towards the expenses their country is at in supporting what we call a necessary defensive war. If we go on thus in our obstinacy and ingratitude, what can we expect but that you should, in your anger, *give a stretch to the Indian forces under your direction, amounting to thousands, to overtake and destroy us;* or which is ten times worse, that you should withdraw your fleets and armies and leave us to our own misery, without completing the benevolent task you have begun, *in restoring to us the rights of the constitution.*

We submit, we submit, *most puissant Colonel of the Queen's regiment of light dragoons, and Governor of Fort William in North Britain!* We offer our heads to the scalping knife and our bellies to the bayonet. Who can resist the force of your eloquence? Who can withstand the terror of your arms? The invitation you have made in the *consciousness of Christianity, your royal master's clemency, and the honor of soldiership,* we thankfully accept. The blood of the slain, the cries of injured virgins and innocent children, and the never-ceasing sighs and groans of starving wretches now languishing in the jails and prison ships of New York, call on us in vain, whilst your sublime proclamation is sounded in our ears. Forgive us, oh our country! Forgive us, dear posterity! Forgive us, all ye foreign powers who are anxiously watching our conduct in this important struggle, if we yield implicitly to the persuasive tongue of the most elegant *Colonel of her Majesty's regiment of light dragoons.*

Forbear then, thou magnanimous *lieutenant-general!* Forbear to denounce vengeance against us! Forbear to *give a stretch to those restorers of constitutional rights, the Indian forces under your direction.*—Let not *the messengers of wrath await us in the field, and devastation, famine, and every concomitant horror,* bar our return to the allegiance of a prince, who, by his royal will, would deprive us of every blessing of life, with all possible clemency.

We are domestic, we are *industrious,* we are *infirm and timid;* we shall *remain quietly at home, and not remove our cattle, or corn, or forage,* in hopes that you will come at *the head of troops in the full powers of health, discipline, and valor,* and take charge of them for yourselves. Behold our wives and daughters, our flocks and herds, our goods and chattels.—Are they not at the mercy of our Lord the King, and of his *lieutenant-general, member of the House of Commons, and governor of Fort William in North Britain?*

July 4

MASSACHUSETTS   This day, being the Anniversary of American Independence, when the thirteen United States publicly and gloriously threw off the shackles forged by George the Third, the British tyrant, and nobly reassumed those rights which God and nature bestowed on man, the same has been noticed by every mark of joy. In the forenoon, the Reverend Mr. Gordon, of Roxbury, at the desire of the assembly sitting at Boston, preached an excellent discourse from 1 Kings xii. 15. After which the General Court having given previous orders for making every preparation for drinking success to the thirteen United States, sent an invitation to General Heath, and the officers of the Continental army and navy; Colonel Crafts and the officers of the train; Colonel Hichborn, of the independent company; Colonel Hatch, the officers of the militia, and many other gentlemen. While the Congress, and other toasts were drank, the guns at Fort Hill, Castle Island, Hull, and the vessels of war in the harbor, fired a grand salute. Also a detachment of Colonel Crafts' regiment of artillery in Congress street, gave thirteen discharges from brass cannon and with powder, both manufactured in the State of Massachusetts. The independent company and the militia, in conjunction with the train of artillery, made a very martial appearance, manoeuvred and performed their firings in view of the General Court, to their full acceptance, and the approbation of the spectators at large.

In the evening Colonel Crafts illuminated his park on the common, threw several shells, and exhibited a number of fireworks. The cheerful appearance of the gentlemen and ladies in the park, and the pleasantness of the eve, closed with universal satisfaction the joys of the day, which so conspicuously appeared in the countenances of every true friend of America.

Pennsylvania Evening Post, July 24

July 5

PENNSYLVANIA   Yesterday, being the first anniversary of the Independence of the United States of America, was celebrated in Philadelphia with demonstrations of joy and festivity. About noon all the armed ships and galleys in the river were drawn up before the city, dressed in the gayest manner, with the colors of the United States and streamers displayed. At one o'clock, the yards being properly manned, they began the celebration of the day by a discharge of thirteen cannon from each of the ships, and one from each of the thirteen galleys, in honor of the thirteen United States.

In the afternoon an elegant dinner was provided for Congress, to which were invited the President and the supreme executive council, and speaker of the assembly of the State, the general officers and colonels of the army, and strangers of eminence, and the members of the several continental boards in town. The Hessian band of music, taken in Trenton the twenty-sixth of December last, attended and heightened the festivity with some fine performances suited to the joyous occasion; while a corps of British deserters, taken into the service of the continent by the State of Georgia, being drawn up before the door, filled up the intervals with *feu de joie*. After dinner a number of toasts were drank, all breathing Independence, and a generous love of liberty, and commemorating the memories of those brave and worthy patriots who gallantly exposed their lives, and fell gloriously in defence of freedom and the righteous cause of their country.

Each toast was followed by a discharge of artillery and small arms, and a suitable piece of music by the Hessian band. The glorious fourth of July was reiterated three times, accompanied with triple discharges of cannon and small arms, and loud huzzas that resounded from street to street through the city. Towards evening several troops of horse, a corps of artillery, and a brigade of North Carolina forces, which was in town on its way to join the grand army, were drawn up in Second street, and reviewed by Congress and the general officers. The evening was closed with the ringing of bells, and at night there was a grand exhibition of fire-works (which began and concluded with thirteen rockets) on the commons, and the city was beautifully illuminated. Every thing was conducted with the greatest order and decorum, and the face of joy and gladness was universal.

Thus may the fourth of July, that glorious and ever memorable day, be celebrated through America by the sons of freedom, from age to age, till time shall be no more. Amen and amen.

Pennsylvania Journal, July 9

July 7

SOUTH CAROLINA   Friday last being the first anniversary of the glorious formation of the American empire, when thirteen colonies, driven by necessity, threw off the yoke and rejected the tyranny of Great Britain by declaring themselves free, independent, and sovereign States, the same was commemorated by every demonstration of joy. Ringing of bells ushered in the day. At sunrise, American colors were displayed from all the forts and batteries, and vessels in the harbor. The Charleston regiment of militia, commanded by the Honorable Colonel Charles Pinckney, and the Charleston artillery company, commanded by Captain Thomas Grimball, were assembled upon the parade, and reviewed by His Excellency the President, who was attended upon this occasion by his honor the Vice-President and the honorable members of the privy council. At one o'clock the several forts, beginning with Fort Moultrie, on Sullivan's Island, discharged seventy-six pieces of cannon, alluding to the glorious year 1776, and the militia and artillery fired three general volleys. His Excellency the President then gave a most elegant entertainment in the council chamber, at which were present all the members of the Legislature then in town, all the public officers, civil and military, the clergy, and many strangers of note, to the amount of more than double the number that ever observed the birthday of the present misguided and unfortunate King of Great Britain.

Pennsylvania Journal, July 30

July 9

RHODE ISLAND   This night, General Prescott, who has held the command of the British forces on Rhode Island, since the departure of Earl Percy, was taken prisoner at his quarters, and carried off by a party of Americans. The following particular account of the manner of his taking, is by a gentleman from Rhode Island:—Lieutenant-Colonel Barton, of Warren, in Rhode Island, is a young gentleman of about twenty-three or twenty-four years of age, of a martial and enterprising disposition, who has signalized himself on several occasions, particularly in attacking and driving the noted pirate, Wallace, and a party of his men, from an island near Newport, which they had been robbing and plundering; and in an expedition last fall, to Long Island, attacking a number of Tories, and bringing them prisoners to New Haven. He was then a captain, having refused a higher post till he had done more to deserve it; and in the body of forces lately raised by the State of Rhode Island for fifteen months, was appointed lieutenant-colonel in Colonel Stanton's regiment, stationed at Howland's ferry, on the west side of the river.

Here Colonel Barton happening to see a deserter from the British army in Newport, who gave him a particular account of the place where General Prescott kept his head-quarters, formed a scheme to surprise and bring him off. It being communicated to and approved of by the commanding officer, Colonel Barton selected and engaged about forty men to go with him on a secret expedition by water in five batteaux. When they were prepared and got to the shore he told them his design, acknowledged it was hazardous, and probably could not be executed without the loss of life to some of those engaged in it; that for his part he was determined to risk his, which would be at least as much exposed as any of theirs; but if any of them were unwilling to engage in the enterprise, they were then at full liberty to decline it, and he should not have the worse opinion of any person for so doing; that he desired no man with him who did not go willingly, and would freely hazard his life to render his country an important service, and obtain honor to himself. On putting the matter to their choice, they unanimously resolved to go with him.

They then set off with muffled oars, crossed the bay, passed Bristol Ferry, where the British have a fort, undiscovered, and went to Warwick Neck on Providence side, near the east side of the island, where the British have several forts but no ships, as they would be exposed to the guns in our forts. They passed the enemy's redoubts on the east side, and when they came to the west, which is guarded all along by the enemy's ships-of-war, they passed between them and the shore till they came opposite to the house where General Prescott kept his head-quarters. Here they landed, about five miles from Newport, and three-quarters of a mile from the house, which they approached cautiously, avoiding the main guard, which was at some distance. The colonel went foremost, with a stout, active Negro close behind him, and another at a small distance; the rest followed so as to be near, but not seen.

A single sentinel at the door saw and hailed the colonel; he answered by exclaiming against and inquiring for rebel prisoners, but kept slowly advancing. The sentinel again challenged him, and required the countersign; he said he had not the countersign, but amused the sentry by talking about rebel prisoners, and still advancing till he came within reach of the bayonet, which, he presenting, the colonel suddenly struck aside and seized him. He was immediately secured and ordered to be silent, on pain of instant death. Meanwhile, the rest of the men surrounding the house, the Negro, with his head, at the second stroke forced a passage into it, and then into the landlord's apartment. The landlord at first refused to give the necessary intelligence; but on the prospect of present death he pointed to the general's chamber, which being instantly opened by the Negro's head, the colonel calling the general by name, told him he was a prisoner. He replied he knew it, and rising from his bed, desired time to put on his clothes. The colonel told him to put on his breeches, and the rest of his clothes should be carried with him, at the same time handing his slippers from the bedside. Meanwhile the general's aide-de-camp got out of the window in his shirt, but was there secured by some of the party, who all went off by the same way they came, carrying with them the general, his aide-de-camp, and the sentinel.

The general was desired to run, but he said he was an old man and could not. He was told that they would help him, and accordingly a stout man taking him under the arm on each side, enabled him to run. As they went through a field of barley, the stalks very much annoying the general's naked legs, he exclaimed, "Gentlemen, do you mean to kill me?" One of them replied, "No, we do not intend to kill you, but to exchange you for General Lee, and after that we do not care how soon the devil has you."

They all embarked in their boats, and rowing back the same way they came, passed all the enemy's ships and forts undiscovered. When they passed the last fort, the general exclaimed, "And is it possible that I am a prisoner of war! Yes, I see I am; but when you set out with me, I had no doubt but that I should have been rescued, and you all have been made prisoners."

When the boats had got almost to Warwick Neck, a sky rocket was sent off, and immediately alarm guns were fired from all the ships and forts on and about the island, and there appeared to be such a general confusion and consternation, that it was thought one thousand men could have taken them all prisoners. From Warwick Neck a flag was sent for the general's clothes.

Thus was this general officer, in the midst of the British army and navy, where he was commander-in-chief, made prisoner, together with his aide-de-camp and the sentinel that guarded his door, by the bravery and judicious conduct of this young colonel and his gallant followers, without the loss of a man, or the fire of a gun, though they did not expect to have accomplished their design without resistance and a pursuit from the enemy, for both of which they were prepared. In the planning and execution of this enterprise, Colonel Barton has given a noble proof of his zeal and ability to render the most important services to his country. In comparison to this action, how contemptible was that of Colonel Harcourt, for which the King, his master, was in raptures, and lavished upon him such extravagant encomiums,—his surprisal, with a large force, of General Lee, unguarded, several miles distant from his army, and betrayed by an ungrateful wretch, on whom he had just before been conferring great and unmerited favors.

Pennsylvania Evening Post, August 7

July 17

NEW YORK   By an express from the northward we learn that the American forces, under the command of General St. Clair, abandoned Fort Ticonderoga and the adjoining lines, on the morning of the 6th instant, and are now encamped in the vicinity of Moses Creek. A letter from an officer at that place, written this day, gives the following account of the retreat and its consequences:—The retreat from Ticonderoga will be a matter of speculation in the country, and the accounts different and confused, a true state of facts will therefore be very satisfactory without doubt.

We were deceived with respect to the strength of the enemy, and our own reinforcements. The enemy have practised a piece of finesse which has too well answered their purpose; they have so conducted that all hands in the United States believed they had drawn their force from Canada to the southward, and designed only to garrison their posts in the northern world; the consequence of this belief has been the ordering eight regiments, destined for Ticonderoga and its environs, to Peekskill, and little attention has been paid to this department. The enemy's condition in Canada has been represented as miserable, confused, scattered and sickly; this has been the general opinion in camp and country, and our situation has been thought perfectly safe.

Our force consisted of about four thousand, including the corps of artillery, and artificers who were not armed, a considerable part of which were militia; we could bring about three thousand fit for duty into the field. General Burgoyne came against us with about eight thousand healthy, spirited troops, with a lake force consisting of three fifty-gun ships, a thunder mounting eighteen brass twenty-four pounders, two thirteen-inch mortars, a number of howitz, several sloops, gun-boats, &c., &c.

Their strength being so very superior to ours obliged us to tamely sit still and see them erect batteries all around us, without hazarding a sally. Two batteries were erected in front of our lines, on higher ground than ours; within half a mile on our left they had taken post on a very high hill overlooking all our works; our right would have been commanded by their shipping and the batteries they had erected on the other side of the lake. Our lines at Ticonderoga would have been of no service, and we must have inevitably abandoned them in a few days after their batteries opened, which would have been the next morning; we then should have been necessitated to retire to Fort Independence, the consequence of which, I conceive, would have been much worse than the mode adopted; for the moment we had left Ticonderoga fort, they could send their shipping by us, and prevent our communication with Skenesborough; then the only avenue to and from Fort Independence would have been by a narrow neck of land leading from the mount to the Grants. To this neck they had almost cut a road; a day more would have completed it. A few troops stationed at Ticonderoga, would have prevented our communication with Lake George, as our own works would have been against us. Their shipping would have destroyed our connection with Skenesborough, and their main body might have been placed on this neck of land, which, by a few works, might have prevented all supplies and reinforcements; we might have stayed at the mount as long as our provisions would have supported us; we had flour for thirty days, and meat sufficient only for a week. Under these circumstances General St. Clair, on the sixth instant, called a council of war, and an evacuation was unanimously agreed upon as the only means of saving the army from captivity.

It was necessary also that our retreat should be precipitate, as the communication was almost cut off, and they would soon be apprised of our designs. It was therefore determined to send the baggage and sick in boats to Skenesborough, and for the army to march by land from the mount to that place, being forty miles. At the dawn of day we left Fort Independence, and I cannot say the march was conducted with the greatest regularity; the front, which was the main body, marched thirty miles to a place called Castleton, about twelve miles from Skenesborough; the militia halted three miles in the rear of the front, and the rear guard, commanded by Colonel Francis, being joined by Colonels Warner and Hale, halted at Hubbardton, about a mile and a half in the rear of the militia. As the march was severe, the feeble of the army had fallen in the rear, and tarried at Hubbardton with the rear guard. This body in rear might consist of near a thousand men. Before I proceed further it may be necessary to give you the enemy's dispositions after they were advised of our retreat: A large body, at least two thousand, were detached to pursue our main body and harass our rear; all the gun boats and some of their shipping were sent after our baggage, came up with it at Skenesborough and took it. The ninth regiment, commanded by Lieutenant-Colonel Hills, was ordered to run down South Bay, and land and march on a by road to Fort Ann, and take that before our troops could reach it; the remainder of the army went on to Skenesborough, except a garrison at Ticonderoga.

The body of the enemy sent to harass our rear, came up with it the next morning at Hubbardton, which was then commanded by Colonel Warner; by the exertions of the officers our little army formed and gave them battle, which continued about twenty-five minutes very severe, when our party were overpowered with numbers and gave way. The loss on both sides was considerable; as our people took to the woods and are daily coming in, it is impossible to ascertain our loss. Colonel Francis, a worthy, brave officer, after signalizing himself, was shot through, and expired instantly; Colonel Hale is missing. It is natural to ask why was not Colonel Warner reinforced? Let me tell you; orders were sent to Colonel ———, who commanded the militia, to go to the assistance of the rear guard, but before they arrived, the action was over and our people dispersed. Our main body being now twelve miles from Skenesborough, and hearing that a large body of the enemy were arrived there, and knowing that a large body were in our rear, the general imagined if we pursued our route, that we must engage both in front and rear under great disadvantage; and to pursue his plan in first retreating, which was to save the army, he thought prudent to file off to the left, and before we reached Hudson River, we marched one hundred and fifty miles; in this march we picked up about thirty prisoners, part British, part Waldeckers, and part Canadians. The party of our men who were at Skenesborough, retreated to Fort Ann; they were twice attacked by the ninth regiment, and both times repulsed them. They took a Captain Montgomery and a doctor, and would probably have taken the whole regiment had their ammunition held out. This is a candid statement of facts, and for this conduct we are told our country calls us either knaves or cowards; I conceive they ought to be grateful to our general, for had we stayed we very certainly should have been taken, and then no troops could have stood between the enemy and the country. Our affairs now are not desperate in this quarter, as they would certainly have been; we have destroyed Fort George and its appendages, and shall soon be able, I hope, to make head against our enemies, as we are gathering strength and re-collecting ourselves.

Pennsylvania Evening Post, August 9

July 27

NEW YORK   General Burgoyne is at Fort Edward, and has with him about six thousand Regulars, three or four hundred Indians, and about two hundred Canadians. The frequent injuries and horrible actions committed by his scouting parties on single unarmed men and defenceless women, are sufficient to give every man a thorough detestation of their whole conduct; and were not the Tories' hearts made of more than iron hardness, it would inspire them with a desire of ridding this world of such a set of villains as their army is in general composed of. Several of our officers and soldiers have been inhumanly shot as they passed from one fort to another unarmed, and scalped while yet alive. It would take too much time to enumerate every action of this kind. One instance which happened yesterday, during a skirmish, may serve for the whole. A young lady, by the name of Miss Jenny M'Crea, of a good family, and some share of beauty, was, by some accident, at Fort Edward when the enemy attacked the picket guard. She and an old woman were taken by the savages, who generally serve as an advance guard or flanking parties to the Regulars, (the latter of whom were drawn up on a hill just above the fort,) and then, with a barbarity unheard of before, they butchered the poor innocent girl, and scalped her in the sight of those very men who are continually preaching up their tender mercies, and the forbearance of their more than Christian King. Is not this sufficient to congeal the heart of humanity with horror, and even oblige a Tory of liberal sentiments to curse the cause which approves or winks at such worse than hell-like cruelties?

The unfortunate maid's corpse was brought to Snook Hill last night, together with a young lieutenant, a Mr. Van Rachter, of Brunswick, who is also scalped, and will be interred to-day. What renders this affair more remarkable is, that Miss M'Crea has a brother an officer in the British service, now at New York, and she herself leaned to that side of the question; but thus they treat their friends as well as their enemies. The young lady has also a brother a senior surgeon in our hospital, a worthy, sensible young fellow, who will not forget the injury, but revenge it tenfold.

Pennsylvania Evening Post, August 12

Polly Wand

At the opening of the Revolutionary War the majority of ballads being sung by Americans were of British origin and composition. These furnished both melodies and models for the new, native American ballads of the revolutionary era; and, of course, people continued to sing the traditional songs during the struggle as well as the new ones currently being produced. "Polly Wand" is an

*excellent example of an imported British broadside ballad, and a
particular favorite of Americans during the Revolution. Variants of
this song have been found in all parts of the United States as well
as in England, Scotland, and Ireland. The melody and the refrain
given here, have been transcribed from the singing of Paul Clayton.
The lyric is from oral tradition, but differs only in minor details from
the broadside version issued by Nathaniel Coverly, Jr. of Boston
shortly after 1800. (Ford, Isaiah Thomas, 211.)*

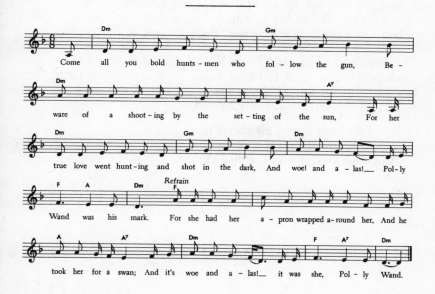

As Polly was walking by the setting of the sun,
She stepped under a green branch the shower to shun;
Her true love was a-hunting, and he shot in the dark,
Alas, and alas! Polly Wand was his mark.

For she had her apron wrapped around her,
    And he took her for a swan;
It's woe and alas! it was she, Polly Wand.

And when he ran to her and found that it was she,
His legs grew weak, and his eyes scarce could see,
He took her in his arms, and he found that she was dead,
And a thousand thousand tears for his own true love he shed.

For you had your apron wrapped about you,
   And I took you for a swan,
But woe and alas! it was you, Polly Wand.

He ran straight home with his gun in his hand,
Saying father, dearest father, I have shot Polly Wand;
I've shot that fair lady in the bloom of her life,
And I always intended to make her my wife.

But she had her apron wrapped around her,
   And I took her for a swan,
But woe and alas! it was she, Polly Wand.

At the height of his trial Polly Wand did appear,
Crying father, dearest father, Jemmy Rander must be clear,
For I had my apron all about me, and he took me for a swan,
Woe and alas! it was I, Polly Wand.

Yes, I had my apron all about me,
   And he took me for a swan,
Woe and alas! it was I, Polly Wand.

———•———

AUGUST

August 17

VERMONT   Yesterday is to be remembered on account
of a signal victory the militia, under the command of General
Stark, obtained over a body of the King's troops, commanded
by Colonel Baum, some account of which is here given by
one who was himself in the action.

It seems that General Burgoyne had detached this corps, consisting of about fifteen hundred men, chiefly Waldeckers and
Brunswickers intermixed with some British troops and Tories, a
motley compound, to penetrate as far as Bennington, and further if it should be found practicable, with a view to increase
the number of his friends, to disperse his protections in the

country, to procure for his army provisions, and to wreak his wrath and vengeance on those who had disregarded his calls of mercy, and slighted with indignity his proffered protection. Colonel Baum had advantageously posted his corps within about five miles of Bennington meeting-house, where in different places they made breastworks for their own security. This digression was of such ill tendency, and savored so much of presumption, that General Stark, who was at that time providentially at Bennington, with his brigade of militia from New Hampshire State, determined to give him battle. Colonel Simond's regiment of militia in Berks County was invited to his assistance; and a part of Colonel Brown's arrived seasonably to attend on the action, and some volunteers from different towns, and Colonel Warner, with a part of his own regiment, joined him the same day.

The general, it seems, wisely laid his plan of operation, and Divine Providence blessing us with good weather, between three and four o'clock P.M. he attacked them in front and flank in three or four different places, at the same instant, with irresistible impetuosity. The action was extremely hot for between one and two hours; the flanking parties had carried their points with great ease, when the front pressed on to their breastwork with an ardor and patience beyond expectation. The blaze of the guns of the contending parties reached each other, the fire was so extremely hot, and our men easily surmounting their breastworks, amidst peals of thunder and flashes of lightning from their guns, without regarding the roar of their field-pieces, that the enemy at once deserted their covers and ran; and in about five minutes their whole camp was in the utmost confusion and disorder, all their battalions were broken in pieces, and fled most precipitately; at which instant our whole army pressed after with redoubled ardor, pursued them for a mile, made considerable slaughter amongst them, and took many prisoners. One field-piece had already fallen in our hands.

At this time our men stopped the pursuit, to gain breath, when the enemy being reinforced, our front fell back for a few rods for conveniency of ground, and being directed and collected by Colonel Rensselaer, and reinforced by Major Stanton, renewed the fight with redoubled ardor. They fell in upon the enemy with great impetuosity, put them to confusion and flight, and pursued them about a mile, making many prisoners. Two or three more brass field-pieces fell into our hands, which are supposed to be the whole of what they brought out with them. At this time darkness came upon us, and prevented our swallowing up the whole of this body. The enemy fled precipitately the succeeding night towards the North River, and, unless they should be met with by a party of our army there, may have reached there without any further molestation. Governor Skeene, in surprise and consternation, took horse and fled.

This action, which redounds so much to the glory of the Great Lord of the heavens, and God of armies, affords the Americans a lasting monument of the Divine power and goodness, and a most powerful argument of love to and trust in God. Our loss is about forty or fifty killed, and more wounded. The enemy's loss is greater, and many more wounded. Their baggage fell into our hands. The number of prisoners taken is said to be about six hundred. Two of their colonels were amongst the prisoners and mortally wounded. A number of inferior officers have also fallen into our hands, and in particular the general's aide-de-camp. A good number deserted and joined us. This victory is thought by some to equal any that has happened during the present controversy; and, as long as prudence, moderation, sobriety and valor, are of any estimation amongst the United States, will not fail to endear General Stark to them. It is the opinion of some, if a large body of militia was now called to act in conjunction with the northern army, the enemy might be entirely overthrown. May all be concerned to give God the glory, whilst we commend the good conduct of the officers and soldiers in general on so important an occasion.

There is adjoining Pittsfield, in Massachusetts, a place called Jericho. From this place forty men marched, under Colonel Brown, for Bennington; on their way eighteen of them deserted and went over to the enemy. After the battle, fifteen of the eighteen were found dead upon the field. The remaining twenty-two were in the action, signalized themselves by their bravery, and came off unhurt. May all villains and traitors meet a similar fate to that of the fifteen.

Account by "a gentleman who was present in the action"
Pennsylvania Evening Post, September 4

August 26

Exclusive of the *natural* character by which mankind are distinguished from each other, there is, in most men, a *secondary* or *artificial* character, through which they present all their actions to the world. I call it artificial, because it is neither produced nor supported by any principle, and is no more than the fashion under which the actors suppose they appear to the most advantage.

This taste is formed very early in life, and frequently by accident either of company or education. Some men are pedantic, and with them every phrase must be technical; others are foppish, and *their* descriptions are always intended to be light and novel; but Burgoyne's turn, or artificial character, is that of a mountebank, in which every thing must be *wonderful*. In this proclamation, which has already been in most of the papers, he has handed himself out under as many titles as a High German doctor, and given as wonderful a detail of enterprises as is to be found in Waltho Van Clutterbank's harangue.

The same pompous complication opens his instructions to Lieutentant-Colonel Baum. "The object (says he) of your expedition is to try the affections of the country, to disconcert the councils of the enemy, mount Reidesel's dragoons, to complete Peter's corps, and—to obtain large supplies of cattle, horses, and carriages."

From this catalogue of orders we may infer, that the instant Burgoyne got into the country, he was at loss how to go *on*, and perhaps by this time he is at as great a loss how to get *out*; that his dragoons were on foot, his army incomplete, and unfurnished with horses and carriages: but the grand secret, and that which engrosses his first thought, and occupies his first line, is "*to try the affections of the country.*" A mountebank may sometimes hit upon the right disease, and

Burgoyne has here given a proof of it; for unless America turns a traitor to herself, *his* efforts will be in vain. The second article in the orders is very judiciously placed, viz., *to endeavor to disconcert our councils;* very happily thrown in! Because it shows us the necessity of attending firmly to business, and the danger of employing our ingenuity to evade or perplex it.

After this introduction of general heads, he lays down the route, the manner of conducting it, with directions for the treatment of the inhabitants. *"All possible care* (says he) *is to be used to prevent plundering."* This seems a very extraordinary order to be given to a plundering party, but is perfectly consistent when we understand that plundering a *country* for *stores* or *supplies* is the general's perquisite, and plundering houses, that of the men. Burgoyne's orders are to bring in *one thousand three hundred horses at least, with all the saddles and bridles that can be found, together with all the wagons, carriages, draft oxen, and cattle fit for slaughter;* for these no money was to be paid, but receipts were to be given, and those to such only as had complied with the terms of his manifesto. Had Burgoyne made the sweep of horses, saddles, bridles, cattle, &c., which he was in hopes of, he would at least have pocketed thirty or forty thousand pounds, *by taking those articles from the country without paying for, and charging them to the treasury as if he had purchased them;* the receipts and the pretended distinction of persons serving as a mask to cover the fraud. As this plundering in the wholesale was the business the party was sent upon, no wonder they were forbidden to spend their time in dividing themselves into parties to rob hen-roosts and cider-cellars, or stealing blankets, breeches, and petticoats.

"As you will," say the instructions, "have *persons with you perfectly acquainted with the abilities of the country,* it may perhaps be advisable to *tax* the several districts with the portions of the several articles, and limit the hours for the delivery; and should you find it necessary to move before such delivery can be made, *hostages* of the most *respectable* people should be taken to secure their following you the ensuing day."

Eng.d by A.H. Ritchie.

J. Burgoyne

Of all the unjust modes of taxation hitherto proposed by our enemies, this is the most summary and the most pernicious. A stranger to the country is to be informed by strangers to him, of the circumstances of the inhabitants; and upon such information a *tax* is to be imposed, for the immediate payment of which the most *respectable people* are to be seized as hostages and carried into captivity! Take care, Americans, how you admit men who practise such wicked methods of taking your property, and such cruel ways of enforcing your compliance.

"You will," say the instructions, "use all possible means to *make the country believe* that the troops under your command are the advanced corps of the army, and that it is intended to pass Connecticut on the road to Boston. You will likewise *insinuate* that the main army from Albany is to be joined at Springfield, by a corps of troops from Rhode Island."

No real, lasting good, Sir John Burgoyne, can come of lying, and if no credit is to be given to your declarations, you cannot expect that any will be given to your proclamation, but that the inhabitants, in all places, will look upon the latter and upon all others which either you or General Howe may put out, as farragoes of threats and delusions, to deter or dissuade them from removing their property till you or he may send parties to plunder and fetch it off. This is the true intent and meaning of all your proclamations.

There is something prophetically pensive towards the conclusion of the instructions. "It is highly probable," he says, "that the corps under Mr. Warner, now supposed to be at Manchester, will retreat before you; but should they, contrary to expectation, be able to collect in great force and post themselves advantageously, it is left to your discretion to attack them or not; *always bearing in mind* that your corps is *too valuable* to let any considerable loss be hazarded on this occasion." *Poor unfortunate John Burgoyne!*

The general, in the next paragraph of his instructions, gives a kind of triumph over his qualmish apprehensions, and putting on the soldiers, assures Colonel Baum, that should the rebels attempt to interrupt him, he, General Burgoyne, "will make *such a movement* as shall put the rebels between two fires." A wonderful piece of firework indeed!—and shows that *one real fire* of ours is better than *two of his* contriving; for the event of this double-barrelled scheme has been, that the colonel and his party are defeated, near a thousand of them made prisoners, and, they say, poor General Burgoyne is gone STARK MAD.

Pennsylvania Evening Post, August 28

SEPTEMBER

September 5

General Washington, our great and illustrious commander, the prop and glory of this western world, issued this day at Wilmington, the following orders, which cannot too much be admired on account of the virtuous and noble sentiments they contain:—

GENERAL ORDERS.—From every information of the enemy's design, and from their movements, it is manifest that their aim is, if possible, to possess themselves of Philadelphia. This is with them a capital object; 'tis what they last year strove to effect, but were happily disappointed. They made a second attempt at the opening of this campaign; but after vast preparation and expense for that purpose, they abandoned their design and totally evacuated the Jerseys. They are now making their last effort. It seems they first intended to come up the Delaware, but from the measures taken against them in the river, judged the enterprise that way too hazardous. At length they have landed on the eastern shore of Maryland and advanced some little way into the country, but the general thinks they will again be disappointed in their views, should they push their design against Philadelphia, on this route. Their all is at stake. They will put the contest on the event of a single battle. If they are overthrown they are utterly undone—the war is at an end. Now, then, is the time for our strenuous exertions; one bold stroke will free the land from rapine, devastation, and burnings, and female innocence from brutal lust and violence. In every other quarter the American arms have been of late rapidly successful; great numbers of the enemy have fallen in battle, and still greater numbers have been taken prisoners. The militia to the northward have fought with a resolution that would have done honor to the oldest soldiers—they bravely fought and conquered, and glory attends them. Who can forbear to emulate their noble spirits? Who is there without ambition to share with them the applause of their countrymen and of all posterity, as the defenders of liberty, and preservers of peace and happiness to millions in the present and future generations?

Two years we have maintained the war and struggled with difficulties innumerable, but the prospect has since brightened and our affairs put on a better face. Now is the time to reap the fruits of all our toils and dangers; if we behave like men this third campaign will be our last. Ours is the main army. To *us* our countrymen look for protection; the eyes of all America and Europe are turned upon us, as on those by whom the event of war is to be determined; and the general assures his countrymen and fellow-soldiers, that he believes the critical, the important time is at hand, which demands their most spirited exertions in the field.

Here glory waits to crown the brave. Peace, freedom, and happiness will be the rewards of victory. Animated by motives like these, soldiers fighting in the cause of innocence, humanity, and justice, will never give way, but with undaunted resolution press on to conquest. And this the general assures himself is the part the American forces, now in arms, will act, and thus acting he will insure them success.

Pennsylvania Journal, September 10

September 11

PENNSYLVANIA   We have had a severe time of it to-day. Early in the morning the Commander-in-chief receiving intelligence that the British were advancing in two columns from their camp at Kennet Square, made a proper disposition to receive them. The first attack was made by Knyphausen, on a party of Americans under General Maxwell, who had crossed the Brandywine, and posted himself in an elevated position on both sides of the main road. In this affair the Americans twice repulsed the British, but the latter receiving a strong reinforcement, General Maxwell was obliged to give way and retreat across the river.

About four o'clock in the afternoon the action became general, and continued very severe until dark, when the British stopped the pursuit, and the Americans retired to Chester, where they are now encamped.

Clift's Diary

PENNSYLVANIA   The following account is given in the journal of a British officer:—"At four o'clock in the morning the army moved in two columns; that under General Howe and Lord Cornwallis to the left, and crossing the river Brandy-wine. Some miles above the direct road and Shad's Ford, came on the right flank and rear of the enemy, who were posted there in great strength, having several batteries and many cannon on exceeding strong ground. Whilst this manœuvre was performing, the column under the commands of Generals Knyphausen and Grant, marched by the usual road to Shad's Ford, and attacked several posts the enemy had on the south side of the Brandywine; these being driven across the river, the cannon were drawn up to the most advantageous situations, and a heavy cannonade kept up. As soon as it was perceived that General Howe had attacked the rebels, the troops passed the river, stormed the batteries, and took their cannon. The rout of the enemy then became general. They were pursued as long as daylight and the fatigued condition of the troops would permit, General Howe's column having marched seventeen miles the day before the engagement. We took ten pieces of cannon, a royal howitzer, several ammunition wagons, &c. It was difficult to ascertain the number of the enemy killed, as they were scattered over a great extent of ground."

Pennsylvania Ledger, December 6

September 17

As the rebels have in their newspapers favored the public with General Burgoyne's orders to Lieutenant-Colonel Baum, it might be interpreted maliciously should we refuse to commit to print any pieces of elegance of their commanders which may fall into our hands. For this reason I send you a copy of some orders for the Jersey militia which we picked up in a late excursion. I hope no invidious comparisons will be drawn between this and General Burgoyne's, for though the latter, to give him his due, writes in a pretty style, and plausibly enough as to military matters, his performance falls infinitely short of that energy, that precision, that sublimity which grace the composition of the Jersey Brigadier. The candid public must consider, that probably poor Burgoyne has not had those advantages of education which have refined the sentiments and expressions of the elegant writer of the following orders. I give them in the original spelling. Probably the brigadier strove to adapt his orthography to the genius of his troops:—

"Mendon Sep. 5 1777.

"Sir you are to keep one man allways with an order already writ to Impres any Horss on the way he shall want that upon the first appearance of the enemy's coming to attack you or yours you are to dispatch the man and tell him to come the nighest road direct to me or my house and he is to call to every man woman and child he sees and desire them to call upon all men to push down whare the enemy is and give them battle. But he is not to stop to tell his story but call out as he rides along and tells his story he is to ride six or seven miles an ower if they have no guns or Ammunison they are to carry pitchforks flailes stones or such weapons as they chuse or think best. But if any man is afraid to goo to battle that hath no gun he is immediately to set out as a Common Cryer towards the back country and desire everyone he sees to come down to the help of the Lord against the mighty and I will keep a becon out so that if you with what will turn out nigh by can keep the enemy in play a few howers I will be down with 1000 or 1500 men. Shew this letter to all men you see and send Coppys of it to all the militia officers you can that live within 15 or 20 miles of the Lines and Shores.—This gentlemen I have writ to the commanding officers down at the shore therefore I desire all men old and young as they regard their lives & properties and all that is dear to them when they hear the a Larm that they a quip themselves as well as they can and march immediately towards the enemy whare I will meet them. Let every man as soon as he is ready stop for no company. But call as they see to come along & they are to send word by some of thare family that cant fight to their next neighbor of the a Larm—and cursed is he that is well & will not turn out when this a Larm comes.

WILLIAM WINDS, B. G."

Pennsylvania Ledger, November 19

September 20

NEW YORK   Yesterday, about noon, the two armies met near Stillwater, and a most obstinate and bloody battle ensued. The advanced parties of the Americans, which were composed of Morgan's riflemen and Dearborn's infantry, received the first fire of the enemy, and a little after two o'clock the action became general. The right wing of the British forces was commanded by Burgoyne in person, the left by Phillips and Reidesel, and the centre, covered by Frazer and Breyman, was supported by the savages, Canadians, and renegade Provincials and Tories. Never was more bravery or determination shown. For upwards of three hours the blaze from the artillery and small arms was incessant, and sounded like the roll of the drum. By turns the British and Americans drove each other, taking and retaking the field-pieces, and often mingling in a hand to hand wrestle and fight. Scammell fought like a hero, leading his regiment where the fire was the hottest, and did not leave his post until he was wounded and taken off the field. The British artillery was well served, and worked with sad havoc among our poor fellows, who are the more to be wept, for their gallantry and devotion to their country. The cannon of the British was lost to us only for the want of horses to draw them off. Arnold rushed into the thickest of the fight with his usual recklessness, and at times acted like a madman. I did not see him once, but S. told me this morning that he did not seem inclined to lead alone, but as a prominent object among the enemy showed itself, he would seize the nearest rifle-gun and take deliberate aim.

During the action a party of our men got up into some trees, and as the clouds of smoke opened, poured in upon the enemy single shot. In this manner several of the officers were killed or wounded. One of Brook's regiment says he silenced two fellows with laced coats, and it is said that Burgoyne had a narrow escape.

At sundown the action was less furious, and a little after dark a greater part of the two armies retired from the field. Some of our men did not come off until near midnight. In the midst of so much destruction, it is a wonder how any of them escaped; "but it is in this cause," as old Emerson used to say about the hens that laid every day in the year but Sunday, *"Providence is with 'em."*

Churchill Papers

September 26

PENNSYLVANIA   Last night, the royal army, under the command of his Excellency Sir William Howe, Knight of the Bath, marched from their encampment, near the Swedish ford, in two grand divisions, one by the Falls of Schuylkill, the other by the road to Germantown, and formed their camp at and near those places. This morning a large detachment, under the command of the Right Honorable the Earl Cornwallis, entered Philadelphia, marched through Second street, and after placing the proper guards, encamped to the southward of the town.

The fine appearance of the soldiery, the strictness of their discipline, the politeness of the officers, and the orderly behavior of the whole body, immediately dispelled every apprehension of the inhabitants, kindled joy in the countenances of the well affected, and has given the most convincing refutation of the scandalous falsehoods which evil and designing men have been long spreading to terrify the peaceable and innocent. A perfect tranquillity now prevails in the city; numbers who have been obliged to hide themselves from the former tyranny and to avoid being forced into measures against their conscience, have appeared to share the general satisfaction, and to welcome the dawn of returning liberty.

Rivington's Gazette, November 8

OCTOBER

October 1

It is unnecessary to say a word of the spirit and numbers of the people of America—of their attachment to their liberty—of the extent and nature of their country—of their resources —and the interest all the powers in Europe have in maintaining the independence of the American States, to show the absolute impracticability of Great Britain's ever subduing this country. I should not despair of the final success of the Americans in the present war, if they were at this time expending their last pound of powder, and their last ounce of ball. Desperation would supply the want of every thing. No force can subdue the hearts of these people; and nine-tenths of them, I am sure, are determined in their opposition to the government of Britain. It is inconceivable to see the exertions of these young republican States. They have done wonders. All the force of the monarchy of Britain in the last war with France, did not produce from the whole continent of America, half the exertions which we sometimes see here in a single state; and yet these republics have as yet put forth but a small part of their strength. I expect to see them, before the close of the war, upon a footing with the oldest monarchies in Europe: and if I was not sure that a love of conquest was incompatible with a love of liberty, I should think they would make some of them tremble from their foundations.

Every part of the conduct of Great Britain, and of her

generals and armies, shows the power of this country, and the absolute impossibility of conquering it. Why has the court of Britain meanly solicited all the courts of Europe to withhold aid of all kinds from the Americans? Why has she bought up twenty thousand foreigners to assist in the reduction of America? Why did she send an army of forty thousand men across the ocean for that purpose last year? Why has the King of Britain proclaimed a fast, and called upon the Almighty to enter into an alliance with him, to assist in conquering his rebellious subjects? Surely all this has been done because they dreaded the power and resources of America.

I believe in no war with the powerful monarchy of France did Britain ever negotiate with more expense—stood more for foreign alliances—lie more for internal support—or fast and pray with more seeming devotion than in the present war with America. An uninformed spectator, from a view of these things, would suppose that the only object of Britain in the prosecution of the war, was not to suppress a rebellion in America, but to defend herself from being subjugated by her American colonies.

But the conduct of her generals in America is all of a piece with the conduct of the court. Read their letters to the British ministry. Observe with what caution they land, how slowly they advance and how circumspectly they march through the country. Their modes of attack and defence in all their battles and skirmishes with the Americans from their own accounts of them, show that they are aware of the skill, and fear the courage, of their generals and armies. Their stratagems (of which they boast) confess that they are contending with a regular army, and not with an undisciplined mob. Even their shouts of victory and the high encomiums they publish of the gallant behavior of their officers and soldiers, declare that they fight with a formidable enemy. The inhumanity of their generals, the insolence of their officers, and the rancor of their soldiers towards the Americans, are all testimonies of the strength of this country. They indicate hatred which can only be exercised towards equals or superiors. The exchange of letters and prisoners between the British and American generals, are further acknowledgments on the behalf of the former, of the stability of the power from whence the latter derive their authority. In spite of all the pains the British generals have taken to destroy the credit of the paper money emitted by the Congress, they have given a sanction to its validity by sending it out from New York to support their prisoners among the Americans. The indiscriminate ravages to which the professed royalists or Tories are exposed in common with the republicans or Whigs, show that the British army believe that a great majority of the people of America are opposed to them, and that all professions of attachment to them are hypocritical, and intended only to save property. But the British generals have gone still farther in declaring by their conduct, that the Americans are invincible. They have, in some measure, thrown down their arms as useless in the present controversy, and have attempted to subdue their enemies by the perfidious arts of a court. They have attempted to surprise the Congress into a negotiation, only for the purpose of deceiving them. They have published proclamations for the encouragement of desertions in the army, and defection among the citizens of America. They have hired printers to traduce the Congress and the army; and to complete all, they have made and attempted to circulate large quantities of counterfeit continental money among the Americans; aiming thereby, at one blow, to cut their sinews of war. Their folly in this manœuvre exceeded their villany; for they weekly advertised their money for distribution, in a New York paper.

I am not so sanguine as some of my friends, as to the issue of the present campaign. By I rest satisfied at all times, that the loss of a battle or of a town will detract nothing, finally, from the Americans; and that the acquisition of victories and of territory will serve only to weaken General Howe's army, and to accelerate the period when America shall establish her freedom and independence, upon the permanent foundation of public virtue and military knowledge.

Letter of a French gentleman
New-Jersey Gazette, January 7, 1778

October 4

PENNSYLVANIA   This morning, before daybreak, (the weather being foggy,) the rebels attempted, with all their force, in six columns, to penetrate on the outposts of our army; they began their attack with three of them on the second light infantry and the fortieth regiment at the end of Germantown, where they were so warmly received that they did not make the least impression for the space of two hours; at length being overpowered with numbers, and risking to be surrounded if longer opposition was made, our two battalions thought it expedient to retire. These columns imagining victory was about to declare in their favor, two of them came into the village, while the third filed off obliquely to our left. Colonel Musgrave having judiciously thrown himself with six companies of the fortieth, into a square house of Mr. Chew's, checked one of the two columns that had followed him, while the other pushed into Germantown. The one at the house immediately invested and riddled it with musketry, grape and cannon shot for a full hour, the colonel defending it most gallantly, killing them by dozens from the windows of every face; but, upon the forty-fourth regiment advancing into the village, supported by the seventeenth, and driving all before them as far Mr. Chew's mansion, both these columns retired precipitately, and would have been totally demolished if the fog had not made it hazardous for so small a body to pursue so rapidly, as it might have done had the weather been clear; the other column, that had filed off towards our left, being drove shortly after by the thirty-third, forty-sixth, and sixty-fourth regiments. Two other columns, that had attacked and obliged the pickets of our right to fall back on their respective corps, were, in their turn, defeated, upon the first light infantry, fourth, fifth, fifteenth, thirty-seventh, forty-ninth, and fifty-fifth regiments attacking them; and the Hessian Jagers repulsed and beat back the column which attacked their post. It now began to clear up, and the Commander-in-chief having perceived a large body (that had rallied) forming itself on Chestnut hill, (apparently to retard our pursuit,) his excellency ordered Major-General Gray to advance upon it with the seventeenth, thirty-third, forty-fourth, forty-sixth, and sixty-fourth regiments, directing the other corps to follow as fast as possible to sustain; but the rebels did not think proper to maintain that ground, retiring precipitately upon the approach of this small corps; and although we pursued for nine miles, till three in the afternoon, we were never able to come up with any considerable body. Thus Mr. Washington's army, consisting of upwards of twelve thousand men, was totally dispersed by a few British battalions, and the Hessian Jagers, (the rest of our army having never had an opportunity of engaging,) and would not only have been cut up had the morning been bright, but all their artillery, &c., must unavoidably have fallen into our hands.

New York Gazette and Weekly Mercury, November 10

October 6

NEW YORK   This day the fortresses Clinton and Montgomery, on the North River, in New York, fell into the hands of the British, under the command of Sir Henry Clinton. A gentleman who was in Fort Montgomery when it was taken, gives the following particulars of the event:—On Saturday night, [4th,]we had advice that a large number of ships, brigs, armed vessels, &c., had arrived at Tarrytown, where they had landed a considerable body of men, supposed to be about one thousand, and had advanced towards the plains. Colonel Lutlington being posted there with about five hundred militia, they sent in a flag to him requiring him to lay down his arms and surrender himself and men prisoners of war. Whilst he was parleying with the flag they endeavored to surround him, which he perceiving, ordered his men to retreat. The British then returned to their shipping, and the next morning we had advice of their being under sail, and coming up as far as King's Ferry. In the afternoon they landed a large body of men on the east side of the river to draw our attention that way, but they re-embarked in the night and next morning landed on the west side.

On Sunday night his Excellency Governor Clinton, who

then commanded at Fort Montgomery, sent out a party of one hundred men, under the command of Major Logan, across the Dunderburg, to watch the motions of the enemy. This party returned in the morning, and reported they had seen about forty boats full of men land below the Dunderburg. The governor sent out another small party of about twenty-eight men, under the command of Lieutenant Jackson. On the road that leads to Haverstraw, two or three miles below Fort Clinton, they fell in with a concealed part of the enemy, who ordered them to club their muskets, and surrender themselves prisoners. They made no answer, but fired on the enemy and hastily retreated. They returned the fire and pursued our people half a mile, but they all got back to the fort without losing a man, though within five rods of the enemy before they were discovered. Upon this intelligence one hundred men were immediately sent off, under Colonel Brown, who fell in with the enemy about two o'clock in the afternoon, when a smart engagement ensued, but the enemy being of much superior force, our people were forced to retreat.

At the same time it was thought proper to send some of the artillery, with a field-piece, to occupy an eminence commanding the road that leads to Orange Furnace, with a party of men to defend it. They were attacked soon after, and our field-piece did great execution; but it soon bursting, our men retreated, and an engagement of small arms was kept up a good while. Most of our men got within the breastworks, when the attack became general on both forts. At the same time the enemy's shipping came in sight, but the wind being light, and the tide against them, none of the vessels could come up, except the galleys and armed sloops, which fired upon us, but did no execution; we, in turn, fired upon them, and believe did them some damage.

The enemy continued a vigorous and incessant attack upon the forts; but notwithstanding their utmost efforts, they were many times repulsed and beaten back from our breastworks with great slaughter. But the smallness of our numbers, (being in both forts but about five hundred,) which required every man to be upon continual duty, and obliged him to unremitted exertions, fatigued our people greatly; while the enemy, whose number was supposed to be at least four thousand, continued to press us with fresh troops.

About four o'clock they sent in a flag, demanding in five minutes a surrender of the forts, and ourselves prisoners of war; or that they would put us all to the sword. An answer was returned by Colonel Livingston, acquainting them that we were determined to defend the forts to the last extremity. The action was renewed with fresh vigor on both sides, and continued till the dusk of the evening, when they stormed our upper redoubt, which commanded the fort, which after a severe struggle, and overpowering us with numbers, they got possession of; and we were obliged to give way. At the same time they stormed and got possession of Fort Clinton, in which were none but militia, who nobly defended it, till they, like the garrison at Fort Montgomery, were obliged to give way to superior force.

The darkness of the evening much favored the escape of our people, the greatest part of whom, with almost all the officers, by some means or other got off, and joined our army, or returned to their places of residence. How those who were so unfortunate as to fall into the hands of the enemy, were treated by them, we have not heard, but have reason to think it was with a cruelty suitable to the wickedness of the cause in which the British are engaged.

New-York Journal, May 11, 1778

October 14

NEW YORK   Yesterday, General Vaughn, having under his command a large body of British, who have committed various acts of vandalism, in their passage up the North River, landed a number of men at Esopus, marched up to the defenceless town of Kingston, about two miles from the river, and immediately set it on fire. The conflagration was general in a few minutes, and in a very short time that pleasant and wealthy town was reduced to ashes; one house only escaped the flames. Thus by the wantonness of power the third town in New York for size, elegance, and wealth, is reduced to a heap of rubbish, and the once happy inhabitants (who are chiefly of Dutch descent) obliged to solicit for shelter among strangers; and those who lately possessed elegant and convenient dwellings, obliged to take up with such huts as they can find to defend them from the cold blasts of approaching winter. We learn that the inhabitants saved the best part of their movable property; but some lost the greatest part of their temporal all. 'Tis said the enemy took little plunder, being told that Governor Clinton was at hand with fifteen hundred men, but unluckily not so near as to save the town. They burnt several houses at Rhynbeck Flats, and proceeded as far as Livingston Manor, where they burnt a few more. Our troops are now up with them. It is hoped they will be able to put a stop to these depredations. Britain, how art thou fallen! Ages to come will not be able to wipe away the guilt, the horrid guilt, of those and such like deeds, lately perpetrated by thee.

New York Packet, October 23

October 17

NEW YORK   General Burgoyne having been defeated in a second trial on the field at Stillwater, and finding himself encircled without the least chance of escape, to-day surrendered to the Americans. General Gates, in a letter to his wife, written from Albany three days after the surrender, says:—

The voice of fame, ere this reaches you, will tell how greatly fortunate we have been in this department. Burgoyne and his whole army have laid down their arms, and surrendered themselves to me and my Yankees. Thanks to the Giver of all victory for this triumphant success. I got here the night before last, and the army are now encamped upon the heights to the southward of this city. Major-General Phillips, who wrote me that saucy note last year from St. John's, is now my prisoner, with Lord Petersham, Major Ackland, son of Sir Thomas, and his lady, daughter of Lord Ilchester, sister to the famous Lady Susan, and about a dozen members of Parliament, Scotch lords, &c. I wrote to T. Boone, by Mr. Fluck, an engineer, whom I permitted to pass to Canada, and who goes immediately from thence to England. I could not help, in a modest manner, putting him in mind of the *fête champêtre* that I three years ago told him General Burgoyne would meet with if he came to America. If Old England is not by this lesson taught humility, then she is an obstinate old slut, bent upon her ruin. I long much to see you, and have therefore sent the bearer to conduct you to Albany by the way of Reading, where you will be received and entertained by Mrs. Potts. Before you leave Reading, you must take advice whether to come by Nazareth or Bethlehem; after that your road up the country by Van Camp's, through the Minnisinks, to Hurley and Esopus, is plain, and well known to the bearer. Don't let Bob's zeal to get to papa, hurry you faster than, considering the length of your journey, you ought to come. If you come by Bethlehem, there is a Mr. Oakley, who holds an office under Mifflin, who will provide you with every thing you may have occasion for, and will introduce you to Madame Langton, and the bishop, and Mrs. Ilsley, &c. Perhaps you may get ruffles to your apron; if they are not finished I desire you will bespeak them.

Tell my dear Bob not to be too elated at this great good fortune of his father. He and I have seen days adverse, as well as prosperous. Let us through life endeavor to bear both with an equal mind. General Burgoyne has promised me to deliver any letters I please to commit to his care in England. I think to send a few to some principal men there. Perhaps they may have a good effect for both countries. I would fain have the mother reconciled to her child, and consent, since she is big enough to be married, to let her rule and govern her own house.

I hope Lady Harriet Ackland will be here when you arrive. She is the most amiable, delicate little piece of quality you ever beheld. Her husband is one of the prettiest fellows I have seen, learned, sensible, and an Englishman to all intents and purposes; has been a most confounded Tory, but I hope to make him as good a Whig as myself before he and I separate. You must expect bad and cold days up the journey, therefore prepare against it. I thank God I am pretty well; have had a bad cold, with loss of appetite from being continually harassed with so much business; but I hope to find some rest in winter and much comfort in yours and Bob's company. I will try to get some good tea for you from some of the English officers. Accept my tenderest wishes for your health and safety, and assure my dear Bob how much I am interested in his welfare. Heaven grant us a happy meeting.

Gates Papers, New-York Historical Society

October 18

NEW YORK   On the morning of the seventh instant, General Burgoyne invited General Frazer to breakfast with him. In the course of their conversation, Frazer told General Burgoyne that he expected in a day or two to be in Albany. "Hold," said General Burgoyne, "the *owners of the land* (meaning the militia) are come out against us. We cannot proceed any farther so fast as we have done." The same day the second battle at Stillwater was fought, in which the militia acquitted themselves like veterans, and the whole British army was routed. The consequence of this defeat is the glorious Convention of Saratoga, which was signed yesterday. A French officer who has served under General Gates during the campaign says: "When dere be no more militia in dis country, I be one very great Tory."

Pennsylvania Packet, September 5, 1778

October 23

The two following advertisements lately appeared, one in the Carolina, and the other in the Virginia newspaper, which show the humanity and great consistency of conduct of the sons of freedom, as the Americans are pleased, in several of their writings, to style themselves:—"Ran away, the tenth instant, a lusty Negro, named Bob; the said fellow is outlawed, and I will give ten pounds for his head, severed from his body, and forty shillings if brought alive."

The second advertisement breathes the same infernal spirit, viz.:—"Ran away from the subscriber, a Negro fellow named Zeb, aged thirty-six; as he is outlawed, I will pay twenty pounds currency, to any person who shall produce his head, severed from his body, and five pounds if brought home alive."

By the most cruel treatment, they make these poor people desperate, and fly from misery; then they are proclaimed, and exposed to be murdered for a reward. The real friends to liberty should be consistent in all their proceedings!

Rivington's Gazette, October 25

A Song Made on the Taking of General Burgoyne

General Burgoyne's Surrender

The Capture of Burgoyne

The surrender of Burgoyne and his entire army at Saratoga on October 17, 1777, was a colossal event in the history of the Revolutionary War. Many songs were written about it. "A Song Made on the Taking of General Burgoyne" is one of the major broadside ballads of this period. It tells the story of Burgoyne's campaign from the departure of the British forces from St. Jean on June 13 to the final capitulation. The ballad survives in the version issued by Nathaniel Coverly, Jr., circa 1810. The melody is a stock tune, "The British Grenadier," reproduced on page 543. (Ford, Check List, 2117; Isaiah Thomas, 252.)

"General Burgoyne's Surrender" is one of the most brilliant songs produced by the war; it is not only a witty and accurate sketch of the British general, but also a profound commentary on the military struggle itself. The melody is an old march tune, "The Girl I Left Behind Me," that would in later years be much used by the Americans. (Moore, Songs and Ballads, 185–187.)

"The Capture of Burgoyne" was first published by William Mc-Carty in a Philadelphia songster of 1842, Songs, Odes, and Other Poems on National Subjects, with the following heading: "from a manuscript furnished the editor by John Ely, now in his eighty-fifth year, a soldier of the Revolution, who was at the capture of Burgoyne." (Harris Collection, Brown University, Old American Songs, No. 5.)

A Song Made on the Taking of General Burgoyne

Come all you gallant heroes, of courage stout and bold,
Who scorn as long as life does last ever to be control'd;
Give ear unto my ditty, for I the truth will tell,
Concerning many a soldier that for his country fell.

Brave General Burgoyne from Canada set sail,
With eight thousand brave Regulars, he thought would never
fail,
With Indians and Canadians, and Tories as we hear,
Besides a fleet of shipping o'er Lake Champlain did steer.

Before Ticonderoga, the first day of July,
Their fleet and army did appear and soon we did them spy:
Their motions we observed, full well both night and day,
And our brave boys prepared all for a bloody fray.

Our garrisons they view'd and straight their troops did land,
When General St. Clair he came to understand,
That the great Mount Defiance they then would fortify,
He found we must surrender or every man must die.

It was on July fifth that we had orders to retreat,
And the next morning left our forts, Burgoyne he thought
us beat,
And closely did pursue us, it was near to Hubbard Town,
Our rear guards he defeated, which he thought great renown.

When our Congress came to hear that we our forts had left,
And that we had retreated near Albany to rest:
Brave General Gates they sent us our country to retrieve,
With shouts and acclamations, with joy we him receive.

Burgoyne sent out a party of fifteen hundred men,
With Hessians and Canadians came near to Bennington,
With Savages and Tories, our cattle for to steal,
Commanded by a Tory, they call'd him Colonel Skeen.

Brave Gates our bold commander, hearing of Skeen's conduct,
He sent out a small party his march for to obstruct;
We took all their artillery, and Skeen his fate may mourn,
For of fifteen hundred men, scarce five hundred did return.

Burgoyne then finding out that his schemes would not succeed,
He then with his artillery and army did proceed,
Thinking for to frighten us and make us for to fly,
Soon he found out his mistake, he found we'd sooner die.

The fifteenth of September, the morning fair and clear,
Brave Gates he said unto his men, my boys be of good cheer,
Burgoyne he now advances, and we will never fly,
But to maintain our country's right, we'll fight until we die.

The news was quickly brought us, their army it was near,
And our brave boys did meet them, all without dread or fear,
It was about Stillwater, we met about noon day,
And quickly you shall hear my boys, began a bloody fray.

We fought them full six hours like valiant hearts of gold,
Each party scorn'd for to give way, we fought like Britons bold,
Until the leaves with blood were stain'd our General then did
    cry.
It is diamond cut diamond, fight on until we die.

The night being coming on, to our lines we did retreat,
Which made the Britons for to think our army it was beat,
But early the next morning they beheld before their eyes,
We were ready to engage again, which did them much surprise.

Then fighting they seem'd tired of, therefore to work they go,
To bury all their dead, and intrenchments up they throw,
Thinking thereby with shot and shells our army to destroy,
But Gates he kept such orders that we did them defy.

They began a cannonading from every mountain hill,
And our brave boys return'd the same, and with a right good
    will,
And then they threw both shot and shells enough to terrify
Our hearts had we been Cæsars, yet neither part would fly.

The great Almighty God he inspir'd great Gate's mind,
To send out General Arnold to see if he could find,
A passage through the enemy, and make them for to flee,
Which he at last completed and set our country free.

They burned all their baggage they fled with haste and fear,
And up to Saratoga, Burgoyne with his troops did steer;
Brave Gates our bold commander soon after him did hie,
Resolving for to take them or every man to die.

Then soon we overtook them, it was near to Saratogue,
Which they had burnt, as they had done all houses on their
        road,
The sixteenth of October was forc'd to capitulate,
Burgoyne and all his army they were our prisoners made.

As for the British soldiers, they fought like hearts of gold,
And scorn'd as long as life does last ever to be control'd;
But as for the proud Hessians they prov'd cowardly of late,
For they refus'd to fight us, which caused their defeat.

Here's a health unto our army, and our commander Gates,
To Washington and Lincoln, but all the Tories hate;
Likewise unto the *Congress,* God send them long to reign,
To do our country justice, our rights for to maintain.

So to conclude my ditty, my song is at an end,
I hope no bold American will slight what I have penn'd,
Our cause is just, in God we trust, therefore my boys ne'er fear,
Brave Gates will clear America before another year.

General Burgoyne's Surrender

When Jack, the King's com-mand-er— bold, Was go-ing to— his— du - ty, Through
all the crowd he smiled and— bow'd To ev - 'ry bloom-ing beau - ty. The

cit - y rung with feats he'd done, In Por - tu - gal and Flan - ders, And

all the town thought he'd_ be_ crown'd The first of Al - ex - an - ders.

To Hampton Court he first repairs,
    To kiss great George's hand, sirs,
Then to harangue on state affairs,
    Before he left the land, sirs.
The Lower House sat mute as mouse
    To hear his grand oration;
And all the peers with loudest cheers
    Proclaimed him to the nation.

Then off he went to Canada,
    Next to Ticonderoga,
And quitting those, away he goes,
    Straightway to Saratoga.
With great parade his march he made,
    To gain his wished for station,
When far and wide his minions hied,
    To spread his "Proclamation."

To such as stayed he offers made,
    Of "pardon on submission;
But savage bands should waste the lands
    Of all in opposition."
But ah, the cruel fate of war!
    This boasted son of Britain,
When mounting his triumphal car,
    With sudden fear was smitten.

The sons of freedom gathered round,
    His hostile bands confounded,
And when they'd fain have turn'd their back,
    They found themselves surrounded!
In vain they fought, in vain they fled,
    Their chief, humane and tender,
To save the rest, soon thought it best
    His forces to surrender.

Brave St. Clair when he first retired,
Knew what the fates portended;
And Arnold and heroic Gates,
His conduct have defended.
Thus may America's brave sons
With honor be rewarded,
And be the fate of all her foes,
The same as here recorded.

The Capture of Burgoyne

When dis-cord had reared her black stand-ard on high, And
sent her hoarse voice through the sky, the sky, Con-vuls-ing all Na-ture with
dread-ful a-larms; Then Free-dom com-mand-ed her he-roes from far, They
heard the proud sum-mons and shout-ed for war! Here might you see,
youth of high spir-it, Of gen-ius and mer-it, in arms.

O'er Champlain, proud Burgoyne all terrible comes,
With thundering cannon, and drums—and drums.
He shook all the neighboring regions around;
Of blustering titles he told a long tale,
And thought pomp and nonsense would turn our cheek pale;
The glory of freemen, he found.

Three times in fierce combat the armies were joined,
But battle went not to his mind—his mind;

For American souls were too gallant to yield.
Amazed from the hill he beheld his hard fate,
And wished to retire, when the hour was too late:
Sighing he saw his hundreds were dying,
    His thousands were flying the field.

While hosts of brave patriots with hearts that beat high,
Rush onward to conquer or die—or die;
    Led by Gates, Morgan, Lincoln, those heirs of bright
    fame:
He saw skill and discipline ever must bend,
Where Freedom, and Virtue, and Glory contend:
Humble and sad, this haughty pretender
    Was forced to surrender, with same.

NOVEMBER

November 20

NEW YORK   The martial spirit which at present shines
forth amongst the inhabitants of New York City, reflects the
highest honor upon them, and is at once a proof of their
loyalty and gratitude. Ever since the arrival of the King's
troops, the greatest harmony and most cordial friendship
have subsisted between them and the citizens, nor has the
martial law been a grievance to any. None have been required to take arms, not even the most apostate amongst
those who have taken the benefit of the proclamation and
come to the city for protection. How different the prospect
if we look where "fraud prevails, and impious men bear
sway," and where the wretched inhabitants have been dragged
to the field to fight against the most glorious constitution in
the universe. The indulgences of the Commander-in-chief
has prompted the principal gentlemen, inhabitants of this
city and refugees from other provinces, to form themselves
into independent companies, twenty of which are nearly
completed.

Last Monday, [17th,] several companies of them paraded on the fields, at the upper end of Broadway, headed by the Worshipful David Matthews, Esq., and made a very fine appearance. These companies, together with the militia, will greatly add to the strength of the city, and relieve the King's troops, who may be employed elsewhere.

Rivington's Gazette, November 22

MASSACHUSETTS   This day arrived at Boston, in Massachusetts, under an escort of American light dragoons, the Honorable John Hancock, Esq., President of the American Congress, and first major-general of the militia of that state. By his coming into town sooner than was expected, he avoided some public marks of respect which would otherwise have been paid him; his arrival was made known by ringing the bells, the discharge of thirteen cannon of Colonel Craft's park of artillery on the common, the cannon on the fortress on Fort Hill, and the shipping in the harbor. The independent and light infantry companies paid him their military salutes. He received the compliments of gentlemen of all orders; and every indication was given of the sense the public has of his important services to the American cause.

Pennsylvania Ledger, January 7, 1778

November 22

PENNSYLVANIA   A gentleman in the American army gives the following account of the late movements of the British forces on and about the Delaware and Schuylkill rivers:

About the 12th of October, the British erected a battery near the mouth of the Schuylkill, in order to prevent our boats going into that river, and then landed a large body of troops on Province Island opposite Fort Mifflin, with intention to erect batteries against that fort.

In the night they threw up one battery within point blank shot directly opposite to the fort, which was attacked the next day by the galleys, who kept up so warm a fire on them for two hours, that one captain, one lieutenant and ensign, with about eighty men, came on the bank with a flag, clubbed their muskets, and surrendered themselves prisoners; but a large body of fresh men coming in through the meadows to rescue them, they were fired at from the block house at Fort Mifflin, and many of those who had submitted, thinking it was them, ran off; that fifty-six privates with Lieutenant Finch and Ensign Hankey were brought off. On the next day the galleys attacked the battery again, but without any effect. The enemy now threw up another battery on the hospital wharf, from which they fired red hot shot, and kept up a firing every day of shells and red hot balls, but to little purpose, having since their first firing to the 9th November killed but two men and wounded a few, though they had thrown some thousand shot and shells.

On Monday, the 10th of November, the enemy had completed five batteries, one on the hospital wharf above mentioned, one on the wharf below that, and three others, one just above the fort, another right opposite, and the third a little below the fort. From all these, about seven o'clock in the morning, they began a most furious can-nonade, with shot, shells, and carcasses, not throwing less than fifteen hundred of them a day. Tuesday morning they began in the same manner, when Captain Treat of the artillery, a brave officer, with two others, were killed, and several wounded; and in the evening Colonel Smith, who commanded the fort, was brought off wounded. Three of the enemy's ships came up the same morning a little above Man-tua Creek, where we had thrown up a small battery, but had that day no guns in it, and kept a continual fire on it for some hours, without the least damage to the battery. Wednesday and Thursday the cannonade of shells, &c., was kept up most violently, which tore the stockades, barracks, &c., all to pieces, and dismounted and broke many of our guns. Friday the fire was also very hot, and the *Vigilant* galley, which had been cut down and carried sixteen twenty-four pounders, got behind Hog Island designing to get up to Fort Mifflin, but could not do it that day.

Saturday the 15th we got three guns in the battery men-tioned above, and that morning the *Somerset* of sixty-four guns, the *Isis*, and another fifty-gun ship, two large frigates, and a galley they brought from New York came up within reach of Fort Mifflin, when the battery began firing on them. This drew the fire from all the men-of-war, which was incessant; so that from the cannonade on the fort and the fire from the enemy, there was one continual roar of cannon. The wind was high, and directly against the galleys, which prevented them from getting to action for some time. In the afternoon the *Vigilant* got through close up to Fort Mifflin and fired most furiously on it. The commodore sent over six galleys to attack her; but she lay so covered by the enemy's batteries that it could not be done to any purpose. The other galleys with the floating batteries, were engaged with the ships; and such a cannonade, I believe, was never seen in America. It continued till the evening, when all the ships fell down and the firing ceased except from the *Vigilant* and the batteries on Province Island against Fort Mifflin, which was by this time torn all to pieces, having scarce a stockade standing, the block houses almost beat down, and every gun dismounted or broken. It now being found impossible to defend it any longer, Major Thayer, who for some days had so bravely defended it, about eleven o'clock at night set fire to the remains of the barracks and brought off his garrison. Thus fell Fort Mifflin after a close siege of near one month, in which time we had on board the galleys only thirty-eight men killed and wounded.

Sunday and Monday the enemy were quite still, and on Tuesday the 18th, in the morning, a large number of transports with troops from New York came up to Billingsport and landed their men; and General Cornwallis came over from Pennsylvania with a number more, in order to attack the fort at Red Bank, where we had not men sufficient to hold a siege. In council it was thought best that it should be evacuated, and on Thursday evening the fort was blown up, and the garrison, with the ammunition, went off.

Our little fleet was now to be preserved; and in consultation with the land and sea officers, it was agreed that it should, if possible, pass by Philadelphia and go up the river. Accordingly, on Wednesday night, the commodore ordered the thirteen galleys to pass close under the Jersey shore, which they all did without a shot being fired at them. It being quite calm, the top-sail vessels could not attempt it. Friday morning, before day, it still being calm, the brig *Convention*, Captain Rice, the schooner *Delaware*, Captain Eyres, with six of the shallops, set off to get by, which they all did, through an exceeding hot fire of shells and shot, except the *Delaware* and one shallop, which were run aground and set on fire. Finding that all the troops were gone, and that there was no wind to carry the continental vessels by, it was thought better to set them on fire, than to let them fall into the enemy's hands; and the same morning before day, the brig *Andria Doria*, the xebecs, *Repulse* and *Champion*, the sloops *Racehorse* and *Champion*, with the two floating batteries and three fire-ships, were accordingly set on fire and destroyed.

New-Jersey Gazette, December 5

DECEMBER

December 1

ENGLAND   We hear from London, that a treaty is to be concluded with Russia for taking thirty-six thousand Russians into pay; and with the King of Prussia, but the contents are not known. It is not for a body of his troops; but twelve thousand more Hessians, Wurtemburgers, Palatines, and Mecklenburgers, are agreed for. Four and twenty new regiments are to be raised in England and Ireland of five hundred men each, so that the army in America, next campaign, will not be short of eighty thousand men.

New-Jersey Gazette, December 5

It is observable that at the opening of every campaign in the spring, the British plunderers, and their Tory emissaries, announce the total reduction of America before the winter. In the fall they find themselves as remote from their purpose as they were in the spring; and then we are threatened with innumerable hosts from Russia and Germany, who will utterly extirpate us the ensuing summer, or reduce us to the most abject submission. They have so beat this beaten track, that for mere sake of variety, I would advise them to explore a new road; and not compel us to nauseate a falsehood, not only because we know it to be one, but for its perpetual repetition without the least variation or alternity. According to custom, therefore, the new lie (that is the old lie reiterated) for next summer is, that we are to be devoured, bones and all, by thirty-six thousand Russians; besides something or other that is to be done to us by the King of Prussia. What this is to be, is still a profound secret; but as it will doubtless be something very extraordinary, and it being impossible to conceive what else he can do to us, after we are swallowed by the Russians, he is probably, by some political emetic or other, to bring us up again. I should think, in common complaisance to human reason, that absurdities so gross, and figments so destitute of probability, could only deceive those who choose to be deceived. The Empress of Russia, though a sovereign in petticoats, knows too well that the true riches of a nation consist in the number of its inhabitants, to suffer such a number of her inhabitants to be knocked in the head in America, for the sake of facilitating the frantic project of a more southern potentate in breeches, deluded by a blundering ministry, and the universal derision of Europe. It is her interest (and I shall wonder if ever princes proceed upon any other principle, before the commencement of the millennium) to have America dismembered from Great Britain, which must of necessity reduce the naval power of the latter, and make Russia a full match for her on the ocean. And as for the King of Prussia, considering that there never was any love lost between him and the family of Brunswick, and that he has long been jealous of the maritime strength of Britain, these artifices of fraud might, with equal plausibility, have introduced the Emperor of Japan as entering into leagues and alliances with our late master at St. James. It is nothing but an impudent forgery from first to last, and merely fabricated to restore to their natural shape and features, the crestfallen countenances of the Tories, and if possible, to intimidate the genuine sons of America.

The utmost they can do, they have already done; and are this moment as far from any prospect of subjecting us to the dominion of Britain, as they were in the ridiculous hour in which General Gage first arrived in Boston. This is no secret with those who have the management of their armies in America, how greatly soever the nation itself it may be deluded by the pompous accounts of their progress. But whatever becomes of Old England at last, these gentlemen are sure of accumulating immense wealth during the war; and are therefore determined to keep up the delusion as long as possible. Burgoyne is the only one of any distinction, who has virtue enough to own the truth; and I am credibly informed, that he has frankly declared, that he was most egregiously deceived in the Americans, that he had been led to believe they would never come to bayoneting, that they behaved with the greatest intrepidity in attacking intrenchments, that although a regiment of his grenadiers and light infantry displayed, in an engagement with Colonel Morgan's battalion of riflemen, the most astonishing gallantry, Morgan exceeded them in dexterity and generalship, and that it was utterly impossible ever to conquer America.

"Hortentius" (Governor William Livingston)
New-Jersey Gazette, December 24

How Stands the Glass Around?

Come Out Ye Continentalers

In December 1777 Washington and his ragged band withdrew from the Philadelphia area and moved into winter quarters at Valley Forge. Through the winter of 1777–8 they would silently keep watch on Howe—and silently starve. As new graves appeared in the frozen earth the rebels began to sing an English soldier's song, "How Stands the Glass Around?" Both a poignant lament and a bitter pro-

test, it was a favorite of General James Wolfe. Dating back at least
to the seventeenth century, it is known in England as "The Duke
of Berwick's March." (William Chappell, Old English Popular Music, London, 1893; re-issued New York, 1961. Ford, Check List,
3127; Isaiah Thomas, 53.)

In spite of the cold, the Continental troops were not idle. All
winter they drilled under the direction of Baron von Steuben, that
they might fight even better in the spring. Tory wits found the
spectacle amusing. "Come Out Ye Continentalers," probably composed in Philadelphia at this time, mocked the efforts of Washington's drill master to make regular soldiers out of country bumpkins.
(Rough and Ready Songster, circa 1848.)

How Stands the Glass Around?

Why soldiers, why,
Should we be melancholy, boys?
Why, soldiers, why,
Whose business 'tis to die!
What sighing, fie!
Drown fear, drink on, be jolly boys,

'Tis he, you or I!
Cold, hot, wet or dry,
We're always bound to follow, boys,
And scorn to fly!

'Tis but in vain—
I mean not to upraid ye, boys,
'Tis but in vain
For soldiers to complain.
Should next campaign
Send us to him who made us, boys,
We're free from pain!
But if we remain,
A bottle and kind landlady
Cure all again.

Come Out Ye Continentalers

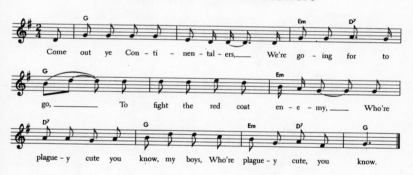

Come out ye Con - ti - nen - tal - ers,___ We're go - ing for to
go,___ To fight the red coat en - e - my,___ Who're
plague - y cute you know, my boys, Who're plague - y cute, you know.

Fix bayonets! That's your sort, my boys,
Now quick time march! that's right!
Just so we'd poke the enemy
If they were but in sight, my boys,
If they were but in sight.

Halt! shoulder whoop! Stop laughing, Nick!
By platoons wheel, right dress!
Hold up your muzzles on the left.
No talking—more or less—my boys,
No talking more or less.

Bill Sneezer keep your canteen down,
We're going for to travel.
"Captain, I wants to halt a bit,
"My shoes are full of gravel, sir,
"My shoes are full of gravel."

Ho! strike up music! forward march!
Come point your toes Bob Rogers.
See, yonder come the redcoat men!
Let's fly upon them soldiers, boys,
Let's fly upon them soldiers.

1778

JANUARY

January 6

PENNSYLVANIA   Philadelphia has been entertained with a most astonishing instance of the activity, bravery, and military skill of the royal navy of Great Britain. The affair is somewhat particular, and deserves notice. Some time last week, two boys observed a keg of a singular construction, floating in the river opposite to the city; they got into a small boat, and attempting to take up the keg, it burst with a great explosion, and blew up the unfortunate boys. Yesterday, several kegs of a like construction made their appearance. An alarm was immediately spread through the city; various reports prevailed, filling the city and the royal troops with consternation. Some reported that the kegs were filled with armed rebels, who were to issue forth in the dead of night, as the Grecians did of old from their wooden horse at the siege of Troy, and take the city by surprise; asserting that they had seen the points of their bayonets through the bung-holes of the kegs. Others said they were charged with the most inveterate combustibles, to be kindled by secret machinery, and setting the whole Delaware in flames, were to consume all the shipping in the harbor; whilst others asserted that they were constructed by art magic, would of themselves ascend the wharves in the night time, and roll all flaming through the streets of the city, destroying every thing in their way.

Be this as it may, certain it is that the shipping in the harbor, and all the wharves in the city were fully manned, the battle began, and it was surprising to behold the incessant blaze that was kept up against the enemy, the kegs. Both officers and men exhibited the most unparalleled skill and bravery on the occasion; whilst the citizens stood gazing as solemn witnesses of their prowess. From the *Roebuck* and other ships of war, whole broadsides were poured into the Delaware. In short, not a wandering ship, stick, or drift log, but felt the vigor of the British arms. The action began about sunrise, and would have been completed with great success by noon, had not an old market woman coming down the river with provisions, unfortunately let a small keg of butter fall overboard, which (as it was then ebb) floated down to the scene of action. At sight of this unexpected reinforcement of the enemy, the battle was renewed with fresh fury, and the firing was incessant till the evening closed the affair. The kegs were either totally demolished or obliged to fly, as none of them have shown their *heads* since. It is said his Excellency Lord Howe, has despatched a swift sailing packet with an account of this victory to the court of London. In a word, Monday, the fifth of January, 1778, must ever be distinguished in history for the memorable BATTLE OF THE KEGS.

Letter from Philadelphia, Pennsylvania
New-Jersey Gazette, January 21

PENNSYLVANIA   The town of Philadelphia not being as fully acquainted with the subject of the letter taken from a Burlington paper, as the ingenious author would have his readers believe them to be, it may be necessary to relate to them the fact. At the time it happened it was so trifling as not to be thought worthy of notice in this paper; and we do not doubt but our readers will allow this letter-writer full credit for the fertility of his invention. The case was, that on the fifth of January last, a barrel of an odd appearance came floating down the Delaware, opposite the town, and attracted the attention of some boys, who went in pursuit of it, and had scarcely got possession of it when it blew up, and either killed or injured one or more of them. So far the matter was serious, and the fellow who invented the mischief may quit his conscience of the murder or injury done the lads, as well as he can. Some days after, a few others of much the same appearance, and some in the form of buoys, came floating in like manner, and a few guns were, we believe, fired at them from some of the transports lying along the wharves. Other than this no notice was taken of them, except, indeed, by our author, whose imagination, perhaps, as fertile as his invention, realized to himself in the frenzy of his enthusiasm the matters he has set forth.

Pennsylvania Ledger, February 11

Battle of the Kegs

Early in January, 1778, David Bushnell, of Connecticut, inventor of a primitive submarine, filled a number of kegs with powder, set fuses to them, and sent them floating down the Delaware, hoping thus to harass the British Navy which was anchored downstream off Philadelphia. The British manned their guns when the kegs came into view, and the mines were neutralized. The incident was soon exploited by Francis Hopkinson, artist, writer, musician, and pamphleteer, in "Battle of the Kegs," one of the most brilliant satirical ballads of the war. The song delighted Washington's troops at Valley Forge, and was even sung in Philadelphia itself. The lady referred to as Mrs. L——g was the wife of Joshua Loring, Howe's Commissary of Prisons. (Ford, Isaiah Thomas, 18; Moore, Songs and Ballads, 209–19.)

Gallants attend, and hear a friend
   Trill forth harmonious ditty:
Strange things I'll tell, which late befel
   In Philadelphia city.
'Twas early day, as poets say,
   Just when the sun was rising,
A soldier stood, on log of wood,
   And saw a sight surprising.

BATTLE OF THE KEGS.

GALLANTS attend, and hear a friend,
   Trill forth harmonious ditty :
Strange things I'll tell, which late befel
   In Philadelphia city.
'Twas early day, as poets fay,
   Juft when the fun was rifing,
A foldier ftood, on log of wood,
   And faw a fight furprifing.

As in a maze, he ftood to gaze,
   The truth can't be deny'd, fir,
He fpy'd a fcore —of kegs, or more,
   Come floating down the tide, fir.
A failor too, in jerkin blue,
   The ftrange appearance viewing,
Firft damn'd his eyes, in great furprife,
   Then faid fome mifchiefs brewing.
Thefe kegs now hold the rebels bold,
   Pack'd up like pickled herring :
And they're come down t'attack the town,
   In this new way of ferrying.

The foldier flew, the failor too,
   And, fcar'd almoft to death, fir;
Wore out their fhoes, to fpread the news,
   And ran till out of breath, fir.
Now up and down, throughout the town,
   Moft frantic fcenes were acted :
And fome ran here, and fome ran there
   Like men almoft diftracted.
Some fire cry'd, which fome deny'd,
   But faid the earth had quaked :
And girls and boys, with hideous noife,
   Ran through the town half naked.

Sir William he, fnug as a flea,
   Lay all this time a fnoring,
Nor dreamt of harm, as he lay warm
   In bed with Mrs. L——g.
Now in affright, he ftarts upright,
   Awak'd by fuch a clatter ;
He rubs both eyes, and boldly cries,
   "For God's fake what's the matter?"
At his bed fide, he then efpy'd
   Sir Erfkine at command, fir,

Upon one foot he had one boot,
   And t'other in his hand, fir.
Arife ! arife ! Sir Erfkine cries ;
   The rebels—more's the pity—
Without a boat, are all on float,
   And rang'd before the city.
The motly crew, in veffels new,
   With fatan for their guide, fir,
Pack'd up in bags, or wooden kegs,
   Come driving down the tide, fir.
Therefore prepare for bloody war ;
   Thefe kegs muft all be routed ;
Or furely we defpis'd fhall be,
   And Britifh courage doubted.

The royal band now ready ftand,
   All rang'd in dread array, fir,
With ftomach ftout, to fee it out,
   And make a bloody day, fir.
The cannons roar, from fhore to fhore ;
   The fmall arms make a rattle :
Since wars began, I'm fure no man
   E'er faw fo ftrange a battle.
The fifh below fwam to and fro,
   Attack'd from ev'ry quarter ;
Why fure, thought they, the devil's to pay
   'Mongft folks above the water.

Thefe kegs, 'tis faid, tho' ftrongly made,
   Of rebel ftaves and hoops, fir,
Could not oppofe their pow'rful foes,
   The conq'ring Britifh troops, fir.
From morn to night, thefe men of might
   Difplay'd amazing courage ;
And when the fun was fairly down,
   Retir'd to fup their porridge:
An hundred men with each a pen,
   Or more upon my word, fir,
It is moft true, would be too few,
   Their valour to record, fir.

Such feats did they perform that day
   Upon thefe wicked kegs, fir,
That years to come, if they get home,
   They'll make their boafts and brags, fir.

Battle of the Kegs. Broadside issued some time after 1800 by Nathaniel Coverly, Jr., of Boston, slightly abridged from Francis Hopkinson's original. Sung to the tune of "Yankee Doodle." Reproduced from the Isaiah Thomas Collection of Broadside Ballads by permission of the American Antiquarian Society, Worcester, Massachusetts.

As in a maze, he stood to gaze,
    The truth can't be denied, sir,
He spy'd a score—of kegs, or more,
    Come floating down the tide, sir.
A sailor too, in jerkin blue,
    The strange appearance viewing,
First damn'd his eyes, in great surprise,
    Then said some mischief's brewing.

These kegs now hold the rebels bold,
    Pack'd up like pickled herring:
And they're come down t'attack the town,
    In this new way of ferrying.
The soldier flew, the sailor too,
    And, scar'd almost to death, sir,
Wore out their shoes, to spread the news,
    And ran til out of breath, sir.

Now up and down, throughout the town,
    Most frantic scenes were acted:
And some ran here, and some ran there
    Like men almost distracted.
Some fire cry'd, which some deny'd,
    But said the earth had quaked:
And girls and boys, with hideous noise,
    Ran through the town half naked.

Sir William he, snug as a flea,
    Lay all this time a-snoring,
Nor dreamt of harm, as he lay warm
    In bed with Mrs. L[orin]g.
Now in affright, he starts upright,
    Awak'd by such a clatter;
He rubs both eyes, and boldly cries,
    "For God's sake what's the matter?"

At his bed side, he then espy'd
    Sir Erskine at command, sir,
Upon one foot he had one boot,
    And t'other in his hand, sir.
Arise! Arise! Sir Erskine cries:
    The rebels—more's the pity—
Without a boat, are all on float,
    And rang'd before the city.

The motley crew, in vessels new,
    With satan for their guide, sir,
Pack'd up in bags, or wooden kegs,
    Come driving down the tide, sir.
Therefore prepare for bloody war;
    These kegs must all be routed;
Or surely we despis'd shall be,
    And British courage doubted.

The royal band now ready stand,
    All rang'd in dread array, sir,
With stomach stout, to see it out,
    And make a bloody day, sir.
The cannons roar, from shore to shore:
    The small arms make a rattle:
Since wars began, I'm sure no man
    E'er saw so strange a battle.

The rebel dales, the rebel vales,
    With rebel trees surrounded,
The distant woods, the hills and floods,
    With rebel echoes sounded.
The fish below swam to and fro,
    Attack'd from every quarter;
Why sure, thought they, the devil's to pay,
    'Mongst folks above the water.

These kegs, 'tis said, though strongly made,
    Of rebel staves and hoops, sir,
Could not oppose their powerful foes,
    The conquering British troops, sir.
From morn till night, these men of might
    Display'd amazing courage;
And when the sun was fairly down,
    Retir'd to sup their porridge.

An hundred men with each a pen,
    Or more upon my word, sir,
It is most true, would be too few,
    Their valor to record, sir.
Such feats did they perform that day
    Upon those wicked kegs, sir,
That years to come, if they get home,
    They'll make their boasts and brags, sir.

January 20

NEW JERSEY   Yesterday, died, in the sixty-sixth year of his age, Francis Furgler, the hermit, who existed alone twenty-five years, in a thick wood about four miles from Burlington, in New Jersey, through all the inclemencies of the season, without fire, in a cell made by the side of an old log in form of a small oven, not high or long enough to stand upright in or lie extended. His recluse manner of living excited the curiosity of strangers, by whom he was often visited. His reasons for thus excluding himself from human society we believe he never communicated to any person in these parts; but it is thought he meant by it to do penance for crimes committed in his own country, for he was a man subject to violent passions. He subsisted upon nuts, and the charity of people in the neighborhood. From whence he came, or who he was, nobody could find out; but appeared to be, by his dialect, a German: yet he spoke that language imperfectly, either through design, or from a defect in his intellect. Just before his death a friend carried him a little nourishment, of which he partook, earnestly praying for his dissolution, and would not suffer himself to be removed to a more comfortable dwelling. Next morning he was found dead in his cell, with a crucifix and a brass fish by his side; and to-day he was decently interred in Friend's burying place at Mount Holly.

New-Jersey Gazette, January 28

January 29

Should the report of General Burgoyne's having infringed the capitulation between Major-General Gates and himself, prove to be true, our superiors will doubtless take proper care to prevent his reaping any benefit from it; and should he be detained as a prisoner for his infraction of any of the articles, I would humbly propose to exchange him in such manner as will at the same time flatter his vanity, and redound to the greatest emolument of America. To evince the reasonableness of my proposal, I would observe that by the same parity of

reason that a General is exchanged for a General, a Colonel
for a Colonel, and so on with respect to other officers of equal
rank, we ought to have for one and the same gentleman, who
shall happen to hold both those offices, both a general and a
colonel. This will appear evident from the consideration that
those exchanges are never regulated by viewing the persons
exchanged in the light of men, but as officers; since otherwise
a colonel might as well be exchanged for a sergeant, as for an
officer of his own rank, a sergeant being undoubtedly equally
a man, and as the case sometimes happens, more of a man
too. One prisoner, therefore, having twenty different offices,
ought to redeem from captivity twenty prisoners aggregately
holding the same offices; or such greater or less number as
shall, with respect to rank, be equal to his twenty offices. This
being admitted, I think General Burgoyne is the most profit-
able prisoner we could have taken, having more offices, or
(what amounts to the same thing in Old England) more titles,
than any gentleman on this side of the Ganges. And as his
impetuous excellency certainly meant to avail himself of his
titles, by their pompous display in his proclamation, had he
proved conqueror, it is but reasonable that we should avail
ourselves of them now he is conquered; and till I meet with a
better project for that purpose, I persuade myself that the
following proposal will appropriate them to a much better
use than they were ever applied to before.

The exchange I propose is as follows:

For John Burgoyne, Esquire: some worthy Justice of the
Peace, magnanimously stolen out of his bed, or taken from
his farm by a band of ruffians in the uniform of British
soldiers, and now probably perishing with hunger and cold in
a loathsome gaol in New York.

For John Burgoyne, Lieutenant-General of his Majesty's
armies in America: two Majors-General.

For John Burgoyne, Colonel of the Queen's regiment of
Light Dragoons: As the British troops naturally prize every
thing in proportion as it partakes of royalty, and undervalue
whatever originates from a republican government, I suppose
a colonel of her Majesty's own regiment will procure at least
three Continental Colonels of horse.

For John Burgoyne, Governor of Fort William in North Britain: Here I would demand one Governor of one of the United States, as his multitulary excellency is Governor of a fort, and two more as that fort is in North Britain, which his Britannic Majesty may be presumed to value in that proportion; but considering that the said fort is called William, which may excite in his Majesty's mind the rebellious idea of liberty, I deduct one upon that account, and rather than puzzle the cartel with any perplexity, I am content with two governors.

For John Burgoyne, one of the Representatives of Great Britain: the first member of Congress who may fall into the enemy's hands.

For John Burgoyne, Commander of a fleet employed in an expedition from Canada: the admiral of our navy.

For John Burgoyne, Commander of an army employed in an expedition from Canada: one commander-in-chief in any of our departments.

For John Burgoyne, &c., &c., &c. Some connoisseurs in hieroglyphics imagine that these three *et ceteras* are emblematical of three certain *occult* qualities in the general, which he never intends to exhibit in more legible characters, viz.: prudence, modesty, and humanity. Others suppose that they stand for King of America; and that had he proved successful, he would have fallen upon General Howe, and afterwards have set up for himself. Be this as it may, (which it however behooves a certain gentleman on the other side of the water seriously to consider,) I insist upon it, that as all dark and cabalistical characters are suspicious, these incognoscible enigmas may portend much more than is generally apprehended. At all events, General Burgoyne has availed himself of their importance, and I doubt not they excited as much terror in his proclamation as any of his more luminous titles. As his person therefore is, by the capture, become the property of the Congress, all his titles, (which some suppose to constitute his very essence,) whether more splendid or opaque, latent or visible, are become *ipso facto* the lawful goods and chattels of the continent, and ought not to be restored without a consideration equivalent. If we should happen to overrate them, it is his own fault, it being in his power to ascertain their intrinsic value; and it is a rule in law, that when a man is possessed of evidence to disprove what is alleged against him, and he refuses to produce it, the presumption raised against him is to be taken for granted. Certain it is that these three *et ceteras* must stand for three *somethings*, and as these three somethings must, at least, be equal to three somethings without rank or title, I had some thoughts of setting them down for three privates; but then as they are three somethings in General Burgoyne, which must be of twice the value of three anythings in any three privates, I shall only double them, and demand in exchange for these three problematical, enigmatical, hieroglyphical, mystic, necromantic, cabalistical and portentous *et ceteras*, six privates.

So that, according to my plan, we ought to detain this *ideal* conqueror of the north, now a *real* prisoner in the east, till we have got in exchange for him, one esquire, two majors-general, three colonels of light horse, two governors, one member of Congress, the admiral of our navy, one commander-in-chief in a separate department, and six privates; which is probably more than this extraordinary hero would fetch in any part of Great Britain, were he exposed at public auction for a day and a year. All which is humbly submitted to the consideration of the honorable the Congress, and his Excellency General Washington.

"Hortentius," *New-Jersey Gazette, December 17, 1777*

FEBRUARY

February 4

The public may be assured it is an undoubted fact that the court of France is positively, and has in earnest determined, that they will show no countenance whatever to the rebellion in America—have given the most satisfactory assurances that they will not assist the Americans in any manner, or suffer their vessels to trade at their ports.

Yesterday a number of the virtuous inhabitants of New Jersey, tired of the oppression of their new government, gave a proof of their loyalty and attachment to his Majesty, by seizing the person of one Wilson, collector of the substitute fines in that province, and bringing him in to the British head-quarters. This example, it is hoped, will be followed by the injured and distressed people of Pennsylvania and New Jersey, as they cannot doubt but their loyalty will meet with every reasonable encouragement.

New York Gazette and Weekly Mercury, February 23

MARCH

March 9

The Southern States are pursuing the most vigorous measures for strengthening the hands of General Washington the ensuing campaign. Virginia has drafted two thousand men to recruit her regiments, who are to serve for one year. They have also set on foot an association for raising five thousand volunteers, to serve six months; North Carolina is exerting herself with equal ardor. The Eastern States, who, in public concerns, always act with a wisdom and vigor that deserves imitation, have already begun to draft, being resolved to fill their regiments *completely*, and to have them early in the field. If the Middle States take the same resolute steps, (and no doubt they will,) the next campaign must be decisive. The strength of the enemy is so much reduced, that nothing but our indolence can prevent their destruction.

We have often thought it strange that America, who could bring three or four hundred thousand men into the field, should so long suffer a paltry banditti to run through her States, and to nestle in her cities. One would be tempted to imagine that we were fond of this destructive war; and yet folly, in her highest delirium, would not wish to protract it. There was a time when protraction and delay were prudent —even necessary; but at this time of day they will certainly be injurious, and may be fatal. Every day the war continues our public debts will increase—our necessities will multiply— and our currency depreciate. Britain knows this—she founds her last hopes upon it; she no longer expects to conquer us by the sword, but she flatters herself that our distresses will sub- due our minds, break the spirit of opposition, and dissolve in time the glorious confederacy in support of freedom. Hence it will be the policy of her generals to possess themselves of our towns, to destroy our manufactures, to block up our harbors, and to protract the war. We should change our measures accordingly—bring our thousands into the field—push the enemy with vigor—drive them from our towns—storm them in their strongholds, and never pause till we force them from our shores. The successes of the last campaign teach us what we are able to do if we exert our strength; and instead of provoking our indolence, should spur our ambition. These rising States should catch the spirit of the gallant Cæsar, and think "that they have done nothing, while any thing remains to do."

Letter from Valley Forge
New-Jersey Gazette, March 18

APRIL

April 15

PENNSYLVANIA   Throughout the whole past winter, with General Washington within twenty miles of them, the British have remained in Philadelphia quite unalarmed and easy. Not a single attack has been attempted; and what is as extraordi- nary, not a single fire has happened, or even a common riot to disturb the peace. It is amazing to think that a garrison so confined in its lines, composed of troops of different nations and languages, together with a motley crew of inhabitants, besides the sailors of the navy, and transports, in all amounting to upwards of fifty thousand people, should have lived together in the most perfect harmony and peace. Nothing reflects more honor on the character of General Howe than this very circumstance, as nothing but the highest attention to good discipline, regularity, and order, could have effected what seems so very incredible. The early support he gave to the police he had established for the government of the city, the public countenance he gave to it on all occasions—never suffering its authority in any one instance to be violated or insulted—and the satisfaction given to the inhabitants by the measure itself, have had the highest good effects, and justly endear him to both army and country. Perhaps there never was a general commanding an army more universally beloved by officers and soldiers, than Sir William; nor in whom, as an officer, a more general confidence has prevailed, both for abilities and spirit.

Upcott, V, 133

April 23

FRANCE   At length we have intelligence from France that the Congress have concluded a treaty of alliance with the King of the French:—His Most Christian Majesty guarantees the independence, sovereignty, liberties, and all the possessions of the United States of America; and they, on their part, guarantee all the dominions of that prince in the West Indies. The part he has acted upon this occasion is truly noble and magnanimous. No monoply of our trade is desired; it is left open to all we choose to trade with. This is wise as it is generous, it being undoubtedly the interest of France that this treaty should be durable, which would not have been so likely had hard terms been exacted of us. We are, moreover, liberally assisted there with all kinds of supplies. The treaties were signed on the sixth of February, but were not publicly known when the frigate which brought them to Congress, sailed; but they were talked of as highly probable, from circumstances: and the English minister to defeat, if possible, this expected union, and recover the dependence of the colonies, has brought in two bills, which he calls conciliatory, but which are a composition of artifice and uncertainty. The *right*, as they are pleased to call it, of laying taxes on us is not given up; the Parliament only declared, that in consideration of some inconveniences found in the exercise of this right, they intend not to exercise it hereafter, except for regulating trade; but the next Parliament may find this declaration inconvenient, and may repeal it, and may resume the right. Commissioners are appointed to treat with any body of men in America, on the means of quieting the disorders there, but can do nothing definite, except granting pardons, declaring and revoking cessation of arms, &c. On this, a gentleman of character says, in one of his letters, "I hope no American will be mean enough to accept their pardons; and I am sure they will not be so weak as to disband or disarm, in the smallest degree, on the faith of their declaring a cessation of arms." He adds, "Believe me, the malice of the British court is as great against us as ever, but they are at present in a great consternation, unable to go on, and dread to give up, and fearing a war with France and Spain, which they see must ruin them. If they can divide and weaken us, or deceive us into a submission, they will punish us at their leisure."

France has this same year renewed her fifty years' alliance with the thirteen United States of Switzerland, which she has faithfully kept for two hundred years. A good omen for us. The accession of Spain to the treaties was not doubted. These events are most important in favor of America; they give us a stability that must support and extend our credit in Europe, while that of Britain is daily sinking. The good will to our cause in Europe is universal; all nations wish, and are ready to concur, in the humiliation of England, as soon as they dare. By returning to their government, we should have them and all Europe against us; we are now, with all Europe, against them. There is no hesitating a moment which to choose of these two situations. The public may rely on the authenticity of the above accounts, which, if improved with wisdom and spirit here, must, by the favor of Heaven, prove decisive for America.

New-York Journal, May 18

MAY

May 1

PENNSYLVANIA   This morning, at daylight, the American camp, which lay near the Crooked Billet, was surrounded with a body of the enemy, who appeared on all quarters. The scouts neglected last night to patrol the roads as they were ordered, but lay in camp till near day, though their orders were to leave it by two o'clock in the morning. On the disobedience of some officers of the scouts we have to lay our misfortunes.

The alarm was so sudden, we had scarcely time to mount our horses before the enemy was within musket shot of our quarters. We observed a party in our rear had got into houses and behind fences; their numbers appearing nearly equal to ours, we did not think it advisable to attack them in that situation, especially as another body appeared in our front to the east of the Billet; and not knowing what numbers we had to contend with, we thought it best to open our way under cover of a wood to the left of our camp, towards Colonel Hart's, for which our little party moved in columns, the baggage following in the rear. We had not passed far before our flanking parties began to change shot with the enemy, but kept moving on till we made the wood, when a party of both foot and horse came up the Biberry road, and attacked our right flank; the party from the Billet fell upon our rear; the horse, from the rear of our camp, came upon our left flank. A body of horse appearing in our front, we made a stand in the wood, and gave them some warm fires, which forced them to retire; their horse suffered considerably as they charged us, and were severely repulsed; their strength gathering from all quarters, we thought it best to move on, which we did with the loss of our baggage, the horse giving way in the front as we advanced.

We continued skirmishing for upwards of two miles, when

we made a turn to the left, which entirely extricated us from them. We came into the York road near the cross roads, and moved slowly down toward the Billet, in hopes to take some advantage of them on that quarter, where they must least expect us, but we found they retired toward the city. Our people behaved well; our loss is upwards of thirty killed and wounded; some were butchered in a manner the most brutal savages could not equal; even while living some were thrown into buckwheat straw, and the straw set on fire; the clothes were burnt on others, and scarcely one without a dozen wounds with bayonets and cutlasses. Fifty-eight are missing. The enemy's loss is not known, but it is currently reported one field officer is among the slain; we took three of their horse, five were left dead on the field, the riders either killed or wounded.

New-York Journal, June 1

May 2

PENNSYLVANIA   Among the slain, near the Crooked Billet, yesterday, fell the gallant Captain John Downey, late schoolmaster in Philadelphia, whose worth entitles him to a place in the annals of America. He took an active and early part in our struggles for liberty. He went as a volunteer to Jersey, last winter was a year, where he behaved gallantly in the battle of Trenton and Princeton. He being chosen captain of a company of Philadelphia militia, served his tour of duty two months last summer at Billingsport, when on account of his superior knowledge in mathematics, the executive council employed him to make a military survey of the river Delaware, which he performed with great exactness; since which time he has performed many very important services to his country, a love to which prompted him to attempt any thing which promised its welfare. He lately acted as an assistant-commissary, and in this capacity was with our brave militia in the attack yesterday. From his known readiness to fight and bleed for his country, it is more than probable that when the attack began he attempted to join his countrymen, when he was shot through the shoulder, and that he lay in his blood till the enemy returned, when they despatched him in a cruel manner; for his body was found with one of his hands almost cut off, his head slashed in several places, his skull cut through, his brains coming out at his nose and scattered all around. He was an enlightened patriot, an affectionate friend, a gallant soldier, a fond husband, and an indulgent parent. He had no inheritance to leave, as his little property was left in Philadelphia; but he has left a sorrowful widow and five helpless children in very indigent circumstances. They are worthy of the notice of the charitable.

New-York Journal, June 1

This day, Mr. Simeon Deane arrived at Congress express from the American plenipotentiaries at the court of France, and delivered his despatches to the President. The important contents are, by a correspondent, thus communicated:

"The news of the defeat and captivity of General Burgoyne was received in France the beginning of December, with as much joy as if a victory by their own troops had been announced. Our plenipotentiaries took this opportunity again to attract the attention of the court of France to the object of their negotiation. On the 16th, Monsieur Gerard, royal syndic of Strasburgh, and secretary of his Majesty's Council of State, waited on our plenipotentiaries, and informed them, by order of the King, 'That after long and full consideration of our affairs and propositions in council, it was decided, and his Majesty was determined to acknowledge our independence, and make a treaty with us of amity and commerce; that in the treaty no advantage would be taken of our present situation to obtain terms from us which otherwise would not be convenient for us to agree to, his Majesty desiring that the treaty, once made, should be durable, and our amity subsist forever, which could not be expected, if each nation did not find its interest in the continuance as well as in the commencement of it. It was therefore his intention that the terms of the treaty should be such as we might be willing to agree to if our state had been long established, and in the fulness of strength and power, and such as we should approve of when that time should come; that his Majesty was fixed in his determination not only to acknowledge, but to support our independence by every means in his power; that in doing this he might probably be soon engaged in war, with all the expenses, risk, and damage usually attending it; yet he should not expect any compensation from us on that account, nor pretend that he acted wholly for our sakes, since besides his real good-will to us and our cause, it was manifestly the interest of France that the power of England should be diminished by our separation from it. He should, moreover, not so much as insist, that, if he engaged in a war with England on our account, we should not make a separate peace for ourselves, whenever good and advantageous terms were offered to us. The only condition he would require and rely on would be this: *That we, in no peace to be made with England, should give up our independence and return to the obedience of that government.'*

"That upon such principles, by virtue of full powers by the King of France, to Monsieur Gerard, royal syndic of the city of Strasburgh, and secretary of his Majesty's Council of State, dated the 30th of January, 1778, this minister, with our plenipotentiaries, signed at Paris on the 6th of February, a treaty of alliance and commerce between the crown of France and the United States of America, almost in the very terms in which the American plenipotentiaries had been instructed by Congress. In the treaty of alliance the following articles are conspicuous:

"Article I. If war should break out between France and Great Britain, during the continuance of the present war between the United States and England, his Majesty and the United States shall make it a common cause, and aid each other mutually with their good offices, their councils, and their forces, according to the exigence of conjunctures, as becomes good and faithful allies.

"Article II. The essential and direct end of the present defensive alliance is, to maintain effectually the liberty, sovereignty, and independence, absolute and unlimited, of the said United States, as well in matters of government as of commerce.

"Article VI. The most Christian King renounces forever the possession of the island of Bermuda, as well as of any part of the continent of North America, which before the treaty of Paris, in 1763, or in virtue of that treaty, were acknowledged to belong to the crown of Great Britain, or to the United States, heretofore called British Colonies, or which are at this time, or have lately been, under the power of the King and crown of Great Britain."

The treaty of commerce stands upon the broad basis of equality; and considering the established great power of France, and the infancy of the United States, is an act without parallel. In a word, the sentiments delivered on the 16th of December by Monsieur Gerard, by order of the King of France, are sentiments rarely entertained by princes, and which, together with these equal treaties, must rank him, not only among the greatest monarchs of France, but in history.

These important advices were brought in the *Le Sensible*, M. Marignie commander, a royal frigate of France, of twenty-eight twelve-pounders, and three hundred men. She left Brest on the eighth of March, and, after a passage of thirty-five days, arrived at Casco Bay, from whence she sailed on her return, after two days' stay to take in water.

Pennsylvania Gazette, May 2

Of this extraordinary publication [says the editor of the *Pennsylvania Ledger*] we doubt not but our readers will think as we do—that we have good reason to suspect it is, what many former publications from the same quarter certainly have been, a *seasonable* piece of *misrepresentation*. There is an art, well known by these adepts, of *mixing* truth and falsehood, or of conveying falsehood in the vehicle of truth.

The hasty resolution of Congress to reject all possible offers of accommodation with Great Britain, was found to alarm the people, who must be supposed to prefer a re-union with the mother country, on the generous terms proposed, before any romantic and hazardous scheme of ambition whatever. It was, therefore, necessary to pacify the popular alarm, and endeavor to reconcile us to the idea of a ruinous connection with France, by representing the terms of that connection in a flattering light. However, supposing this to be a true and faithful account, it certainly ought the more to alarm every true friend to the future peace and prosperity of America. Surely we have reason to distrust the restless and enterprising spirit of France, and of those other commercial powers who are said to favor the project of American independency! And, if the French King has agreed to such a treaty as this, of which, however, a *sample* only is given us, we must be madly credulous indeed if we believe it proceeds from any other motives than, at all events, to prevent our enjoying now the benefits of a happy reconciliation, and with a view, when the times will bear it, to bring us into such a state of domestic expense and foreign dependence, as must make us forever repent our folly in not having embraced the opportunity, now presented, of securing our civil and religious freedom, peace, and safety, against the arts or violence of all the world, by a cordial re-union with our mother country!

Is it possible that we can *now* wish for a final separation from Britain, the ancient and chief support of the Protestant religion in the world, for the sake of upholding a little longer, at the expense of our lives and fortunes, the arbitrary power of that Congress, who without even asking our consent, have *disposed* of us, have *mortgaged* us like vassals and slaves, by refusing to treat with Britain, and by entering into a treaty with that ambitious and treacherous power, whose religious and political maxims have so often disturbed the peace and invaded the rights of mankind? The Congress have wonderfully altered their tone of late. The time was when the bare *toleration* of the Roman Catholic religion in Canada, though stipulated for by articles of capitulation, was treated as a wicked attempt to establish "a *sanguinary* faith, which had for ages filled the world with blood and slaughter!" But now the Congress are willing to make us the instruments of weakening the best friends, and of strengthening the most powerful and ambitious enemies of the Reformation to such a degree as must do more than all the world besides could do, towards the universal re-establishment of Popery through all Christendom. It will be said that the French are no longer such a bigoted people as they were in the day of the St. Bartholomew massacre, and that we need not fear imbibing any improper sentiments from her maxims of religion or government. That

France is not so blindly bigoted to her religious faith as formerly, we readily grant—indeed, her religion is little more at this day than an outside show to cover a general infidelity; but there is, for this very reason, the more cause to fear and distrust her views, as the less real religion she has at heart, the more will she be disposed to encourage the political tenets of the Church of Rome, on account of the advantages they afford to her ambition, in the pious work of enslaving mankind. As to Spain, the confederated ally of France, we know how zealously she continues to support the horrid authority of an inquisition for the same reasons.

Judge, then, what we have to hope or expect from such an alliance! We do not only run a manifest risk of becoming slaves ourselves, under the treacherous title of independency, but we are doing every thing in our power to overturn the Protestant religion, and extinguish every spark, both of civil and religious freedom, in the world! These sentiments, no doubt, will be ridiculed by those who are interested in supporting the measures of Congress; but they surely demand the serious attention of every distinterested friend of this country, and of every man who wishes well to the right of humanity and conscience in every part of the world.

Pennsylvania Ledger, May 13

May 5

PENNSYLVANIA   This afternoon, the Commander-in-chief issued, from head-quarters at Valley Forge, the following after orders: It having pleased the Almighty Ruler of the Universe, propitiously to defend the cause of the United American States, and finally, by raising up a powerful friend among the Princes of the Earth, to establish our Liberty and Independence upon lasting foundations—it becomes us to set apart a day for gratefully acknowledging the divine goodness and celebrating the important event which we owe to his benign interposition.

The several brigades are to be assembled for this purpose, at nine o'clock to-morrow morning, when their chaplains will communicate the intelligence in the postscript to the *Penn-*

sylvania Gazette of the second instant, and offer up a thanks-giving, and deliver a discourse suitable to the occasion.

At half after ten o'clock a cannon will be fired, which is to be a signal for the men to be under arms.

The brigade inspectors will then inspect their dress and arms, form the battalions according to instructions given them, and announce to the commanding officers of brigades that the battalions are formed.

The brigadiers will then appoint the field officers to command the battalions, after which each battalion will be ordered to load and ground their arms. At half-past eleven another cannon will be fired as a signal for the march, upon which the several brigades will begin their march by wheeling to the right by platoons, and proceed by the nearest way to the left of their ground, in the new position that will be pointed out by the brigade inspectors. A third signal will be given, upon which there will be a discharge of thirteen cannon; when the thirteenth has fired, a running fire of the infantry will begin on the right of Woodford's, and continue throughout the whole front line; it will be then taken up on the left of the second line, and continue to the right. Upon a signal given the whole army will *Huzza! long live the King of France!*

The artillery then begins again, and fires thirteen rounds. This will be succeeded by second general discharge of musketry in a running fire—*Huzza! long live the friendly European powers!* Then the last discharge of thirteen pieces of artillery will be given, followed by a general running fire—*Huzza for the American States!*

New-Jersey Gazette, May 13

May 6

PENNSYLVANIA   Agreeably to the special orders issued yesterday at head-quarters, the alliance has been splendidly celebrated. A writer gives the following minute account of the festivities, in a familiar letter to a friend:

"How often have you told me that a man of my contemplative turn, so fond of the shades of retirement and the

Engraved by Geo R Perine, N.Y.

LAFAYETTE.

endearments of domestic life, could find but little felicity amidst the uncontrollable vicissitudes of war. You did not recollect that there is in nature a principle much stronger than the passion for ease, and more powerful than the incitements to pleasure, which operates like the strength of a Samson in drawing us from our retirements, and breaking asunder the silken cords of our Helens or Delilahs. I have long since discovered that pleasures of the most agreeable kind may be found even in the bustle of a camp. What do you think, my dear friend, does the soldier feel, in reviewing the dangers he has passed—in planning or executing the overthrow of tyranny—or celebrating the exploits of heroes? And what spectacle can you imagine more splendid, than an army of freemen drawn up, within hearing of their enemy, to celebrate the acknowledgment of our independence, and alliance with the first monarch in the world; and who can you conceive more happy than those who have borne no inconsiderable part in the struggles and adversities that served to produce an event so favorable to the interests of mankind? I wished for you more than once, during our *feu de joie*, to have shared with me in the festivity of the day. It would have given you new ideas of military pleasures, and helped the poem on our independence, which you have promised, to some elegant strokes of the epic. Heretofore we have celebrated the day in which a prince was vested with the power to kill and enslave us; but this was the day of rejoicing at the interment of tyranny, and the coronation of American Independence.

"After the chaplains had finished their discourses, and the second cannon was fired, the troops began their march to the lines in the following order:—Each major-general conducted the first brigade of his command to the ground; the other brigades were conducted by their commanding officers in separate columns. Major-General Lord Stirling commanded on the right, the Marquis de Lafayette on the left, and the Baron de Kalb the second line. But this arrangement can convey no adequate idea of their movements to their several posts—of the appearance of his excellency during his circuit round the lines—of the air of our soldiers—the cleanliness of their dress—the brilliancy and good order of their arms, and the remarkable animation with which they performed the necessary salute as the general passed along. Indeed, during the whole of the review, the utmost military decorum was preserved, while at the same time one might observe the hearts of the soldiery struggling to express their feelings in a way more agreeable to nature.

"The Commander-in-chief, his suite; the Marquis de Lafayette, his train; Lord Stirling, General Greene, and the other principal officers, who had joined his excellency, having finished the review, retired to the centre of the encampment, to a kind of amphitheatre, which had been formed to entertain the officers of the army, who were invited to partake of a collation with his excellency, after the *feu de joie*.

"On firing of the third signal gun, the *feu de joie* commenced. It was conducted with great judgment and regularity. The gradual progression of the sound from the discharge of cannon and musketry, swelling and rebounding from the neighboring hills, and gently sweeping along the Schuylkill, with the intermingled huzzas—to long live the King of France—long live the friendly European powers, and long live the American States, composed a military music more agreeable to a soldier's ear than the most finished pieces of your favorite Handel.

"The *feu de joie* being over, and the troops marched back to their different quarters, the officers came forward to the entertainment provided by his excellency. But I must not pass over the description of their order of march.

"Some of the ancients were not more attached to their mystical figures than many of the moderns. We of America have our number THIRTEEN. The officers approached the place of entertainment in different columns, thirteen abreast, and closely linked together in each other's arms. The appearance was pretty enough. The number of officers composing each line, signified the thirteen American States; and the interweaving of arms a complete union and most perfect confederation.

"The amphitheatre looked elegant. The outer seats for the officers were covered with tent canvas stretched out upon poles; and the tables in the centre shaded by elegant marquees, raised high, and arranged in a very striking and agreeable style. An excellent band of music attended during the entertainment; but the feast was still more animating by the discourse and behavior of his excellency to the officers, and the gentlemen in the country (many of them our old Philadelphia acquaintances) who were present on this occasion. Mrs. Washington, the Countess of Stirling, Lady Kitty her daughter, Mrs. Greene, and a number of other ladies, favored the feast with their company, amongst whom good humor and the graces were contending for the pre-eminence. The wine circulated in the most genial manner—to the King of France —the friendly European powers—the American States—the honorable Congress, and other toasts of a similar nature, descriptive of the spirit of freemen.

"About six o'clock in the evening the company broke up, and his excellency returned to head-quarters. The French gentlemen of rank and distinction seemed peculiarly pleased with this public approbation of our alliance with their nation. The general himself wore a countenance of uncommon delight and complacence. I wish that you, who are so great an adept in preserving the expressions of nature, had been here to have done justice to him and the army. The latter, in particular, never looked so well, nor in such good order, since the beginning of the war. And here I cannot forbear mentioning a little anecdote that I am told happened during the review. An officer was called to one side in order to know what was to be done with a spy who was making observations on the army. But the officer coolly observed to the gentleman who gave the information, that he thought it best to take no further notice of the spy, but suffer him to return to his employers, as they must feel more pain from his account of the army, than grief on hearing of his detection and death.

"What may be reckoned somewhat remarkable, not one accident happened to lessen or disturb the joy of the day; and the whole was closed by the officers returning to the duties of their several stations with hearts filled with the warmest sensations to the great cause of their rejoicings."

New-York Journal, June 15

May 19

PENNSYLVANIA   Yesterday the British army, anxious to give Sir William Howe the most public and splendid testimony of the high esteem they entertain of him as a general, and of the affection and attachment which his popular conduct has secured to him from all ranks, both of officers and men, prepared a magnificent entertainment to grace his departure from Philadelphia. It consisted of a variety of parts, and was therefore called the MISCHIANZA. The admission tickets were decorated with a sun just verging towards the horizon, with this inscription, *Luces descedens aucto splendore resurgam*. On the lower part of the shield was the sea—at top the general's crest, with the words *Vive, vale*, and at the bottom and all round, different military trophies. The fête began at four o'clock in the afternoon, by a grand procession on the Delaware, consisting of three divisions—a galley and ten flat-boats in each division. In the centre division was the *Hussar* galley, with the general, the admiral, General Sir Henry Clinton, and the ladies of their party. Three flat-boats, with bands of music in each, led the procession.

They set out from Knight's wharf at a signal from the *Vigilant*, and proceeded till they arrived off the Market Place, where the *Fanny* armed ship was drawn off into the stream, and beautifully decorated with a variety of colors. Here they lay on their oars while the music played "God save the King." They then proceeded to the Old Fort, where a landing place was prepared, and as soon as the general landed he was saluted with nineteen guns from the *Roebuck*, and the same number from the *Vigilant*. The company, as they quitted the boats, formed themselves into a line of procession, and advanced between two files of grenadiers till they came to a square of four hundred yards on every side, railed in and prepared for the tournament. In front of the square was Sir Harry Colder's house, appearing through two triumphal arches, erected, one in honor of Lord Howe, the other of Sir William. Two sofas, in form of amphitheatres, formed the advanced wings of one of these arches. On these the ladies took their places, advancing to them through the centre of the square. On the lowest seat of each were seven young ladies dressed in the Asiatic habits, and wearing the different colors of the knights who chose them for their damsels. Here the tournament commenced, when the elegance and richness of the different dresses of the knights and squires, their horses' trappings and caparisons, the taste displayed in their mottoes and devices, the various evolutions and feats of arms they performed, exhibited altogether a spectacle as new, as it surpassed the most sanguine expectations of the beholders.

As soon as the tournament ended, the knights and squires, two and two, moved through the first triumphal arch, which was decorated with naval ornaments. At the top was the statue of Neptune with his trident; in the interior were the attributes of that god, and in a niche on each side stood a sailor with his sword drawn; on the two wings were plumes of feathers, with this description on the entablature, *Laus illi debetur, et alme gratia major*. An avenue of three hundred yards in length, and thirty-five in breadth, lined with troops, and decorated with the colors of the different regiments, planted at proper distances, led to the second triumphal arch. Between these colors the knights with their attendants ranged themselves, and the company, preceded by all the music of the army, advanced in procession. They were led into the house through the second arch, erected in honor of the general. This arch was of the Tuscan order; on the pediment was Fame with her trumpet; in the interior was a plume of feathers, and military trophies, and on the entablature, *I, bone, quo virtus vocat tua, I pede fausto*. The house within side was painted in a light elegant style, with festoons, and several emblematical figures; mirrors, girandoles and chandeliers, decorated with wreaths of different colored gauze, adorned the walls. The company were entertained with tea and refreshments, and then danced till half after ten o'clock; the windows being then suddenly thrown open, a grand and beautiful display of fireworks was exhibited.

Towards the conclusion, the triumphant arch next the house appeared magnificently illuminated, and Fame blew from her trumpet in letters of light, "Thy laurels shall never fade."

After the fireworks the company sat down to a supper consisting of a thousand and twenty-four dishes, in a magnificent apartment built for the occasion, decorated in the same style and elegance as the rooms in the house. The herald of the *blended rose*, in his robes of ceremony, announced by sound of trumpet the King's health; the Queen and Royal Family; the Army and Navy, and their respective commanders; the Ladies. A salute of music and three cheers graced each of these toasts. After supper the company returned to the ball room, and at four o'clock they all withdrew.

Pennsylvania Ledger, May 23

May 31

RHODE ISLAND   Last week, a party of British troops, from Rhode Island, made a descent upon the towns of Bristol and Warren, and after plundering and destroying all they could lay their hands on, they made a hasty retreat. This morning, about daybreak, another party from the same place, consisting of one hundred and fifty men, under the command of Major Eyre, landed at the mouth of Fall River, with a design to burn Tiverton and the mills. They set fire to the lower mill, and a house that stood on the shore; but the town, and upper mills, by the vigilance of the inhabitants, were saved. Apprised of the enemy's intention, they took up the bridge, and posted themselves behind a wall that commanded it, from whence they kept up so brisk a fire, that after an engagement of nearly an hour and a half, the enemy were compelled to retire, leaving behind them one killed and another mortally wounded. Five muskets and as many hats have since been found, and from every circumstance it appears that their loss was considerable. The militia turned out with great alacrity, and repaired to the place of action; but the precipitate retreat of the enemy deprived those spirited fellows of an opportunity to revenge the injuries they have repeatedly received, and of treating the detestable conflagrators as they justly deserved.

The enemy's boats and shipping, in passing down the river, received considerable annoyance from the American fort on Bristol Neck. A galley that came up to cover them from the well-directed fire of the fort, was driven on the Rhode Island shore, and the men were obliged to abandon her; a sloop that attempted to assist her shared the same fate. The Americans had not a man killed or wounded.

New Hampshire Gazette, June 16

JUNE

June 5

PENNSYLVANIA   The last accounts from Philadelphia are, that the transports with the baggage have fallen down the river—that the British have begun to destroy some of their outworks—that they have broken off the trunnions of the heavy cannon which are not put on board, and that the whole army is ordered to be in readiness to march at a minute's warning.

A flag came out from the city yesterday, with a packet for Congress, containing the *acts* for appointing commissioners and other purposes. The commissioners are Lord Carlisle, Governor Johnston, and William Eden, Esquire. There was also a letter from General Clinton to his Excellency General Washington, proposing an exchange of the prisoners who are in Philadelphia, the others to remain until a cartel is settled. The British officer informed General Lee, who received him, that the British intended to leave Philadelphia soon, and *that he had permission to mention it.*

The commissioners mentioned in the above arrived at Philadelphia on Sunday morning last. Lord Cornwallis also arrived at the same time, but without troops.

Letter from Valley Forge
New-Jersey Gazette, June 10

June 17

This day the Congress agreed to an answer to the letters and inclosures sent to them by the commissioners lately arrived at Philadelphia, to treat of reconciliation, of which the following is an extract:—"The acts of the British Parliament, the commission from your sovereign, and your letter, suppose the people of these States to be subjects of the crown of Great Britain, and are founded on the idea of dependence, which is utterly inadmissible. I am further directed to inform your excellencies, that Congress are inclined to peace, notwithstanding the unjust claims from which this war originated, and the savage manner in which it hath been conducted. They will therefore be ready to enter upon the consideration of a treaty of peace and commerce, not inconsistent with treaties already subsisting, when the King of Great Britain shall demonstrate a sincere disposition for that purpose. *The only solid proof of this disposition will be an explicit acknowledgment of the independence of these States, or the withdrawing his fleets and armies.*"

Broadsides, I, 30
Gordon, II, 366

June 19

PENNSYLVANIA   The British army, early yesterday morning, completed their evacuation of Philadelphia, having before transported their stores and most of their artillery into Jersey, where they had thrown up some works, and several of their regiments were encamped. They manned the lines the preceding night, and retreating over the common, crossed at Gloucester Point. It is supposed they will endeavor to go to New York. A party of the American light horse pursued them very close, and took a great number of prisoners, some of whom were refugees. Soon after the evacuation, the Honorable Major-General Arnold took possession of Philadelphia, with Colonel Jackson's Massachusetts regiment.

Pennsylvania Evening Post, June 20

June 29

NEW JERSEY   His Excellency General Washington, having early intelligence of the intended movement of the enemy from Philadelphia, detached a considerable body of troops under the command of Major-General Lee, on order to support General Maxwell's brigade of Continental troops already in New Jersey, and the militia under Generals Dickinson and Heard. These troops were intended to harass the enemy on their march through the state to Amboy, and retard them till General Washington, with the main body, could get up. In the mean time several small skirmishes happened between the enemy and General Maxwell's troops, joined by the militia, but without any considerable execution on either side.

The march of the enemy being by this means impeded, and the main army having crossed the Delaware at Coryell's ferry on the 20th and 21st ultimo, proceeded by the way of Hopewell, Rocky Hill, Kingston, and Cranbury, and on the 27th overtook the enemy at Monmouth Court House, whither they retired from Allentown on the approach of our troops, leaving their intended route to Amboy.

It having been previously determined to attack the enemy on their march, a suitable disposition was made the same evening. General Lee, with a detachment of picked men, consisting of about fifteen hundred, and reinforced by a strong body of Jersey militia, advanced to English Town, (about six miles from Monmouth Court House;) the militia then proceeded to the meeting-house, the main army, under General Washington, being about four miles in the rear of English Town. In this position the whole halted until advice could be received of the enemy's motion.

At three o'clock yesterday (Sunday) morning, their first division, under General Knyphausen, began their march, of which we had intelligence in about two hours, when General Lee had orders to advance and begin the attack, the main army at the same time advancing to support him. About half a mile beyond the court house, General Lee began his attack, and drove the enemy for some time, when they being reinforced, he was obliged to retreat in turn, till met by General Washington with the main army, which formed on the first advantageous ground. In the mean time two field-pieces, covered by two regiments of the detachment, and commanded by Colonels Livingston and Stewart, were advanced to check the enemy's approach, which they performed with great spirit and considerable loss on both sides. This service being performed, they retired with the pieces to the front line, then completely formed, when the severest cannonade began that it is thought ever happened in America. In the mean time, strong detachments marched and attacked the enemy with small arms, with various success. The enemy were finally obliged to give way, and we took possession of the field covered with dead and wounded. The intense heat of the weather, and the preceding fatigue of the troops, made it necessary to halt them to rest for some time; the enemy, in the mean time, presenting a front about one mile advanced beyond the seat of action. As soon as the troops had recovered breath, General Washington ordered two brigades to advance upon each of their flanks, intending to move on in front at a proper time to support them, but before they could reach their destination, night came on, and made any further movements impracticable.

The British left on the field the Honorable Colonel Monckton with several other officers, and a great number of privates, which cannot yet be ascertained with precision. About twelve o'clock last night they moved off with great precipitation, towards Middletown, leaving at the court house five wounded officers, and above forty privates. They began the attack with their veteran grenadiers and light infantry, which renders their loss still more important. On our side Lieutenant-Colonel Bonner, of Pennsylvania and Major Dickinson, of Virginia, are slain. Colonel Barber, of New Jersey, is wounded by a musket ball, which passed through the right of his body; but it is hoped will not prove mortal. Our troops behaved with the greatest bravery, and opposed the flower of the British army. Our artillery was well served, and did amazing execution. Before, during, and after the action, deserters came over to us in great numbers, and still continue so to do. Of the enemy's dead many have been found without any wound, but being heavily clothed, they sank under the heat and fatigue. We are well assured the Hessians absolutely refused to engage, declaring it was too hot. Their line of march from the court house was strewed with dead, with arms, knapsacks, and accoutrements, which they dropped on their retreat. They had the day before taken about fifteen prisoners, whom in their haste they left behind. Had we been possessed of a powerful body of cavalry on the field, there is no doubt the success would have been much more complete, but they had been employed in harassing the enemy during the march, and were so detached, as to give the enemy a great superiority in number, much to their advantage. Our success, under Heaven, is to be wholly ascribed to the good disposition made by his excellency, supported by the firmness and bravery of both officers and men, who were emulous to distinguish themselves on this occasion. The great advance of the enemy on their way, their possession of the strong grounds at Middletown, added to the exhausted state of our troops, made an immediate pursuit ineligible; and the American army now remains about one mile advanced from the field of battle, having been since employed in collecting the dead and wounded, and burying the former.

New-York Journal, July 13

JULY

July 11

PENNSYLVANIA   Early this afternoon, His Excellency Monsieur Gerard, ambassador from his Most Christian Majesty to the United States, arrived at Philadelphia. He was accompanied from Chester to an elegant apartment provided for him in Market street, by a committee of Congress, appointed for that purpose. On his entrance into the city, he was saluted by Colonel Proctor's artillery. It is impossible to describe the joy that appeared in every good man's countenance on this auspicious event. His excellency came in a frigate, part of a fleet of twelve ships of the line from Toulon, under the command of Count D'Estaing.

Upcott, V, 139

July 13

NEW JERSEY AND NEW YORK   General Washington's army is now encamped at Elizabethtown, Newark, Hackensack, &c., in New Jersey; and the following regiments are at the White Plains, viz.: Putnam's, Webb's, Enos', Mieg's, Sheldon's, Nixon's, Sherburn's, Graham's, and Willis's, with some light horse. They occupy the ground on which General Howe engaged General Washington in the year 1776, and are commanded by Generals Gates, McDougall, Parsons, and two other brigadier-generals.

New York Gazette and Weekly Mercury, July 13

July 20

PENNSYLVANIA   During the past week many of the distressed refugees from the Wyoming settlement on the Susquehannah, who escaped the general massacre of the inhabitants, have passed through Poughkeepsie, in New York. From them we have collected the following account, viz.:— Previous to the narrative, it may be necessary to inform some of our readers, that this settlement was made by the people of Connecticut, on a grant of lands purchased by the inhabitants of that colony, under sanction of the government, of the Indian proprietors; and that these lands, falling within the limits of the Pennsylvania claim, a dispute concerning the right has arisen, between the two governments, and proceeded to frequent acts of hostility. When it was at a height that threatened the disturbance of the other governments, Congress interposed, by whose recommendation and authority the decision of the dispute was suspended till that with Great Britain, equally interesting to every American State, was concluded, when there might be more leisure to attend to the other, and consider the justice of each claim.

On this footing the dispute has lain dormant for two or

three years; the inhabitants lived happily, and the settlement increased, consisting of eight townships, viz.: Lackawanna, Exeter, Kingston, Wilkesbarre, Plymouth, Nanticoke, Huntington, and Salem, each containing five miles square. The six lower townships were pretty full of inhabitants, the two upper ones had comparatively but few, thinly scattered. The lands are exceeding good, beautifully situated along both sides of the Susquehannah, navigable for flat-bottomed boats, and produced immense quantities of grain of all sorts, roots, fruits, hemp, flax, &c., and stock of all kinds in abundance. The settlement had lately supplied the Continental army with three thousand bushels of grain, and the ground was loaded with the most promising crops of every kind. The settlement included upwards of a thousand families, which had furnished our army with a thousand soldiers, besides the garrisons of four forts, in the townships of Lackawanna, Exeter, Kingston, and Wilkesbarre. One of these forts was garrisoned by upwards of four hundred soldiers, chiefly of the militia, the principal officers in which were Colonels Dennison and Zebulon Butler.

The Tories and Indians had given some disturbance to these settlements last year, before General Herkimer's battle at Oneida Creek, near Fort Stanwix, and our skirmishes soon after with parties of the enemy at and near Schoharie, when they were dispersed, and the Tories concealed themselves among our different settlements; the people here remained undisturbed during the rest of the year.

About this time the inhabitants having discovered that many of these villanous Tories who had stirred up the Indians, and been with them in fighting against us, were within the settlements, twenty-seven of them were, in January last, taken up and secured. Of these, eighteen were sent to Connecticut, the rest after being detained some time and examined were, for want of sufficient evidence, set at liberty; they immediately joined the enemy, and became active in raising in the Indians a spirit of hostility against us. This disposition soon after began to appear in the behavior of the Tories and Indians, which gave the people apprehensions of danger, and occasioned some preparations for defence.

The people had frequent intimations that the Indians had some mischievous design against them, but their fears were somewhat abated by the seeming solicitude of the Indians to preserve peace; they sent down at different times, several parties with declarations of their peaceable disposition toward us, and to request the like on our part towards them. They were always dismissed with assurances that there was no design to disturb them. But one of those Indians getting drunk, said he and the other messengers were only sent to amuse the people in the settlement, but that the Indians intended, as soon as they were in order, to attack them. On this the Indian men were confined, and the women sent back with a flag. In March, appearances became more alarming, and the scattered families settled for thirty miles up the river, were collected and brought into the more populous parts. In April and May, strolling parties of Indians and Tories, about thirty and under in a company, made frequent incursions into the settlement, robbing and plundering the inhabitants of provision, grain, and live stock. In June, several persons being at work on a farm from which the Tory inhabitants had gone to the enemy, were attacked, and one man of them killed; soon after, a woman (wife of one of the twenty-seven Tories before mentioned) was killed, with her five children, by a party of these Tories and Indians, who plundered the house of every thing they could take away, and destroyed the rest.

On the first instant (July) the whole body of the enemy, consisting, it is supposed, of near sixteen hundred, (about three hundred of whom were thought to be Indians, under their own chiefs, the rest, Tories, painted like them, except their officers, who were dressed like Regulars,) the whole under the command of Colonel John Butler, (a Connecticut Tory, and cousin to Colonel Zebulon Butler, the second in command in the settlement,) came down near the upper fort, but concealed the greatest part of their number; here they had a skirmish with the inhabitants, who took and killed two Indians, and lost ten of their own men, three of whom they afterwards found killed, scalped, and mangled in the most inhuman manner.

Thursday, July 2.—The enemy appeared on the mountains,

back of Kingston, when the women and children then fled
into the fort. Most of the garrison of Exeter fort were Tories,
who treacherously gave it up to the enemy. The same night,
after a little resistance, they took Lackawanna fort, killed
Squire Jenkins and his family, with several others, in a barbarous manner, and made prisoners of most of the women
and children; a small number only escaped.

  Friday, July 3.—This morning Colonel Zebulon Butler,
leaving a small number to guard the fort, (Wilkesbarre,)
crossed the river with about four hundred men, and marched
into Kingston fort. The enemy sent in a flag, demanding a
surrender of the fort in two hours. Colonel Butler answered
he should not surrender, but was ready to receive them. They
sent in a second flag, demanding an immediate surrender,
otherwise that the fort should be stormed, plundered, and
burnt, with all its contents, in a few hours, and said that they
had with them three hundred men. Colonel Butler proposed
a parley, which, being agreed to, a place in Kingston was
appointed for the meeting, to which Colonel Z. Butler repaired with four hundred men well armed, but finding nobody
there, he proceeded to the foot of the mountain, where at a
distance he saw a flag, which, as he advanced, retired, as if
afraid, twenty or thirty rods; he following, was led into an
ambush, and partly surrounded by the enemy, who suddenly
rose and fired upon them. Notwithstanding the great disproportion of sixteen hundred to four hundred, he and his men
bravely stood and returned the fire for three-quarters of an
hour, with such briskness and resolution, that the enemy
began to give way, and were upon the point of retiring, when
one of Colonel Z. Butler's men, either through treachery or
cowardice, cried out that the colonel ordered a retreat. This
caused a cessation of their fire, threw them into confusion,
and a total rout ensued. The greatest part fled to the river,
which they endeavored to pass, to Fort Wilkesbarre; the
enemy pursued them with the fury of devils; many were lost
or killed in the river, and no more than about seventy, some
of whom were wounded, escaped to Wilkesbarre.

  Saturday morning, July 4.—The enemy sent one hundred

and ninety-six scalps into Fort Kingston, which they invested on the land side, and kept up a continual fire upon it.

This evening Colonel Z. Butler, with his family, quitted the fort, and went down the river.

Colonel Nathan Dennison went with a flag to Exeter fort, to know of Colonel John Butler what terms he would grant on a surrender. Butler answered, *the Hatchet.* Colonel Dennison returned to Fort Kingston, which he defended till Sunday morning, when his men being nearly all killed or wounded, he could hold out no longer, and was obliged to surrender at discretion. The enemy took away some of the unhappy prisoners, and shutting up the rest in the houses, set fire to them, and they were all consumed together. These infernals then crossed the river to Fort Wilkesbarre, which in a few minutes surrendered at discretion. About seventy of the men, who had listed in the continental service to defend the frontiers, they inhumanly butchered, with every circumstance of horrid cruelty; and then shutting up the rest, with the women and children in the houses, they set fire to them, and they all perished together in the flames.

After burning all the buildings in the fort, they proceeded to the destruction of every building and improvement (except what belonged to some Tories) that came within their reach, on all these flourishing settlements, which they have rendered a scene of desolation and horror, almost beyond description, parallel, or credibility; and were not the facts attested by numbers of the unhappy sufferers, from different quarters of the settlement, and unconnected with each other, it would be impossible to believe that human nature could be capable of such prodigious enormity.

When these miscreants had destroyed the other improvements, they proceeded to destroy the crops on the ground, letting in the cattle and horses to the corn, and cutting up as much as they could of what was left. Great numbers of the cattle they shot and destroyed, and cutting out the tongues of many others, left them to perish in misery.

The course of these truly diabolical proceedings was marked by many particular acts of distinguished enormity, among which were the following, viz.:

The Captains James Bedlock, Robert Duryee, and Samuel Ransom, being made prisoners by the enemy, they stripped Captain Bedlock, tied him to a tree, and stuck him full of sharp splinters of pine knots, then piling a heap of pine knots round him, they set all on fire, put Duryee and Ransom into the fire, and held them down with pitchforks.

Thomas Hill, (whose father was killed by the Indians last Indian war,) with his own hands killed his own mother, his father-in-law, his sisters, and their families.

Partial Terry, the son of a man who bore a very respectable character, had several times sent his father word that he hoped to wash his hands in his heart's blood. Agreeable to such a horrid declaration, the monster, with his own hand, murdered his father, mother, brother and sisters, stripped off their scalps, and cut off his father's head.

Colonel Dennison was seen surrounded by the enemy, and was doubtless murdered. Colonel Zebulon Butler is supposed to be the only officer who escaped.

It is said he had several times written letters to the Congress and General Washington, acquainting them with the danger the settlement was in, and requesting assistance, but that he received no answer, except that he had no cause to fear, since the Indians were all for peace and quite averse to war. However, he lately received a letter from Captain Spaulding, acquainting him that neither the Congress nor General Washington had received any of his letters, which had been intercepted by the Pennsylvania Tories, who, in all probability, acted in concert with those execrable miscreants, against Wyoming. It is reported that these wretches, after completing their horrid business at Wyoming, are going or gone to Cherry Valley, and the parts adjacent.

We hear that a party of infernals, of the like kind, have, within this week or two, infested the parts about Leghawegh, near Rochester, on the Minisink road to Philadelphia, where a party of them, about forty in number, have plundered and burnt several houses, abused some people, and carried off three men. It is hoped speedy and effectual measures will be taken to punish and extirpate these monsters in human shape, from the face of the earth.   *New-York Journal, July* 20

AUGUST

August 6

PENNSYLVANIA   This being the day appointed by Congress for the reception of Sieur Gerard, Minister Plenipotentiary from his Most Christian Majesty, that Minister received audience accordingly. In pursuance of the ceremonial established by Congress, the Honorable Richard Henry Lee, Esquire, one of the Delegates from Virginia, and the Honorable Samuel Adams, Esquire, one of the Delegates from Massachusetts Bay, in a coach and six provided by Congress, waited upon the Minister at his house. In a few minutes, the Minister and the two delegates entered the coach, Mr. Lee placing himself at the Minister's left hand on the back seat, Mr. Adams occupying the front seat. The Minister's chariot being behind, received his Secretary. The carriages being arrived at the state house, Philadelphia, the two members of Congress, placing themselves at the Minister's left hand, a little before one o'clock, introduced him to his chair in the Congress chamber, the President and Congress sitting; the chair was placed fronting the President. The Minister being seated, he gave his credentials into the hand of his Secretary, who advanced and delivered them to the President. The Secretary of Congress then read and translated them, which being done, Mr. Lee announced the Minister to the President and Congress; at this time, the President, the Congress, and the Minister rose together: he bowed to the President and Congress, they bowed to him; whereupon the whole seated themselves. In a moment the Minister arose and made a speech to the Congress, they sitting. The speech to the Congress being finished, the Minister sat down, and giving a copy of his speech to his Secretary, he presented it to the President. The President and the Congress then rose, and the President pronounced their answer to the speech, the Minister standing.

The answer being ended, the whole were again seated, and the President giving a copy of the answer to the Secretary of the Congress, he presented it to the Minister. The President, the Congress, and the Minister then again arose together. The Minister bowed to the President, who returned the salute, and then to the Congress, who also bowed in return. The Minister, having again bowed to the President, and received his bow, he withdrew, and was attended home in the same manner in which he had been conducted to the audience.

Within the bar of the house, the Congress formed a semi-circle on each side of the President and the Minister: the President sitting at one extremity of the circle, at a table upon a platform elevated two steps, the Minister sitting at the opposite extremity of the circle, in an arm chair, upon the same level with the Congress. The door of the Congress chamber being thrown open, below the bar, about two hundren gentlemen were admitted to the audience, among whom were the Vice-President of the Supreme Executive Council of Pennsylvania, the Supreme Executive Council, the Speaker and Members of the House of Assembly, several foreigners of distinction, and officers of the army.

Thus has a new and noble sight been exhibited in this new world—the representatives of the United States of America, solemnly giving public audience to a Minister Plenipotentiary from the most powerful prince in Europe. Four years ago, such an event, at so near a day, was not in the view even of imagination: but it is the Almighty who raiseth up; he hath stationed America among the powers of the earth, and clothed her in robes of sovereignty.

The audience being over, the Congress and the Minister, at a proper hour, repaired to an entertainment by Congress, given to the Minister, at which were present, by invitation, several foreigners of distinction, and gentlemen of public character. The entertainment was conducted with a decorum suited to the occasion, and gave the most perfect satisfaction to the whole company.

New-York Journal, August 24

August 17

NEW YORK   The following oath is part of an act lately passed by the New York Congress at the Fishkills, which is to be taken by every subject, agreeable to the new constitution established by the Congress:—"I A. B. do solemnly, and without any mental reservation whatever, swear and call God to witness, (or, if the people called Quakers, affirm,) that I believe and acknowledge the State of New York to be of right a free and independent State, and that no authority or power can of right be executed in or over the said State, but what is, or shall be granted by, or derived from the people thereof; and further, that as a good subject of the said free and independent State of New York, I will, to the best of my knowledge and ability, faithfully do my duty, and as I shall keep or disregard this oath, so help and deal with me Almighty God."

The first person who was cited before the commissioners to take the oath, was Cadwallader Colden, Esq., of Coldenham, in Ulster County, New York, and eldest son of the late lieutenant-governor of that province. This gentleman showed an unshaken attachment to his sovereign and the constitution, from the first of the present rebellion. He had been a prisoner among the rebels for above two years, great part of the time closely confined in a common jail, or on board a sloop in the Hudson River, (in company with many other loyal sufferers,) for no other cause than avowing his sentiments with candor, modesty, and firmness, against independency. Determined to adhere to the good old constitution under which he and his fellow subjects enjoyed so much happiness, he persevered calmly, though resolutely, to oppose each innovation, for which he was ignominiously treated from time to time, and suffered every wanton indignity that malice could invent. When desired to take the above oath, he nobly refused it, returning a decent, spirited answer, in writing, which does him great honor; whereupon he was ordered to depart, and go within the British lines. On Monday last he arrived at New York in a flag of truce sloop, leaving behind him his wife, and a numerous family of children, to the insults, and a large estate to the depredations of a blind, infatuated people.

New York Gazette and Weekly Mercury, August 17

August 20

RHODE ISLAND   A gentleman who went on board the French fleet at Sandy Hook, gives the following account of their principal transactions during the time he was on board:

On the 30th of July the fleet arrived off, and anchored before the light-house, at the entrance of the harbor of Newport, in Rhode Island, except two frigates, that were ordered to the east end of the island, in order to prevent any vessels from getting out through Seconnet passage. On the frigates' arrival there, the English set fire to one twenty-gun ship and two galleys, which lay in that passage. The next morning one ship of fifty guns was sent up the west side of Conanicut Island, and after exchanging a few shots with the battery, the English thought proper to evacuate that island, after blowing up their fortifications, which were said to be guarded by about fifteen hundred men; they likewise blew up some of their outworks on Rhode Island, and burnt some dwelling-houses. The same day we sent up the west passage, one ship of sixty-four guns. The weather for the several following days was very foggy, which gave our fifty-gun ship an advantage of passing, without being seen, around the north end of Conanicut, and anchoring between a small bay or cove, on the west side of Rhode Island, (in which lay three British frigates,) and the harbor of Newport. On the fog's clearing away, the people, finding the frigates could not return to Newport, immediately left them after setting them on fire.

On the 8th of August, a signal was made for the fleet to weigh anchor and get in a line, which was done, and about three o'clock in the afternoon, we stood in for the harbor of Newport, under topsails lowered down. The Admiral being the first of the line, as soon as he came within about two miles, the battery on Brenton's Neck began a brisk cannonade on the *Languedoc*, which was not returned till she came within about three-quarters of a mile of the battery, when she began such a cannonade as I could not have conceived to have been possible from on board one ship, the consequence of which was, the battery was silenced in two or three broadsides, and the fleet passed in through the fire of the cannon from Fort Island, and two forts on the north end of the town of Newport, and anchored between Gold Island and Conanicut, without receiving any damage. On the ninth, a fleet of thirty-four sail of ships appeared off the harbor, which, we were informed, were a fleet from New York, commanded by Lord Howe; the wind being to the southward, we could not get out of the harbor. On the tenth, in the morning, the wind came round to the northward; a signal was made for the fleet to cut their cables, which was immediately done, and all came to sail except the frigates, which were all in Seconnet passage. On our coming to sea, the wind became very small. The enemy appeared to have been much alarmed on seeing our fleet under sail, as they all either cut or slipped their cables, cut many of their boats from their sterns, and hove many things overboard, in order to lighten their ships. On the 11th, in the morning, we found them at a much greater distance than they were the night before, but the wind springing up, we continued the chase. The British fleet now bearing about south-east by east, the wind at north-east, they hauled close upon a wind, but finding we came up with them, they altered their course from east south-east to south-east and to the southward, and from that to south-west, but all without effect, as we could outsail them very easily; the wind still continuing to blow a very fresh gale, and constantly increasing. At about five o'clock in the afternoon, both fleets drew in a line. The English fleet now consisted of only twenty-four sail, and ours of twelve. Our headmost ship in the line got up abreast with the sternmost of the English, but the sea running so high, we could not engage; we intended to have continued along side of them till the wind abated, but about sunsetting, a very heavy gale coming on, we were obliged to bring to, which we did with our heads to the southward; the English then hauled to the north-west, and the night coming on, we lost sight of them. On the 12th, at daylight, we discovered the *Languedoc* about a league distant, without a mast standing, and at about eight o'clock saw the *Marseilles* without a foremast or bowsprit. The gale continued extremely hard all this day and night following, and the greater part of the thirteenth, in the afternoon of which it abated. We then made sail and stood in about north-west, under what sail we could carry. In the morning of the 14th, at daylight, saw the *Languedoc* at about two leagues distance, which, when we came up with her, informed us she had been attacked the night before, by a ship of fifty guns, but had obliged her to sheer off, although she had neither mast nor rudder. At about nine o'clock discovered the *Marseilles*, who had been attacked early in the morning by a sixty gun ship, and one other coming down on her, but our fleet coming in sight, they quitted her. In the afternoon we took the *Thunder Bomb*; and in the morning of the fifteenth, saw the *Senegal* sloop of war, of sixteen guns, commanded by Captain Inglis, which we very soon came up with, and made a prize of. The fleet then anchored in latitude thirty-nine, in about forty fathoms water, where we lay till we got up jury masts on board the *Languedoc* and *Marseilles*. The *César*, of seventy-four guns, had not joined the fleet since the gale on the seventeenth. In the evening we weighed anchor and came to sail, and arrived off Rhode Island this afternoon.

New-York Journal, September 7

August 22

PENNSYLVANIA   A correspondent in Philadelphia offers the following hint, with the hope that it will be improved upon:—"I have labored under many difficulties, for my principles are such, that I would not willingly purchase any article (except in absolute necessity) of a Tory. To be asking always who are Whigs who have to sell, is troublesome, and, I am sorry to say, uncertain. I wish the same mark were put upon the houses of our well-known enemies, as the Turks use to designate the residences of liars, that is, by painting them black. This might be done with a very small expense, and I am firmly convinced that every well-wisher to his country would willingly contribute towards paying the expense. The lower story blackened might be sufficient."

Pennsylvania Packet, n.d.

This suggestion, says another writer, does well enough as far as it goes, but we would propose a still more prominent designation of a Tory, that is, let the right side of the face and the right hand be dyed black, and if that don't answer, it will not be any great loss if the whole body be set to dying.

Clift's Diary

August 23

RHODE ISLAND   The French fleet returned to Rhode Island on Thursday last, (20th,) but had suffered so considerably in the late storm, together with some slight engagement with the enemy, that they judged it necessary to retire in order to refit; in consequence of which resolution, the whole fleet sailed for Boston yesterday. General Sullivan, with the other general officers, were of opinion that they had not suffered to such a degree but that they were capable of sufficiently co-operating with the Americans in the reduction of Newport, without danger to the fleet; consequently the general, in the name of all the general officers of his army, protested against the count's withdrawing with his fleet and army at this critical juncture, as this expedition would not have been undertaken at this time, had it not been for the assurance he had given of assisting the American army to the utmost of his power.

New York Gazette and Weekly Mercury, September 21

August 29

MASSACHUSETTS   Yesterday, the fleet of his Most Christian Majesty, commanded by Admiral Count D'Estaing, arrived safe in Nantasket Road, and this morning three of his frigates anchored off Boston. The fleet has received considerable damage in the late storm; the count's ship (the *Languedoc*, of ninety guns) is particularly much damaged, her masts and bowsprits being carried away, and her rudder injured. In this condition she was attacked by a British ship of fifty guns, when, to her mortification, she could bring but five or six of her guns to bear upon the enemy. After firing four hours upon the *Languedoc*, the British man-of-war left her, having made very little addition to the damage she sustained in the storm, and killed only one man and wounded two or three. The damaged ships are repairing with the utmost expedition, and in all probability will soon be in a condition to give the dastardly Britons a drubbing, should they have the effrontery to attempt to stand before them.

This afternoon the Count D'Estaing, with his suite, came up to Boston in his barge. He was saluted on his landing by the cannon of the American fortresses and ships in the harbor, and all respects were paid him that time and circumstances would allow. The count and his officers, General Heath, the Marquis de Lafayette, the principal officers of the American marine, and other gentlemen, dined with General Hancock.

New Hampshire Gazette, September 8

RHODE ISLAND   Since the departure of the French fleet from Rhode Island, the operations of the Americans against the enemy's strongholds in that quarter have been carried on with great vigor; and last night it was unanimously determined by the general officers in council to change the position of the army from the advanced batteries before the enemy's lines, and to take post on Butt's Hill, at the north end of the island, till the return of the fleet. This was effected before two o'clock this morning, with the greatest order, the picket, commanded by Colonel Wigglesworth, remaining on Quaker Hill, a mile in front of the main body, and Livingston's and Lauren's corps advanced on the east and west roads, a mile beyond the picket. At seven o'clock the advanced corps were attacked by the enemy, and after returning the fire briskly, retired skirmishing to the picket on Quaker Hill. Here the whole made a stand, and were reinforced on the left by a regiment from Glover's brigade, commanded by Lieutenant-Colonel Sprout, and on the right by a regiment from Varnum's brigade, commanded by Lieutenant-Colonel Livingston. The action now became severe; the Americans were well posted, and twice repulsed the enemy on their left, but they being strongly reinforced, and a general action not intended on this ground, the advanced corps were ordered to retire, which they did with the greatest order and regularity, having five killed and sixteen wounded on the left, and bringing off a lieutenant of grenadiers and seven privates prisoners. The enemy, about nine in the morning, began a cannonade, which was returned with great spirit, and skirmishing continued between the advanced parties until near ten, when their two ships of war and some small armed vessels, having got up the river on the right flank of the Americans, the enemy bent most of their force that way, and endeavored to turn their right under cover of their ships. They were twice driven back in much confusion, when a third effort was made with greater numbers. General Sullivan now ordered the right to be reinforced, and a sharp conflict of near an hour succeeded, in which the artillery of both armies played briskly from the hills. The enemy were at length routed, and fled in great confusion to a hill where they had cannon and works to cover them, leaving their dead and wounded on the field. We took about sixty prisoners. The action must have ended in the ruin of the British army, had not the redoubts on the hill covered them from a close pursuit. Immediately after the repulse of the enemy on the right, they appeared advancing on the left, in consequence of which, Glover's brigade and General Tyler's militia, supported by Titcomb's brigade, were ordered to advance and form in a cross road within half a mile of the enemy. They accordingly took post, and a cannonade, with skirmishing, ensued, and continued till dark. It was not judged advisable to attack them in their works, as the Americans, inferior in number to the enemy, were much fatigued, and had been without provision or refreshment of any kind for thirty-six hours.

Too much praise cannot be given to the officers and soldiers in general for their exemplary bravery. The whole of the troops that were engaged received the thanks of the general in orders. The Americans killed, wounded, and missing, are two hundred and eleven; about sixty supposed to be killed. The enemy's loss is computed at three hundred killed and wounded, of which number forty or fifty of the latter fell into our hands, and about one hundred and sixty were left dead on the field.

Mr. Walker, of Massachusetts Bay, who acted as brigade major, is among our slain. Major Sherburne, of the same state, unfortunately lost his leg by a cannon ball. Young Mr. Henley, of Boston, is wounded in his wrist and through the body. Lieutenant-Colonel William Livingston received two contusions on his breast, from balls whose force was too far spent to penetrate his body, and had his horse killed under him by a cannon shot. There are three or four more officers of Colonel Jackson's regiment slightly wounded. The whole of his corps distinguished themselves.

New-York Journal, September 14

August 30

RHODE ISLAND   This morning the American army pitched their tents on the front of Butt's Hill, on Rhode Island, when a heavy cannonade commenced, and has continued through the whole day. At seven this evening a picket was posted in advance of the first line, and a chain of sentinels formed from the east to the west river. In consequence of authentic intelligence received, that Lord Howe, with his fleet, had sailed from Sandy Hook, and that from the best information one hundred and fifty sail of transports were in the Western Sound, with five thousand troops, bound to Newport, a council was called, who were unanimously of opinion, (considering the situation of the army, the absence of the fleet, and the momentary expectation of the enemy's receiving a strong reinforcement of troops, with a number of ships,) that the island should be evacuated, which has been completed in perfect order and safety, not leaving behind the smallest article of provision, camp equipage, or military stores.

New Hampshire Gazette, September 15

Yankee Doodle's Expedition
to Rhode Island

———•———

This witty song was published in Rivington's Gazette, October 3, 1778, and was received with glee by Tories on both sides of the Atlantic. The song lampoons the pomp that accompanied Louis Gerard's arrival in Philadelphia as French ambassador to the United States; mocks the French promises of aid to the embattled colonists; and chortles with delight at the failure of the Franco-American expedition against Rhode Island, August 1778. Melody: Yankee Doodle. (Moore, Songs and Ballads, 231–6; Diary, 617–8.)

———

From Louis, Monsieur Gerard came
    To Congress in this town, sir,
They bowed to him, and he to them,
    And then they all sat down, sir.
"Begar," said Monsieur, "one *grand coup*
    You shall *bientôt* behold sir;"
This was believed as gospel true,
    And Jonathan felt bold, sir.

So Yankee Doodle did forget
    The sound of British drum, sir,
How oft it made him quake and sweat
    In spite of Yankee rum, sir.
He took his wallet on his back
    His rifle on his shoulder,
And vowed Rhode Island to attack
    Before he was much older.

In dread array their tattered crew,
    Advanced with colors spread, sir,
Their fifes played Yankee-doodle-doo,
    King Hancock at their head, sir.
What numbers bravely crossed the seas,
    I cannot well determine,

A swarm of rebels and of fleas
   And every other vermin.

Their mighty hearts might shrink, they thought,
   For all flesh only grass is,
A plenteous store they therefore brought
   Of whisky and molasses.
They swore they'd make bold Pigot squeak,
   So did their good ally, sir,
And take him prisoner in a week,
   But that was all my eye, sir.

As Jonathan so much desired
   To shine in martial glory,
D'Estaing with *politesse* retired
   To leave him all the glory.
He left him what was better yet,
   At least it was more use, sir,
He left him for a quick retreat
   A very good excuse, sir.

To stay unless he ruled the sea,
   He thought would not be right, sir,
And Continental troops, said he,
   On islands should not fight, sir.
Another cause with these combined,
   To throw him in the dumps, sir,
For Clinton's name alarmed his mind,
   And made him stir his stumps, sir.

———— •—• ————

NOVEMBER

November 11

NEW YORK   This day, a party of Tories, Indians, and Regulars, under the command of Colonel Butler, made a descent on the fort at Cherry Valley. An officer who was in the fort, gives the following account of the affair:

On Saturday night, 7th of November, an express arrived

from Fort Stanwix, informing that an Oneida Indian had acquainted them that he sat in council in the Seneca country with the Six Nations, and other tribes, and that they had concluded to attack Fort Alden, in Cherry Valley. On Sunday morning a sergeant and twelve men were sent on the road by Beaver Dam, towards the enemy, to continue five days; another scout, with a non-commissioned officer, and five men, were sent on the road to Springfield, to continue four days; these two roads being the only avenues from the enemy's country to this place, except an old Indian path that had been neglected by us. At the same time, we sent by the same roads scouts in the morning, which returned at night. On Wednesday, the 11th, it rained very hard; the enemy came by the above-mentioned path, past by two houses, and lodged themselves in a swamp a small distance back of Mr. Wells' house, head-quarters; at half-past eleven, A.M., Mr. Hamlin came by and discovered two Indians, who fired upon him, and shot him through the arm; he rode to Mr. Wells', and acquainted the colonel, the lieutenant-colonel, major, and adjutant being present; the two last (the house at this time being surrounded by Indians) got to the fort through their fire; the colonel was shot near the fort. The enemy, eight hundred in number, consisting of five hundred Indians, commanded by Brant, fifty Regulars under Captain Colvill, and another captain with some of Johnson's Rangers, and above two hundred Tories, the whole under Colonel Butler's command, immediately surrounded the fort, excluding several officers who were quartered out of the garrison, and had gone to dinner; they commenced a very heavy fire upon the fort, which held three and a half hours, and was as briskly returned; they were so near as to call to the fort and bid the "damn'd rebels" to surrender, which was answered with three cheers, and a discharge of cannon and musketry. At four P.M., the enemy withdrew. Captain Ballard sallied out with a party, which the enemy endeavored to cut off, but were prevented by a reinforcement.

The next day they made it their whole business to collect horses, cattle, and sheep, which they effected, and at sunset left the place. The enemy killed, scalped, and most barbarously murdered, thirty-two inhabitants, chiefly women and children, also Colonel Alden, and the following soldiers of this regiment, viz.: Robert Henderson, Gideon Day, Thomas Sherridan, Pelletiah Adams, Simeon Hopkins, Benjamin Worcely, Thomas Holden, Daniel Dudley, Thomas Knowles, and Oliver Deball. The following officers were taken prisoners, viz.: Lieutenant-Colonel Stacey, Lieutenant Aaron Holden, Ensign Garret, Surgeon's Mate Francis Souza De Bierve, and thirteen privates; burnt twenty-four houses with all the grain, &c., took above sixty inhabitants prisoners, part of whom they released on going off. They committed the most inhuman barbarities on most of the dead. Robert Henderson's head was cut off, his skull bone was cut out with the scalp. Mr. Willis' sister was ripped up, a child of Mr. Willis', two months old, scalped, and arm cut off; the clergyman's wife's leg and arm cut off, and many others as cruelly treated. Many of the inhabitants and soldiers shut out from the fort, lay all night in the rain with the children, who suffered very much. The cattle that were not easy to drive, they shot. We were informed by the prisoners they sent back, that the lieutenant-colonel, all the officers and Continental soldiers, were stripped and drove naked before them.

The fort was commanded by the brave Major Whiting, of Dedham, in Massachusetts, and the two cannon under the direction of the brave Captain Hickling, of Boston, who was chief engineer in building the fort, and whose assistance contributed in saving it.

New-Jersey Gazette, December 31

November 25

GEORGIA   A correspondent in Charleston, South Carolina, says:—"A body of armed men, supposed to be about five hundred, chiefly on horseback, with four pieces of artillery, from St. Augustine, in Florida, have made a very sudden and rapid incursion overland, by way of the Alatamaha, into the neighboring State of Georgia, burning all the houses, and destroying every thing in their way. It does not appear that they were discovered before last Friday, yet by Sunday they had advanced to within four miles of Sunbury, and burnt every house on the other side of Newport Ferry, but not without receiving some check from a body of militia collected under Colonel Screven, together with the continentals of the third and fourth battalions, who had retreated in order to receive reinforcements, to Midway meeting-house, where they were intrenching to make a stand, but having disputed every inch of ground against a superior enemy, they lost a few men, and had some of their most valuable officers wounded. We since learn that the militia have every where turned out with the greatest alacrity, and that such vigorous measures are pursuing as, with the co-operation of South Carolina, will probably not only disappoint the designs of the enemy, but also cut off their retreat. The opinion of some is, that this expedition has been contrived by Governor Tonyn on purpose to pacify or get rid of the clamorous Tories and horse thieves which he has, by intimidating suggestions and lavish promises, for years past, drawn from South Carolina, and other states, to strengthen the province under his government."

Rivington's Gazette, January 20, 1779

November 27

GEORGIA   The British have as suddenly abandoned the State of Georgia as they invaded it, and retired into East Florida. Their hasty retreat was occasioned by an express sent to Colonel Prevost, advising him of a naval and land force coming against him from South Carolina, who might cut off his retreat, and by the sudden appearance of some vessels at the same time off Sunbury, which they apprehended to be the American fleet. Previous to their going off, they sent away near one thousand head of cattle, some sheep, about three hundred horses, two hundred Negroes, and other plunder. Although the enemy have destroyed almost every thing in their way, within a mile of each side of the road south of Ogeechie, yet many buildings and other property, supposed to have been burnt and destroyed, are, since their departure, found untouched. Colonel Prevost, in many instances, has shown that humanity and generosity for which British officers were formerly distinguished. The land force which came against Georgia consisted of eighty-six Regulars, and about five hundred Scofelites and rangers in one body, who entered the country at Fort Howe, and marched on by land under Colonel Prevost; while between four and five hundred Regulars, in another body, commanded by Colonel Fuser, landed upon Colonel's Island near Sunbury, (fordable at low water,) and marched into that town. Their naval force consisted of no more than the ship *Lord Germaine,* of twenty guns, (two and three-pounders,) the brig *Spitfire* of sixteen, the sloop *Musquito* of ten, the sloop *Tonyn's Revenge* of eight, a large galley with two twelve or eighteen-pounders in her bow, a large flat, and a number of boats, &c., most of them mounting one or two swivels, and generally lay at St. Simon's inlet. After Colonel Fuser withdrew from Sunbury, the two bodies joined at Newport Ferry, where they intrenched, to cover and give time to their hunters to get off with the cattle, and when that was accomplished they followed.

A great variety of conjectures having been formed concerning this expedition. One is, that they came only to forage. Another, that it was undertaken merely to pacify the clamors of the discontented Scofelites, by giving them an opportunity to plunder, till the grand scheme in which it was intended to employ them should be ripe. Another, that they had some more extensive object in view, and a part of their plan had failed them; perhaps their scalping brethren and the numerous bands of Tories they expected to co-operate with them, did not appear at the time appointed. Another, that it was a project to stop the sale of estates of attainted persons, and endeavor to get off their slaves. Another, that the enemy were impelled by the want of a sufficient supply of provisions, and the consequent dread of a famine, to risk their whole strength to procure cattle. But the opinion that seems to be most probable is, that the late expedition is only part of one, long since projected by that restless, artful, specious and aspiring deserter and betrayer of his country, the well-known Moses Kirkland, improved by Governor Tonyn, the Indian agent, and General Grant, for the conquest of the Southern States, with a view to share the spoil among them, and with the LOYAL REFUGEES, as they style themselves, who have basely deserted their country, and put themselves under the protection of the British generals at New York. That General Sir Henry Clinton, when convinced by experience that it would not be possible for all the force of Britain to subjugate America, finding these people both troublesome and expensive, willing to get rid of them as decently as possible, and desirous at the same time to prevent an increase of pensions on the British government, at last so far adopted Mr. Kirkland's plan, as to form them into regiments, furnish them with arms, and the means for an embarkation and invasion of these States, with full liberty to spread devastation and ruin to the extent of their inclination and ability, and a promise, if they can conquer, of the best plantations and most valuable gangs of slaves, in proportion as they shall distinguish themselves, together with a government on the British establishment, and such officers (from among themselves) as the King shall be pleased to approve of. That to forward these purposes, orders have been sent to the troops and banditti in East Florida, to make a rapid incursion into Georgia at a fixed period, for securing the most advantageous posts to favor future operations; and to the Indian superintendent, at the same time, to pour the savage allies of Britain, with all the horrors of their warfare, into the heart of the settlements, under the guidance of Richard Pearis, &c., while the emissaries of Britain, dispersed through these states under a variety of disguises, from the eastern shore of Maryland quite to Florida, should prepare the ignorant, and the wicked outcasts of each, to repair to their standard. But, that the East Floridans, too eager to carry their part of the plan into execution, had penetrated into the country rather precipitately; being, perhaps, deceived by their reliance on the Indians, and the Tory embarkation providentally delayed, dispersed by a storm, or prevented by the unexpected news of the Marquis de Bouille's operations in the West Indies. Be these conjectures well founded or not, it certainly behooves us to be spiritedly active, and thoroughly guarded, against every possible evil that may be brought upon us, by our declared, or infinitely more dangerous, concealed enemies.

Pennsylvania Packet, January 30, 1779

DECEMBER

December 30

GEORGIA   Early yesterday morning the British, under the cover of several armed vessels, landed at Brewton's plantation, about a mile from Savannah. The Continental troops were drawn up on an eminence about half a mile from the town, near Tatnal's gate, their right extending to the swamp and river, their left across the road; and a morass, crossed by the road, in their front. The morass was thought impracticable for near two or three miles up. The militia were near the barracks, meant to cover the right of the Regulars; their whole force scarcely amounting to five hundred men.

The British, under feint of attacking us by the main road, filed off to the left, and found means to cross the morass, about a quarter of a mile above our right; this, as soon as it was known, obliged our Regulars to retreat, which was effected at the same time that the militia were attacked, and obliged to retire through the town. Our troops sustained a very hot fire on their retreat between the town and barracks; but by that means gained the road which leads out by the spring house; while the only alternative left the militia was to surrender or swim McGilvray's Creek. Those who could not swim were made prisoners, among whom were Colonel Walton of the militia (wounded in the action) and Major Habersham of the Georgia Regulars. Colonels Elbert and Harris saved themselves by swimming.

At present our loss cannot be ascertained; and I am inclined to think it not near so considerable as many apprehend.

Colonel Roberts, with four pieces of artillery, was posted near the Continental troops, and made good his retreat, with the loss of one of his pieces. All accounts agree that the Georgians are the most considerable sufferers.

New-Jersey Gazette, February 10, 1779

1779

JANUARY

American Taxation: A Song of Seventy-Nine

This song, by Peter St. John of Norwalk, Connecticut, antedates the Revolution. In 1779 the author revised it to produce a coherent and connected history of the struggle, a ringing appeal for renewed effort in a time of threatened stalemate, an articulate, classic ballad of the war. A later generation would also draw inspiration from this piece. At least five different versions survive in broadside form, each with its own textual variations. All texts have been compared to give the corrected version that is printed here. (Moore, Songs and Ballads, 1–16; Ford, Check List, 2121–2124; Isaiah Thomas, 8, 9.)

Whilst I relate my story, Americans give ear,
Of Britain's fading glory you presently shall hear;
It is a true relation, attend to what I say,
Concerning the taxation in North America.

The cruel Lords of Britain, who glory in their shame,
The project they had hit on they joyfully proclaim;
'Tis what they're striving after to take our rights away,
And rob us of our charter in North America.

There are two mighty speakers that rule in Parliament,
Who always have been seekers some mischief to invent,
'Twas North, and Bute his father, a horrid plan did lay,
A mighty tax to gather in North America.

They search'd the gloomy regions of the infernal pit,
To find amongst those legions one who excell'd in wit,
To ask of him assistance to tell them how they may
Subdue without resistance this North America.

Old Satan, the arch traitor, resolv'd a voyage to make,
Who rules sole navigator on the infernal lake,
For the Britannic ocean he launches fast away,
To land he had no notion in North America.

He takes his seat in Britain, it was his sole intent
Great George's throne to sit on and rule the parliament;
His comrades were pursuing a diabolic way,
For to complete the ruin of North America.

They try'd the arts of magic to bring their schemes about
At length this gloomy project was artfully found out,
The plan was long indulg'd in a clandestine way,
But lately was divulg'd in North America.

These subtle arch combiners address'd the British court,
All three were undersigners to this obscene report,
There is a pleasant landscape that layeth far away,
Beyond the wide Atlantic in North America.

There is a wealthy people who sojourn in that land,
Their churches all with steeples most delicately stand,
Their houses like the tulip are painted red and gay,
They flourish like the lily in North America.

Their land with milk and honey continually doth flow,
The want of food or money they seldom ever know;
They heap up gold and treasure, they have no debts to pay,
They spend their time in pleasure in North America.

On turkey, fowls and fishes most frequently they dine,
With gold and silver dishes their tables always shine,
They crown their feasts with butter, they eat and rise to play,
In silks the ladies flutter in North America.

With gold and silver laces they do themselves adorn,
The rubies deck their faces refulgent as the morn;
Wine sparkles in their glasses, they spend each happy day
In merriment and dances in North America.

Let not our suit affront you when we address your throne,
O King, this wealthy country and subjects are your own,
And you their lawful sovereign they surely must obey,
You have a right to govern this North America.

O King, conceive the sequel, from what we here prescribe,
Is it not just and equal to tax this wealthy tribe?
The question being asked, his Majesty did say,
My subjects shall be taxed in North America.

Invested with my warrant my publicans shall go,
The tenth of all their current they shall on us bestow;
If they indulge rebellion or from my precepts stray,
I'll send my war battalions to North America.

I'll rally all my forces by water and by land,
My light dragoons and horsemen shall go at my command;
I'll burn both town and city, with smoke becloud the day,
I'll shew no human pity in North America.

Go on, my hardy soldiers, you need not fear of ill,
There's Hutchinson and Rogers their function will fulfil,
They tell such ample stories, believe them sure we may,
That one half will turn Tories in North America.

My gallant ships are ready to waft you o'er the flood,
Then in my cause be steady, it is supremely good!
Go, ravage, steal and plunder, and yours shall be the prey,
They quickly will knock under in North America.

The laws I have enacted I never will revoke,
Although they are neglected, my fury to provoke;
I will forbear to flatter, I rule with mighty sway;
I'll take away the charter from North America.

O George, you are distracted, by sad experience find,
The laws you have enacted are of the blackest kind;
I'll make a short digression and tell you by the way,
We fear not your oppression in North America.

Our fathers were distressed while in their native land,
By tyrants were oppressed, as we do understand;
For freedom and religion they were resolv'd to stray,
And try the desert regions of North America.

Heaven was their sole protector while on the raging tide,
Kind fortune their director, and Providence their guide;
If I am not mistaken, about the first of May,
This voyage was undertaken for North America.

If rightly I remember, this country to explore,
They landed in November on Plymouth's desert shore;
The savages were frighten'd, with fear they fled away,
In peace our fathers settled this North America.

We are their bold descendents, for liberty we'll fight,
The claim to independence we challenge as our right,
'Tis what kind Heaven gave us, who then shall take away:
Kind Heaven soon will save us in North America.

We never will knock under, O George, we do not fear
The rattling of your thunder, nor lightning of your spear;
Though rebels you declare us, we're strangers to dismay,
Therefore you cannot scare us in North America.

To what you have commanded we never will consent,
Although your troops are landed upon our continent;
We'll take our swords and muskets and march in bright array,
And drive the British red coats from North America.

We have a bold commander that fears not sword nor gun,
A second Alexander, his name is Washington;
His men are all collected and ready for the fray,
To fight they are directed for North America.

We've Greene, and Gates, and Putnam to manage in the field,
A gallant train of footmen who'd rather die than yield;
A noble troop of horsemen, train'd in the martial way,
For to augment our forces in North America.

Proud George, you are engaged all in a dirty cause,
A cruel war you've waged repugnant to the laws;
Go tell the savage nations you're crueler than they,
To fight your own relations in North America.

Ten millions you've demanded and twice ten millions more,
Our riches you intended should pay the mighty score;
Who now will stand your sponsor your charges to defray,
For sure you cannot conquer this North America.

I'll tell you, George, in metre, if you'll attend a while,
We forced your Sir Peter from Sullivan's fair isle;
At Monmouth town we gained the honors of the day,
The victory obtained for North America.

We truly were your betters hard by the Brandywine,
We led him fast in fetters whose name was John Burgoyne,
We made your Howe to tremble with terror and dismay,
True heroes we resemble in North America.

Confusion to the Tories, that black infernal name,
In whom Great Britain glories, forever to their shame;
We'll send each foul revolter to smutty Africa,
Or noose him with a halter in North America.

Here's health to all our footmen that handle sword and gun,
To Warren, Gates and Putnam, and conq'ring Washington,
Their names are wrote in letters which never shall decay,
Whilst sun and moon shall glitter in North America.

Success unto our allies, in Holland, France and Spain,
Who arm'd their ships and gallies our freedom to maintain,
May they subdue the rancor of proud Britannia,
And drive them from their anchors in North America.

Success unto the Congress of these United States,
Who triumph in the conquest of Washington and Gates,
To all both land and seamen who glory in the day,
When we shall all be freemen in North America.

Success to legislation that rules with gentle hand,
To trade and navigation by water and by land;
May all with one opinion our wholesome laws obey,
Throughout the vast dominion of North America.

FEBRUARY

February 2

PENNSYLVANIA   This morning, his Excellency General Washington set off from Philadelphia to join the army in New Jersey. During the course of his short stay, (the only relief he has enjoyed from service since he first entered into it,) he has been honored with every mark of esteem which his accomplished fortitude as a soldier, and his exalted qualities as a gentleman and a citizen, entitle him to. Among other instances, he was welcomed at his first coming by an address from the Supreme Executive Council and the magistrates of the city, and politely entertained by the President of Congress, the President of the State, his Excellency the Minister of France, Don Juan Marrailles, a Spanish gentleman of distinction and amiable character, besides the numerous testimonials of regard shown to him by private gentlemen. The council of this State being desirous of having his picture in full length, requested his sitting for that purpose, which he politely complied with, and a striking likeness was taken by Mr. Peale of Philadelphia. The portrait is to be placed in the Council Chamber. Don Juan Marrailles has ordered five copies, four of which, we hear, are to be sent abroad. His excellency's stay was rendered the more agreeable by the company of his lady, and the domestic retirement which he enjoyed at the house of the Honorable Henry Laurens, Esquire, with whom he resided.

Pennsylvania Packet, February 4

February 4

NEW YORK   It is painful to repeat the indubitable accounts we are continually receiving, of the cruel and inhuman treatment of the subjects of these States from the Britons in

New York and other places. They who hear our countrymen, who have been so unfortunate as to fall into the hands of those unrelenting tyrants, relate the sad story of their captivity, the insults they have received, and the slow, cool, systematic manner in which great numbers of those who could not be prevailed on to enter their service, have been murdered, must have hearts of stone not to melt with pity for the sufferers, and burn with indignation at their tormentors. As we have daily fresh instances to prove the truth of such a representation, public justice requires that repeated public mention should be made of them. A cartel vessel lately carried about one hundred and thirty American prisoners from the prison ships in New York to New London, in Connecticut. Such was the condition in which these poor creatures were put on board the cartel, that in that short run, sixteen died on board; upwards of sixty, when they were landed, were scarcely able to move, and the remainder greatly emaciated and enfeebled; and many who continue alive, are never likely to recover their former health. The greatest inhumanity was experienced by the prisoners in a ship of which one Nelson, a Scotchman, had the superintendence. Upwards of three hundred American prisoners were confined at a time on board this ship. There was but one small fireplace allowed to cook the food of such a number. The allowance of the prisoners was, moreover, frequently delayed, insomuch that in the short days of November and December, it was not begun to be delivered out till eleven o'clock in the forenoon, so that the whole could not be served till three o'clock. At sunset the fire was ordered to be quenched; no plea for the many sick, from their absolute necessity, the shortness of the time, and the smallness of the hearth, was allowed to avail. The known consequence was, some had not their food dressed at all; many were obliged to eat it half raw. On board this ship, no flour, oatmeal, and things of like nature, suited to the condition of infirm people, were allowed to the many sick; nothing but ship bread, beef and pork.

This is the account given by a number of prisoners, who are credible persons; and this is but a part of their sufferings; so that the excuse made by the enemy, that the prisoners were emaciated, and died by a contagious sickness, which no one could prevent, is futile. It requires no great sagacity to know, that crowding people together without fresh air, and feeding, or rather starving them in such a manner as the prisoners have been, must unavoidably produce a contagion. Nor is it want of candor to suppose, that many of our enemies saw with pleasure this contagion, which might have been so easily prevented, among the prisoners who could not be persuaded to enter their service. Some of them, no doubt, thought they acted in all this with the true spirit of the British Parliament, who began hostilities against America by shutting up the port of Boston, interdicting the fishery and those branches of trade that were deemed necessary to our subsistence; and when some members objected to the cruelty of such acts, some well-known friends to the ministry had the face to ring in the ears of others, Starvation, starvation to the rebels—starvation is the only thing that will bring them to their senses! In short, the inhumanity of the Britons, from the beginning of this war, and through every stage of it, is without a parallel in the annals of any civilized nation.

These things ought never to be forgotten, though some would fain wink them out of sight. We are not, indeed, to resolve never to make peace with our enemies, but never to make a peace that will leave it in their power to act over again their intolerable oppressions and cruelties. We can never secure ourselves against this, but by maintaining, at all adventures, the sovereignty and independence of these States. Nothing but this can effectually prevent the present generation from enduring the severest punishment for their noble resistance to the tyranny of Britain, nor our posterity from groaning throughout all generations under the most abject and cruel bondage.

New Hampshire Gazette, February 8

February 7

Yesterday being the anniversary of forming the alliance between France and the United States, the honorable the Congress at Philadelphia gave a public entertainment to his Excellency the Minister Plenipotentiary of his Most Christian Majesty, at which the following toasts were drank, under the discharge of cannon:

1. May the alliance between France and the United States be perpetual. 2. The United States. 3. His Most Christian Majesty. 4. The Queen of France. 5. His Most Catholic Majesty. 6. The Princes of the House of Bourbon. 7. Success to the allied arms. 8. General Washington and the army. 9. The friends of liberty in every part of the world. 10. May the new constellation rise to the zenith. 11. May the American stripes bring Great Britain to reason. 12. The memory of the patriots who have nobly fallen in defence of the liberty and independence of America. 13. A safe and honorable peace.

The cheerfulness which existed in the company upon the happy occasion of their being assembled was not to be exceeded, and a thousand brilliancies, alluding to the alliance, were uttered. There can be no doubt but that every true American and every true Frenchman will contribute his efforts to preserve that connection which is formed by the alliance, and which is so necessary to the happiness and aggrandizement of both nations. Their mutual interests dictate such a conduct in the strongest and most affectionate terms. The principles of the alliance are founded in true policy and equal justice; and it is highly probable that mankind will have cause to rejoice in this union which has taken place between two nations; the one the most puissant in the old, and the other the most powerful in the new world.

New-Jersey Gazette, February 17

February 10

NEW JERSEY   Last Tuesday, about three o'clock in the morning, a party of the new levies from Staten Island went into Woodbridge, New Jersey, and marched up into the town, undiscovered, to the house of Charles Jackson, in which there happened to lay that night a scout of Continental troops from Bonamtown, consisting of twelve men. The sentinel did not discover them till they had well-nigh surrounded the house, it being very dark, when he fired and ran off, making his escape; the rest being unfortunately asleep, were taken by surprise without making any resistance. Their principal object was Captain Nathaniel Fitz Randolph, who lived at this house. He had just returned from Staten Island, having been over there with a small party, chief of the night, and was but a few minutes in the house before he was alarmed by the firing of the sentinel, when they instantly rushed into the house and seized him and Mr. Jackson, with the scout. The party had gone before the inhabitants had time to collect, without doing any other damage except plundering the house of a few trifling articles, taking the shoe buckles out of the women's shoes, which was as little, or more than could be expected, considering the usual practice of the British troops, as the men were restrained from plundering by their officer, said to be a Captain Ryerson, of Buskirk's regiment, who seemed actuated by principles of honor and humanity; and upon this occasion imitated the laudable example of Captain Randolph, who has not only distinguished himself by his activity and bravery, but by his politeness and generosity towards such as he hath taken prisoners, never allowing his men to plunder—a practice most ignominious and base, by which Britons have, in the present contest with America, greatly disgraced themselves, and deserve to be forever despised, in which their principal officers have joined, and so sunk themselves to a level with the meanest pilfering soldier.

New-Jersey Gazette, February 17

February 18

NEW JERSEY   This day, the anniversary of the alliance with France was celebrated at Pluckemin, in the Jerseys, at a very elegant entertainment and display of fireworks given by General Knox, and the officers of the corps of artillery. It was postponed to this late day on account of his Excellency General Washington's absence from camp.

General Washington, the principal officers of the army, Mrs. Washington, Mrs. Greene, Mrs. Knox, the gentlemen and ladies for a large circuit round the camp, were of the company. Besides these, there was a vast concourse of spectators from every part of the Jerseys.

New-Jersey Gazette, March 3

February 26

NEW JERSEY   Yesterday morning a body of the British, consisting of the 42d and 33d regiments, and the light infantry of the guards, in number about a thousand, commanded by Lieutenant-Colonel Stirling, attempted to surprise the troops and inhabitants of Elizabethtown. They embarked at Long Island the evening before, about seven o'clock, and landed on the Salt Meadows, better than a mile to the left of Crane's ferry, between two and three in the morning. From thence they were conducted through a very difficult marsh to Woodruff's farm, which lies directly to the left of the town.

The guard at Crane's ferry having discovered their landing, immediately despatched the intelligence to town, where the alarm being sounded, the troops were afforded an opportunity to collect. The number and movements of the enemy remaining doubtful by reason of the darkness, the troops were marched to the rear of the town, where the Whig inhabitants likewise retired.

A detachment of the enemy was despatched to the governor's house [Governor William Livingston], while the main body advanced to the skirts of the town, and from thence proceeded along the rear until they fell into the Brunswick road on the right. The governor happened to be absent from home that night, but if he had not, they would have been unsuccessful in this instance likewise, as the family received timely notice of their approach.

Finding themselves completely disappointed in every expectation, they made their visit in town very short; however, during their small halt, they set fire to the barracks, the schoolhouse, (in which were stored some few articles of provision,) and a blacksmith's shop. So soon as they began their retreat to their boats, General Maxwell marched such of his troops as were yet in reserve against their rear; the number of

Engraved by Geo.E.Perine, N.York.

WASHINGTON.

these, however, was small, several parties having been detached at different times to hang upon them.

About half way between the town and ferry, the enemy perceiving their rear in danger, from the sudden advance of our troops, and the assembling of the militia, faced about and paraded, as if for action. A few well-directed shot from our artillery induced them to renew their retreat, leaving two dead on the field. Perceiving an embarkation at the ferry would be attended with considerable hazard, their boats were moved better than a mile up Newark Bay, while the troops marched along the meadow's edge, in many places up to their middles in mud and mire. A galley and two or three gun boats covered their retreat at this place.

The American loss, exclusive of a few aged inhabitants whom the British took with them, but have since sent back, are, one private killed, two officers, to wit, Brigade Major Ogden and Lieutenant Rencastle, with four privates wounded, and seven privates missing. Major Ogden, who was reconnoitering the enemy shortly after their landing, very narrowly escaped being made prisoner; he was wounded in his right side by a bayonet, but we hope not dangerously.

The Rev. Mr. Hunter, chaplain to the brigade, on returning from the governor's house, where he had been to give the alarm, was made prisoner by them in the night, but he had the address very soon after to make his escape.

The enemy's loss we cannot ascertain, except the two killed, whom they left behind, two made prisoners, and one boat taken. Cornelius Hetfield, Smith Hetfield, and Captain Luce, late of Elizabethtown, were their principal guides. They had collected a considerable number of horned cattle and horses, but their retreat was so precipitate, that they were obliged to leave them behind.

New-Jersey Gazette, March 3

MARCH

March 4

GEORGIA   Yesterday, the British forces, under the command of Colonel Prevost, defeated a party of General Lincoln's army, under General Ashe, near the junction of Briar Creek and the Savannah River. The following is the British account of the affair:—"The rebel army having penetrated, with near two thousand men, partly Continentals and partly militia, as far as Miller's burnt bridge, on Briar Creek, Colonel Prevost thought prudent to allow them to repair it, and to draw them on the south side of the creek before they were attacked; but information being received that they had sent off all their carts and wagons to Burton's ferry, over Savannah River, and proceeding but slowly in the repairs of the bridge, the colonel concluded that they had no further object in view, and that they meant to return shortly, in consequence of which, he ordered the first battalion of the 71st regiment, with about one hundred and fifty of the Carolina volunteers, to proceed to Buck Creek, three miles south of the burnt bridge, in order to mask the advance corps, with which he took a circuit of fifty miles in order to come on their rear, and attack them with five field-pieces, about eight hundred and fifty Regulars, and about one hundred and eighty or two hundred of the Carolina volunteers and rangers. The march was begun privately on the first day of March, in the evening. The troops marched all night, and arrived about ten o'clock the next day, at a place where the rebels had lately destroyed a bridge. A temporary one was constructed, but for want of grapnels and cables, could not stand the strength of the current, the creek being both wide and rapid. A pontoon was then substituted, and though it occasioned considerable delay, the troops and artillery were carried over before daybreak on the third instant. The light infantry and the horse had been sent forward the preceding evening, to prevent the retreat of the enemy, and to conceal the intended movement. The scouts gave advice that they had discovered some parties of the enemy, when they were reinforced with a view to attack them, and at the same time to conceal the march of the Regular troops. In the attack, part of them escaped over the river, having a ferry there, a few of them were taken, and some saved themselves by the great speed of their horses; but as they had not discovered the troops, it gave no kind of apprehension that it would alarm them, otherwise than to induce them to send a party in quest of the scout we had shown in the rear.

"The prisoners we had taken concurred in their declaration, that the rebels were unapprised of the vicinity of any enemies, and trusting much to their superiority in numbers, were in the most perfect security. They also said that Major Ross, with three hundred light horse, had joined their army the preceding evening.

"The troops continued their march, and by half after four in the afternoon, the flying parties of horse drove in the enemy's picket, and took some prisoners, who informed us that they knew not of any number of troops but only a few scouters coming. The troops were rapidly formed, with the light infantry on the right, and two field-pieces were ordered to penetrate by a road leading towards the left of the rebel army. The centre was composed of the 2d battalion 71st, with some rangers, and Carolina foot on their left, and one howitzer and two six-pounders in their front. About one hundred and fifty horse were ordered to take the left of the whole, to turn the right flank of the enemy. A reserve was formed about four hundred yards to the rear, and consisted of three companies of grenadiers from Florida, and a troop of dragoons. About forty or fifty riflemen were posted to ambuscade a place through which the rebels might attempt, under cover of a swamp and thicket, to attack our left and rear.

"The enemy began a scattering fire of musketry, and fired some cannon, but were put to flight in an instant. They could not stand the spirited attack of Sir James Baird's light infantry on our right, and from that instant the success of the day was decided. They were pursued to the creek, into which, after throwing away their arms, the most active plunged and escaped by swimming; their right had no means of escaping, but over a lagoon very deep and broad, and then to cross the river Savannah. In that place, numbers have been drowned and perished, many were killed in the pursuit, and about one hundred taken prisoners. General Ashe, the commanding officer of their army, with some other officers of note, were mistaken by the 2d battalion 71st for some of our own people, as they passed by them and took off their hats. Brigadier-General Elbert, Colonel M'Intosh, two other colonels, and twenty-three more officers have been taken, seven pieces of cannon, several stand of colors, their baggage, arms, ammunition, and every thing, in short, fell into the hands of the brave, victorious troops. Not a whole platoon of the rebel army escaped together, on our right or left. The panic occasioned by the terror of the bayonet, left them no alternative but that of plunging into the water, many of which, we are since informed, have been met without any other clothes but a shirt and breeches, and without arms, numbers of them badly wounded; few would have escaped if night had not come on so soon.

"The loss on our side was one officer wounded, five privates killed, and ten wounded; that of the enemy, about one hundred and fifty killed in the pursuit, vast numbers were drowned, and the rest rendered useless, having lost their arms and clothes.

"The coolness and intrepidity of the troops was conspicuous; not a word was heard but what was expressive of a wish to come up with the enemy; a cheerful, smiling countenance appeared on every side; the confidence of the troops was, to a degree, a sure and certain sign of the success they met with. Notwithstanding every fatigue, and even want of provisions for the whole day of the engagement, the troops formed, advanced rapidly, changed their disposition, and manœuvred with as much ease as they could have done on the same ground had no enemy been in sight."

New York Gazette and Weekly Mercury, March 29

March 18

NEW YORK   Yesterday, the anniversary of Saint Patrick, the tutelar saint of Ireland, was celebrated in New York by the natives of that kingdom, with their accustomed hilarity. The volunteers of Ireland, preceded by their band of music, marched into the city, and formed before the house of their colonel, Lord Rawdon, who put himself at their head, and, after paying his compliments to his Excellency General Knyphausen, and to General Jones, accompanied them to the Bowery, where dinner was provided, consisting of five hundred covers. After the men were seated, and had proceeded to the enjoyment of a noble banquet, the officers returned to town, and dined with his lordship. The soldierly appearance of the men, their order of march, hand in hand, being all natives of Ireland, had a striking effect.

This single battalion, though only formed a few months ago, marched four hundred *strapping fellows*, neither influenced by Yankee or Ague; a number, perhaps, equal to all the recruits forced into the rebel army in the same space of time, which shows how easily troops may be formed on this continent, from the people who have been seduced into America, and spurn at the treason and tyranny of the Congress, providing proper measures are followed, and they are headed by men of their choice. And, also, that such men, however long they may have remained in the haunts of hypocrisy, cunning, and disaffection, being naturally gallant and loyal, crowd with ardor to stand forth in the cause of their King, of their country, and of real, honest, general liberty, whenever an opportunity offers.

New York Gazette and Weekly Mercury, March 22

APRIL

April 24

NEW YORK   This afternoon, the detachment sent out last
Monday on an expedition against the Indians at Onondaga,
returned to Fort Schuyler. The following account of it is
given by a writer in the *New York Packet:*—"An enterprise
against the Onondaga settlements of the Indians having been
projected and approved of by His Excellency General Washington, and the direction of it committed to Brigadier-General James Clinton, commanding in the northern department,
he, on the seventh of April, issued his orders, and gave the
execution of them to Colonel Van Schaack, commander of
the 1st battalion of New York Continental troops, appointing
as second and third in command Lieutenant-Colonel Willet
and Major Cochran, of the 3d New York battalion, all officers of approved courage and abilities. The detachment for
the service consisted of six companies of New York, one of
Pennsylvania, one of Massachusetts troops, and one of riflemen, amounting, in the whole, to five hundred and four rank
and file, and fifty-one officers.

"Fort Schuyler being appointed the place of rendezvous,
from thence, early on Monday morning, the nineteenth of
April, the whole party began their march, provision for eight
days having been previously sent off in twenty-nine batteaux
into Wood Creek.

"After a march of twenty-two miles, the troops arrived
about three o'clock in the evening at the old Scow Place, but
the boats having much farther to come, did not arrive till ten
o'clock. As soon as the boats arrived, the whole of the troops
embarked, and, upon entering the lake, were much impeded
by a cold head wind.

"At eight o'clock in the morning of the twentieth, the
troops halted at Pisser's Bay till all the boats came up, and

then proceeded to the Onondaga landing, opposite to old Fort Brewerton, which they reached at three o'clock in the afternoon. From thence, after leaving all their boats with a proper guard, they marched eight or nine miles on their way to the Onondaga settlement, and, not being able to continue their march in the dark, lay on their arms all night, without fire.

"Very early on the twenty-first they proceeded to the Salt Lake, an arm of which (two hundred yards over, and four feet deep) they forded, with their pouches hung to their fixed bayonets, and advanced to the Onondaga Creek, where Captain Graham took prisoner an Onondaga warrior. The creek not being fordable, the troops crossed it on a log, and as soon as they were over, the utmost endeavors were used to surround the settlements, but as they extended eight miles, besides some scattered habitations lying back of the castles, it was impossible; and on the opposite side of the creek, though our troops entered their first settlement wholly undiscovered by them, they soon discovered some of our advanced parties, and took the alarm in all their settlements. The colonel, however, ordered different routes to be taken by different parties, in order to surround as many of their settlements as possible at the same time; but the Indians fled precipitately to the woods, not taking any thing with them. Our troops took thirty-three Indians and one white man prisoners, and killed twelve Indians. The whole of their settlements, consisting of about fifty houses, with a large quantity of corn and beans, were burnt, a number of fine horses, and every other kind of stock were killed. About one hundred guns, some of which were rifles, were among the plunder, the whole of which, after the men were loaded with as much as they could carry, was destroyed, with a considerable quantity of ammunition; one swivel, taken at the council house, had the trunnions broken off, and was otherwise much damaged, and, in fine, the destruction of all their settlements was complete.

"After this, the troops began to march on their return, recrossed the creek, and forded the arm of the lake, on the side of which they encamped on a good ground. They had only been once interrupted by a small party of Indians, who fired upon them from the opposite side of the creek, but were soon beaten back by Lieutenant Evans' riflemen, who killed one of them.

"On the twenty-second the troops marched to the landing, embarked in good order, and rowed to Seven Mile Island; on the twenty-third crossed the lake, and landed two miles up Wood Creek. On Saturday, the twenty-fourth, at twelve o'clock, the whole detachment returned in safety to Fort Schuyler, having been out five days and a half."

New-Jersey Gazette, May 12

April 27

NEW JERSEY   Yesterday, the British, in two divisions, landed in the county of Monmouth, in New Jersey; one party at Shoal Harbor, which marched to Middletown, and entered the village at daybreak; the other went in flat-bottomed boats, into Shrewsbury River, landed at Red Bank, and then proceeded to Trenton Falls. Colonel Ford, with the Continental troops, retired to Colt's Neck. Near the middle of the day the party which had landed at Shrewsbury River, crossed the river and went to Middletown, where both the divisions formed a junction. They sent their boats round to the bay shore, near one Harber's plantation, where they had thirteen sloops ready to take them off. At eight o'clock, Captain Burrows, who had mustered twelve men, gave them to understand that they were surrounded by the militia. They continued in the village till three o'clock, when they began their retreat. Captain Burrows was then joined by three other men, and kept a constant fire upon them for two miles, when Colonel Holmes, of the militia, with about sixty of his men, reinforced Captain Burrows, and then the enemy's retreat was precipitate; they were drove on board at sunset, and immediately set sail for New York.

Their numbers were about eight hundred, commanded by Colonel Hyde. We had but two men slightly wounded. The enemy left three dead behind them, their wounded they carried off, as their rear made a stand at every hill, house, and barn in their route. One of the inhabitants says fifteen wounded were carried on board their boats. In their progress, or rather flight, they plundered the inhabitants, and burnt several houses and barns. Had they landed in the day, or stayed till the militia could be collected to half their number, (which we always reckon sufficient to drub them,) they would doubtless have repented their invasion. But ever choosing, like their brother thieves, the hours of darkness to perpetrate the works of darkness, they generally land in the night, and before the militia can be collected, flee to their vessels with precipitation, snatching up in their flight what plunder they can, and then magnify in their lying Gazettes, one of those sheep-stealing nocturnal robberies, into one of the Duke of Marlborough's victories in Flanders.

New Hampshire Gazette, May 25

———•———

MAY

May 29

SOUTH CAROLINA A correspondent in Charleston, South Carolina, gives the following account of the late movements of the two armies at the southward:—"On the twenty-eighth of April, a party of the British army, under the command of Major Fraser, landed nine miles below Purysburg, and on the next morning, Lieutenant-Colonel Maitland, with the light infantry of the line and a battalion of the 1st, landed four miles higher up Savannah River. Colonel McIntosh, who commanded at Purysburg, having only two hundred men, the major part of whom were militia, (after calling in all his outposts,) was obliged to retire as the enemy advanced towards the town, of which they took possession that afternoon.

"General Moultrie was at this time posted at Black Swamp, with about eight hundred men. The enemy's drawing more of their forces on this side the river, and advancing higher up, evidently indicated an intention of attacking the general before he could be joined by Colonel McIntosh. General Lin-

coln, with the main body of the army, being then eighty miles
further up the country, should the enemy have succeeded in
the attempt, there would be no obstacle in their march to
Charleston, and as their force was treble General Moultrie's,
the worst was to be apprehended. These considerations induced the general to retire on the thirtieth, and that night he
met Colonel McIntosh on his march to join him at Black
Swamp. The event proved the propriety of the movement, as
next morning the British were in possession of the ground
the Americans had evacuated.

"The general halted at Coosawhatchie that night, and
having marched over the bridge, before daylight next morning
proceeded to Tulifinny, and took post there. A field-officer's
guard was left at the bridge.

"Early in the morning of the second of May, advice was
received that the enemy were in motion, and about two
o'clock in the afternoon an attack was commenced by their
advanced party of light infantry at the bridge, where the
guard had been reinforced by one hundred and fifty riflemen.
Their superior numbers rendered it impossible to stop their
progress. Little other loss was sustained in this skirmish than
Colonel John Laurens being wounded in the right arm, which
deprived the army of that gallant officer's services.

"The general's army being chiefly composed of militia,
whose families and effects lay in the way of the enemy, was
every moment diminishing, and laid him under the necessity
of retiring, which he did by the Saltketcher road, having destroyed the bridges of Tulifinny and Pocotaligo in his way.
The army halted for a few hours at the meeting-house, and
then marched to Ashepoo. They passed the bridge in the
forenoon of the fourth, and took post for the rest of the day
on the high grounds near Mr. Pinckney's house. Intelligence
was this night received that the enemy's advanced party had
reached Godfrey's, near Savannah, and that their main body
had found means to cross Saltketcher River, notwithstanding
the Americans had taken the precaution to destroy the bridge;
this, joined to the inferior number of our army, which was
considerably less than when it left Black Swamp, and the
nature of the country, which rendered it impossible to make

a stand without being exposed, obliged the general to quit Ashepoo between three and four o'clock in the morning of the fifth.

"At night the enemy halted at Mr. Ferguson's plantation, called Spring Grove, having destroyed Jacksonborough Bridge on their way, and reached Bacon's Bridge next night, when General Moultrie left the army, and proceeded to Charleston.

"Major Butler, who joined the army at Jacksonborough, with a party of horse, on the sixth, fell in with a foraging party of the enemy, sixteen miles to the southward of Parker's ferry. Three of them, belonging to the 71st light infantry, were taken prisoners, and a few horse killed and wounded.

"Part of Count Pulaski's legion arrived on the eighth; on the ninth, Colonel McIntosh, with the troops left at Bacon's Bridge, and a detachment from Orangeburgh, arrived in town. And next day, Colonel Harris, who had been detached by General Lincoln, with two hundred Continental troops, to reinforce General Moultrie, and Colonel Neal, with three hundred men from Orangeburgh, also arrived.

"In the evening of the tenth, intelligence was received of the royal army being encamped on the south side of Ashley Ferry, where they appeared so suddenly as to prevent the ferry boats being destroyed. The troops stationed in town, Regulars and militia, were under arms the whole night.

"The enemy began to cross Ashley Ferry at ten in the forenoon of the eleventh. Their advanced party, composed of light infantry, cavalry, and savages, took post half a mile from the ferry. General Pulaski, after reconnoitring them, left a detachment to watch their motions, and repaired to town in order to confer with the council. During this interval, the enemy had completed their passage of the river, and were advancing in three columns towards the town. Their advanced guard consisted of two hundred horse, four hundred Highlanders, and some Indians; their rear guard of cavalry.

"At the distance of five miles from town, some of the count's party were ordered to fire, principally with a view of announcing the enemy's approach. The enemy made frequent halts in order to explore the ground over which they were to pass.

"The count, who had ordered the infantry of his corps to form an ambuscade, and directed a detachment of volunteer horse which he fell in with to second his infantry, advanced and made his disposition for inducing the enemy to detach their cavalry from the head of their column. A close fire began, when both our cavalry and infantry charged; but the latter were exceedingly embarrassed and confined in their movements by the volunteer horse, owing to a misapprehension of orders. Notwithstanding these difficulties, and the superiority of the enemy's numbers, the ground was obstinately disputed. But at length the order for retreat became necessary, and the enemy, by their prudence in not advancing, escaped the fire of the artillery from our works. The British loss was forty-five soldiers and officers, and ours thirty in all.

"About ten o'clock at night, an alarm being given by one of our sentinels, occasioned a general fire of cannon and musketry from the lines and armed vessels stationed on the flanks. Major Benjamin Huger, who has been sent out with a party to fill up a gap in the abatis, and three privates, were unfortunately killed. He was a gentleman whose memory will be ever dear to all those who had the happiness of knowing him; and whether considered as a citizen, as a soldier, as the father of a family, or as a friend, is universally regretted. The enemy had several men killed, they say chiefly from the shipping.

"On the morning of the twelfth, Major Gardner, of the 60th regiment, was met with at some distance from the lines, bearing a flag from General Prevost. Several others passed and repassed, but in the afternoon all further intercourse of that kind was discontinued, and every preparation made for vigorously repelling a general assault, expected at night, which, however, was never attempted.

"Early in the morning of the thirteenth, Count Pulaski went out with a small party of horse to reconnoitre; and the surprise was scarcely to be conceived which was occasioned by his sending intelligence of the enemy having decamped and recrossed Ashley River. Eleven deserters, and about as many prisoners, were brought into town during the course of the day. The sudden departure of the enemy gave rise to a variety of conjectures. The most probable appeared to be their being misinformed respecting the strength of the garrison and works, and their having some intimation of General Lincoln's approach. They were, for several days after their retreat, encamped in different places in the neighborhood of Ashley Ferry, and on James' Island. On General Lincoln's coming to Ashley Ferry, they drew in force towards Wappoo, and it was imagined meant to hazard an action; but they suddenly decamped on the night of the twenty-seventh, and passed over to John's Island, where, by the last accounts, they are at present. Some are of the opinion that they intend proceeding through the islands to Port Royal.

"As some movements of the enemy gave reason to imagine they intended attacking Fort Johnson, and the greater part of the forces then in this neighborhood being required for the defence of the works in town, that fortification was blown up on the twelfth. Great part of the ball, &c., have been since brought off. Thirty of Captain Matthew's company of the Charleston militia being sent down to cover a party employed in bringing off some more of the iron work, were attacked on Saturday by Major Gardner, with a superior number of men, but were fortunate enough to escape with the loss of seven wounded and one taken prisoner."

New York Gazette and Weekly Mercury, July 26

SOUTH CAROLINA   An officer of distinction in the British army gives the following "authentic account" of the foregoing operations in South Carolina:—"The success which his Majesty's army has met with in South Carolina, by penetrating, without any loss of men, to the very gates of Charleston, and obliging the enemy to burn its beautiful suburbs, will hardly be credited. The natural difficulties of the country were thought a sufficient barrier, with General Moultrie's army, to stop us from penetrating any distance into the province, but the spirit shown by the troops, their patience and perseverance under the severest fatigues, were such as would have surmounted greater obstacles than the resistance of the enemy.

"We arrived before Charleston on the eleventh, in the evening, after almost totally destroying or taking that famous legion of Pulaski's, by forty-five of our gallant dragoons, under

the command of the brave Captain Tawes. Amongst the killed
of the enemy, was Count Pulaski's colonel, and several privates, besides a great number of prisoners taken. The enemy
sent next morning to know what terms we would grant. Four
hours were allowed them to surrender prisoners of war, or
take the oaths of allegiance to his Majesty, and be protected
in their persons and property, and return to the class of peaceful citizens. But an express having arrived in the mean time
from General Lincoln, with an account of his approach, and
that a reinforcement would be in town that day, the enemy
grew more confident, and began to talk in higher terms; however, they proposed a neutrality for the province until the war
between Great Britain and America was determined; but it
being a proposition which the general could not agree to,
they were informed that nothing could be granted but the
most favorable terms, as to security of persons and property
if the place was surrendered; this they declined on the encouragement received from General Lincoln, the arrival of
their armed vessels to flank their works, and the number of
guns mounted on them. The storming of the place was the
next point to be considered, but though it was not doubted
but it might be carried in that way, yet, as it would probably
have been attended with the loss of a considerable number
of men, which may be avoided by proceeding on another plan,
(where the success will be at least equally certain, and the
risk less,) it was therefore determined to keep the field, as we
were so situated as to insure a communication with our shipping, receive the necessary supplies, and from thence act as
circumstances should require. This measure is now pursued,
and the army are in possession of James' and John's Islands,
the enemy having precipitately abandoned the very strong
fort situated on the former island, called Fort Johnson."

                              Georgia Gazette, June 10
              New York Gazette and Weekly Mercury, July 12

May 31

NEW YORK   Day before yesterday, fifteen hundred men,
consisting of British and Hessian grenadiers, light infantry,

volunteers of Ireland and Jagers, landed on Teller's Point, eight miles below Peekskill, on the North River, and the following day another party landed on the west side of the river, where they burnt some houses, and opened two small batteries, from which they threw shells, and cannonaded Fort de Lafayette across the river, all day; at the same time two galleys kept up a severe fire on the fort. They have continued their firing till eleven o'clock to-day. Meanwhile their army marched from Teller's to Verplanck's Point, on which the fort stands. By a flag they demanded a surrender; the parley continued two hours, when Captain Armstrong thought fit to surrender. General McDougall has not yet received a justifiable reason why the fort was given up.

This little fort was built on purpose to secure King's Ferry from the insults of the enemy's vessels, which frequently interrupted the American boats in crossing. It was small, and would contain, with conveniency, about a company of men. The redoubt was strong, and covered a barbette battery, mounting three pieces of cannon. We had in the barbette a company of artillery; they were all drawn off but a sergeant, a corporal, and twelve privates. In the redoubt were a captain, two subalterns, three sergeants, and forty-four rank and file. They had provisions and water sufficient to serve them thirty days.

New-Jersey Gazette, June 9

NEW YORK   A British officer gives the following account of this affair:—"On Monday morning, the thirty-first of May, part of the army, under the command of Major-General Vaughan, landed on the east side of Hudson River, about eight miles below Verplanck's Point. The corps intended to land on the west side, under his excellency the Commander-in-chief, with Major-General Pattison, proceeded up within three miles of Stony Point, where they landed, about which time the rebels, who had a block-house and some unfinished works on a height of that point, commanding the ferry, as well as Fort de Lafayette on the east side of the river, set fire to the block-house, and ran off to the mountains. That corps, about four o'clock in the afternoon, continued their march

round, and took possession of the heights; during this time
the galleys fired some shot at Fort de Lafayette, on the east side
of Verplanck's Point; these were returned from the fort,.
which was a small but complete work. Artillery was now
necessary in order to expedite the business; his excellency
the general ordered Major-General Pattison to command the
troops and carry on the attack. In the night, the artillery for
that service, notwithstanding great difficulties from a bad
landing place and a very steep precipice, were got up, and
batteries completed by five o'clock in the morning, when
orders were given for firing upon the enemy's works; which,
notwithstanding the great distance, was soon perceived to be
effectual. The galleys and batteries continued the cannonade
about two hours, when the main body, under Major-General
Vaughan, having made a detour and approached the fort, the
Commander-in-chief being there in person, sent orders to
General Pattison and the galleys to cease firing, the enemy
having surrendered; they laid down their arms, became prisoners of war, and on Thursday morning arrived in New York.

"The commodore had, previous to the attack, ordered up
the *Vulture* sloop-of-war above the fort, with a row-galley,
which prevented the enemy's retreat from the fort."

New York Gazette and Weekly Mercury, June 7

———— ◆ • ◆ ————

JUNE

June 1

Among the many errors America has been guilty of during
her contest with Great Britain, few have been greater, or attended with more fatal consequences to these States, than
her lenity to the Tories. At first it might have been right, or
perhaps political; but is it not surprising that, after repeated
proofs of the same evils resulting therefrom, it should still
be continued? We are all crying out against the depreciation
of our money, and entering into measures to restore it to its
value; while the Tories, who are one principal cause of the

depreciation, are taken no notice of, but suffered to live quietly among us. We can no longer be silent on this subject, and see the independence of the country, after standing every shock from without, endangered by internal enemies. Rouse, America! your danger is great—great from a quarter where you least expect it. The Tories, the Tories will yet be the ruin of you! 'Tis high time they were separated from among you. They are now busy engaged in undermining your liberties. They have a thousand ways of doing it, and they make use of them all. Who were the occasion of this war? The Tories! Who persuaded the tyrant of Britain to prosecute it in a manner before unknown to civilized nations, and shocking even to barbarians? The Tories! Who prevailed on the savages of the wilderness to join the standard of the enemy? The Tories! Who have assisted the Indians in taking the scalp from the aged matron, the blooming fair one, the helpless infant, and the dying hero? The Tories! Who advised and who assisted in burning your towns, ravaging your country, and violating the chastity of your women? The Tories! Who are the occasion that thousands of you now mourn the loss of your dearest connections? The Tories! Who have always counteracted the endeavors of Congress to secure the liberties of this country? The Tories! Who refused their money when as good as specie, though stamped with the image of his most sacred Majesty? The Tories! Who continue to refuse it? The Tories! Who do all in their power to depreciate it? The Tories! Who propagate lies among us to discourage the Whigs? The Tories! Who corrupt the minds of the good people of these States by every species of insidious counsel? The Tories! Who hold a traitorous correspondence with the enemy? The Tories! Who daily sends them intelligence? The Tories! Who take the oaths of allegiance to the States one day, and break them the next? The Tories! Who prevent your battalions from being filled? The Tories! Who dissuade men from entering the army? The Tories! Who persuade those who have enlisted to desert? The Tories! Who harbor those who do desert? The Tories! In short, who wish to see us conquered, to see us slaves, to see us hewers of wood and drawers of water? The Tories!

And is it possible that we should suffer men, who have been guilty of all these and a thousand other calamities which this country has experienced, to live among us! To live among us, did I say? Nay, do they not move in our Assemblies? Do they not insult us with their impudence? Do they not hold traitorous assemblies of their own? Do they not walk the streets at noon day, and taste the air of liberty? In short, do they not enjoy every privilege of the brave soldier who has spilt his blood, or the honest patriot who has sacrificed his all in our righteous cause? Yes—to our eternal shame be it spoken—they do. Those very men who wish to entail slavery on our country, are caressed and harbored among us. Posterity will not believe it; if they do, they will curse the memory of their forefathers for their shameful lenity. Can we ever expect any grateful return for our humanity, if it deserves that name? Believe not a spark of that or any other virtue is to be found in the Tory's breast; for what principle can that wretch have who would sell his soul to subject his country to the will of the greatest tyrant the world at present produces? 'Tis time to rid ourselves of these bosom vipers.

"A Whig," Pennsylvania Packet, August 5
[Abridged]

June 20

SOUTH CAROLINA   This day the South Carolina troops attempted to force the British lines at Stono Ferry. The numbers within and without were rather too nearly equal for the enterprise. The Americans attacked boldly, fought gallantly, and retired in soldierly order. It had been preconcerted that seven hundred men should be detached from Charleston to James' Island, where a show should be made of a design to land on John's Island, in order to attract the enemy's attention, while General Lincoln should attack their redoubts and trenches. By some unlucky accident the appointment was not kept, and the seven hundred did not reach James' Island till afternoon. This failure enabled the British to draw a large reinforcement from John's Island to the main, and brought their number to be nearly equal to that of General Lincoln's troops. Maugre this balk or blunder, the general, at half-past seven in the morning, began to assault. The order of the battle was as follows: General Huger, with the two Continental brigades, and 2d battalion of light infantry, commanded by Colonel Henderson, on the left, where the most strenuous efforts were to be made, opposed to the Highlanders; General Sumter, with the North and South Carolina brigades of militia, and 1st battalion of light infantry, commanded by Colonel Malmadie, on the right; the Virginia brigades of militia formed a corps of reserve.

Colonel Malmadie began the action. On the extension of General Huger's division to the left, two hundred Highlanders sallied out, and his warm discharge of musketry was exchanged, but on our light infantry's quick advance to the charge, the Highlanders shrunk into the works, leaving twenty-seven dead, and several wounded on the ground, among the latter a Captain Bennet. The action continued with great warmth fifty-six minutes. The enemy's works being found much stronger than was expected, the American field-pieces making no impression on them, and intelligence being likewise received that the enemy had drawn in a reinforcement of five hundred men from John's Island, General Lincoln gave orders for retreating, which the troops performed in good order, carrying off their dead and wounded. The light infantry covered the rear, and maintained so good a countenance, that the enemy did not attempt to follow more than four hundred yards, and at a respectable distance.

New Hampshire Gazette, August 10

Should America continue firmly to oppose the tyranny of Britain, says a correspondent, may not the promise of the present day sanctify a conjecture, that in a few years the rising grandeur of this new world will invite every man from Europe who is not attached to it by landed property or other similar cause. There is a field opening for every species of manufacture, art and science, trade and commerce. Finely situated for the encouragement and cultivation of business, every artificer will fly here and transplant with him the art he possesses. Secure from tyrannical burdens, he will apply himself assiduously in the prospect of reaping what he sowed, and will assist in rearing this new republic to a pitch of grandeur superior, perhaps, to any state now existing.

New Hampshire Gazette, June 29

Last week died, at Hammersmith, in England, Mrs. Ross, celebrated for her beauty and constancy. Having met with opposition in her engagement with Captain Charles Ross, she followed him, in men's clothes, to America, where, after such a research and fatigue as scarce any of her sex could have undergone, she found him in the woods lying for dead, after a skirmish with the Indians, and with a poisoned wound. Having previously studied surgery in England, she, with an ardor and vigilance which only such a passion could inspire, saved his life by sucking his wound, the only expedient that could have effected it at the crisis he was in, and nursing him with scarce a covering from the sky for the space of six weeks. During this time she remained unsuspected by him, having dyed her skin with lime and bark; and keeping to a man's habit, still supported by the transport of hearing his unceasing aspirations of love and regret for that dear though (he then thought) distant object of his soul, being charged by him with transmitting to her (had the captain died) his remains, and dying asseverations of constancy and gratitude for the unparalleled care and tenderness of his nurse, the bearer of them; but, recovering, they removed into Philadelphia, where, as soon as she had found a clergyman to join her to him forever, she appeared as herself, the priest accompanying her. They lived for the space of four years in a fondness almost ideal to the present age of corruption, and that could only be interrupted by her declining health, the fatigue she had undergone, and the poison not properly expelled which she had imbibed from his wound, undermining her constitution. The knowledge he had of it, and piercing regret of having been the occasion, affecting him still more sensibly, he died with a broken heart last spring at John's Town, in New York. She lived to return and implore forgiveness of her family, whom she had distressed so long by their ignorance of her destiny. She died, in consequence of her grief and affection, at the age of twenty-six.

New York Gazette and Weekly Mercury, October 4

June 30

That wretched tool of a brutish tyrant, Sir Harry Clinton, in a proclamation, dated this day, has declared, "That all Negroes taken in arms, or upon any military duty, shall be purchased, and the money paid to the captors." He likewise invites all Negroes to desert the States, and "take refuge with his army;" meaning, no doubt, (like the noted Negro thief, *Lord Dunmore*,) to put such refugees in his pocket. However, I am not much concerned, nor is the cause of freedom much interested, how Sir Henry and his *black* and *white* refugees, settle their accounts; as they are all villains, it matters little which may prove in the end the *greatest*. But justice, honor, and freedom, are concerned for all men, of whatever nation or kindred, who are in the service of the United States, and fight under the banners of freedom; therefore I have long expected some notice from authority, would have been taken of that insulting and villanous proclamation. Justice demands retaliation for every man in the service of these States who may be injured by the ruffian tyrant or any of his slaves; and his slave Sir Harry ought to be told what retaliation he is to expect from the insulted majesty of our nation in this instance.

"American Soldier," New York Packet, November 18

JULY

July 2

NEW YORK   Last night, Lieutenant-Colonel Tarleton marched out with a detachment of cavalry, and early this morning attacked a party of the rebel Nags, commanded by a Colonel Sheldon, in the neighborhood of Bedford. The

Americans' situation was in a wood, with a morass on each
side, which was intersected by a road, along which they, with
great precipitancy, retreated. The rebel officers and men
quitted their jades, and threw themselves over the fences to
gain the swamp. By so sudden a flight, in such a narrow road,
no great impression could be made, only on the rear, of whom
about twenty-two were killed and wounded. Two corps of
rebel militia, which had formed on their rear, at the approach
of the legion, quitted their post, retreating to the morass. The
colonel, finding it impracticable, with his fatigued horses, to
pursue them further, returned to the camp of the rebels, burned
and destroyed their whole baggage, and brought off a standard,
about an hundred helmets, and seventeen prisoners, with the
loss of one corporal of the legion killed, and one light horse-
man wounded by some skulking militia firing from the fences
on his return. They were cautioned by the commanding officer
to desist from firing, on pain of their houses being consumed,
but still foolhardily persevering in their hostility, he was constrained to carry his menaces into execution, and several
houses were accordingly destroyed.

Among the prisoners is one of the Vantassels, from near
Tarrytown, of a pedigree partly Indian and partly Batavian.
This despicable caitiff has of late amused himself with cruelly
flagellating numbers of inoffensive women, whom he had suspected of frequenting the New York markets. Four of this
hardy varlet's brothers are also in safe custody, held as hostages
for four men of the provincial corps who have been made prisoners on the North River, tried and *destined to the cord* by
their new republican legislature. The Yankees have been formally apprised that the fate of the Vantassel fraternity will
depend immediately upon that of the loyal provincials; when
once the gallows of castigation shall be erected on the side of
loyalty, a period to the public and wanton murder of the
King's friends will most assuredly follow.

One Hunt, formerly a breeches maker of New York, but
of late a vender of the confiscated estates of loyal refugees, an
orator, and a messenger employed by the Congress, was at the
same time delivered to the custody of Mr. Cunningham, to
sympathize at leisure, en provost, with his mongrel friend

Vantassel on the disastrous condition of their paper piastres, the dwindled number of Mr. Washington's scaled miserables, and the chop-fallen countenance of each delegate at this time composing the distracted Continental Congress.

Rivington's Gazette, July 7

July 5

PENNSYLVANIA   Yesterday being the anniversary of the day which gave freedom to the vast republic of America, the Congress, the President, and the Council of the State, with the other civil and military officers, and a number of principal gentlemen and ladies, at twelve o'clock, attended at the Roman Chapel, in Philadelphia, agreeable to invitation received from the Minister Plenipotentiary of his Most Christian Majesty. A *Te Deum* was performed on the occasion to the great satisfaction of all present, and His Excellency's chaplain delivered a short and elegant address to his audience, of which we have been favored with the following translation:

"GENTLEMEN:—We are assembled to celebrate the anniversary of that day which Providence had marked in his eternal decrees to become the epocha of liberty and independence to the thirteen United States of America. That Being whose almighty hand holds all existence beneath its dominion, undoubtedly produces in the depth of his wisdom those great events which astonish the universe, and of which the most presumptuous, though instrumental in accomplishing them, dare not attribute to themselves the merit. But the finger of God is still more peculiarly evident in that happy, that glorious revolution, which calls forth this day's festivity. He hath struck the oppressors of a people, free and peaceable, with that spirit of delusion, which renders the wicked artificers of their own proper misfortunes. Permit me, my dear brethren, citizens of the United States, to address you on this occasion. It is that God—that all-powerful God who hath directed your steps, when you knew not where to apply for counsel—who, when you were without arms, fought for you with the sword of eternal justice—who, when you were in adversity, poured into your hearts the spirit of courage, of wisdom, and of fortitude, and who has at length raised up for your support a youthful sovereign whose virtues bless and adorn a sensible, a faithful, and a generous nation. This nation has blended her interests with your interests, and her sentiments with yours. She participates in all your joys, and this day unites her voice to yours at the foot of the altars of the eternal God, to celebrate that glorious revolution which has placed the sons of America among the free and independent nations of the earth!

"We have nothing to apprehend but the anger of Heaven, or that the measure of our guilt should exceed the measure of his mercy. Let us then prostrate ourselves at the feet of the immortal God, who holds the fate of empires in his hands, and raises them up at his pleasure, or breaks them to dust— let us conjure him to enlighten our enemies, and to dispose their hearts to enjoy that tranquillity and happiness which the revolution we now celebrate has established for a great part of the human race—let us implore him to conduct us by that way which his Providence has marked out for arriving at so desirable an end—let us offer unto him hearts imbued with sentiments of respect, consecrated by religion, by humanity and patriotism. Never is the august ministry of his altars more acceptable to his divine Majesty than when it lays at his feet homages, offerings, and vows so pure, so worthy the common parent of mankind. God will not reject our joy, for he is the author of it; nor will he reject our prayers, for they ask but the full accomplishment of the degrees he hath manifested. Filled with this spirit, let us in concert with each other, raise our hearts to the Eternal—let us implore his infinite mercy to be pleased to inspire the rulers of both nations with the wisdom and force necessary to perfect what it hath begun. Let us, in a word, unite our voices to beseech him to dispense his blessing upon the counsels and arms of the allies, that we may soon enjoy the sweets of a peace which will cement the Union, and establish the prosperity of the two empires. It is with this view that we shall cause that canticle to be performed which the custom of the Catholic Church hath consecrated, to be at once a testimonial of public joy, a thanksgiving for benefits received from Heaven, and a prayer for the continuance of its mercies."

New-York Journal, July 26

Siúbhail a Ghrádh

This lament came to America with Irish immigrants during the eighteenth century. It records the anguish of the Irish people who saw the flower of their youth and leadership sent into exile after the abortive rebellion of 1689–91 against the British Crown. The haunting sorrow of the melody has echoed down American history; it has been sung here, in one form or another, for two hundred years. First used to bewail the loss of colonial militiamen who had departed to fight the French (French and Indian Wars) or the British (American Revolution), the song won popularity in the nineteenth century under the title "Johnny Has Gone for a Soldier." (Oral tradition, Eire and the United States. The Gaelic refrain is translated by John Anthony Scott and Samuel Prescott Bayard.)

I wish I were on yon green hill, 'Tis there I'd sit and cry my fill, And ev - 'ry tear would turn a mill, For the lad that I love has gone a - way. *Refrain* Gone, gone, gone a - way, Now death a - lone can end my woe, Don't leave me here to mourn a - lone, My dar - ling and my life, I love you so.

I'll sell my rack, I'll sell my reel,
I'll sell my only spinning wheel,
To buy my love a sword of steel,
My darling and my life, I love you so.

Gone, gone, gone away,
Now death alone can end my woe,
Don't leave me here to mourn alone,
My darling and my life, I love you so.

But now my love has gone to France,
To try his fortune to advance,
If he come back, 'tis but a chance,
My darling and my life, I love you so.

Gone, gone, gone away,
Now death alone can end my woe,
Don't leave me here to mourn alone,
My darling and my life, I love you so.

I'll dye my petticoat, I'll dye it red,
And round the world I'll beg my bread,
For the lad that I love from me is fled,
My darling and my life, I love you so.

Gone, gone, gone away,
Now death alone can end my woe,
Don't leave me here to mourn alone,
My darling and my life, I love you so.

Siúbhail, siúbhail, siúbhail a ghrádh,
Ní leigheas le fagháil acht leigheas an bháis.
Ó d'fhág tu mise, is bocht mo chás,
Is go dteidhidh tu a mhúirnin slán.

July 7

CONNECTICUT   On Sunday night last, (4th,) a fleet of
British ships and vessels were observed in Long Island Sound,
standing towards New Haven, and about two o'clock the next
morning the fleet, consisting of the *Camilla* and *Scorpion*
men-of-war, with tenders, row-galleys, and transports, to the

number of forty-eight, commanded by Sir George Collier, anchored off West Haven. They had on board, it is said, between two and three thousand land forces, commanded by Governor Tryon, who, a little after sunrise, landed most of the troops on West Haven Point. The alarm guns were fired, the drums beat to arms, and every preparation which the confusion and distress of the inhabitants (on the near and sudden approach of so terrible an enemy) would permit, was made for defence and resistance. The bridge on the western road was taken up, and a number of field-pieces were placed and served to such advantage as prevented the enemy's approaching the town by that route. They then proceeded on the west side of the creek, in order to cross at the bridge on the Amity road, but were bravely opposed by small parties of Americans, particularly by about twenty-five under the command of a lieutenant of the militia, who drove upwards of two hundred of the enemy for near half a mile, and retarded their getting into the town for about three hours, giving all the women, except those who entertained too favorable an opinion of them, time to escape.

The British intended to have destroyed the powder and paper mills, the latter of which several of them entered, but were obliged to retire (before they had time to do any mischief) by a party of Americans posted there and at the bridge, who made fourteen of them prisoners. The main body of the enemy in a column, and two flanking parties, then forded the stream, some distance below the bridge, and proceeded through the enclosed grounds to the town. The people, though yet assembled in very small numbers, kept up a scattering fire with them all the way to the entrance of the town, and several were killed and wounded on each side. Between twelve and one o'clock the enemy entered the town in the most malignant disposition, enraged by the opposition from a number much inferior to their own, proud of their superiority, ashamed of the difficulty of overcoming the resistance of so small a number, and cruel in their resentment. They vented their fury upon the persons and effects of all who unfortunately fell under their power. They plundered the houses of every thing they could carry away or convert to their own use, and broke or destroyed every whole article of household goods and furniture, together with the window glass and sashes.

A few houses, however, escaped plunder, and a few persons abuse. These were such as were either noted Tories, or those that had been particularly recommended by such of those at whose houses the officers happened to put up, or who were spared through caprice or accident. Some few of the inhabitants both male and female; were noted Tories, who stayed in through choice, and were glad of such visitants. Some others, though professing to be Whigs, had conceived a good opinion of the enemy, and believed they would behave well and politely to those who were peaceable and did not oppose them. These, too, stayed in of choice; a very small number, and no women among them that we have heard of, were unwillingly caught in town, having no opportunity to get out. The few men who stayed in town, most of whom were old, infirm, or Tories, were treated with the greatest abuse and insolent ferocity—stripped and plundered of every thing valuable about them, and on the slightest pretences, or even without any pretence at all, inhumanly stabbed with bayonets, shot, or otherwise murdered, with circumstances of savage and wanton cruelty.

One Kennedy, a noted Tory who rejoiced at their coming, they plundered of his buckles, &c., and on his expressing some resentment, immediately stabbed him to death. A very old man of the name of English, (whose daughter was busy in providing for their entertainment,) on expression of reproof, uttered in the most gentle, inoffensive manner, they murdered by running through the body several times with bayonets; and as he lay on his back bleeding on the floor in the agonies of death, his daughter coming in, exclaimed— "Oh! how could you murder my poor old father so cruelly?" One of them asking, "Is he your father?" to which she answered, "Oh! yes, he is my father," the inhuman villain immediately stood and stamped on his breast, and then upon his face, crushing down his nose.

Mr. Bears, the elder, a man of a most respectable and inoffensive character, had been entertaining them in his own house, in the most liberal and obliging manner, treating them with good wine and punch, one of them who had been out, came in, and charged him with having fired a gun out of the window, and presenting a gun, swore he would kill him for it immediately. Mr. Bears seeing by the ruffian's motions that he intended to murder him, denied that he had fired any gun, or knew or believed that any had been fired out of the house; and said, "You see I am an old, infirm man; I am not able to do you any hurt, and have done nothing to oppose you; all I have is in your hands—why should you take away my life?" Unmoved by this remonstrance, the villain immediately shot him, giving him a mortal wound.

One Tuttle, (a man who on some late very great losses and misfortunes, occasioned by his having espoused the cause of the British tyrant, had lost his senses and been in a state of distraction, not having spoken a word for above six weeks before the time,) being met by some of the British cut-throats, they asked him a question, which he not regarding, and making no answer, they stabbed with a bayonet, which some person of the town seeing, told them the man was crazy, and had not spoken a word these six weeks. "Damn him," replied the murderer, "it is time he should be made to speak;" and forcing the point of the bayonet into his mouth, thrust it into his tongue, drew it out and cut it off. The man died in a few hours.

So firmly were these British miscreants possessed of the diabolical spirit of murder, that it did not quit them in the last stage of life, but went with them into eternity, to attend them at their appearance before their Judge! One Mr. Gilbert, a man advanced in years, having faithfully attended his duty in the field, in defence of the just rights and liberty of his country against the invasion of the bloody tyrants, happened to give a mortal wound to one of their officers, and afterwards was taken prisoner by the enemy, and brought to the man he had wounded. The dying wretch, instigated by infernal malice and revenge, said to the men under his command, "That man has murdered me; kill him, kill him!" And this murderous order was instantly executed accordingly; so that both spirits took their departure nearly together, and might, perhaps, together be summoned to make their appear-

ance before the awful tribunal. What a contrast in their circumstances!

The behavior of this crew of British miscreants to the unhappy women, who conceiving too favorable an opinion of
them, and confiding in their politeness and generosity, had
stayed in town and trusted themselves in their hands; to these
they behaved with worse than savage cruelty, and though
most, if not all of them, were reputed of Tory principles, yet
very few, if any, of the young women, (except some who fled
for protection to a few protected persons) nor not all the old,
or even the Negroes, escaped violation—some in the presence
of their husbands, and others by great numbers successively.
Some of these unhappy victims they carried off with them in
their vessels. These are some of the exploits of Britons (long
famous for justice and generosity, but now, alas! how fallen)
at New Haven.

After keeping possession of the town all night, (and a night
of horror it was to the inhabitants,) pretty early yesterday
morning a considerable body of militia, being collected under
the command of General Ward, General Hart, and other
officers, and great numbers continually coming in from every
quarter, the enemy unexpectedly and with great stillness and
despatch, retreated with their vessels, taking with them about
twenty of the inhabitants prisoners, with three or four families, and a few other persons who chose to accompany them.

While the British General Garth, with his division, plundered New Haven, Sir George Collier brought his fleet into
the harbor, landed Governor Tryon with the rest of the troops,
at East Haven, and then began a heavy cannonade on the
little fort at Black Rock, which was handsomely defended as
long as it was tenable, and then evacuated. On Tuesday afternoon the militia collected in such numbers, and pressed so
close upon Governor Tryon that he thought best to retreat on
board his fleet, and before morning had set sail to the westward.

The abusive and cruel treatment of the inhabitants of New
Haven, the wanton and malicious destruction of that part of
their property that could not be carried away, and the burning
of the warehouses on the wharf with the vessels that lay there,

as also part of the houses at East Haven, sufficiently prove that it was not owing to good will that the town of New Haven was not burned. The most probable conjecture is, that it was spared for the sake of the plunder.

The American loss at New Haven is twenty-three killed and fifteen wounded; that of the enemy cannot be exactly ascertained, but is known to exceed one hundred, and some report one hundred and fifty, among which are two adjutants, and some other officers they much lament. The number of Americans killed, exceeding that of the wounded, has been uncommon in former wars, but has frequently happened in this between Britain and America, and can only be accounted for by supposing that they generally murder our wounded men that fall into their hands.

New-York Journal, July 19

CONNECTICUT   The British fleet, with the same accursed crew of abandoned, bloody miscreants who left New Haven yesterday, arrived at Fairfield this afternoon, and continued their plundering and destruction. A correspondent gives the following account of their ravages:—"About four o'clock on the morning of the seventh of July, the approach of the fleet was announced by the firing of a gun from a small fort on Grover's Hill, contiguous to the Sound. They seemed, however, to be passing by. About seven o'clock we with pleasure beheld them all to the westward of us, steering, as we thought, for New York. A very thick fog came on which deprived us of them till between the hours of nine and ten, when, the mist clearing away, we beheld the whole fleet right under our western shore, and some of them close in with Kinzie's Point. They presently came to anchor, and lay till about four in the afternoon, when they began to land the troops a little to the eastward of Kinzie's Point, at a place called the Pines. From thence the troops marched along the beach until they came to a lane opposite the centre of the town, through which they proceeded, and in about an hour paraded in three divisions on the green between the meeting-house and court house. From thence they detached their guards, and then dividing into small parties, proceeded on their infernal business. Their com-

manding officers were Sir George Collier by sea, Generals
Tryon and Garth by land.

"The approach of the fleet was so sudden that but a few
men could be collected, though the alarm guns were fired immediately upon the dissipation of the fog. There was no
thought of opposing their landing, as our force was nothing
to theirs. Our little party, however, posted themselves so as
to annoy them to the best advantage, expecting that they
would land at the Point. When our people found them landing on their left, and marching in their rear to take possession
of the town, they retreated immediately to the court house
green; and as the enemy advanced through the beach lane,
they gave them such a warm reception with a field-piece,
which threw both round and grape shot, and with their musketry, as quite disconcerted them for some time. The column,
however, quickly recovered its solidity, and advancing rapidly,
forced our small body to retreat to the heights back of the
town, where they were joined by numbers who were coming
in from the country. The enemy were likewise galled very
much, as they turned from the back of the lane, by the cannon which played from Grover's Hill.

"The town was almost cleared of inhabitants—a few women,
some of them ladies of the most respectable families and
character, tarried with a view of saving their property. They
imagined that their sex and character would avail to such a
purpose; they put such confidence in the generosity of an
enemy who were once famed for humanity and politeness, and
thought that kind treatment and submissive behavior from
them would secure them against harsh treatment and rough
usage. Alas! they were miserably mistaken; they every one
bitterly repented their confidence and presumption.

"The parties that were first set loose for rapine and plunder,
were the Hessians. They entered the houses, attacked the
persons of Whig and Tory indiscriminately, breaking open
desks, trunks, chests, closets, and taking away every thing of
value; they robbed women of buckles, rings, bonnets, aprons,
and handkerchiefs; they abused them with the foulest and
most profane language, threatened their lives, presenting bayonets to their breasts, not in the least regarding the most

earnest cries and entreaties; there was likewise heard the dashing of looking glasses, furniture, china, and whatever came in their power. A nursing infant was plundered of part of its clothing, while the bayonet was held to his mother.

"Another party that came on were the American refugees, who, in revenge for their confiscated estates, carried on the same business. They were not, however, so abusive to the women as the former, but appeared very furious against the town and country.

"The Britons were the least inveterate. Some of the officers seemed to pity the misfortunes of the country, but in excuse said they had no other way to gain their authority over us. Individuals among the British troop were exceedingly abusive, especially to women. They solicited, they attempted their chastity; and though no rape was committed, yet some were forced to submit to the most indelicate and rough treatment. They exerted their utmost strength in the defence of their virtue, and some still bear the scars and bruises of the horrid conflict.

"Just about an hour before sunset the conflagration began at the house of Josiah Jennings, which was consumed, with the neighboring buildings. In the evening, the house of Elijah Abel, Esq., sheriff of the county, was consumed, with a few others. In the night, several buildings were burnt in the main street. General Tryon was in various parts of the town—the good women begging and entreating him to spare their houses. Mr. Sayre, the Church of England's missionary, a gentleman firmly and zealously engaged in the British interest, and who has suffered considerably in their cause, joined the women in their entreaties, begged the general to spare the town; but his request was denied. He then begged that a few houses might be kept as a shelter for some who could provide habitations nowhere else; this was likewise denied him. At length Mr. Tryon consented to spare the buildings and property of Mr. Burr and the writer of this epistle. They had both been plundered ere this. He likewise said that the houses of public worship should be spared. He was far from being in a good temper of mind during the whole affair. General Garth, at the other end of the town, treated the inhabitants with as much humanity as his errand would admit of.

"At sunrise, some considerable part of the town was standing; but in about two hours the conflagration became general. The burning pirates carried on their business with horrible alacrity, headed by two or three persons who were born and bred in the neighboring towns. All the town, from the bridge towards Stratford to the Mill River, (a few houses excepted,) were consumed.

"About eight o'clock the enemy sounded a retreat. The meeting-house and a few other houses were standing, which afforded some pleasure amidst our·woe; but the rear guard, consisting of a banditti of the vilest that was ever let loose among men, set fire to every thing which General Tryon had left—the large and elegant meeting, the ministers' houses, Mr. Burr's, and other houses which had received protection. They tore Tryon's protections in pieces, damn'd "General Tryon and his protections," and abused women most shamefully; they ran off in a very disgraceful manner. Happily our men came in, and extinguished the flames in several houses, so that we are not entirely destroyed. The Church of England building was destroyed; but by whom, or at what time, I am not able to say.

"The rear guard, which behaved in such a scandalous manner, were chiefly Germans called Jagers, which carry a small rifle-gun, and fight in a skulking manner, much like our Indians. They may emphatically be called the sons of plunder and devastation.

"Our fort yet stands. The enemy sent a row galley to silence it, and there was a constant firing between them all night. One or two attempts were made to take it by parties of troops, but it was most bravely and obstinately defended by Lieutenant Isaac Jarvis, who had but twenty-three besides himself. The militia followed the bloody incendiaries to the place of embarkation, where they galled them considerably. The embarkation took place about twelve o'clock, and the cruel foe set sail for Long Island about two o'clock in the afternoon. Many were killed on both sides; the number cannot be ascertained. They carried with them several prisoners, but no person of distinction. Old Mr. Solomon Sturgis, an Irish servant belonging to Mr. Penfield, and an old Negro man belonging to Mr. Jonathan Lewis, were put to the bayonet. Mr. Job Bartram was shot through the breast; the ball came out just under his shoulder-blade; he fought bravely, as did also many others."

New London Gazette, August 4

CONNECTICUT   A British writer gives the following account of the burning of Fairfield:—"About five o'clock in the afternoon the British troops landed about a mile and a half west of the fort at Fairfield. One division, consisting of Jagers, flank companies of guards, Fanning's corps, and the regiment of Landgrave, with General Tryon, moved up in columns to gain the right of the town, and were cannonaded from the fort hill above it, without suffering any loss. The advanced corps drew up a little short of the town, where they proposed remaining; but the enemy bringing a six-pounder on their left to enfilade them, they were obliged to move towards, and drive the enemy from the lower heights in front of the town, which they occupied with this field-piece. This they effected with little loss and difficulty, Jonathan very prudently removing himself to the upper heights, at a very decent distance, where he amused himself with firing long shot till about eight o'clock; when, upon the approach of General Garth with another division, he thought proper to retire entirely, after a narrow escape of being cut off by the forces under that general. Not a single house was touched, as the generals had taken some pains the two days before to circulate their address and proclamation [to the inhabitants of Connecticut]; and New Haven, though so fine a town, and of so much use to the rebellious colonists, was spared, in hopes these deluded people would at last be made sensible that lenity, whilst it could be shown without prejudice to ourselves, was the wish of British souls and British commanders. New Haven, except one or two storehouses and one or two small vessels, was left unhurt.

"Uninfluenced by this gentle treatment, their hearts seemed hardened like the hearts of Pharaoh's servants. Fairfield, till

six in the evening, remained as before, when an order came
for the advanced troops to retire a little nearer the town.
Jonathan, imagining the dread of him had inspired this motion,
felt very bold, and advancing nearer, got in behind some
houses in front of the town, and flattering himself he was then
in security, threw his shot something thicker about him. The
troops faced about, drove Jonathan from his fancied fortress,
and then set fire to these few alone which had emboldened
and afforded cover to their enemies; these houses were in
front of the town. General Tryon then sent a flag to them by
the clergyman of the place, offering, if they would return to
their allegiance, the town should be spared, and those who
would come in should remain unmolested. This generous offer
Jonathan did not think fit to comply with, but cannonaded
his own town all night; the consequence of which was, in the
morning the troops set it on fire, and they re-embarked,
leaving their conduct in these two instances to inspire proper
reflections in their enemies."

Rivington's Gazette, July 14

July 16

NEW YORK   This morning, General Wayne, with the
light infantry, consisting of about twelve hundred men, drawn
from the whole of the American army on each side of the
North River, surprised the British garrison, consisting of five
hundred men, commanded by a Colonel Johnson, in their
works at Stony Point, on the west side of King's Ferry, and
made the whole prisoners, with the loss of four Americans
killed, and General Wayne slightly wounded.

Nothing can exceed the spirit and intrepidity of our
brave countrymen in storming and carrying the British fortress at Stony Point. It demonstrates that the Americans
have soldiers equal to any in the world; and that they can
attack and vanquish the Britons in their strongest works.
No action during the war, performed by the British military,
has equalled this *coup de main*. The generosity shown by our
men to the vanquished, when the parties of our enemy are
repeating their savage barbarities, whenever they come by

surprise, is unexampled. How much more honorable and manly is it to carry fortresses sword in hand, than to burn defenceless towns, and distress unarmed citizens, and even women and children? What action has Clinton to boast of, this campaign, that may be compared with this master-piece of soldiership by General Wayne? And how much provocation had he to have bayoneted the whole British garrison, when he recollected how cruelly the British had massacred the men he commanded some time ago, who fell into their merciless hands? How many of these brave men were killed in cold blood, after they could make no resistance? Clinton must be highly chagrined at this conquest, and employ some good pen to disguise and palliate this affair at the court of London. He has exceeded Howe in the ferocity and savageness of his exploits; but perhaps will not succeed better than he in accomplishing the designs of Britain.

New Hampshire Gazette, July 27

July 20

NEW YORK   We have just seen a rebel newspaper which contains a very curious article relative to the late attack on Stony Point. The article is written in that turgid style, and in that little spirit of triumph, which distinguish almost all the rebel publications, on the acquisition of any trifling advantage; and is at once a just sample of the eloquence and temper of the rebels. It begins thus: "Our gallant light infantry, who, under the brave, intrepid General Wayne, have gained immortal honor by storming the British garrison at Stony Point, were composed of drafts from each State. The firm coolness with which they marched," &c. It proceeds in the same style of bombast and exaggeration to describe the *amazing* fortitude, *wonderful* prowess, and *astonishing* humanity which marked the conduct of the rebel troops, from the beginning to the end of the whole business.

Far be it from me to detract from any bravery or humanity which may have been shown by the rebels on this occasion. I respect those qualities even in an enemy; and so far as the rebels exhibited either, or both, at Stony Point, (of which, however, I am unable to judge at present,) I give them full credit.

But the writer of the above article was not aware that by extolling the bravery and humanity of General Wayne and his men so extravagantly, he induces his readers to conclude that such instances are very rare among the rebels. People who would make a figure, and have but slender means, must make the most of the little they possess. This writer tells us that the men destined for the attack at Stony Point "were composed of drafts from each State;" and we are elsewhere assured that they amounted to upwards of twelve hundred— some say to double that number. Is it so extraordinary a matter that all the States, as he calls them, should furnish twelve hundred men, (reckoning them at the lowest calculation, and of whom many were Europeans,) who, in the dead of the night, and after taking every precaution to conceal their design—even killing all the dogs in the neighborhood of Stony Point to prevent an alarm—is it extraordinary, I say, that such a body of men, thus picked, and culled, and circumstanced, would venture to attack about four hundred men? for, if my information be right, the effective men at Stony Point did not exceed that number. Among troops accustomed to face and meet their enemies, I am sure this would not be esteemed any mighty affair. When the British troops, not amounting to twelve hundred men, really stormed the rebel forts at the Highlands, in open day—forts that were defended by a garrison three times as numerous as that at Stony Point— there was not half so much said about it as there is said here of General Wayne's exploit. Such things are expected from British troops: there is nothing unusual in it, and therefore little is said about it.

Our writer reminds me of a passage in De Solis's history of the conquest of Mexico. While Cortez was subduing that empire, a Spaniard was killed in a fray with the natives. The Mexicans got possession of the corpse, and viewed it with a mixture of admiration and joy; admiration at their own prowess in killing a Spaniard, and joy to find that the Spaniards were vulnerable and mortal! Similar to this is an incident related by Josephus, when Titus besieged Jerusalem. The Roman general constructed works, and planted engines on them to batter the walls. The Jews made a sally, destroyed the works, and burnt the engines. They exulted most extravagantly on this little success, which only served to confirm their obstinacy, hasten their ruin, and stimulate them to greater cruelties against their wretched brethren, who groaned under all the horrors of foreign and domestic war.

This writer is so hugely elevated with the affair at Stony Point, that he thinks Britain should now confirm the independency of America publicly! Can any one be so stupid as to imagine that such a trifling affair could be any way decisive at present, or influence the conduct of Britain? Or are incidents of this kind unusual in the course of war? I could mention several instances where outposts belonging to the greatest generals that ever led armies into the field, have been attacked and carried; and in wars, too, where those generals have been most successful. People who are so easily elevated, betray their own weakness, both in judgment and resources, and generally are easily depressed. Their minds, like a pendulum, will vibrate to either extreme equally, as circumstances occur; and it is an indubitable proof how low the affairs of the rebels are sunk, when so trivial an advantage is puffed off with so much parade. It evidently shows that they are obliged to seize every little incident which can serve, by exaggeration, to support the flagging spirits of their party.

Our writer goes on to extol the "humanity of the rebels," and contrasts it with the "savage barbarity of burning unguarded towns, deflowering defenceless women," &c. As far as truth will permit, I am willing to believe, for the honor of America, that the rebels on this occasion relaxed in their usual barbarity. As it is the first instance, it should be recorded, though it would have lost nothing had it been expressed in less exaggerated terms.

The rebels have hitherto been infamous for their wanton cruelties. Their brutal treatment of Governor Franklin, and many other persons of distinction whom I could mention,— their barbarity to loyalists in general, and at this present hour —hanging men for acting according to the dictates of conscience—whipping men almost to death because they will not take up arms—publicly whipping even women, whose husbands would not join the militia—their confiscations, fines, and imprisonments; these things which they daily and indubitably practice, very ill agree with the character of humanity so lavishly bestowed on them by this writer. Nothing but a long, very long series of conduct the reverse of this can wipe off the infamy which they hereby incurred.

The charge of "deflowering defenceless women" is one of those deliberate, malicious falsehoods which are circulated by the rebels, purely to incense the inhabitants against the British troops. As to burning "unguarded towns," this writer should know that the King's troops burn no houses except public magazines, and those from which they are fired at, or otherwise annoyed. This was lately the case at Fairfield and Norwalk, the towns to which, I suppose, the author alludes; and when houses are thus converted into citadels, it is justifiable to burn them by the rules of war among all civilized nations.

New Haven was in the possession of the King's troops, yet they did not burn it. The reason was, they were not fired at from the houses during their approach to, or retreat from, the town. Some of the inhabitants, however, did what would have justified the British troops in consigning it to the flames. Sentries placed to guard particular houses have been fired at from those very houses, and killed. An officer of distinction took a prisoner who was on horseback, and had a gun; the prisoner apparently submitted, but watching for an opportunity, he discharged his gun at the officer, and wounded him. The wounded officer was carried into an adjoining house to have his wound dressed; the owner of the house seemed to be kind and attentive to the officer; the latter, in gratitude for his attention, ordered the soldiery, on his departure, to be particularly careful of the house, that no injuries should be offered to it. Yet, no sooner was the officer gone, and at the distance of fifty yards, than this very man discharged a loaded musket at him. These are samples of rebel humanity, which *sweetly harmonize* with our writer's sentiments.

In fine, this writer, and all others of his stamp, should remember that the colonies are now in a state of revolt and rebellion against their rightful sovereign. The British legislature is unalterably determined to bring them back to their allegiance. The most generous overtures have been made to them—*a redress of grievances, an exemption from taxes, and a free trade, have been offered.* These liberal terms would indubitably make America the happiest, freest, and most flourishing country in the world. But the American Congress have madly and insolently rejected these terms. The Congress, therefore, and their partisans, are justly chargeable, before God and the world, with all the calamities which America now suffers, and with all those other and greater calamities which it will probably hereafter suffer in the course of this unnatural contest.

"Candidus," New York Gazette and Weekly Mercury, August 16

AUGUST

August 3

MASSACHUSETTS   This morning, arrived at Boston, in Massachusetts, a French frigate of thirty-two guns, from France, in which came passengers his excellency the Chevalier de la Luzerne, Plenipotentiary from his most Christian Majesty, to the United States, with his secretary, &c.; as also the Honorable John Adams, Esquire, late a commissioner from the United States to the Court of France. His excellency and suite landed on General Hancock's wharf, about five o'clock this afternoon, where they were received by a committee from the honorable Council of the State, who were waiting with carriages for their reception. They were conducted to the house late the residence of the Continental general. He was saluted by a discharge of thirteen cannon, on his landing, from the fortress on Fort Hill, and every other mark of respect shown him which circumstances would admit.

Pennsylvania Packet, August 17

August 25

MASSACHUSETTS   Yesterday evening, the Chevalier de
la Luzerne, accompanied with M. de Valnais, Consul of
France, M. de Marbois, counsellor of parliament, M. de
Chavagnes, captain in the royal navy of France, and a number of other gentlemen of distinction, both French and
Americans, made a visit to Harvard College, at the invitation
of the president and corporation. The Chevalier and company having alighted from their carriages, passed through
the college yard between two lines of students in their academ-
ical habits, their heads uncovered, to the door of Harvard
Hall, where they were received by the president, corporation, professors, and tutors, and conducted to the library.
Soon after they were seated, the president rose, and in the
name of the corporation and the whole university, addressed
the Chevalier in the Latin language, congratulating his safe
arrival, making the most respectful mention of our illustrious
ally, his most Christian Majesty; expressing the warmest
wishes for the perpetuation of the alliance, and the completion of its important and happy design, and for the prosperity
of religion and learning throughout the world.

The Chevalier replied in the most polite manner, and in
the same language, assuring his audience that his wishes had
been most fortunately crowned by seeing a country, once indeed the region of ignorance and barbarity, now the seat of
freedom, commerce, virtue, and the liberal arts; and expressing, at the same time, the uncommon joy he should derive
from finding the turbulent scenes of war, and the public negotiation in which he was engaged, preparing the way for a closer
alliance between the arts and sciences in distant nations, to
their mutual improvement, and the common benefit of mankind. After amusing themselves among the rich variety of
books deposited in the library, the company were conducted
into a large and elegant philosophy room, where a very decent
entertainment was provided. After dinner they viewed the
curiosities of the museum, and the philosophical apparatus
fabricated by some of the best artists in Europe.

Every countenance indicated pleasure, and every circumstance of the day testified the joy that was diffused through the whole university upon this agreeable occasion.

New Hampshire Gazette, September 7

———•———

SEPTEMBER

September 16

PENNSYLVANIA   The expedition of General Sullivan against the Indians has been crowned with complete success. Forty of their towns have been reduced to ashes: one of them (Genesee) contained about one hundred and twenty-eight houses; all of their corn destroyed, computed to amount to one hundred and sixty thousand bushels, besides large quantities of other articles. The whole country of the Senecas, and other tribes of the Six Nations, have been overrun and destroyed, and they compelled to fly to Niagara for security; and all this done with the loss of less than forty men on our part, including killed, wounded, taken, and those who died natural deaths. In course of the expedition, it became necessary to lessen the issues of provisions to half the usual allowance, in which the troops acquiesced with the greatest cheerfulness, being determined to prosecute the enterprise to a complete and successful issue.

Colonel Brodhead, who commanded a party from Fort Pitt, has penetrated the Indian country, lying on the Alleghany River, one hundred and eighty miles, burnt ten of the Mingo, Munsey, and Seneca towns in that quarter, containing one hundred and sixty-five houses, and destroyed all the fields of corn, computed to be five hundred acres, with the only loss on our side of three men slightly wounded. Forty-three of their warriors were met by Lieutenant Harding and an advance party of twenty-two men, who attacked the savages, and routed them, killed five on the spot, and took all their canoes and blankets.

New Hampshire Gazette, November 2

PENNSYLVANIA   A gentleman who attended Colonel
Brodhead, gives the following particular account of the expedition:—"The many savage barbarities and horrid depredations committed by the Seneca and Munsey nations upon the
western frontiers, had determined Colonel Brodhead, as the
most effectual way to prevent such hostilities in future, and
revenge the past, to carry the war into their own country, and
strike a decisive blow at their towns.

"On the 11th of August, our little army, consisting of only
six hundred and five rank and file, marched from Pittsburg
with one month's provision. At Mahoning, fifteen miles above
the Old Kittanning, we were detained four days by the excessive rains, from whence (leaving the river, which flows in a
thousand manners) we proceeded by a blind path leading to
Cuscushing, through a country almost impassable by reason
of the stupendous heights and frightful declivities, with a
continued range of craggy hills, overspread with fallen timber,
thorns, and underwood; here and there an intervening valley,
whose deep, impenetrable gloom has always been impervious
to the piercing rays of the warmest sun. At Cuscushing (which
is fifteen miles above Venango) we crossed the Alleghany, and
continued our route upon its banks. But here our march was
rendered still more difficult by the mountains, which jutted
close upon the river, forming a continued narrow defile, allowing us only the breadth of an Indian path to march upon.

In the midst of these defiles, our advanced party, consisting
of fifteen white men and eight Delawares, discovered between
thirty and forty warriors landing from their canoes, who having
also seen part of our troops, immediately stripped themselves and prepared for action. Lieutenant Harding, who commanded our advance, disposed his men in a semi-circular
form, and began the attack with such irresistible fury, tomahawk in hand, that the savages could not long sustain the
charge, but fled with the utmost horror and precipitation,
some plunging themselves into the river, and others, favored
by the thickness of the bushes, made their escape on the main,
leaving five dead on the field, without any loss on our side
except three men slightly wounded. Upon the first alarm,
supposing it to be more serious, the army was arranged for

fight; both officers and men, enraged at their former cruelties, animated by the calmness, resolution, and intrepidity of the commandant, showed the utmost ardor to engage; and had the action been general, we had every prospect of the most ample success from a brave commander at the head of brave men.

Continuing our march, we arrived the same day at Buchan, where, leaving our baggage, stores, &c., under a guard, we proceeded to their towns with the utmost despatch, which we found at the distance of about twenty miles further, with extensive cornfields on both sides of the river, and deserted by the inhabitants on our approach. Eight towns we set in flames, and committed their pagoda, and war posts to the river. The corn, amounting in the whole to near six hundred acres, was our next object, which in three days we cut down and piled into heaps, without the least interruption from the enemy.

"Upon our return, we several times crossed a creek about ten miles above Venango, remarkable for an oily liquid which oozes from the sides and bottom of the channel and the adjacent springs, much resembling British oil, and if applied to woollen cloth burns it in an instant.

"After burning the old towns of Conauwago and Mahusquachinkocken, we arrived at Pittsburg, the fourteenth instant, with the scalps we had taken, and three thousand dollars' worth of plunder; having, in the course of thirty-three days, completed a march of near four hundred miles, through a country the Indians had hitherto thought impenetrable by us, and considered as a sufficient barrier for the security of their towns; and, indeed, nothing but the absolute necessity of such a measure, and a noble spirit of enterprise, could be a sufficient inducement to undertake so arduous a task, and encounter those difficulties and obstacles which require the most consummate fortitude to surmount."

Letter from Pittsburg, Pennsylvania, September 16
New York Gazette and Weekly Mercury, November 1

Paul Jones's Victory

The great naval duel between the American and British sea captains, Paul Jones and Richard Pearson, was fought off Flamborough Head, Yorkshire, in the evening of September 23, 1779. Pearson, commanding the Serapis (50 guns), and Captain Piercy, with the Countess of Scarborough (20 guns), were convoying a merchant fleet from the Baltic. At noon on September 23 they sighted Paul Jones's squadron, which included the Bonhomme Richard *and* Pallas. *The battle was joined the same evening as the moon was rising, and it lasted about three hours, in the form of a duel between* Bonhomme Richard *and* Serapis *on the one hand, and* Pallas *and* Countess of Scarborough *on the other. Paul Jones's two other ships, the* Alliance *and* Vengeance, *played no positive role in the encounter. Paul Jones was the victor, thanks to his indomitable will. The* Bonhomme Richard *was so badly battered that she sank two days later; most of her guns had been disabled at the very first encounter.*

The engagement was commemorated in a broadside written in England in 1779; the song soon found its way to America, enjoyed a wide popularity, and has remained in oral tradition ever since. Strange to say, this great sea ballad rarely finds its way into modern song books. For a detailed account of the fight and the words of the 1779 edition of the broadside, see S. E. Morison, John Paul Jones *(Boston: Little Brown, 1959), 221–42. The lyric reproduced here is from oral tradition, and differs in detail from the early nineteenth-century broadside reproduced on page 396. The melody is transcribed from the singing of Frank Warner, who learned it from C. K. Tillett, of Wanchese, North Carolina. (Ford, Isaiah Thomas, 203, 4.)*

An A - mer - i - can frig - ate, a frig - ate of fame, With guns mount - ed for - ty, the Rich - ard by name,___ For to

cruise in the chan - nel of old Eng - land, And a

val - iant com - mand - er, Paul Jones is the man.

We had not sailed long before we did spy
A large forty-four, and a twenty so nigh,
With fifty bold seamen well laid in with store,
In consort pursued us from the old English shore.

About twelve at noon Pearson came alongside,
With a speaking trumpet; "Whence came you?" he cried,
"It's now give an answer, I hail'd you before,
Or this moment a broadside into you I will pour."

Paul Jones then he says to his men every one,
"Let every bold seaman stand true to his gun;
We'll receive a broadside from these bold Englishmen,
And like true Yankee heroes return it again."

The contest was bloody, both decks ran with gore,
The sea seemed to blaze when the cannon did roar;
"Fight on my brave boys," then Paul Jones he cried,
"We will soon humble this bold Englishman's pride."

We fought them eight glasses, eight glasses so hot,
Till seventy bold seamen lay dead on the spot,
And ninety bold seamen lay bleeding in gore,
While the pieces of cannon like thunder did roar.

Our gunner in a fright to Paul Jones he came;
"We make water quite fast, and our side's in a flame;"
Then brave Jones he said in the height of his pride,
"If we can't do no better boys, sink alongside."

The *Alliance* bore down while the *Richard* did rake,
Which caused the heart of poor Pearson to ache;
Our shot flew so hot they could not stand us long,
And the flag of proud Britain was forced to come- down.

Captain Paul Jones of the ſhip Poor Richard of 40 guns, took an Engliſh ſhip called the Serapis of 44, and the Lion a 20 gun ſhip at one engagement.

PAUL JONES'S VICTORY.

AN American frigate, a frigate of fame,
With guns mounted forty, the Richard by name,
For to cruiſe in the channel of old England,
And a valiant commander, Paul Jones is the man.

We had not fail'd long before we did eſpy
A large forty-four, and a twenty ſo nigh,
With fifty bold ſeamen well laid in with ſtore,
In conſort purſu'd us from the old Engliſh ſhore.

About twelve at noon Percy came along ſide,
With a ſpeaking trumpet, whence came you ? he cry'd,
Its now gave an anſwer, I hail'd you before,
Or this moment a broadſide into you I'll pour.

Paul Jones then he ſays to his men every one,
Let ev'ry bold ſeaman ſtand true to his gun ;
We'll receive a broadſide from theſe bold Engliſh men,
And like true yankee heroes return it again.

The conteſt was bloody, both decks ran with gore,
The ſea ſeem'd to blaze when the cannons did roar ;
Fight on my brave boys, then Paul Jones he cry'd,
We will ſoon humble this bold Engliſhman's pride.

Stand firm to your quarters, your duty don't ſhun,
The firſt man that quits them, thro' his body I'll run,
Tho' their force is ſuperior, yet they ſhall know
What true brave American ſeamen can do.

we fought them eight glaſſes, eight glaſſes ſo hot,
Till ſeventy bold ſeamen lay dead on the ſpot,
And ninety bold ſeamen lay bleeding in their gore,
while the pieces of cannon moſt wretched did roar,

Our gunner in a fright to Paul Jones he came,
we make water quite faſt, and our ſide's in a flame ;
Then brave Jones he ſaid in the height of his pride,
If we can't do no better boys ſink along ſide.

The Lion bore down while the Richard did rake,
which cauſed the heart of poor Percy to ake ;
Our ſhot flew ſo hot they cou'd not ſtand us long,
'Till the undaunted union of Britain came down.

To us they did ſtrike, their colors pull'd down ;
The fame of Paul Jones will be heard with renown ;
His name will be rank'd among heroes ſo brave,
who fought like a freeman our country to ſave.

Now all you brave ſeamen whoever you be,
who hear of this battle that's fought on the ſea,
May you all do like them, when call'd to the ſame,
And your names be enroll'd on the pages of fame.

Your country will boaſt of Tars that's ſo brave,
And to you ſhe will look in dangers to ſave ;
She'll call you dear Sons, your names they will ſhine,
And about your brave brows bright laurels entwine.

So now my brave boys we have taken a prize,
A large forty-four, and a twenty likewiſe ;
Then God bleſs the mother, that cauſe has to weep
For the loſs of her ſon in the ocean ſo deep.

STERRET's Sea Fight.

STAND to your guns my hearts of oak,
Let not a word on board be ſpoke,
Victory ſoon will crown the joke ;
    Be ſilent and be ready.
Ram down your guns and ſpunge them well,
Let us be ſure that the balls will tell,
The cannons' roar ſhall ſound their knell ;
    Be ſteady boys, be ſteady.

Not yet, nor yet—reſerve your fire,
Says brave Sterret—Fire !
And ſink thoſe Mooriſh Tropolines,
All were amaz'd who beheld the ſcenes.
    A broadſide my boys.

See the blood in purple tide,
Trick down her batter'd ſide ;
wing'd with fate the bullets fly,
Conquer boys—or bravely die,
Be ſteady and defend your rights.
    She's ſilent—huzza !
To Columbia's flag ſhe ſtrikes.

So now my brave boys, you have taken a prize,
A large forty-four and a twenty likewise,
Both noble vessels well laden with store,
We'll bend on all canvas for New England once more.

God bless the widows who shortly must weep
For the loss of their husbands now sunk in the deep;
Here's a health to Paul Jones, a sword in his hand,
Who led us to battle and gave the command!

The Deserter

European fighting forces of the eighteenth century were composed in part of mercenaries, in part of "pressed" men conscripted by force and disciplined by the lash. "The Deserter" dates from the mid-eighteenth century, and is from the Such Collection. It illuminates the unspeakable brutality that in all European armies, under most commanders, was inflicted upon the common soldier. On the very eve of the Revolution Americans had witnessed the horrors of military punishment; during the occupation of Boston in 1768 they had seen British soldiers flogged to death for "desertion." Patriots did not belittle the bravery of British troops, and they had compassion for their sufferings. But they insisted that love of country and home would prove a higher morale factor than the motivation that the other side had to offer—lash and the love of loot.

This fine example of a British broadside is transcribed here from the singing of Ewan McColl.

As I _____ was a - walk - ing a - long Rad - cliff high - way, The re - cruit - ing _____ par - ty come a - beat - ing _____ that way: I was list ed _____ and at - test - ed, and be - fore _____ I did know, _____ It's to the King's _____ du - ty I was forced for _____ to go.

When first I deserted I thought myself free,
When my cruel companions informed against me:
I was quickly followed after, and brought back with speed,
With chains I was loaded, heavy irons on me.

Court martial! court martial! they held upon me,
And the sentence they passed was three hundred and three:
May the Lord have mercy on their souls for their sad cruelty,
For now the King's duty lies heavy on me.

Then again I deserted and I thought I was free,
When my cruel sweetheart informed against me:
I was quickly followed after and brought back with speed,
With chains I was loaded, heavy irons on me.

Court martial! court martial! I very soon got,
And they quickly gave verdict that I should be shot;
Now the Lord have mercy on their souls for their sad cruelty,
For now the King's duty lies heavy on me.

Brave Wolfe he come a-riding, and as he passes by:
"Bring to me that young man whose death is so nigh;
Strike off those heavy chains, and let him go free,
He'll make a clever soldier in far America."

OCTOBER

October 22

GEORGIA   On the first day of last month (September) Count D'Estaing arrived off the coast of Georgia, in order to co-operate with the Americans under the command of General Lincoln, in the reduction of Savannah. Upon the fifteenth, says a correspondent, the Count summoned the town to surrender, in the true style of a Frenchman. A proper answer was returned. In the mean time Moncrieffe was indefatigable in putting the place in a proper state of defence. A few days afterwards, the French and rebels began to throw up works upon the hill to the left of Tatnall's, within about three or four hundred yards of the British lines, when three companies of light infantry were sent out in hopes of drawing on a general action; but were obliged to retire, being opposed by ten times their number, after fighting like lions in the sight of the whole army. The British loss was Lieutenant M'Pherson killed, and about fifteen privates killed and wounded; and it is beyond doubt that the French had upwards of fifty killed, and a considerable number wounded. Major Graham commanded in this little affair. After this, the British never attempted to interrupt the Monsieurs, who could be heard working like devils every night.

About one o'clock in the morning of the third instant, they began a most dreadful cannonade and bombardment, which continued with very little intermission until the ninth, when the town was very much shattered, and two houses burnt by carcases. Notwithstanding there were thirty pieces of heavy cannon and ten mortars incessantly playing upon us, it is astonishing the little loss we sustained; the only officer killed was our worthy friend Captain Simpson, of Major Wright's corps.

About daybreak on the ninth, the united forces of France and America, consisting of upwards of four thousand French, and the Lord knows how many rebels, attempted to storm our lines. The principal attack was made in three columns, who intended to unite and attack the works at the redoubt upon the Ebenezer road. The count, in person, began the attack with great vigor, but was soon thrown into confusion by the well-pointed fire from our batteries and redoubts. A choice body of grenadiers came on with such spirit to attack the old redoubt upon the Ebenezer road, that if Tawse, with a number of his men, had not thrown himself in very opportunely, it must have been carried; upwards of sixty men were lying dead in the ditch after the action. Poor Tawse fell bravely fighting for his country. The rebels could not be brought to the charge, and in their confusion are said to have fired upon their allies, and killed upwards of fifty of them. It is almost incredible the trifling loss we sustained; the only officer killed was poor Tawse, and there were not twenty privates killed and wounded. The enemy's loss was astonishing. I never saw such a dreadful scene, as several hundreds lay dead in a space of a few yards, and the cries of many hundreds wounded was still more distressing to a feeling mind. The exact loss of the enemy cannot be ascertained; but Mr. Robert Baillie, who was a prisoner with the French during the whole of the siege, says they own a loss of near fifteen hundred. The count, in the action of the ninth, was wounded in the arm and thigh, and Pulaski very dangerously by a grape shot in the groin. Two days ago the last of the French troops embarked; the rebels have been gone some time, and we are now in as much tranquillity as we have been for any time these six months past. Mutual animosity and reviling have arisen to such a height between the French and rebels since they were defeated, that they were almost ready to cut one another's throats.

Letter from Savannah, Georgia
Rivington's Gazette, November 20

October 26

RHODE ISLAND   Last evening the invincible troops of
Britain, having evacuated Newport, in Rhode Island, embarked on board the transports which lay ready to receive
them; and soon after the whole fleet sailed, it is said, to New
York, to assist in defending that last asylum of British
tyranny in the thirteen United States. The American troops
took possession of the town this morning.

New Hampshire Gazette, November 9
[Abridged]

NOVEMBER

November 11

MASSACHUSETTS

The Dying Criminal:

POEM, by ROBERT YOUNG, on his own Execution, which
is to be on this Day, November 11th, 1779, for RAPE committed on the Body of Jane Green, a Child, eleven years of
age, at Brookfield, in the County of Worcester, on the third
Day of September last. Corrected from his own Manuscript.

---

*The execution of a condemned felon was an event of great
importance in colonial America. Crowds gathered from far and near
on the appointed day to see justice done. The chief role in the
drama, of course, was played by the condemned man himself; not
infrequently he rose magnificently to the occasion. Standing on the
rim of oblivion, during his last moments on earth, he gave a passionate harangue, exhorting the people to live righteously and to
avoid his course of action and his fate. Inevitably these scenes gave*

*rise to ballads; such broadsides would find a ready sale when
hawked about at the place of execution. Some of these, as in the
case of Robert Young, might actually be based upon the criminal's
own confession. "The Dying Criminal," given here, is brilliantly
representative of this type of gallows literature. (Ford, Check List,
2211, 2212.)*

Attend, ye youth! if ye would fain be old,
Take solemn warning when my tale is told;
In blooming life my soul I must resign,
In my full strength, just aged twenty-nine.

But a short time ago I little thought
That to this shameful end I should be brought;
But the foul fiend, excepting God controuls,
Dresses sin lovely when he baits for souls.

Could you the Monster in true colours see,
His subject nor his servant would you be;
His gilded baits would ne'er allure your minds,
For he who serves him bitter anguish finds.

Had I as oft unto my Bible went,
As on vain pleasures I was eager bent,
These lines had never been compos'd by me,
Nor my vile body hung upon the tree.

Those guilty pleasures which I did pursue,
No more delight—they're painful to my view;
That monster, Sin, that dwells within my breast,
Tortures my soul, and robs me of my rest.

The fatal time I very well remember,
For it was on th' third day of September,
I went to Western, thoughtless of my God,
Though worlds do tremble at his awful nod.

With pot companions did I pass the day,
And afterwards to Brookfield bent my way,
The grand deceiver thought it was his time,
And lead me to commit a horrid crime.

Just after dark I met the little fair,
(O Heav'n forgive, and hear my humble pray'r)
And thou, dear Jane, wilt thou forgive me too,
For I most cruelly have treated you.

I seiz'd th' advantage of the dark'ning hour,
(And savage brutes by night their prèy devour)
This little child, eleven years of age,
Then fell a victim to my brutal rage:

Nor could the groans of innocence prevail,
O pity, reader, though I tell the tale;
Drunk with my lust [on] cursed purpose [bent]
Severely us'd th' unhappy innocent.

Her sister dear was to have been my wife,
But I've abus'd her and must lose my life;
Was I but innocent, my heart would bleed
To hear a wretch, like me, had done the deed.

Reader, whoe'er thou art, a warning take,
Be good and just, and all your sins forsake;
May the almighty God direct your way
To the bright regions of eternal day.

A dying man to you makes this request,
For sure he wishes that you may be blest;
And shortly, reader, thou must follow me,
And drop into a vast eternity!

The paths of lewdness, and the base profane,
Produce keen anguish, sorrow fear and shame;
Forsake them then, I've trod the dreary road
My crimes are great, I groan beneath the load.

For a long time on sin should you be bent,
You'll find it hard, like me, [for to] repent;
The more a dangerous wound doth mortify,
The more the surgeon his best skill must try.

These lines I write within a gloomy cell,
I soon shall leave them with a long farewell;
Again I caution all who read the same,
[And] beg they would their wicked lives reclaim.

[Last verse illegible.]

1780

JANUARY

January 1

An American gentleman, now in London, who is well acquainted with General Washington, gives the following account of him:—"That, though advanced in years, he is remarkably healthy, takes a great deal of exercise, and is very fond of riding on a favorite white horse. He is very reserved, and loves retirement; when out of camp, he has only a single servant attending him, and when he returns within the lines, a few of the light horse escort him to his tent. When he has any great object in view, he sends for a few of those officers of whose abilities he has a high opinion, and states his present plan among half a dozen others to all which they give their separate judgments; by these means he gets all their opinions, without divulging his intentions. He has no tincture of pride, and will often converse with a sentinel with more freedom than he will with a general officer. He is very shy and reserved to foreigners, although they have letters of recommendation from the Congress. He punishes neglect of duty with great severity, but is very tender and indulgent to recruits until they learn the articles of war and their exercise perfectly. He has a great antipathy to spies, although he employs them himself, and has an utter aversion to all Indians. He regularly attends divine service in his tent every morning and evening, and seems very fervent in his prayers. He is so tender-hearted that no soldier can be flogged nigh his tent; or, if he is walking in his camp and sees a man tied to the halberds, he will either order him to be taken down, or walk another way to avoid the sight. He has made the art of war his particular study; his plans are in general good and well digested; he is particularly careful always of securing a retreat, but his chief qualifications are courage, steadiness, perseverance, and secresy. Any act of bravery he is sure to reward, and make a short eulogium on the occasion to the person and his fellow-soldier (if it be a soldier) in the ranks. He is humane to the prisoners who fall into his hands, and orders every thing necessary for their relief. He is very temperate in his diet, and the only luxury he indulges himself in, is a few glasses of punch after supper."

New Hampshire Gazette, March 4

January 10

NEW YORK   The very remarkable and long-continued severity of the weather at New York, (the like not having been known, as we are informed, by the oldest man living,) has stopped all the avenues of intelligence, and almost cut off all social intercourse between people of the same neighborhood. The incessant intenseness of the cold, the great depth and quantity of the snows, following in quick succession one on the back of another, attended with violent tempests of wind, which for several days made the roads utterly impassable, has put a stop to business of all kinds, except such as each family could do within itself. And as many were slenderly provided with necessaries for subsistence, we have reason to apprehend that we shall shortly hear many melancholy accounts of private distress in the country, and that from the sea-coasts and vessels at sea, the accounts will be dreadful.

Pennsylvania Packet, January 27

January 19

NEW YORK   Yesterday, the anniversary of her Majesty's birthday was celebrated at New York with uncommon splendor and magnificence. At noon, a royal salute was fired from Fort George, and repeated by his Majesty's ships-of-war at one o'clock. The public rooms were, on this occasion, entirely new painted and decorated in a style which reflects honor on the taste of the managers. A Doric pediment was erected

over the principal entrance, enclosing a transparent painting
of their Majesties, at full length, in their royal robes, over
which was an emblematical piece, encircled with the motto
of "BRITONS STRIKE HOME"—the whole illuminated with a
beautiful variety of different colored lamps. In the evening,
a most splendid ball was given by the general, field, and staff-
officers of the army, to the garrison and principal ladies and
gentlemen of the city. The ball was opened at eight o'clock
by the Baroness de Riedesel and Major-General Pattison,
commandant of the city and garrison. Country dances commenced at half-past nine, and at twelve the company adjourned
to supper, prepared in the two long rooms. The tables exhibited a most delightful appearance, being ornamented with
parterres and arbors, displaying an elegant assemblage of
natural and artificial flowers, china images, &c. The company
retired about three o'clock this morning, highly satisfied with
the evening's entertainment, which abounded with so many
scenes equally new and agreeable.

                                    Rivington's Gazette, January 19

January 22

NEW JERSEY   A writer in the American camp at Baskenridge, in New Jersey, in a letter of this date, says:—"We
have had a fast lately in camp, by general constraint, of the
whole army, in which we fasted more sincerely and truly for
three days than ever we did from all the resolutions of Congress put together. This was occasioned by the severity of the
weather, and drifting of the snow, whereby the roads were
rendered impassable, and all supplies of provisions cut off,
until the officers were obliged to release the soldiers from
command, and permit them to go in great numbers together
into the country to get provision where they could find it.

"The inhabitants of this part of the country discovered a
noble spirit in feeding the soldiers; and to the honor of the soldiery, *they received what they got with thankfulness*, and did
little or no damage. As soon as the roads were broken, and
the brave fellows *got their bellies full*, they went, with amazing alacrity, on the Staten Island expedition; but the British

getting intelligence, our people, after reconnoitring their strength, returned *not a little disappointed*. They did little more than burn a large fortified house and five small vessels, after stripping them of every thing valuable."

Maryland Journal, February 8

January 27

NEW JERSEY Last Tuesday night, [25th,] a party of the enemy, consisting of about three hundred infantry, under the command of Colonel Van Buskirk, of the new levies, and about sixty dragoons, said to be under the command of Captain Steward, of the seventeenth light dragoons, with several refugees—the whole in number nearly four hundred—crossed on the ice from Staten Island to Trembly's Point, about three miles from Elizabethtown. From thence they were conducted by Cornelius Hetfield, Job Hetfield, and Smith Hetfield, their principal guides, by the nearest and most retired route into Elizabethtown. They entered the town in two divisions, before the alarm was sounded. As soon as the troops that were in the town (consisting of about sixty men) perceived their danger, they retreated; however, they took a major who was commandant of the place, two or three captains that lodged in the town that night, and a few troops. They then set fire to the Presbyterian meeting and court house, which were consumed; plundered, insulted, and took off some of the inhabitants, and retreated, with great precipitation, by the way of De Hart's Point, whose house they likewise burned.

The same night another party of the enemy, consisting of drafts from the different regiments stationed in New York, passed over the North River in sleighs, to Powle's Hook; from thence through Bergen, the nearest way to Newark. They entered the town in three divisions, and proceeded to the academy, where they surprised and took about fifteen men, being all the troops that were on duty in the town—a lieutenant, notwithstanding he was twice a prisoner with the enemy, by his vigilance, effected his escape. They then set fire to the academy, which they consumed, during which time a party was detached to several of the inhabitants' houses, which they rifled of the most valuable effects; that which was not portable they destroyed. They took off Justice Hedden and Robert Neil, jun., two of the inhabitants. The former gentleman was taken out of his bed, and without any of his clothes on except his shirt and a pair of stockings, carried off, notwithstanding the strongest solicitations of Mrs. Hedden to the officers, for permission for her husband to dress himself. She received two wounds with a bayonet, one in the face, the other in the breast.

They continued in town about fifteen or eighteen minutes. A few militia being hastily collected, pursued their rear, by which means five of the enemy fell into their hands. Two of them died a short time after from the intense cold. Justice Hedden is so frost-bitten, that it is thought he will lose both his legs.

New-Jersey Journal, February 2

NEW JERSEY   A correspondent of *Rivington's* thus refers to this affair:—"Seeing in your last Wednesday's *Gazette* an extract taken from a rebel paper of the second instant, giving an account of the taking and bringing Justice Hedden and Robert Neil prisoners from Newark to this city, treating Mr. Hedden with great cruelty, and reflecting on the officer who commanded that party, you may inform the public that the apprehending of Justice Hedden was no part of the object of the King's officers; but that one Walker, a volunteer with them, who with many others had been most inhumanly and barbarously treated by Justice Hedden, went with a few of the privates to his house and took him, without waiting long for him to put on his clothes, which he intentionally delayed; when the officers perceived, on their march, his want of more clothing, they provided him with some.

"If Mrs. Hedden was wounded, it is what she merited, by her assaulting and opposing all in her power, the carrying away her husband. There was no intent to hurt Mrs. Hedden, but to make her desist in her violence; if any harm happened to her, she must blame her own fury. Mr. Hedden and his friends may, if they have any sense of justice remaining, find that justice hath in part overtaken him, when they reflect on the acts of barbarity he has frequently committed on many of his Majesty's loyal subjects for not perjuring themselves in abjuring their lawful sovereign, and swearing allegiance to the Congress, and to the State of New Jersey. Among many of his persecutions were imprisonments, reducing others to bread and water only, stripping many women and children of their clothing, beds, and household furniture, and then banishing them without the necessaries of life, and seizing and selling the estates of a great number of his Majesty's subjects, to his no small emolument.

"Robert Neil is also notorious in his way. A bankrupt four years past, since acting under the pretence of a sub-deputy quarter-master to the rebel army, made it his constant practice to take and dispose of, on his own account, to the Continental troops, the wheat, corn, and other grain, and also the firewood he cut from many valuable lots of land, belonging to those he pleased to call Tories and enemies to the State of New Jersey, whereby both Hedden and Neil have amassed large estates with the properties of others. Common justice, it is hoped, will prevent their discharge, till they have made full satisfaction to his Majesty's faithful subjects for the injuries they have done them."

Rivington's Gazette, February 16

FEBRUARY

February 1

NEW YORK   The sound, between Long Island and Connecticut, is almost frozen over in the widest part; and some persons have passed over from Long Island to Norwalk and other parts in Connecticut on the ice. Wood is brought from Long Island to New York on sleighs. It is almost passable from Powle's Hook to New York.

Rivington's Gazette, February 16

February 15

SOUTH CAROLINA   The following sketch of the present situation of affairs in Charleston, South Carolina, is communicated by Colonel John Laurens:—"The British army, said to be under the command of Sir Henry Clinton, are distributed on Port Royal Island, John's Island, Stono Ferry, and a detachment last night landed upon James' Island. The headquarters are at Fenwick's house, on John's Island. Four of their galleys have been seen between John and James' Island. The number of troops not known, supposed to be much diminished since the embarkation at New York. About twelve deserters from the fleet and army have come into Charleston, and as many prisoners are taken by our light horse. Different deserters from the fleet and army agree in reporting very heavy losses at sea. Three ships foundered, many dismasted, one brig, two ships are taken, and brought into Charleston; a brig is carried into North Carolina. One of the deserters informs, that thirteen sail were left on the rocks of Bermuda. There is undoubtedly some grand impediment to the enemy's progress. All their horses perished at sea, and much of their furniture was captured. Three days ago, passed by Charleston bar, in a hard gale of wind, a sixty-four gun ship, a frigate, and some transports. These may be gone to New York for further supplies; but all is conjecture. Near the bar of Charleston daily appears a frigate and other ships of war, reconnoitring and blocking up the harbor. We have four Continental frigates, two French armed ships, two State armed ships, six other armed vessels, some of them carrying very heavy cannon. The enemy's delay has afforded an opportunity for strengthening the lines of Charleston, which will be in pretty good order to-morrow. *The number of men within the lines uncertain; but by far too few for defending works of near three miles in circumference, especially considering many of them to be citizens, and unaccustomed to the fatigues of a besieged garrison, and many of the Continental troops half naked.*

"Reinforcements are expected—General Hogan is within a

few miles. *The Virginia troops are somewhere!—assistance from that sister state has been expected these eighteen months.* General Moultrie is forming a camp at Bacon Bridge, where he has about five hundred horse belonging to South Carolina —Baylor's and Bland's regiments of Virginia. General Williamson is encamped at Augusta—a thousand men are expected from his brigade. General Richardson and Colonel Carlen are raising the militia at and about Camden. At this moment the escape of the Americans depends on further delay on the enemy's part: two or three weeks more will make this garrison strong. The inhabitants in general are in good spirits; competent judges say that Sir Henry Clinton will then have cause to repent his enterprise. This affords encouragement, but events in war are uncertain; and if we do not receive assistance, the next intelligence may be quite contrary."

Maryland Journal, March 21

THE SIEGE OF CHARLESTON

March 19 – May 12

For a journal of the Siege see May 12 below.

MAY

May 12

SOUTH CAROLINA   This morning the garrison of Charleston, after sustaining a siege of over a month's duration, surrendered prisoners of war to the combined fleet and army of Great Britain. The following is a journal of the siege, from the day previous to the British fleet's crossing the bar, to the present hour:—

"*March* 19.—The British under General Clinton, now encamped on James Island, seem to wait for the shipping which lay off the bar, and have been disappointed at the last springs by south-west winds, which kept down the tides so that they cannot get over. This day the springs are at the highest, but the weather so hazy that they will scarcely attempt it, and it will probably clear up with unfavorable winds. We begin to hope that Province has interposed a second time to prevent their getting over until we are ready. If they should get over either now or hereafter, there will probably be the hottest contest that has happened this war, just off Fort Moultrie. The British ships destined to come in are said to be the *Renown*, fifty guns; *Roebuck*, forty-four; *Blond*, thirty-two; *Perseus*, twenty and *Camilla*, twenty. These, and some say another frigate with some galleys, are to force their way past the town, and cut off the communication between Charleston and the country. To oppose their passing the fort, the Americans have thrown a boom of cables across the channel at the fort, and stationed the *Providence*, of thirty-two guns; *Boston*, twenty-eight; *Bricole*, twenty-eight; *Adventure*, twenty; French vessel, twenty; *Queen of France*, eighteen; *Truite*, twenty, and three galleys, (seven guns;) so that either the fort or they must rake the enemy as they pass, and with the boom they hope to detain them so long as to do it effectually.

"As the enemy's chance of success depends entirely on getting up their shipping, and the American hopes of defending the town greatly depend on preventing it, they seem determined to sell the passage immensely high. The commodore, in sailor language, swears if he cannot defeat them he will run both them and himself ashore, and all shall perish together; and every officer in the navy is ready to second his resolution. Colonel Laurens commands the marines on board the *Providence*.

"*March* 20.—This morning the British got their ships over the bar. They consist of ten vessels of force, from twenty guns to a sixty-four, as some say, others a fifty. However, ours appeared so inadequate to oppose them by Fort Moultrie, that they were all ordered up to town. On the first alarm of the arrival of the enemy, the *Eagle* pilotboat was despatched to the Savannah to solicit assistance from Spain. Colonel Tonant went with the despatches, and has this evening returned. Report says that he has succeeded, and that we may expect three seventy-fours and thirteen frigates every hour, with three thousand land forces. Nothing has yet transpired from authority. I am just come from the general's, but can learn nothing without being too inquisitive. It is now left to a stand in the town, which I trust will remain until Woodford arrives with the Virginia line. The enemy have not yet summoned the town, nor made any movement indicating an immediate attack. It is said that Lord Cornwallis is against it entirely, and that the army seems much dispirited; but Clinton is bent on it. This is the most of our present intelligence. Our lines round the whole town are nearly completed, except by Gadsden's wharf, where the works on the bay should join those on the land. Our people are hard at work there now, as we dread the enemy's shipping on that quarter. We have on the Ashley River, or south side of the town, six batteries —some ten guns, some six, some four, none less, so that no vessel can lay before them. Four of them cross-fire the only landing-place on that quarter, besides field-pieces at proper distances all along the line. On the bay side we have four batteries of Palmetto, and a line of Palmetto. On the Neck we have seven batteries along the line, some redoubts to the left, a regular fort to the right, and a horn work by the gateway. In front of the line is a good line of abatis, a canal, most of it filled with water, and the side of the canal is abatied also. Only the north-east corner, rather than a side, by Gadsden's wharf, is unprovided with proper defense. This, I trust, we will have time to fortify. Four pieces of cannon scour the canal in front of the lines.

"*March* 27.—This morning Colonel Washington, with a party of horse reconnoitring, came up with a light party of the British, on which an engagement ensued, when the Americans took a Colonel Hamilton of the North Carolina refugees, a Doctor Smith, and seven privates, and it is said they had seven killed. The Americans had only one man badly wounded. This action happened within one hundred yards of the British flying army, consisting of light infantry and grenadiers, whose marching across the field to get in the rear of the Americans obliged Colonel Washington to order a retreat; otherwise their whole party would have been cut to pieces."

Pennsylvania Packet, April 25 and May 2

"*March* 30.—Yesterday, a large body of British grenadiers and infantry crossed Ashley River, and to-day they appeared before the American lines, where they are now encamped. As the enemy approached, Colonel John Laurens, with a small party, had a brush with the advance body, in which Captain Bowman, of the North Carolina forces, fell, much lamented; Major Herne and two privates were wounded. The enemy's loss is reported to be from twelve to sixteen killed. A French gentleman, who was volunteer in the action, says he counted eight and a Highland deserter says a Colonel St. Clair was mortally wounded."

Letter from Charleston, South Carolina
Pennsylvania Packet, April 25

"*April* 7.—This afternoon, about three o'clock, General Woodford and his brigade arrived in town, after a most rapid march of five hundred miles in thirty days, in perfect health, and high spirits.

"*April* 8.—This afternoon, between three and five o'clock, the British fleet passed Fort Moultrie, in a heavy gale, and anchored between Fort Johnson and Charleston, just out of reach of the guns from the town, where they now continue. They were so covered with the thunder storm as to be invisible near half the time of their passing. One of their frigates had a fore-topmast shot away by a cannon at the fort, and a store ship was so injured, in her rudder, as to be incapable of working, and the gale being fresh she went on shore, under the guns of our half-moon battery, on the point of the island, which obliged them to burn her, to prevent her falling into our hands. After burning a while she blew up. We had not a man hurt at the fort, though they kept up a brisk fire as they passed.

"Our garrison is in good health and high spirits, the town well fortified and defended by a numerous artillery; Sir Henry approaching very slowly, and our men longing for the hour in which he may afford them the opportunity of teaching the temerity of the present expedition."

Pennsylvania Packet, May 2

"*April* 12.—Day before yesterday, the British having completed their first parallel, summoned the town to surrender, of which General Lincoln took no notice; and to-day Clinton opened his batteries, which are answered by the Americans with spirit, but not with the effect that will insure success, the enemy's fire being far superior to ours. Governor Rutledge has taken post in the country between the Cooper and Santee rivers. A work is ordered to be thrown up on the Wando, nine miles from town, and another at the point of Lamprieres, to preserve the communication with the country by water."

Clift's Diary
Gordon, III, 47

"*April* 18.—The cannonading on both sides still continues. General Clinton received a reinforcement from New York yesterday, and it is probable he will make a further advance on us soon. He is very cautious, and moves with all the care and deliberation of an old Roman, which he certainly is not. Our men are in good spirits, although it seems to be the general opinion that we must at last succumb; not without a hard fight, however.

"Last Friday, (14th,) the party of Americans, posted to preserve the communication between the country and the town, were surprised at Monk's Corner by a body of British under the command of Lieutenant-Colonel Tarleton."

Elliot Manuscript

"A Negro slave, for a sum of money, conducted the British from Goose Creek, in the night, through unfrequented paths. Although the commanding officer of the American cavalry had taken the precaution of having his horses saddled and bridled, and the alarm was given by his videttes, posted at the distance of a mile in front; yet, being entirely unsupported by the infantry, the British advanced so rapidly, notwithstanding the opposition of the advanced guard, that they began their attack upon the main body before the men could put themselves in a posture of defence.

"*April* 21.—The British have completed their second parallel, which is within three hundred yards of the American lines. At a council of war held this morning, it was decided that offers of capitulation should be made to the British commander, 'which may admit of the army's withdrawing, and afford security to the persons and property of the inhabitants.'

"*April* 24.—Sir Henry Clinton rejects the American offers of capitulation, and is actively pushing forward his third parallel, which is not more than three hundred feet from our lines. This morning Lieutenant-Colonel Henderson led out a party of Americans, and attacked the advance working party of the British, killed several, took eleven prisoners, and returned to the lines victorious. In this sally, Captain Moultrie, a brother of the general, was killed."

Gordon, III, 48

"*May* 6.—This afternoon, the garrison at Fort Moultrie was summoned to surrender by Captain Charles Hudson, commander of his Majesty's ship *Richmond*. The commander of the fort answered, 'it should be defended to the last extremity;' but the officer carrying the refusal had proceeded but a little way on his return, when he was called back and told that the storm which was threatened by Captain Hudson must prove a very serious affair, and therefore the garrison had consented to submission."

Rivington's Gazette, May 31

"*May* 12.—Yesterday the British advanced within thirty yards of the American lines, and commenced preparations for a combined assault by sea and land. The reduced state of the garrison, the urgent solicitations of the inhabitants, and the clamors of the soldiery, compelled General Lincoln to renew negotiations with the British commanders; and to-day the articles of capitulation have been signed. It is stipulated that the Continental troops and sailors shall remain prisoners of war until exchanged, and be supplied with good and wholesome provisions, in such quantity as is served out to the British troops. The militia are to return home as prisoners on parole, which, as long as they observe, is to secure them from being molested in their property by British troops. The officers of the army and navy are to keep their swords, pistols, and baggage, which is not to be searched, and are to retain their servants. The garrison, at an appointed hour, is to march out of the town, to the ground between the works and the canal, where they are to deposit their arms. The drums are not to beat a British march, nor the colors to be uncased. All civil officers and citizens who have borne arms during the siege, are to be prisoners on parole, and with respect to their property within the city, they are to have the same terms as the militia. All persons in the town, not described in any article, are, notwithstanding, to be prisoners on parole. It is left to future discussion whether or no a year shall be allowed to all such as do not choose to continue under the British government, to dispose of their effects real and personal, in the state, without any molestation whatever, or to remove such part thereof as they choose, as well as themselves and families, and whether, during that time, they, or any of them, shall have it in their option to reside occasionally in town or country. The French consul, the subjects of France and Spain, with their houses, papers, and other movable property, are to be protected and untouched; but they are to consider themselves as prisoners on parole."

Gordon, III, 49

May 20

MASSACHUSETTS   Yesterday we were visited by a most unusual and uncomfortable phenomenon. As early as ten o'clock in the morning, a thick darkness came over the face of the country, so that it was impossible to move about the house without the assistance of a candle. Many persons were much frightened at the sudden darkness, and some thought that judgment-day had come. The cause of this strange appearance is now explained.

A writer in the *Boston Country Journal* gives the following particular account of the phenomenon:—"As the darkness which happened on last Friday was unusual, and to many people surprising, it will no doubt gratify the public to have the observations which have been made in various parts, communicated. In this way we may learn the extent, and perhaps ascertain the cause, of so remarkable a phenomenon. With these views I send you the enclosed.

"The observations from the first coming on of the darkness to four o'clock P.M., were made by several gentlemen of liberal education, at the house of the Rev. Mr. Cutler, of Ipswich Hamlet. There are some things worth noticing before and after this time. The hemisphere for several days had been greatly obscured with smoke and vapor, so that the sun and moon appeared unusually red. On Thursday afternoon and in the evening, a thick cloud lay along at the south and south-west, the wind small. Friday morning early, the sun appeared as it had done for several days before, the wind about south-west, a light breeze, and the clouds from the south-west came over between eight and nine o'clock; the sun was quite shut in, and it began to shower, the clouds continuing to rise from the south-west, and thicken from the thickness of the clouds, and the confusion which attended their motions. We expected a violent gust of wind and rain; the wind, however, near the earth, continued small, and it rained but little. About eleven o'clock the darkness was such as to demand our attention, and put us upon making observations. At half-past eleven, in a room with three windows, twenty-four panes each, all opened towards the south-east and south, large print could not be read by persons of good eyes. About twelve o'clock, the windows being still open, a candle cast a shade so well defined on the wall, as that profiles were taken with as much ease as they could have been in the night. About one o'clock, a glimpse of light which had continued till this time in the east, shut in, and the darkness was greater than it had been for any time before. Between one and two o'clock, the wind at the west freshened a little, and a glimpse of light appeared in that quarter. We dined about two, the windows all open, and two candles burning on the table. In this time of the greatest darkness, some of the dunghill fowls went to their roost; cocks crowed in answer to each other, as they commonly do in the night; wood-cocks, which are night birds, whistled as they do only in the dark; frogs peeped; in short, there was the appearance of midnight at noon-day. About three o'clock the light in the west increased, the motion of the clouds more thick, their color higher and more brassy than at any time before; there appeared to be quick flashes or coruscations, not unlike the aurora borealis. Between three and four o'clock we were out and perceived a strong, sooty smell; some of the company were confident a chimney in the neighborhood must be burning; others conjectured the smell was more like that of burned leaves. About half-past four, our company, which had passed an unexpected night very cheerfully together, broke up. I will now give you what I noticed afterwards. I found the people at the tavern near by much agitated. Among other things which gave them much surprise, they mentioned the strange appearance and smell of the rain water, which they had saved in tubs. Upon examining the water, I found a slight scum over it, which, rubbing between my thumb and finger, I found to be nothing but the black ashes of burnt leaves. The water gave the same black, sooty smell which we had observed in the air, and confirmed me in my opinion that the smell mentioned above was occasioned by the smoke, or very small particles of burnt leaves, which had obscured the hemisphere for several days past, and were now brought down by the rain. The appearance last mentioned served to confirm the hypothesis on which we had endeavored to account for the unusual darkness. The vast body of smoke from the woods, which had been burning for many days, mixing with the common exhalations from the earth and water, and condensed by the action of winds from opposite points, may perhaps be sufficient causes to produce the surprising darkness.

"The wind in the evening passed round further north, where a black cloud lay, and gave us reason to expect a sudden gust from that quarter. The wind brought that body of smoke and vapor over us in the evening, (at Salem, Massachusetts,) and perhaps it never was darker since the children of Israel left the house of bondage. This gross darkness held till about one o'clock, although the moon had fulled but the day before.

"Between one and two, the wind freshened up at northeast, and drove the smoke and clouds away, which had given distress to thousands, and alarmed the brute creation."

"Viator," Boston Country Journal, May 29
New-Jersey Gazette, June 21

A Few Lines Composed on the Dark Day, of May 19, 1780

Since ancient times natural disasters or epidemics—earthquakes, plagues, volcanic eruptions, tidal waves, and the like—have been interpreted by man as divine retribution for wickedness and as a warning against continuing in the path of sin. On May 19, 1780, as reported in the press, a dark cloud spread over the Boston area and blotted out the daylight. "Viator," in the Country Journal, *identified the phenomenon as smog. A more traditional reaction was expressed in the broadside reproduced below in full. The cloud, in the writer's opinion, was sent by God as a sign of his anger. Sinners should make haste to repent; if not, the vengeance of God would take a more permanent form, and their souls would burn in hell for eternity. (Ford, Check List, 2268–70; Isaiah Thomas, 194.)*

Let us adore, and bow before
The sovereign Lord of might,
Who turns away the shining day,
Into the shades of night.

All nature stands, when he commands,
   Or changes in its course;
His mighty hand rules sea and land—
   .He is the Lord of Host.

Nineteenth of May, a gloomy day,
   When darkness veil'd the sky;
The sun's decline may be a sign
   Some great event is nigh.

Let us remark, how black and dark,
   Was the ensuing night;
And for a time the moon's decline,
   And did not give her light.

Can mortal man this wonder scan?
   Or tell a second cause?
Did not our GOD then shake his rod,
   And alter nature's laws?

What great event, next will be sent
   Upon this guilty land?
He only knows, who can dispose
   All things at his command.

Our wickedness, we must confess,
   Is terrible and great;
Sin is the thing that we should shun,
   The thing GOD's soul doth hate.

Our mighty sins, GOD's judgment brings
   But still we hard'ned grow;
Then judgments great, may not abate,
   Until our overthrow.

How sin abounds in all our towns,
   Now in these gospel days;
How vice prevails and virtue fails,
   And godliness decays.

If we reflect, can we expect,
   According to our doing—
But that we are, as we may fear,
   Just on the brink of ruin.

A few Lines compofed on the *Dark Day*, of *May* 19, 1780.

I.

LET us adore, and bow before,
The fovereign LORD of might ;
Who turns away the fhining day,
Into the fhades of night.

II.

All nature ftands, when he commands,
Or changes in its courfe ;
His mighty Hand rules fea and land,
He is the LORD of Hoft.

III.

Nineteenth of *May*, a gloomy Day,
When darknefs veild the fky ;
The fun's decline may be a fign,
Some great event is nigh.

IV.

Let us remark, how black and dark,
Was the enfuing night ;
And for a time the moon decline,
And did not give her light.

V.

Can mortal man, this wonder fkan ?
Or tell a fecond caufe ?
Did not our GOD, then fhake his rod,
And alter nature's laws ?

VI.

What great event next will be fent,
Upon this guilty land ?
He only knows, who can difpofe,
All things at his command.

VII.

Our wickednefs we muft confefs,
Is terrible and great :
Sin is the thing, that we fhould fhun,
The thing GOD's Soul doft hate.

VIII.

Our mighty fins, GOD's judgment brings,
But ftill we heard'ned grow ;
Then judgments great, may not abate,
Until our overthrow.

IX.

How fin abounds, in all our towns,
Now in thefe Gofpel Days ?
How vice prevails and virtue fails,
And godlinefs decays ?

X.

If we reflect, can we expect,
According to our doing ?
But that we are, as we may fear,
Juft on the brink of ruin.

XI.

Awake, awake, your fins forfake,
And that immediately ;
If we don't turn, his wrath will burn,
To all eternity.

XII.

This is the day, that finners may
Repent, and turn to GOD ;
If they delay and won't obey,
Then they muft feel His rod.

XIII.

How good and kind, would finners find
Their great REDEEMER now ;
If they'd awake, their fins forfake,
And to his Sceptre bow.

XIV.

The gofpel Call, is unto all ;
Repent, why will you die ?
Why will you go to endlefs woe ;
And pafs my mercy by ?

XV.

Come unto me, JESUS doth fay,
All ye that weary are ;
Ye fhall find reft, ye fhall be bleft,
For fo his words declare.

XVI.

If after all, this gracious call,
You utterly refufe ;
And ftop your ear, and will not hear,
But your own ruin choofe ;

XVII.

Mercy abufe, and grace refufe,
Juftice then takes the throne ;
And in fome hour Almighty Power,
Will make his vengeance known.

XVIII.

O dreadful ftate, when 'tis too late,
For finners to return ;
When life and breath is loft in death,
The Soul in Hell muft burn.

XIX.

What mortal tongue, what human pen,
The terrour can declare,
That finners all in Hell, who fhall
That dreadful torments bear ?

XX.

Eternity ! Eternity !
Behold there is no end ;
Where finners lie, and wifh to die,
Who into Hell defcend.

XXI.

And now let all, who hear this call,
And faw the day fo dark ;
Make hafte away without delay,
And get into the Ark.

XXII.

Then fafe fhall he, forever be,
That doth to JESUS come,
He need not fear tho' death be near,
Since Heaven is his home.

A *Few Lines Composed on the Dark Day, of May 19, 1780.* A contemporary broadside. Reproduced by courtesy of The New-York Historical Society, New York City.

Awake, awake, your sins forsake,
  And that immediately;
If we don't turn, his wrath will burn,
  To all eternity.

This is the day, that sinners may
  Repent, and turn to God!
If they delay and won't obey,
  Then they must feel his rod.

How good and kind, would sinners find
  Their great Redeemer now;
If they'd awake, their sins'forsake,
  And to his sceptre bow.

The gospel's call, is unto all—
  Repent! why will you die?
Why will you go to endless woe,
  And pass my mercy by?

Come unto me! Jesus doth say!
  All ye that weary are;
Ye shall find rest! ye shall be blest!
  For so his words declare!

If after all, this gracious call,
  You utterly refuse;
And stop your ear, and will not hear,
  But your own ruin choose.

Mercy abuse, and grace refuse,
  Justice then takes the throne;
And in some hour Almighty Power,
  Will make his vengeance known.

O dreadful state, when 'tis too late,
  For sinners to return;
When life and breath is lost in death,
  The soul in hell must burn.

What mortal tongue, what human pen,
  The terror can declare,
That sinners all in hell who shall
  That dreadful torments bear?

Eternity! Eternity!
   Behold there is no end;
Where sinners lie, and wish to die,
   Who into hell descend.

And now let all, who hear this call,
   And saw the day so dark!
Make haste away without delay,
   And get into the Ark!

Then safe shall he, forever be,
   That doth to JESUS come,
He need not fear though death be near,
   Since heaven is his home.

JUNE

June 8

NEW YORK   By the latest intelligence from Schenectady, in New York, we are informed that Sir John Johnson, (who styles himself lieutenant-colonel commanding the King's Royal Yorkers, in the paroles given to some of the prisoners,) on Lord's day evening, the twenty-first of last month, (May,) made his first appearance at Johnson Hall, undiscovered by any but his friends, who, no doubt, were in the secret. On Monday, about daybreak, they began to burn all the houses except those of the Tories; beginning at Aaron Putnam's, below Tripe's Hill, and continued burning to Anthony's Nose, or Acker's house, except a few which, by the vigilance of the people, were put out after the enemy had set them on fire. There are burnt, thirty-three houses and out-houses, and a mill; many cattle were killed in the field, and sixty or seventy sheep burnt in a barn. Eleven persons were killed. Colonel Fisher and his two brothers fought with great bravery, when the two brothers were killed and scalped. The colonel went up stairs and there defended himself; but, being overpowered, was knocked down and scalped, on which they plundered the house, set it on fire, and then went off. The colonel reviving a little, though he was left by the enemy for dead, pulled one of his dead brothers out of the house, then in flames; the other was consumed in the house. It is said the mother had a narrow escape for her life, being knocked on the head by an Indian; but she is like to do well. Captain Hansen was killed by an Indian, who had formerly been used by him with kindness, and professed much gratitude. Old Mr. Fonda was cut in several parts of his head with a tomahawk. Had it not been for the alertness of Mr. Van Vrank, probably more would have been butchered by their savage hands. He alarmed the people along the way to Caughnawaga, who, by crossing the river, saved their lives.

Having done all the mischief to the distressed inhabitants they possibly could, they returned to Johnson Hall in the afternoon, when Johnson dug up his plate, and about sundown marched for the Scotch Bush, about four miles, that evening. He took with him fifteen or twenty of his Negroes, who had been sold. Several of his tenants and others, are gone with him. He has permitted some of his prisoners to return on parole. His whole force when he landed at Crown Point, is said to be about five hundred men —two hundred of them British, part of his own regiment, and Indians. Captain Putnam and four men followed them in their retreat four days, on their way to Lake Champlain. He saw him twenty-four miles from Johnson Hall. Some think they will take their route to Oswagatchie; but this seems improbable, as they have not provisions sufficient with them. His excellency the governor has collected a body of militia to intercept their way to Lake Champlain; a number have also marched from New Hampshire Grants (Vermont) for the purpose. Colonel Van Schaick, with eight hundred men, is in pursuit of him by the way of Johnstown. We hear the enemy had their feet much swelled by their long march; and being greatly fatigued, it is hoped our people may come up and give a good account of the lieutenant-colonel and his murdering banditti.

New-Jersey Gazette, June 21

June 9

NEW JERSEY   Last Tuesday night, (6th,) between eleven
and twelve o'clock, a body of the British, commanded by
General Knyphausen in person, landed at Elizabethtown
Point, in Jersey, who, being timely discovered by the American guards, gave the troops that were in town, commanded
by Colonel Dayton, an opportunity to assemble; but, on
reconnoitring them, their force was found inadequate for an
attack. Of course a retreat became indispensable, which was
performed in good order, with the enemy in their rear, until
they arrived at Connecticut Farms, where they fell in with the
Jersey brigade; and being joined by a few militia, posted
themselves on an advantageous piece of ground, thinking it
advisable to check the advance of the enemy, which, with
singular bravery, they effectually did, and annoyed them considerably, driving them back some distance. The British then
brought up some field-pieces which played briskly, but happily without any effect. The Americans kept them here about
two hours, until they were reinforced by the second division,
which had landed some time after the first, and had marched
up hastily. They then gained that ground, though not without considerable loss, and some wounded on that of the
Americans. Their advance after that was very tardy; yet they
seemed to show an inclination to possess themselves of Springfield, until they received a few shot from a piece of cannon,
not without some effect; which obliged them again to retreat,
and the day was spent in continual skirmishing, by which
they suffered amazingly. Since their retreat, forty or fifty of
their dead, which they had secretly buried, have been found.
Among the number it is said, is a son of Count Donop, who
has met the fate of his hapless father.

As soon as they came to Connecticut Farms, seven miles
from the place of their landing, they began the exercise of
their awful cruelty. Although they observed great discipline
and decorum in Elizabethtown, yet at the Farms every step
was marked with wanton cruelty and causeless devastation.
They set fire to, and entirely destroyed, the Presbyterian

Church, and fourteen dwelling-houses and barns, so that there are but two dwelling-houses remaining in that fertile settlement. But, alas! this is only one part of the horrid scene.

In this neighborhood lived the Rev. Mr. James Caldwell, whose zeal and activity in the cause of his country had rendered him an object worthy of the enemy's keenest resentment. His vigilance and attention had always evaded every attempt to injure him, and therefore it was now determined to wound him in any unguarded part. Following the absurd principles of too many of our incautious countrymen, he left his wife and family at home, trusting to the politeness and humanity of the enemy towards an amiable woman, and a number of helpless and innocent children, though he did not think it prudent to trust them with his own safety. He had been warned of their utmost hatred to him, and therefore dissuaded from leaving his family in their power; but, alas! his confidence in their benevolence towards the helpless has been his destruction.

Soon after their possessing themselves of the neighborhood, a soldier came to the house, and putting his gun to the window of the room where this worthy woman was sitting, (with her children, and a maid with an infant in her arms, along side of her,) he shot her through the lungs dead on the spot. Soon after an officer with two Hessians came in, and ordered a hole dug and her body thrown in, and the house to be set on fire. At the earnest request of an officer of the new levies, and with some difficulty, the body was suffered to be carried to a small house in the neighborhood, and Mr. Caldwell's dwelling-house immediately set on fire, and every thing belonging to him consumed together. The only comfort arising to this afflicted family is, that the wretch who served as the executioner of this murdered lady, (who, from her excellent character, deserved a better fate,) did his business so effectually that she lost her life without distress or pain. Thus it is, that even the tender mercies of the wicked are cruelty. This melancholy affair, with their cruel burnings, has raised the resentment of the whole country to the highest pitch. They are ready almost to swear an everlasting enmity to the very name of a Briton. So far is this cruelty and devastation from terrifying them to submission, that it rouses the most timid to feats of desperate heroism. A most worthy man, who has for four years past devoted himself to the service of his country, is thus left with nine small children, destitute even of a shift of clothes to comfort them. Many of the inhabitants are in a similar situation; some widows, some aged, some infirm.

The British being opposed by a regiment of Colonel Dayton's, and such militia as could be suddenly collected, made a slow advance till they came to a bridge at the entrance of Springfield, where the militia had an old iron four-pound field-piece, which they used to such purpose that the enemy were driven back for some considerable distance. Being thus encouraged, Colonel Dayton's regiment, and the militia together, pressed upon them, and killed and wounded many of them: the general estimate is about one hundred. As our people were reinforced they gained firmness, and at night the enemy had secured no farther than Connecticut Farms. In the night, having received an express from General Clinton in South Carolina, they immediately began a retreat; and by ten o'clock on Thursday, they had gained Elizabethtown Point, from whence they sent off all their wagons, a part of their artillery, and some of their cavalry. Lord Stirling, with General Hand's brigade, and the militia, was detached close on their rear, and between Elizabethtown and the Point had a very severe skirmish, with some loss on both sides. From what we can collect from the inhabitants of the Farms, many of whose houses were filled with their wounded, they must have suffered considerably. General Stirling had his thigh broken. Never did troops behave better than the Americans. The militia behaved beyond any thing that could have been expected. The Continental officers gave them the greatest credit. It is said the enemy had been persuaded that after the taking of Charleston, the militia would all submit, and the Continental troops would desert. It seems as if the militia had known these suggestions. Never did they so universally turn out on such short notice, and never with better spirits. This morning at least two thousand of them were below the mountains, and more flocking down continually. Colonel

Dayton deserves the greatest credit, as do all his officers, who behaved unexceptionably.

The British were all day yesterday manœuvring to bring on a general engagement, and General Washington was trying to draw them from their strong position on the Point, where it was impossible to attack them with advantage. Both have failed, and General Washington hath drawn back the main body of the army above Springfield to refresh them, as they are exceedingly fatigued with two days and two nights lying on their arms. Every thing has been carried on with great propriety, and we are in hopes their gentry will be obliged to retire, notwithstanding their sanguine expectations. General Knyphausen, it is said, brought over his carriage, expecting to have considerable use for it. There is a brigade left to watch their motions at Elizabethtown, with a number of the militia. They are in such force that it is supposed they intend to penetrate the country, and from some hints that have dropped, they have Pennsylvania in their eye, if they can beat General Washington.

Pennsylvania Packet, June 13

NEW JERSEY   A British officer gives the following account of the recent operations of the royal army in New Jersey:—"On Tuesday night, (6th,) the British troops made their first landing upon Elizabethtown meadows, and were crossed over by divisions in succession from Staten Island, with some light artillery, taking their route by Elizabethtown and Connecticut Farms, towards Springfield.

"Dayton's regiment receiving intimation of our approach, retired with precipitation, as did also the other Jersey regiments which compose Maxwell's brigade, from their position near Camp's. The militia of the country, although incapable of making any fixed resistance, did their utmost to incommode the troops upon their march; and collecting from different quarters, they assembled in some force in the vicinity of Springfield, forming a junction with the Jersey brigade at that place; and it is said that in the course of Wednesday, the seventh instant, they were supported by another brigade detached from Morristown.

"The troops halted upon some heights beyond Connecticut Farms, where they were ordered to take post till such time as the remainder of the artillery, the provision and other wagons, with the corps which brought up the rear, joined the army. From this circumstance it is probable the rebels conceived that whatever might have been the original plan, it was intended to penetrate no farther. Increasing in numbers, they used every exertion in their power, in flying parties, to fire upon the advanced pickets; and during the course of the day they made different attacks upon a body of Jagers, which was advanced upon the Springfield road. This produced much firing upon both sides.

"During the course of the evening, it is reported that information was received from the southward, which rendered it expedient to defer the object in agitation; and about two hours afterwards the troops returned towards Elizabethtown, without a single shot being fired, taking post upon the heights near the Point.

"On Thursday the eighth instant, the rebels advanced in some force to Elizabethtown, and made an attack upon the twenty-second regiment, which was posted some little distance in front of the line. This regiment was ordered to fall back, and the rebels conceiving it was the rear guard of the army, they advanced with some rapidity, but were soon checked, and retired with precipitation.

"The loss sustained during the course of this service is inconsiderable; nor can that of the rebels be determined, as they conceal it.

"Whilst the troops were advancing to Connecticut Farms, the rebels fired out of the houses, agreeable to their usual practice, from which circumstance Mrs. Caldwell had the misfortune to be shot by a random ball. What heightens the singularity of this lady's fate is, that upon inquiry, it appears beyond a doubt that the shot was fired by the rebels themselves, as it entered the side of the house from their direction, and lodged in the wall nearest to the troops, when advancing. The manner in which the rebels aggravate this unfortunate affair in their publications, is of a piece with their uniform conduct—plausible, but fallacious; nor is it to be wondered at, if a rebellion which originated in falsehood, is prosecuted with deceit. The soldiery received with smiles one moment, and the following instant butchered (for in a military view it merits no other name) by a set of people, who, by their clothing and appointments, cannot be distinguished from the quiet inhabitants of the country, may well be supposed to be exasperated; nor need we be surprised at their using the torch to dwellings which they find hourly occupied by armed men, who either want the generosity or the spirit to close the present unhappy contest by a manly, open, soldier-like decorum. Whatever may be the humane wishes of the commanders, human nature at times steps over the barrier of discipline, and men of judgment and wisdom, in the great scale of political reasoning, do not wonder at occurrences which their private feelings shrink at; such are the effects of intestine divisions. Miserable is the fate of that country which is the theatre of such a quarrel; and accursed is the man, or the set of men, who, from motives of private lucre or inordinate ambition, have fanned a flame which, if they were willing, they are now, perhaps, unable to extinguish."

Rivington's Gazette, June 21

JULY

July 1

The *Gazette* of to-day contains the following *"Sentiments of a Lady in New Jersey:"*—The war carried on by the British nation against my native country, cannot fail to excite in the humane and virtuous mind sentiments very unfavorable to the authors and instruments of such a variety of complicated evils and misfortunes as we have suffered in the course of it.

The contest began on their part without principle—has been prosecuted without humanity. Devoid of those sentiments and that conduct which do so much honor to the civi-

lized nations of Europe, even in the time of war, they have
thrown off all restraint, and fully displayed, in their military
operations in this part of the world, the true characteristics of
their country—a fierce and barbarous spirit, resisting, contrary
to the common rule, the ordinary effects which refinement of
manners and a high degree of polish usually have on the
minds of men in softening them to humanity, constitutes their
real character.

Were I unconnected with Americans by ties of friendship
or blood,—were I not attached by that love of one's country
which is inherent in some degree in every breast, and partakes
of the nature of that instinctive affection which we bear to
our parents and kindred,—were I situated in a distant part of
the world, unagitated by the incidents of the day which are the
more interesting the nigher we are to the scene of war, the
bare recital of their unjust claims, their cruelties, and their
crimes, would fill my soul with horror, and I should regard
them not only as unprovoked aggressors, but as enemies by
principle and example to mankind in general.

But as if it were not enough unjustly to spill the blood of
our countrymen, to lay waste the fields, to destroy our dwellings, and even the houses consecrated and set apart for the
worship of the Supreme Being, they have desolated the aged
and unprotected, and even waged war against our sex. Who
that has heard of the burning of Charlestown, in New England—of the wanton destruction of Norfolk and Falmouth—
of their wasting the fine improvements in the environs of
Philadelphia—of the tragical death of Miss M'Crea, torn from
her house, murdered and scalped by a band of savages hired
and set on by British emissaries—of the melancholy fate of
Mrs. Caldwell, put to death in her own house in the late incursion of the enemy, and the general havoc which at this
time marks their footsteps in their route through a part of this
state—but would wish to avert from themselves, their kindred,
their property, and their country in general, so heavy misfortunes.

These are truths sufficiently affecting to touch with pity
and compassion even hearts hard as marble, and cannot fail to
make a deep and lasting impression in the minds of all.

These feelings and these sentiments have been particularly manifested by the ladies of Philadelphia in their liberal contributions of money towards rendering the situation of the soldiery of the Continental army more convenient and comfortable. It is to this class of men we more immediately owe our defence and protection; they have borne the weight of the war, and met danger in every quarter; and what is higher praise, they have with Roman courage and perseverance suffered the extremes of heat and cold, the attacks of hunger, and the pain of long and fatiguing marches through parts before unexplored by armies, and which had scarcely ever before borne the print of human feet.

It was enough for these brave men to reflect they were engaged in the best and most glorious of all causes—that of defending the rights and liberties of their country—to induce them to behave with so much resolution and fortitude. Their many sufferings so cheerfully undergone, highly merit our gratitude and sincere thanks, and claim all the assistance we can afford their distresses. If we have it not in our power to do from the double motive of religion and a love of liberty what some ladies of the highest rank in the Court of France every day perform from motives of religion only, in the hospitals of the sick and diseased, let us animate one another to contribute from our purses in proportion to our circumstances towards the support and comfort of the brave men who are fighting and suffering for us on the field. We ought to do this if we desire to keep the enemy from our borders—if we wish that there may not be occasion to call forth our husbands, our children, and our dearest friends, to risk their lives again in our defence. I can truly say that I have experienced the most heart-rendering anxieties when my friends and relations have been called upon as free citizens to march against the enemy; and the pangs I have suffered on such occasions have made it easy for me to give credit to the account we have in the history of ancient Rome, of the two matrons who died for joy, one at the gate of the city, the other at her own house, at the sight of their sons, who returned in safety after the battle at the Lake of Thrasymene. When I say this, I mean only to express the feelings of a woman, my sentiments being ever in

favor of that spirit which my countrymen have so often manifested when their services have been required.

New-Jersey Gazette, July 12

July 10

NEW JERSEY   On Thursday last, (6th,) the brig *Admiral
Rodney*, of sixteen carriage-guns and eighty-three men, commanded by Captain Daniel Moore, sailed from Sandy Hook
on a cruise, and on Saturday, (8th,) in latitude 39° 26′, longi-
tude 74°, fell in with a rebel brig, (supposed to be the *Kolker*,
of Philadelphia,) of sixteen guns, two cohorns, and a tier of
swivels, and full of men. At four o'clock in the afternoon, a
very close and furious engagement commenced between them,
and in about twenty minutes after the action began, the gallant Captain Moore was mortally wounded in the head by a
swivel-shot, while issuing his orders with that coolness and
composure of mind which ever characterize the brave, and,
by his spirited conduct, exciting the crew to follow so good
an example. The action, which lasted three glasses, was continued with great spirit by the officers who succeeded to the
command, and every individual on board behaved with that
intrepidity and valor which has ever distinguished British
seamen. So much justice should be done the rebel crew as to
say that, though in an infamous cause, they did not exhibit
any symptoms of cowardice until half-past five o'clock; when,
after receiving a well-directed broadside from the *Rodney*,
they uttered a dreadful scream, made sail, and ran off.

The *Rodney* chased about an hour; but totally disabled in
her rigging, her mainsail and boom overboard, and not a single
brace standing, she was reluctantly obliged to give over a vain
pursuit and make the best of her way for New York, where she
arrived the following evening. Captain Moore expired at four
o'clock this morning, to the inexpressible grief of his gallant
crew, and deservedly lamented by all who knew him. This
last and melancholy proof was not wanting to evince his zeal
in the service of his King and country. He had early taken an
active part towards the suppression of a rebellion which he
uniformly detested, and which, while he had life, he was

determined to oppose. In a few words, it may with truth be said, that he died as he had ever lived—a faithful subject, a good citizen, an honest man.

His remains were interred this evening in the family vault in Trinity church-yard, New York, attended by a numerous and respectable company—the Marine Society—together with the owners and officers of the brig; and as many of the gallant crew as could be spared ashore showed their respect to his memory by attending the funeral.

New York Gazette and Weekly Mercury, July 17

AUGUST

August 1

Arguments at this period of the war to prove the justice of our cause, or the importance of the controversy, would be useless, nay, would be insults to our understandings. But our successes in arms and in gaining the powerful alliances of foreign nations, have lulled us into a dangerous security. We neither want wisdom to conduct, nor courage to finish, what we have carried so far with unequalled reputation. But as the bravest minds are the most tender and gentle, our soft feelings have betrayed us too soon into a forgiving indolence, and led us to hope that the war may be finished without those vigorous exertions which may prove bloody to us, and must end in the total destruction of our enemies. Save Britain! has been the common cry. It was our own. The Britons have schooled us out of our error, and taught us that we must entirely put out the flame, or lose the building.

Britain hath long seen that the conquest of America, by force alone, is impracticable. She has therefore had recourse to stratagems, by which she hopes to gain an accommodation, if not a victory; an accommodation that will give such power to neutrals and Tories as will gain a slower, but not less certain, nor less fatal, victory in the end. To accomplish this she has too well succeeded in depreciating our money, by her emissaries both without and within our lines and councils. But she can never accomplish her design unless our zeal and vigor are depreciated with our money. This is now attempted by various means. Some they endeavor to crush by making rapid excursions and cruelly and totally divesting them of their property; others are stolen from their beds into captivity; others are allured by hopes and fears, to trade and parole submission. By thus gradually removing from the lines such spirits as they cannot tame, and enlarging their connections among the meaner sort, they hope gradually to make their way into the country. We are, therefore, often told by their abettors that they can go where they please, and take whom they will. One to save his house will declare, "That no rebel gun was ever fired from behind it;" another to save his person, seeks a parole, or refuses to take any active part. The calamities of war are held up in magnified prospects on the one hand, and the mild terms offered by the enemy more falsely trumpeted upon the other. The most horrid murders, and other barbarities committed by them, are attributed to accident, or the error of some irresponsible individual. And from Lord North downward, they are all declaring they do not mean to injure America, but to watch the favorable movement of the war to give the Americans peace and order. That all their barbarity in the field, the destruction of our property, and the far more cruelly slow murders of thousands in their prisons, is only designed for our good, and to prepare us for the olive branch. By such pretensions some are imposed upon, and by the same, our public danger is increased. Yet how little reason there is for the imposition, reflection will soon convince.

The death of our paper currency and the fall of Charleston (S. C.) happening near together, flushed the hopes of the British, and, in their opinions, gained them the point which Lord North deemed proper for extending the olive branch. But what was their conduct? In the south, their cruelty, and the high demands of Clinton's proclamations, were sufficient to draw the pale ghosts from the graves of their former fears, resolved to check the tyrant or deliver themselves by an honorable death in arms. And amongst us their barbarities rose with their hopes, till they have proved to us, by the strong language of plunder, flames, and murder, that they only waited for power wholly to desolate the friends of liberty. Our dwelling-houses and temples in flames before our eyes; the aged, the widow, the fatherless, insulted, beaten, and plundered without pity, are arguments we understand and feel.

And oh! that unequalled act of guilt and cruelty! We cannot forget it, nor are we willing it should be forgotten. Defended by every personal charm; protected by a complete collection of the softest and most charming virtues; guarded by a sucking infant and a large family of depending babes, and who, sitting still in her own house, might thereby claim, at least, life from the enemy in whose power she had put hers;—yet she [Mrs. Caldwell] falls by the deliberate aim of an instigated soldier! What then can we expect if fully in their power? Some of the enemy affect to say her death was accidental. There is sufficient proof to the contrary. But suppose some of the enemy thought so, did they show one mark of grief, pity, or humanity? Did one officer, or one soldier, protect the corpse, or save any property for the bereaved babes? Not one; General Robertson's wagon was brought to the door, and loaded by his own servants with the beds and family goods. General Skinner knew the lady and her family. He had many years pleaded at the bar where her father was judge—long sat a fellow-member with him in the legislature; but the plunder of the house was more in his eyes than the murdered person of his old friend's daughter. And her corpse, which was in part stripped, must have been consumed in the flames had it not been for the humanity of some persons who were not of the army.

The enemy have also insulted our understanding by assigning as a reason why they burned our houses that *we fired out of them*. Had it been convenient to have used our houses as forts, we should have been justified in it, and could the enemy have fired them at that time, they would also have been justified. But after they were not, and could not again be used for that purpose, the reason for burning ceases. But the whole story is false in fact. We know but of one house out of which a gun was fired at the Connecticut Farms or Springfield. If there are any more instances they are very few. And did not the enemy avail themselves of our houses in Elizabethtown while they lay in it, and fire upon us out of the windows?

From every view, then, of the enemy's conduct, it is evident we have nothing to expect from them but the effects of pride and malice heightened by resistance. Many may now be flattered by them, and a few villains may be finally protected to answer their purposes. But if they could conquer this country for the present, they could not hold the conquest without crushing us. That necessity will favor their dispositions to prosecute the object. As a warning, we give an extract, which is genuine, from the journal of a principal officer of their own when speaking of a number of persons of considerable note who came into General Howe, from Philadelphia. He says, "They are all very politely received for the present, but their several characters are particularly known to the general, and a day of reckoning is to come hereafter."

In these circumstances, Divine Providence is rousing to action by the most favorable prospects, our allies are gaining the superiority by sea in the different quarters of the globe, and at the same time have sent a very powerful aid to us. The remains of this campaign are big with important events. The danger and expense of one liberal supply, of one vigorous effort, will be much less than a lingering war. While in the one case our success is morally certain, and in the other doubtful. Rouse then all at once to action, and flash the final shock upon all those who disgrace humanity. Nay, humanity cannot live till they are dead. Give the necessary supplies, with your personal services. We shall either gain an honored death or secure a fine country in circumstances more advantageous to posterity than our fathers found it at first, even if we lose our movable property. Let us free ourselves from the hope of reunion with such men.

The Tories are now returning to their original—horse thieves, night robbers, and murderers. They are banding themselves together for the execution of their plan. Rise, then, to extirpate those wretches, root and branch, from this continent, which was given to freemen! The late militia law is favorable beyond others to us who only deserve the country because we fight for it. And as the government is fully in our own power, we need nothing but watchful zeal to have all our own. Look back on what we have done and gained, and also consider what we have at stake. Let not the want of a last brave effort sacrifice the whole. Do not so much as please the Tories' ears by a groan under the complicated difficulties we have to struggle with. The greater they are, the more honor we shall gain by cheerfully surmounting them. In a future day we shall enjoy pleasing reflections, and feel rich, in proportion to the losses we have sustained in preserving our country. He that has lost nothing will not dare to be seen amongst freemen. Let affection, strengthened by suffering, fears roused by dangers, and fortitude supported by the greatest prospects, unite and invigorate the grand struggle, that we may soon be in full liberty and peace, each enjoying all that is contained in the character of A *Citizen*.

New-Jersey Journal, August 2

August 16

SOUTH CAROLINA Early this morning the advanced parties of the British under Cornwallis, and the Americans under General Gates, met in the woods near Camden. The result is not altogether known, but from every quarter we hear of the total rout of Gates and his ragamuffins.

Andrew Helm to P. Van Schaak

SOUTH CAROLINA A correspondent at Salisbury, in North Carolina, gives the following account of Gates's defeat, together with a sketch of the movements of the American army during the few days preceding the battle: "It is natural for mankind, who have lost their country and property, to be too anxious in their pursuits to regain them, and while they partially grasp at the shadow, lose the substance. Men of this complexion, constantly surrounding the Commander-in-chief, lessening his difficulties, the number of the enemy, and pointing out the certainty of success, excite measures which in the event become fatal. We marched from Hillsborough about the 1st of July, without an ounce of provision being laid in at any one point, often fasting for several days together, and subsisting frequently upon green apples and peaches; sometimes by detaching parties, we thought ourselves feasted, when by violence they seized a little fresh beef, and cut, threshed out, and ground a little wheat; yet, under all these difficulties, we had to press forward.

"Just before, and on the arrival of General Gates, both he and the Baron De Kalb seemed disposed to give the army a little respite, but General Caswell, with the North Carolina militia, having moved over the Pedee, we were obliged to make a six days' hard march, before we could form a junction with him; this effected, our march was rapidly continued for six days longer, when we arrived at Clermont, within thirteen miles of Camden, on the 13th instant.

"Our supplies here began to come in more amply, and had we waited a few days, our forces must have been considerably augmented, which would have enabled us to have harassed the enemy, and in a great measure cut off their resources; this must have effected our purpose in the event without risking a general engagement, the last step in my opinion to be taken, where so much was to be risked. We were ordered down on the evening of the 15th to attack the enemy, and General Sumpter was to proceed down to the ferry opposite to Camden, to create a diversion in that quarter, to facilitate our making an impression on Camden. Here the British had collected their whole force, and gaining intelligence of our position, moved out at nine o'clock in the evening to meet us; forming an ambuscade on the road, they surprised us about one o'clock in the morning on our march. Our advanced and flanking parties endeavored to resist the shock, but were broken, and this threw the Continental brigades into disorder; but they rallying immediately, advanced, engaged and forced the enemy to give way in turn; this gave respite to the troops to form, and so we remained in anxious expectation till near daybreak, nothing material occurring, but partial firings from the advanced and reconnoitring parties of each army, when the general ordered the first Maryland brigade to form a *corps de reserve*, about two hundred yards in the rear of the centre of the line; this was immediately effected, and the troops rested upon their arms till a little after daybreak, when the action recommenced.

"The attack was made by Lord Cornwallis from the right and centre, on the centre and left wing of the front line of the Americans, which was altogether composed of militia, who upon the first fire gave way, and were pursued by the British. This threw the *corps de reserve* into disorder; but they rallying immediately under a very hot fire, charged the British so warmly, that they entirely broke their centre. By this time the fire commenced very hot on the right, where the second Maryland brigade behaved with great gallantry and firmness, but the enemy's line of Regular troops being far more extensive on the right than the Americans on the left, after the militia had given way, exposed the left flank and rear of the first brigade, notwithstanding which they manfully maintained their ground, till the left wing was ordered to retreat to a point in view, about eighty yards in the rear, at the extremity of the flanking party. Here it instantly formed, renewed, and continued the attack with great vigor; but being again hard pressed in front, flank, and rear, retreated a second time, formed, and disputed the ground with great obstinacy, till, borne down by numbers, they were obliged generally to retreat. At this time the second brigade, which before had not been so hard pressed, was also borne down by superior numbers, after behaving with the greatest firmness and bravery. The retreat now became general, and the militia by this time had got six or eight miles in the rear, some of whom, together with our camp women, wagoners, and some scattering light horse, plundered all our baggage.

"General Smallwood endeavored to cover the retreat, and is collecting the remains of our scattered troops, for which purpose he has established posts at Salisbury and Charlotte, and has prevailed on a considerable body, not less than one thousand volunteers, to make a stand at Charlotte."

New-Jersey Journal, September 17

SOUTH CAROLINA   "The British loss hath been much more considerable than the Americans. Lord Cornwallis, or some other British General, *it is conjectured*, is amongst the slain. Notwithstanding this misfortune, General Gates, whose head-quarters are at Hillsborough, is collecting a force much superior to his late army, and appears resolved to try the fortune of another day."

Pennsylvania Gazette, September 6

August 31

SOUTH CAROLINA   In the *Royal Gazette Extraordinary* of this day, is published the following account of the different actions which have lately happened in South Carolina. Lord Cornwallis having received intelligence that General Gates had arrived at Deep Creek, in North Carolina, the twenty-fourth of July last, and taken upon him the command of the troops which had been collecting there since the surrender of Charleston, and that he was putting them in motion, set out for Camden on the evening of the tenth, and arrived there early in the morning of the fourteenth instant. General Gates had already penetrated into South Carolina, and was advanced as far as Rugely's, about twelve miles distance from Camden. His lordship having informed himself of the strength and position of the rebels, resolved to attack them, (although they had been joined on the fifteenth by about fifteen hundred militia, under General Scott, from Virginia,) and accordingly about ten in the evening of that day the army began their march, and after they had proceeded about eight miles, the advanced guards of both parties fell in with each other, and a skirmish ensued in which several were killed and wounded on both sides; Colonel Porterfield, of the rebels, had his leg broken, and afterwards fell into our hands, as also did an ammunition wagon, which they left upon the field. From the prisoners and deserters, Lord Cornwallis was informed that the whole rebel army was upon the march to attack him. In order to avoid the confusion of an action in the night, his lordship halted on ground which was favorable for his small numbers, and in the mean time took measures to oblige the rebels to fight him on it. At daybreak in the morning, he formed his army into one line with a reserve, and the cavalry behind the reserve. The line consisted of two divisions; that on the right consisted of the light infantry, the twenty-third and thirty-third regiments, under the command of Lieutenant-Colonel Webster; the left, the volunteers of Ireland, infantry of the legion, and part of Colonel Hamilton's North Carolina Corps, under Lord Rawdon, with two six and two three-pounders; the reserve was composed of the seventy-first regiment, and two six-pounders, to whom the cavalry was ordered to keep close; the North Carolina refugees and militia were directed to attend to the rear, and a swamp upon the left.

About twenty minutes after day, finding the rebels formed near him, Lord Cornwallis ordered their left to be attacked, and the action soon became general. After a short conflict, which was sustained about three-quarters of an hour, the rebels were thrown into utter confusion, and gave way, when they lost a great number of men; the cavalry were ordered immediately to fall upon them, which they did with great slaughter. The pursuit was continued for upwards of twenty-two miles, and many men were killed in the course of it; seven pieces of brass cannon and all their ammunition were taken in the field, and the baggage of their general officers, and all their other baggage and camp equipage, were taken in the pursuit by the cavalry, together with one brass field-piece, the carriage of which was damaged in the skirmish in the night, and, with the seven before mentioned, was the whole they had with them. A General Gregory was killed in the field, and General De Kalb, who is since dead of his wounds, and General Rutherford, who is also wounded, were made prisoners. Upwards of nine hundred officers and men were killed in the field, and in the pursuit, and about nine hundred were prisoners, many of whom are wounded. The loss sustained by the royal army in killed and wounded, amounts to three hundred and twenty men, including ten officers, three of which were killed, and two more dangerously wounded.

Some days before the action, General Sumpter was detached over the Wateree River, with twelve or fifteen hundred men, to cut off the communication between Lord Cornwallis and Charleston, and the Congaree. He fell in with, and took several wagons which were bringing flour, &c., to the British army, together with their escort and some sick men. On the morning of the seventeenth, Lieutenant-Colonel Tarleton was detached with the cavalry and light infantry of the legion to attack him. He conducted his march with so much skill that he surprised the Americans in the middle of the day on the eighteenth, totally defeated them, killed upwards of one hundred and fifty, took two pieces of brass cannon, and three hundred prisoners; he at the same time retook the wagons which had been taken, and about one hundred men who had been made prisoners, and also relieved one hundred and fifty inhabitants who had been taken up by Sumpter. The British loss on this occasion is six men killed, including Captain Charles Campbell of the light infantry, and eight or ten wounded.

After the victory, it was discovered that amongst the prisoners there were some persons who had lately received protections and enrolled themselves in the militia, to serve under and support his majesty's government, and one who was a prisoner upon parole, notwithstanding which, they were taken fighting on the part of the rebels. Two of them were hanged upon the spot, and we hear that wherever such instances of perfidy and treachery are discovered, they will constantly be punished with the utmost severity. Two deserters from the royal army were taken at the same time and executed in the same manner.

In marching the prisoners taken by Lord Cornwallis and Colonel Tarleton, from Camden to Charleston, the first division of them consisting of one hundred and fifty Continentals, escorted by a party of the sixty-third regiment, were met by Colonel Marion, with one hundred and fifty or two hundred militia. Our party were made prisoners, and those they were conducting were rescued; but it was an event so little agreeable to them that within two days afterwards upwards of one-half of them came of their own accord to deliver themselves up; and since that time the whole of them have surrendered themselves either to Lord Cornwallis or our party on this side of Santee; nor were the rebels able to carry away the party of the sixty-third, all of whom are since come in. So the only consequence of the insurrection is the discovery of the perjury and perfidy of a set of people, who, without hesitation, have broken through engagements which are always deemed so sacred and inviolable that the most severe punishment for the breach of them is not only warranted but required by the laws of nations and of arms. The prisoners, especially those called Continentals, appear to be highly disgusted with, and disaffected to the cause they have been engaged in, and which many of them were obliged to enter into by absolute necessity, and the persecuting tyranny of a set of men who, without the least remorse or scruple, see hundreds every day sacrificed to attain their wicked and ambitious purposes.

New York Gazette and Weekly Mercury, September 25

SEPTEMBER

September 26

NEW YORK   Treason of the blackest dye was yesterday discovered. General Arnold, who commanded at West Point, lost to every sentiment of honor, of public and private obligation, was about to deliver up that important fort into the hands of the enemy. Such an event must have given the American cause a deadly wound if not a fatal stab. Happily the scheme was timely discovered to prevent the fatal misfortune. The providential train of circumstances which led to it, affords the most convincing proofs that the liberties of America are the object of divine protection. At the same time the treason is so regretted, the General cannot help congratulating the army on the happy discovery.

Our enemies, despairing of carrying their point by force, are practising every base art to effect, by bribery and corruption, what they cannot accomplish in a manly way. Great honor is due to the American army, that this is the first instance of treason of this kind, where many were to be expected from the nature of the dispute, and nothing is so high an orna-

Eng^d by W. G. Jackman.

Major Andre

ment to the characters of the American soldiers as their with-standing all the arts and seductions of an insidious enemy.

Arnold the traitor has made his escape to the enemy, but Mr. André, Adjutant-General to the British army, who came out as a spy to negotiate the business, is our prisoner.

His Excellency the Commander-in-chief has arrived at West Point, from Hartford, and is now doubtless taking proper steps to unravel fully so hellish a plot.

General Greene's Orders of the Day
Pennsylvania Packet, October 10

NEW YORK   A gentleman at the American camp, in a letter dated Robinson's House, gives the following account of the discovery of Arnold's plot:—"I make use of the present express to acquaint you with a scene of villany which happened in this quarter. A very singular combination of circumstances has preserved to us West Point and its dependencies. General Arnold, who was the commanding officer, has been bought over to the interest of the enemy, and the place in a few days must have become theirs. They had a part of their army in readiness to act on this occasion, and could not have failed of success from the concert of Arnold within the fort.

"Such was the situation of this important post, when a providential event discovered the traitor. Major André, the British Adjutant-General, a person of great talents, appears to have been the principal actor with Arnold. In his return to New York, after an interview with Arnold, he was stopped near Tarrytown by a few militia, (notwithstanding a pass written and signed by General Arnold, by which André was permitted to proceed as a John Anderson,) and detained as a spy. As they were conducting him to a party of Continental troops, he offered them a large sum of money for his release, which they rejected with as much virtue as Arnold received his with baseness.

"The state of the garrison, arrangements for its defence in case of attack, a council of war, &c., were found on André, in Arnold's own handwriting.

"Colonel Jameson, of the light dragoons, to whom he was conveyed in the first instance, and before a detection of these papers, despatched an account to Arnold that he had a spy in his care, and described him in such a manner, that Arnold knew it to be André. His Excellency General Washington, the Marquis de Lafayette, General Knox, and their aids, were within a few miles of his quarters at this juncture. I had preceded them with a Major Shaw, to give notice of their coming. Arnold, I think, must have received the advice while we were present, as I observed an embarrassment, which I could not at that time account for. The approach of his Excellency left him but an instant to take measures for his own safety, or it is likely he would have attempted that of André's, and the matter might have remained in obscurity. He ordered his barge, and passing King's Ferry as a flag boat, fell down to the *Vulture* sloop of war, which lay below at a short distance. In the mean time, an officer arrived with the papers which were discovered, and a letter from André to his Excellency, in which he endeavors to show that he did not come under the character of a spy. Upon this Colonel Hamilton and myself rode to King's Ferry, but he had before this gained the enemy's vessel.

"We expect André here every minute. I lament Arnold's escape, that we might have punished such a high piece of perfidiousness, and prevented the enemy from profiting by his information. André has ventured daringly for the accomplishment of a great end; fortunate for us his abilities failed him, as it was on the point of being finished, and he must in all human probability submit to the fate of a common spy."

Pennsylvania Packet, October 3

September 30

PENNSYLVANIA   This afternoon the people of Philadelphia and vicinity made a demonstration somewhat unfavorable to the late commander at West Point, by carting that notorious conspirator through the streets of the city. The exhibition was as follows:—A stage raised on the body of a cart, on which was an effigy of General Arnold sitting; this was dressed in regimentals, had two faces, emblematical of his traitorous conduct, a mask in his left hand, and a letter in his right from

Beelzebub, telling him that he had done all the mischief he could do, and now he must hang himself.

At the back of the general was a figure of the Devil, dressed in black robes, shaking a purse of money at the general's left ear, and in his right hand a pitchfork, ready to drive him into hell as the reward due for the many crimes which his thirst for gold had made him commit.

In the front of the stage, and before General Arnold, was placed a large lantern of transparent paper, with the consequences of his crimes thus delineated, i.e.: On one part General Arnold on his knees before the Devil, who is pulling him into the flames; a label from the general's mouth with these words, "My dear sir, I have served you faithfully;" to which the Devil replies, "And I'll reward you." On another side, two figures hanging, inscribed, "The Traitor's Reward," and written underneath, "The Adjutant-General of the British Army, and Joe Smith; the first hanged as a spy, and the other as a traitor to his country." And on the front of the lantern was written the following:—

"MAJOR-GENERAL BENEDICT ARNOLD, LATE COMMANDER OF THE FORT WEST POINT. THE CRIME OF THIS MAN IS HIGH TREASON.

"He has deserted the important post WEST POINT, on Hudson River, committed to his charge by his Excellency the Commander-in-chief, and has gone off to the enemy at New York.

"His design to have given up this fortress to our enemies, has been discovered by the goodness of the Omniscient Creator, who has not only prevented him carrying it into execution, but has thrown into our hands ANDRÉ, the adjutant-general of their army, who was detected in the infamous character of a spy.

"The treachery of this ungrateful general is held up to public view, for the exposition of infamy, and to proclaim with joyful acclamation, another instance of the interposition of bounteous Providence.

"The effigy of this ingrate is therefore hanged (for want of his body) as a traitor to his native country, and a betrayer of the laws of honor."

The procession began about four o'clock in the following order:—Several gentlemen mounted on horseback; a line of Continental officers; sundry gentlemen in a line; a guard of the city infantry; just before the cart, drums and fifes playing the Rogue's March; guards on each side.

The procession was attended with a numerous concourse of people, who after expressing their abhorrence of the treason and the traitor, committed him to the flames, and left both the effigy and the original to sink into ashes and oblivion.

Pennsylvania Packet, October 3

OCTOBER

October 1

NEW JERSEY   Yesterday the board of general officers appointed by General Washington for the trial of the unfortunate Major André, having fully considered the facts belonging to his case, reported that he "ought to be considered as a spy from the enemy, and that agreeably to the law and usage of nations, in their opinion he ought to suffer death." General Washington approved of this opinion, and ordered the execution to take place this afternoon, but owing to the arrival of a flag from the enemy, it is postponed until to-morrow at noon.

Mss. letter from Charles Wilson to Timothy Paine
Clift's Diary

NEW JERSEY   The following is a copy of a letter from Major André to his Excellency General Washington, received to-day:

"Sir:—Buoyed above the fear of death, by the consciousness of a life spent in the pursuit of honor, and fully sensible that it has at no time been stained by any action which, at this serious moment, could give me remorse, I have to solicit your Excellency, if there is any thing in my character which excites your esteem, if aught in my circumstances can excite you with compassion, that I may be permitted to die the death of a soldier; it is my last request, and I hope it will be granted. I have the honor to be, &c."

New-Jersey Journal, October 25

October 2

NEW YORK   Arnold's conduct since he went to New York, is a greater proof of his villany (if greater villany is possible) than his late treason. At his arrival with the British, says a gentleman in the American army, he had upwards of fifty of our warmest friends in New York taken up, and put into dungeons and other places of confinement. But there is a Providence attending the unhappy friends to their country, that puts it out of his power to injure them, other than imprisonment. Such was the precipitate flight he made, to save his neck from the halter, that he had no time to move off a single paper, or any other matter which can be a testimony against those he would otherwise ruin in person and estate.

Letter from camp, Tappan, October 2
Pennsylvania Packet, October 10

NEW YORK   General Robertson, of the British army, came up yesterday to Dobb's Ferry with a flag, which was soon dismissed, it being of so trite a nature, viz., to entreat his Excellency General Washington, at the request of Sir Harry Clinton, to use lenity to Major André; it had the effect to respite him for some hours, as the flag did not return till five o'clock, which was the hour fixed in general orders for his execution. This day at twelve o'clock it took place, by hanging him by the neck. Perhaps no person (on like occasion) ever suffered the ignominious death, that was more regretted by officers and soldiers of every rank in our army; or did I ever see any person meet his fate with more fortitude and equal conduct. When he was ordered to mount the wagon under the gallows, he replied: "He was ready to die, but wished the mode to have been in some more eligible way;" preferring to be shot. After he had opened his shirt collar, fixed the rope, and tied the silk handkerchief over his eyes, he was asked by the officer commanding the troops, if he wished to say any thing? He replied: "I have said all I had to say before, and have only to request the gentlemen present, to bear testimony that I met death as a brave man."

The flag mentioned to have come out with General Robertson, was received by General Greene and Colonel Hamilton; and what is curious, Arnold sent his resignation, with desire that General Washington should forward it to Congress, with an insolent letter, intimating he would never serve Congress any more, nor need they expect it. And, moreover, that if Major André should be executed by order of General Washington, that he would strike a blow on some of his friends on the continent, that should sufficiently retaliate for his loss to his Prince. General Greene, when he read the letter, treated it with contempt, and threw it on the ground before General Robertson, that he might return it to the traitor if he thought proper. The hanging of Major André, one of the most eminent officers and polite men in the British army, and the *second life* of Clinton, shows we are not deterred by great menaces, but determined to extirpate our enemies one by one, until peace shall be restored to our country.

Pennsylvania Packet, October 10

The Ballad of Major André

This striking ballad appeared soon after the death of Major John André, and is considered to be one of the classic broadsides of the Revolutionary War. Various versions survive; the one offered here is a composite utilizing the resources of all of them. The melody is a stock one—a variant of the "Bonny Boy"—often used by American singers with stories that told of a young man's untimely death. (Moore, Songs and Ballads, 316–21; and a broadside in the possession of the Harris Collection of Brown University, entitled "Death of Major André"; not listed by Ford.)

Come all ye brave A-mer-i-cans, and un-to me give ear, I'll
sing you now a dit - ty, that__ will your spir - its cheer, Con -
cern - ing a young gen - tle - man, whose__ age was twen - ty - two; He__
fought for North A - mer - i - ca, his heart was just and true.

They took him from his dwelling, and did him close confine,
They cast him into prison, and kept him there a time;
But he being something valiant, resolved not long to stay,
He set himself at liberty and soon did run away.

And when that he had returned home to his own country,
There was a plan contriving to undo America
Plotted by General Arnold and his bold British crew,
Who thought to shed our innocent blood, and America sub-
    due.

He with a scouting party went down to Tarrytown,
Where they met a British officer, a man of high renown;
Who said unto these gentlemen "You're of the British cheer,
I trust that you can tell me if there is danger near?"

Then up spoke this young hero, John Paulding was his name;
"Oh tell us where you're going, sir, and also whence you
    came?"
"I bear the British flag, sir, I've a pass to go this way,
I'm on an expedition, I have no time to stay."

Then round him came this company, and bade him to dis-
    mount;
"Come, tell us where you're going, give us a strict account;
For now we are resolved, that you shall ne'er pass by."
On a strict examination they found he was a spy!

Death of Major Andre.

COME all you brave Americans I pray you lend an ear,
I will sing you a short ditty your spirits for to cheer,
Concerning a young gentleman whose age was twenty-two,
He is fit for North America, with a heart that's just and true.

The British took him from his lodging and did him close confine
They in strong prison bound him & kept him there sometime,
But he being something valient resolv'd there not to stay,
He got himself at liberty and from them come away.

And when that he had returned home to his own country,
There was many a plan contriving to undo America;
Plotted by General Arnold, and his bold british crew,
They tho't to shed our innocent blood and America to undue.

It was of a scouting party that sail'd from Tarrytown,
They met a British officer of fame and high renown ;
And sail to this young gentleman you are of the british core,
And I trust that you can tell me if the dangers are all o'er.

O then up steps John Spalding saying you must dismount,
And where you are agoing you must give a strict account ;
I am a British flag sir, I've a pass to go this way,
Upon an expedition in North America.

O then up steps John Spalding saying you must dismount,
And where you are agoing give me a more strict account ;
For I will have you searched before that you pass by—
On a strict examination he was found to be a British Spy !

" There take my gold and silver and all I have in store,
And when down to New. York I come will send you thousands more !
I scorn your gold and silver, I've enough of it in store,
And when my money it is gone I will bodily fight for more.

O then he found that all his plans were like to be bro't to light,
He call'd for pen and paper and begged leave to write
A line to General Arnold to let him know his fate,
He begged of him assistance but alas, it was too late !

When Arnold he this letter read it made his heart relent,
He called for his barge, down to New York quickly went ;
There he is amongst the Britons a fighting for his king
He has left poor Major Andre on the gallows for to swing!

If you are a man from Britain with courage stout and bold,
He fear no man of valour tho' he be cloth'd in gold ;
This place it is improper our valour for to try,
And if we take the sword in hand one of the two must die!

When he was executed he being both meek and mild,
Around on the spectators most pleasantly did smile,
I fill'd each one with terror and caus'd their hearts to bleed,
They wished that Andre was set free and Arnold in his stead.

Success unto John Spalding, let his health be drank around,
Likewise to those brave heroes who fough against the crown
Here is a health to every Soldier who fought for liberty,
And to the brave and gallant Washington of North America.

Printed and Sold at NO, 25, High Street, PROVIDENCE, where may be obtained 100 other kinds.

Death of Major André. Early nineteenth century broadside. Reproduced from the Harris Collection of Brown University, by permission.

He begged for his liberty, he pled for his discharge,
And oftentimes he told them, if they'd set him at large,
"Here's all the gold and silver, I have laid up in store,
And when I reach the city I will send you ten times more."

"We scorn your gold and silver, you have laid up in store,
And when you reach the city, you need not send us more."
He saw that his conspiracy would soon be brought to light,
He begg'd for pen and paper, and asked for to write.

The story came to Arnold, commanding at the Fort:
He called for the *Vulture*, and sailed for New York;
Now Arnold to New York has gone, a-fighting for his King,
And left poor Major André on the gallows for to swing.

André was executed, he book'd both meek and mild;
Around on the spectators most pleasantly he smiled;
It moved each eye to pity, and every heart there bled,
And everyone wished him releas'd, and Arnold in his stead.

He was a man of honor, in Britain he was born,
To die upon the gallows most highly he did scorn:
And now his life has reached its end, so young and blooming
     still,
In Tappan's quiet countryside he sleeps upon the hill.

A bumper to John Paulding! Now let your voices sound,
Fill up your flowing glasses, and drink his health around;
Also to those young gentlemen who bore him company,
Success to North America, ye sons of liberty!

October 9

When we see a man who has formerly attracted esteem, at
once falling into the greatest contempt, and becoming the
opprobrium and shame of his country, we feel a mixture of
passions in striking him off the list of honest men to degrade
him with the most infamous. The good citizen is ready to
reproach himself for having misplaced his esteem, and would
fain strip the wretch even of those qualities that had the
semblance of good and occasioned the error. It is thus we
regard Arnold, whose name must now go down to posterity

with the epithet traitor. We see the traitor Arnold in his degradation and misery, deprived even of the honor of having been brave. But why should we contest this advantage? Have not robbers and assassins who take from the passenger his purse and his life; have not incendiaries, parricides, and traitors, a certain species of bravery? We may leave, then, to the traitor Arnold this quality, which can only serve to place his crimes in a stronger point of light. His treason, avarice, hypocrisy, ingratitude, barbarity, falsehood, deception, peculation, and robbery, all these are the base and black crimes of this conspirator.

1. *Treason.* He solicited the command of the bulwark of America on purpose to deliver it, with his benefactor and general, into the hands of the enemy.

2. *Avarice.* Should we give a particular account of the bargain he concluded, and the disputes about the price at which he sold himself and country, even Britons themselves must blush at the infamy.

3. *Hypocrisy.* The traitor Arnold had the face to speak of religion in his address to the Americans. He had so totally sold himself to the English, and was so entirely lost to every moral sentiment, as not to perceive that Providence itself had patronized the cause of our independence, by discovering his plots in a manner next to miraculous.

4. *Ingratitude.* He aimed to plant a dagger in the bosom of his country, which had raised him from the obscurity in which he was born, to honor which never could have been the object even of his most sanguine hopes.

5. *Barbarity.* He intended to deliver up the fortress of America to the Britons, and at the same time, to cover his own perfidy, he designed there should be all the appearance of a sincere assault, in which many brave men must have fallen victims to his treason, and only to screen him from the shame of it.

6. *Falsehood.* Falsehood to his own officers and troops, falsehood to his general, falsehood to his country, false passports, and false oaths, from the beginning to the end of this horrid business.

7. *Mean deception.* What subtleties and dissemblings,

what evasions and lies did he employ to conceal his plot! A villain who had stolen the purse of his master could not be reduced to so ignominious a situation. If the fortune of war should ever throw him into our power, he would doubtless protest that his design in going over to New York, was only to deceive the Britons, and to obtain a command by which he might better serve the Americans by betraying their enemies.

8. *Peculation.* His papers contain the most authentic and incontestable proofs of this crime; and that he never regarded his important employments but only as power which enabled him to pillage the public with impunity.

9. *Robbery.* He robbed his country at the time of her deepest distress. He robbed his own soldiers when they wanted necessaries. He robbed a poor helpless woman of a pittance she had earned by service for his army. He robbed his own friends, who trusted and had greatly served him.

This is the man to whom we are told the Britons have given the rank of a general in their army. This may be true, perhaps they are capable of such an act. But if there is an officer of honor left in the British army, he will sooner resign his commission, or die by his own sword, than serve under, or rank with, Benedict Arnold.

Independent Chronicle, December 8

October 30

NORTH CAROLINA   Colonels Campbell and Sevier have taken a great part of Cornwallis' army, and a precious crew of Tories, at King's Mountain. The battle took place on the 7th instant, and lasted more than an hour. The following is the formal account:—"On receiving intelligence that Major Ferguson had advanced up as high as Gilbert town, in Rutherford County, and threatened to cross the mountains to the western waters, Colonel William Campbell, with four hundred men from Washington County in Virginia, Col. Isaac Shelby, with two hundred and forty men from Sullivan County in North Carolina, and Lieut.-Col. John Sevier, with two hundred and forty men of Washington County, North Carolina, assembled at Wattango, on the 25th of September, where they were joined by Col. Charles McDowell with one hundred and sixty men from the counties of Burke and Rutherford, who had fled before the enemy to the western waters. We began our march on the 26th, and on the 30th we were joined by Col. Cleveland, on the Catawba River, with three hundred and fifty men from the counties of Wilkes and Surrey. No one officer having properly a right to the Command-in-chief, on the 1st of October we despatched an express to Major-General Gates, informing him of our situation, and requesting him to send a general officer to take command of the whole. In the mean time, Colonel Campbell was chosen to act as commandant, till such general officer should arrive. We marched to the Cowpens on Broad River, in South Carolina, where we were joined by Colonel James Williams, with four hundred men, on the evening of the 6th of October. He informed us that the enemy lay encamped somewhere near the Cherokee ford of Broad River, about thirty miles distant from us.

"By a council of the principal officers it was there thought advisable to pursue the enemy that night, with nine hundred of the best horsemen, and leave the weak horse and footmen to follow as fast as possible. We began our march with nine hundred of the best men about eight o'clock the same evening, and marching all night, came up with the enemy about three o'clock P.M. of the 7th. They were encamped on the top of King's Mountain, twelve miles north of the Cherokee ford, in the confidence that they could not be forced from so advantageous a post. Previous to the attack, on our march, the following disposition was made: Colonel Shelby's regiment formed a column in the centre on the left; Col. Campbell's another on the right; part of Col. Cleveland's regiment, headed in front by Major Winston, and Colonel Sevier's, formed a large column on the right wing; the other part of Cleveland's regiment, headed by Col. Cleveland himself, and Colonel Williams's regiment, composed the left wing. In this order we advanced and got within a quarter of a mile of the enemy before we were discovered. Col. Shelby's and Col. Campbell's regiments began the attack, and kept up a fire on the enemy, while the right and left wings were advancing to surround them, which was done in about five minutes, and the fire became general all around. The engagement lasted an hour and five minutes, the greatest part of which time a heavy and incessant fire was kept up on both sides. Our men, in some parts where the Regulars fought, were obliged to give way a small distance two or three times, but rallied and returned with additional ardor to the attack. The troops upon the right having gained the summit of the eminence, obliged the enemy to retreat along the top of the ridge to where Col. Cleveland commanded, and were there stopped by his brave men; a flag was immediately hoisted by Captain Depeyster, the commanding officer, (Major Ferguson having been killed a little before,) for a surrender. Our fire immediately ceased, and the enemy laid down their arms, the greatest part of them loaded, and surrendered themselves prisoners to us at discretion. It appears from their own provision returns for that day, found in their camp, that their whole force consisted of eleven hundred and twenty-five men, out of which they sustained a very heavy loss."

New York Packet, November 23

NOVEMBER

November 6

A writer in London, says:—The incredible fall of continental currency in America, may be understood from the following notorious fact, viz.: Ten thousand pounds of Maryland currency *was* worth six thousand sterling; ten thousand pounds continental money *is* worth one hundred pounds. The difference makes a loss of five thousand nine hundred pounds sterling, being as sixty to one.

This was the exchange at Philadelphia in June last, and as they had not then heard of Gates's defeat, it must be now lower. Actions commenced for considerable sums by creditors, have been obliged to be withdrawn, or a non-suit suffered; a

lawyer of eminence not opening his mouth in a trial of consequence, under a fee of *one thousand pounds,* though the
legal fee is about forty, and the debt, if recovered, being paid
in continental money, dollar for dollar, worth now but a
penny, the difference between a penny and 4s. 6d. sterling, is
lost to the receiver. The Congress having called in the former
emissions, forty dollars for one, and giving that *one* in paper,
cuts off every hope it will hereafter *appreciate.* The freight of
a hogshead of tobacco is three hundred pounds, or one hogshead for the carriage of another; instead of the creditor pursuing the debtor with an arrest, the debtor pursues the creditor with a *tender* of continental money, and forces the bond
out of his hand. Hence it appears what the best fortunes in
that country are reduced to; an unpleasing reflection it must
be! for time, which lightens all other losses, aggravates the
loss of fortune. Every day we feel it more, because we stand
more in want of the conveniences we have been used to. On
the other hand, new fortunes are made on the ruin of old
ones. War, which keeps the spirits in motion, has diffused a
taste for gayety and dissipation. The French Resident at
Philadelphia gives a rout twice a week to the ladies of that
city, amongst whom French hair-dressers, milliners, and
dancers are all the *ton.* The *Virginia Jig* has given place to the
Cotillon, and *minuet-de-la-cour.* The Congress are fallen into
general contempt, for their want of credit and power; the
army is absolute, and has declared it will not submit to a
peace made by Congress; the people grumble, but are obliged
to surrender one piece of furniture after another, even to their
beds, to pay their taxes. After all, a power drawn from such
distant and dissonant parts cannot form a permanent union.
The force of this kingdom, moving uniformly from one centre,
must in all human probability ultimately prevail; or an accident may produce, in an instant, what the most powerful
efforts require time and perseverance to accomplish.

No source

DECEMBER

December 5

NORTH CAROLINA   A letter of this date from Charlotte, in North Carolina, says:—"Although some pains have been taken to asperse the militia of this, as well as our sister states, on account of what happened on the memorable 16th and 18th of August, yet I hope that an impartial world will not lose sight of those striking marks of heroism displayed at Ramsour's, on the 20th of June, where Colonel Locke commanded; at Packolet in the night of the 15th of July, where Colonel McDowel commanded; at Coleson's, the mouth of Rocky River, on the 21st of July, where Colonel, now General Davidson commanded, and in which he was wounded; at Rocky Mount, on the 23d of July, where the heroic General Sumpter commanded; at Hanging Rock, on the 6th of August, where General Sumpter commanded; at Enoree, the 19th of August, where the late intrepid Colonel Williams commanded; at Augusta, in Georgia, on the 12th of September, where Colonel Clarke commanded; at King's Mountain, on the 7th of October, where Colonel Campbell commanded; at Broad River, on the 9th of November, where General Sumpter commanded, and where Major Weymss was made prisoner; at Black Stocks, on Tygar River, on the 20th of November, where General Sumpter commanded, and was unfortunately wounded; besides several other rencounters. Such a train of important victories, obtained by raw militia, has no parallel in history.

"The firmness of the people in Mecklenburg and Rowan counties, when the enemy advanced to Charlotte, evince that they possess the most genuine principles; they were left to defend themselves against the whole force of the enemy. His lordship took post at Charlotte with amazing pomp. Proclamations were issued, peace and protection were offered to all returning and penitent rebels, and death, with all its terrors, threatened to the obstinate and impenitent. Governor Martin with great solemnity assumed the Government, and conceived himself reinstated. The people generally abandoned their habitations, some fled with such of their property as they could carry, others took the field, determined to dispute every foot of ground, and some assembled in small parties, in their respective neighborhoods, determined to harass the enemy's foraging parties. His lordship soon discovered that he was in an enemy's country, without provisions, without forage, without friends, without intelligence, without a single humble servant except Peter Johnston and McCafferty, who at last deserted him in the night, and came to make peace with us; his communication with Camden cut off, and his despatches intercepted; in the mean time our friends joined issue with Ferguson at King's Mountain.

"These are stubborn facts, and will do immortal honor to the militia. Lord Cornwallis' aid, in a letter to Colonel Balfour, which was intercepted, says:—'Charlotte is an agreeable village, but in a d——d rebellious country.' Oh! had we a well-appointed, well-disciplined, permanent force, what a delightful back country dance we should have led his lordship at Charlotte."

New-Jersey Gazette, January 31, 1781

December 19

ENGLAND   Early in September last, Mr. Henry Laurens was taken prisoner by the British frigate *Vestal*, on his way from Congress to the Court of Holland, and is now confined in the Tower of London. A correspondent at Portsmouth, England, gives the following account of his capture:—"Mr. Keppel, the captain of the *Vestal*, was on a cruise off the coast of America, when he fell in with the ship which carried Mr. Laurens, the President of the American Congress. It was a Dutch vessel, laden with tobacco, and bound for Holland. As soon as Mr. Laurens perceived the English armed boat make up to the vessel in which he was, he threw the box that contained his letters overboard, but the lead that was annexed to it proving insufficient for sinking it immediately, one of the daring tars belonging to the *Vestal*, leaped from the boat, and kept it afloat till the rest assisted him in lifting it.

"Mr. Laurens was bound to Holland with a commission from the Congress, and the tenor of his business was certainly of such a nature as must have produced immediate hostilities between England and the States, if this accident had not intervened to protect us against this farther misfortune. The papers which have been found in the box above mentioned are of the utmost consequence; they contain an explicit detail of his business with the States, and a full description of his powers and commission there. Some secret correspondence is said to be discovered between the members of the Congress and certain great inhabitants of England, but we do not mention this with any degree of confidence, it having been an old and favorite device of a disappointed Minister to insinuate the imputation of treason against those men who have the fortitude to discover a steady opposition to his measures.

"Government have sent word that Mr. Laurens should be brought to London under a strong guard. They have ordered one lieutenant to come in the chaise with him, and two more in another vehicle behind. How he is to be disposed of, is as yet a doubt with administration. They are in a puzzle whether he should be received only as an American captive, or be sent to Newgate as a rebel."

Upcott, VI, 59

December 23

ENGLAND   The firmness of Mr. Laurens, whatever opinions may have been conceived of the nature of his past conduct, was certainly such, in his examination before the Secretaries of State, as must extort admiration from the most attached and enthusiastic partisan. Besides the three Secretaries of State, who sat in solemn council for the purpose of interrogating him, there were present Mr. Frazer, the Secretary of Lord Stormont, Mr. Thompson, the Secretary of Lord George Germaine, and Mr. Mansfield, the present Solicitor-

General. Their lordships commenced the business by severally putting such questions to him as seemed to them of most peculiar importance. The spirited American, in reply to their repeated interrogatories, bowed, and thanked their lordships for the civilities and attention he had received since the misfortune of his captivity, but in all matters respecting his country he was determined on the most inviolable silence. He then addressed himself to the Under Secretaries, who attended with pen, ink, and paper, ready to commit every expression to record, and observed to them, (our readers may depend upon it, these are his own words,) "Your paper, gentlemen, will certainly retain its original purity for any thing that falls from me, for on this subject I neither can nor will give the smallest information." Mr. Mansfield then held a conference with their lordships, the result of which was, an injunction upon the subtle civilian to practise a little of his profession upon the wary American, and to endeavor, by first asking trifling questions, and so proceeding gradually to more material inquiries, to seduce him into an inadvertent reply on some subjects of consequence. This artifice was accordingly carried into execution, but the same effect attended the lawyer's finesse, as had before accompanied the more open proceedings of their lordships, and Mr. Laurens kept strictly to his first determination of total taciturnity. He was five hours under examination.

All the material papers taken in the possession of Mr. Laurens, have, by command, been sent to Windsor, to undergo the inspection of a great personage.

Mr. Laurens' black servant, who was prohibited from attending his master some days ago, has been permitted, by an order from the Secretary of State, to go to the Tower. The order, however, is very limited, as it is an express injunction that he shall never be left alone with Mr. Laurens, but that the warder of the Tower is to be present at every interview that passes between them.

When the above celebrated captive first arrived in the metropolis, he was by accident carried into a house in Scotland Yard, in which Sir William Meredith was at that time a lodger. Sir William and he had been acquainted some time ago, so that as soon as Mr. Laurens had rested a little from the fatigue of his journey, he sent up his name and compliments, offering his services, and requesting an interview. Mr. Laurens returned his best thanks to Sir William, for his obliging intentions respecting him, but as he had received every attention and civility that his unhappy circumstances would admit of from the hands of his captors, he did not think it would be altogether honorable to indulge himself in any interview with a gentleman, however he might otherwise wish it, whose professed political principles were in a direct opposition to theirs. Sir William had good sense enough to admit the propriety of the apology, and as an indication that he felt no chagrin from the rejection of his application, that same evening sent Mr. Laurens a present of a pine-apple.

Upcott, VI, 67

December 27

A soldier in the American army being unfortunately surprised at a game of cards by a sergeant who owed him an old grudge, was carried before the colonel of the regiment, that he might be punished for gaming, against which general orders were very severe. The soldier being asked what he had to say in his defence, replied: That having been religiously educated, and well instructed in the Bible by his parents, and his pay so small that with the greatest economy he had not been able to save enough to buy one, he had therefore purchased an old pack of cards for a few dollars of one of his comrades, which not only served him for a Bible, but made a most excellent almanac besides; then taking out his cards he proceeded thus: "When I see a one, it reminds me that there is but one God; a two, of the Father and Son; a three, of the Father, Son, and Holy Ghost; a four, calls to my remembrance the four evangelists, Matthew, Mark, Luke, and John; a five, the five wise and five foolish virgins; a six, that in six days God created the heavens and the earth; a seven, that the seventh was to be kept holy; an eight, of the eight righteous persons that were preserved from the flood, viz.: Noah, his wife, his three sons and their wives; a nine, the nine ungrateful lepers cleansed by our Saviour; a ten, of the Ten Commandments; the queen reminds me of Queen Sheba, who came from the uttermost parts of the earth to hear the wisdom of Solomon; and the king, of the great King of Heaven." The colonel told him he had forgot the knave. "That," replied he, "used to represent Judas; but from this time, when I see the knave, I shall always think of the sergeant who brought me before your honor." "I don't know," interrupted the colonel, smiling, "whether he is the greatest of the two, but I am sure he is the greatest fool."

The soldier then continued as follows: "When I count the number of dots on a pack of cards they are three hundred and sixty-five, for so many days there are in a year; when I count how many cards are in a pack, I find fifty-two, so many weeks are there in a year; when I reckon how many picture cards are in a pack, I find there are twelve, so many months are there in a year; when I reckon how many tricks are won by a pack, I find there are thirteen, this reminds me of the duty I owe to the thirteen United and Independent States of America. Thus they serve both for Bible and almanac." The colonel called his servant, told him to treat the soldier well, and dismissed him, saying he was a very clever fellow.

Reader, be not ashamed of cards, since they may be applied to the best of purposes; the scandal consists not in the use, but in the abuse of them.

New-Jersey Journal, December 27

1781

JANUARY

January 1

As the manumission of slaves has become a topic of general conversation, we beg permission to offer a few sentiments on the subject:—The merits of almost every case of litigation generally turns upon one or two points. In the present instance the question is, we conceive, whether law, justice, and policy, warrant the retaining our slaves in their present situation?

That we became legally possessed of them, or that they were introduced into this country agreeable to its laws, no one will presume to deny, and that we cannot constitutionally be divested of them by legislative authority, is, we humbly imagine, as evident as that white is not black, or that slavery is not freedom. Our most excellent constitution admits not the subject to be deprived of his life, liberty, or property, but by a trial by a jury of his equals; and lest this inestimable privilege, the glory of freemen, should be infringed on, the constitution expressly requires that no member of the Legislature shall possess a seat in the House, until he has solemnly sworn that he will maintain this immunity inviolate. It becomes, therefore, one of the unalterable particulars of our rights, and cannot be relinquished by the guardians of our liberties but at the expense of perfidy, and even of perjury itself. The liberation of our slaves, therefore, without the concurrence of their possessors, we apprehend, is an object infinitely further distant from the legal attention of our assembly, than are the heavens above the earth.

Whether, as individuals, justice permits the detention of our Negroes, is next to be considered. The Divine Saviour of men hath been pleased to give a summary of our duty towards each other in a single sentence, viz.: "To do to others as we would they should do to us;" or, "To love our neighbor as ourselves." As we profess to believe in a future judgment, that we shall one day give an account to the Supreme Governor of the world of our actions, it highly concerns us to be attentive that they be conformable to the heavenly law. That barbarity to our slaves is repugnant to this law, cannot be controverted; but whether the divine precept enjoins us to free them or not is the dispute. Were we in their situation, it is more than probable we should pant after freedom; and so does the poor debtor desire a release from his creditor; but the injunction "to do unto others as we would be done to," does not oblige the latter to free the former of the debt, if it hath not been contracted by injustice. Nor can this command oblige us to liberate our slaves unless they were sinfully obtained, or are thus held in bondage. If the usages of the nations in Africa justify the foreign and domestic slavery of their captives, they can be purchased and retained without iniquity.

But let us suppose our Negroes were stolen from their country, divested of that natural liberty given to them by heaven, and reduced to vassalage, it may be asked whether the whole of the guilt devolves not on the perpetrators of the deed? Whether any of the sin rests on those who have purchased of the posterity of the slaves, or inherit them by the gift or will of parents? The people of Africa were formerly and lawfully exposed here for sale as articles of commerce, and it may be queried if in conscience we were bound to inquire whether the Guinea merchant became more rightfully possessed of his slaves than of his gold dust, or any other commodity of Africa? Is it possible an African will part with his liberty for temporary considerations, as many Europeans have exchanged their freedom, for a few years, for a passage only to America; and the purchasers of such servants never, perhaps, thought it incumbent on them to inquire whether they were stolen or decoyed away by their masters, (which we believe was often the case,) or received an equivalent for their loss of liberty. We do not conceive that slavery in itself is iniquitous. The Jews were suffered to have slaves; and our very sons are such; that is, perfectly subject to the will of their fathers and at their disposal until they attain the age of twenty-one years; till then they are not free; and what is slavery but an entire submission to the commands, disposal, or will of another? But this vassalage we endure without repining, as we esteem ourselves helpless and incapable of self-government during our state of legal infancy, or nonage.

It may be said, if our slaves were unjustly obtained, it must be unjust to hold them in bondage. We readily grant it would be so for an unjust importer of them, or the heirs of the importer who received them without paying what is deemed an equivalent for the property; and we freely declare we would not retain a slave under the circumstances, or be instrumental in reducing a freeman to slavery for any consideration. But as the slaves are among us; as the sale of them among ourselves does not cause a farther importation of their countrymen, and if it is not disadvantageous to the slave, we are as free to declare we cannot comprehend why, without any injustice to him, he may not now be purchased and possessed.

Humanity, indeed, wishes they could enjoy liberty and happiness, consistent with justice to those who have honestly bought them, and we, in truth, consider our liberty as a preclude to their release from slavery. The love of freedom, in due season, we trust, will be so predominant, that either the individuals whose property they are, will, for their emancipation, disregard their cost; or the public, by subscription or donation and not by law, (for we know of no just authority the Legislature have to command the property of their constituents for this purpose, without express permission,) will cheerfully defray it, and put them on an equal footing with ourselves. But a measure so important cannot be adopted without the approbation of our Assembly; for though, we conclude, they have not the right to free our slaves without the consent of their owners, they are judges of the propriety of receiving them as freemen of the State. Taking it for granted this disposition of benevolence now prevails either in their proprietors among the people, or, if the reader pleases, that justice demands the freedom of our Africans, for we wish not to contend for the negative in this particular, the other inquiry is, whether the present is a proper period to effect so laudable a design?

That there is "a time for all things," is an indisputable truth. A small error in the execution of schemes, in point of time only, has been productive of the most unhappy effects. A potion of medicine administered unseasonably, may occasion the death of a patient, or the word of command given by a general a moment too soon, may not only lose a victory, but be productive of ruin to his army. If we desire the freedom of our Negroes may not be injurious to ourselves, or render them more miserable than at present, we should duly attend to this circumstance of time as well as to the mode of their release. A premature attempt of this sort may be productive of the most serious consequences. That the present day would be improper for the execution of this business, must, we think, appear evident to every one, on the least reflection. Should our slaves be freed, they must either continue with us or inhabit some territory by themselves. If the freemen of the country find it difficult to support themselves and families at the present time, is it reasonable to suppose that our slaves, naturally indolent, unaccustomed to self-government, destitute of mechanical knowledge, unacquainted with letters, with a peculiar propensity to spirituous liquors, destitute of property, and without credit, would pay their taxes and provide for themselves, in the path of integrity, the necessaries and comforts of life? Is it not more rational to infer, from these considerations, that many of them would soon revert to their former state, more wretched than before; that great numbers would become pests to society; by plunder and rapine add to the horrors of war, and that dire necessity would compel us to deprive some of them not only of liberty, but also of life? Their sloth alone might be sensibly felt by the community at this juncture, and on their arms, we are of opinion, for several obvious reasons, there could not be any just dependence. Our state of war forbids their removal to any exterior part of the country, not only in regard of safety, but also in other respects.

Whenever they shall be emancipated, on mature deliberation, perhaps it will be thought that small settlements of them, in different parts of the continent, under proper regulations, will be most compatible with our safety and their felicity. They may thus become useful members of the body politic, enjoy the sunshine of freedom, together with the cheering rays of the light of the gospel. Some compensation will this be for their servitude! A striking exhibition, too, of the goodness of the Divine Being towards them, and of the wisdom of his holy providence in bringing good out of evil; in causing the inhumanity of their brethren, like that of the sons of Jacob to their brother Joseph, to terminate in honor, glory, and happiness! Until that day shall arrive, it is to be hoped the possessors of slaves will revere the sacred precept, "to do as they would be done by;" mollify the hardness of slavery by acts of kindness; but above all, be particularly anxious to have them freed by instruction, admonition, and example, from spiritual thraldom, and "brought into the glorious liberty of the children of God." The effecting of this will not only be paying a tribute to justice, but also an advancement of our temporal emolument; for experience will decide, that it will not be less politic and wise than humane and Christian.

"Impartial," New-Jersey Gazette, January 10

January 13

VIRGINIA   A correspondent gives the following narrative of the late incursion made by the British under Arnold, to Richmond, in Virginia:—"On the 31st of December last, a letter from a private gentleman to General Nelson, reached Richmond, notifying that on the morning of the preceding day, twenty-seven sail of vessels had entered the capes, and from the tenor of the letter, there was reason to expect, within a few hours, farther intelligence whether they were friends or foes, their force, and other circumstances. General Nelson went immediately into the lower country, with power to call on the militia in that quarter, or to act otherwise as exigencies should require. The call of the militia from the middle and upper counties, was not made till intelligence could be received that the fleet was certainly hostile. No farther intelligence came till the second instant, when the former was confirmed; it was ascertained that they were enemies, and had advanced up James' River to Warrasqueak Bay. All arrangements were immediately taken for calling in a sufficient body of militia for opposition. In the night of the third, advice was received that they were at anchor opposite Jamestown. Williamsburg was then supposed to be their object; the wind, however, which had hitherto been unfavorable, shifted fair, and the tide being also in their favor, they ascended the river to Kennon's that evening, and with the next tide came up to Westover, having on their way taken possession of the battery at Hood's, by which two or three of their vessels had received some damage, but which was of necessity abandoned by the small garrison of fifty men placed there on the enemy's landing to invest the works. Intelligence of the enemy's having quitted the station at Jamestown, from which it was supposed they meant to land for Williamsburg, and that they had got in the evening to Kennon's, reached Richmond at five o'clock in the morning of the fourth. This was the first indication of their meaning to penetrate towards Richmond or Petersburg. As the orders for drawing the militia thither had been given but two days, no opposition was in readiness. Every effort was therefore necessary to withdraw the arms and other military stores, and records, and accordingly every exertion was made to convey them to the foundry and laboratory, till about sunset of that day, when intelligence was received that the enemy had landed at Westover. From this it appeared that Richmond, not Petersburg, was their object; and it became necessary to remove every thing which remained there, across the river, as well as what had been carried to the foundry and laboratory; which operation was continued till the enemy approached very near. They marched from Westover at two o'clock in the afternoon of the fourth, and entered Richmond at one o'clock in the afternoon of the fifth. A regiment of infantry and about fifty horse continued on without halting to the foundry; they burnt that, the boring-mill, the magazine, and two other houses, and proceeded to Westham, but nothing being in their power there, they retired to Richmond. The next morning they burnt some buildings of public, and some of private property, with the stores which remained in them; destroyed a great quantity of private stores, and about twelve o'clock retired towards Westover, where they encamped within the Neck the next day. The loss sustained is not yet accurately known. At Richmond about three hundred muskets, some soldiers' clothing to a small amount, sulphur, some quartermasters' stores, of which one hundred and twenty sides of leather was the principal article, part of the artificers' tools, and three wagons; besides five brass four-pounders, which had been sunk in the river, were discovered to them, raised, and carried off. At the foundry about five tons of powder was thrown into the canal, of which there will be a considerable saving, by re-manufacturing it. Part of the papers belonging to the Auditor's office, and the books and papers of the Council office, which were ordered to Westham, but in the confusion carried by mistake to the foundry, were also destroyed. The roof of the foundry was burnt, but the stacks of chimneys and furnaces are not at all injured. Within less than forty-eight hours of the time of their landing, and nineteen from our knowing their destination, they had penetrated thirty-three miles, done the whole injury, and retired. Our militia dispersed over a large tract of country, can be called in but slowly. On the day the enemy advanced to Richmond, two hundred only were embodied; they were of that town and neighborhood, and were too few to do any thing effectual. The enemy's forces are commanded by the parricide Arnold."

New-Jersey Gazette, January 31

January 15

NORTH CAROLINA   The North Carolina boys have returned from the expedition against the Cherokees crowned with success. Colonel Arthur Campbell, who commanded them, in his report to Mr. Jefferson, dated this day, gives the following circumstantial account of their experience:—"On reaching the frontier, I found the Indians meant to annoy us by small parties, and carry off horses. To resist them effec-

tually, the apparently best measure was to transfer the war
without delay into their own borders. To raise a force sufficient, and provide them with provisions and other necessaries,
seemed to be a work of time that would be accompanied with
uncommon difficulties, especially in the winter season. Our
situation was critical, and nothing but an extraordinary effort
could save us and disappoint the views of the enemy. All
the miseries of 1776 came fresh in remembrance, and to avoid
a like scene men flew to their arms, and went to the field.
The Wattago men, under Lieutenant-Colonel Sevier, first
marched to the amount of about three hundred; the militia
under Campbell, with those of Sullivan, made four hundred
more. The place of rendezvous was to be on this side the
French River. Colonel Sevier with his men got on the path
before the others, and by means of some discoveries made by
his scouts, he was induced to cross the river, in pursuit of a
party of Indians that were coming towards our settlements. On
the 16th of December he fell in with the party, since found
to consist of seventy Indians, mostly from the town of Chote,
killed thirteen, and took all their baggage, &c., in which were
some of Clinton's proclamations, and other documents expressive of their hostile designs against the Americans.

"After this action, the Wattago corps thought proper to retreat to an island in the river. On the 22d I crossed the French
River, and found the Wattago men in great want of provisions. We gave them a supply from our small stock, and the
next day made a forced march towards the Tenasse. The success of the enterprise seemed to rest on our safely reaching the
further bank of that river, as we had information that the Indians had obstructed the common fording places, and had a
force ready there to oppose our crossing. The morning of the
24th I made a feint towards the island town, and with the
main body passed the river at Timothee. We were now discovered; the Indians we saw seemed to be flying in consternation. Here I divided my force, sending a part to attack the
towns below, and with the other I proceeded towards their
principal town Chote. Just as I passed a defile above Toque,
I observed the Indians in force, stretching along the hills below Chote, with an apparent design to attack our van, then

within their view; but the main body too soon came in sight for me to succeed in decoying them off the hills; so they quietly let us pass on in order, without firing a gun, except a few scattering shot at our rear, at a great distance from the cliffs. We soon were in possession of their beloved town, in which we found a welcome supply of provisions. The 25th, Major Martin went with a detachment to discover the route the enemy were flying off by. He surprised a party of Indians, took one scalp, and seventeen horses loaded with clothing, skins, and household furniture. He discovered that most of the fugitives were making towards Telico and the Hiwasse. The same day, Captain Crabtree, of the Virginia regiment, was detached with sixty men to burn the town of Chilhowee. He succeeded in setting fire to that part of it which is situated on the south side of the river; although he was attacked by a superior force, he made good his retreat.

"The 26th, Major Tipton, of the Carolina corps, was detached with one hundred and fifty mounted infantry, with orders to cross the river, dislodge the enemy on that side, and destroy the town of Telassee. At the same time Major Gilbert Christian, with one hundred and fifty foot, were to patrol the hills on the south side of Chilhowee, and burn the remaining part of that town. This party did their duty well, killed three Indians, and took nine prisoners. The officer of the horse, by an unmilitary behavior, failed in crossing the river. This trip took two days. In the mean time the famous Indian woman, Nancy Ward, came to camp. She gave us various intelligence, and made an overture in behalf of some of the chiefs for peace; to which I then evaded giving an explicit answer, as I wished first to visit the vindictive part of the nation, mostly settled at Hiwasse and Chistowee, and to distress the whole as much as possible by destroying their habitations and provisions. The 28th we set fire to Chote, Sietogo, and Little Tuskeego, and moved our whole force to a town on Telico River, called Kai-a-tee, where I established a post to secure a retreat, and to lay up provisions. In the evening, Major Martin, on returning from a patrol, attacked a party of Indians, killed two, and drove several into the river. The same evening, in another skirmish, we lost Captain James Elliot, a gallant young officer, being the first and only man the enemy had power to hurt on the expedition; the Indians lost three men on the occasion.

"The 29th I set out for Hiwasse, distant about forty miles, leaving at Kai-a-tee, under Major Christian, a garrison of one hundred and fifty men. The 30th we arrived at the Hiwasse, and found the town of the same name abandoned. In patrolling the environs, we took a sensible young warrior, who informed us that a body of Indians, with McDonald, the British Agent and some Tories, were at Chistowee, twelve miles distant, waiting to receive us. I had reason to believe that the enemy had viewed us from the hills above Hiwassee, for which reason I ordered our camp to be laid off, fires kindled, and other shows made, as if we intended to stay all night. At dark we set out with about three hundred men, (the Wattago men refusing to go farther,) crossed the river at an unexpected ford, and that night got near the town. Early in the morning of the 31st, we found that the enemy had fled in haste the evening before, leaving behind them as they had done at the other towns, almost all their corn and other provisions, together with many of their utensils for agriculture and all their heavy household furniture, with part of their stocks of horses, cattle, and hogs. These towns I expected would have been contended for with obstinacy, as most of the Chickamogga people had removed thither after their visitation in 1779. Our troops becoming impatient, and no other object of importance being in view, it was resolved to return homewards. Major Martin, with a detachment, was ordered to pass by Saltoga, and the other towns on the Telico River. In his route, he took four prisoners, from whom he learned that several of the chiefs had met a few days before, to consult on means of procuring peace. As I found the enemy were humbled, I took the liberty to send the chiefs a message, as follows:—

"CHIEFS AND WARRIORS,—We came into your country to fight your young men; we have killed not a few of them, and destroyed your towns. You know you began the war by listening to the bad counsels of the King of England and the falsehoods told to you by his agents. We are now satisfied with what is done, as it may convince your nation that we can distress them much at any time they are so foolish as to engage in a war against us.

"If you desire peace, as we have understood you do, we, out of pity to your women and children, are disposed to treat with you on that subject, and take you into friendship once more. We therefore send this by one of your young men, who is our prisoner, to tell you if you are also disposed to make peace, six of your head men must come to our agent, Major Martin, at the Great Island, within two moons. They will have a safe passport, if they will notify their approach by a runner with a flag, so as to give him time to meet them with a guard on Halstein's River, at the boundary line. The wives and children of those men of your nation that protested against the war, if they are willing to take refuge at the Great Island until peace is restored, we will give a supply of provisions to keep them alive.

"Warriors, listen attentively: If we receive no answer to this message until the time already mentioned expires, we shall then conclude you intend to continue to be our enemies, which will compel us to send another strong force into your country, who will come prepared to stay a long time, and take possession thereof as conquered by us without making any restitution to you for lands.

"Signed at Kai-a-tee, the fourth day of January, 1781, by

"ARTHUR CAMPBELL, Colonel,

"JOHN SEVIER, Lieutenant,

"JOSEPH MARTIN, Agent and Major of Militia.

"Our whole loss on this expedition was, one man killed by the Indians, and two wounded by accident. It would have been very pleasing to the troops to have met with the whole force of the nation at once on equal ground, but so great was the panic that seized them after seeing us in order over the Tenasse, that they never ventured themselves in sight of the army, but on rocky cliffs, or other ground inaccessible to our mounted infantry. By the returns of the officers of different detachments, we killed twenty-nine men, and took seventeen prisoners, mostly women and children; the number of wounded is uncertain. Besides these we brought in the family of Nancy

Ward, whom for their good offices we do not consider as prisoners. The whole are in Major Martin's care at the Great Island, until the sense of Government is known how they are to be disposed of. We have destroyed the towns of Chote, Sietogo, Tuskeego, Chilhowee, Toque, Micliqua, Kai-a-tee, Saltoga, Telico, Hiwassee, and Chistowee, all principal towns, besides some small ones, and several scattering settlements, in which were upwards of one thousand houses, and not less than fifty thousand bushels of corn, and large quantities of other kinds of provisions, all of which, after taking sufficient subsistence for the army whilst in the country and on its return, were committed to the flames, or otherwise destroyed. No place in the Over Hill country remained unvisited, except the small town of Telassee, a scattering settlement in the neighborhood of Chickamogga, and the town of Calogee, situated on the sources of the Mobile. We found in Okanastota's baggage, which he left behind in his fright, various manuscripts, copies of treaties, commissions, letters, and other archives of the nation, some of which show the double game that people have been carrying on during the present war. There seemed to be not a man of honor among the chiefs, except him of Kai-a-tee, whom I would willingly have discriminated, had it been in my power. Never did a people so happily situated, act more foolishly, in losing their livings and their country at a time an advantageous neutrality was held out to them; but such are the consequences of British seduction. The enemy in my absence did some mischief in Powell's Valley, and on the Kentucky path, near Cumberland Gap, besides three children that they scalped on Halstein; one of the perpetrators of which we killed on our return, and retook a number of horses. The Botetourt and Montgomery militia were too slow in their movements to do any service."

New-Jersey Gazette, March 21

January 16

PENNSYLVANIA   The following is an authentic account of the disorders that have lately taken place among the soldiers of the Pennsylvania line, which are now happily settled: —A discontent arose among them on the first of this month about the period of their enlistments, which many of them contended were expired. Some invidious comparisons were also made between the large bounty given to enlist those whose time was confessedly out, and the condition of those who were engaged during the war. Endeavors were used by the officers to quiet them, but without success. One officer was unfortunately killed, and a great part of the soldiers marched off from their encampment towards the Delaware. They were under the conduct of their sergeants; but General Wayne, with some other officers, determined to follow and keep with them, at all events, though the general could not prevail upon them to stop till they came to Princeton. They marched through the country with great regularity and good conduct, and perhaps less damage than is common on the passing of troops. While they continued at Princeton, a sergeant of the British army with one Ogden, an inhabitant of New Jersey, for a guide, came to them, and made proposals from General Clinton. These they rejected with so much honor and indignation, that they seized the messengers and delivered them to General Wayne, who put them under guard. Soon after this a Committee of the Council of Pennsylvania together with a Committee of Congress met the soldiery. Their grievances were redressed, particularly by giving an interpretation favorable to the soldier of the enlistments which were for three years, or during the war; declaring them to expire at the end of the three years. They marched from Princeton on Tuesday the ninth. On Wednesday the tenth, the two spies were tried, and executed next day at the cross roads near the upper ferry. Commissioners were appointed to hear and settle the claims of the soldiers, who are now going through them with all possible despatch; and on Monday the Committee of Congress returned to Philadelphia.

Upon the whole, this affair, which at first appeared so alarming, has only served to give a new proof of the inflexible honor of the soldiery, and their inviolable attachment to American liberty; and will teach General Clinton, that though he could bribe such a mean toad-eater as Arnold, it is not in his power to bribe an American soldier.

New-Jersey Gazette, January 17

A New Song, Written by a Soldier

Throughout the war the lot of the common soldier—little food, scanty clothing and scantier pay, lack of boots and blankets in the freezing winter—was an unenviable one. Such grievances, long accumulating, came to the explosion point among the Pennsylvania troops on New Year's Day, 1781. A march from Morristown to Trenton was followed by a revolt of the Jersey Line. Order was not restored until the ringleaders had met with summary execution. This song expresses clearly the bitter sense of injustice that led to the revolt. The precise date of composition, the author, and place of origin are unknown. The revolt, as the song so well shows, was not directed against the Revolution or George Washington, but only against the authorities whom the soldiers considered directly responsible for their unnecessary sufferings. (Harris Collection broadside, Brown University; unlisted by Ford.)

My time it has expired all on the tenth of June,
Where the pretty birds were singing, and flowers in their
     bloom,
Where the pretty birds were singing, so sweet from every
     tree,
Farewell unto the army where they beat the revillee.

And to you my lovely officers, a word I have to say,
Before you go to battle, consider well I pray,
See how you kept our wages back, and rob'd us of our clothes,
That we so dearly paid for in hard fatiguing blows.

NEW SONG.

WRITTEN BY A SOLDIER.

MY time it has expired all on the tenth of June,
Where the pretty birds were singing, and flowers in their bloom,
Where the pretty birds were singing, so sweet from every tree,
Farewell unto the army where they beat the reville.

And to you my lovely officers, a word I have to say;
Before you go to battle, consider well I pray,
See how you kept our wages back, and rob'd us of our clothes,
That we so dearly paid for in hard fatiguing blows.

And to you my lovely officers, those lines were written for,
I'd have you to pray for a short and moderate war,
Pray for the strength of Sampson and great King David slight,
For there's scarcely one to twenty of you that's courage enough to fight.

Hear a word unto our counsel, that rules through every state,
I pray be honest hearted, for knavery I hate,
Try for once to do justice, be liberal and free,
Deal fairly with a soldier, and he'll deal fair with thee.

What think you of a soldier that fights for liberty,
Do you think he fights for money, or to set his country free ?
I'd have you consider, and bear it on your mind,
Lest you should want their help again, it might be hard to find.

Our officers on the right of us, our country on the left,
Our enemy in front of us a firing at our breasts,
The devil he comes up behind, and brings up the rear,
And a soldier that escapes them all has never need to fear.

My time it has expired, my song is at an end,
Here's a health to General Washington and every soldiers friend,
And he that cheats a soldier out of his little pay,
May the devil take him on his back, to hell with him straghtway.

＊＊＊＊＊＊＊＊＊＊＊＊＊＊＊＊＊＊＊＊＊＊＊＊＊＊＊＊＊＊＊＊＊＊＊＊

Printed by Nathaniel Coverly, Jun.---Milk-Street,

And to you my lovely officers, those lines were written for,
I'd have you to pray for a short and moderate war,
Pray for the strength of Sampson and great King David slight,
For there's scarcely one to twenty of you that's courage enough
    to fight.

Hear a word unto our counsel, that rules through every state,
I pray be honest hearted, for knavery I hate,
Try for once to do justice, be liberal and free,
Deal fairly with a soldier, and he'll deal fair with thee.

What think you of a soldier that fights for liberty,
Do you think he fights for money, or to set his country free?
I'd have you consider, and bear it on your mind,
Lest you should want their help again, it might be hard to find.

Our officers on the right of us, our country on the left,
Our enemy in front of us a firing at our breasts,
The devil he comes up behind, and brings up the rear,
And a soldier that escapes them all has never need to fear.

My time it has expired, my song is at an end,
Here's a health to General Washington and every soldier's
    friend,
And he that cheats a soldier out of his little pay,
May the devil take him on his back, to hell with him straight-
    way.

January 17

SOUTH CAROLINA   This morning, after a very severe
action, General Morgan, with a detachment of the southern
army, obtained a complete victory over Colonel Tarleton at
the Cowpens, with eleven hundred and fifty men, the flower
of Cornwallis's army. Tarleton, that enterprising, though inhuman young officer, advanced to the attack about sunrise.
General Morgan was apprised of his approach, and had time
to form his troops in a manner which would have done honor
to the most experienced general. His whole force, including
the Georgia, South and North Carolina militia, amounted to
but eight hundred men. The conflict was severe, and the
Americans at first were yielding to the impression. A critical

manœuvre was performed in the height of the action. The Continental infantry were obliged to change their front, to prevent their being flanked by the enemy; it was done with coolness and activity, and terminated the fate of the day. When formed, a close and well-directed fire was given, which threw the enemy into confusion. Embracing the fortunate moment, a general charge was directed, a total route ensued, and no opposition was made afterwards. About eight hundred, including the wounded, with twenty-nine commissioned officers, were taken prisoners, and near one hundred and fifty left dead on the field; two field-pieces, the same which General Morgan took in 1777, upon Bemis Heights, two stands of colors, thirty-five baggage wagons, and eight hundred stands of excellent arms, together with all their music, were among the trophies of victory; and what adds to its importance, it was obtained with the loss of but ten killed and fifty-three wounded of the Americans.

This is but the prelude to the era of 1781, the close of which, we hope, will prove memorable in the annals of history, as the happy period of peace, liberty, and independence to America.

New-Jersey Gazette, February 21

January 31

VIRGINIA   This morning, his Majesty's ship *Iris* arrived at New York from the Chesapeake, with the following account of the proceedings of the British forces in Virginia, under Brigadier-General Arnold:—"The fleet having been separated by a hard gale of wind on the 26th and 27th December, rejoined off the capes of Virginia, and arrived in Hampton road on the 30th, except three transports and one armed vessel, with upwards of four hundred troops.

"On the 31st of December the troops were embarked in small vessels and boats, (part of which were captured on their arrival,) and proceeded up James River, with the *Hope* and *Swift* armed vessels. On the 3d of January, in the evening, they anchored at Flour de Hundred, about half a mile from a battery of three eighteen and one twenty-four pounders, and one brass eight-inch howitzer, which only killed one man. Lieutenant-Colonel Simcoe, with two hundred men, landed and took possession of the battery, without opposition, spiked the iron guns, and brought off the howitzer. On the 4th the fleet proceeded to Westover, about one hundred and forty miles from the capes of Virginia, where the troops were immediately landed, and marched to Richmond, which they reached without opposition; the militia that was collected having everywhere fled on their approach. From hence Lieutenant-Colonel Simcoe marched with a detachment of the army to Westham, where the troops burnt and destroyed one of the finest foundries for cannon in America, and a large quantity of cannon, stores, &c. General Arnold, on his arrival at Richmond, found there large quantities of tobacco, salt, rum, sail cloth, and merchandise, and that part which was public property he destroyed.

"The public stores, &c., said to be at Petersburg, being found on inquiry not an object worth attention, the ships only were sent up within six miles of that place, from whence they brought off some vessels, several having been previously sunk by the rebels.

"The troops having effected this service, marched back with five very fine brass field-pieces, six-pounders, which they had taken, and arrived at Westover on the 7th, having performed a march of sixty-three miles, through very heavy roads and excessive rains, in three days, in an enemy's country where they were sometimes retarded for hours by the destruction of bridges, &c.

"The 8th, in the evening, Lieutenant-Colonel Simcoe was detached with forty-two cavalry to Charles City Court House, nine miles from Richmond, where, with his usual address, he surprised about two hundred of the enemy's cavalry and foot, killed about twenty, and took eight prisoners, with the loss of one man killed and three wounded. Captain Shanks, of the Queen's Rangers, behaved on this, as on every other occasion, with great bravery.

"On the 9th the army was joined by the troops in the missing transports, and on the 10th the whole fell down the river to Flour de Hundred, where the general being informed there was a party of six or eight hundred rebels, under the command of Baron Steuben, he landed with part of his troops, and sent Lieutenant-Colonel Simcoe, with three hundred men, about two miles to the cross roads, where the enemy were posted; Captain Hatch, who commanded the van-guard, having with great gallantry drove in their picket on the main body. A very heavy fire from the rebels killed three men, and wounded Captain Hatch, Ensign Sword, and about twenty privates of the loyal American regiment, whose conduct on this occasion does them great honor. They then charged the enemy with such firmness and resolution, that they instantly fled on all sides, and were pursued about two miles, but the darkness of the night, badness of the roads, and a heavy shower of rain falling about the time, put an end to the pursuit. On their return, three pieces of heavy, and some light cannon, with a quantity of stores taken from the enemy, were put on board, and the troops embarked at four next morning. On the 11th, fell down the river, taking some stores on their way. On the 14th they anchored at Harding's ferry, the troops, horses, and artillery were landed, and on the 15th the army marched to Smithfield, on Pagan Creek, seventeen miles from thence, where a quantity of provisions was collected.

"On the 16th, Lieutenant-Colonel Simcoe, with two hundred men, was detached to Mackie's Mills, three miles from Smithfield, to dislodge about two hundred of the enemy who had taken post there, and who fled upon his approach. Major Gordon was at the same time thrown over the creek to cut off their retreat, but they took the woods. On the 18th the army moved to Sleepy Hole on Nansemond River, which Lieutenant-Colonel Simcoe passed with his men, and at two o'clock in the morning they began to cross the ferry. They were all over by eleven, and marched fifteen miles. When they were within five miles of Portsmouth, Lieutenant-Colonel Simcoe was detached thither, and arrived at ten the next morning, time enough to prevent the town from being burnt, as threatened by the rebels; and on the 20th, in the morning, the whole army, to the great joy of the inhabitants, marched into Portsmouth in good health and high spirits.

"General Arnold expresses himself much indebted to Commodore Symonds, Captain Evans, and the other officers of his Majesty's ships on this service, for the great assistance he has received from them. And he at the same time speaks in the highest terms of the behavior of the officers and men of both navy and army during the whole expedition."

Rivington's Gazette, February 7

MARCH

March 1

PENNSYLVANIA   This day will be memorable in the annals of America to the last posterity, for the final ratification in Congress of the articles of confederation and perpetual union between the States.

This great event, which will confound our enemies, fortify us against their arts of seduction, and frustrate their plans of division, was announced to the public at twelve o'clock, under the discharge of the artillery on the land and the cannon of the shipping in the Delaware. The bells were rung, and every manifestation of joy shown on this occasion. The *Ariel* frigate, commanded by the gallant Paul Jones, fired a *feu de joie*, and was beautifully decorated with a variety of streamers in the day, and ornamented with a brilliant appearance of lights in the night.

At two o'clock in the afternoon his Excellency the president of Congress received the congratulations of the legislative and executive bodies of Pennsylvania, of the civil and military officers, and many of the principal citizens, who partook of a collation provided on this happy occasion. The evening was ushered in by an elegant exhibition of fireworks.

Thus has the union, began by necessity, been indissolubly cemented. Thus America, (like a well-constructed arch, whose parts harmonizing and mutually supporting each other, are the more closely united the greater the pressure upon them,) is growing up in war into greatness and consequence among the nations. But Britain's boasted wealth and grandeur are crumbling to pieces, never to be again united. Her empire of the ocean is dividing among her insulted neighbors; and if she persists in her present self-destroying system, there will be a time when scarcely a monument of her former glory will remain. The fragments of her empire, and its history, will then be of little other use to mankind, but like a landmark to warn against the shoals and rocks on which her political navigators had ship-wrecked that infatuated nation.

Pennsylvania Packet, March 3

March 16

NORTH CAROLINA   Yesterday morning an engagement was brought on near Guilford Court House, between a small part of the American regulars, joined by a very considerable body of militia, and most of General Cornwallis's army.

Letter, New-Jersey Gazette, April 4

NORTH CAROLINA   Early in the morning, the American reconnoitring parties reported the enemy advancing on the Great Salisbury road. The army was drawn up in three lines: the front line was composed of the North Carolina militia, under the command of Generals Butler and Eaton; the second line of Virginia militia, commanded by Generals Stevens and Lawson, forming two brigades; the third line, consisting of two brigades, one of Virginia, and one of Maryland Continental troops, commanded by General Huger and Colonel Williams. Lieutenant-Colonel Washington, with the dragoons of the first and third regiments, a detachment of light infantry, composed of Continental troops, and a regiment of riflemen under Colonel Lynch, formed a corps of observation for the security of the flank; Lieutenant-Colonel Lee, with his legion, a detachment of light infantry and a corps of riflemen, under Colonel Campbell, formed a corps of observation for the security of the left flank.

The greater part of the country is a wilderness, with a few cleared fields interspersed here and there. The army was drawn up upon a large hill of ground surrounded by other hills, the greater part of which was covered with timber and thick underbrush. The front line was posted, with two field-pieces, just on the edge of the woods, and the back of a fence which ran parallel with the line, with an open field directly in their front. The second line was in the woods, about three hundred yards in rear of the first, and the Continental troops about three hundred yards in the rear of the second with a double front, as the hill drew to a point where they were posted, and on their right and left were two old fields.

In this position the Americans waited the approach of the enemy, having previously sent off the baggage to the iron works, (about ten miles from Guilford Court House,) appointed to rendezvous at in case of a defeat. Lieutenant-Colonel Lee, with his legion, his infantry and part of his rifle-men, met the enemy, on their advance, and had a very severe skirmish with Lieutenant-Colonel Tarleton, in which the enemy suffered greatly. Captain Armstrong charged the British legion, and cut down near thirty of their dragoons, but as they reinforced their advanced party, Lieutenant-Colonel Lee was obliged to retire, and take his position in the line.

The action commenced by a cannonade, which lasted about twenty minutes, when the enemy advanced in three columns; the Hessians on the right, the guards in the centre, and Lieu-tenant-Colonel Webster's brigade on the left. The whole moved through the old fields to attack the North Carolina brigades, who waited the attack until the enemy got within about one hundred and forty yards, when part of them began to fire; but a considerable part left the ground without firing at all. The generals and field-officers did all they could to induce the men to stand their ground, but neither the advantage of the position nor any other consideration could induce them to stay. Generals Stevens and Lawson, and the field-officers of those brigades, were more successful in their exertions. The Virginia militia gave the enemy a warm reception, and kept up a heavy fire for a long time, but being beaten back, the action became general almost everywhere. The corps of observation under Washington and Lee were warmly engaged and did great execution. In a word, the conflict was long and severe, and the enemy only gained their point by superior discipline.

The enemy having broken the second Maryland regiment, and turned our left flank, and got into the rear of the Virginia brigade, and appearing to be gaining our right, which would have encircled the whole of the Continental troops, General Greene thought it most advisable to order a retreat. About this time Lieutenant-Colonel Washington made a charge with the horse upon a part of the brigade of guards, and the first regiment of Marylanders, commanded by Colonel Gunby, and seconded by Lieutenant-Colonel Howard, followed the horse with their bayonets; near the whole of this party fell a sacrifice. General Huger was the last that was engaged, and gave the enemy a check.

The Americans retreated in good order to the Reedy Fork River, crossed at the ford, about three miles from the field of action, and there halted, and drew up the troops, until they collected most of their stragglers. They lost their artillery and two ammunition wagons, (the greater part of the horses being killed before the retreat began,) it being impossible to move the pieces but along the great road. After collecting their stragglers, they retired to the iron works, where they now are.

From the best information, we learn the British loss is very great, not less in killed and wounded than six hundred men, besides some few prisoners that the Americans brought off.

General Greene's letter to Samuel Huntington
New-Jersey Journal, April 11

NORTH CAROLINA   Cornwallis, in his despatches to the British government, gives the following detailed account of this battle:—"In pursuance of my intended plan, I had encamped on the 13th instant, at the Quaker Meeting, between the forks of Deep River. On the 14th I received information that General Butler, with a body of North Carolina militia, and the reinforcements from Virginia, said to consist of a Virginia State regiment, a corps of Virginia eighteen-month men, three thousand Virginia militia and recruits for the Maryland line, had joined General Greene, and that the

whole army, which was reported to amount to nine or ten
thousand men, were marching to attack the British troops.
During the afternoon intelligence was brought, which was
confirmed in the night, that he had advanced that day to
Guilford, about twelve miles from our camp. Being now
persuaded that he had resolved to hazard an engagement,
(after detaching Lieutenant-Colonel Hamilton with our wagons and baggage, escorted by his own regiment, a detachment
of one hundred infantry, and twenty cavalry, towards Bell's
Mill, on Deep River,) I marched with the rest of the corps
at daybreak, on the morning of the 15th, to meet the enemy,
or attack them in their encampment. About four miles from
Guilford our advanced guard, commanded by Lieutenant-
Colonel Tarleton, fell in with a corps of the enemy, consisting
of Lee's legion, some back mountain men, and Virginia
militia, which he attacked with his usual good conduct and
spirit, and defeated; continuing our march, we found the
rebel army posted on rising ground, about a mile and a half
from the court house. The prisoners taken by Lieutenant-
Colonel Tarleton, having been several days with the advanced
corps, could give me no account of the enemy's order or
position, and the country people were extremely inaccurate
in their description of the ground. Immediately between the
head of the column and the enemy's line, was a considerable
plantation, one large field of which was on our left on the
road, and two others, with a wood of about two hundred
yards broad between them, on our right of it; beyond these
fields, the road continued for several miles to our right. The
wood beyond the plantation in our front, in the skirt of which
the enemy's first line was formed, was about a mile in depth,
the road then leading into an extensive space of cleared
ground about Guilford Court House. The woods on our right
and left were reported to be impracticable for cannon; but,
as that on our right appeared to be most open, I resolved to
attack the left wing of the enemy, and whilst my disposition
was making for that purpose, I ordered Lieutenant-Colonel
McLeod to bring forward the guns, and cannonade their
centre. The attack was directed to be made in the following
order:

"On the right, the regiment of Bose, and the 71st regiment, led by Major-General Leslie, and supported by the 1st battalion of guards; on their left the 23d and 33d regiments, led by Lieutenant-Colonel Webster, and supported by the grenadiers and 2d battalion of guards, commanded by Brigadier-General O'Hara; the Jagers and light infantry of the guards remained in the wood, on the left of the guns, and the cavalry in the road, ready to act as circumstances might require. Our preparations being made, the action began about half-past one in the afternoon. Major-General Leslie, after being obliged by the great extent of the enemy's line, to bring up the 1st battalion of guards to the right of the regiment of Bose, soon defeated every thing before him. Lieutenant-Colonel Webster having joined the left of Major-General Leslie's division, was no less successful in his front, when, on finding that the left of the 33d was exposed to a heavy fire from the right wing of the enemy, he changed his front to the left, and being supported by the Jagers and light infantry of the guards, attacked and routed it; the grenadiers and 2d battalion of guards moving forward to occupy the ground left vacant by the movement of Lieutenant-Colonel Webster.

"All the infantry being now in the line, Lieutenant-Colonel Tarleton had directions to keep his cavalry compact, and not to charge without positive orders, except to protect any of the corps from the most evident danger of being defeated. The excessive thickness of the woods rendered our bayonets of little use, and enable the broken enemy to make frequent stands with an irregular fire, which occasioned some loss, and to several of the corps great delay; particularly on our right, where the first battalion of guards and regiment of Bose were warmly engaged in front, flank, and rear, with some of the enemy that had been routed on the first attack, and with part of the extremity of the left wing, which by the closeness of the woods had been passed unbroken. The 71st regiment and grenadiers, and 2d battalion of guards, not knowing what was passing on their right, and hearing the fire advance on their left, continued to move forward, the artillery keeping pace with them on the road, followed by the cavalry. The 2d battalion of the guards first gained the clear ground, near

Guilford Court House, and found a corps of Continental infantry, much superior in number, formed in the open field on
the left of the road. Glowing with impatience to signalize
themselves, they instantly attacked and defeated them, taking
two six-pounders, but pursuing into the wood with too much
ardor, were thrown into confusion by a heavy fire, and immediately charged and driven back into the field, by Colonel
Washington's dragoons, with the loss of the six-pounders they
had taken. The enemy's cavalry was soon repulsed by a well-
directed fire from two three-pounders just brought up by
Lieutenant McLeod, and by the appearance of the grenadiers
of the guards, and of the 71st regiment, which, having been
impeded by some deep ravines, were now coming out of the
wood on the right of the guards, opposite to the court house.
By the spirited exertions of Brigadier-General O'Hara, though
wounded, the 2d battalion of guards was soon rallied, and,
supported by the grenadiers, returned to the charge with the
greatest alacrity. The 23d regiment arriving at that instant
from our left, and Lieutenant-Colonel Tarleton having advanced with part of the cavalry, the enemy were soon put to
flight, and the two six-pounders once more fell into our hands;
two ammunition wagons, and two other six-pounders, being
all the artillery they had in the field, were likewise taken.
About this time the 33d regiment and light infantry of the
guards, after overcoming many difficulties, completely routed
the corps which was opposed to them, and put an end to the
action in this quarter. The 23d and 71st regiments, with part
of the cavalry, were ordered to pursue; the remainder of the
cavalry was detached with Lieutenant-Colonel Tarleton to
our right, where a heavy fire still continued, and where his
appearance and spirited attack contributed much to a speedy
termination of the action. The militia, with which our right
had been engaged, dispersed in the woods; the Continentals
went off by the Reedy Fork, beyond which it was not in my
power to follow them, as their cavalry had suffered but little.
Our troops were excessively fatigued by an action which lasted
an hour and a half; and our numerous wounded, dispersed
over an extensive space of country, required immediate attention. The care of our wounded, and the total want of provi-

sions in an exhausted country, made it equally impossible for me to follow the blow next day. The enemy did not stop until they got to their iron works on Troublesome Creek, eighteen miles from the field of battle.

"From our own observation, and the best accounts we could procure, we did not doubt but that the strength of the enemy exceeded seven thousand men; their militia composed their line, with parties advanced to the rails of the field in their front; the Continentals were posted obliquely in the rear of their right wing. Their cannon fired on us, whilst we were forming, from the centre of the line of militia, but were withdrawn to the Continentals before the attack.

"I have the honor to inclose your lordship the list of our killed and wounded. Captain Schutz's wound is supposed to be mortal, but the surgeons assure me that none of the officers are in danger, and that a great number of the men will soon recover. I cannot ascertain the loss of the enemy, but it must have been considerable; between two and three hundred dead were left upon the field; many of their wounded that were able to move, while we were employed in the care of our own, escaped and followed the routed enemy; and our cattle drivers and foraging parties have reported to me, that the houses in a circle of six or eight miles round us are full of others; those that remained we have taken the best care of in our power. We took few prisoners, owing to the excessive thickness of the woods facilitating their escape, and every man of our army being repeatedly wanted for action.

"The conduct and actions of the officers and soldiers that composed this little army, will do more justice to their merit than I can by words. Their persevering intrepidity in action, their invincible patience in the hardships and fatigues of a march of about six hundred miles, in which they have forded several large rivers and numberless creeks, many of which would be reckoned large rivers in any other country in the world, without tents or covering against the climate, and often without provisions, will sufficiently manifest their ardent zeal for the honor and interests of their sovereign ' and their country.

"I have been particularly indebted to Major-General Leslie,

for his gallantry and exertion in the action, as well as his assistance in every other part of the service. The zeal and spirit of Brigadier-General O'Hara merit my highest commendations, for, after receiving two dangerous wounds, he continued in the field whilst the action lasted; by his earnest attention on all other occasions, seconded by the officers and soldiers of the brigade, his Majesty's guards are no less distinguished by their order and discipline, than by their spirit and valor.

"The Hessian regiment of Bose deserves my warmest praise for its discipline, alacrity, and courage, and does honor to Major du Buy, who commands it, and who is an officer of superior merit.

"I am much obliged to Brigadier-General Howard, who served as volunteer, for his spirited example on all occasions. Lieutenant-Colonel Webster conducted his brigade like an officer of experience and gallantry. Lieutenant-Colonel Tarleton's good spirit and conduct in the management of his cavalry, was conspicuous during the whole action; and Lieutenant McLeod, who commanded the artillery, proved himself upon this as well as all former occasions, a most capable and deserving officer. The attention of my aide-de-camp, and of all the other public officers of the army, contributed very much to the success of the day.

"I have constantly received the most zealous assistance from Governor Martin, during my command in the southern district. Hoping that his presence would tend to excite the loyal subjects to take an active part with us, he has cheerfully submitted to the fatigues and dangers of our campaign; but his delicate constitution has suffered by his public spirit, for, by the advice of the physicians, he is now obliged to return to England for the recovery of his health.

"This part of the country is so totally destitute of subsistence, that forage is not nearer than nine miles, and the soldiers have been two days without bread; I shall therefore leave about seventy of the worst of the wounded cases at the New Garden Quarter Meeting House, with proper assistance, and move the remainder with the army to-morrow morning, to Bell's Mill. I hope our friends will heartily take an active part with us, to which I shall continue to encourage them, still approaching our shipping by easy marches, that we may procure the necessary supplies for further operations, and lodge our sick and wounded where proper attention can be paid to them."

London Gazette, June 5
Rivington's Gazette, August 11

March 28

VIRGINIA Chevalier d'Astouches, with the French fleet, lately returned to Rhode Island from an unsuccessful encounter with the British squadron in the Chesapeake. The subjoined relation of his recent operations, is given by a writer at Newport:—"The gale of wind on the 21st of January, having consequences which put some equality in the naval forces of France and Great Britain, in North America, the Chevalier d'Astouches took advantage of the circumstance to stop the depredations and plunders of the British on the coast of Virginia. For that purpose he sent with the greatest speed a sixty-four gun ship and two frigates, under the orders of Mons. de Tilly, captain of the navy. His orders were to go to Chesapeake Bay, and to endeavor to destroy the little British fleet there, and the frigates which protected it. The enemy having taken the precaution to put their vessels out of danger in the small river of Elizabeth, Mons. Tilly could not completely carry out the object of his mission; his expedition, however, was not fruitless; he took or destroyed ten ships, and carried into Newport, Rhode Island, the *Romulus*, of forty-four guns, which he had taken at the entrance of the bay.

"The success of this undertaking, and the great desire of Mons. d'Astouches to give an efficacious succor to the State of Virginia, made him take the resolution to renew the attempt with greater force. He fitted out his squadron, armed the *Romulus*, and to insure as much as it was possible the success of the expedition, the Count de Rochambeau sent on board his men-of-war and the *Fantasque*, a detachment of his army, under the orders of the Baron de Viomenil.

"On the 8th of March, in the evening, the fleet got under way; the contrary winds drove it the following days to the south-east; however, they took the advantage of the variety of the winds, approached the coast, and on the 14th, in the morning, discovered Cape Charles, in Chesapeake Bay. The south winds which blew very hard, did not allow them to rise in the wind so as to go into Cape Henry; on the contrary, they were driven northward, and tacked about two whole days. On the 16th, at daybreak, the wind still continuing to blow from the same quarter, but with less force, and the weather foggy, the fleet having their larboard tacks on, a frigate was discovered two gunshots to windward; the admiral made signals for chasing, but a short time after, many large ships appearing through the fog, he did not in the least doubt but the British had got intelligence, by some enemy to America, of his going out, and that the west and north-west winds having made them run more rapidly, they had arrived almost as soon as the French fleet on the coast of Virginia. In consequence of that reflection, he called back the chase, and the wind shifting to the north-east in the same instant, he made signal to form the line, with the larboard tacks on. The British fleet were then two leagues off to the southward, steering the same course. At nine o'clock the French fleet wore round ahead by the counter march, and in half an hour after, the British did the same. At half-past ten the admiral, seeing that the wind increased, and that he was approaching the shallows on the north coast of Virginia, made signals to take the larboard tacks on board, and to wear round before the wind by the counter march.

"The Chevalier d'Astouches was conscious that not having got into the Chesapeake before the British, his expedition could not take place; he knew it was impossible to land his troops, even from the men-of-war, under the fire of a superior fleet; his only care was for the glory of the arms of his King, without endangering his fleet.

"The British taking advantage of their superiority in sailing and force, continued to rise in the wind, crowding a great deal of sail, having their starboard tacks aboard. At noon they were in the French fleet's wake; a little before one, their van approached within half a league of the rear of the French line and they seemed to have a mind to attack to the leeward. Till then the Chevalier d'Astouches had worked his ships so as neither to avoid nor seek the engagement, because he was sure that even the happiest issue of it would hinder him from fulfilling his principal object; but the honor of the King's arms, which he must sustain before America, would not let him give room to the British to boast that they had pursued him, even with a superior force, and he took the resolution of attacking by falling on their van, wearing round by a counter march, and fighting them on opposite tacks to leeward, that his ships might with facility make use of their lower deck guns.

"At one o'clock, the headmost ship of the French line was within gunshot of the British, and a few minutes after the engagement began. The van of the British fell to leeward, and the van of the French fleet did the same, to keep up with the enemy, so that those two parts of the fleet fought for some time, running before the wind. A little before two o'clock, the admiral seeing that the manœuvre of the British van did not allow it to run more to leeward, made his fleet haul in the wind, with larboard tacks aboard by a successive motion, which made his whole line file off upon the van of the enemy. This manœuvre had a complete success; their foremost ship had scarce received the fire of the fifth French ship, when she fell to leeward, took the wind on his starboard side, and left the line, accompanied by a frigate which came to her relief; however, the rear of the British fleet had kept to windward, and was near enough to fight the French rear while it was making a motion to get in the wake of the head of the line. This attack of the enemy's van did very little damage to the ships that sustained it. The *Conquerant*, how-ever, suffered a great deal, because, after having fought with the British van, she sustained all the fire of the centre. She especially fought with a three-decker, the loss of whose main-topsail yard, and of a great part of her rigging, compensated the damage done the *Conquerant*.

"A quarter before three, the fire having ceased on both sides, and the French fleet being ahead and to leeward of the British, the admiral made signal to form promiscuously the line, larboard tacks aboard. In a short time this was done, and the fleet ran under small sail in expectation that the enemy would attack a second time. The admiral then proposed to wear round them, and fall upon their van, but they had been so ill-used in the first encounter, that they did not think it prudent to expose themselves to a second, and during the rest of the day they kept to windward and astern, without taking advantage of their superiority in sailing, to renew the fight.

"In the beginning of the night the British fleet fell to leeward, and the French fleet continued to run to the south-east with very little sail, and all its lights hung out. The next day the British were not to be seen, and the Chevalier d'Astouches, though the advantage was on his side, was obliged to renounce his hopes of succoring Virginia. Consequently he steered towards Newport, to repair his ships that had been damaged, and to put them in a condition of undertaking new operations.

"Too much praise cannot be given to the intrepid firmness shown by the captains, officers, crews, and troops; their courage has made a compensation for the number and superior strength of the enemy's ships, and the expedition would have been successful had it been depending on the superiority of courage. The loss of the fleet amounts to eighty men killed, or dead of their wounds, and one hundred and twenty wounded. Among the first are sincerely lamented, M. de Cheffontaine, captain of the navy, and Mons. de Kergu, ensign."

Newport Mercury, March 31
Rivington's Gazette, April 18

APRIL

April 25

SOUTH CAROLINA   Yesterday morning the American forces under General Greene, encamped on Hobkirk's Hill, about a mile from Camden, (S. C.,) where they remained unmolested until this forenoon, at which time Lord Rawdon, who had been in possession of Camden for some time past, attacked them unexpectedly, and after a furious fight, compelled them to retire from the field, leaving a large number of killed and wounded.

In the action Colonel [William Augustine] Washington, with more address than usual, captured a party of the British, but was obliged to relinquish a great portion of them on the retreat. Much dissatisfaction is expressed by the general with the conduct of the officers, but we (the soldiers) are loaded with honor.

No source

April 28

NEW YORK   Last Wednesday night a party of Indians, consisting of twenty-five, with two Tory pilots, crossed the river Delaware opposite Minisink, the principal settlement of that country. At daybreak they proceeded to the house of Thomas Brink, whom they made prisoner, with his two little sons, then plundered and destroyed every thing of any value in the house. From thence they went to the widow Brink's, distant about one hundred yards, robbed her of every valuable thing in the house, and destroyed all her provisions; then marched to a house near by, where lived two young men by the names of Westbrook and Job. They entered the house while the family were asleep; the men waked in a surprise, sprung out of bed, and made all the resistance possible, but being greatly overpowered by numbers, fell a sacrifice to savage Indians and Tories, and experienced that torture in death, which nothing but British and savage cruelty could invent. At this house they made Job's wife, and a girl about thirteen years old, prisoners. They next proceeded to Captain Shimer's, where they made three of his Negroes prisoners; six rushed into a room next to where Captain Shimer lay, while the rest surrounded the house. An old Negro woman ran to her master's bedside, and cried out, "The Indians are all around the house, and the next room is full of them." Upon which information he left his bed in a moment, seized his rifle, ran to the front door of the room, opened it, and saw about ten Indians before the piazza, when he presented his piece briskly from one to another which induced the whole to run to the rear of the house; he then, by the same stratagem, drove the whole out of his house. In the mean time, two of his Negroes got clear, whom he fixed at the two front doors of the house, each with an axe, with orders to defend them to the last extremity, then ran up to the second story, and began to fire out of the windows, when he soon got the assistance of a man who lay in one of the upper bed-rooms; they continued a brisk fire for near an hour, running from window to window, and making all the parade possible. The Indians continued a sharp fire upon the house during the whole time, but such was the unparalleled bravery and good conduct of Captain Shimer, that they despaired of effecting their cursed design, and began to retreat with their prisoners and plunder. At this moment Captain Shimer got a reinforcement of four good marksmen, when he put on his breeches and shoes, (having fought all the morning in his shirt,) and pursued them to the river, near a mile from his house, where he found that about one-half had crossed. He continued his pursuit with a brisk fire after the others, crying out: "Rush on, my brave boys; we'll surround them!" which so terrified the cowardly murderers, though double in number, that they ran into a swamp, leaving behind them their plunder, Mrs. Job, her little girl, and a Negro man belonging to Captain Shimer. They took Mr. Brink and his two boys over with the first party. Captain Shimer, going into a back bedroom to discharge his piece, providentially prevented his two daughters, one a young woman, the other Captain Bonnel's wife with a child in her arms, from jumping out of the window, as they were just lifting up the sash for that purpose, which was at least eighteen feet from the ground. The loss of the enemy we cannot ascertain. During the action they were seen to carry off one on a board, and several were carried away from the Pennsylvania shore; there was likewise a considerable quantity of blood seen where they passed.

New-Jersey Journal, May 16

MAY

May 1

When rebel writers write, and rebel printers print, all good rebels must believe. Walsingham's inquiry into the causes of the depreciation of the paper money of the United States, is an honest display, to say the least, and will effect a change in the sentiments of those who have been the real supporters of the Congress measures.

> *Mss. letter from Edward Bagot, May 20*
> *Winslow*

That writer says:—"The Continental money was issued in 1775, at a time when America was without trade, without allies, and above all, without any system of government. At no period of the present revolution were the malice and arts of dissaffection employed with more industry to prevent the circulation of this money, than for the first year after its emission; and yet, under all these complicated disadvantages, it passed near a twelvemonth upon a par with gold and silver; nor did it suffer the least depreciation, until it felt the operation of that cause which would have depreciated the gold of Ophir; I mean an excess in its quantity. Here, then, we have fixed the first cause of the depreciation of the paper money of the United States. This cause affected its value only, but had no effect upon its credit. The lower it depreciated, until it fell to four to one, the more extensively and freely it circulated, insomuch that many of the most acknowledged Tories sold gold for it at the above exchange, and put it into the funds, or locked it up in their chests.

"The second cause which produced a depreciation in our money, must be sought for in those acts of government which affected its credit. These were:

"1. *The resolve of Congress for calling the emissions of*

May 1777 *and* 1778 *out of circulation.* This was the first shock the money received. Hundreds suffered by it, and although its quantity was diminished by it, yet it fell in a few weeks from four to ten, and in a few months to twenty to one.

"2. *The laws for making the Continental money a legal tender for old debts.* This made it the interest of every man who had debts or even taxes to pay, to depreciate the money. It moreover excited the disgust and opposition of everybody who had been injured by it.

"3. *Laws for regulating the prices of goods.* These, from the instability of the paper currency, were unjust and incapable of execution, and hence specie or barter were introduced in many places in the room of paper money. This affected the money in two ways. By diminishing the number of people among whom it circulated, it sunk its value, and the authority of the laws which compelled its circulation at a given rate, for articles at all times fluctuating in their prices, necessarily struck at its credit.

"4. *The embargo upon provisions.* This depreciated the money in two ways: First, it lessened the objects of money, particularly among the farmers; and secondly, it obliged our merchants to purchase specie often at a high exchange to send abroad, which exchange afterwards stamped a similar value upon every article of life.

"5. *The resolve of the eighteenth of March,* 1780, *for redeeming the money at forty for one.* This resolve, from being compared with the tenor of every bill, and above all, from being compared with the circular letter which preceded it only a few months, destroyed all faith in the promises and declarations of government. I should as soon think of trusting a man with a cargo of goods who had ruined my family by bankruptcy, as think of giving a credit to a new emission of money, from a body of men who had acted so contrary to every principle of sound policy.

"6. *The neglect of Congress to pay the interest of the moneys borrowed since March.* This, like number five, helped to destroy the confidence of the public in the promises of Congress.

"7. *The payment of public debts in depreciated money.*

This, like numbers five and six, has destroyed the faith of individuals in our governments. The scale of depreciation lately adopted by the State of Pennsylvania, for the settlement of old debts, is both impolitic and unjust. The first payment of the money due, for depreciation, to the officers and soldiers of the Pennsylvania line, is obviously calculated to promote resignations and mutiny.

"8. *The laws for investing executive bodies with a power to alter the exchange of money.* The edict of the council of Pennsylvania, of the second of May, was the death-blow of paper currency of all kinds. As Mark Antony says of the wound inflicted by Brutus upon the body of Cæsar, 'it was the most unkindly stab of all.'

"Thus have I enumerated the principal causes and circumstances which have reduced and nearly ruined the paper money of the United States. I think it is evident, from what has been said, that the arts of the Tories, sharpers, speculators, and money-changers, so often mentioned by weak politicians, have had no more to do in depreciating it than the patriotism of the Whigs, or the exertions of officers of government have been effectual in raising its value or restoring its credit. It is high time to seek for the causes of our misfortunes, in other sources than the disaffection of a few *tame* animals, who are peaceably submitting to our governments, and contributing their share of industry in agriculture, arts, and commerce, towards establishing our independence. This country groans at present only beneath the folly of weak, ambitious, and interested Whigs, from whom we have more to fear than all the Tories on the continent, or even from the power of Britain.

"It becomes rulers to learn, from the catastrophe of our Continental currency, that money is upon a footing with commerce and religion. They all three refuse to be the subjects of law. It becomes the rulers of freemen to learn further, that money is property, and that the least attempt to lessen its value in our pockets or chests, is taxing us without our consent. It is the highest act of tyranny. We have tried every art and device to keep up the credit of paper money, except one. We have never yet tried the effects of being honest.

"I shall conclude by proposing two plans for the emission of paper money, which no arts of Tories or Whigs will be able to depreciate:

"1. Institute a bank where specie may be lodged in safety; let bills be issued, signed by the Financier-General, subject to be exchanged at the pleasure of the holder, for specie at this bank. One million of Spanish dollars, under the management of a gentleman of established credit and ample fortune, would serve as a fund for ten millions of paper dollars. Or,

"2. Let our government emit money, and let a tax be imposed at the same time to the exact amounts of the emission to be paid in three, six, nine, or twelve months in specie, or the said bills only. This will necessarily bring the paper money into universal circulation, and preserve its equality to gold and silver.

"It has been said, that the war may be carried on by taxes and loans in specie. Perhaps this may be necessary until we forget the frauds and deceptions of our paper currency. It is certain there is more specie in the country than there was ten years ago. But while contracts for specie may be cancelled with paper, (but little more valuable than oak leaves,) it will be difficult to draw it from the coffers of those who hold it in the largest quantity.

"The Americans deserve the highest praise for the fortitude with which they have borne the sacking of their towns, and the desolation of their country, from the hands of the British army. But let Europe and posterity admire them chiefly for the patience with which they have borne the more complicated evils and losses of tender laws, regulations of trade and exchange, and a depreciating paper currency. In spite of them all, I hope my countrymen will part with their republican forms of government and their independence only with their lives."

Pennsylvania Journal, May 16

May 7

PENNSYLVANIA   The Congress is finally bankrupt! Last Saturday a large body of the inhabitants with paper dollars in their hats by way of cockades, paraded the streets of Philadelphia, carrying colors flying, with a DOG TARRED, and instead of the usual appendage and ornament of feathers, his back was covered with the Congress' paper dollars. This example of disaffection, immediately under the eyes of the rulers of the revolted provinces, in solemn session at the State House assembled, was directly followed by the jailer, who refused accepting the bills in purchase of a glass of rum, and afterwards by the traders of the city, who shut up their shops, declining to sell any more goods but for gold or silver. It was declared also by the popular voice, that if the opposition to Great Britain was not in future carried on by solid money instead of paper bills, all further resistance to the mother country were vain, and must be given up.

Rivington's Gazette, May 12

May 12

SOUTH CAROLINA   Lord Rawdon having on the 7th instant been reinforced by the corps under Lieutenant-Colonel Watson, marched out with the hope of bringing General Greene to action; but that wary officer, rendered still more so by the event of the 25th of April, chose to remain in a strong position, behind Swansey Creek, from which no efforts of his lordship could draw him; he rather preferring to see his enemy manoeuvre in his front, with all the confidence of a victorious army, than contest a point, of which former experience must have rendered him so very cautious. Lord Rawdon, therefore, finding it impossible to draw on an action, but on terms highly disadvantageous, and by assailing a position which gave the rebels their only security, returned to Camden, having convinced General Greene how futile were his ideas of blockading that place, when obliged himself to seek shelter in the recesses of the country, and even there to suffer that blockaded garrison to taunt him with daily defiance.

Thus finding all efforts to engage General Greene in a fair field were ineffectual, Lord Rawdon removed with the King's troops from Camden, induced thereto by the approaching

season, when that part of the country proves destructive to
the soldiery.

Pennsylvania Packet, July 12

May 20

SOUTH CAROLINA   A writer in the British army at
Charleston, South Carolina, in a letter to his friend in London, says:—"The retrograde progress of our arms in this
country, you have seen in your newspapers, if they dare tell
you the truth. This precious commodity is not to be had in
the government paper which is printed here, for a fell li-
censer hangs over the press, and will suffer nothing to pass
but what is palatable; that is, in plain terms, what is false.
Our victories have been dearly bought, for the rebels seem to
grow stronger by every defeat, like Antæus, of whom it was
fabled, that being the son of the goddess Tellus, or the earth,
every fall which he received from Hercules gave him more
strength, so that the hero was forced to strangle him in his
arms at last. I wish our ministry could send us a Hercules to
conquer these obstinate Americans, whose aversion to the
cause of Britain grows stronger every day.

"If you go into company with any of them occasionally,
they are barely civil, and that is, as Jack Falstaff says, by
compulsion. They are in general sullen, silent, and thought-
ful. The King's health they dare not refuse, but they drink it
in such a manner as if they expected it would choke them.

"The assemblies which the officers have opened, in hopes
to give an air of gayety and cheerfulness to themselves and
the inhabitants, are but dull and gloomy meetings; the men
play at cards, indeed, to avoid talking, but the women are
seldom or never to be persuaded to dance. Even in their
dresses the females seem to bid us defiance; the gay toys which
are imported here they despise; they wear their own homespun
manufactures, and take care to have in their breasts knots,
and even on their shoes something that resembles their flag
of the thirteen stripes. An officer told Lord Cornwallis not
long ago, that he believed if he had destroyed all the men in
North America, we should have enough to do to conquer the

women. I am heartily tired of this country, and wish myself at home."

Pennsylvania Packet, December 11

———— •••• ————

JUNE

June 6

NEW YORK   This day arrived at New York, Ebenezer Hathaway and Thomas Smith, who, on the 18th of May last, made their escape from Simsbury Mines, after a most gallant struggle for their liberty. These men declare, that they were two of eight belonging to the privateer boat *Aventure*, which was duly commissioned; that they were taken in Huntington Bay, Long Island, on the 7th of April, by seven rebel whale-boats, manned with seventy-three men, and that night carried across the Sound to Stamford, in Connecticut; that the next day they were carried to what they called headquarters, before General Waterbury, who with the air of a demagogue, ordered them to Hartford Gaol, and told the guard they had his liberty to strip them even of the clothes remaining on their backs; but the captors had left them so bare, that all they had about them was not now an object even to a Yankee soldier; there they lay until the 27th following, when their trial came on before the Superior Court; that they were brought before the court and directed to plead not guilty, and offered for council Colonel Sention, one of the justices, then on the bench, in order that they might by law bring them in guilty; but aware of their knavish tricks, they declared themselves British subjects, and refused to plead either guilty or not guilty, therefore they were ordered to Newgate Gaol, or rather to that inquisition, Simsbury Mines, which, from the following description, exceeds any thing amongst their allies in France or Spain.

These poor unfortunate victims relate, that they were taken from Hartford Gaol, and marched under a strong guard to

Simsbury Mines, distant about seventy-four miles.' In approaching this horrid dungeon, they were first conducted
through the apartments of the guards, then through a trap-
door down stairs into another upon the same floor with the
kitchen, which was divided from it by a very strong partition
door. In the corner of this outer room, and near to the foot of
the stairs, opened another huge large trap-door, covered with
bars and bolts of iron, which was hoisted up in two guards by
means of a tackle, whilst the hinges grated as they turned
upon their hooks, and opened the jaws and mouth of what
they call Hell, into which they descended by means of a
ladder about six feet more, which led to a large iron grate or
hatchway, locked down over a shaft of about three feet diam-
eter, sunk through the solid rock, and which they were told
led to the bottomless pit. Finding it not possible to evade this
hard, cruel fate, they bid adieu to the world, and descended
the ladder about thirty-eight feet more, when they came to
what is called the landing; then marching shelf by shelf, till
descending about thirty or forty feet more, they came to a
platform of boards laid under foot, with a few more put over
head to carry off the water, which keeps continually dropping. Here, say they, we found the inhabitants of this woeful
mansion, who were exceedingly anxious to know what was
going on above. We told them that Lord Cornwallis had beat
the rebel army, and that their money was gone to the
d——l, with which they seemed satisfied, and rejoiced at the
good news.

They were obliged to make use of pots of charcoal to dispel
the foul air, which in some degree is drawn off by the means
of a ventilator or auger hole, which is bored from the surface
through at this spot, said to be seventy feet perpendicular.
Here they continued twenty days and nights, resolved, however, to avail themselves of the first opportunity to get out,
although they should lose their lives in the attempt. Accordingly, on the 18th, eighteen of them, being let up to the
kitchen to cook, found means to break the lock of the door,
which kept them from the foot of the ladder leading up to
the guard-room. They now doubly resolved to make a push
should the door be opened; which, fortunately, was the case

about ten o'clock at night, (to let down a prisoner's wife who had come there and was permitted to see him.)

Immediately they seized the fortunate moment and rushed up, but before any, except one, got out, the door was slammed down on the rest, and he, the brave Captain Hathaway, who commanded the adventure, scuffled with the whole of them for a few minutes, and was wounded in three different places; when he was nobly assisted by his trusty friend Thomas Smith, and afterwards by the other eight. They then advanced upon the guard, consisting of twenty-four in number, and took the whole prisoners. This was no sooner accomplished than they brought their companions from out of the bottomless pit, and put the guard down into their room, then marched off with their arms and ammunition, but were soon afterwards obliged to disperse.

Rivington's Gazette, June 9

June 14

ENGLAND   This morning, died in Forton Prison, near Portsmouth, England, Mr. William Hines, an officer of the General Gates' private ship of war, from Danvers, near Boston, Massachusetts; after having with much patience, and with the most irreproachable conduct, sustained a three years' captivity. He was a man of eminent religion and virtue. Finding death swiftly advancing, he called to him his two sons, Francis and William, the one in the eighteenth and the other in the fifteenth year of his age, and said: "My dear boys, I cheerfully submit to my lot, for it is appointed for all men once to die. I meekly resign unto the Providence of God, for I see infinite mercy toward me in this dispensation. Indeed, why should I repine? I shall now speedily obtain that release which my eyes have often failed me in looking after. Oh! wretched man that I was! that my faith had almost failed me, as to my temporal deliverance, at the moment my God was about to give me my grand discharge! Who, or what shall now confine me! I shall soon be free as a celestial. Farewell, farewell bolts, bars, and prisons! Adieu ye dungeons! adieu ye tents of clay! welcome fair daylight and liberty! The time of my redemption draweth nigh. But, my dear boys, how shall I bid farewell to you? That final parting which would have been easy, which would have been blissful in our cottage at Danvers, gives pungent grief to my spirits. I leave you, alas! in this abode of sorrow and of wretchedness, but I charge you 'to pray unto God from this far country and cry unto him from this strange land.' I hope it will be given to you to revisit the land of your nativity, and to enjoy peace and prosperity for the days wherein ye have seen evil. Let a high and genuine sense of liberty direct and animate your whole conduct. I give no directions concerning my bones. They indeed must lie in this region of oppression and cruelty. O that I had been buried in some part of the American world! then would the clods of the valley have been sweet to me. It is done—my children, weep not for me, 'but weep for yourselves, and for the slain of your people.' If ever you mourn, let it be for the calamities of your country, highly beloved, because greatly injured. Francis, give me thine hand—slender as thine arm is, it may shield thy brother. The God of Abraham, Isaac, and Jacob, bless the lads."

New York Packet, November 1

June 16

Our correspondents beyond the lines, says *Rivington*, give us a most melancholy description of the wretchedness of the inhabitants of all parts of the country. The increase of the numbers who are for peace and the re-union, by driving the rest who are a great minority of the whole to despair, excites them to practise every barbarous exertion for the preservation of their tyranny.

The mob legislature of New York, by a late law, have enacted treasons into felonies, that they may take away life with only one witness, or presumptive evidence, instead of two witnesses to each overt act, as their own republican constitution requires; and that they may the more easily get jurymen to attend in criminal cases, and thus abate the dread of falling within the exception contained in the Declaration of the Royal Commissioners, by being exempted from pardon for putting loyal subjects to death. The new act passed by the usurpers at Albany, gives power to send such as they convict for certain offences *before* treasonable, and *now* made felony, to serve in the *French fleet*.

Their laws for taxing the people, and forcing them from home into military services, are intolerably severe and cruel. Among others they have one called the Black Act, under which they plunder the loyalists for every thing lost or taken from any independent partisan, and by this they have found means so to manage matters as greatly to enrich themselves. There is an instance in Duchess County, of about five hundred pounds in value in hard money, raised to pay for a *single horse*. Others again profit by robberies of the loyalists, whose houses are entered by armed parties at midnight, calling themselves *Tories*, and who, of course, go clear, because the persons robbed will not prosecute on the Black Act, nor would succeed if they did, the law (as is expressed) being made only for *good Whigs*.

That they may not be embarrassed by the backwardness or conscientious qualms of jurymen, certain classes of people obnoxious to the ruling party, are made triable by courts-martial, and many perish by these military tribunals, under the imputation of spies, or concealers, or comforters of spies. To the credit of the main body of the people, it is observed, that few, and in some districts none, attended at the late elections for the officers of the usurpation, and many have removed to Vermont and other places, not yet so miserable as those they fly from. In some counties there would be tolerable ease to the inhabitants, but for ten or twelve of the ringleaders in the vicinity in all the wicked work of oppression, plunder, and blood-shedding. It is with difficulty the unhappy sufferers restrain themselves under their complicated calamities, and only through their present dread of the rebel garrison at West Point.

Of the tyrants against whom the complaints of the people run highest as the most unfeeling malefactors, we find in the latest letters in general, those acting as Commissioners for conspiracies, and sequestrations, and sheriffs, with the names in particular of William Duer, Egbert Benson, Robert Harper, Henry Williams, a fellow vulgarly called at Poughkeepsie, *the Bishop*, a Doctor Van Wyck, Judge Platt, Squire Van Ness, old Wisner, Squire Stewart, Joseph Wood, William Holly, Gill Cooper, Judge Call, Squire Rye, and Captain Crompond Drake.

Some Connecticut friends assert that there appears to be such an abhorrence of the present system, and so general a turn in the minds of the people, that if any patriot should stand forth, and call out all those who wish to preserve the charter, and enjoy immediate peace, he would be instantly joined by a vast majority of the colony, in a resolution to withdraw from the Congress, and oppose the pernicious councils by which they so often have been cheated of their property.

Very judicious intelligencers also inform us, that the disgusts and impatience of the main body of the people are as great in Massachusetts and New Hampshire, and especially in all that part of the former to the west of Connecticut River. A few months ago, Deerfield ordered her delegate in the general court at Boston, to move for instructions to the province of Delegates in Congress, to make overtures for peace with the mother country; and so much alarmed were the zealots for independency, lest this should prove a match to a train, as instantly to violate their new constitution, by suspending the privilege of habeas corpus; after which the tyrants threw Messrs. Williams, Catlin, and Ashley into jail, as chief promoters of the Deerfield instructions.

Rivington's Gazette, June 16

June 22

SOUTH CAROLINA   Information being received that Lord Rawdon had received a reinforcement from England, and that he was advancing to the relief of Ninety-Six, General Greene determined to make an attack upon the British fortifications, before he raised the siege, commenced against that post on the twenty-second of last month. Accordingly, on the morning of the 18th, the necessary dispositions were made, and about twelve o'clock the action commenced. The fire from the American battery on the right, where Lieutenant-Colonel Lee commanded, was so warm that the British were soon driven from their redoubt in that quarter, which the colonel immediately took possession of, and pointed the cannon against the town. At that moment, Lieutenant Selden, of the Virginia, and Lieutenant Duval of the Maryland line, made a lodgment in the fosse of the star redoubt, against which our principal approaches were directed without the loss of a man. The working party were pulling down the sand bags, and there was a great probability of their making a breach in the parapet in a very little time, when the British being reinforced from the right, charged the Americans in their fosse to the right and left, and were driven back three times with very considerable loss; but Lieutenant Selden, having received a wound in his arm, and being obliged to retire, the men were pressed in upon the Marylanders, and the whole thrown into confusion, which induced Lieutenant Duval, who had likewise received a wound, to bring off the party. These two young gentlemen displayed great gallantry upon this occasion, and merit the particular respect of their country.

During the attempt, a very heavy fire was kept up by the American troops in the front parallel, and the riflemen upon the advanced battery, with considerable execution; and though they had the misfortune to fail in their first effort, such was the spirit and eagerness of the men to engage, that if their situation and circumstances would have justified the general in sporting with the lives of two hundred men, they could have carried the place. The Americans continued before it until the morning of the 20th, (when his lordship was within twelve miles of the American camp,) and then retired across the Saluda River.

His lordship is now at Ninety-Six, and the Americans are about fifteen miles off. The military of the country are turning out, and when drawn to a point, we think we shall be able to put him in a retrograde to Monk's Corner; at any rate he cannot live where he is, and must either retire to the neighborhood of Charleston or take post at the Congaree. Should he take post there without superior cavalry and mounted militia, we can cut off his supplies, and render his situation very critical. We are prepared for all events, and let what will happen, we are determined to do every thing in our power to promote the interest and honor of our country.

New-Jersey Journal, August 1

June 28

The United States of America have at this moment a fair prospect of establishing their peace and independence, which may soon be realized, if the Americans be not wanting to themselves. The Britons, by turning their arms to the Southern States, have experienced what the wise and sagacious predicted from this measure; they have greatly exhausted and dissipated their army, and found it easier with a collected force, covered by a superior navy, to penetrate into a thin settled country, than to spread themselves over it, and maintain their conquests. The climate, and the brave persevering efforts of the patriots in that quarter, have almost ruined the army of Cornwallis, which having been drawn from New York, must have greatly weakened that important post. The Spaniards have greatly distressed the British settlements in the Floridas, and have taken Pensacola. A great part of Georgia is recovered from the British, and almost the whole of South Carolina is at this hour in the possession of the United States. Virginia, under particular disadvantages at its first invasion, is now collecting its whole force to co-operate with the assistance it has received, and to which it is entitled, and the prospect there is far from being discouraging. Britain has received an unexpected and terrible shock in the late account from the East Indies, where the loss of a large share of her settlements, and the tottering state of the rest, threatens the total ruin of her finances; at the same time she cannot but look with anguish on the good condition of the finances of France, where not a single new tax has been levied during the war; but the whole charge of it defrayed by the mere savings of economy. These, and many other circumstances that might be mentioned, must induce Britain to be very serious in her desires of peace. Accordingly she has consented, if not primarily, and secretly moved a convention of the belligerent powers at Vienna for that purpose, under the mediation of the Emperor of Germany and the Empress of Russia. To suppose that nothing is to be said in this convention respecting America, or that even Britain has forbidden it, is too ridiculous to require a serious answer. It is to suppose all the powers convened in this business are fools; for how can they confer upon a pacification, and at the same time leave out America, the source and principal seat of the war? In the nature of things, America must be the chief subject in their deliberations, and Britain will doubtless keep her eye principally upon that continent during the negotiations, and will rise and fall in her demands, will accede to, or recede from the proposals made, according to the events of war in that quarter.

The present, then, is the critical day for America. Dissensions, languor in our councils or conduct, would revive the hopes of Britain, and might be an irreparable injury to the Americans and their latest posterity. Union and vigor through the present campaign, may lay a stable foundation of liberty and happiness to these States. Having expended already so much blood and treasure in their glorious cause, it should be a first principle in the mind of every free citizen, that the only way to reap the fruits of all, and to make a safe and honorable peace, is to conduct the remainder of the war with vigor. This, and this alone, will make it short. The most noble negotiator in Europe will find himself greatly embarrassed if the measures we take here do not give force to his demands on our behalf, and an edge to his arguments and persuasions. A good army in the field, and well provided, is absolutely necessary to give the finishing stroke to the establishment of America's invaluable rights. One signal defeat of the British will have more effect on the negotiations at Vienna, than all the eloquence of the most accomplished plenipotentiaries.

Pennsylvania Packet, July 14

JULY

July 1

SOUTH CAROLINA   Last Thursday night a small party
of mounted rebel militia surrounded the house of Andrew
Williamson, Esq., formerly brigadier-general of the South
Carolina militia, about seven miles from Charleston, and
without allowing him time to put on his clothes, carried him
off prisoner. On intelligence being received of this, Major
Frazer, with ninety of his dragoons, was detached next day in
quest of them. After having effected a circuitous march of
more than seventy miles through the woods, with the most
profound secrecy, on Saturday morning the major surprised
their main body in their camp at the Horse Shoe, killed fourteen on the spot, wounded several, took Colonel Isaac Hayne,
their commander, prisoner, and released General Williamson
from his confinement at a house in the neighborhood.

The anxiety to rescue General Williamson, and the rebels
not making the smallest show of resistance, but betaking
themselves to the woods in every direction, prevented their
sustaining a greater loss. Their numbers before that morning
were estimated at more than two hundred; their own accounts
made them much stronger. Among the killed was the second
in command, Lieutenant-Colonel McLaughlan; his brother
Captain McLaughlan was dangerously wounded. Colonel
Hayne was brought into Charleston to-day, and is now lodged
in the provost.

Rivington's Gazette, August 1

July 4

NEW YORK   The imagination can scarcely conceive of a
more miserable condition than that of the inhabitants of
New York, between the Highlands and Albany. The persons

favoring independency, which consist only of such as despair of escaping the vengeance of their countrymen, abandon themselves to all the cruelty of cowardice. Alive to suspicion, the general consideration is about spies and harborers of spies, and in the extremity of their terrors, the slightest preparations pass with the tyrants in office for demonstrative proof. Hence women are committed to their jails, capital executions grow more frequent, and to the reproach of humanity, there was an instance within a month past of a man under public condemnation, being hanged *in his prison* to gratify the pride of the sheriff, who (obliged to be executioner himself) was ashamed to perform the office of hangman in the fields. Albany was reserved for this first and rare instance of infamy.

And though the credit of paper money is totally extinct in all parts of the continent, (and for that reason the late mint of *specie or hard money paper* not wholly issued, but withheld if possible to increase its value, or rather the demand for it,) their late mob assembly have published a tax law, to oblige every man to give a bushel of wheat for every sixty dollars of his former assessment, in old continental, and if he has no wheat, then twelve shillings in lieu of a bushel of wheat, and on failure in ten days, two bushels or twenty-four shillings. This wheat, it is said, is for the supply of Washington's army, but really intended to be sold to the French for hard money; and what will be done with that, no person is at a loss to conjecture. *Miserable people, the prey of plunderers of their own creating!* "How long, O Lord!" is the cry of the oppressed!

By the abandoning of Fort Stanwix, all the western country is deserted down to Schenectady, and the persecutors who dare to continue in Kingston have fortified and drawn ditches around their houses, in expectation of the Indians as soon as the harvests are in stack.

The advocates for peace and the re-union, and who have been so ever since the fatal Declaration of Independence, and who are a vast majority, grow every day more numerous, and it is remarkable that not a single instance can be assigned of the apostasy of a loyalist to the wicked and interested views of the usurpers.

There is a new set of mob legislators met at Poughkeepsie; a little time will show whether they mean to expose themselves to all the vengeance of which the majority of the late assembly and senate live in constant dread, many of them changing their lodgings, to elude the search of the avengers of the innocent blood they have shed. Mr. Clinton, the titular governor, has fortified his huts against a sudden surprise, and the rebel slaves of Poughkeepsie guard it every night.

Rivington's Gazette, July 4

From the commencement of the present war, the British Ministry, their agents and tools, have depended more upon the base arts of deceit and corruption, than the justice of their cause or the power of arms. It is a fact well established, that in the course of the last year, the British government expended upwards of fifty thousand guineas on hirelings employed to tell lies in pamphlets and in the newspapers in Europe and America. The present year will probably cost them double that sum, as their affairs are in a more critical state, and we may expect to see marks of redoubled industry in the trade of misrepresentation and falsehood. The newspapers begin to abound with this species of intelligence. We are told that fleets of ships and armies of men are coming to America; that all the powers of Europe are against us; that the rupture with Holland is to be made up; that a peace is about to be concluded among the European belligerent powers, and the United States are to be left to shift for themselves; with a thousand tales of this stamp, so shallow and absurd, that any man who has the least reflection or the slightest means of information, and believes them, almost deserves to be duped and imposed upon. It is to be lamented that the uninformed, the unwary, and the timid, are sometimes deceived, notwithstanding the whole experience of the war. *Beware, Americans, that they who cannot fight you out of your liberties, be not suffered to lie you out of them.*

New-Jersey Gazette, July 4

July 8

VIRGINIA   Lafayette and Wayne are leading the British in Virginia through a very intricate path. The latest operation is that of Wayne, with a handful of Pennsylvanians, frightening the whole of Cornwallis's army of "undaunted Britons." The Tories say it is only "another version of the deceit and unfairness practised by the little Frenchman last May."

Letter from Colonel Alexander Scammel, dated King's Ferry,
New York, August 20

VIRGINIA   Cornwallis having encamped near Jamestown, in Virginia, the Marquis de Lafayette sent General Wayne, with the Pennsylvania line, to take their station within a small distance of the British army, and watch their motions. About three hundred riflemen occupied the ground between General Wayne and Lord Cornwallis, who were directed to scatter themselves in the woods, without order, and annoy the enemy's camp. This they did with such effect, that a small party was sent out against them, to dislodge them; each side continuing to reinforce, at length the whole of General Wayne's division were engaged; they drove the advance detachment back to their lines, and, without stopping there, attacked the whole British army, drawn up in order of battle, and charged them with their bayonets. The action was obstinate for the little time it lasted, but the disproportion of numbers was too great. The marquis arrived, in person, time enough to order a retreat, and to bring off the Pennsylvania troops before they were surrounded, which the enemy were endeavoring to effect, being able greatly to outflank them. Cornwallis did not pursue them more than half a mile in the retreat, apprehending that the rest of the Americans were near enough to support them, and not choosing to risk a general engagement.

The Americans lost two field-pieces, which could not be brought off, all the horses belonging to them being killed. Captain Savage did great execution with a third field-piece under his command, situated in such a manner as to rake, with grape-shot, a solid column of the enemy on their march, with which he cut lanes through them, and repeatedly drove them back with the utmost confusion. The riflemen and light-infantry were of great service, and gave the British some well-directed and very heavy fires. The whole of the American troops which were engaged that day, did not amount to more than eleven hundred. Wayne's division lost one hundred and seven privates and non-commissioned officers, killed, wounded, and missing, and twelve commissioned officers, among the last, Captain Stakes, wounded in the leg, and Captain Cunningham, in the foot, both slightly. The Americans suffered no loss of any consequence, except in General Wayne's division.

The British, immediately after the action, which ended about nine o'clock in the evening, crossed James River. The whole army were crossed over in the morning, excepting a part of their light-horse, for which they had boats ready to bring them over instantly, in case of an emergency. Saturday afternoon, or evening, they crossed also.

Those of the wounded Americans who were left on the field, to the number of about twenty-five, were treated by the British with more humanity than usual, and were left behind.

Cornwallis, finding among the killed and wounded none but the Pennsylvania line, and from that circumstance, and the information of his prisoners, having learned that only that line, with a few riflemen and light-infantry, had been in the action, found greater cause of chagrin that such a handful of men should have made so spirited an attack upon his army, than of exultation for having repulsed them.

It is said a part of the British troops are embarking for New York, that a garrison will be left at Portsmouth, and the rest probably go to the southward. The marquis is moving up James River.

Letter from a soldier dated Holt's Forge, Kent County, July 11
New-Jersey Gazette, August 8

July 26

VIRGINIA   Lord Cornwallis has returned over James River to Portsmouth, Virginia, having detached all his cavalry to Carolina. Most disgracefully has he finished a plundering excursion into the heart of Virginia. It is now clear that all ideas of conquest are ended with his lordship. To the immortal honor of Virginia, scarcely a citizen of that state joined the enemy; they abandoned and lost all, sooner than take refuge under the standards of the British.

New-Jersey Gazette, August 15

AUGUST

August 1

NEW YORK   An American, now confined on board the *Jersey* (vulgarly called Hell) prison-ship at New York says:—
"There is nothing but death or entering into the British service for me. Our ship company is reduced to a small number (by death and entering into the British service) of nineteen. There is a partial cartel arrived which brought eleven prisoners, and the names of so many as make up that number, sent from Boston by somebody. Damn the villain that trades that way, though there are many such that are making widows and fatherless children—a curse on them all! The commissary told us one and all, to the number of four hundred men, that the whole fault lays on Boston, and we might all be exchanged, but they never cared about us; and he said the commissaries were rogues and liars.

"I am not able to give you even the outlines of my exile; but thus much will I inform you, that we bury from six to eleven men in a day; we have two hundred more sick and falling sick every day; the sickness is the yellow fever, small-pox, and in short every thing else that can be mentioned. I had almost forgot to tell you, that our morning's salutation is, 'Rebels, turn out your dead!' "

Pennsylvania Packet, September 4

August 17

NORTH CAROLINA   A correspondent at Salisbury, in North Carolina, thus refers to the commander of the southern army:—"Future ages will celebrate the name of that illustrious hero, who, by his activity and superior military talents, has, for more than eight months past, so often baffled the British, always superior in numbers and every thing else except valor and military talents. The Carolinas will never forget General Greene, and the North State in particular will always acknowledge that it is to his abilities and perseverance we owe our present promising condition. He has inspired our people with a spirit and confidence that rises greatly above every opposition and distress. Our civil government has now acquired a better tone.

"Major Burnet and Colonel Morris, two of the general's aids-de-camp, have gone to the northward, I presume on business of great importance; those two young gentlemen are an honor to their profession, and their names ought never to be forgotten. Indeed, all that little army have done and suffered more in the defence of their country than can be expressed."

New-Jersey Journal, September 19

August 24

In the present unsettled state of things in America, when the British are in possession of a part of the southern states, and when men's minds are distracted between a love of property, and that attention which should ever be paid to the solemn agreements entered into by them at the commencement of the war, it may not be amiss to throw the following remarks respecting our situation, upon paper, convinced that it is not the case with us, (as we believe it to be with the people of England,) that we are unable to bear full liberty. In a republic where its powers are well poised, liberty may be better preserved, than by any monarchial government we know of, whatever forms may exist in imagination. Those who have already enjoyed, in any degree, the benefits of this establishment, will not, we presume, easily give it up, and run infinite hazards in endeavoring to obtain one a little better, even if they have the prospect of attaining it.

The American government is a good one, and must be much better as soon as we have expelled the British from it, and buried in oblivion those prejudices which have done infinitely more harm than any thing else. From our unhappy divisions, our enemies have derived more benefit than they have ever done from the success of their arms; they have taken the advantage of our internal contentions, and endeavored to crush us in this moment of adversity. These unfortunate dissensions have contributed upon every occasion to deprive us of that strength which is ever the attendant of national union. It is ridiculous to suppose that we can ever entertain the same affection for the people of Great Britain we formerly did, or even to expect the renewal of those blessings we enjoyed under that government, previous to the Stamp Act. While their manners remained entire, they corrected the vice of their laws and softened them to their own temper, but in all their late proceedings we see very few traces of that generosity, humanity, and dignity, which formerly characterized them. War seems to have suspended all the rules of moral obligation; civil wars strike deeply into the manners of the people, vitiate their politics, corrupt their morals, and even pervert the natural taste and relish of equity and justice; the very names of affection and kindred, which were the bond of union while we agreed, are now become incentives to rage and hatred.

It is too late to flatter ourselves that we shall not fall into this misfortune. Experience has convinced us that we are not exempt from the ordinary frailties of our nature, and that we have nothing to hope for but from *perseverance*, that pillar of fire, which can alone conduct us to the promised land.

The affairs of Britain are certainly at this time in a most distressing situation; at war with France, Spain, Holland, and America. She seems tamely to acquiesce in the loss of her East and West India possessions, in the destruction of her commerce, and in the diminution of her credit, merely to cherish the delusive idea of reducing America; but after all her exertions, she must be convinced it is now wholly impossible that America can ever be conquered. Not a single district throughout our extensive continent has yet voluntarily submitted. Even in Carolina and Georgia (where from the loss of the army in Charleston, they had the fairest opportunities) they now only occupy the spot they encamp on, and no more. Wherever they move they spread devastation and horror, and their perfidy and cruelties invariably tend to unite the people more firmly in their opposition.

At a time when we are insulted by enemies, long accustomed to conquer, when some of our governments are not so well established as we could wish, and their existence endangered, it is too late to inquire minutely into the causes which have brought us into this situation. The conjuncture calls for the immediate exertion of whatever wisdom or vigor is left among us, and the man who withholds his assistance, on any pretence, is an enemy to his country. It is a common cause, in which every one is concerned, and in which all should be engaged; the blunders of the ruling powers should be overlooked, and the gratification of personal animosities should give way to the public good of the community. At such a crisis, to arouse the drooping spirit of the people, to encourage the timid, to revive the desponding, and to animate the brave, is the duty of every friend to his country; for by vigorously resenting the injuries, and avenging the insults we have received, we lay the most solid foundation of peace, independence, and safety.

"A Carolina Planter," Pennsylvania Packet, August 28

VIRGINIA   The last division of the Portsmouth garrison arrived last evening at Yorktown, in Virginia. Gloucester Point is strongly fortified, where Colonel Dundas commands, having with him the 80th regiment, that of the Hessian Prince Hereditaire, and Colonel Simcoe's. The rest of the army are encamped immediately in front of the town. At eight o'clock last night all the light infantry and the legion, marched towards Williamsburgh. It is conjectured they have fallen in with a certain Lieutenant-Colonel Innes before this, who commands the advance corps of the Marquis de Lafayette's people. He has been very busy of late in collecting vast numbers of cattle for the American army, and it is not improbable that the Colonels Abercrombie and Tarleton before sunset may release a tolerable portion of them, if they can only overtake that body of freebooters. The marquis's main body is about twenty miles from Williamsburgh; a party of four hundred of them have been routed, about twenty killed, and as many made prisoners by Colonel Tarleton.

Letter from an officer, Yorktown, Virginia, August 24
Rivington's Gazette, September 1

August 26

SOUTH CAROLINA   Colonel Isaac Hayne was, by a mandate of Balfour's, ignominiously hanged in Charleston, South Carolina, on the fourth instant. After the execution, his young son was permitted to carry his father's body and inter it at his plantation at Ponper, which was done on Sunday evening last, (19th.) Colonel Hayne was a most amiable character, highly respected, and had a most extensive influence. Nothing could strike deeper at the root of independence than this measure, if suffered to pass without retaliation; General Greene therefore has stopped all further exchanges, avowed his intention of retaliation, and issued a proclamation, setting forth his reasons, let them lead to what consequences they may. Our countrymen breathe nothing but revenge on this cruel occasion; it will now unite them stronger than ever, in prosecuting the war with the greatest vigor and spite. Could the diabolical Balfour fall into our hands to suffer the same ignominious death, it would be but a small recompense for the loss of our worthy countryman; but he keeps close in his strongholds in Charleston.

New-Jersey Gazette, September 26 and October 10

August 29

SOUTH CAROLINA   A correspondent at Camden, in South Carolina, says:—"Every officer in the line of the south-

ern army, that was present, has addressed General Greene on
the late execution of Colonel Hayne, praying that the *lex
talionis* shall follow. In consequence of which the general
has issued his proclamation to that purpose, and by a flag
sent to the commandant of Charleston, has forwarded him
copies of the address and proclamation, which sets forth:
'That retaliation shall immediately take place, not on the
Tory militia officers, but it shall fall on the heads of regular
British officers.' This will now open a new scene of bloodshed, which in the end the British will have reason sorely to
repent. We have three British officers with us prisoners, who
are quaking with fear, on the result of this proclamation, but
they are not of sufficient rank to become objects; they tell us
that Colonel Balfour was very averse to the measures taken
against Colonel Hayne, and throw all the blame on Lord
Rawdon and Colonel Gould. However, this gains little credit
here, as the character of the commandant for his cruelty,
persecution, and hypocrisy is so well established, that we are
certain that he would not have foregone the great pleasure of
giving his fiat to the execution of an American for the universe, as this cruel piece of baseness will the more endear him
to his sovereign."

The following is General Greene's proclamation:—A PROC-
LAMATION.—Whereas on the fourth day of the present month,
Colonel Isaac Hayne, commanding a regiment of militia in
the service of the United States, was captured by a party of
British troops, and after a rigorous confinement in the provost
of Charleston, most cruelly and unjustifiably condemned and
executed, in open violation of the cartel agreed upon between
the commanders of the two armies for the relief and exchange of prisoners of war.

And whereas, it is no less the duty than the inclination of
the army to resent every violence offered to the good citizens
of America, and disclaim those distinctions set up for dis-
criminating between different orders of men found in arms,
in support of the independence of the United States, and as
these violences are intended to deter the good people from
acting agreeably to their political interest and private inclination, and as the mode of trial and punishment which follows

these discriminations are no less opposite to the spirit of the British constitution, than they are an unwarrantable attack upon the laws of humanity, and the rights of free citizens of these United States; I have therefore thought fit to issue this my proclamation, expressly declaring it to be my intention to retaliate for all such inhuman insults, as often as they may occur.

And whereas the enemy seem willing to expose a few deluded inhabitants who adhere to their interest, if they can but have the opportunity of sacrificing the many who appear in support of our cause; I do further declare it my intention to make BRITISH REGULAR OFFICERS, and not the deluded inhabitants who have joined their army, subjects of retaliation. But while I am determined to resent every insult that may be offered to the United States, for supporting their independence, I cannot but regret the necessity of appealing to measures so hurtful to the feelings of humanity, and so contrary to those liberal principles on which I would choose to carry on the war.

Given at head-quarters at Camden, the 26th day of August, 1781, and in the sixth year of American Independence.

NATHANAEL GREENE.

By the General's command,
  Will Pierce, Jr., Aid and Secretary.

New York Packet, October 4

August 31

PENNSYLVANIA   Yesterday, at one o'clock in the afternoon, his Excellency the Commander-in-Chief of the American armies, accompanied by the Generals Rochambeau and Chastellux, with their respective suites, arrived in Philadelphia. The general was received by the militia light horse in the suburbs, and escorted into the town. He stopped at the city tavern, and received the visits of several gentlemen; from thence he proceeded to the house of the Superintendent of Finance, where he now has his head-quarters. About three o'clock he went up to the State House, and paid his respects to Congress. He then returned to the superintendent's, where his Excellency the President of Congress, with the generals before mentioned, General Knox, General Moultrie, and several other gentlemen, had the pleasure of dining with him. After dinner, some vessels belonging to the port, and then lying in the stream, fired salutes to the different toasts which were drank. In the evening the city was illuminated, and his Excellency walked through some of the principal streets, attended by a numerous concourse of people, eagerly pressing to see their beloved general.

> *Pennsylvania Packet, September 1*
> *New York Gazette and Weekly Mercury, September 10*
> *Thacher's Military Journal, p. 326*

SEPTEMBER

September 5

This day an engagement between the British fleet, under Admiral Graves, and the French, commanded by de Grasse, took place off the Chesapeake. The first certain notice Admiral Graves received of the French fleet being actually upon the coast, was from the advanced ships of his fleet, this morning, when the French were seen at an anchor, extending from Cape Henry to the centre of the middle ground, (a shoal so called, which confines the entrance into the Chesapeake,) apparently in three divisions.

As the British fleet advanced with a fair wind, the French got their ships under sail, and extending themselves in a line of battle ahead, stretched out to seaward. The British ran down upon an east and west line, with the wind at N.N.E., formed, and put themselves into order and preparation for battle. As they advanced toward the shoal of the middle, they were prepared to veer by signal, the whole fleet together, to bring them upon the same tack with the French, who were all this time forming the line as they advanced to sea.

The moment it was no longer safe for the British van to

advance further, on account of the shoal, the fleet wore together, and came to the same tack with the French, and formed a line ahead nearly parallel with them, with their main top-sails square, to let the French van-guard advance until the British could operate to advantage.

The French came forward slowly, and showed twenty-four large ships of their line of battle. The British formed nineteen in theirs.

The French van had extended themselves considerably too much from their own centre, and seemed to present the favorable moment for attack, while the British line had been continually pressed down to approach them as near as possible; and the moment the French van betrayed their apprehension of our design by bearing away, the signal for a close action was made, and the signal for the line was taken down, that nothing might cross the opportunity.

Rear-Admiral Drake's division composed the van of the British line; Rear-Admiral Sir Samuel Hood, Bart., that of the rear.

The action began at a quarter after four, about the fourth or fifth ship, and in a few minutes extended from the van to the second ship astern of the centre. In the van the fight was very close and sharp for some time, and continued so until the French ships put before the wind to prevent being cut up. Their centre and rear then pushed forward and kept much from the wind as they approached the British centre, appearing to have little more in view than to advance far enough to receive their own van, who were nearly before the wind, and the better to effect this purpose, they constantly declined close action with the centre of the British fleet.

Every necessary signal was made to urge a close as well as general action, which Count de Grasse appeared desirous to decline, and he did not permit the British rear to close with him, which prevented that part of the fleet from having any share of the action.

All firing ceased on both sides soon after sunset. About ten o'clock it was made known to the British admiral by two frigates, which had been sent throughout the line, that several of the ships of the van were not capable of keeping extended with the enemy, having suffered so much in their masts and rigging, they must attend to their security or be dismasted; that two of the ships which came very leaky from the West Indies, had aggravated their complaints, and one of them could only be kept free with all her pumps.

New York Gazette and Weekly Mercury, September 24

September 6

CONNECTICUT   This morning about daybreak, twenty-four sail of British shipping appeared to the westward of the harbor of New London, in Connecticut. By many they were supposed to be a plundering party, after stock. Alarm guns were immediately fired, but the discharge of cannon in the harbor has become so frequent of late, that they answered little or no purpose. A few of the inhabitants who were equipped, advanced towards the place where the enemy were thought likely to make their landing, and manœuvred on the heights adjacent, until the British, at about nine o'clock, landed in two divisions of about eight hundred men each, one of them at Brown's farm, near the light-house, the other at Groton Point. The division that landed near the light-house, marched up the road, keeping out large flanking parties, who were attacked in different places on their march by the inhabitants, who had spirit and resolution enough to oppose their progress; the main body proceeded to New London, and set fire to the stores on the beach, and immediately after to the dwelling-houses lying on the mill cove. The scattered fire of the little parties of Americans, unsupported by their neighbors more distant, galled them so that they soon began to retire, setting fire to stores and dwelling-houses promiscuously in their way; the fire from the stores communicated to the shipping that lay at the wharves; a number were burnt, others swung to singly and remained unhurt. At four o'clock they began to quit the town in great precipitation, and were pursued with the spirit and ardor of veterans and driven on board their boats. Five of the British were killed, and about twenty wounded; among the latter is a Hessian captain, who is a prisoner, as are seven others. The Americans lost four killed, and ten or twelve wounded, none mortally.

The most valuable part of New London is reduced to ashes, with all the stores. Fort Trumbull not being tenable on the land side, was evacuated as the British advanced, and the few men in it crossed the river to Fort Griswold on Groton Hill, which was soon after invested by the division that landed at the point. The fort having in it only about one hundred and twenty men, chiefly militia hastily collected, was defended with the greatest resolution and bravery, and the British were once repulsed; but the fort being out of repair, could not be defended by such a handful of men, though brave and determined, against so superior a number. They did all that men of spirit and bravery, in such a situation, could do; but after having a number of their party killed and wounded, they found that further resistance would be in vain, and resigned the fort. Immediately on their surrender, the valiant Colonel Ledyard, whose fate in a particular manner is much lamented, and seventy other officers and men, most of whom were heads of families, were murdered. The British lost a Major Montgomery, and forty-one officers and men in the attack; they were found buried near the fort; their wounded were carried off.

Soon after the British got possession of the fort, they set fire to and burnt a number of dwelling-houses and stores on Groton Bank, and embarked about sunset, taking with them sundry of the inhabitants of New London and Groton. A Colonel Eyre, who commanded the division at Groton, was wounded, and, it is said, died on board the fleet. About fifteen sail of vessels with effects of the inhabitants of New London, retreated up the river on the approach of the enemy, and were saved, while four others remained in the harbor untouched. The troops were commanded by that infamous traitor to his country, Benedict Arnold, who headed the division which marched into New London.

By this calamity, it is judged that more than one hundred families are deprived of their habitations, and most of them of their all. The neighborhood feels sensibly the loss of many deserving citizens, and though deceased, cannot but be highly indebted to them for their spirit and bravery in their exertions and manly opposition to the merciless enemies of our country in their last moments.

New-York Journal, September 24

September 7

VIRGINIA   A correspondent now in the camp of La-fayette's army in Virginia, says:—"Let me make you ac-quainted with Major-General the Marquis de St. Simon, and the French army; you have seen the British troops and the troops of other nations, but you have not seen troops so uni-versally well-made, so robust, or of such an appearance, as those General St. Simon has brought to our assistance. These are all under the command of our general. They now en-camp nearly on the ground the British occupied before they evacuated Jamestown. I do not pretend to know the secrets of our commander, or I would tell you what is to be done; I pretend, however, to see a great general in the Marquis de St. Simon, an affectionate politeness in his officers toward ours, and a general impatience in the French army to com-plete the Gordian knot, in which our second Fabius Fayette has been entangling his lordship; some of its cords already press him, and, I believe, if there were hopes of succeeding, he would attempt to cut it. But notwithstanding his lordship is, perhaps, the first officer in the British service, yet he may not be in possession of the sword of Alcides.

"The light infantry are advanced to Williamsburgh; the Pennsylvanians lay near us, and it is the talk of the camp that the French troops will take their position to-morrow in its vicinity. The French ships lay in James River, to prevent a retreat in York River, and at the capes. You are a soldier as well as a philosopher, and will experience our feelings on the present occasion. We have a brave army to contend against, furnished in provisions, with all the necessaries for a gallant resistance, and in number fully sufficient for the defence of their post; but we shall do very well, for to the common mo-tives of our profession will be joined an emulation arising from the fighting by the side of our allies.

"The British are intrenching at York with great industry.

Every thing is landed from their shipping, and dispositions made for their destruction. A *propos*, yesterday evening a patrol of nine or ten militia fell in with a patrol of Colonel Tarleton's legion, of an equal number, and commanded by a lieutenant, the whole of which the militia captured; it is a trifle, but it is a trifle that was very prettily done."

Pennsylvania Packet, September 18

September 9

SOUTH CAROLINA   General Greene has added another to the number of *rebel* victories. Yesterday morning at four o'clock, having been joined by the forces under General Marion, he made the following disposition of his army, and marched from the encampment at Burdell's plantation, to attack the British at Eutaw Springs. His front line was composed of four small battalions of militia, two of North and two of South Carolinians; one of the latter was under the immediate command of General Marion, and was posted on the right, who also commanded the front line; the two North Carolina battalions, under the command of Colonel Malmady, were posted in the centre, and the other South Carolina battalion, under the command of General Pickens, was posted on the left. The second line consisted of three small brigades of Continental troops, one from North Carolina, one from Virginia, and one from Maryland. The North Carolinians were formed into three battalions, under command of Lieutenant-Colonel Ash, Majors Armstrong and Blount, the whole commanded by General Sumner, and were posted on the right. The Virginians consisted of two battalions, commanded by Major Snead and Captain Edmonds, and the whole by Lieutenant-Colonel Campbell, and were posted in the centre. The Marylanders also consisted of two battalions, commanded by Lieutenant-Colonel Howard and Major Hardman, and the brigade by Colonel Williams, deputy adjutant-general to the army, and were posted upon the left. Lieutenant-Colonel Lee, with his legion, covered the right flank, and Lieutenant-Colonel Henderson, with the state troops, commanded by Lieutenant-Colonels Hampton, Middleton, and Polk, the left. Lieutenant-Colonel Washington, with his horse, and the Delaware troops under Captain Kirkwood, formed a *corps de reserve*. Two three-pounders, under Lieutenant Gaines, advanced with the front line, and two sixes under Captain Brown with the second. The legion and state troops formed the advance, and were to retire upon the flanks upon the British forming.

In this order the Americans moved on to the attack. The legion and state troops fell in with a party of British horse and foot, about four miles from their camp, who, mistaking the Americans for a party of militia, charged them briskly, but were soon convinced of their mistake by the reception they met with. The infantry of the state troops kept up a heavy fire, and the legion in front, under Captain Rudolph, charged them with fixed bayonets, when they fled on all sides, leaving four or five dead on the ground, and several more wounded. As this was supposed to be the advance of the British army, the front line of the Americans was ordered to form and move on briskly in line, the legion and state troops to take their position upon the flanks. All the country is covered with timber, from the place where the action began to the Eutaw Springs. The firing began again between two and three miles from the British camp. The militia were ordered to keep advancing as they fired. The British advanced parties were soon driven in, and a most tremendous fire began on both sides, from right to left, when the legion and state troops were closely engaged. General Marion, Colonel Malmady, and General Pickens, conducted the troops with great gallantry and good conduct, and the militia fought with a degree of spirit and firmness that reflects the highest honor on that class of soldiers. But the enemy's fire being greatly superior to the Americans', and continuing to advance, the militia began to give ground. The North Carolina brigade, under General Sumner, was then ordered up to their support. These were all new levies, and had been under discipline little more than a month; notwithstanding which, they fought with a degree of obstinacy that would do honor to the best of veterans, and it was hard to tell which to admire most, the gallantry of the officers, or the bravery of the troops. They

kept up a heavy and well-directed fire, and the enemy returned it with equal spirit, for they really fought worthy of a
better cause, and great execution was done on both sides. In
this stage of the action, the Virginians, under Lieutenant-
Colonel Campbell, and the Maryland troops under Colonel
Williams, were led on to a brisk charge with trailed arms,
through a heavy cannonade and a shower of musket balls.
Nothing could exceed the gallantry and firmness of both officers and soldiers upon this occasion; they preserved their order, and pushed on with such unshaken resolution, that they
bore all down before them. The British were routed in all
quarters. Lieutenant-Colonel Lee had, with great address,
gallantry, and good conduct, turned their left flank, and was
charging them in rear at the same time the Virginians and
Maryland troops were charging them in front. A most valuable officer, Lieutenant-Colonel Henderson, was wounded
early in the action, and Lieutenant-Colonel Hampton, who
commanded the state cavalry, and who, fortunately, succeeded Lieutenant-Colonel Henderson in the command,
charged a party of the enemy, and took upwards of one hundred prisoners.

Lieutenant-Colonel Washington brought up the *corps de
reserve* upon the left, where the British seemed disposed to
make further resistance, and charged them so briskly with the
cavalry and Captain Kirkwood's infantry, as gave them no
time to rally or form. Lieutenant-Colonels Polk and Middleton, who commanded the state infantry, were no less conspicuous for their good conduct than their intrepidity; and the
troops under their command gave specimens of what may be
expected from men naturally brave, when improved by proper
discipline. Captain-Lieutenant Gaines, who commanded the
three-pounders with the front line, did great execution till
his pieces were dismounted.

The Americans kept close at the enemy's heels after they
broke, until they got into their camp, and a great number of
prisoners were continually falling into their hands, while some
hundreds of the fugitives ran off towards Charleston. But a
party threw themselves into a three-story brick house which
stands near the Spring, others took post in a picketed garden,

and in the impenetrable shrubs, and the rear also being secured by the Springs and deep hollow-ways, the British renewed the action.

Every exertion was made to dislodge them. Lieutenant-Colonel Washington made most astonishing efforts to get through the thicket to charge them in the rear, but found it impracticable, had his horse shot under him, and was wounded and taken prisoner.

Four six-pounders were ordered up before the house, two of the Americans' and two of the enemy's which they had abandoned, and they were pushed on so much under the command of the fire from the house, and the party in the thickets, as rendered it impracticable to bring them off again when the troops were ordered to retire. Never were pieces better served; most of the men and officers were either killed or wounded.

Washington failing in his charge upon the left, and the legion baffled in an attempt upon the right, finding the infantry galled by the fire of the British, and the ammunition mostly consumed, though officers and men continued to exhibit uncommon acts of heroism, General Greene thought proper to retire out of the fire of the house, and draw up the troops at a little distance from the woods, not thinking it advisable to push his advantages further, being persuaded the enemy could not hold the post many hours, and that his chance to attack them on the retreat was better than a second attempt to dislodge them, which, if he succeeded, must be attended with considerable loss.

After collecting all the wounded, except such as were under the command of the fire of the house, the Americans retired to the ground from which they marched in the morning, there being no water nearer, and the troops ready to faint with the heat and want of refreshment, the action having continued near four hours. A strong picket was left on the field of action, and early this morning, General Greene detached General Marion and Lieutenant-Colonel Lee, with the legion horse between Eutaw and Charleston, to prevent any reinforcements from coming to the relief of the British, to retard their march should they attempt to retire, and give time for the army to fall upon their rear, and put a finishing stroke to the work. The Americans left two pieces of artillery in the hands of the enemy, and brought off one of theirs.

General Greene thinks himself principally indebted for this victory to the free use of the bayonet made by the Virginians and Marylanders, the infantry of the legion, and Captain Kirkwood's light infantry; and though few armies ever exhibited equal bravery with the Americans in general, yet the conduct and intrepidity of these corps were peculiarly conspicuous. Lieutenant-Colonel Campbell fell as he was leading his troops to the charge, and though he fell with distinguished marks of honor, yet his loss is much to be regretted. He was the great soldier and the firm patriot.

The American loss in officers is considerably more from their value than their number, for never did either men or officers offer their blood more willingly in the service of their country. "I cannot help acknowledging my obligations to Colonel Williams," says General Greene, "for his great activity on this and many other occasions, in forming the army, and for his uncommon intrepidity in leading on the Maryland troops to the charge, which exceeded any thing I ever saw. I also feel myself greatly indebted to Captains Pierce and Pendleton, Major Hyrne, and Captain Shubrick, my aide-de-camp, for their activity and good conduct throughout the whole of the action."

Letter from General Greene to the President of Congress
New-Jersey Gazette, October 24
Carver, 140

September 27

VIRGINIA The American army and their allies, near Williamsburg, in Virginia, formed the line of battle to-day. To-morrow morning they expect to march to a position near York, to commence a siege. They make a brilliant appearance as to numbers, and are fifteen thousand strong, not including the Virginia militia. General Wayne was wounded in the thigh the 2d instant, by a sentinel, who conceived him to be an enemy, but has since recovered.

We congratulate our friends upon the prospect of reducing his lordship, and restoring peace and liberty to our country.

Letter from camp
New York Gazette and Weekly Mercury, October 22

OCTOBER

October 1

VIRGINIA   A gentleman who left the American army in Virginia, on the afternoon of the 30th of September, gives the following account of transactions in that quarter:—"On Friday, September 28th, the whole army marched from Williamsburg to within one mile of the enemy's works at York, and formed the first line of circumvallation without any loss. On the 29th the Americans had a few skirmishes with the enemy, but little damage done on either side. In the night the British evacuated Pigeon Quarter, and three other redoubts, which are so high as to be able to command the town. These were taken possession of on Sunday morning at sunrise, under a heavy cannonade from Yorktown. The enemy next fled from a stockade, when the French grenadiers had advanced within fifteen yards of it, and retreated under cover of their shipping with the loss of ten taken prisoners. It was expected our troops would break ground on the 1st instant. Cornwallis's forces in York are supposed to be six thousand troops, including refugees, besides one thousand armed Negroes. He has possession of the river and Gloucester, strongly fortified and garrisoned by about one thousand men. These are hemmed in by General Weedon with fifteen hundred men, the Duke de Lauzun with his legion, and two thousand mariners from the fleet to prevent any escape that way. One ship of forty-four guns, two frigates, and a twenty-gun packet lie at Burwell's Landing, in James River; one of fifty, one of forty, two frigates and a storeship in the mouth of that river; five ships of the line off Cape Henry; thirty-two ships of the

Yours most truly

Cornwallis

line and several frigates are drawn up across the mouth of York River, and three ships of considerable force are in that river below the town, which were to proceed onward with the first fair wind. General Washington sent in a flag to Lord Cornwallis, directing him not to destroy his shipping or war-like stores, as he would answer it at his peril. The easy capture of the outposts will greatly accelerate the future operations of our army. Lieutenant-Colonel John Conolly was taken near Yorktown, by two militia men, and is paroled to Hanover in Virginia."

Pennsylvania Packet, October 9

October 9

VIRGINIA   The British in Yorktown and Gloucester, in Virginia, are now completely invested by land and water. The allied army, under his Excellency General Washington's command, commenced operations against the enemy in those towns, on Thursday, the 27th ultimo, and we are assured that the French and American batteries were playing successfully against the enemy, on that and the three following days.

New York Gazette and Weekly Mercury, October 22

October 19

VIRGINIA   Be it remembered, that on the seventeenth of October, 1781, Lieutenant-General Earl Cornwallis, with above five thousand British troops, surrendered prisoners of war to his Excellency General George Washington, Commander-in-chief of the allied forces of France and America! *Laus Deo!*

New York Packet, October 25

VIRGINIA   Yesterday commissioners were appointed to adjust the etiquette of the capitulation; the Viscount de Noailles, and Lieutenant-Colonel Laurens, aide-de-camp to the Commander-in-chief, on the part of the allied army, and Colonel Dundas and Major Ross, aide-de-camp to Lord Cornwallis, on that of the enemy. To-day, about one o'clock, the articles of capitulation were signed and interchanged, and about two o'clock, P.M., the British garrison of York, led on by General O'Hara, (Lord Cornwallis being *indisposed*,) were conducted by General Lincoln through the combined army, drawn up in two lines to a field, where, having grounded their arms, and stripped off their accoutrements, they were reconducted through the lines, and committed to the care of a guard. At the same time and in the same manner the garrison of Gloucester was surrendered to the command of the Duke de Lauzun. Previous to this, a detachment of French, and one of American troops, took possession of the British horn works, and planted on the epaulements the standards of the two nations. The brilliant appearance of the allied army, the joy which diffused itself from rank to rank, contrasted with the mortification, the despondence, and unsoldiery behavior of the British troops, formed one of the most pleasing prospects a patriot can behold, or even his fancy depict.

In justice to the brave, the unfortunate garrison of Charleston, the terms imposed on them were made the basis of the present capitulation, and on the worthy General Lincoln was conferred the supreme delight of giving laws to those men, who had treated him with the insolence of conquerors. The garrisons are prisoners of war, to be disposed of in America at our option, to march out with cased colors, and to play no French or American tune. All plundered property to be restored to its owners; private baggage secured to the officers, and private property to the British merchants and traders, the continent having the right of pre-emption.

No returns have been handed in, but from the accounts of the British officers, there are between five and six thousand prisoners, including sick and wounded. Their military stores are trifling; their commissary stores do not exceed six hundred barrels of pork, and about one thousand barrels of bread and flour. Near one hundred vessels, with their sailors and marines, have fallen into the hands of the French fleet under the capitulation. The British loss during the siege, they allow to be very considerable; the loss of the allied army does not exceed three hundred killed and wounded, a small portion of whom are officers.

Never was a plan more wisely concerted, or more happily and vigorously executed, than the present. The wisdom, perseverance, and military talents of our illustrious commander, shone with superior lustre on this occasion, and if possible, must increase the love and veneration of his countrymen. The well-concerted and animated support of the Count de Grasse, was essentially conducive to the completion of this glorious event, and deserves the warmest thanks of his own country, and the grateful plaudits of every American.

The exertions of the Count de Rochambeau, and all the officers and soldiers of the French army, can never be excelled, and only equalled by their American friends, who glowed with the laudable ambition of imitating the achievement of the finest body of men in the world. The only contention which subsisted during the siege between the troops of the two nations, was the glorious one of excelling each other in operations against the common enemy, and in doing justice to each others' merits. An army, thus cemented by affection, created by a union of interests and the intercourse of good offices, and animated by an attachment to the rights of mankind, could not fail of triumphing over a body of troops, enlisted under the banners of despotism, and led on by the hopes of plunder; who, made insolent by partial victories, gave loose to the greatest licentiousness and brutality that ever disgraced a disciplined corps. The expiring groans of thousands, who in vain begged Cornwallis for protection, and whom he inhumanly starved, have ascended to the throne of Almighty justice, and must bring down vengeance on his guilty head. It is sincerely to be wished, for the sake of humanity, that his lordship had made a more obstinate defence, that the allied army, obliged to storm his works, might have offered up him and his troops as a sacrifice to the violated rights of humanity!

New-York Journal, November 12

Lord Cornwallis's Surrender

The debacle at Yorktown produced a number of triumphal odes, of which the one reproduced here is perhaps the most impressive; it gives a vivid picture of the scene and captures the mood of American elation. The melody to which the lyric was set made the British humiliation more complete: it was "The British Grenadier," one of the proudest marching songs of the British Army. (Ford, Isaiah Thomas, 150.)

Come all you brave A - mer - i - cans, The__ truth to you__ I'll__ tell, 'Tis of a sad mis - for - - tune, To__ Brit - ain late__ be - fell, 'Twas all in the heights of York -- town, Where can - nons loud__ did__ roar,_____ They sum - moned Lord Corn - wal - lis To__ fight or else__ give__ o'er.

The summons then to be served,
    Was sent unto my Lord,
Which made him feel like poor Burgoyne,
    And quickly draw his sword,
Say, must I give these glitt'ring troops,
    These ships and Hessians too,
And yield to Gen'ral Washington,
    And his bold rebel crew?

A grand council then was called,
  His Lordship gave command,
Say, what think you now my heroes,
  To yield you may depend—
For don't you see the bomb shells fly,
  And cannons loud do roar,
Count de'Grasse lies in the harbour,
  And Washington's on shore.

'Twas the nineteenth of October,
  In the year eighty-one,
Lord Cornwallis he surrender'd
  To General Washington:
They marched from their posts brave boys,
  And quickly grounded arms,
Rejoice, ye brave Americans,
  With music's sweetest charms.

Six thousand chosen British troops,
  To Washington resign'd,
Besides some ships and Hessians,
  That could not stay behind;
With refugees and blackamores;
  O what a direful crew!
It was then he had some thousands,
  But now he's got but few.

My Lord has gone unto New York,
  Sir Harry for to see;
For to send home this dreadful news
  Unto his Majesty;
To contradict some former lines,
  That once to him was sent,
That he and his bold British troops,
  They conquer'd where they went.

Here's a health to great Washington,
  And his brave army too,
And likewise to our worthy Green,
  To him much honour's due.
May we subdue those English troops,
  And clear the eastern shore,
That we may live in peace my boys,
  Whilst wars they are no more.

LORD CORNWALLIS'S SURRENDER.

COME all you brave Americans,
   The truth to you I'll tell,
It is of a sad misfortune,
   To Britain late befell,
'Twas all in the heights of York-town,
   Where cannons loud did roar,
They summoned Lord Cornwallis
   To fight or else give o'er.

The summons then to be served,
   Was sent unto my Lord,
Which made him feel like poor Burgoyne,
   And quickly draw his sword,
Say, must I give these glitt'ring troops,
   These ships and Hessians too,
And yield to Gen'ral Washington,
   And his bold rebel crew?

A grand council then was called,
   His Lordship gave command,
Say, what think you now my heroes,
   To yield you may depend—
For don't you see the bomb-shells fly,
   And cannons loud do roar,
Count de'Grasse lies in the harbour,
   And Washington's on shore,

'Twas the ninteenth of October,
   In the year eighty-one,
Lord Cornwallis he surrender'd
   To General Washington:
They marched from their posts brave boys,
   And quickly grounded arms,
Rejoice, ye brave Americans,
   With music's sweetest charms.

Six thousand chosen British troops,
   To Washington resign'd,
Besides some ships and Hessians,
   That could not stay behind;
With refugees and blackamores;
   O what a direful crew!

It was then he had some thousands,
   But now he's got but few.
My Lord has gone unto New-York,
   Sir Harry for to see;
For to send home this dreadful news
   Unto his Majesty;
To contradict some former lines,
   That once to him was sent,
That he and his bold British troops,
   They conquer'd where they went.

Here's a health to great Washington,
   And his brave army too,
And likewise to our worthy Green,
   To him much honour's due.
May we subdue those English troops,
   And clear the eastern shore,
That we may live in peace my boys,
   Whilst wars they are no more.

The Sailor Boy.

THE sea was calm, the sky serene,
   And gently blew the eastern gale;
When Anna seated on a rock,
   Watch'd the Lovina's lessning sail.
To heaven she thus her prayer address'd—
   Thou who can'st save, or can'st destroy,
From each surrounding danger guard,
   My much lov'd little sailor boy.

When tempests o'er the ocean howl,
   And even sailors shrink with dread,
Be some protecting angel near,
   To hover round my William's head:
He was belov'd by all the plain,
   His father's pride, his mother's joy,
Then safely to their arms restore
   Their much lov'd little sailor boy.

October 20

VIRGINIA　　This morning, Cornwallis, in a letter to Sir Henry Clinton, gives the following account of the siege, which terminated yesterday in his surrender to the allied forces of France and America:—"I never saw Yorktown in any favorable light, but when I found I was to be attacked in it in so unprepared a state, by so powerful an army and artillery, nothing but the hopes of relief would have induced me to attempt its defence, for I would either have endeavored to escape to New York, by rapid marches from the Gloucester side, immediately on the arrival of General Washington's troops at Williamsburg, or I would, notwithstanding the disparity of numbers, have attacked them in the open field, where it might have been just possible that fortune would have favored the gallantry of the handful of troops under my command. But being assured by your Excellency's letters, that every possible means would be tried by the navy and army to relieve us, I could not think myself at liberty to venture on either of those desperate attempts. Therefore, after remaining two days in a strong position in front of this place, in hopes of being attacked, upon observing that the enemy were taking measures which could not fail of turning my left flank in a short time, and receiving on the second evening your letter of the 24th of September, informing me that the relief would sail about the 5th of October, I withdrew within the works on the night of the 29th of September, hoping, by the labor and firmness of the soldiers, to protract the defence until you could arrive. Every thing was to be expected from the spirit of the troops, but every disadvantage attended their labors, as the works were to be continued under the enemy's fire, and our stock of intrenching tools, which did not much exceed four hundred when we began to work in the latter end of August, was now much diminished.

"The enemy broke ground on the 30th, and constructed on that night, and the two following days and nights, two redoubts, which, with some works that had belonged to our outward position, occupied a gorge between two creeks or ravines, which come from the river on each side of the town. On the night of the 6th of October they made their first parallel, extending from its right on the river to a deep ravine on the left, nearly opposite to the centre of this place, and embracing our whole left, at the distance of six hundred yards. Having perfected this parallel, their batteries opened on the evening of the 9th against our left, and other batteries fired at the same time against a redoubt advanced over the creek upon our left, and defended by about one hundred and twenty men of the 23d regiment, and marines, who maintained that post with uncommon gallantry. The fire continued incessant from heavy cannon, and from mortars and howitzers, throwing shells from eight to sixteen inches, until our guns on the left were silenced, our works much damaged, and our loss of men considerable. On the night of the 11th they began their second parallel, about three hundred yards nearer to us. The troops being much weakened by sickness, as well as by the fire of the besiegers, and observing that the enemy had not only secured their flanks, but were proceeding in every respect with the utmost regularity and caution, I could not venture so large sorties as to hope from them any considerable effect, but otherwise I did every thing in my power to interrupt their work, by opening new embrazures for guns, and keeping a constant fire with all the howitzers and small mortars that we could man.

"On the evening of the 14th they assaulted and carried two redoubts, that had been advanced about three hundred yards, for the purpose of delaying their approaches, and covering our left flank, and during the night included them in their second parallel, on which they continued to work with the utmost exertion. Being perfectly sensible that our works could not stand many hours after the opening of the batteries of that parallel, we not only continued a constant fire with all our mortars, and every gun that could be brought to bear upon it, but a little before daybreak in the morning of the 16th, I ordered a sortie of about three hundred and fifty men, under the direction of Lieutenant-Colonel Abercrombie, to attack two batteries which appeared to be in the greatest forwardness, and to spike the guns; a detachment of guards, with the

8oth company of grenadiers, under the command of Lieutenant-Colonel Lake, attacked the one, and one of light infantry
under the command of Major Armstrong attacked the other,
and both succeeded in forcing the redoubts that covered them,
spiking eleven guns, and killing or wounding about one
hundred of the French troops, who had the guard of that
part of the trenches, and with little loss on our side.

"This action, though extremely honorable to the officers
and soldiers who executed it, proved of little public advantage,
for the cannon having been spiked in a hurry, were soon
rendered fit for service again, and before dark the whole
parallel and batteries appeared to be nearly complete.

"At this time we knew that there was no part of the whole
front attacked in which we could show a single gun, and our
shells were nearly expended; I had therefore only to choose
between preparing to surrender next day, or endeavoring to
get off with the greatest part of the troops, and I determined
to attempt the latter, reflecting that though it should prove
unsuccessful in its object, it might at least delay the enemy in
the prosecution of further enterprises. Sixteen large boats
were prepared, and upon other pretexts were ordered to be in
readiness to receive troops precisely at ten o'clock; with those
I hoped to pass the infantry during the night, abandoning our
baggage, and leaving a detachment to capitulate for the
town's people, and for the sick and wounded, on which subject a letter was ready to be delivered to General Washington.
After making my arrangements with the utmost secrecy, the
light infantry, the greatest part of the guards, and part of the
23d regiment, embarked at the hour appointed, and most of
them landed at Gloucester, but at the critical moment, the
weather from being moderate and calm, changed to a most
violent storm of wind and rain, and drove all the boats, some
of which had troops on board, down the river.

"It was soon evident that the intended passage was impracticable, and the absence of the boats rendered it equally
impossible to bring back the troops that had passed, which I
had ordered about two o'clock in the morning. In this situation, with my little force divided, the enemy's batteries
opened at daybreak. The passage between this place and

Gloucester was much exposed, but the boats having now returned, they were ordered to bring back the troops that had passed during the night, and they joined us in the forenoon without much loss. Our works in the mean time were going to ruin, and not having been able to strengthen them by abatis, nor in any other manner than by a slight friezing, which the enemy's artillery were demolishing whenever they fired, my opinion entirely coincided with that of the engineer and the principal officers of the army, that they were in many places very assailable in the forenoon, and that by the continuance of the same fire for a few hours longer, they would be in such a state as to render it desperate with our numbers to maintain them. We at that time could not fire a single gun, only one eight-inch, and little more than one hundred cohorn-shells remained; a diversion by the French ships of war that lay at the mouth of York River was to be expected, our numbers had been diminished by the enemy's fire, but particularly by sickness, and the strength and spirits of those in the works were much exhausted by the fatigue of constant watching and unremitting duty.

"Under all these circumstances I thought it would have been wanton and inhuman to the last degree, to sacrifice the lives of this small body of gallant soldiers who had ever behaved with so much fidelity and courage, by exposing them to an assault, which, from the numbers and precautions of the enemy, could not fail to succeed. I therefore proposed to capitulate.

"I sincerely lament that better terms of capitulation could not be obtained, but I have neglected nothing to alleviate the misfortunes and distress of both officers and soldiers. The men are well clothed, and provided with necessaries, and I trust will be regularly supplied by the means of the officers that are permitted to remain with them. The treatment in general that we have received from the enemy since our surrender, has been perfectly good and proper, but the kindness and attention that has been shown to us by the French officers in particular, their delicate sensibility of our situation, their generous and pressing offers of money both public and private to any amount, has really gone beyond what I can possibly describe, and will, I hope, make an impression on the breast of every British officer whenever the fortune of war should put any of them into our power.

"Although the event has been so unfortunate, the patience of the soldiers in bearing the greatest fatigues, and their firmness and intrepidity under a persevering fire of shot and shells, that I believe has not often been exceeded, deserves the highest commendation and praise; a successful defence, however, in our situation, was perhaps impossible, for the place could only be reckoned an intrenched camp, subject in many places to enfilades, and the ground in general so disadvantageous, that nothing but the necessity of fortifying it as a post to protect the navy, could have induced any person to erect works upon it. Our force diminished daily by sickness and other losses, and was reduced, when offered to capitulate, on this side to little more than three thousand two hundred rank and file, fit for duty, including officers, servants, and artificers, and at Gloucester, about six hundred, including cavalry. The enemy's army consisted of upwards of eight thousand French, nearly as many Continentals, and five thousand militia. They brought an immense train of heavy artillery, most amply furnished with ammunition, and perfectly well-manned.

"The constant and universal cheerfulness and spirit of the officers in all hardship and danger, deserve my warmest acknowledgments, and I have been particularly indebted to Brigadier-General O'Hara, and to Lieutenant-Colonel Abercrombie, the former commanding on the right, and the latter on the left, for their attention and exertion on every occasion. The detachment of the 23d regiment and marines in the redoubt on the right, commanded by Captain Apthorpe, and the subsequent detachments commanded by Lieutenant-Colonel Johnston, deserve particular commendation; Captain Rockport who commanded the artillery, and indeed every officer and soldier of that distinguished corps, and Lieutenant Sutherland the commanding engineer, have merited in every respect my highest approbation, and I cannot sufficiently acknowledge my obligations to Captain Symmonds, who commanded his Majesty's ships, and the other officers and seamen of the navy, for their zealous and active co-operation."

Rivington's Gazette, November 24

After an attentive perusal of Lord Cornwallis's letter to Sir Henry Clinton, containing an account of the reduction of his post and army in Virginia, we think the following observations are equally just and natural:—

I. *That his lordship is no general.* This is evident:—1. From the nature of the posts he occupied; 2. From the structure of his works; 3. From his presuming it impracticable to escape to New York by land; 4. From his neglecting to obtain earlier intelligence of the approach of General Washington, at the head of the allied army.

II. *His lordship is no soldier.* This is evident:—1. From his neglecting to attack the Marquis de Lafayette and the French troops, before the arrival of General Washington; 2. From his evacuating his outposts at the approach of the French grenadiers; 3. From his not daring to make a sortie, by which he might have injured our works, and protracted the siege for several weeks.

III. *His lordship is no politician.* This is evident:—1. From his neglecting to take notice of the conduct of the German troops during the siege. This impolitic omission will probably be resented by large and immediate desertions from the German corps who are now in captivity among us. 2. From his accounts of the strength of the American army. The powers of Europe must soon see the impossibility of conquering America, when they perceive from Lord Cornwallis's letter that only one of our armies consisted, after a war of nearly six years, of eight thousand regulars and five thousand militiamen.

IV. *His lordship is no gentleman.* This is evident from his ungrateful silence as to the noble and generous conduct of General Washington and the American officers to him and his army after the capitulation.

The magnanimity, humanity, and politeness of the commander-in-chief of the American armies would have extorted expressions of gratitude and respect from an Indian savage, a Tartar, or a Turk. A British General and an English noble-man is the *only* human being that could have treated such superlative virtue with sullen disrespect.

"A Subaltern," New York Packet, December 27

APPENDICES

Appendix A

PRINCIPAL SOURCES USED BY MOORE IN THE PREPARATION OF THE *Diary*

(1) *Newspapers*

During the Revolutionary War, newspapers encountered many difficulties in continuing regular publication. Numerous changes in title, ownership, and place of publication occurred.

The following listing is a summary of the newspapers that published during the war with dates and places of publication. The original title is followed immediately by information about subsequent titles, but each title is also listed separately with cross-references given for each.

A fundamental and exhaustive source for American newspapers at this time is Clarence Brigham, *History and Bibliography of American Newspapers, 1690–1820* (Worcester, Massachusetts: American Antiquarian Society, 1947, 2 vols.) to which the reader is referred for further information.

BOSTON GAZETTE AND COUNTRY JOURNAL
Boston, 1763–1775 / Watertown, 1775 / Boston, 1776–1783

CONNECTICUT GAZETTE AND UNIVERSAL INTELLIGENCER
New London, 1773–1783

CONNECTICUT JOURNAL
New Haven, 1767–1783

CONSTITUTIONAL GAZETTE
New York, 1775–1776

DUNLAP'S PENNSYLVANIA PACKET (*See:* PENNSYLVANIA PACKET)

FREEMAN'S JOURNAL
Portsmouth, N.H., 1776–1778

NEW HAMPSHIRE GAZETTE
Portsmouth, N.H., 1778–1783

GEORGIA GAZETTE
Savannah, 1763–1776

INDEPENDENT CHRONICLE
Boston, 1776–1783

MARYLAND JOURNAL
Baltimore, 1773–1783

MIDDLESEX JOURNAL
London, England

NEW ENGLAND CHRONICLE
Cambridge, 1775–1776

NEW HAMPSHIRE GAZETTE (*See:* FREEMAN'S JOURNAL)

NEW-JERSEY GAZETTE
Burlington and Trenton, 1777–1783

NEW-JERSEY JOURNAL
Chatham, 1779–1783

NEW YORK GAZETTE AND WEEKLY MERCURY (*Hugh Gaine, editor*)
New York, 1768–September 9, 1776 / New Jersey, September 21–November 2, 1776 / New York, November 11, 1776–1783
A New York edition, edited by Ambrose Serle, was published by the British while Gaine was issuing his New Jersey edition. New York, September 30–November 11, 1776

NEW-YORK JOURNAL
New York, 1766–1776 / Kingston, 1777–1778 / Poughkeepsie, 1778–1782

NEW YORK PACKET
New York, 1776 / Fishkill, 1777–1783

NEWPORT MERCURY
Newport, R.I., 1763–1776; 1780–1783

PENNSYLVANIA EVENING POST
Philadelphia, 1775–1783

PENNSYLVANIA GAZETTE
Philadelphia, 1765–1777 / York, 1777–1778 / Philadelphia,
1779–1783

PENNSYLVANIA JOURNAL
Philadelphia, 1766–1777; 1778–1783

PENNSYLVANIA LEDGER
Philadelphia, 1775–1778

PENNSYLVANIA PACKET
Philadelphia, 1771–1777 / Lancaster, 1777–1778 / Phila-
delphia, 1778–1783
Published as DUNLAP'S PENNSYLVANIA PACKET, 1733–1776

RIVINGTON'S GAZETTE (James Rivington, editor)
RIVINGTON'S NEW-YORK GAZETTEER
April 22, 1773–November 23, 1775

RIVINGTON'S NEW-YORK GAZETTE
October 4–18, 1777

RIVINGTON'S NEW YORK LOYAL GAZETTE
October 18–December 6, 1777

ROYAL GAZETTE
December 18, 1777–November 19, 1783

VIRGINIA GAZETTE
Williamsburg, 1766–1781 / Richmond, 1780–1781
Three separate papers were published during this period
under the same title.

(2) Miscellaneous

BARBER'S COLLECTIONS
John Warner Barber. *Historical Collections of Connecticut.*
New Haven, 1838.

BROADSIDES
Refers probably to the Broadside Collection of The New-York Historical Society.

CHURCHILL PAPERS
Untraced

CARVER
Untraced

CLIFT'S DIARY
This diary, available to Moore, has vanished and remains untraced. One authority attributes it to a Solomon Clift. The Clifts were a shipbuilding family from Marshfield, Massachusetts.

CURWEN'S JOURNAL
Journal and Letters of the Late Samuel Curwen, ed. G. A. Ward, New York, 1842.

ELLIOT MS
Untraced

GATES PAPERS
The Papers of Horatio Gates. New-York Historical Society, New York Public Library.

GORDON'S *American Revolution*
William Gordon. *History of the Rise, Progress, and Establishment of the Independence of the United States of America.* London, 1794.

MARKOE TO OSWALD
Untraced

PARK'S DIARY
Untraced

SMYTHE'S DIARY (JOURNAL)
Untraced

THACHER'S MILITARY JOURNAL
James Thacher. A *Military Journal during the Revolutionary War.* Boston, 1823.

UPCOTT

Refers to the collection of the antiquarian, William Upcott (1802–45) in The New-York Historical Society. These materials have been reorganized and are not now available for examination under this classification.

WINSLOW, Job
Untraced

WHITE'S COLLECTIONS
Rev. George White. *Historical Collections of Georgia.* New York, 1855.

Appendix B

THE PRINCIPAL WORKS OF FRANK MOORE

THE AMERICAN REVOLUTION

SONGS AND BALLADS OF THE AMERICAN REVOLUTION
New York: Appleton and Co., 1856; and Hurst and Co., 1905. The 1856 edition was re-issued in facsimile by the Kennikat Press, Port Washington, N.Y., in 1964.

DIARY OF THE AMERICAN REVOLUTION: *From Newspapers and Original Documents*
New York: Scribner's, 1860 and 1863, 2 volumes; privately printed in 100 copy edition, New York, 1865; re-issued in one volume as a centennial edition, Hartford, Connecticut: J. B. Burr and Co., 1876, under the title *The Diary of the Revolution*.

THE CORRESPONDENCE OF HENRY LAURENS
Issued in a 250 copy edition for the Zenger Club, New York, 1861 under the general heading *Materials for History Printed from Original Manuscripts*.

PATRIOT PREACHERS OF THE AMERICAN REVOLUTION 1763–83
New York: printed for the subscribers, 1861; Evans, 1862.

ILLUSTRATED BALLAD HISTORY OF THE AMERICAN REVOLUTION, 1763–83
Originally designed as thirty separate issues, six issues only, bound in one volume, New York: 1876.

THE CIVIL WAR

THE REBELLION RECORD: *A Diary of American Events, with Documents, Narratives, Illustrative Incidents, Poetry,* etc.
New York: Putnam, 1861–3, and Van Nostrand, 1864–8. Ten vols. and a supplement.

ANECDOTES, POETRY AND INCIDENTS OF THE WAR, NORTH AND SOUTH: 1860–65
New York: Collier's, 1867 and 1882; re-issued in 1889 under the title *The Civil War in Song and Story.*

HEROES AND MARTYRS: *Notable Men of the Time*
New York: Putnam, 1862.

WOMEN OF THE WAR: *Their Heroism and Self-Sacrifice*
Hartford, Conn.: S. S. Scranton, 1867 and 1869.

The Red, White and Blue song series, composed of SONGS OF THE SOLDIERS, LYRICS OF LOYALTY, and PERSONAL AND POLITICAL BALLADS, published New York: Putnam, 1864.

REBEL RHYMES AND RHAPSODIES
New York: Putnam, 1864.

SPEECHES OF ANDREW JOHNSON, PRESIDENT OF THE UNITED STATES
Boston: Little Brown, 1866.

SONGS AND BALLADS OF THE SOUTHERN PEOPLE, 1861–5
New York: Appleton, 1886.

ALSO

AMERICAN ELOQUENCE: *A Collection of Speeches and Addresses by the Most Eminent Orators of America*
New York: Appleton, 1858 and 1871. 2 vols.

RECORD OF THE YEAR: *A Reference Scrap Book, Being the Monthly Record of Important Events Worth Preserving*
New York: Carleton, 1876. 2 vols.

Appendix C

BIBLIOGRAPHICAL NOTES

The purpose of these Notes is to provide for the librarian, student, and general reader, a guide to reliable materials on the American Revolution that are actually in print and easily available either in hardcover or paperback editions. Some of these works, as indicated below, contain useful guides to further source and secondary materials. * Indicates out of print, but for which we may hopefully expect a new issue, in view of its importance.

The series of events leading directly to the Revolution is outlined briefly but with precision in Edmund S. Morgan, *The Birth of the Republic, 1763–89* (Chicago: University of Chicago Press, 1956; hardcover and paperback). A fuller treatment is contained in Laurence Henry Gipson, *The Coming of the Revolution* (New York: Harper and Bros., 1954; Torchbook paperback, 1962); and John C. Miller, *Origins of the American Revolution* (Boston: Little Brown, 1949, re-issued by Stanford University Press, 1959). Both books contain guides to the sources for original study.

A number of useful monographs amplify the various episodes. Particularly useful are Howard H. Peckham, *Pontiac and the Indian Uprising* (Chicago: University of Chicago Press, 1947; Phoenix paperback, 1961); Edmund S. and Helen M. Morgan, *The Stamp Act Crisis* (Chapel Hill, N.C.: University of North Carolina Press, 1953); John Richard Alden, *General Gage in America* (Baton Rouge, La.: University of Louisiana Press, 1948); Benjamin Woods Labaree, *The Boston Tea Party* (New York: Oxford University Press, 1964); and Arthur M. Schlesinger, *The Colonial Merchants and the American Revolution* (New York: Frederick Ungar, 1957).

The origins of the Revolution in the economic and political relationships of the mother country and the colonies in the eighteenth century have been subjected to analysis in a number of important recent works. *O. M. Dickerson, *The Navigation Acts and the American Revolution* (Philadelphia: University of Pennsylvania Press, 1951) demolishes a longstanding tradition of the role of the Navigation Acts in causing the Revolution. Bernard Knollenberg, *Origin of the American Revolution 1759–66* (New York: The Macmillan Company, 1960; Collier paperback, 1961) argues that the clash was precipitated by British provocations that challenged and undermined colonial autonomy. See also Charles M. Andrews, *Colonial Background of the American Revolution* (New Haven: Yale University Press, 1931; paperback, 1961). The intellectual origins of the Revolution may best be studied in the debates, sermons, pamphlets, and press polemics of this period. Of the first order of importance for the modern reader is a new series, *Pamphlets of the American Revolution 1750–76*, edited by Bernard Bailyn (Cambridge, Mass.: the Belknap Press of Harvard University Press, 1965). Vol. I covers the years 1750–65. See also *Frank Moore, ed., *Patriot Preachers of the American Revolution* (New York: Evans, 1862). The role of the colonial press in the struggle against Great Britain before the outbreak of the military conflict is carefully described in Arthur M. Schlesinger, *Prelude to Independence, 1764–76* (New York: Alfred A. Knopf, 1958). This work constitutes a guide to the history of revolutionary journalism, and provides the immediate background for an understanding of the scope and significance of journalistic effort during the revolutionary war itself. Alice Baldwin's monograph, *The New England Clergy and the American Revolution* (New York: Frederick Ungar, 1958) should be read in conjunction with Moore's *Patriot Preachers* cited above.

The question of the origins of the Revolution in all its complex facets finds a focus of unique importance in the Declaration of Independence. The Declaration's philosophy is analyzed in Carl Becker, *The Declaration of Independence* (New York: Alfred A. Knopf, 1922; Vintage paperback, 1958). Jefferson's *Summary View of the Rights of British America,* which provides major insights into the basic issues underlying the Declaration, is available in John Anthony Scott, ed., *Living Documents in American History* (New York: Washington Square Press, 1964; hardcover and paperback). Thomas Paine's classic pamphlet *Common Sense,* proving both the desirability and the feasibility of independence, is available in a number of paperback editions (e.g., New York: Doubleday Dolphin paperback, n.d.).

Two useful general surveys are available for the period of the revolutionary war, 1775–83: John R. Alden, *The American Revolution* (New York: Harper and Bros., 1954; Torchbook paperback, 1962); and John C. Miller, *Triumph of Freedom* (Boston: Little Brown, 1948; Atlantic paperback, 1965). Both books have guides to the sources. The imperial framework of the American revolutionary struggle—its relationship to the worldwide battle of the European Empires—is illuminated brilliantly in Piers Mackesy, *The War for America, 1775–83* (Cambridge, Mass.: Harvard University Press, 1964). For American diplomacy's exploitation of the international situation, see Samuel Flagg Bemis, *The Diplomacy of the American Revolution* (New York: American Historical Association, 1935; Indiana University Press paperback, 1957).

The development of political parties in the revolutionary period, and the role of Whig and radical groups in the formation of State governments and constitutions, is surveyed by Elisha P. Douglass, *Rebels and Democrats* (Chapel Hill, N.C.: University of North Carolina Press, 1955). An older monograph is available that supplements this study, Carl L. Becker's first-rate *History of Political Parties in the Province of New York, 1760–76* (Madison, Wis.: University of Wisconsin Press paperback, 1960); and see also Schlesinger's *Colonial Merchants,* cited above. The Tories during the Revolution are the subject of a pioneer essay by Lorenzo

Sabine, *The Loyalists of the American Revolution* (Spring-field, Mass.: The Walden Press, 1957); and a modern study, William H. Nelson, *The American Tory* (New York: Oxford University Press, 1961; Beacon paperback, Boston: Little Brown, 1964).

The role and history of the Continental Congress receives definitive treatment in Edmund Cody Burnett, *The Continental Congress* (New York: The Macmillan Co., 1941; Norton paperback, 1964). The origins and the nature of the federal union forged during the war years is examined in Merrill Jensen, *The Articles of Confederation* (Madison: University of Wisconsin Press paperback, 1962).

Books on the military history of the Revolution continue to trickle from the presses in a steady stream. The best of the recent general surveys are, in our opinion, *Lynn Montross, *Rag, Tag, and Bobtail* (New York: Harper and Bros., 1952), and R. Ernest and Trevor N. Dupuy, *The Compact History of the Revolutionary War* (New York: Hawthorn Books, 1963). Both these works have good sketch-maps, the *sine qua non* of books presuming to explain the story of battle, but neither is yet in paperback. Paperback surveys are as deplorable in quality as they are abundant in quantity; among the best are Howard H. Peckham, *The War for Independence* (Chicago: University of Chicago Press, 1958; cloth and paper-bound), a careful work handicapped by a lack of proper maps and excessive brevity; and Willard Wallace, *Appeal to Arms: a Military History of the Revolution* (New York: Harper and Bros., 1951; Chicago: Quadrangle paperback, 1964). George F. Scheer and Hugh F. Rankin's *Rebels and Redcoats* (New York: New American Library, Mentor paperback, 1959) is long on local color but short on analysis, inadequately mapped, and poorly printed.

Some important original sources for the study of the war years are available; notably Joseph Plumb Martin, *Narrative of Some of the Adventures, Dangers and Sufferings of a Revolutionary Soldier, Interspersed with Anecdotes of Incidents That Occurred within His Own Observation*, which has been edited by George F. Scheer, and issued under the title *Private Yankee Doodle* (New York: Popular Library paperback, 1963);

The Narrative of Ethan Allen (New York: Corinth paper-
back, 1961); Captain Thomas Dring, *Recollections of the
Jersey Prison Ship*, ed. Albert Greene (New York: Corinth
paperback, 1961); Baron Ludwig Von Closen, *Revolutionary
Journal*, 1780–83, translated and edited by Evelyn M. Acomb
(Chapel Hill, N.C.: University of North Carolina Press,
1958); and Baroness Riedesel, *Journal and Correspondence
of a Tour of Duty*, 1776–83, ed. Marvin L. Brown, Jr. (Chapel
Hill, N.C.: University of North Carolina Press, 1965). Sir
Henry Clinton's journal, *The American Rebellion*, edited by
William B. Willcox, was published by Yale University Press in
1954, but is out of print. A general source book is available
in paperback, *The American Revolution*, ed. Hugh F. Rankin
(New York: Capricorn paperback, 1964), but its usefulness
is diminished by editorial mutilation.

A number of recent works concentrate on separate battles
and campaigns. Arthur Tourtellot, *Lexington and Concord*
(New York: Norton paperback, 1963), makes excellent reading. Thomas J. Fleming and Richard Ketchum have both
produced fine studies entitled *Bunker Hill*, the former being
a Collier paperback (1962), the latter a Doubleday book
(1963). A comparison of these studies in terms of style,
sources and analysis, is both amusing and instructive. Alfred
Hoyt Bill, *Valley Forge: The Making of an Army* (New
York: Harper and Bros., 1952), and *The Campaign of Princeton*, 1776–77 (Princeton, N.J.: Princeton University Press,
1948) are first-rate; Bruce Bliven's *Battle for Manhattan*
(New York: Holt, 1955), and Harrison Bird, *March to Saratoga* (New York: Oxford University Press, 1963), are also to
be recommended. Paul H. Smith, *Loyalists and Redcoats*
(Chapel Hill, N.C.: University of North Carolina Press,
1964), is a fine study of the impact of loyalism on British
military policy See also various monographs of Donald B.
Chidsey, notably, *Valley Forge*, and *Victory at Yorktown*
(New York: Crown Press, 1959 and 1962 respectively).

First-rate biographical studies of military and naval leadership are of great importance because they add depth to the
study of war and enable us to investigate the political and
social estimates, as well as the military calculations, that un-

derlay the conduct and behavior of the participants. William B. Willcox, *Portrait of a General* (New York: Alfred A. Knopf, 1964), is a major study of Sir Henry Clinton's role in the War of Independence, and a model of its kind. *Chalmer G. Davidson scores also with *Piedmont Partisan: the Life and Times of Brigadier General William Lee Davidson* (Davidson, N.C.: Davidson College, 1951). Theodore Thayer, *Nathanael Greene* (New York: Twayne Publishers, 1960), must be mentioned, but it is not the definitive study of Greene or his military role. Surprisingly, no one-volume work is available on George Washington that even remotely measures up to the need or the opportunity. Esmond Wright, *Washington and the American Revolution* (New York: Collier paperback, 1962) is a stopgap. Samuel Eliot Morison, *John Paul Jones* (Boston: Little Brown, 1959; Atlantic paperback, 1963) is an important biography that does full justice to its subject. Lord George Germain, who was in effect Britain's minister for war during the revolutionary struggle, is the topic of a biography bearing his name by Alan Valentine (New York: Oxford University Press, 1962); this book makes a contribution though it is not to be compared, for breadth of approach or grasp of its subject, to the works of Mackesy or Willcox cited above.

American civilization at the outset of the revolutionary struggle is the subject of a survey by Carl Bridenbaugh, *Cities in Revolt, 1743–76* (New York: Alfred A. Knopf, 1955), and this may be complemented by Evarts Boutell Greene's *The Revolutionary Generation, 1763–90* (New York: The Macmillan Company, 1943). J. Franklin James, *The American Revolution Considered as a Social Movement* (Boston: Beacon paperback, 1962), is an attempt to assess the impact of revolutionary change on American society. Dan Lacy, *The Meaning of the American Revolution* (New York: New American Library, 1964) is a first-rate summary of the achievements of the revolutionary era, and their significance.

Appendix D

BIBLIOGRAPHICAL NOTES
ON SONGS, BALLADS, AND VERSE

For general surveys of this topic, see John Anthony Scott, "Ballads and Broadsides of the American Revolution," *Sing Out!* (April–May, 1966, 18–23); and the same author's *Ballad of America* (New York: Bantam Book, 1966; Grosset and Dunlap, 1967, chapter 3). Many surviving broadsides are listed, with respect to title and location, in Worthington C. Ford, *Check List of Massachusetts Broadsides* (Boston: Massachusetts Historical Society, 1922). The same editor's *The Isaiah Thomas Collection of Ballads* is a catalogue of the great collection in the possession of the American Antiquarian Society (Worcester, Mass.: American Antiquarian Society, 1924). Both works are out of print. Frank Moore, *Songs and Ballads of the American Revolution* has been re-issued (Port Washington, N.Y.: Kennikat Press, 1964). Broadsides of British origin are listed in G. Malcolm Laws, Jr. *American Balladry from British Broadsides* (Philadelphia: American Folklore Society, 1957). A number of the ballads included in this edition of the *Diary* are sung by Bill and Gene Bonyun and John Anthony Scott on an Heirloom Record, *The American Revolution through Its Songs and Ballads* (Brookhaven, N.Y.: HL 500, 1960).

INDEX

Lewis, Jonathan, of Fairfield. Conn., 383

"Lexington March, The," *see* "Yankee Doodle"

Lexington, Mass.: battle of, 24-26; reception of news of, at Williamsburg, Va., 30-31; route of news of, from Watertown to Baltimore, 30-31

Lillington, Colonel, at battle of Moore's Creek, N.C., 101

Lincoln, Benjamin, General: at Boundbrook, N.J., 212; in South Carolina maneuvers, 357-58, 361, 362; at Stono Ferry, 366-67; at Charleston, S.C., 415-17; conducts British troops at surrender of Cornwallis, 541

Lindley, Lieutenant-Colonel, at Punk Hill, N.J., skirmish, 211

Lippitt, Christopher, Colonel, at Newport, R.I., 136

Lispenard, Colonel, Washington lands at seat of, 52

"Little Phil" sings new campaign song at dinner to Washington in New York, 117

Little Tuskeego, Indian town of, 475

Livingston, Colonel: at Fort Clinton, 259; at battle of Monmouth, 311

Livingston, H. B., Lieutenant-Colonel, at Quaker Hill, R.I., 326, 328

Livingston, Henry, Colonel, at attack on Quebec, 90

Livingston, William: writings of, *see* "Hortentius"; British raid house of, 347

Locke, Colonel, at Ramsour's, 461

Logan, Major, at Fort Montgomery, 258

Long Island: British land on, 144; battle of, 144-47; Washington's ejaculation at battle, 146; General Howe's account of battle of, 148-52; recruiting speech for British delivered on, 152-54

"Lord Cornwallis' Surrender," 543-44

Loring, Joshua, commissary of prisoners at New York, 281

Lovell, James: in Boston jail, 58, 59; exchange of, for Governor Skeena, 135-36, 181

Low, Isaac, notice of, 30

Loyal Refugees, under protection of British, 334-35

Lucas, Captain, at battle of Long Island, 146

Luce, Captain, guides British into Elizabethtown, N.J., 348

Lutlington, Colonel, at Tarrytown, 257

Luzerne, Chevalier de la: arrives at Boston, 389; visits Harvard College, 390-91

Lynch, Colonel, at Guilford Court House, 487

Lying: "no real lasting good can come from," 246; English pamphleteers and newspapers given to, 518

Magaw, Colonel, surrenders Fort Washington to British, 181

Maitland, Lieutenant-Colonel, lands at Savannah River, 357

Malmady, Colonel: at Stono Ferry, 367; at Eutaw Springs, 533-37

Manumission of slaves, 467-71

JOHN ANTHONY SCOTT

Born in England of English and Scottish parents, John Anthony Scott attended St. Paul's School in London and received B.A. and M.A. degrees from Oxford University. He came to the United States on a graduate research fellowship at Columbia University, and enlisted in the United States Army at the start of World War II. On his return to the United States he received his Doctorate degree in French history and political theory from Columbia.

In 1951, after teaching modern European history at Columbia and Amherst College, Mr. Scott was appointed Chairman of the History Department at Fieldston School, Riverdale, New York. Since then he has concentrated on the study and teaching of American history—especially Colonial history, the Constitution, and slavery. He is currently also a visiting faculty member in the History Department and Law School of Rutgers University.

Mr. Scott has collected the results of his intense search for documentary material for direct use in the classroom in *Living Documents of American History: From Earliest Colonial Times to the Civil War*. A second volume, from the Emancipation Proclamation to the outbreak of World War I, is in preparation. *The Ballad of America: The History of the United States in Song and Story* reflects his avid interest in collecting folk songs embodying the essence of the American national experience.

Mr. Scott has also edited a new edition of F. A. Kemble's *Journal of a Residence on a Georgian Plantation, 1838–39* issued in 1961 as a contribution to the Centennial of the Civil War, and has translated and edited *The Defense of Gracchus Babeuf before the High Court of Vendôme*, a work designed by Leonard Baskin, illustrated by Thomas Cornell, and issued in both limited hardcover and paperback editions.

605